CADOGANguides

VENICE, VENETIA & THE DOLOMITES

'The Bard may never have visited the cities where he set many of his plays, but there's something very Shakespearean about them – something gorgeous and poetic, full of character and Renaissance swagger'

Dana Facaros & Michael Pauls

About the Guide

The full-colour introduction gives the author's overview of the country, together with suggested itineraries and a regional 'where to go' map and feature to help you plan your trip.

Illuminating and entertaining cultural chapters on local history, art, architecture, colourful characters, and food and drink give you a rich flavour of the country.

Planning Your Trip starts with the basics of when to go, getting there and getting around, coupled with other useful information, including a section for disabled travellers. The Practical A–Z deals with all the essential information and contact details that you may need while you are away.

The regional chapters are arranged in a loose touring order, with transport information and driving instructions. The author's top 'Don't Miss' ⓧ sights are highlighted at the start of each chapter and there are also short-tour itineraries. At the back of the book you'll find a useful colour touring atlas. All chapters have personal recommendations for places to stay and eat.

A language and pronunciation guide, a glossary of cultural terms, ideas for further reading and a comprehensive index can be found at the end of the book.

Although everything we list in this guide is personally recommended, our authors inevitably have their own favourite places to eat and stay. Whenever you see this Author's Choice ★ icon beside a listing, you will know that it is a little bit out of the ordinary.

Hotel Price Guide

Luxury	€€€€€	€250 and above
Very Expensive	€€€€	€160–250
Expensive	€€€	€100–160
Moderate	€€	€70–100
Inexpensive	€	€70 and under

Restaurant Price Guide

Very Expensive	€€€€	€50 and above
Expensive	€€€	€35–50
Moderate	€€	€25–35
Inexpensive	€	€25 and under

About the Authors

Dana Facaros and Michael Pauls are professional travel writers. They spent three years in a tiny Italian village, where they suffered massive overdoses of food, art and wine, and enjoyed every minute of it. They reckon they could whip 98 per cent of the world's non-Italian population at Trivial Pursuit (except for the sports questions). They now live in southwest France.

4th Edition Published 2007

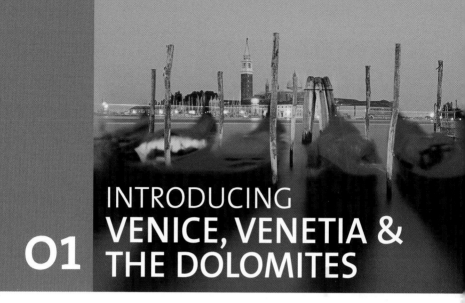

INTRODUCING
VENICE, VENETIA &
THE DOLOMITES

01

Above: Gondolas at dusk, Venice, pp.105–68

How often have you come across a place promising 'something for everyone', which behind the brochure-speak means a water park for the tots, a club or two for the frisky, a spa for the arthritic and enough monuments to fill a postcard rack? The striking thing about Northeast Italy, or Venetia, is not that it promises 'something for everyone', but that its 'somethings' are 24-carat gold. The Dolomites aren't just mountains, they are the Most Beautiful Mountains. Venice is the Most Beautiful City; Lake Garda, the Palladian villas, the Renaissance paintings, the frescoes by Giotto, all *i più belli del mondo*, as the Italians say. You want to argue, except that they're probably right. The region that gave the world Bellini, Giorgione, Titian and Tiepolo may not have that clear Mediterranean quality of places further south, but it has an extra dimension that no photograph of Piazza San Marco, La Rotonda, or Lake Garda ever conveys; this region is sumptuous, sensuous, lush, worldly – at times magnificent.

Venetia has roughly the same borders that it had as the Roman Tenth Augustine Region of *Venetia et Histria*. The Italians call it the *Tre Venezie* for its three modern regions: the Veneto, Trentino-Alto Adige and Friuli-Venezia Giulia. The last two only joined Italy after the First World War; the frontier at Trieste was settled only in 1972. This has left the northeast the most cosmopolitan pocket of Italy, by a long shot. German often prevails in the Alto Adige/Süd Tirol, Slovenian in eastern and northern Friuli, while languages you may never have heard of, such as Ladin, Friul and Cimbro, are still spoken and undergoing a revival. Even Italian is beginning to lose out to Venetic, its colourful cousin (call it a 'dialect' at the risk of starting

Above: Polenta, pp.69–71

Opposite: Danieli Hotel interior, Venice, p.159

an argument). Religious traditions, folk customs, music, cuisine and national dress have not been forgotten or homogenized. If Venetia is a melting pot, it's a pot full of polenta, 'dust as beautiful as gold', according to Goldoni, a dish that crosses all its cultures, but one that can be grilled, fried, sliced and served in a thousand different ways.

Variety may be in its genes. Venice, the leading player in these parts for over a thousand years, was always the most cosmopolitan state in Europe, and influenced Venetia economically and culturally even before it became part of the *Serenissima* in the early 15th century. You can still sense her presence; winged lion memories of her industry, her *dolce vita*, her fears and dreams have seeped into the land. In Italo Calvino's *Invisible Cities*, Marco Polo tells Kublai Khan of the cities he has visited. After hearing countless places described, Kublai Khan asks him why he never speaks of one city – his own, Venice. Polo replies, 'Every time I describe a city I am saying something about Venice.' For him, Venice was implicit in everything. And so, too, in Venetia, like a gentle sigh. But along with its beauty and the magnificent villas dotted around the countryside, be warned that Venetia also possesses some equally magnificent sprawl and industry. This is nothing new: in the *Inferno*, Dante vividly describes the proto-Industrial Revolution goings-on in Venice's Arsenale. Since the Second World War, Venetia has re-established its historic position as one of the wealthiest regions in Italy, a place where people grow and make things: wine, apples, cheese, maize (source of all that polenta), clothes, furniture, gold jewellery, ceramics, chandeliers. With the great exception of Venice, of course, where hosting the world has been a way of life for about three centuries now, tourism is only a sideline here.

Venice and her pearly lagoon are only a few hours from the jagged, wind-clawed towers of the Dolomites. You can attend a ballet in Vicenza, in Europe's oldest theatre, and the next night hear *Aïda* in Verona's Roman arena, or top off a lazy day on the beach with a romantic evening in Asolo. The gold you seek is never far away.

Where to Go

As with Marco Polo, **Venice** is the place to start, not only for its intrinsically fascinating self, but to help understand the rest, especially the **Veneto**. Here Venice's sweet sisters, **Padua**, **Vicenza**, **Verona** and **Treviso**, are among Italy's richest art cities, each with a strong personality, each surrounded by a constellation of villas and smaller jewels – Monselice, Este, Asolo, Marostica, Bassano del Grappa, Rovigo, Oderzo and Feltre. The south of the Veneto is defined by the flatlands and mystery-laden delta of the Po, interrupted by little clusters of volcanic bumps, the fabled Euganean Hills and Monti Berici. To the west the Veneto is framed by **Lake Garda**, the most dramatic of the Italian lakes, rimmed by the Dolomites and the lovely towns of Sirmione, Gardone, Salò, Malcesine, Riva and Torri del Benaco.

The Veneto town of **Belluno** and its glittering resort of **Cortina d'Ampezzo** are the gateway to the strange and fabulous **Dolomites**. Each group of peaks is as different and beautiful as the next – if you have time for a short stay, you can see them at their most breathtaking along the Great Dolomites Road between Cortina and Bolzano. To the west lies the autonomous province of **Trentino**, where the delightful city of Trento hosted the famous Counter-Reformation council. It encompasses the westernmost Dolomites, the Brenta Group, lush valleys of orchards and vineyards, two resorts in gorgeous settings, **Madonna di Campiglio** and **San Martino di Castrozza**, as well as a score of beautifully preserved medieval castles with courtly frescoes. There are just as many fairy-tale castles up in bilingual **Alto Adige/Süd Tirol**, on the border of Austria and Switzerland, where strudel meets pasta head on. You could easily spend a day in and around **Bolzano**, the arty modern capital, or the celebrated watering hole of **Merano**; among its many secrets are some of Europe's best-preserved Carolingian churches. Much of the western part of the province lies within the confines of **Stelvio**, Italy's largest national park, where you can ski year-round.

Off to the east towards Slovenia, **Friuli-Venezia Giulia** was the centre of action in Roman times, when **Aquileia** was the capital of *Venetia et Histria*; today it's the most important archaeological site in northern Italy. **Cividale del Friuli** has rich souvenirs of its days as the capital of an 8th-century Lombard duchy, while **Trieste** is an intriguing bit of Mitteleurope on the Med. Its other attractions are just as diverse: the sandy beaches at **Grado**, the Tuscan-like wine-growing hills of the **Collio**, the karst and Grotta Gigante, Italy's largest forest around Tarvisio, and **Udine**, the city of Tiepolo.

Above: Casa Mazzanti, Piazza delle Erbe, Verona, p.244; Trieste, pp.371–8

Chapter Divisions

SWITZERLAND

AUSTRIA

Lake
Garda

Verona

Trento

Bolzano

10
THE DOLOMITES
p.291

Vicenza

09
THE VENETO
p.169

Padua

Cortina
d'Ampezzo

Laguna

Belluno

Venice

08
VENICE
p.105

Pordenone

11
FRIULI-VENEZIA
GIULIA
p.357

N

Udine

40 km
20 miles

Trieste

AUSTRIA

CROATIA

SLOVENIA

Cities Seeped in Art

The historic cities of Venetia have a rich, sumptuous Shakespearean swagger, with no false modesty, their buildings lavishly swathed in frescoes, coloured marbles, and ornament. Their *piazzas* are perfect stage sets for drama and romance, harmonious even when Gothic and Baroque churches are standing cheek to jowl with Renaissance *palazzi* and Roman walls. They are not only filled with art, but are works of art themselves built on a human scale.

Right: San Zaccaria ceiling, Venice, p.141

From top: Sirmione, pp.263–4; Lagoon, Friuli-Venezia Giulia, pp.357–92

Waterscapes

You're never far from the wet stuff in Northeast Italy. Dramatic waterfalls, rushing streams and impossibly azure lakes enliven the stony fortresses of the Dolomites all the way down to Garda, a sheet of water so vast that it has its own lemon- and olive-growing microclimate. Rivers such as the mighty Adige, Piave, Brenta and Tagliamento weave through the landscapes of vineyards and end in lagoons. Moods vary widely. There's the Po Delta, luminous, wild and melancholy; the tidy civilized Brenta Canal, linking Venice to Padua, a road of water lined with villas, and the Adriatic itself, skirted by endless sandy lidos, where Middle Europe comes to play.

Above: Skiing, Alto Adige, pp.330–56

Right: Passo Pordoi, p.341

In the Hall of the Mountain King

From top: the Dolomites, pp.291–356; Cortina d'Ampezzo, pp.298–300

Europe's loveliest mountains, the Dolomites, are a crystallized coral garden thrust out of a primordial sea, sculpted by millennia of wind and ice into fantastical fairytale forms – great clusters of pinnacles, sheer cliffs and mesas pierce the clouds and tickle the stars. Remarkably pale as mountains go (the locals say they are covered in fairy webs woven of moonbeams), they reflect the changing light over the course of the day, and blush as the sun goes down – most famously the mighty mass of Rosengarten, the enchanted realm of Lauren, king of the Dwarves.

Above: Miramare,
Friuli-Venezia
Giulia, pp.378–80

The Land of Palladian Dreams

Up until the *Quattrocento*, when the Venetians acquired their mainland *terra firma* empire, all their investments and energy were concentrated in their fleet, trade and defence. The lure of real estate on the mainland, however, proved an irresistible temptation for Venice's tough old mercantile soul, and the overweening drive and ambition that had characterized the Most Serene Republic in the Middle Ages slowly lost its edge. Being Venetians, however, the splendid villas they built were more than functional farmhouses or summer retreats in the hills: they were places to entertain and display one's exquisite taste. And thanks to Andrea Palladio and his daydreams of antiquity, they also changed the course of Western architecture.

Food and Wine, with a Difference

With Austria and Slovenia as neighbours, Northeast Italy has firm multicultural roots in the kitchen. Here cooks invented fusion cuisine before there was even a name for it – there's pasta, to be sure, but a strong preference for heartier polenta, gnocchi and rich risottos, sauerkraut in various forms, goulash, sausage, hams and game dishes. The land produces an equally varied array of wines, that are fun to explore on wine roads and at *enoteca*s. The Veneto produces Italian classics such as Valpolicello, Bardolino, and sparkling Prosecco, while Trentino/Alto Adige and Friuli produce excellent single grape DOC wines, mostly white (Chardonnay, Pino Grigio, Reisling and so on), and specialities such as Gewürtztraminer *aromatico*, a legendary aphrodisiac.

Above: Bottle of Livio Felluga Terre Alte, Brazzano di Cormons, the Collio, pp.380–82; Prosciutto di San Daniele, p.71

Right: the Wine Road, pp.333–5

Itineraries

A Two-Week Immersion in Art and Beauty

Note: For the most popular sights, book tickets in advance

Days 1–2 Get lost in Venice – it's easy. If it's your first time, be sure to do the truly dazzling main sights – St Mark's, the Doge's Palace and the Accademia. On the evening of Day 2, take a train to Padua and check into a central hotel.

Day 3 In Padua, visit Giotto's Scrovegni Chapel and Mantegna's Eremitani, the Palazzo della Ragione, and the Basilica di Sant'Antonio. In the evening take the train to Vicenza.

Day 4 See Vicenza's Palladian palaces, Teatro Olimpico, La Rotonda and Villa Valmarana. In the evening take the train to Verona.

Days 5–6 You'll need two days in Verona for the Roman Arena (and ideally an opera, in season), the great medieval churches, the Scaliger tombs, Juliet's house and Castelvecchio Museum. Be sure to try the gnocchi.

Day 7 Hire a car for a week and head west to Sirmione, then make the magnificent drive up Lake Garda's east shore. Stop often for the views and, in Malcesine, to take the revolving cable car to the top of Monte Baldo. Overnight in Riva del Garda.

Day 8 Follow the SS45bis north, past baby lakes and castles into the Dolomites. Check into a hotel in Trento and visit the charming frescoes at Castello del Buonconsiglio, the Duomo (scene of the famous Council of Trent) and Museo Diocescano.

Day 9 From Trento, drive east to Lake Carezza, then continue up the SS24 to the Passo di Costalunga and Vigo di Fassa; pick up the Great Dolomites Road, stopping often to drink in the views on the way to Cortina d'Ampezzo.

Days 10–11 Spend a couple of days exploring the mountains and lakes around Cortina – the options are many.

Day 12 Drive south and turn west at Conegliano to visit the exquisite Villa Barbaro at Maser, then spend the night in lovely Asolo.

Day 13 See the great Giorgione in the cathedral of Castelfranco Veneto, and Palladio's Villa Cornaro in Piombino Dese, then drive along the Brenta Canal, stopping at the Villa Nazionale Pisani at Strà. Return the car, and have a last romantic night in Venice; spring for a midnight boat taxi tour.

Day 14 Home again.

Above: The Doge's Palace, Venice, pp.130–33

Below: Roman Arena, Verona, p.243

Left: Lake Garda, pp.260–80

01

Introduction | Itineraries

Above: Bolzano/Bozen,
pp.335–9

Below: Palazzo, Corso
Vittorio Emanuele,
Pordenone, pp.330–32

The Best of Alto Adige in a Week

Day 1 Start in Bolzano and visit 5,000-year old Ötzi the Ice Man in the archaeology museum and the frescoed Castel Roncolo. Have a traditional Sud Tyrolean feast at Pra Meisa.

Day 2 Hire a car and take the SS42 towards Appiano, a town of 40 castles, and make a loop on the lovely Strada del Vino to Caldaro, Termeno, Egna and Ora. Head back towards Bolzano, taking the road up the Val d'Ega to watch the magical sun set on Rosengarten. Overnight in Nova Levante.

Day 3 Drive up the Val di Fassa, then take in the sublime Passo di Sella and Passo di Gardena; carry on north on the S244 to the frescoed town of Brunico; stay overnight.

Day 4 Visit Brunico's Museo Civico and Renaissance Casteldarne at Chienes, then follow the road towards the Brenner Pass, stopping at Vipiteno; see the ancient Roman Mithraeum in the Municipio and the Castel Tasso.

Day 5 Head south to Bressanone – see the cloister and baptistery and Museo Diocesano. Continue south to Chiusa to visit the Monastero di Sabonia. In the late afternoon drive west past Bolzano to Merano.

Days 6–7 Spend a couple of days exploring the lovely Val Venosta and its idiosyncrasies – the typewriter museum, the Yeti collection in Reinhold Messner's Castel Juvale, the Trapp family's Castel Coira, and perhaps the Carolingian frescoes at Müstair before heading back to Bolzano.

A Week in Friuli-Venezia Giulia

Days 1–2 Begin in Trieste, absorbing the unique atmosphere of its historic cafés, piazzas, and museums; visit the Capitoline hill and Basilica di San Giusto, and take city buses out to the Carso's Grotto Gigante, the Habsburg folly at Miramare, and nearby beaches.

Day 3 Hire a car and tour the Collio, the pretty wine region around Gorizia on the way to Cividale di Friuli; visit its unique Lombard sites and museums.

Day 4 Hop over to Udine, a pretty Venetian town full of Tiepolos.

Day 5 Drive west to San Daniele di Friuli: see the fresco cycle in Sant'Antonio Abate and try some of its famous prosciutto; after lunch drive down to Codroipo to visit the Villa Manin, residence of Venice's last doge. Have a looked at the planned town of Palmanova, then check in at Grado.

Day 6 Spend a day wandering the excavations, basilica and museum at Aquileia, then relax in the sands at Grado and dine on the local seafood.

Day 7 Visit Grado's 5th-century churches and go birdwatching on horseback before heading home.

CONTENTS

Contents

History

Corsica

02

Prehistory, and the Rather Mysterious Palaeoveneti

Some of the most creative cultures grow up from some of the messiest historical composts. The Mediterranean is a case in point, and Italy an extreme case, and its northeast corner as historically messy and creative as any place on this planet. Venetia's earliest inhabitants (5th–4th millennium BC) were shepherds, but little else was known about them until 1991 and the sensational discovery of the '**Ice Man**', who met a violent end on the mountainside some 5,300 years ago; his frozen, miraculously intact mummy is now on display in Bolzano, complete with all his gear and the stone statue steles carved by his Neolithic/early Copper Age contemporaries. Many of the Ice Man's contemporaries were lake dwellers, who built their houses on piles in the water – an art their descendants would one day perfect when they turned the mud flats in a lagoon into Venice. You can see how they lived at Lake Ledro, just above Lake Garda, where one of their lake houses has been reconstructed.

The Ice Man's world was invaded in the Bronze Age (2nd millennium BC) by proto-Celtic tribes from the Caucasus, some of whom settled on the Black Sea in Paphlagonia (now part of Turkey) and others in northeast Italy, settling in the fertile lands between the Alps and the Adriatic. These invaders seem to have been the first of the **Palaeoveneti** (aka the ancient Veneti or even Heneti in some accounts). They maintained contact with their Veneti kinfolk back in Paphlagonia, and the Mycenaean Greeks traded with them and others along the Po near Adria.

Catastrophic floods, war and migrations in the 12th–9th centuries, symptomatic of the great upheavals plaguing the entire Mediterranean at this time, brought the onset of the Western world's first Dark Age. According to Titus Livy, the great Roman historian from Padua, the Veneti living in Paphlagonia had fought as allies of the Trojans under their leader **Antenor**, and in the turmoil after the fall of Troy (c. 1180 BC) Antenor brought his tribes to the promised lands of their cousins, and founded Padua in the same way that Aeneas founded Rome. Livy, of course, wanted to give his folk a pedigree as good as the Romans, and whether or not Antenor and company ever fought at Troy, it is true the Veneti were long considered a race apart, of 'Illyrian' origin, different from the other Italic tribes; in their own myths they were raisers of horses from a place called 'Tessalia'. They were certainly more advanced than Venetia's natives, at least in an equine way: they had light, fast chariots, and knew how to ride.

By the 9th century BC, the Veneti of the coastal areas began to trade again with their old acquaintances across the Adriatic and Black Sea, most notably acting as agents between the Greek world and the wealthy Etruscans of Felsina (Bologna). The inland Veneti became known for their vineyards, cloth and bronze working. The intricate working and detail of their artefacts places them firmly in the Celtic tradition, evidence of Polybius' description, that 'the Veneti differed only slightly from the Gauls in their customs and dress, but had a different language'.

This different language, the Indo-European-based **Venet** or **Venetic**, has been the subject of much debate. Once widespread in Venetia and eastern Lombardy, from

Bergamo as far east as Istria and into the Dolomites, it was first written in the Etruscan alphabet in the 6th century BC. According to some linguists, its closest cousin is Latin prior to its infiltration by Etruscan. Pliny the Elder confirms a bond between the two, and cites the link between people of the Veneti and the ancient (pre-Rome) Latin league of Alba Longa. It makes sense, if Livy and Virgil are to be believed, and the Veneti and Latins both washed ashore in Italy from the east, if not all as glorious descendants of Trojan warriors.

The original Veneti capital was **Ateste** (Este); by the time of their first contact with Rome in the 5th century BC, the Veneti had at least 50 towns, a population reckoned at a million and a half, and a new capital at Padua. This was their golden age, enjoyed even as trouble appeared in this same century, in the shape of **Gauls** who came from over the Alps in wave after wave – and stayed, infiltrating south of Venetia into Etruscan lands north of the Apennines. Extremely talented in art and metalworking, they present the singular paradox of a nomadic people caring little for the comforts of home, and everything for their freedom, yet culturally and technologically up to date.

The Gauls invented one significant though often overlooked military advance – horseshoes – and carried better swords than most of their foes. The native Veneti allied themselves with Rome against them, but got little thanks for it; on the Roman map, everything north of the Rubicon was lumped together as **Cisalpine Gaul**.

The Romans, Rise and Fall

More rumblings came, this time from the south, as **Rome** gradually subjugated the Etruscans, Latins and neighbouring tribes. The little republic with the military camp ethic was successful on all fronts, and a sack by marauding Gauls in 390 BC proved only a brief interruption in Rome's march to conquest. Their archenemies, the Samnites, formed an alliance with the Northern Etruscans and Celts, leading to a general Italian commotion in which the Romans beat everybody, annexing almost all of Italy by 283 BC.

All the while, the Romans had been diabolically clever in managing their new demesne, maintaining most of the tribes and cities as nominally independent states (among them Verona, Trieste, Oderzo, Este, Adria, Treviso, Vicenza, Feltre, Belluno and Padua), while planting Latin colonies at important transport nodes (Aquileia, Chioggia, Concordia, Cividale del Friuli, Trento and Altinum, which became the region's biggest port and something of a Roman holiday resort). A major Roman contribution was the great network of roads, beginning with the Via Postumia (148 BC) from Genoa to Verona and Aquileia, and the Via Popilia, linking the Adriatic coast as far south as Rimini, all of which made a truly united Italy seem close to reality.

The northeast, the Roman Tenth Augustine Region of **Venetia et Histria**, 'the flower of Italy, that ornament of the people of Rome', as Cicero once flattered it, actually turned out to be one of the sleepier corners. The famous men it contributed (the poet Catullus, architect-author Vitruvius, the historian Livy) and the events it saw, such as the meeting of Augustus and Herod the Great in Aquileia, made their mark elsewhere. What the Romans loved best about Venetia was its lagoons, a major source of salt (an imperial monopoly). The Veneti preserved fish in salt to create those favourite Roman condiments, *garum* and *allec*, which must have tasted something like Vietnamese fish sauce; they produced it all along the coast from the Po to the River Timavo on an ancient industrial scale, and exported it all over the empire.

The sparsely populated northern section of what is now Alto Adige was conquered in AD 15 by Augustus' stepson, Nero Drusus, as a buffer between Italy and the hostile Germanic tribes. These mountains were divided into the Imperial provinces of **Raetia** (along with Switzerland) and **Norico** (along with Austria) which, if anything, were even sleepier than Venetia et Histria. The Romans did, however, busy themselves with more roadworks in the Dolomites, laying out the originals of the modern *autostrade* that link Italy with the great Alpine passes.

The 2nd century AD saw the emergence of the well-known north–south economic divide in Italy. The south – the former lands of Magna Graecia – ruined by Hannibal, impoverished by the Roman Republic, now sank deeper into decline, wrecked by foreign competition. In the north, a sounder economy led to the growth of new centres; in Venetia Padua, Verona and Aquileia were among the most prominent. On balance, though, Italy was becoming an increasingly less significant part of the empire, both politically and economically. Of the 2nd-century emperors, fewer came from Italy than from Spain, Illyria or Africa.

By the 3rd century, the legions were no longer the formidable military machine of Augustus' day. In 256 the **Franks** and **Alemanni** invaded Gaul descending as far as the Adige, and in 268 much of the east detached itself from the empire under the leadership of Odenathus of Palmyra. Somehow Rome recovered and prevailed, under four soldier–emperors led by **Diocletian**, who completely revamped the structure of the state and economy, replacing it with a gigantic bureaucracy. Taxes reached new heights as people's ability to pay them declined, and society became increasingly militarized. The biggest change was the division of the empire into halves, each ruled by a co-emperor called 'Augustus'; the Western Emperors after Diocletian usually kept their court at army headquarters in Milan, and Rome itself became a marble-veneered backwater.

The confused politics of the 4th century are dominated by **Constantine** (306–37), who ruled both halves of the empire, and favoured Christianity, by now the majority religion in the east but largely identified with the ruling classes and urban populations in Italy and the west. But even the new faith wasn't able to stay the disasters that began in 406. Visigoths, Franks, Vandals, Alans and Suevi overran Gaul and Spain. Italy's turn came in 408, when Western Emperor **Honorius**, ruling from the empire's new capital of Ravenna, had his brilliant general Stilicho (who himself happened to be a Vandal) murdered. A Visigothic invasion followed, including Alaric's sack of Rome in 410. St Augustine, probably echoing the thoughts of most Romans, wrote that the end of the world must be near. Rome should have been so lucky; judgement was postponed long enough for **Attila the Hun** to pass through Italy in 451, decimating Venetia, uprooting its vineyards and burning Padua and Altinum to the ground.

So completely had things changed, it was scarcely possible to tell the Romans from the barbarians. By the 470s, the real ruler in Italy was a Goth general named **Odoacer**, who led a half-Romanized Germanic army and thought of himself as the genuine heir of the Caesars. In 476, he decided to dispense with the lingering charade of the Western Empire, and had himself crowned King of Italy at Pavia. In the confusion, Venetia was left as a province of the Eastern Empire, but a faraway and fairly autonomous one. The fall of Rome was to prove its big chance; Attila in his rampage had indirectly founded a new city of refugees called **Venice**.

The Dark Ages

In Italy, the Dark Ages were never as dark as common belief would have it. One key to understanding the period is that the Roman cities never entirely disappeared. A few expired totally, like Altinum, but most of the rest shrank to provincial market centres, their theatres, arenas and aqueducts abandoned. Amidst the confusion of Rome's fall, popes and monks and battling barons, Goths, Greeks and Lombards were weaving a strange cocoon for Roman Italy. From its silence, centuries later, would be born a new Italian people, suddenly bursting with talent and energy.

Odoacer's government was a peaceful parenthesis for Italy until Byzantine Emperor Zeno, in 488, commissioned young **King Theodoric of the Ostrogoths** to invade, a ploy meant to take Ostrogoth pressure off Constantinople. Odoacer's army was waiting, but the Goths defeated them decisively near Verona. Most of the peninsula was speedily occupied, though Odoacer held out in impregnable Ravenna for another three years. At last Theodóric tricked him out with a promise to share Italy with him, then performed the traditional murder at what was supposed to be a reconciliation banquet.

Despite that black mark, Theodoric – a strapping fellow with long Asterix moustaches, typical of the half-cultured, half-barbaric protagonists of the Roman twilight – reorganized his new dominions with remarkable sophistication. Inheriting a civil service that had come down from Odoacer, and before him the empire, Theodoric used it well to stabilize his realm. The Church was a harder nut to crack. In the disorders of the first barbarian invasions, the Roman pope and scores of local bishops had achieved a great degree of temporal power, filling the vacuum left by the collapse of the Roman system. This temporal power gave the Church a diabolical incentive to oppose any strong government in Italy – especially one of heretical Arian Christians. Theodoric, himself, had no use for theological disputes, but his policy of religious tolerance proved as intolerable to the Church as his Arianism. Most of his subjects, at least, were thankful for it.

The old guard Romans and Veneti, however, continued to regard the Goths as usurpers; religious bigotry grew, and many looked towards Constantinople in hopes of a restoration of legitimate government. Embittered and increasingly paranoid, Theodoric died in 526, leaving as heir a young grandson named Athalaric, who, with his good Gothic warrior's upbringing, drank himself to death. His mother Amalasuntha was then forced to marry her cousin Theodahad, who had her murdered. With no strong hand in control, the kingdom was ripe for mischief. There was no doubt in anyone's mind: the next move would come from Constantinople.

The Eastern Empire had just the right sort of emperor to take up the challenge: the great **Justinian**. Amalasuntha's murder in 536 gave him his excuse to invade Italy, in the person of his young and brilliant general **Belisarius**. The historical irony was profound; in the ancient homeland of the Roman Empire, Roman troops now came not as liberators, but as foreign, largely Greek-speaking, conquerors. Belisarius, and his successor, the eunuch Narses, ultimately prevailed over the Goths in a series of terrible wars that lasted until 563, but the damage to an already stricken society and economy was incalculable.

Italy's total exhaustion was exposed a mere five years later, when the **Lombards**, a Germanic tribe who drank out of their enemies' skulls and otherwise worked hard to earn the title of barbarians, overran the north, setting up their capital at Cividale del Friuli. Although first sharing Italy with semi-independent Byzantine dukes, the Exarchs (Byzantine Viceroys) of Ravenna, and the remarkable new trading city of Venice, the Lombards, under the ruthless and crafty **King Aistulf**, saw their chance to go for the whole boot. Aistulf conquered almost all of the Byzantine Exarchate; in 753, even the old Imperial capital of Ravenna fell into his hands. If the Lombards' final solution were to be averted, the popes would need help from outside. The logical people to ask were the Franks.

At the time, the popes had something to offer in return. For years, the Mayors of the Palace had wanted to supplant the Merovingian dynasty, but lacked the appearance of legitimacy that only the pageantry of the papacy could provide. At the beginning of Aistulf's campaigns, Pope Zacharias quickly gave his blessing to the change of dynasties, and **Pepin**, the new king of the Franks, sent his army over the Alps, in 753 and 756, to foil Aistulf's designs. His unsuccessful attempt to tame Venice, which refused to take sides, helped set the city on its idiosyncratic track.

By 773 the conflict remained the same, though with a different cast of characters. The new Lombard king was Desiderius, the Frankish; his cordially hostile son-in-law **Charlemagne**, who also invaded Italy twice (in 775 and 776), deposed his father-in-law and took the Iron Crown of Italy for himself. In 799, Pope Leo III set an imperial crown on his head, resuscitating not only the idea of empire, but of an empire that belonged to the successors of St Peter, to dispose of as they wished. It changed the political face of Italy for ever, beginning the contorted *pas de deux* of pope and emperor that was to be the mainspring of Italian history through the Middle Ages.

With the disintegration of Charlemagne's empire, Italy reverted to a finely balanced anarchy. In Venetia, forests and marshes replaced the ravaged and abandoned farmland, creating a physical as well as a psychological barrier between the precocious maritime city of Venice and the people who remained on the mainland. For the latter, the 9th and early 10th centuries were a bad time of endless wars of petty nobles and battling bishops, forcing many cities to look to their own resources, defending their interests against Church and nobles alike. An invasion by the Magyars from Hungary in the early 10th century forced the cities to build their first walls and the rural nobles their first castles, which became a source of control over the populations who sought their shelter – hence the origins of the fabulous Este family, and the demonic Ezzelini.

A big break for the cities came in 961, with the invasion of the German **Otto the Great**, the conqueror of the Hungarians, at the request of the powerful Count of Tuscany at Canossa. Otto deposed the last feeble King of Italy, Berengar II, married his widow and was crowned Holy Roman Emperor in Rome the following year. Not that any of the Italians were happy to see him, but the strong government of Otto and his successors beat down the great nobles, gave more power to the bishops, and allowed the growing cities to expand their power and influence. A new pattern was established; the Germanic emperors would be meddling in Italian affairs for centuries, not powerful enough to establish total control, but at least usually able to keep out important rivals.

The Rise of the *Comuni*

Like the rest of Christendom, Italy looked ahead to the year 1000 fearing nothing but the worst – the old legends prophesied that this nice round number would bring with it the end of the world. Perhaps only historical hindsight could see the sprouts of new life and growth that were appearing everywhere on Italian soil at this time, perhaps most remarkably symbolized by the building of St Mark's in Venice. In the towns, business was very good, and the political prospects even brighter. The first mention of a truly independent *comune* (a term used throughout this book, meaning a free city-state; the best translation might be 'commonwealth') was in Milan, in 1024; before long similar *comuni* appeared in Verona, Padua, Vicenza and Treviso.

Throughout this period the papacy had declined greatly in power. In the 1050s, a remarkable monk named Hildebrand controlled papal policy, working behind the scenes to reassert the influence of the Church. When he became pope himself in 1073, **Gregory VII** immediately set himself in conflict with the emperors over the issue of investiture – whether the church or secular powers would appoint church officials. Fifty years of intermittent war followed, including the famous penance in the snow of **Emperor Henry IV** at Canossa (1077) and his donation, that same year, of the lands of Friuli, from the Cadore to Slovenia and Istria, to the **Patriarchate of Aquileia**. Elsewhere, the cities of the north used the long struggle between pope and emperor as an opportunity to increase their influence, and in some cases achieve outright independence.

A different fate was in store for the Dolomites. Keen to keep the road to Rome open and well disposed for their all-important papal coronations, the German emperors in the 1020s made powerful feudal princes of the bishops at the crossroads towns of **Trento** and **Bressanone**. As time went on, the vassals of the bishop-princes were equally keen to escape their overlords' clutches, and they littered the mountains with castles to defend their relatively autonomous fiefs.

Guelphs and Ghibellines

While all this was happening, of course, the **First Crusade** (1097–1130) occupied the headlines, partially a result of the new militancy of the papacy begun by

Gregory VII. For Italy, and especially for Pisa and Genoa, with plenty of boats to help ship Crusaders, the affair meant nothing but pure profit. Venice sat this Crusade out, not wanting to disrupt its own trade in the East, but it quickly moved to get in on the new action. It also financed the continued independence of the *comuni*, with a big enough surplus for building projects like Verona's San Zeno and Padua's Palazzo della Ragione. After a thousand years, Venetia and the other cities of the north were as prosperous as they had been in Roman times. Nor had those good old days ever been forgotten. Free *comuni* in the north called their elected leaders 'consuls' or 'senators', and artists and architects turned ancient Roman styles into the Romanesque.

Emperors and popes were still embroiled in the north. **Frederick I Barbarossa** of the Swabian dynasty of the Hohenstaufen was strong enough back home in Germany, and he made it the cornerstone of his policy to reassert imperial power in Italy. Beginning in 1154, he crossed the Alps five times, molesting free cities that asked nothing more than the right to fight one another continually. After he brutally sacked and pillaged Lodi and Milan, the cities forgot their differences and formed a united front called the **Lombard League**, and joined up with **Pope Alexander III** (whom Frederick had exiled from Rome in favour of his antipope) to defeat him in 1176. Frederick was forced to recognize Italian freedoms and, equally galling, he was forced to kiss Alexander's foot in Venice. For all that, Frederick triumphed south of the Alps when he arranged a marriage that left his grandson **Frederick II** not only emperor but King of Sicily, thus giving him a strong power base in Italy itself.

The second Frederick's career dominated Italian politics for 30 years (1220–50). With his brilliant court, in which Italian was used for the first time (alongside Arabic and Latin), his half-Muslim army, his processions of dancing girls, eunuchs and elephants, he provided Europe with a spectacle the like of which it had never seen. The popes excommunicated him at least twice, while all Italy divided into factions: the **Guelphs**, under the leadership of the popes, supported religious orthodoxy, the liberty of the *comuni*, and the interests of their emerging merchant class. The **Ghibellines** stood for the emperor, state economic control, the interests of the rural nobles, and religious and intellectual tolerance.

When fierce family feuds tore Verona apart (the germ of the Romeo and Juliet story), Frederick appointed his lieutenant in the region, **Ezzelino III da Romano**, as *podestà* to restore order. As he dragged the rebellious Guelph *comuni* of Padua, Vicenza and Treviso back into the imperial fold, Ezzelino, the first of the Italian self-made despots, or *signori*, was so wickedly effective that he earned the nickname 'the son of Satan' (*see pp.54–5*). Frederick's other campaigns and diplomacy in the north met with very limited success; nothing he gained was secure, revolts were frequent, and the Bolognese defeated and captured his son, Enzo, in 1249. Frederick died the next year.

To fight Frederick's other son, Manfred, Pope Urban IV set an ultimately disastrous precedent by inviting in foreign assistance, in the person of **Charles of Anjou**, brother of the King of France. As protector of the Guelphs, Charles defeated Manfred (1266) and murdered the last of the Hohenstaufens, Conradin (1268). He held unchallenged sway over Italy until 1282, creating the perfect conditions to produce a whole new crop of Ezzelino wannabes in every town, until the revolt of the **Sicilian Vespers** started the wars up again. By now, however, the terms Guelph and Ghibelline had ceased to have much meaning; men and cities changed sides as they found expedient, and the old parties began to seem like the black and white squares on a chessboard. If your neighbour and enemy were Guelph, you became for the moment Ghibelline, and if he changed so would you.

Some real changes did come out of all this sound and fury. In 1208 Venice hit its all-time biggest jackpot when it diverted the **Fourth Crusade** to the sack of Constantinople, winning for itself a small empire of islands in the Adriatic and Levant. Other cities fell under the rule of military despots, the *signori*, whose descendants would be styling themselves counts and dukes – the da Carrara of Padua, the della Scala of Verona, the da Camino in Treviso. Everywhere the freedom of the *comuni* was in jeopardy; after so much useless strife the temptation to submit to a strong leader often proved overwhelming. Still, trade and money flowed as never before; cities built new cathedrals and incredible skyscraper skylines, with the tall tower-fortresses of the now urbanized nobles. Above all, it was a great age of culture. The time of Guelphs and Ghibellines was also the time of Dante (*b.* 1265) and Giotto (*b.* 1266).

Renaissance Italy

This paradoxical Italy continued into the 14th century, with a golden age of culture and an opulent economy alongside continuous war and turmoil. With no serious threats from any other foreign power, the myriad Italian states were able to menace each other joyfully without interference. By now most wars had become a sort of game, conducted on behalf of cities by bands of paid mercenaries, led by a hired captain called a *condottiere*, who were never allowed to enter the cities themselves. The arrangement suited everyone well. The soldiers had lovely horses and armour, and no real desire to do each other serious harm. The cities were usually free from grand ambitions; everyone was making too much money to want to wreck the system. Best of all, the worst schemers and troublemakers on the Italian stage were fortuitously removed from the scene. With the election of the French **Pope Clement V** in 1303, the papacy moved to Avignon, a puppet of the French king and temporarily without influence in Italian affairs.

By far the biggest event of the 14th century was the **Black Death** of 1347–8, in which it is estimated that Italy lost one-third of its population. The shock brought a rude halt to what had been 400 years of almost continuous growth, though its effects did not prove a permanent setback to the economy. In fact, the plague's grim joke was that it actually made life better for most who survived; working people in the cities, no longer overcrowded, found their rents lower and their labour worth more, while in the country farmers were able to increase their profits by tilling only the best land.

By now the peninsula was split into long-established, cohesive states pursuing different ends and often warring against each other. Italian statesmen well understood the idea of a balance of power long before political theorists invented the term, and most of them probably believed Italy was enjoying the best of all possible worlds. Foremost among the major states was Venice, the oldest and most glorious, with its oligarchic but singularly effective constitution, and its exotic career of trade and contacts with the East (*see* Venice 'History' pp.110–16). The Venetians waged a series of wars against archrival Genoa, finally exhausting her after the **War of Chioggia** in 1379. Once serenely aloof from Italian politics, Venice then added to her sea realms a small land empire, including by 1428 Udine, Treviso, Verona, Padua, Vicenza, Belluno, Brescia and Bergamo. One city she subdued but never captured was Adriatic rival Trieste, which in 1382 had come under the protection of the Austrian emperors. Meanwhile in the north, the independent bishop-princes of Trento ruled what was in effect a demilitarized zone between Venice's ambition and the formal vassals of Trento who had managed to achieve real independence: the Counts of Tyrol, and their soon to be dominant 14th-century successors, the **Habsburg** dynasty.

Meanwhile, the Renaissance – the new art and scholarship that began in Florence in the 1400s from a solid foundation of medieval accomplishment – found a happy home in northeast Italy. Masters like Giotto (back in 1309), Donatello, and Antonello da Messina spent time in the region, leaving seeds of the imagination for Venetia's artists. Asolo, under the exiled Queen of Cyprus, became a courtly ideal of Renaissance art and literature, and the University of Padua led Europe in the study of medicine.

The Wars of Italy

The Italians brought the trouble down on themselves, when Duke Lodovico of Milan invited the French King **Charles VIII** to cross the Alps and assert his claim to the throne of Milan's enemy, Naples. Charles did just that, and the failure of the combined Italian states to stop him (at the inconclusive Battle of Fornovo, 1495) showed just how helpless Italy was at the hands of emerging new nation-states like France or Spain. When the Spaniards saw how easy it was, they, too, marched in, and before long the German emperor and even the Swiss entered this new market for Italian real estate. The popes did as much as anyone to keep the pot boiling. Alexander VI and his son, Cesare Borgia, carried the war across central Italy in an attempt to found a new state for the Borgia family, and Julius II's madcap policy saw him unite the emperor and the Italian states in the **League of Cambrai**, which soundly defeated Venice in 1508, sapping her strength just when it was most needed to fight the Turks. Julius egged on the Swiss, French and Spaniards in turn, before finally crying 'Out with the barbarians!' when it was already too late.

By 1516, with the French ruling Milan and the Spanish in control of the south, it seemed as if a settlement would be possible. The worst possible luck for Italy, however, came with the accession in Spain of the insatiable Habsburg megalomaniac **Charles V**, who got enough loans from the Fugger banks to buy himself the crown of the Holy Roman Empire in 1519, making him the most powerful ruler in Europe since Charlemagne. As soon as he had emptied Spain's treasury, driven her to revolt and plunged Germany into civil war, he turned his tender attentions to Italy. The wars began anew, bloodier than anything Italy had seen for centuries.

Italy in Chains, but Venice Recovers

Two years after the dramatic 1527 **Sack of Rome** by Imperial troops and German mercenaries, Charles V met Pope Clement VII in Bologna for his fateful coronation as Holy Roman Emperor (he was to be the last ever crowned by a pope) and to draw the map of Italy, which, save only the Republic of Venice, was at the mercy of the Spaniards.

It also marked the beginning of the bitter struggles of the **Counter-Reformation**. In Italy, the Spaniards found a perfect ally in the papacy. One had the difficult job of breaking the spirit of a nation that, though conquered, was still wealthy, culturally sophisticated and ready to resist; the other saw an opportunity to recapture by force the hearts and minds it had lost long before.

The job of re-educating Italy was put in the hands of the new Jesuit order; their schools and propaganda machine bored the pope's message deeply into the Italian mind. The Church's **Council of Trent** (1545–63) provided long-needed reforms, and although it was too little too late to bring the Protestants back to the fold, it initiated the creation of sumptuous new churches, spectacles and dramatic sermons that helped redefine Catholicism.

Protected by its lagoon, and clever enough to avoid the Spaniards and most of the Jesuits, Venice quickly recovered its conquered territories of the Veneto lost in the War of Cambrai and went about perfecting a way of life that came to be the envy of Italy (*see* pp.63–6). Venetian artists attained a brilliance and virtuosity never seen before, just in time to embellish the scores of new churches, palaces and villas of the mid-16th-century building boom. On one issue, however, Venice combined with Spain – in turning back the Turkish threat at the **Battle of Lepanto** (1571), a victory that provided a tremendous boost to morale throughout Christendom.

The Age of Baroque

Palladio's country villas for the magnates of the Veneto are landmarks in architecture but were also an early symptom of decay. The old mercantile economy was failing, and the wealthy began to invest their money less productively in land instead of risking it in business. Despite Lepanto, Venice's position in the east continued to be eroded, damaged by the Portuguese discovery of the spice route to the Indies, and by endless warfare with the Turks and the Austrian-backed pirates, the Uskoks, in the north Adriatic. Yet when the chips were down, Venice had the spirit to stand up to Pope Paul V and his Spanish allies during the **Great Interdict** (1606), striking an irreversible blow to papal temporal authority while all Europe watched. It was her last starring role in European affairs, but the Venetians kept their heads and made their decline remarkably serene and a great deal of fun.

Decline was not limited to Venice. After 1600 nearly everything started to go wrong for Italy across the board. The textiles and banking of the north, long the engines of the economy, both withered in the face of foreign competition; the popes soaked whomever they could for money to redecorate Rome. Bullied, humiliated and impoverished, 17th-century Italy tried hard to keep up its prominence in the arts and sciences. Galileo looked through telescopes and taught at Padua, Monteverdi wrote the first operas, and hundreds of talented though uninspired artists cranked out pretty pictures to meet the continuing high demand. Baroque art – the florid, expensive coloratura style that serves as a perfect symbol for the age itself – impressed everyone with the majesty of Church and State. Baroque impresarios managed the wonderful pageantry of Church holidays, state occasions and carnivals that kept the crowds amused; manners and clothing were decorously berserk.

By the 18th century, there were very few painters or scholars or scientists. There were no more heroic revolts either. Italy in this period hardly has any history at all; with Spain's increasing decadence, the great powers decided the futures of Italy's major states, and used the minor ones as a kind of overflow tank to hold surplus princes. Gambling revenues became one of the main props of the Venetian state. The carnival there was extended to six months in order to bring in decadent aristocrats from around Europe; this was the age of blundering spies and scamps like Casanova, of the glittering brilliance of Vivaldi, of Grand Tourists, opera at La Fenice, and Canaletto.

Napoleon and Austrians

Napoleon (that greatest of Italian generals) arrived in 1796 on behalf of the French Revolutionary Directorate, winning at Rivoli north of Verona and sweeping away Austrians, Spaniards, the pope, the bishop-princes of the Dolomites and the doge, replacing them with the '**Cisalpine Republic**' and '**Kingdom of Illyria**' in the east. Italy woke up with a start from its Baroque slumbers, and local nobles gaily joined the French cause. In 1799, however, while Napoleon was off in Egypt, the advance through Italy by an Austro-Russian army, aided by Nelson's fleet, restored the status quo.

In 1800 Napoleon returned in a campaign that saw the great victory at Marengo, which gave him the opportunity once more to reorganize Italian affairs as the nation's self-crowned king. Napoleonic rule only lasted until 1814, but in that time important public works were begun and laws, education and everything else reformed after the French model; immense Church properties were expropriated, and medieval relics everywhere put to rest – including the Venetian Republic, which Napoleon for some reason took a special delight in liquidating.

The French, however, soon outstayed their welcome. Besides hauling much of Italy's artistic heritage off to the Louvre, implementing high war taxes and conscription (some 25,000 Italians died on the Russian front), and brutally repressing a number of local revolts, they systematically exploited Italy for the benefit of the Napoleonic élite and the crowds of speculators who came flocking over the Alps. When the Austrians and English came to chase all the little Napoleons out, no one was sad to see them go.

But the experience had given Italians a taste of the opportunities offered by the modern world, as well as a sense of national feeling that had been suppressed for centuries. The 1815 **Congress of Vienna** put the clock back to 1796; indeed the Habsburgs and Bourbons thought they could pretend the Napoleonic upheavals had never happened, and the political reaction in the territories was fierce. The only major change from the *ancien régime* was that all of Venetia now unwillingly (except for the South Tyrol) belonged to **Austria**.

The Risorgimento and United Italy

Simmering discontent kindled into action across Italy in the revolutionary year of 1848. On 22 March, the fire spread to Venice. The Austrian authorities simply fled, and the Venetian Republic was back in business. Within a few days, a democratic assembly was elected; leadership passed to **Daniele Manin**, a lawyer who had distinguished himself in liberal struggles in Venice for a decade. A day after the events in Venice, **King Carlo Alberto** of Piedmont-Savoy declared war on Austria.

At first, the odds seemed to favour Piedmont, the strongest state and leading force in Italian unification. Austria's army was disorganized and outnumbered, and for the time being it could expect little help from Vienna. The Piedmontese won early victories, but under the timid leadership of the king they failed to follow them up. The Austrians fell back to the firm base of their defences in Italy, the circuit of fortresses called the Quadrilateral (Peschiera, Verona, Mantua and Legnano, in the western Veneto). Here they won a resounding victory, at Custozza, on 25 July, that knocked Piedmont ingloriously out of the war.

Shutting out the disappointments of 1848, Venice put up a brave and determined resistance. Though blockaded by the Austrian fleet, the Venetians nevertheless had a large quantity of arms and men to complement the natural protection of their lagoon in withstanding a siege. The Austrians bombarded the city continuously from May of 1849. An outbreak of cholera, as much as a total absence of outside support, decided the issue. The city surrendered on 22 August.

Despite failure on a grand scale, at least the Italians knew they would get another chance. Unification was inevitable, but there were two irreconcilable contenders for the honour of accomplishing it. On one side, the democrats and radicals dreamed of a truly reborn, revolutionary Italy, and looked to the popular hero **Garibaldi** to deliver it; on the other, moderates wanted the Piedmontese to do the job, ensuring a stable future by making **Vittorio Emanuele II** King of Italy. Vittorio Emanuele's minister, the polished, clever Count Camillo Cavour, spent the 1850s getting Piedmont into shape for the struggle, building its economy and army, participating in the Crimean War to earn diplomatic support, and plotting with the French for an alliance against Austria.

War came in 1859, just as a rebellion chased the pope's troops out of Bologna. The French and Piedmontese defeated Austria in two inconclusive, extremely bloody battles, at Magenta and Solferino. Piedmont annexed Lombardy and the Marches, and the armistice of 1850 was arranged so that France picked up Nice and Savoy, while Tuscany, Emilia-Romagna and the duchies of Parma and Modena went to

Piedmont. These gains were increased in the next two years, when Garibaldi and his Thousand picked up Sicily and the south.

With Austria still in control of Venetia, most Italians felt that the first duty of the nation was to complete the work of unification. The logical place to look for an ally against Austria was with Bismarck and **Prussia**, then preparing for the climax of their own nation's struggle for unification. In April 1866, Italy and Prussia signed a treaty, proposing the Veneto as reward for Italian aid in the imminent war with Austria. That war was not long in coming. Hostilities began in June, and before the year was out the Italians had been decisively defeated on land, at Custozza (again) and on sea, at Lissa. Fortunately for them, Von Moltke's Prussian army was causing even greater embarrassments to the Austrians up north. The Veneto and western Friuli joined Italy – a gift from Prussia.

Despite popular feeling, and its conquest by Garibaldi, Trentino remained a part of Austria, as did eastern Venezia Giulia. In these regions secret revolutionary committees for unity with Italy soon gave politics a new word: 'irredentism', from *irredenta* or 'unredeemed'. Unfortunately the price of their 'redemption' as part of Italy was to cost the country dear – its entrance into the First World War.

After 1900, with the rise of a strong socialist movement, strikes, riots and police repression often occupied centre stage in Italian politics. But at the same time new industries, at least in the north, made the country a fully integral part of the European economy. The 15 years before the war, prosperous and contented ones for many, came to be known by the slightly derogatory term *Italietta*, the 'little Italy' of modest bourgeois happiness, an age of sweet Puccini operas, the first motorcars, blooming 'Liberty'-style architecture, and Sunday afternoons on the beach.

War, Fascism and War

Besides the hope of gaining Trentino, Trieste and Istria, Italy's blind leap into the **First World War** was influenced by a certain segment of the intelligentsia who found *Italietta* boring and disgraceful: followers of the artistic Futurists and the perverse, idolized poet **Gabriele D'Annunzio**. Venetia saw the bulk of the fighting – especially along the Piave and Isonzo rivers, at Asiago and at Monte Grappa. Italian armies fought with their accustomed flair, masterminding an utter catastrophe at Caporetto (October 1917) that any other nation but Austria would have parlayed into a total victory. No thanks to their incompetent generals, the poorly armed and equipped Italians somehow held firm for another year, until the total exhaustion of Austria allowed them to prevail at **Vittorio Veneto**, capturing some 600,000 prisoners in November 1918.

In return for 650,000 dead, a million casualties, severe privation on the home front and a war debt higher than anyone could count, Italy received Trieste, Gorizia, Trentino, and the South Tyrol up to the natural frontier of the Brenner Pass, where many German-speakers, who suddenly found themselves Italian, began in turn a new Irredentist movement, yearning to be reunited with Austria.

Led somehow to expect much more, Italians felt they had been cheated, and nationalist sentiment increased, especially when D'Annunzio led a band of freebooters to seize the half-Italian city of Fiume in September 1919, after the peace conferences had promised it to Yugoslavia. The Italian economy was a shambles and, at least in the north, revolution was in the air. The trouble had encouraged extremists of both right and left, and many Italians became convinced that the liberal state was finished.

Enter **Benito Mussolini**, a professional intriguer with bad manners and no fixed principles. Before the war he had found his real talent as editor of the Socialist Party paper *Avanti!* – the best it ever had, tripling the circulation in a year. When he decided that what Italy really needed was war, he left to found a new paper, and contributed mightily to the jingoist agitation of 1915. In the postwar confusion, he found his opportunity. A little bit at a time, he developed the idea of Fascism, at first less a philosophy than an astute use of mass propaganda and a sense of design. With a little discreet money supplied by frightened industrialists, Mussolini had no trouble finding recruits for his black-shirted gangs, who had their first successes bashing Slavs in the city of Trieste.

The basic principle, combining left- and right-wing extremism into something the ruling classes could live with, proved attractive to many Italians, and a series of weak governments chose to stand by while the fascist *squadre* cast their shadow over more and more of Italy. Mussolini's accession to power was the result of an improbable gamble. In the particularly anarchic month of October 1922, he announced that his followers would march on Rome. **King Vittorio Emanuele III** refused to sign a decree of martial law to disperse them, and there was nothing to do but offer Mussolini the post of prime minister. At first, he governed Italy with undeniable competence. Order was restored, and the economy and foreign policy handled intelligently by non-fascist professionals. Mussolini increased his popularity by singling out especially obnoxious unions and corrupt leftist local governments for punishment. However, in the 1924 elections, despite the flagrant rigging and intimidation, the Fascists won by only a slight majority.

Mussolini evolved a new economic philosophy, the 'corporate state', where labour and capital were supposed to live in harmony under a syndicalist government control. But the longer Fascism lasted, the more unreal it seemed, a patchwork government of Mussolini and his ageing cronies, magnified and rendered heroic by cinematic technique – stirring rhetoric before oceanic crowds, colourful pageantry, magnificent, larger-than-life post offices and railway stations built of travertine and marble, dashing aviators and winsome gymnasts from the Fascist youth groups on parade. In a way it was the Baroque all over again, and Italians tried not to think about the consequences. In the words of one of Mussolini's favourite slogans, painted on walls all over Italy: 'Whoever stops is lost.'

Mussolini couldn't stop, and the only possibility for new diversions lay with the chance of conquest and empire. His invasion of Ethiopia and his meddling in the Spanish Civil War, both in 1936, compromised Italy into a close alliance with Nazi Germany. Under Hitler's prodding, Mussolini invited all the unhappy German-speakers in the Alto-Adige to leave, which they immediately did, in droves. Nevertheless, Mussolini's confidence and rhetoric never faltered as he led an entirely unprepared nation into the biggest war ever. The Allies invaded; the Germans poured in divisions to defend the peninsula. In 1943 they set Mussolini up in a puppet state called the Italian Social Republic at **Salò** on Lake Garda. In September, the Badoglio government finally signed an armistice with the Allies, too late to keep the war from dragging on another year and a half, as the Germans made good use of Italy's difficult terrain to slow the Allied advance. Meanwhile Italy finally gave itself something to be proud of: a determined, resourceful Resistance that established free zones in many areas, and harassed the Germans with sabotage and strikes. The *partigiani* caught Mussolini in April 1945, while he was trying to escape to Switzerland; after shooting him and his mistress, they hung him by the toes from the roof of a petrol station in Milan.

1945–the Present

Postwar Italy *cinema-verità* – Rossellini's *Rome, Open City*, or De Sica's *Bicycle Thieves* – captures the atmosphere better than words ever could. In a period of serious hardships that older Italians still remember, the nation slowly picked itself up and returned things to normal. The eastern border with Yugoslavia was the most lingering problem in the north – **Trieste**, as the major bone of contention, was made a neutral zone from 1947 to 1954, when it was finally given to Italy in exchange for what bits of Istria it still controlled.

A referendum in June 1946 made Italy a republic, but only by a narrow margin. The first governments fell to the new **Christian Democrats** under Alcide de Gasperi, the party that would run the show for decades in coalitions with a preposterous band of smaller parties. The main opposition was provided by the Communists, surely one of the most remarkable parties of modern European history. With the heritage of the only important socialist philosopher since Marx, Antonio Gramsci, and the democratic and broadminded leaders Palmiere Togliatti and Enrico Berlinguer, Italian Communism took the moral high ground and stayed there.

Modern Venetia

In Venetia, with its history of separateness from the rest of Italy, there is a growing interest in reviving the glories of the *Serenissima*. New groups such as the Società Filologica Veneta have sprouted up, with the goal of defending the Veneto language and culture, and there's a Liga Veneta for greater regional autonomy and greater recognition for the German-speakers in the Süd Tirol. As of 1998, it has been possible for anyone to take classes in Venetic, and listen to long-winded arguments about how the Palaeoveneti were Celts (one of Bossi's favourite topics), in the hopes of showing that they aren't like the rest of the Italians and should therefore go their separate ways.

But, truer to the spirit of the once great cosmopolitan Republic of Venice, the natives seem rather more impressed with their economy. The Veneto has become a vast metropolis of four and a half million people, connected by the A4 highway. Its economy, with a gross domestic product of over $95 billion, is larger than that of Israel and Greece; its exports are worth more than those of Portugal and Argentina. People talk of the 'Veneto model' that has evolved since the war, creating a climate that encourages small, mainly family-run businesses (some 65 per cent are of recent origin) aimed towards the export market, employing a devoted workforce making something that is unique or at least better than foreign competition: Benetton is a case in point. Luxury goods (fashion, jewellery, housewares and everything else related to the cleverly promoted mystique of Italian design) are a mainstay, just as they were during the Renaissance and Middle Ages. Before the war, 60 per cent of the work was in agriculture; today only six per cent of the population are farmers, while the unemployment rate, at a measly 5 per cent – microscopic in European terms – has brought emigrants from around the world in search of a job. As a result, this has restored some of Venetia's old international feel, which is especially noticable the further east you go. If old Venice is cosmopolitan because of international tourism, Trieste can also be thought of in the same way as a result of its unique and new-found status as Mitteleurope on the Med.

Trieste and the border country of Friuli remains very much torn between its Italian, Austrian and Slovenian identities with a veneer of tolerance disguising a deep and lasting distrust and sometimes hate, left over from the dictatorships of Mussolini and Tito, two world wars and one civil war. When the Bishop of Gorizia dared to say a prayer in Slovenian during a Mass at San Giusto, many of the congregation started to stamp their feet to express their disapproval of his gesture of conciliation and he was urged to stop the reading by one of his peers. Old feelings die hard.

The same goes for Alto Adige: many German speakers do not react well to your speaking Italian and may be resentful and unhelpful, and the German version of place names is the norm. At times speaking English is often better than struggling on in pigeon Italian.

The economic miracle that began in the 1950s continues today, propelling the Italians into sixth place among the world's national economies. 'God made the world and Italy made everything in it,' was the slogan of the 60s. The rotten Christian Democratic corruption behind the glittering mask was revealed in the early 1990s, when a small group of judges and prosecutors in Milan took a minor political kickback scandal and from it unravelled the golden string that held together the whole tangle of Italian political depravity – what the Italians call the *tangentopoli*, or 'bribe city'. The Christian Democrats and the Socialists, the two leading parties, collapsed like a house of cards, leaving a vacuum filled by a jostling array of new parties and personalities, none of whom so far has been able to put the brakes on the merry-go-round of Italian politics: noisiest of all was media tycoon **Silvio Berlusconi**'s rightest Forza Italia, which won Mr Television a brief tenure as prime minister in 1994.

Plagued by allegations of scandals and bribery, Berlusconi was soon forced out by the more enduring, middle-of-the-road Olive Tree coalition of **Romano Prodi**, with the support of the former Communists. Prodi's stringent economic measures allowed Italy to squeak into Euroland in January 1999, but led to the Communists' withdrawing their support of his government in late 1998, and giving it to **Massimo d'Alema**'s DS (Democratici di Sinistra) party. But the D'Alema government did not last long either, and was replaced by yet another coalition of the left headed by former Craxian minister Giuseppe Amato. Berlusconi returned to power in 2001, with no obviously strong rival, but in a delicately balanced coalition with Fini and Bossi, both far-right politicians. While a regular figure of fun, Berlusconi remains extremely powerful, with a finger in every pie: no one seems to want to admit voting for him, but millions did and probably would again. Berlusconi is known for his double-breasted suits, hair transplants and crocodile smile.

Alberto Fini, the frontman of the former neo-Fascist MSI party, now heads the **Alleanza Nazionale** (name changed, line-up hasn't) and is one of the jokers in the Italian deck alongside Milanese lawyer Umberto Bossi, the on–off ally of Berlusconi as well as the only Italian political figure to dress badly since the time of King Aistulf. Bossi's new Lombard League, or **Lega Nord**, was around even before the *tangentopoli*, breaking through in the 1990 elections in Lombardy; by 1994 he had united with similar northern leagues to form the Lega Nord. Although many of the Lega's positions change by the hour, its basic tenet of federalism, to cut out the voracious politicians and bureaucrats of Rome and allow the wealthy north of Italy to keep more of its profits for itself, has understandably struck a deep chord in Venetia. In September 1996, Bossi attracted a lot of attention by declaring the north (as far south as Umbria and the Marches) as the independent Republic of Padania, and made a three-day march down the Po to Venice. Unlike Mussolini's march on Rome, the whole affair turned out to be a badly staged comedy, although it did put federalism, perhaps on the Spanish model, a little higher up on the politicians' agenda.

In September 2003 Bossi launched a highly publicized campaign to make Milan Italy's capital city instead of Rome, which caused uproar. Meanwhile, Fini, flying in the face of Fascist tradition, despite representing the former far-right MSI party, brought in a controversial bill to give legal immigrants the right to vote. Xenophobic Bossi was outraged by the very idea. The proposal has now been sidelined. In July 2004 Bossi suffered a serious stroke and quit his post.

In May 2006, Romano Prodi was elected as prime minister following the narrow victory of his **l'Unione** coalition over the Casa delle Libertà, led by Silvio Berlusconi. Giorgio Napolitano was voted in as the new President. Massimo D'Alema is the acting Foreign Secretary. There have now been 60 governments since the end of the Second World War.

Art and Architecture

03

Venetia produced one of the three great schools of Italian art – not a spiritual or intellectual school like the Tuscan, or anything half as imposing or classical as the Roman, but an art of visual delight and sensuality. A love of decoration, of gold and glitter and gorgeous colours is the thread that links the glimmering richness of the 11th-century Byzantine-style mosaics of St Mark with the effervescent sparkle of Tiepolo in the 18th century.

Architecture was showy too – you'll find little of that sombre, rusticated stone monumentality that characterizes Tuscany or Rome, but palaces meant to dazzle, and villas set like gems in the landscape.

Palaeoveneti (8th–2nd centuries BC)

The mysterious Palaeoveneti excelled in metalwork, and many of their artefacts are indistinguishable from Celtic styles of production. The museums in Este and Adria have the most extensive collections of Palaeoveneti and other pre-Roman objects, but all the archaeology museums in Venetia contain evocative bits and bobs. Among the most striking works of this period are the little metal plaques, or *laminette*, from the 5th century BC, engraved with warriors and women and displayed in the Santa Corona museum, in Vicenza.

Roman Art (3rd century BC–5th century AD)

Roman art may have been derivative of Etruscan and Greek models, but it showed a special talent for mosaics, portraiture, wall paintings and glasswork; architecturally, the Romans were brilliant engineers, grand exponents of the arch and inventors of concrete. **Verona** is one of the best places in Italy to admire their ability to build large and well, with the Ponte della Pietra, the ancient theatre, Porta dei Borsari, and especially the Arena, a pink marble oval that rivals the Colosseum in size and grandeur. The city was the birthplace of Vitruvius, the only classical writer on architecture whose works have come down to us.

Aquileia was one of the few great Roman cities that died completely in the early Middle Ages. Although its marbles were pillaged by the Venetians and others, it still remains the most evocative Roman and Early Christian archaeological site in the region, with beautifully preserved Roman and palaeo-Christian mosaics and a fine museum.

The so-called 'Villa of Catullus' (actually a bath complex) at **Sirmione** on Lake Garda is one of Italy's most poetic ruins. Other Roman odds and ends remain in **Trieste** (theatre, gate, museum), and in the museums of **Padua**, **Oderzo** and **Venice**. The latter has a fair share of Greek originals as well, donated by collectors, although none that can match Venice's finest Greek work – the four horses of St Mark, the only surviving bronze *quadriga* from antiquity.

Dark and Early Middle Ages (5th–10th centuries)

Artistically, at least, the decline of Rome was a bonus for Venetia, especially when Emperor Honorius transferred the capital of the Western Empire to nearby Ravenna. Although Roman sculpture and painting were already degraded, mosaics thrived, as they were a decorative art patronized by the rich. It was a strange time; a 5th-century chronicle declares: 'Those who are alive perish from thirst, while corpses float in the water…priests practise usury and Syrians sing psalms…eunuchs learn the art of war and barbarian mercenaries study literature.'

The Greek artists working in Ravenna drifted into Venetia – the 7th-century frescoes in the cathedral crypt in **Adria** are a rare record of their migration. Their still, 'hieratic' art, really an inheritance from decadent Rome, was to remain prominent until the 13th century, and found its greatest expression in mosaics, where highly stylized, spiritual beings live in a gold-ground paradise, with no need of shadows or perspective or other such worldly tricks. Beautiful examples remain at **Aquileia** and **Grado**, and at **Torcello** in Venice, where the style lingered long enough to adorn St Mark's. In architecture, forms that originated in the time of Constantine prevailed – basilican churches, derived directly from Roman law courts and octagonal baptistries.

In the 7th–10th centuries, while Byzantine artists painted and mosaiced their ethereal, almond-eyed creatures, the native population under the Lombards produced works in a vigorous style that had little use for Roman or Byzantine models. Instead of mosaics, the Lombards' talent lay in architecture, sculpture and metalwork. The churches and museum of **Cividale del Friuli**, the capital of a Lombard duchy, contain unique sculptures and reliefs from the 8th century. More art from the period awaits in the Castelvecchio museum in **Verona**, and in the Dolomites: rare 8th-century Lombard frescoes in the church of San Procolo at **Naturno**, along with Carolingian churches and frescoes in an unusually excellent state of preservation, in the **Val Monastero** and in **Malles Venosta**, hugging the Swiss frontier.

Veneto-Byzantine and Romanesque (11th–12th centuries)

By the 11th century, Venice had taken over the artistic crown in northeast Italy from Ravenna, in a typically lavish if rather conservative way: the Veneto-Byzantine style of the magnificent mosaics and Pala d'Oro in St Mark's basilica is still ninety per cent Byzantine. But influences from other parts of Italy were seeping into the heart of the lagoon: the vigorous reliefs of the Labours of the Months on St Mark's central portal, St Mark's campanile and the church of SS. Maria e Donato in Murano are in the new Romanesque style from Lombardy.

Lombard Romanesque churches are characterized by broad, triangular façades, blind arcading, gabled porches, rib vaulting, and presbyteries raised above the nave and crypt. The best examples are in **Trento** (the Duomo) and in **Verona**, near the Lombard frontier (the Palazzo della Ragione, S. Fermo, S. Lorenzo, the Duomo and, most magnificently, San Zeno, with its superb Romanesque decoration and unique bronze doors, a 'poor man's Bible' that predates the church by a century). Other architects in the 12th century opted for a Veneto-Byzantine and Romanesque compromise, as in the Friulian abbey of Santa Maria in Sylvis in **Sesto al Reghena**, the hodgepodge S. Giusto in **Trieste**, and Santa Sofia in **Padua**. In the next century Padua would witness the most amazing Veneto-Byzantine-Romanesque wedding of all, in the fabulous multidomed basilica of St Anthony.

The 11th and 12th centuries also saw the erection of urban skyscrapers by the nobility: family fortresses and towers built when the *comuni* forced the barons to move into the towns. Larger cities once had hundreds of them, and although municipal authorities gradually succeeded in having most of them demolished, **Rovigo** still has two of the oldest and crookedest. This same period is marked by an epidemic of castle building, especially in the Dolomites; some have charming courtly frescoes from medieval romances (Castel Sabbionara, at **Avio**; Castel Roncolo, **Bolzano**; Castel Rodengo, near **Rio di Pusteria**).

Gothic and Early Renaissance (13th–14th centuries)

The Italians never really appreciated Gothic; trapped in their Roman sensibilities and snobbishness, they looked on the soaring flying-buttressed cathedrals from the Île-de-France as barbaric. Still, they weren't entirely immune to its charms. Bonino's ornately chivalric Scaliger tombs in **Verona** are a prime example of what they could do when they bothered. Most Italian Gothic, however, is austere, coinciding with back-to-basics Franciscan and Dominican religious revivals of the 13th century, and resulting in piously plain Gothic-barn churches that loom over city rooftops like beached whales. Among them are S. Nicolò in **Treviso**, Santa Corona in **Vicenza**, the Frari and SS. Giovanni e Paolo in **Venice**, and the most beautiful, the Dominican Santa Anastasia in **Verona**.

At that time the Venetians were rolling in riches gained from the Fourth Crusade (1204), and for their secular buildings they took Gothic and twisted it merrily round to suit their flamboyant, cosmopolitan tastes. Gothic arches took on Byzantine and Islamic designs, and plain walls were enlivened with coloured marbles in different shapes and patterns, reliefs, round *paterae* of semi-precious stones, and even gold. The resulting hybrid, Venetian Gothic, became the city's own distinct style, seen in scores of magnificent palaces from the Fondaco dei Turchi to the Ca' d'Oro, and culminating in the Palazzo Ducale. Venetian Gothic became so closely identified with Venice that the style took on a second life in the 16th century, in public buildings designed to mark the Republic's presence on the *terra firma* (**Udine**'s Piazza della Libertà and **Belluno**'s Palazzo dei Rettori).

In painting, the colourful, decorative fairy-tale style called International Gothic also lingered longer in Venetia than elsewhere in Italy. The great Pisanello of Pisa and Stefano da Verona were its major exponents in **Verona**; in **Venice** painters like Paolo Veneziano, Jacobello del Fiore and Michele Giambono and the Vivarini family remained popular into the 15th century. Other jewels of the period to seek out include the delightful fresco cycles in **Trento**'s Castello di Buonconsiglio and the cathedral cloister at **Bressanone**.

The Gothic spirit endured for centuries in the Dolomites, especially in polychrome sculpture and ornate altarpieces that often combine a powerful expressiveness with a love of rich decoration; the two greatest masters, Michael Pacher and Hans Klocker, are represented in the excellent collections at **Bolzano** and **Bressanone**. In Trentino, the joys of Gothic were prolonged into the 16th century by the Baschenis family; Simone's striking *Dance of Death* on the cemetery church of **Pinzolo** is as memorable as it is retro, even by Venetian standards.

In Tuscany, the 14th century was one of the most exciting and vigorous phases in Italian art, when great imaginative leaps occurred in architecture, painting and sculpture. In 1308, the most influential of all early Tuscans, Giotto, left the Veneto the seeds of the future in the Cappella degli Scrovegni or Arena Chapel in **Padua**, teaching local artists about forms in space, composition, and a new, more natural way to paint figures. His chief followers of the Paduan school, Altichiero and Menabuoi, frescoed Padua's baptistry, oratory of San Giorgio and the Eremitani Church; another, Tommaso da Modena, left beautiful works in **Treviso** and almost nowhere else. Other anonymous Giottoesque painters roamed as far afield as **Bolzano** (the Domenicani Church) and **Feltre** (SS. Vittore e Corona).

The Renaissance of the *Quattrocento* (15th century)

The visit to **Padua** by Giotto was followed up in the next century by the prolonged stay of another Tuscan genius, Donatello; the perfect harmony and classical calm of his great equestrian statue of Gattamelata, and his complex reliefs in the Basilica of Sant'Antonio, were a formative influence on Venice's Lombardo and Bon families, as well as on Antonio Rizzo of Verona. The Lombardi and Bons went on to create an overwhelming share of **Venice**'s best Renaissance churches, palaces, sculptures and tombs, along with Mauro Codussi, who instilled a certain amount of Tuscan order and classicism into the Venetian imagination.

The great revolution in Venetian painting began in the mid-15th century, and owes much to the brothers-in-law Andrea Mantegna and Giovanni Bellini. Mantegna influenced generations of artists and sculptors with his strong interest in antiquity, his scientific perspective, and his powerfully sculpted figures, while Giovanni Bellini (*see* pp.55–7) perfected a luminous oil painting technique used to express natural light and rich, autumnal colours. Other major figures of the *quattrocento* include narrative masters Gentile Bellini and Vittore Carpaccio, the more rustic Cima da Conegliano, and the more elegant Carlo Crivelli.

The Venetian High Renaissance and Mannerism (16th century)

While the rest of Italy, increasingly oppressed by reaction and war, followed the artists of Rome in learning drawing and anatomy, the Venetians followed Giovanni Bellini and his obsession with the expressive qualities of atmosphere and colour. The shooting star among his many pupils was Giorgione of Castelfranco, a major if tragically short-lived figure in the new manner; his *Tempest* in the Accademia is a remarkable study in brooding tension. Giorgione is credited with inventing 'easel painting' – art that served neither Church nor State nor the vanity of a patron, but stood on its own for the pleasure of the viewer.

Another Bellini alumnus, Titian, the High Renaissance master of the Venetian school, was a revolutionary in his own right. He was one of the first painters to put the 'art' into art with his dramatic compositions and striking tonal effects produced by large brushstrokes, or even finger-painting. His contemporary, Tintoretto, took these Mannerist tendencies to extremes, while Paolo Veronese painted lavish canvases that are the culmination of all that Venice had to teach in decoration and magnificence. Veronese's followers, Zelotti, Battista Franco and others, laboured beaverishly across the Veneto, filling patrician villas with allegories, mythologies and virtues.

One of the greatest sculptors in *cinquecento* Venice was Jacopo Sansovino, who adapted his training in Tuscany and Rome to create a distinctive Venetian architectural style, richly decorated with sculpture and classical motifs. He was greatly admired by Andrea Palladio, whose creamy white temple-fronted villas – as characteristic of the rural Veneto as Venetian Gothic is of Venice – would inspire architects as far away as England and colonial America (*see* pp.59–63). Palladio's colleague and artistic heir, Vincenzo Scamozzi, added a Mannerist touch that became the rage for the following century in the Veneto, even when the more populist Baroque style squashed Mannerism and its intellectual fancies elsewhere in Italy.

Baroque and Rococo (17th and 18th centuries)

Art shall move to devotion the heart of the beholder.
The Council of Trent

As an art designed to induce temporal obedience and psychological oblivion, Baroque's effects are difficult to describe. On the whole, however, history saw that little of its most excessive moods (as in Rome or Naples) touched Venetia; the Venetians kicked the Jesuits out, and the Spaniards had little influence in the Republic. In short, the 17th century saw more of the same Palladian villas, Venetian palaces, atmospheric painting and decorated churches, but squared into Baroque. The age does provide some exceptions to the rule that in art, less is more: the churches of La Salute in **Venice** and the Inviolata in **Riva del Garda**, or the uncanny paintings of Francesco Maffei of **Vicenza**, the furniture of Andrea Brustalon (Ca' Rezzonico, in **Venice**) or the gardens of the Villa Barbarigo in **Valsanzibio**.

In the 18th century Venice bloomed like Camille on her death bed, when its charming, elegant school of painting was in demand across Europe, thanks almost entirely to one figure: Giambattista Tiepolo. Tiepolo's buoyant ceiling art and narrative frescoes, shimmering with light, added a fresh, scintillating rococo fizz to Veronese's grandeur. If Giotto's Cappella degli Scrovegni is the majestic overture in the art of Italian fresco, Tiepolo's Villa Valmarana in **Vicenza** and the Palazzo Labia in **Venice** are the grand finale.

Less majestic but extremely popular 18th-century figures include Antonio Canaletto, who produced countless views of Venice snapped up by English and French travellers on the Grand Tour; another now famous painter of views, proto-Impressionist Francesco Guardi, had to wait until the 19th century to gain recognition. Pietro Longhi, their contemporary, devoted himself to little genre scenes that offer an insight into the Venice of 200 years ago; Rosalba Carriera's pastel portraits were the rage of Europe's nobility. While Venetian architect Giorgio Massari translated their rococo sensibility into stone, specializing in churches that doubled as concert halls, in the countryside neo-Palladian villas grew bigger and bigger in Venice's hectic *Götterdämmerung*: Villa Pisani on the **Brenta Canal** and Villa Manin near **Passariano** in Friuli are monsters of the genre.

Neoclassicism, Romanticism and Other -isms (19th and 20th centuries)

Whatever artistic spirit remained at the end of the 18th century evaporated with Napoleon and remained evaporated for a long time. Although Europe's greatest neoclassical sculptor, Antonio Canova, hailed from **Possagno** in the northern

Veneto, he left very few of his pseudo-Greeks and Romans in the region. The Habsburgs built an entire new neoclassical quarter for **Trieste**, and Giuseppe Jappelli left his famous coffeehouse in **Padua** and designed romantic gardens for villas. Good collections of 19th-century art can be seen in Palazzo Pesaro (**Venice**) and the Museo Revoltella (**Trieste**).

Italians began to regain some of their artistic panache in the 20th century. The first years saw new grand hotels built on Venice's **Lido** and **Lake Garda**, many with a delightful Liberty-style (Italian Art Nouveau) touch. Other artistic trends also came from elsewhere. There was Futurism, an artistic movement that made dynamism, velocity and modernity its creed (**Rovereto**'s museums) and at the same time, the so-called Metaphysical school led by Giorgio de Chirico and Carlo Carrà, filled with a hallucinatory nostalgia and stillness; the Peggy Guggenheim museum in **Venice** has a good representative collection.

The Fascist style (Art Deco at the service of Mussolini's illusions of grandeur) often makes us smile, but as the only Italian school in the last two hundred years to achieve a consistent sense of design it presents a challenge to all modern Italian architects. Venetia has only a few examples: the Palazzo del Cinema on the Lido in **Venice**, war monuments in **Trieste**, **Trento** and **Rovereto**. **Bolzano** for its part got the very mixed blessing of a whole new Fascist quarter – Mussolini's way of asserting Italian domination over the German-speaking population.

In 1946, Renato Guttuso and Emile Vedova founded an avant-garde group in Venice, the Fronte Nuova, but without much noticeable improvement in the local art scene, then or now. Misplaced atavism prevented the construction of Frank Lloyd Wright's palace on the Grand Canal (although, when the same authorities vetoed a hospital designed by Le Corbusier, even Corby agreed they were right).

But **Venice** does get its share of contemporary art, in special exhibitions and at the Biennale, although at times the latter has all the panache of a Eurovision art contest. Besides the Peggy Guggenheim, northeast Italy reveals some excellent collections of modern and contemporary art – most notably in **Trento**, **Verona**, **Udine** and **Rovereto** – and a new museum is being developed in Bolzano.

Artists' Directory

This short list of the principal architects, painters and sculptors of Venetia is bound to exasperate partisans of some artists and do scant justice to the rest, but we've tried to include those who produced the most representative works in the region.

Altichiero (da Zevio; 1320–95): top Veronese painter of his day, and a talented follower of Giotto (S. Anastasia, S. Stefano, Verona; Oratorio de S. Giorgio, Padua).

Antonello da Messina (*c.*1430–79): a Sicilian painter who visited Venice. Antonello became one of the first Italians to perfect the Van Eyckian oil-painting techniques of Flanders; his compelling mastery of light, shadows, and the simplification of forms was a major influence on Giovanni Bellini (see the great but damaged Pietà in the Museo Correr, Venice).

Basaiti, Marco (1470–*c*. 1530): student and collaborator of Alvise Vivarini (Accademia, Venice).

Baschenis, Simone (*c*. mid-16th century): precise, expressive Lombard painter with a Gothic sensibility; undeservedly obscure, only because he left his best work in tiny Alpine villages (*Cycles of Dance of Death* at Pinzolo and Carisolo in the Val di Non).

Bassano, Jacopo (da Ponte; 1510–92): son of village painter Francesco senior and head of a clan of artists working mainly from Bassano del Grappa, from where they took their name. Jacopo began by painting in the monumental style of Parmigianino, but is better known for cranking out a succession of religious night scenes in rustic barnyards that became increasingly dramatic *à la* Tintoretto. Of his four painter sons, Francesco the Younger (1549–92) was his most skilled assistant and follower, until he jumped out of a window; the more prolific Leandro, less so (Palazzo Ducale, Venice; Cartigliano; also the museums in Vicenza and Bassano).

Bastiani, Lazzaro (*c*. 1420–1512): probably Carpaccio's master, and the painter responsible for the charming 'Baby Carpaccios' in Venice's S. Alvise.

Bella, Gabriel (1730–99): painter of city scenes, a valuable source of information about 18th-century Venice despite their sublime ineptitude (Palazzo Querini-Stampalia).

Bellini, Gentile (1429–1507): elder son of Jacopo, famous for his meticulous depictions of Venetian ceremonies and narrative histories (*Miracles of the True Cross*, Accademia, Venice). Unfortunately, his histories painted for the Doge's Palace were lost in the fire.

Bellini, Giovanni (1435–1516): the greatest early Renaissance painter of Northern Italy. No artists before him painted with such sensitivity to light, atmosphere, colour and nature; none since has approached the almost magical tenderness and empathy he conveyed in his Madonnas and other religious works (Accademia, San Zaccaria and the Frari in Venice; S. Corona, Vicenza). *See* also 'Still the Best: Giovanni Bellini', pp.55–7.

Bellini, Jacopo (1400–70): pupil of Gentile da Fabriano, father of Giovanni and Gentile, father-in-law of Mantegna, all of whom were influenced by Jacopo's beautiful drawings from nature (in the Louvre and British Museum); in Venetia his best works are his Madonnas, more natural and lifelike than others of his generation (Accademia, Venice; Castelvecchio, Verona).

Bon, Bartolomeo (*d*. 1464): prolific Venetian sculptor and architect, who worked with his brother Giovanni to produce some of Venice's most lavishly decorative work (Porta della Carta and statues of the Ducal Palace, Ca' d'Oro).

Bonifazio, Veronese (Bonifazio de' Pitati; 1487–1553): native of Verona who moved to Venice and fell under the spell of Titian and company; as he rarely signed anything, secondary paintings in their style have been so often attributed to him that he has become posthumously one of the most prolific painters of his generation.

Bonino (*c*. 1335–75): flamboyant Gothic sculptor from Campione (Lake Lugano), the cradle of northern builders and sculptors; in Verona he carved most of the Scaliger tombs.

Bordone, Paris (1500–71): from Treviso, a pupil of Titian and follower of Giorgione, whose pastoral landscapes were a seminal influence on his work and earned him commissions from across Europe (*The Presentation of the Ring of St Mark to the Doge*, Accademia, Venice, is his masterpiece; a close second is *Scuola del Carmine*, Padua).

Brustalon, Andrea (1662–1732): from Belluno, rococo sculptor and furniture maker of imagination and whimsy (Ca' Rezzonico, Venice; Museo Civico, Belluno).

Campagnola, Domenico (1500–50s): adopted son and pupil of the great Paduan engraver Giulio Campagnola, a student of Mantegna; like Giulio he made bucolic landscapes a speciality (Scuola di S. Rocco and Scuola del Carmine, Padua).

Canaletto, Antonio (Giovanni Antonio Canal; 1697–1768): master of meticulous, colourful and postcard-accurate Venetian *vedute*, or views, but the best place to see them is in England – there is only one in the Accademia, and two in the Ca' Rezzonico (Venice).

Canova, Antonio (1757–1821): born in Possagno near Asolo, a neoclassical celebrity sculptor – the favourite of Napoleon and Benjamin Franklin and everyone in-between, including the popes, one of whom made him Marchese d'Ischia. The Museo Correr in Venice has a naturalistic early work, *Daedalus and Icarus*, but most of his sculptures went elsewhere; his studio in Possagno is now a museum of casts, while the village is crowned with a huge temple he built to hold his ashes. The Museo Civico in Bassano del Grappa features many of his cartoons and studies.

Caroto, Giovanni (1480–1555): not the greatest Veronese artist, but an endearing one; the Big Carrot is best known for his portrait of a child in the Castelvecchio; also works in S. Fermo, both in Verona.

Carpaccio, Vittore (*c.* 1465–1525): a probable student of Gentile Bellini and the most charming of Venetian artists, with fairy-tale paintings full of documentary details from his life and times. The distinctive red tones he loved gave his name to paper-thin slices of raw beef fillet (major cycles at Scuola di S. Giorgio Schiavone and the Accademia; also the *Two Courtesans*, in the Museo Correr, all in Venice).

Carriera, Rosalba (1675–1757): a Venetian portraitist and miniaturist, and the first woman to make a good living as an artist; her soft, pastel portraits were the rage of the powdered wig set not only in Venice, but in Paris and Vienna, until she lost her eyesight in 1749 (Accademia and Ca' Rezzoni, Venice).

Castagno, Andrea del (1423–57): a Tuscan master of striking form and composition, who visited Venice in 1445 and left the city some Renaissance food for thought in St Mark's and S. Zaccaria.

Catena, Vincenzo (1480–1531): a well-born Venetian merchant, humanist and friend of Giorgione who painted as a hobby, increasingly well as time went on (*Judith*, in the Palazzo Querini-Stampalia in Venice, is his masterpiece).

de Chirico, Giorgio (1888–1978): a Greek–Italian who was one of the founding fathers of the Metaphysical School (1916–18), best known for his enigmatic, often uncanny empty urban landscapes, dotted with classical odds and ends and dressmakers' mannequins (Peggy Guggenheim, Venice).

Cima da Conegliano, Giovanni Battista (1459–1518): whose luminous autumnal colours and landscapes were inspired by Bellini – as Bellini was inspired by several of his compositions (Madonna dell'Orto and Accademia in Venice; Duomo, Conegliano).

Codussi, Mauro (*c.* 1420–1504): architect from Bergamo, who worked mainly in Venice; a genius at synthesizing traditional Venetian styles with the classical forms of the Renaissance (S. Michele in Isola, Venice's first Renaissance church; also S. Zaccaria, staircase at the Scuola di S. Giovanni Evangelista, Palazzo Vendramin-Calergi).

Crivelli, Carlo (*c.* 1435–95): meticulous Venetian enamoured of luminous, perspective, crystalline forms, garlands and cucumbers in his exclusively religious work; he spent most of his time in the Marches (Accademia, Venice; Castelvecchio, Verona).

Depero, Fortunato (1892–1960): a Futurist who moved to a colourful poster-like style (Museo Depero, Rovereto). Examples of his work can be seen in MART in Rovereto.

de Pisis, Filippo (1896–1956): a neo-Impressionist from Ferrara who spent a long period in Venice (Peggy Guggenheim, Venice).

Donatello (1386–1466): from Florence, the greatest European sculptor of the *quattrocento*, never equalled in technique, expressiveness or imaginative content. He spent 1443–50 in Padua, casting his Gattamelata statue and sculptures and reliefs for the high altar for the Basilica di S. Antonio, a major inspiration to young Andrea Mantegna; also a statue in the Frari, Venice.

Falconetto, Giovanni Maria (1468–1534): a Veronese architect who built in a charming antiquarian style that inspired Palladio, leading the way in the transformation of Gothic Padua (especially the Loggia della Gran Guardia and Loggia Cornaro) into a Renaissance city; he also designed the villa at Luvigliano in the Euganean Hills.

Fogolino, Marcello (1480–1550): a fine painter originally from Vicenza, who became court artist to prince-bishop Bernardo Cles, introducing the Renaissance to Trento (Palazzo delle Albere and Castello di Buonconsiglio, Trento; Santa Corona, Vicenza).

Giambono, Michele (*c.* 1420–62): one of the princes of Venetian retro; while everyone else moved on to the Renaissance, Giambono was still cranking out rich paintings in International Gothic style (Accademia, altarpieces in St Mark's, Venice).

Gianfrancesco da Tolmezzo (*c.* 1450–1510): was the top *quattrocento* painter in his native Friuli (Castel d'Aviano, San Giorgio della Richinvelda, and Forni di Sopra – his masterpiece).

Giorgione (Giorgio da Castelfranco; *c.* 1478–1510): got his nickname 'Big George' not only for his height, but for the huge influence he had on Venetian painting. Although he barely lived past 30 and only a few paintings are undisputedly by his hand, his poetic evocation of atmosphere and haunting, psychological ambiguity was echoed not only by Titian and Sebastiano del Piombo, his followers, but by his master Giovanni Bellini (paintings in the Accademia in Venice).

Giotto di Bondone (*c.* 1267–1337): a Florentine, one of the most influential painters in history, the first Italian to break away from stylized Byzantine forms in favour of a more 'natural' and narrative style. Although associated with Florence and Assisi, he painted his masterpiece in Padua: the Cappella degli Scrovegni.

Giovanni da Udine (1487–1562): pupil and leading assistant of Raphael, as well as an architect and master of graceful stuccoes and grotesques. In 1552 he was made city architect of his native Udine, and designed the Torre dell'Orologio and fountain in Piazza Matteotti, among other projects.

Giovanni da Verona (1457–1525): a Dominican friar and greatest marquetry artist of the century (S. Maria in Organo, Verona).

Guardi, Francesco (1712–93): brother-in-law of Giambattista Tiepolo and younger brother of Gianantonio (1699–1760) with whom he worked, making early attributions difficult. Guardi's favourite subject was Venice, but his views, unlike Canaletto's, are suffused with light and atmosphere; many canvases approach Impressionism in their handling – hence his revival in the 19th century, after a life of obscurity and poverty (Ca' d'Oro, Accademia, church of Angelo Raffaele, all in Venice).

Guariento (14th century): a follower of Giotto and founder of the Paduan school. His masterpiece, a massive fresco of Paradise in Venice's Ducal Palace, burned in a fire, though fragments hint at what was lost. His work has much of the same humane quality as Giotto (Eremitani, Padua; Museo Civico, Bassano del Grappa).

Jacobello del Fiore (c. 1370–1439): Venetian master of International Gothic, fond of raised gold embossing (Accademia, Venice).

Jappelli, Giuseppe (1783–1852): stylish Paduan neoclassical/eclectic architect and romantic landscape gardener; designed the Caffè Pedrocchi and several other buildings around Padua; Villa Valmarana, Saonara; Villa Selvatico-Capodilista, Rivella; Grand Hotel Orologio in Abano Terme).

Liberale da Verona (c. 1445–1529): genteel painter of frescoes, the Carpaccio of Verona (Duomo, Castelvecchio, S. Fermo).

Lombardo, Pietro (c. 1455–1516): native of Lombardy and founder of Venice's greatest family of sculptors and architects, strongly influenced by the Tuscan Renaissance and antique models (SS. Giovanni e Paolo, S. Giobbe, S. Francesco della Vigna, and his masterpiece, S. Maria dei Miracoli, all in Venice).

Lombardo, Tullio (c. 1455–1532): son of Pietro, with whom he often worked. Lombardo was an exquisite marble-sculptor, best known for his tombs, especially the Vendramin tomb in Venice's SS. Giovanni e Paolo. His brother Antonio (c. 1458–1516) assisted him in the classical reliefs in the basilica of S. Antonio, in Padua.

Longhena, Baldassare (1598–1682): Venetian architect, a student of Scamozzi, whose best work was one of his first commissions: the church of the Salute (also Ca' Pesaro, both in Venice).

Longhi, Pietro (1702–85): there weren't photographers in 18th-century Venice, but there was Pietro Longhi dutifully portraying society's foibles (Ca' Rezzonico, Accademia, Querini-Stampalia, all in Venice; also Palazzo Leoni Montanari, Vicenza). His son Alessandro (1733–1813) was official portrait painter of the Accademia, and in 1762 he published a biography of historical Venetian painters, with portraits of each.

Lorenzo Veneziano (active 1356–79): disciple of Paolo Veneziano (no relation) and painter in a luxuriant, golden International Gothic style (Duomo, Vicenza; Accademia, Venice).

Lotto, Lorenzo (c. 1480–1556): a neurotic Venetian, trained under Giovanni Bellini, best known for religious paintings – some great, some uninspired – and portraits that seem to catch their sitters off guard, capturing on canvas his own restless energy. Lotto was run out of Venice by Titian and Aretino and spent much of his life in the Marches (Accademia, Venice; S. Cristina at Quinto; Pinacoteca and S. Nicolò, Treviso).

Maffei, Francesco (c. 1600–60): from Vicenza, a dissonant and unorthodox Baroque painter, whose nervous brush often brings out the dark side of the age of curlicues (Museo Civico and Oratorio di San Nicola, Vicenza; Castelvecchio, Verona).

Mansueti, Giovanni (c. 1465–1527): an underrated student of Giovanni Bellini and a talented painter of narrative histories (Accademia, Venice; Museo Civico, Vicenza).

Mantegna, Andrea (c. 1420–1506): remarkable painter born near Padua, whose use of antiquity, sculptural forms as hard as coral, and unusual perspectives dominated art in the Veneto until the rise of his brother-in-law Giambellini (Eremitani Church, Padua; San Zeno and Castelvecchio, Verona; Accademia, Venice).

dalle Masegne, Jacobello and **Pier Paolo**: 14th-century Venetian architects and sculptors, influenced by the works of the great Tuscan Nicolò Pisano, creator of a new, realistic, classically inspired style (S. Marco, Venice).

Massari, Giorgio (1687–1766): Venetian architect who collaborated with G. B. Tiepolo and Vivaldi to create some of the most delightful Baroque churches in Venice (La Pietà and Gesuati; also Villa Cordellina-Lombardi in Montecchio Maggiore).

Mazzoni, Sebastiano (1611–78): irrepressible Florentine Baroque master who loved to go over the top (Museo Civico, Padua; Pinacoteca, Rovigo).

Menabuoi, Giusto de' (d. 1397): Florentine painter who followed Giotto to Padua, where his masterpiece is the Baptistry (also the frescoes in the Palazzo della Ragione).

Montagna, Bartolomeo (1450–1523): a painter of heavy dignity inspired by Antonello da Messina, founder of the Vicentine school (Monte Berico; Museo Civico, Vicenza).

Morto da Feltre (Lorenzo Luzzo; 1467–1512): the Dead Man got his unfortunate nickname from his pale complexion, but painted with Giorgione's colours (Museo Civico, Feltre).

Muttoni, Francesco (1668–1747): architect from Como and one of the most talented proponents of the Palladian revival in the Veneto (Palazzo Valmarana-Trento, Vicenza; Villa Da Porto, near Lonigo; Villa Fracanzan-Piovene, Orgiano).

Pacher, Michael (c. 1430–98): of Brunico, one of the leading late Gothic painters and sculptors of the day (Museo Diocesano, Bressanone; Nostra Signora at Gries, Bolzano).

Palladio (Andrea di Pietro della Gondola; 1508–80): the Veneto's most influential architect, not only for his buildings, but for his books and drawings that imaginatively reinterpreted the classics to fit the needs of the day (major buildings in Vicenza, Venice, Piombino Dese, Maser, and on the Brenta Canal). *See* also 'The Gentle Art of Building Villas: Palladio and his Heirs', pp.59–63.

Palma Giovane (Jacopo Palma; 1544–1628): the most prolific painter of his day, the great-nephew of Palma Vecchio and a pupil of Titian, who specialized in large but usually vapid narrative paintings (every church in Venice seems to have at least one).

Palma Vecchio (Jacopo Negretti; *c.* 1480–1528): a student of Giovanni Bellini who successfully adopted the new, sensuous style of Giorgione and young Titian, and is best known for his voluptuous Venetian blondes, often disguised as saints (S. Maria Formosa, Venice; S. Stefano, Vicenza).

Paolo Veneziano (*c.* 1290–1360): the leading painter of his day, a powerful Byzantine influence in Venetian art that would linger longer in the lagoon than elsewhere (Accademia, Venice; Museo Civico, Padua).

Pellegrino da San Daniele (Martin da Udine; 1467–1547): a little-known Renaissance talent from Udine, because he spent much of his life frescoing one church, San Antonio, in San Daniele del Friuli; also look out for the altarpiece in the basilica, Aquileia.

Piazzetta, Giambattista (1683–1754): Venetian Baroque painter extraordinaire, who went to extremes in his use of light and dark, favouring the latter. An early influence on Giambattista Tiepolo, he became the first director of the Accademia (Accademia, SS. Giovanni e Paolo, and other churches, Venice).

Pisanello, Antonio (*c.* 1395–*c.* 1455): originator of the Renaissance medal and one of the leading and most graceful painters of the International Gothic school; he collaborated with Gentile da Fabriano on the lamented lost frescoes in the Doge's Palace (Castelvecchio, S. Fermo, and S. Anastasia, Verona; medals in Ca' d'Oro, Venice).

Pittoni, Giovanni Battista (1687–1767): one of the most popular painters of his day in Venice, who like many went from dark Baroque to a lighter rococo mood under the influence of Tiepolo (S. Corona, Vicenza).

Pordenone (Giovanni de' Sacchis; 1484–1539): Titian's main rival, with a more monumental, Roman style inspired by Michelangelo, combined with quick brushstrokes and often bizarre iconography and expressions; Vasari claims that he was self-taught (S. Giovanni Elemosinario, Venice; Museo Civico, Pordenone; Duomo, Treviso).

Ricci, Sebastiano (1659–1734): decorative painter from Belluno inspired by the scenographic monumentality of Roman Baroque; his work at its best is fresh and colourful, while at other times it shows slapdash haste – Ricci was a terrible womanizer and often had to flee jealous husbands (S. Giustina, Padua; Museo Civico, Vicenza; S. Pietro, Belluno). He often worked with his nephew Marco Ricci (1670–1730; landscapes in the Accademia, Venice).

Il Riccio (Andrea Briosco; *c.* 1470–1532): High Renaissance sculptor and architect and great friend of Humanist scholars, famous for his intricate bronze work and statuettes (Museo Civico, S. Antonio – where the Pascal candelabrum is his masterpiece, also S. Giustina, Padua).

Rizzo, Antonio (*c.* 1445–98): pure Renaissance sculptor and architect from Verona, who worked mostly in Venice (Tron monument, Frari, courtyard of the Palazzo Ducale).

Sammicheli, Michele (1484–1559): born in Verona, sometimes heavy-handed Renaissance architect and sculptor, as well as the Serenissima's masterbuilder of walls and fortifications (walls, Padua; also palaces in Treviso; walls, S. Bernardino and Palazzo Bevilacqua, Verona; Palazzo Grimani, Venice).

Sansovino, Jacopo (Jacopo Tatti; 1486–1570): sculptor and architect from Florence who took his name from his master Andrea Sansovino. Jacopo fled the Sack of Rome in 1527 and came to Venice, where he became chief architect to the Procurators of St Mark's and a good buddy of Titian and poison pen master Aretino. Sansovino created a new Venetian High Renaissance style – the rhythmic use of columns, arches, loggias and reliefs, with sculpture playing an integral role (Venice, where he rebuilt St Mark's Square and designed the famous Library; sculptures in the Ducal Palace; also Villa Garzoni-Michiel, Pontecasale).

Scamozzi, Vincenzo (1552–1616): from Vicenza, Palladio's closest collaborator who completed many of his projects according to his own imagination, and a brilliant Mannerist architect in his own right (villas, palaces and Teatro Olimpico, Vicenza; Procuratie Nuove, Venice; Rocca Pisani, at Lonigo; Via Sacra, Monselice).

Sebastiano del Piombo (Sebastiano Luciani; 1485–1547): a pupil of Giorgione, and a rich autumnal colourist. Sebastiano went to Rome when Giorgione died, and became the chief notary of the Vatican (hence his nickname, for the lead seals that still haunt the Posta Italiana); most works are in Rome, but see S. Giovanni Grisostomo, Venice.

Squarcione, Francesco (*c.* 1394–1474): a Paduan tailor who became a self-taught painter, one of the first antique dealers, and teacher of Mantegna; unfortunately, not much of his documented work survives beyond a polyptych in the Museo Civico, Padua.

Stefano da Verona (or da Zevi; *c.* 1375–1450): delightful International Gothic master, lead painter in Verona in the generation after Turone (S. Fermo Maggiore, Castelvecchio, Verona).

Tiepolo, Giambattista (1691–1770): Venice's rococo wizard, generally considered the greatest European painter of the 18th century. He initially worked in the style of Piazzetta, but soon left all that gloomy *chiaroscuro* behind for one of the most colourful palettes in art; Tiepolo's subjects, many mythological, live in the delightful warm afterglow of Venice's decline (Palazzo Labia, Scuola dei Carmini and Gesuati, Venice; Villa Valmarana, Vicenza; Oratorio della Purità and Museo Diocesano, Udine; Villa Pisani, Strà).

Tiepolo, Giandomenico (1727–1804): son of Giambattista, with whom he frescoed Villa Valmarana. While he could imitate his father's grand heroic manner to the point that attribution of some frescoes could go either way, Giandomenico's work tends to be more introspective and often wistful, especially his masquerades (Ca' Rezzonico, S. Polo, Venice; parish church, Desenzano del Garda).

Tintoretto (Jacopo Robusti; 1518–94): was given his name 'little dyer' because of his father's profession. A proud, ill-tempered workaholic, his ideal was to combine Michelangelo's drawing with the colouring of Titian, but his most amazing talent was in his visionary, unrestrained and original composition, often delighting in startling sleight-of-hand foreshortening. His most talented follower was a Greek who ended up in Spain – El Greco (Scuola di S. Rocco series; the world's largest painting, in the Palazzo Ducale; Accademia and S. Giorgio Maggiore, all in Venice; also Museo Civico, Vicenza).

Titian (Tiziano Vecellio; *c.* 1480s–1576): from Pieve di Cadore in the Dolomites; he became, with the death of Giovanni Bellini, official painter to the Venetian Republic. Generally regarded as the greatest painter of the Venetian school, Titian was a pupil of Giovanni Bellini at the same time as Giorgione, and followed the latter so closely that many of his early works have often been attributed to his colleague. Titian made his reputation with the monumental altarpiece of the *Assumption* in Venice's Frari, a bold handling of form and colour that cast a spell on Tintoretto, Veronese and countless others. In his long career, his work evolved through several phases, influenced by Mannerism in the 1540s after a trip to Rome, and then in his last years, taking his revolutionary free brushwork to an extreme, most violently in his last unfinished work, the *Pietà* in the Accademia. Although Titian spent most of his life in Venice, his international reputation saw most of his canvases scattered across Europe: Emperor Charles V was such an admirer that he made Titian a Count Palatine, an extraordinary honour for a painter. Besides the Frari altarpieces, Venice keeps a few of his works in S. Salvatore, the Accademia, the Salute; also the cathedrals of Treviso and Verona.

Tommaso da Modena (*c.* 1325–76): delightful, humane 14th-century painter, a follower of Giotto who worked for a long period in Treviso (church and seminary of S. Nicolò, also S. Caterina); also in Castelvecchio, Verona.

Troger, Paul (1698–1762): Tirolese rococo painter, trained by Giuseppe Maria Crespi in Bologna and Piazzetta in Venice, before he returned to decorate his native valleys with colourful airy frescoes (Bressanone cathedral, his masterpieces; also altars at Monguelfo, his birthplace).

Tura, Cosmè (*c.* 1430–90): of the Ferrara school, whose singularly intense, craggy and weirdly tortured style is immediately recognizable and, for many, an acquired taste (Museo Correr, Venice).

Turone (active in the 1360s): Veronese master influenced by German miniaturists, teacher of Altichiero (Castelvecchio and S. Anastasia, Verona).

Veronese (Paulo Caliari; 1528–88): the most sumptuous and ravishingly decorative painter of the High Renaissance, fond of striking illusionism, shimmering colours, and curious perspectives, set in Palladian architectural fancies (Villa Barbaro at Maser; Accademia, Ducal Palace, and S. Sebastiano, Venice; S. Corona, Vicenza).

Verrocchio, Andrea del (Andrea di Cioni; 1435–88): painter, sculptor and alchemist nicknamed 'true eye', Verrocchio was a follower of Donatello and teacher of Leonardo da Vinci. The greatest bronze sculptor of the day, he was hired by Venice to create the dynamic equestrian statue of Colleoni.

Vitale da Bologna (active 1330–59): a disarming and guileless fellow who set the tone for Bolognese painting, celebrated in part for the lack of mental effort it requires from the beholder (Museo del Duomo, Udine).

Vittoria, Alessandro (1525–1608): Venetian sculptor, a student of Sansovino and famous for his elegant bronze statuettes and portrait busts (S. Francesco della Vigna, Frari, Ca' d'Oro, Venice).

Vivarini: 15th-century clan of painters from Murano, the chief rivals of the Bellini dynasty in Venice, noted for their rich, decorative and retro style. Antonio (c. 1415–76/84) collaborated with Giovanni d'Alemagna to paint altarpieces (S. Giobbe, Venice); brother Bartolomeo (1432–99) was more imaginative in his use of colour and rhythm (S. Maria Formosa, Frari, Venice); Alvise (1446–1503), son of Antonio, was influenced by Antonello da Messina (Frari, S. Giovanni in Bragora, Venice).

Zelotti, Giambattista (1526–78): from Verona, a collaborator of Veronese who became one of Palladio's chief and most interesting interior decorators (Villa Godi Malinverni, Lonedo di Lugo; Villa Emo, Fanzolo; La Malcontenta, on the Brenta Canal; Il Catajo, Battaglia Terme).

Tales of Tyranny and Harmony

Corsica

04

The Son of Satan

In stark contrast to the benign flock of winged lions left behind by Venice, in Venetia you'll find older, darker relics – walls, castles, towers, prisons and torture chambers – recalling one of the meanest *hombres* who ever lived. The very name Ezzelino still evokes a shiver in this part of the world, even though he's been frying in hell for over 700 years. Medieval Italy was precocious in so many ways, in banking, in trade, in art, in architecture, in literature – the list goes on and on. Ezzelino III da Romano was another first: Europe's first self-made tyrant.

He lived in interesting times. Two generations previously, in 1176, the Lombard League, including Verona, Vicenza, Padua, Belluno and Treviso, had battled to win the guarantee of their civic freedoms from the German Holy Roman Emperor, Frederick I Barbarossa. This came as a blow to the Ezzelini, the feudal lordlings of what is now northern Vicenza province and staunch members of the Emperor's Ghibelline party. Now the pro-papal Guelph *comuni* were open rivals, especially Vicenza, which had taken advantage of its new freedoms to snatch a chunk of Ezzelino turf.

Ezzelino hopes rose again with the advent of Barbarossa's grandson, Emperor Frederick II, *Stupor Mundi*, 'the wonder of the world'. A man with a brilliant mind, a poet fluent in six languages, Frederick was the first 'Italian' emperor, having grown up in cosmopolitan Arab-Greek-Norman Sicily. This also made him singularly open-minded and tolerant. But these were the tub-thumping days of the Crusades, and the popes hated him from the start; when he regained Jerusalem in 1229, by treaty rather than by massacring the infidels, the popes excommunicated him.

Frederick hated the popes right back. They presented the biggest obstacle to his plans for a modern centralized empire, and it came as a major blow in 1230 when the *comuni* of northern Italy re-formed the Lombard League, declaring themselves the allies of Pope Gregory IX. It was an act that many *comuni* soon regretted, as Gregory made them prove their allegiance by accepting the Church's new weapon, the Inquisition, to roust out the Paterini and Cathar heretics they had hitherto tolerated. Many of these heretics belonged to the nobility, including Ezzelino II da Romano. Gregory demanded that his son, Ezzelino III, then serving as *podestà* (feudal mayor, or imperial representative) of Verona, turn his father over for burning. The younger Ezzelino refused; it was the only good deed of his life.

Ezzelino III was born in 1194, the same year as Frederick. He was the most skilled military commander of his day, ruthless and ambitious, a bachelor who despised luxury and women. He was also completely devoted to the emperor. In 1234, when Frederick amassed a Saracen army from Sicily (immune from papal bans and excommunications) to attack the *comuni* of the Lombard League, he naturally chose Ezzelino as his lieutenant in Venetia and, in Verona in 1236, put 3,000 German cavalry and his Saracens under his command.

Ezzelino, advised by his astrologers, at once pounced on Vicenza and Padua, then the most powerful city on the *terra firma*. He did this with a brutality shocking even by the standards of the day, torturing his victims to death to extract names of other potential enemies, flinging others into dungeons to starve to death, then killing all their relatives. Stories of his cruelty dominate the literature of the 13th century and feature prominently in the *Cento Novelle Antiche*, gathered together in 1525. His subjects called him the 'Son of Satan'.

Although Frederick regained much of northern Italy, it was at the price of taking the blame for Ezzelino's atrocities and another excommunication. The emperor's colleagues, fearful for their own souls, began to abandon and betray him, and Frederick grew increasingly bitter. If he was alarmed by the monster he had created in the Veneto, he could at least trust him. In 1250, *Stupor Mundi* died of dysentery while preparing to crusade with St Louis in the hope of returning to the pope's good graces. Ezzelino, for his part, was never bothered by remorse. In Padua alone he kept eight overflowing prisons 'notwithstanding the incessant toil of the executioner to empty them'. In 1256 Pope Alexander IV preached an anti-Ezzelino Crusade, offering all who fought him the same indulgences offered to Crusaders in the Holy Land. The offer attracted all the riffraff in Italy, who took Padua by sheer numbers; the gates were opened to welcome the 'liberators' who then raped and pillaged the city for a week. In revenge for that open gate, Ezzelino tortured and killed all but 200 of the 11,000 Paduans in his army.

The Pope's Crusaders were so incompetent that Ezzelino actually grew stronger and gained Brescia when the Ghibellines there delivered their *comune* to him, free of charge. This gave Ezzelino a bad case of hubris, and in 1259, aged 65, he decided to take all of Lombardy and Milan itself, believing the nobles there, as in Brescia, would hand their city to him. Off he marched with the most splendid army of his career, but the Brescians, by now disgusted with his cruelty, had secretly dealt with the Guelphs of Milan, Cremona, Ferrara and Mantua; when Ezzelino was well into Lombardy, at Cassiano on the Adda, the Brescians abandoned him and his enemies closed in. Ezzelino fought until he was severely wounded in the foot. The Guelphs chained him up in the castle at Soncino, where he refused to speak or accept any aid, but furiously tore his bandages off with his teeth and died eleven days later.

His brother, the *podestà* of Treviso, and all his family were slain to make sure the family never plagued Venetia again. But in reality Ezzelino had more than his share of heirs: the mafia-like *signori*, the Carrara of Padua, the Scaligers of Verona, the Visconti of Milan, and the Medici of Florence. In *The Civilization of the Renaissance in Italy* (1860) Jacob Burckhardt wrote Ezzelino's chilling epitaph:

> *The conquests and usurpations which had hitherto taken place in the Middle Ages rested on real or pretended inheritance and other such claims... Here for the first time the attempt was openly made to found a throne by wholesale murder and endless barbarities, by the adoption, in short, of any means with a view to nothing but the end pursued. None of his successors, not even Cesare Borgia, rivalled the colossal guilt of Ezzelino; but the example once set was not forgotten, and his fall led to no return of justice among nations, and served as no warning to future transgressors.*

Still the Best: Giovanni Bellini

Renaissance artists tended to be pernickety proud individualists, not averse to pulling a pistol on one another, and their lives often make for colourful reading.

One great exception to the rule was Giovanni Bellini, who apparently never quarrelled, married, travelled, designed buildings, wrote letters or poetry, hobnobbed with princes, or in brief did anything at all except paint during a career that lasted for 65 years. In most art histories he gets a nod as the father of the Venetian school and master of Giorgione and Titian, but many visitors to the Veneto overlook him, bedazzled by the greater fireworks of the Three Ts (Titian, Tintoretto and Tiepolo). Next to theirs, Bellini's work is very still, but like many quiet voices he often has more to say at the end of the day.

Giambellino, as our ancestors liked to call him, was born in Venice around 1430, with a paintbrush in his baby fist. His father, Jacopo, a student of the great International Gothic master Gentile da Fabriano, was an innovator in his own way; one of the first artists to draw from nature, he also did a number of perspectivist studies in his notebooks. Giovanni and his older brother Gentile learned their craft at their father's knee, but early on they went their separate ways: Gentile inherited Jacopo's workshop and style, while Giovanni inherited his love of the natural world. His heaven was on earth, in the Veneto; his saints were human, and his faith, while pure, was above all humane, and expressed itself not through halos and gold paint, but through a warm and sensuous empathy. Only Raphael, that other great painter of madonnas, had a similar gift. But while Raphael's are beautiful, tender loving mammas bursting with charm, Bellini's have the balance and measure of the *quattrocento*. They are women doing their bit in the divine scheme, brave yet wistful, perhaps knowing what's in store for their *bambino*. They never emote, or appeal for the viewer's sympathy, which makes them all the more poignant.

In 1453, family played another formative role in Bellini's development, when his older sister married Andrea Mantegna. Mantegna, already the top master of perspective in Italy, showed Giovanni how to place solid figures in three-dimensional settings, lessons revealed in a number of works now in Venice's Museo Correr: *Transfiguration*, the *Frizzoni Madonna*, *Crucifixion*, and the *Dead Christ Supported by Two Angels*. Some time around 1460, Andrea and Giovanni both produced paintings from a drawing of *The Agony in the Garden* in old Jacopo's notebooks. Both are in London's National Gallery: Mantegna's landscape is as precise as his figures, while Bellini has a more lyrical bent in his use of colour and light. His most important work of the period, the *Polyptych of S. Vincenzo Ferreri* in Venice's SS. Giovanni e Paolo (1464–8), shows his rapid progress – the pediment, which he painted first, is awkward, but the last figure he added, the Angel Gabriel, is exquisite.

The last key ingredient for Bellini came to Venice with Antonello da Messina in 1475. Antonello had just learned the art of oil painting from Jan Van Eyck, and among the Italians Bellini led the way in adopting the new medium, then mastering it to a degree that few painters since have ever equalled, painstakingly building up colour and depth in transparent glazes, enabling him to achieve a remarkable richness of tone and luminosity. Critics call Bellini's mature style 'tonalism', for its emphasis on light and colour and atmosphere at the expense of design and line. In his experiments, the borders between solids and space begin to dissolve, replaced by melting transitions of light and shadow. Backgrounds and landscapes play a larger role in the composition than they ever had before, until they become as integral to the meaning as the central figures. An early example is the *Saint Francis* (1480, Frick Collection, New York City), while the *Pala Barbarigo* (1484, San Pietro Martire, Murano), the *Pala di San Giobbe* and *Madonna of the Little Trees* (1487, both in the Accademia) represent the culmination.

Bellini's splendid late style dates from around 1500, when he was 70 and could count nearly every young Venetian painter of distinction as a pupil. He was the Official Painter of Venice and had singlehandedly brought his home town into the first ranks of the Renaissance alongside Florence and Rome. But he never stopped learning or innovating. His *Portrait of Doge Leonardo Loredan* (National Gallery, London, 1501) shows the first use of *impasto* (the building up of paint to produce texture) – the first individualist use of a brushstroke and the first step in the great revolution in Western art that would separate art from the object represented. Other beautiful examples of Bellini's late style are the *Baptism of Christ* (Santa Corona, Vicenza) and the sublime *Sacra Conversazione* (San Zaccaria, Venice), where the complex shadings of colour and glazings are sheer wizardry – Leonardo da Vinci's famous *sfumato* technique but in colour, all merging to create a perfect lyrical unity.

And he still had time for young artists. Albrecht Dürer wrote home from Venice in 1507, 'Giambellino praised me in front of many gentlemen. He wanted something done by me, and he came in person to ask me, telling me he would pay me well. And everyone said that it really was very gracious of him to have favoured me in this way. He is very old, but he's still the best in painting.'

And he still had nine good years in him. He greatly admired the work of his pupil Giorgione, who had taken his tonalism a step further by emphasizing mood over matter, and painted for the delight of private patrons. Bellini, after 60 years of painting for Church and State, was ready for a change. Five of his small mythologies remain in Venice's Accademia, while the others are abroad, including the *Feast of the Gods* (1514) in the National Gallery, Washington DC. Perhaps most remarkable of all is his *Lady with a Mirror* (1515) in Vienna's Kunsthistorisches Museum – possibly the most touchingly optimistic and dreamily sensuous work ever painted by an artist in his late 80s, a year before his death.

The Council of Trent

In the 1520s Emperor Charles V, haughty ruler of much of Europe and the Americas, found his Germanic possessions in the throes of the Reformation, and his Catholic domains bracing themselves for a hysterical reaction. A staunch Catholic himself, Charles sought to heal the rift by asking the pope to call a council – an idea first suggested by Luther himself – to look into some urgently needed reforms in the Church. Pope Clement VII refused point blank (the last thing any pope wanted was a revival of Counciliarism, with the threat that papal authority could be overruled in a general council), but after Charles V taught him a lesson by sacking Rome in 1527, Clement agreed that perhaps a council wasn't such a bad idea after all.

His successor, Paul III, let the uncongenial idea slide until 1538, when the Germans threatened to call a national council of their own, minus the pope. But where to convoke it? Charles insisted that it take place on Imperial turf, while the pope wanted an Italian city where he could influence the outcome. Eventually, Trento, an Italian city ruled by a prince-bishop under the Holy Roman Empire, proved to be the perfect compromise. After more delays, the Council finally convened in Trento in December 1545 to study the three goals Paul III had placed before it: to reunite Christendom, reform the Church's administration and procedures, and form a league of Christian princes against the Turks.

The Council had hardly begun when a typhus epidemic sent the prelates scurrying off to Bologna for safety, and it was another six years before a new pope, Julius III, ordered them back to Trent. Other events in Germany, such as the military advance of the Protestant princes, soon caused a new break-up. The last session of the Council, under Pius IV, met for two years, from January 1562 to December 1563, when a long list of decrees were promulgated and approved by the pope.

If the Council of Trent had signally failed to unite the Christians (after all the dithering, it was far too late for compromise) or unite their princes against the Turks, it did result in a new, unified, clear-cut doctrine to confront the Protestant threat. This provided for vast improvements in pastoral care and the education of priests, and an end of clerical concubinage; there was to be a new edition of the Bible and a new catechism. In the face of Protestant doubt, the rites of the Seven Sacraments in themselves were confirmed as signs of grace (the spiritual state of the minister or recipient being incidental), and the Office of Propaganda was created to convert Protestant (and other) unbelievers.

The Council's last salvos, decided at the last minute during the last session, were aimed straight at the Protestants, confirming the existence of Purgatory, the veneration of saints, images and relics, and the value of indulgences. The Counter-Reformation had blasted off, and the 'Jesuit style', precursor of the Baroque, incorporating all the richness, pomp and sensuality that the Protestants hated, inspired a wave of church building to provide a visual symbol for the new Catholicism. It was a hothouse orchid that blossomed on a scorched and increasingly fearful Christendom.

In his famous *History of the Council of Trent* (first published in 1619, in London), Paolo Sarpi, the great Venetian monk and historian, called the controversies in Trent 'the *Iliad* of our age' and believed that the resulting Council's doctrines were an unmitigated disaster. According to Sarpi, the original goal of its well-meaning leaders – the restoration of the primitive Church, poor and democratic, to coax back the Protestants – had been distorted by the political intrigues of the Roman Curia, Jesuits and Spaniards.

This Council, which pious men desired and procured to reunite the Church (which was beginning to split apart), has, on the contrary, made the split a permanent one and the parties to it irreconcilable. It was planned by the princes to reform the Church; but it has brought about the greatest corruption of the Church since the name of 'Christian' was first heard.

Paolo Sarpi, *History of the Council of Trent*

Sarpi's *Iliad* analogy was certainly right in one respect. Instead of making peace, the Council of Trent turned out to be a Trojan horse for an ever grander, ever more militant Church, re-armed with its most fearful weapon, the Inquisition (reinstated by Paul III), an excess soon followed by the Wars of Religion and the even more horrific Thirty Years War – the worst Europe would see until the 20th century.

The Gentle Art of Building Villas: Palladio and His Heirs

The man who would change the face of Western architecture could not have had a more unlikely background. Andrea di Pietro della Gondola was born in 1508 into a poor family in Padua, who apprenticed him to a stonecutter at the age of 13. Treated harshly, he ran away 18 months later, taking refuge in Vicenza, where he found a job as an assistant with a kinder family of stonecutters. And so he would have remained, chiselling away, had not Dame Fortune smiled on him in 1537 and sent him to the humanist scholar Giangiorgio Trissino, to work on the villa he was redesigning at Crioli, just outside Vicenza.

Able to see a spark in Andrea that no one else had bothered to notice, Trissino became his fairy godfather, teaching him the essentials of a Renaissance education and the principles of classical architecture, especially *De Architectura* of Vitruvius, a treatise that had been rediscovered in the 1400s. The 30-year-old stonecutter blossomed. Trissino proudly introduced him to his humanist cronies in Vicenza, Padua and Venice. He got him his first commission as an architect, designing the Villa Godi at Lonedo di Lugo (1538). At the same time Trissino was working on an epic poem, 'L'Italia liberata dai Goti' (Italy freed from the Goths), with Justinian's General Belisarius and his guardian angel Palladio (from Pallas Athena, the goddess of wisdom) as the heroes. Trissino was so pleased with both the name he invented and his protégé that he united the two for ever in 1540.

To complete Palladio's education, Trissino took him on a two-year study tour of Rome (1540–1), giving him first-hand knowledge not only of the ancients, but of the pioneer architects of his day – Michele Sammicheli, Giulio Romano, Giovanni Maria Falconetto and Sebastiano Serlio. Palladio would return to Rome four times, measuring and analysing; he even wrote a best-selling guidebook to the ruins. Yet rather than direct inspiration, ancient Rome and Vitruvius would act primarily as emotional reference in all his work, as he created idylls that reflected an antiquity that was partly real (notably in Italy, where Roman ruins were everywhere), and partly the dream antiquity that infused the Renaissance. Palladio liked to flatter his villa clients by comparing them to Pliny and Seneca, philosophizing in their country retreats.

But there was far more to Palladio than Roman play-acting; more than any other architect of that talented age, he was able to invent a style that was at once imposing yet sensuous, perfect for his time and place. Venetia's patrician élite, increasingly unable to risk their fortunes in new trade ventures or Middle Eastern derring-do, now sought to escape city business in the summer, seeking a life of balance and harmony in the country, enjoying the beauties of nature while

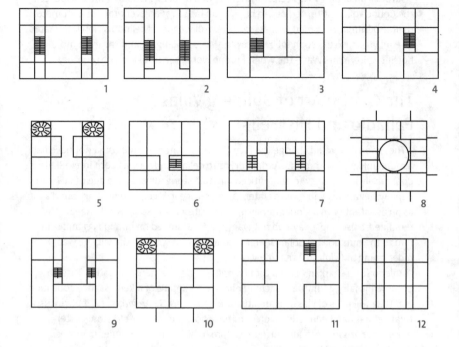

1 Villa Thiene
2 Villa Sarego
3 Villa Badoera, p.199
4 Villa Zeno
5 Villa Pisani, Montagnana
6 Villa Emo, p.203
7 Villa Pisani, Bagnolo
8 La Rotonda, p.232
9 Villa Pojana, p.235
10 Villa Cornaro, p.204
11 La Malcontenta, p.188
12 General pattern of villas

supervising their new-found interests in agriculture. While they required the structures necessary for a working farm (*barchesse*), defence was no longer a consideration, even in the open country; by the time Palladio came on the scene, Venetia had recovered from the War of the Cambrai and was at peace. He led the way in abandoning the old fortified country residence in favour of light and comfort. His famous temple fronts and airy double loggias, derived from his mistaken notions of Roman domestic architecture, were revolutionary in the 16th century and lend the villas an openness and serenity that feel at home in the surrounding countryside.

There are over three thousand of these villas in the Veneto alone. But why are Palladio's eighteen surviving houses the most satisfying? One lesson from Vitruvius that Palladio engraved on his heart was the ideal of harmony and proportion. According to his own writings, the elements of a building must correspond to the whole and to each other, the careful consonance of parts and dimensions that was the original meaning of the word *symmetry*. Within those restrictions, what he called 'the certain truth of mathematics which is final and unchangeable', he managed a subtle variation of size and shape according to each commission, although always with the idea that no matter where one stood inside a villa, the whole would be immediately comprehensible. Rudolf Wittkower, in his *Architectural Principles in the Age of Humanism* (1949), noted that Palladio's dimensions are based on the harmonic proportions of music, as in Pythagoras' musical scale. This was no accident – in the 16th century, music and architecture were praised as the most artificial of arts, based on science alone, and free from attempts to imitate or better nature. The country villa, more than any other building, was an isolated ideal that united the artificial and natural in perfect harmony (*see* below).

Because of the innate classical grandeur of his designs, Palladio didn't need to rely as much as past architects on expensive stone, marbles, reliefs, exterior frescoes and gilding for effect; his finest villas are endowed with a serene clarity and geometric simplicity, all white surfaces and columns, set against lush green lawns and gardens. And as buildings go they were bargains; what looks like stone is cheap brick coated with a sheen of stucco-like material called *intonaco* (one imagines Palladio had seen enough stone for a lifetime in his former career). Most of the capitals crowning the brick columns are made of terracotta, while other features that look like marble are nearly always wood, coated with straw and stucco. Because the villas were only for the summer, there was no need to worry about heating them and no need for expensive tapestries to insulate the walls; frescoes were the answer, a nice family allegory perhaps, or mythological allusions to suit the owner's private fancy.

Architecture Mirrors Music

...in all works it is requisite that their parts should correspond together, and have such proportions, that there may be none whereby the whole cannot be measured, and likewise all the other parts.

I Quattro Libri dell'Architettura Book IV, chapter 5

Based on Pythagoras' musical scale, and the Renaissance concept that architecture can mirror music to reveal the universal harmonic ratios inherent in nature, Palladio proposes seven sets of beautiful and harmonious proportions for rooms:

1 Circular
2 Square (1:1)
3 The diagonal of the square for the room length (1:$\sqrt{2}$)
4 A square plus a third (3:4)
5 A square plus a half (2:3)
6 A square plus two-thirds (3:5)
7 Double square (1:2)

The double square is the *diapason*, or octave, as a lyre string of a given length will produce a note one octave above the note of a string half its size. Two strings of lengths in the ratio of 2:3 will produce harmony, a *diapente*, or musical fifth. If the ratio is 3:4, you get a different harmony, a *diatesseron*, or fourth.

The ratio of 3:5 isn't musical, but it is extremely close to the famous proportion called the Golden Section, found throughout nature and in much ancient and medieval architecture. All of these relationships are commensurable – expressible in whole numbers, and easy for an architect to work with. The non-musical, incommensurable exception, the diagonal of a square, or $\sqrt{2}$, comes straight out of Vitruvius, and is believed to hark straight back to ancient Greek theories of proportions. The Romans never used it in building, and to tell the truth Palladio didn't either.

Unlike Alberti, Michelangelo, Raphael, Sansovino, Giulio Romano and the other great architects of the Renaissance, Palladio was the first who did nothing but build. He was the first professional architect. But he also found the time to pass his knowledge on. Besides his very popular guide to Rome, he illustrated Daniele Barbaro's annotated edition of Vitruvius' *De Architectura*, and then, in 1570, published his own monumental *I Quattro Libri dell'Architettura*, offering practical advice for builders, illustrated with fine woodcuts of his own buildings. *I Quattro Libri* has never gone out of print, with good (and perhaps not so good) reason: 'With the touch of pedantry that suited the times and invested his writings with a fallacious air of scholarship, he was the very man to summarize and classify, and to save future generations of architects the labour of thinking for themselves,' as Sir Reginald Blomfield wrote in his *Studies in Architecture*.

These future generations would give Palladio a curious afterlife. The first foreign president of his fan club was Inigo Jones, who came to the Veneto in 1613, toured the villas and met Palladio's collaborator, Vincenzo Scamozzi. Smitten, Jones returned to England and designed stage sets in the Italian manner, collaborating on elaborate masques with Ben Jonson. By 1615, he had worked his way up to the post of Surveyor of the King's Works, in effect the court architect. Even after that, he still had time for theatrical work. The very first masque he staged after gaining his royal post was called *The Golden Age Restored*, and this proved a fitting motto for what was to follow.

Jones may have brought the Renaissance in building to Britain, but he was hardly a slavish follower. His Banqueting House at Whitehall, the Queen's House at Greenwich and Covent Garden were highly original interpretations of the Palladian style. They induced a revolution in British tastes; Jones even had the effrontery to tack a Palladian façade onto the old Gothic St Paul's in London, which so embarrassed the old cathedral that it burned up along with the rest of London in 1666. After the fire, Jones's precocious Vitruvian visions were bumped aside for Christopher Wren's more genial mix of Renaissance and Continental Baroque. For a whole century, British fashion would ignore Inigo Jones; even in the Veneto, Palladio's reputation took a nosedive in the 1600s, his fame entirely eclipsed by that of Scamozzi.

But in the early 18th century change was again in the air, and as John Charlton put it 'a new architectural religion was born, with Palladio as Mahomet, his *Four Books of Architecture* as the sacred text, and Inigo Jones as a major prophet. Of the new cult Lord Burlington was to be high priest and Chiswick House the temple.' After reading *Vitruvius Britannicus* by Colen Campbell (1715) and Venetian Giacomo Leoni's 'translation' of Palladio's *Four Books of Architecture* (1715), the young aristocrat-architect Burlington went to Vicenza in 1719 to study the master's works in person and to purchase every drawing by Palladio he could lay his hands on. The fresh interest by foreigners inspired a Palladian revival in Venetia itself, just when the booming economy ignited a veritable villa-building spree. But while the architects of the *settecento* packed their houses with Palladian decorative elements, few tried to follow the old master's recipes for harmonic proportions.

Neither did any of his foreign followers. Burlington, who loved Palladio for his re-interpretation of the ancients, was dogmatically more Palladian than Palladio (forgetting that Palladio himself often broke his own rules), and his greatest work, Chiswick House, seems cold compared with its model, La Rotonda. Burlington's strict interpretations influenced 18th-century domestic architecture in England more than Palladio himself, both through his own designs and the books he financed, especially *The Designs of Inigo Jones* by William Kent (1727).

Other influential works that followed, *Palladio Londinensis: Of the London Art of Building* by William Salmon (1738) and *The City and Country Builders and Workman's Treasury of Designs* by Batty Langley (1740), were sent to colonial America as pattern books, illustrated with Anglo-Palladian designs. There, in the more congenial climate and landscapes of Virginia and the Carolinas, Palladian architecture was to find its true home. The planters' houses and public buildings of the Old South in the 18th century are still revered as some of America's finest buildings, and Palladio's stamp is on most of them.

The northern colonies' first accomplished architect, Peter Harrison, carried the fashion up to Newport, Rhode Island, but the crowning achievement of Palladian architecture in America was to come courtesy of the copy of the *Quattro Libri* in the library of Thomas Jefferson. Jefferson once wrote to an architect friend, 'Palladio is the Bible. You should get it and stick close to it.' His three great works, the State Capitol at Richmond, his home at Monticello and the august rotunda of the University of Virginia, stand as reminders that, in architecture, America's first national style was a gift from Venice.

A Most Serene Civilization

Esto perpetua (May it last forever).
Paolo Sarpi's last words

There was nothing quite like the *Serenissima*, and there never will be again. The eight centuries in which the lagoon city kept her own counsel, plus the three and a half centuries when her government embraced the *terra firma* of Venetia, are marked by a way of life so distinct and original as to be a civilization apart. It wasn't perfect, but the last 200 years of Italian history would have been far different, and probably far happier, had Venice rather than Rome had been put in charge of the show. Of course the Italians themselves never considered any such thing; even today, in their national family, Venice is the quirky cousin born on the wrong side of the blanket who spent most of her life in exotic lands. She stands apart, proud and diffident and perhaps a little misunderstood. Modern Italians tend to find Rome far more beautiful.

Although Venetia was fragmented after the fall of Rome, and separated throughout the Middle Ages into two distinct camps, the precocious seagoing Republic and the more traditional states of the *terra firma*, there was always a close relationship between the sea Venetians and the land Venetians. They shared a common ancient history and language – Venet, the official language of the *Serenissima* until the Austrian occupation. And even though Venice remained aloof from mainland politics for centuries, avoiding the Ghibelline–Guelph gang rumbles that troubled the rest of the peninsula, her famous network of spies kept a close eye on potentially troublesome tyrants like Ezzelino da Romano and the Carrara of Padua. Protected by her impenetrable lagoon, Venice intervened only when it suited her interest or pleasure.

It was not exactly an attitude that won her many friends in Italy, but there wasn't much anyone could do about it, either – until the pincer-like siege by Genoa and its ally, Padua, cut off Venice's food supplies in the Battle of Chioggia (1379). This scared the pants off Venice, and changed her mind; holding her nose, she plunged into the murk of mainland affairs. By 1454 she had conquered (mostly by diplomacy) all of the present Veneto, Friuli, the Dolomites as far as Belluno, as well as Bergamo, Brescia and Istria. It proved to be an act of some prescience: as Venice's sway grew on the mainland, her traditional livelihood, trade in the East, was being drained away by Ottoman conquests, the opening of new markets in the Americas and, after Vasco da Gama, the opening up of alternative trade routes around the Horn of Africa.

Unlike most empires, the *terra firma* cities were given the choice of whether or not they wanted to stay in or get out. Pope Julius II, who had the artistic foresight to muscle Michelangelo into painting the Sistine Chapel ceiling, was an imbecile at statecraft. Rather than support Venice as Europe's main bulwark against the Turks, he grew jealous and raised the international League of the Cambrai against her in 1509. In face of the massive invasion, Venice released the *terra firma* from its oaths of allegiance. And as soon as the coast was clear, every last *comune* returned to St Mark's.

This hate and envy by outsiders gave the people of Venetia a strong sense of solidarity with one another – a bond strengthened by the law that compelled the mainlanders and overseas colonists to buy and sell with Venice alone. That this monopoly actually ran smoothly is testimony to the spirit of internal harmony in the Republic; outside conspirators and instigators found it notoriously difficult to latch on to a discontented citizen to work their schemes. People were happy and proud to be part of the Most Serene Republic. You can see it in the lions of St Mark that remain in place on gates and portals, columns and towers from Asiago to Udine. No two lions are alike; the symbol was never standardized, true to the Republic's unity in plurality. Veronese's banquet scenes are prototypes of UN cocktail parties. Even women, notoriously absent from Venetian life in the Middle Ages, increasingly distinguished themselves: Cassandra Fedele was one of Italy's first female poets, followed by Gaspara Stampa and Veronica Franco, while Elena Lucrezia Corner Piscopia became the first woman in Europe to earn a degree (a doctorate in philosophy, from Padua, in 1678).

Another source of solidarity arose from the sincere if quaint Venetian conviction that their destiny was mystical and divine. Like the Blues Brothers, they were on a mission from God. They had in Mark (never mind that they shanghaied him from Alexandria) a saint as good as Peter, not to mention all the other holy relics they swiped from Constantinople and elsewhere, in which they placed the most naïve and credulous belief. Other Italians commented in astonishment on the masses the Venetians held before going into battle; the doge was not only a secular ruler but high priest, the vicar of the Republic. The Venetians credited all their victories to heaven and all their defeats to the bungling of their leaders, whom more often than not they tossed in the clink. Failure was against the law.

Yet at the same time, religious fanaticism was as alien to their pragmatic nature as nationalism; throughout their history the Venetians would be condemned for doing business with Muslims. They bear the shame for having invented the Ghetto, yet Venetia was considered Europe's safest refuge for Jews. Under their spiritual leader Fra Paolo Sarpi, the Venetians hemmed and hawed over the Reformation, until many Protestants thought they would join them. The Jesuits were banned outright or strictly controlled. At the Council of Trent, it was Venetia's special ambassador who defended the rights of the Orthodox Christians in the West. Papal interference in the Republic was kept to a minimum, and the Venetians defied the pope to keep it that way, even when he laid an Interdict on the whole Republic that lasted nearly two years (1606–1607).

For all their superstition, the Venetians didn't entirely rely on the bones of St Rocco to keep away the plague and epidemics (and they had perhaps more than their share, with 70 major outbreaks in 700 years). The Republic was famous for its hospitals – the University at Padua was the chief medical school of the Renaissance – and in times of war the Venetians astonished the world by caring not only for their own wounded, but the enemy's. In the 18th century, Venice was the first state in Europe to abolish torture.

The Venetians accumulated power and wealth with the aim of enjoying life, spending what they made on luxuries and spices and courtesans; they were besotted by music (a well-sung aria was about the only thing that could shut them up), and little bothered by intellectual debates, philosophical speculations or literature. They may have been proud that Petrarch, a Tuscan, had chosen to retire in the Euganean Hills south of Padua, but they absent-mindedly misplaced the great library he left them; they were far more interested in imitating his pioneering country-villa lifestyle than reading any of his books.

But the Venetians also planned ahead for future generations in ways that shame modern democracies. Programmes such as diverting the River Brenta into canals to prevent the silting up of the lagoon took centuries to complete; special forests such as Cansiglio, deemed essential to future shipbuilding, were protected to the extent that it was death to chop down a tree. The Venetians put their considerable energy into land-reclamation schemes and the draining of pestilent marshes; even in their decadent 18th century, when the State derived much of its income from gambling, they managed to find the money to build the wide quay of the Riva degli Schiavoni and the *Murazzi*, the great sea walls that shielded the lagoon from catastrophic floods, at least until 1966. Their villas were not just the pleasure domes most of them have become, but were working agricultural estates that fed the growing population of the cities. Although Columbus is a villain in Venetian eyes, they could thank him for a new crop – maize from the New World; Villa Emo, near Castelfranco, was one of the first places in Europe to sow it. Smart investments in silk and wool paid off with an economic boom in the late 17th and 18th century. Even in 1790, when the rest of the world looked at Venice as a nonstop party, it had the guts to teach the Barbary pirates a lesson, when even the English were paying them tribute.

All of this happened, of course, without the people having the slightest voice in politics. Yet they enjoyed more social justice than any one else in Italy, if not Europe. The mercantile oligarchy understood that the best way to maintain their exclusive grip on power and privilege was to keep the people happy and secure and to that end they, by their own strict laws, devoted themselves to the public good, paying heavy taxes and serving at the state's beck and call from the age of 16 until the grave. Other aristocrats in Europe thought they were nuts; the Republic's biggest social problem was what to do with all the bankrupt noblemen.

As for the people, by contemporary standards they had it made. The government encouraged cooperative, independent guilds and confraternities (*scuole*): at the fall of the Republic, there were over 300 of these – either large religious charitable confraternities (the *scuole* connected to the churches), or guilds, from the arsenal workers down to the greengrocers. These *scuole* were the backbone of society; each had its own constitution, senate and 'doge'; they regulated pay, set standards of craftsmanship, settled disputes and selected apprentices. Members paid dues to their *scuole* according to their earnings, and in return had access to the guild hospital and school, old age pensions, and the knowledge that the *scuola* would support their widows and orphans. Napoleon, busily melting the priceless treasure of St Mark's to pay his troops and stripping the Veneto of its art to beautify Paris, thought the whole system was a load of anachronistic rubbish, and he destroyed it along with everything else.

Food and Drink

05

There are those who eat to live and those who live to eat, and then there are the Italians, for whom food has an almost religious significance, unfathomably linked with love, *la Mamma* and tradition. In this singular country, where millions of otherwise sane people spend much of their waking hours worrying about their digestion, standards both at home and in restaurants are understandably high. Few Italians are gluttons, but all are experts in the kitchen. To serve a meal that is not properly prepared and more than a little complex is tantamount to an insult in Italy.

For the visitor, this culinary obsession comes as an extra bonus to the senses – along with Italy's remarkable sights, music and the warm sun on your back, you can enjoy some of the best tastes and smells the world can offer. Eating *all'italiana* is delicious and wholesome, and now undeniably trendy. Foreigners flock here to learn not only the secret of Italian cuisine, but of how the Italians can live surrounded by such delights and still fit into their sleek Armani trousers.

Riva del Garda has a famous cooking school open to foreigners wanting to know about Trentino cuisine. Details from Riva tourist office (*see* p.276) or *www.trentino.to*.

Restaurant Generalities

Breakfast (*colazione*) in Italy is an early-morning wake-up shot to the brain: a cappuccino (espresso with hot foamy milk, often sprinkled with chocolate – incidentally, first thing in the morning is the only time of day any self-respecting Italian will touch the stuff), a *caffè latte* (white coffee) or a *caffè lungo* (a generous portion of espresso), accompanied by a croissant-type roll (a *cornetto* or *brioche*) or a fancy pastry. This repast can be consumed in any bar and repeated during the morning as often as necessary. Breakfast in most Italian hotels seldom represents great value.

Lunch (*pranzo*), generally served around 1pm, has traditionally been the most important meal of the day, with a minimum of a first course (*primo piatto* – any kind of pasta dish, broth or soup, or rice dish or pizza), a second course (*secondo piatto* – a meat dish, accompanied by a *contorno* or side dish – a vegetable, salad or potatoes, usually), followed by fruit or dessert and coffee. You can, however, begin with a platter of *antipasti* – beautiful appetizers ranging from warm seafood delicacies, to raw ham (*prosciutto crudo*), salami in a hundred varieties, lovely vegetables, savoury toasts, olives, pâté and many more. There are restaurants that specialize in *antipasti*, and it's usually acceptable to forget the pasta and meat and just nibble on these scrumptious hors d'oeuvres (though in the end they may well cost more than a full meal). Most Italians accompany their meals with wine and mineral water – *acqua minerale*, sparkling (*frizzante*) or still (*acqua naturale* or *liscio*) – concluding with a *digestivo* liqueur.

Cena, the **evening meal**, is usually eaten around 8pm – earlier in the north and later in the south. This is much the same as *pranzo* although lighter, without the pasta; a pizza and beer, eggs or a fish dish. In restaurants, however, they offer all the courses.

In Italy the various terms for types of **restaurants** – *ristorante*, *trattoria* or *osteria* – have been confused. A *trattoria* or *osteria* can be just as elaborate as a restaurant, though rarely is a *ristorante* as informal as a traditional *trattoria*. Unfortunately, the old habit of posting menus and prices in the windows has fallen from fashion, so it's often difficult to judge variety or prices. Invariably the least expensive eating place is the *vino e cucina*, a simple establishment serving simple cuisine for simple everyday prices.

It is essential to remember that the fancier the fittings, the fancier the **bill**, though neither of these points has anything at all to do with the quality of the food. If you're uncertain, do as you would at home – look for lots of locals.

People who haven't visited Italy for years and have fond memories of eating full meals for under a pound will be amazed at how much **prices** have risen, though in some respects eating out in Italy is still a bargain, especially when you figure out how much all that wine would cost you at home. In many places you'll often find restaurants offering a *menu turistico* – full meals of usually meagre inspiration for a reasonable set price. More imaginative chefs often offer a *menu degustazione* – a set-price gourmet meal that allows you to taste their daily specialities and seasonal dishes. Both of these are cheaper than if you had ordered the same food *à la carte*.

As the pace of modern urban life militates against lengthy home-cooked repasts with the family (followed by a siesta), alternatives to sit-down meals have mushroomed. Many office workers now behave much as their counterparts elsewhere in Europe and consume a quick snack at lunchtime, returning home after a busy day to throw together some pasta and salad in the evenings.

The original Italian fast-food alternative, a buffet known as the 'hot table' (*tavola calda*) is becoming harder to find among the fast-food franchises; a bar may well double as a *paninoteca* (which make sandwiches to order, or serve *tramezzini*, little sandwiches on plain, square white bread that are much better than they look); outlets selling pizza by the slice (*al taglio*) are common in city centres. At any grocer's (*alimentari*) or market (*mercato*), you can buy the materials for countryside or hotel-room picnics; at some (notably at a *salumeria*), you can choose the bread and they will make the sandwiches for you.

Regional Specialities

Forget the Italian stereotypes; olive groves are rare in Venetia (except around Lake Garda), so many dishes are prepared with butter. Tomatoes and oregano are used more sparingly here than in the south, and many dishes are served with polenta (pudding or cake of yellow maize flour), brick-heavy in character and suited to the colder climate.

Venice

Venetian cuisine is delicious, although in Venice itself you'll have to pay way over the odds to have it done properly; quality and price are much better on the *terra firma*. In seaside or lagoonside restaurants (where seafood tends to be garlicky or highly spiced as it's not generally Italy's freshest or most flavoursome), a typical meal might include oysters from Chioggia or *sarde in saor* (marinated sardines) for *antipasti*, followed by the classic *risi e bisi* (rice and peas, cooked with Parma ham and Parmesan) or the Veneto's favourite pasta, *bigoli in salsa* (thick spaghetti, served with a piquant onion, butter and anchovy sauce). Other choices for *primo* are various types of risotto: *di mare*, with seafood, *in nero*, with cuttlefish cooked in its own ink, or *alla sbirraglia*, with vegetables, chicken and ham. For *secondo*, liver and onions (*fegato alla veneziana*) share top billing with seafood dishes like scampi, cuttlefish in its own ink (*seppie alla veneziana*), and lobster (*aragosta*), or the equally pricey Venetian crab, *granceola*. Top it all off with a tiramisù, the traditional Veneto mascarpone, coffee and chocolate dessert.

Candied fruit plays an important role in the sweet category, recalling Venice's long rule over the island that gave us both the name and Europe's first sugar cane – Candia (Crete). An enduring taste for sultanas and pine nuts was acquired from the Byzantines and Turks, studding not only pastries but dishes such as *stoccafisso* (salt cod) and fish prepared in *carpione* (fried or grilled, then marinated with vinegar, wine and fried onions – a favourite of Venetian sailors).

The Veneto

Elsewhere along coastal areas look for fish soup, *brodetto di pesce*, often served with polenta. Catfish and other freshwater creatures are the speciality at Rovigo, served fried or in ragouts. Treviso's little River Sile yields the star ingredient of *anguilla* (or *bisato*) in *umido* (eel stew), while the province is renowned for its *radicchio*, red chicory, a favourite in winter salads. Since Roman times the Trevigiano has been famous for its *soppressa* (salted meats) and spicy *divina lucanica tarvisiana*, a sausage better known as *luganega*. A traditional first course, *sopa coada*, is a rich chicken broth.

In springtime gastronomes flock to feast on white asparagus in Bassano del Grappa and the deep red cherries of Marostica, while in the autumn wild mushrooms, especially from the hills of Montello, hold pride of place, along with game dishes served with *peverada* (a traditional sauce made of giblets, anchovies and lemons). Padua is the land of pumpkin dishes and poultry 'of the courtyard' – chicken and geese mainly, usually served roasted; if it's cooked *alla Padovana* it will be spit-roasted and very spicy. Vicenza is famous for its dried cod, *bacalà*, and tops its *bigoli* with duck sauce. Montagnana produces sweet hams, Verona is synonymous with gnocchi, tall golden Pandoro cakes and all kinds of fruit and peaches served in red wine; it also produces more cabbage than anywhere else in Italy. The latter features in the classic Veronese dish, *patissada de cavolo con gnocchi*. The Veneto's best-known cheese is strong-flavoured Asiago; another, Formaggio Monte Veronese DOC, is made at the Lessinia, north of Verona, and hard to find outside the Veneto.

Trentino-Alto Adige

In the Dolomites, look for hearty Austrian influences and plenty of calories (and polenta) to keep you warm in the mountains. Nearly every menu features gnocchi, various kinds of ravioli such as *alla trentina* (filled with meat or vegetables and curds), *Schlutzkrapfen* (little ravioli), *canederli* (Italianized *Knödeln*, gnocchi made with breadcrumbs, egg, cheese and bacon, served with a sauce or in a broth) and, biggest of all, *strangolapreti* ('priest stranglers'), a 16th-century tradition in the Trentino – gnocchi made of bread, eggs and spinach topped with melted butter. Other first courses include the wine soup of the Val d'Isarco, *zuppa acida* (a soup of pickled tripe – an acquired taste), and *risotto ai frutti di bosco* (with woodland berries – delicious but rather rare). Speck, a cured ham, is found on pizzas, in *tortellini*, in sandwiches, or as *antipasti*, where it may share the plate with goose, ham and various other meaty treats. Main courses range from goulash, fresh trout and grilled meats, omelettes packed with potatoes and meat, *lepre alla trentina* (jugged hare), *Würstel con crauti* (sausage and sauerkraut), *osei scampai* (veal 'birds', i.e. *involtini*, filled with bacon and sage), *Wienerschnitzel* (*cotoletta alla milanese*, in Italian), sweet and sour venison dishes, and the Trentino classic with a funny name, *smacafam*, a pie filled with game and salted meats and baked in a wood oven. Local cheeses include *Trentingrana*, a hard cheese similar to Parmesan, and ricotta, served fresh or smoked. *Apfelstrudel*, often with pine nuts and raisins, is everywhere. Also try *fortaies*, 'sweet snails' – not snails really, but snail-shaped fritters with powdered sugar.

Friuli-Venezia Giulia

Little Friuli has one of the most cosmopolitan kitchens and most complicated menus in Italy, where you'll find the Austrian influences of Trentino and Alto Adige matched by dishes with a Slovene slant, which makes for an often surprising fusion cuisine – where else in Italy can you find a poppy-seed risotto or gnocchi with plums?

On a more traditional level, polenta, 'the bread of the mountains', is by far the favourite stodge, often served hot and creamy with tomatoes and pepper, sausages, game, fish or garden vegetables, or with cheese (*toc in braide*). The single most famous Friulian comestible is *prosciutto di San Daniele*, a rival to Parma's famous hams. In Udine ravioli are called *cialsons*; also try *frico* (a fried cheese wafer) served with polenta and potatoes.

Around Trieste, menus feature *jota* (a soup of sauerkraut, beans, potatoes, garlic, cumin and olive oil), potato gnocchi flavoured with herbs, goulash, tripe dishes, hot Prague ham, and *porzina* (pork) with mustard; also look for *blijeki alla carsolina* (the *alla carsolina* part means with rocket) and *palacinke* (crêpes) filled with ricotta. Grado takes a great deal of pride in its fish soup, or *boretto alla gradese*. Among the cheeses, Montasio is the best known, with the local *formai salat* from the Valcosa, Val d'Arzino and Valcellina.

The cosmopolitan pastries and desserts of Friuli-Venezia Giulia command equal status on the menu with the other courses. Taste a wide choice of strudels (not only apple, but poppy-seed, pear, grape and cherry) and *krapfens*, Viennese-style *Sachertorte*; Hungarian *rigojanci* (all whipped cream and chocolate) and *dobos*, Slovenian filo pastry and cheese *presniz*, *gibanica* (full of ricotta, honey, poppy seeds and pine nuts) and *strukiji kuhani* (filled with walnuts, raisins and rum).

The Wines of Northeast Italy

If Italy has an infinite variety of regional dishes, there is an equally bewildering array of regional wines, many of which are rarely exported because they are best drunk young. Unless you're dining at a restaurant with an exceptional cellar, do as the Italians do and order a carafe of the local wine (*vino locale* or *vino della casa*). Most Italian wines are named after the grape and the district they come from.

If the label says DOC (*Denominazione di Origine Controllata*), it means that the wine comes from a specially defined area and was produced according to a certain traditional method. DOCG (*Denominazione di Origine Controllata e Garantita*) is allegedly a more rigorous classification, indicating that the wines are tested by government-appointed inspectors.

Classico means that a wine comes from the oldest part of the zone of production, though is not necessarily better than a non-*Classico*. *Riserva*, *superiore* or *speciale* denotes a wine that has been aged longer and is more alcoholic; *Recioto*, a favourite in the Veneto, is a wine made from the outer clusters of grapes ('the ears') with a higher sugar and therefore alcohol content.

Other Italian wine words are *spumante* (sparkling), *frizzante* (pétillant), *amabile* (semi-sweet), *abboccato* (medium dry) and *passito* (strong sweet wine made from raisins). *Rosso* is red, *bianco* white; between the two extremes lie *rubiato* (ruby), *rosato*, *chiaretto* or *cerasuolo* (rosé). *Secco* is dry, *dolce* sweet, *liquoroso* fortified and sweet. *Vendemmia* means vintage, a *cantina* is a cellar, and an *enoteca* is a wine shop where you can taste and buy wines.

The **Veneto**, one of Italy's top three wine regions (along with Tuscany and Piedmont), has made massive strides in improving quality. Verona's Valpolicella is now one of Italy's most prestigious reds, followed in fame by its lesser cousin Bardolino, from the shores of Lake Garda. Other lesser known reds worth seeking out in the region include Pramaggiore Cabernet and Merlot, Venegazzù della Casa and Piave Raboso. Of the whites, Soave is the most abundant, if not the most reputable, although small Soave estates have been producing wines of quality; dry white Bianco di Custoza is a more flavoursome bet, while Tocai di Lison from the border of Friuli has an excellent reputation. Most of the house wine in Venice is Piave, and the favourite aperitif throughout the region is Prosecco, that charming sparkler from Conegliano. Then there's grappa, a mighty, schnapps-like *aquavit* drunk in black coffee after a meal (*caffè corretto*) or for breakfast if it's chilly; Bassano del Grappa has Italy's oldest distillery.

Trentino-Alto Adige may have two personalities, one Italian and one Teutonic, but both make plenty of wine, predominately whites, and nearly all from a single grape variety. The Chardonnays, Rhinerieslings, Sauvignons, Pinot Bianco and Grigio, and Gewürztraminers are excellent; the various dry and sweet Moscatos are also worth a try. For a red, you'll generally do well with a Cabernet Franc and Sauvignon, or the more exotic Lagrein or rosé-scented Rosenmuskateller.

Similar to Trentino-Alto Adige, **Friuli-Venezia Giulia** abstains from blending and produces mono-grape wines from seven different DOC regions: Latisana, Isonzo, Grave del Friuli (the biggest), Aquileia, Carso, Collio Goriziano and Colli Orientali. The region's finest wines are Pinot Grigio, Riesling Renano, Traminer, and the native Tocai, which apparently has nothing to do with the famous Hungarian grapes. The Colli Orientali also produce a notable sweet wine called Picolit, in tiny precious amounts, prized by connoisseurs. Friulian reds have a mostly French pedigree: Pinot Noir, Cabernet Franc and Merlot rule the roost, while the Colli Orientali produce an excellent wine from a local variety, Refosco.

Italian Menu Reader

Antipasti

These before-meal treats can include almost anything; the most common include:

antipasto misto mixed *antipasto*
bruschetta garlic toast (often with tomatoes)
carciofi (sott'olio) artichokes (in oil)
frutti di mare seafood
funghi (trifolati) mushrooms (with anchovies, garlic and lemon)
gamberi ai fagioli prawns (shrimps) with white beans
mozzarella (in carrozza) cow or buffalo cheese (fried with bread in batter)
prosciutto (con melone) cured ham (with melon)
salsicce sausages

Minestre (Soups) and Pasta

These dishes are the principal first courses (*primi*) served throughout Italy.

agnolotti ravioli with meat
cacciucco spiced fish soup
cappelletti small ravioli, often in broth
crespelle crêpes
fettuccine long strips of pasta
frittata omelette
gnocchi potato dumplings
minestra di verdura thick vegetable soup
minestrone soup with meat, vegetables and pasta
orecchiette ear-shaped pasta, often served with turnip greens
panzerotti ravioli filled with mozzarella, anchovies and egg
pappardelle alla lepre pasta with hare sauce
pasta e fagioli soup with beans, bacon and tomatoes
pastina in brodo tiny pasta in broth
penne all'arrabbiata quill-shaped pasta with tomatoes and hot peppers
polenta cake or a kind of savoury pudding of corn semolina
risotto (alla Milanese) risotto (served with saffron)
spaghetti all'Amatriciana with spicy sauce of salt pork, tomatoes, onions and chilli

spaghetti alla Bolognese with minced/ground meat, ham, mushrooms, etc.
spaghetti alla carbonara with bacon, eggs and black pepper
spaghetti al pomodoro with tomato sauce
spaghetti al sugo/ragù with meat sauce
spaghetti alle vongole with clam sauce
stracciatella broth with eggs and cheese
tagliatelle flat egg noodles
tortellini al pomodoro/panna/in brodo small pasta parcels filled with meat and cheese with tomato sauce/with cream/in broth

Carne (Meat)

abbacchio milk-fed lamb
agnello lamb
anatra duck
animelle sweetbreads
arista pork loin
arrosto misto mixed roast meats
bocconcini veal fried with ham and cheese
bollito misto stew of boiled meats
braciola chop
brasato di manzo braised beef with vegetables
bresaola dried raw meat similar to Parma ham
capretto kid
capriolo roebuck
carne di castrato/suino mutton/pork
carpaccio thin slices of raw beef served with a piquant sauce
cassoeula winter stew with pork and cabbage
cervello (al burro nero) brains (in black butter sauce)
cervo venison
cinghiale boar
coniglio rabbit
cotoletta (alla milanese/alla bolognese) veal cutlet (fried in breadcrumbs/with ham and cheese)
fagiano pheasant
faraona guinea fowl
fegato alla veneziana liver (usually of veal) with filling
involtini sliced, stuffed slices of meat
lepre (in salmì) hare (marinated in wine)
lingua tongue
lombo di maiale pork loin

lumache snails
maiale (al latte) pork (cooked in milk)
manzo beef
osso buco braised veal knuckle with herbs
pajata calf's or lamb's intestines
pancetta rolled pork
pernice partridge
petto di pollo (sorpresa) boned chicken breast
   (stuffed and deep-fried)
piccione pigeon
pizzaiola beef steak with tomato and
   oregano sauce
*pollo (alla cacciatora/alla diavola/alla
   Marengo)* chicken (with tomatoes and
   mushrooms grilled/fried with garlic and
   wine)
polpette meatballs
quaglie quails
ragù meat sauce
rane frogs
rognoni kidneys
saltimbocca veal escalope with prosciutto, sage,
   wine, butter
scaloppine thin slices of veal sautéed in butter
spezzatino beef or veal pieces, usually stewed
spiedino meat on a skewer or stick
stracotto slow-cooked beef with wine, herbs
   and vegetables
stufato beef in white wine with vegetables
tacchino turkey
uccelletti small birds on a skewer
vitello veal
zampone pig's trotter

Pesce (Fish)

acciughe or *alici* anchovies
anguilla eel
aragosta lobster
aringa herring
baccalà dried salt cod
bonito small tuna
branzino sea bass
brodetto fish stew
calamari squid
cappesante scallops
cefalo grey mullet
coda di rospo angler fish
cozze mussels
dentice dentex (perch-like fish)
dorato gilthead
fritto misto mixed fried delicacies,
   mainly fish
gamberetto shrimp
gamberi prawns
gamberi di fiume crayfish
granchio crab
insalata di mare seafood salad
lampreda lamprey
merluzzo cod

nasello hake
orata bream
ostriche oysters
pesce azzurro various small fish
pesce di San Pietro John Dory
pesce spada swordfish
polipi/polpi octopus
rombo turbot
sarde sardines
seppie cuttlefish
sgombro mackerel
sogliola sole
squadro monkfish
stoccafisso wind-dried cod
tonno tuna
triglia red mullet (rouget)
trota trout
trota salmonata salmon trout
vongole small clams
zuppa di pesce mixed fish in sauce or stew

Contorni (Side Dishes, Vegetables)

aglio garlic
asparagi alla fiorentina asparagus with
   fried eggs
broccoli broccoli
capperi capers
carciofi (alla giudea) (deep-fried) artichokes
cardi cardoons/thistles
carote carrots
cavolfiore cauliflower
cavolo cabbage
ceci chickpeas/garbanzo beans
cetriolo cucumber
cipolla onion
fagioli white beans
fagiolini French (green) beans
fave broad beans
finocchio fennel
funghi (porcini) mushrooms (boletus)
insalata (mista/verde) salad (mixed/green)
lattuga lettuce
lenticchie lentils
melanzane aubergine/eggplant
patate potatoes
patate fritte chips, French fries
peperoncini hot chilli peppers
peperoni sweet peppers
peperonata stew of peppers, onions, etc.
piselli (al prosciutto) peas (with ham)
pomodoro(i) tomato(es)
porri leeks
radicchio red chicory
radice radish
rapa turnip
rucola rocket
sedano celery

spinaci spinach
verdure greens
zucca pumpkin
zucchini courgettes

Formaggio (Cheese)

Bel Paese a soft white cow's cheese
cacio/caciocavallo pale yellow, sharp cheese
caprino goat's cheese
fontina rich cow's milk cheese
gorgonzola soft blue cheese
groviera mild cheese (gruyère)
mozzarella soft cheese
parmigiano Parmesan cheese
pecorino sharp sheep's cheese
provolone sharp, tangy; dolce is
   less strong
ricotta creamy white cheese
stracchino soft white cheese

Frutta (Fruit, Nuts)

albicocche apricots
ananas pineapple
arance oranges
banane bananas
cachi persimmon
ciliege cherries
cocomero watermelon
datteri dates
fichi figs
fragole (con panna) strawberries
   (with cream)
lamponi raspberries
limone lemon
macedonia di frutta fruit salad
mandarino tangerine
mandorle almonds
melagrana pomegranate
mele apples
mirtilli bilberries
more blackberries
nespola medlar fruit
nocciole hazelnuts
noci walnuts
pera pear
pesca peach
pesca noce nectarine
pinoli pine nuts
pompelmo grapefruit
prugna/susina prune/plum
uva grapes

Dolci (Desserts)

amaretti macaroons
cannoli crisp pastry tubes filled with ricotta,
   cream, chocolate or fruit
coppa gelato assorted ice cream
crema caramella caramel-topped custard
crostata fruit flan

gelato (produzione propria) ice cream
   (home-made)
granita water ice, usually lemon or coffee
monte bianco chestnut pudding
   with cream
panettone sponge cake with candied fruit
panforte dense cake of chocolate, almonds and
   preserved fruit
saint honoré meringue cake
semifreddo refrigerated cake/dessert
sorbetto sorbet/sherbet
spumone a soft ice cream
tiramisù layers of sponge, mascarpone, coffee
   and chocolate
torrone nougat
torta cake, tart
torta millefoglie layered pastry and
   custard cream
zabaglione hot dessert made with eggs and
   Marsala wine
zuppa inglese trifle

Bevande (Beverages)

acqua minerale mineral water
   con/senza gas sparkling/still
aranciata orange soda
birra (alla spina) beer (draught)
caffè coffee
caffè freddo iced coffee
caffè macchiato espresso with a drop of milk
cioccolata calda hot chocolate
cioccolata con panna chocolate with cream
gassosa lemon-flavoured soda
ghiaccio ice
granita iced drink (with fruit or coffee)
latte milk
latte macchiato milk with a drop of coffee
latte (intero/scremato) milk (whole/skimmed)
limonata lemon soda
spumante sparkling wine
succo di frutta fruit juice
tè tea
tè freddo tea (sweet, iced)
tisana herbal tea
tonica tonic water
vino (rosso/bianco/rosato) wine (red/
   white/rosé)

Snacks

biscotti biscuits
caramelle sweets, candy
cioccolato chocolate
grissini bread sticks
patatine crisps/potato chips
pizzetta small pizza with cheese and tomato

Cooking Terms (Miscellaneous)

aceto (balsamico) vinegar (balsamic)
affumicato smoked

aglio garlic
alla brace on embers
bicchiere glass
burro butter
cacciagione game
conto bill
costoletta/cotoletta chop
coltello knife
cucchiaio spoon
filetto fillet
forchetta fork
forno oven
fritto fried
ghiaccio ice
griglia grill
in bianco without tomato
magro lean meat/pasta without meat
marmellata jam
menta mint
miele honey
mostarda candied mustard sauce
olio oil

pane bread
pane tostato toasted bread
panini sandwiches (in rolls)
panna cream
pepe pepper
piatto plate
prezzemolo parsley
ripieno stuffed
rosmarino rosemary
sale salt
salmì wine marinade
salsa sauce
salvia sage
senape mustard
tartufi truffles
tavola table
tazza cup
tovagliolo napkin
tramezzini triangular sandwiches
umido cooked in sauce
uovo egg
zucchero sugar

Planning Your Trip

06

When to Go

Climate

O Sole Mio notwithstanding, Italy isn't permanently sunny; believe it or not, it rains just as much in Rome every year as it does in London.

Summer comes on humid and hot in Venetia, especially along the Po; the Dolomites stay blessedly cool, though the valleys just below can be little ovens and, while the coasts are often refreshed by breezes, Venice in its lagoon tends to swelter through the sultry months. You can get by without an umbrella, but take a light jacket for cool evenings.

For average touring, August is probably the worst month. Transport facilities are jammed to capacity, prices are at their highest, and the large cities are abandoned to hordes of tourists while the locals take to the beach. As compensation, summer is prime festival time (*see* 'Festivals' and 'Calendar of Events', opposite).

Spring and autumn are the loveliest times to visit this corner of Italy. In spring the blossoming apple orchards around Trento and cherry orchards of Treviso and Modena rival the wild flowers of Italy's countryside and mountains; by May and June the gardens are at their peak.

But in many ways the best and certainly the most soulful season of northeast Italy is autumn, when the landscapes match the colours of Venetian art; the Po Delta and lagoon are at their most haunting, the sumac on Trieste's karst bursts into scarlet flames and the vineyards are heavy with grapes. The weather is mild, places aren't crowded, and you won't need your umbrella too much, at least until November.

During the winter the happiest visitors are either skiing the slopes, in the opera house, or at the table eating wild mushrooms and *radicchio*. It's the best time to go if you want the churches and museums to yourself, or want to meet Italians. Beware, though, that it can rain and rain in winter, and mountain valleys can lie under banks of fog and mist for days.

Festivals

There are literally thousands of festivals answering to every description in Venetia. Every *comune* has at least one or two, celebrating a patron saint; others are sponsored by the political parties (especially the Communists and Socialists), where everyone goes to meet their friends and enjoy masses of cheap food.

No matter where you are, look at the posters; Italy is swamped with culture, and best of all, remains refreshingly unsnobbish about it all. On the other hand, don't expect anything approaching uninhibited gaiety. Italy is a rather staid place these days, and festivals are largely occasions to dress up, hear some music, re-enact a historic event or have a pleasant outdoor supper. If you ever see Italians at a festival laughing too loudly, drinking too much or dancing too hard, drop us a line. We'd love to see it.

Have a look through the 'Calendar of Events', opposite, for a list of popular annual events in northeast Italy. The list is far from exhaustive; check with the local tourist offices for more comprehensive listings and for precise dates – they tend to change year on year.

For 'National Holidays', *see* the **Practical A–Z** chapter, p.100.

Average Temperatures in °C (F)

	Jan	April	July	Oct
Trieste	5 (41)	14 (57)	24 (75)	16 (61)
Venice	3 (37)	12 (54)	21 (69)	14 (58)
Lake Garda	3 (37)	13 (56)	23 (74)	13 (56)
Cortina	−2 (27)	5 (41)	15 (59)	7 (45)
Merano	1 (33)	12 (53)	22 (72)	13 (55)
Treviso	3 (37)	13 (55)	23 (73)	14 (57)

Average Rainfall in millimetres (inches)

	Jan	April	July	Oct
Trieste	71 (2.8)	87 (3.4)	71 (2.8)	87 (3.4)
Venice	33 (1.3)	59 (2.3)	68 (2.7)	94 (4)
Lake Garda	43 (1.7)	55 (2.1)	79 (3.1)	78 (3)
Cortina	28 (1.1)	46 (1.8)	109 (4.3)	56 (2.2)
Merano	26 (1)	53 (2.1)	92 (3.6)	56 (2.2)
Treviso	67 (2.6)	68 (2.7)	66 (2.6)	81 (3.2)

Calendar of Events

January

1 Parade of folk costumes and horse-drawn sleighs, at Ortisei (Bolzano).

5–6 Feast of the *pignarul*, Tarcento (Udine), 14th-century costumes in a torchlit parade of the Three Kings, followed by bonfires.

6 Mass of the Sword, Cividale del Friuli, where the priest wears a sword in memory of the town's famous 14th-century patriarch; Taller Mass, at Gemona del Friuli, in which the mayor presents a *'taller'* (coin) to the priest, symbolizing homage to the Church's authority.

Mid-month Gold and silver fair, Vicenza.

February

First week Dobbiaco–Cortina Cross Country Ski race, ending at Cortina d'Ampezzo; *Padovanti-quaria*, week-long antiques fair, Padua.

Carnival Venice is the place to see the most beautiful masks and costumes, and to attend big-name events as the Lagoon city strives to recreate the old magic; Sappada (Belluno) celebrates with three weeks of parades and traditional events featuring a personage called *Rollate*, dressed in furs and hood, and wearing a carved wooden mask. On Carnival Friday, Verona celebrates the *Bacanal del gnocco*, a parade with the king of gnocchi and a feast, all in 15th-century costume. Other Carnival celebrations take place in Arco (Trento), Muggia (Trieste) and Ora/Auer (Bolzano).

18 *Festa della Renga*, feasting on local specialities, Concordia Sagittaria (Venice).

March

19 *Lis cidulis*, at Forni Avoltri (Udine), in which burning logs are rolled down the hillside.

Good Friday Passion play, performed since 1600, at Erto (Pordenone).

Easter Mon Parades in costume and horse races at Merano.

Middle of Lent Trial of the *Vecia*, the old year, Cavaso del Tomba (Treviso).

25 Traditional horse fair, Lonigo (Vicenza).

End month *Vinitaly*, wine, spirits and olive oil fair, Verona.

April

2 *Antica Festa della Madonna Addolorata*, processions and spectacles draw some 50,000 to Belluno.

Mid-month *Sagra del Gnocco*, eating and dancing, in Teolo (Padua); flower festival, Lignano Sabbiadoro (Udine).

3rd week Asparagus festival, San Zeno di Cassola (Vicenza); kite-flying festival, Badia Polesine (Padua).

End month Giant antiques fair, and Città di Padova Rugby Tournament, both in Padua.

May

First week *Sagra di Sansonessa*, country fair of food, games and dancing, Caorle (Venice).

10 *Palio della Valle dei Frassini*, 19th-century fun and games at Frassinelle Polesine (Rovigo).

Ascension *La Sensa*, or re-enactment of the Doge's Wedding of the Sea, Venice; cross-kissing ceremony, at Zuglio (Udine), in which all the crosses from the countryside are decorated and brought to the church of San Pietro.

Mid-month *Festa Medievale del Vino Bianco*, Soave.

End month Cherry festival, Marostica (Vicenza); Fiera Maggio Arquatese, Arquà Polesine (Rovigo), with costumes, races, parades, fireworks; flower markets, Bolzano.

June

12–13 *Sant'Antonio*, Padua, the historic re-enactment of the transition of saint's relics from Arcella, and torchlight procession along the Bacchiglione.

Mid-month *Palio di Noale* (Venice), with 14th-century costumes, market, games; Migration of the flocks, at Senales (Bolzano), in which the sheep cross the glaciers to the Giogo Alto.

3rd Sun *Palio della Marciliana*, Chioggia, celebrating the 14th-century Battle of Chioggia.

Third week San Vigilio, folklore, music and stealing of the polenta pot at Trento.

24 San Giovanni Battista, with fireworks, Lugo di Vicenza.

June–July Festival of Herbs, Forni di Sopra (Udine).

End of June International Summer Curling competitions, Cortina d'Ampezzo; Toti del Monte International contest for aspiring opera singers, Treviso.

July

July–Aug Opera at the Arena, and Shakespeare in the Roman theatre, Verona; Operetta festival, Trieste; *Festival delle Ville*, theatre and other events in the villas along the Brenta Canal, Mira (Venice); *Mura Sotto le Stelle*, jazz and blues under the stars, Cittadella; music festival at the Villa Manin, Passariano (Udine); Veneto Jazz Festival, (throughout Veneto)

Mid-month International wood sculpture competition, Recoaro Terme (Vicenza); international choral singing competitions, Gorizia.

All month *Mittelfest*, celebrating Central Europe with music, etc. Cividale del Friuli.

Full moon *Sardellata*, midnight fishing and huge fireworks on Lake Garda, Pal del Vò.

1st Sun *Perdon de Barbana*, nautical procession to the island monastery, Grado.

2nd Sun Historical pageant, Palmanova (Udine).

Mid-month *Sagra del Pesce*, seafood festival, folklore and fireworks, Chioggia.

3rd week *Fiera della Maddalena*, thousand-year-old fair with events, songs, food and races, Oderzo.

3rd Sun Feast of the Redentore, Venice, celebrating the end of the 1576 plague, with a tremendous fireworks show followed by a procession over a bridge of boats.

August

All month *Folkest*, international folk music festival with concerts throughout Friuli; *Agosto Medievale*, costumes and performances evoke the Middle Ages, at Gemona (Udine).

1st weekend *Palio* and pageant at Feltre, celebrating the city's gift of itself to Venice in 1404; fish festival, parades and food at Porto Tolle (Rovigo).

First week *Pavana d'Estate*, festival of popular and ethnic music, Teolo (Padua); *Aria Festa*, ham and wine fest, San Daniele del Friuli.

15 *Palio delle Contrade*, at Garda, with fishing boat regatta and historical parade; songbird market, Vittorio Veneto.

Mid-Aug–Sept International piano competitions at Bolzano; musical festival, Portogruaro.

19–21 Traditional festival of Santa Augusta, Vittorio Veneto, with fireworks.

Last Sat *Giro delle Mura*, race around the walls of Feltre.

Last Sun Medieval songbird festival, Sacile (Pordenone).

End Aug–early Sept International Film Festival, Venice; *Sagra di Santa Colomba*, Piazzola sul Brenta (Padua), popular folk festival, with a donkey *palio*, dances, food, etc.

September

Sept–Dec *Autunno Musicale Trevigiano*, ballet, opera and concerts, Treviso

1st Sun Historical regatta in costume and gondola races in Venice; *palio* in Montagnana; *Coppa d'Oro delle Dolomiti*, historic sportscar race, Cortina d'Ampezzo; *Preludio e Dama Castellana*, Conegliano Veneto, Renaissance costumes and checkers played with living pieces between the neighbourhoods; *Gioco*

dell'Oca in Piazza, playing of the medieval Goose Game, in costume, Mirano (Venetia).

2nd week Human chess game at Marostica (Vicenza), even-numbered years only; autumn festival at Tirolo (Bolzano).

Mid-month *Vivistoria*, re-enactment of 10th-century nabbing of the 12 Venetian brides by pirates on their wedding night, Caorle (Venice).

3rd Sun *Gran Prix de Merano* horse race and lottery; *Festa Regionale dell'Uva*, Vò (Padua), festival of grapes, with a parade and plenty of wine; wine festival, Gambellara (Vicenza).

October

1st two weeks International Silent Film Festival, Sacile (Pordenone).

1st week *Festa della Giuggiola*, food, medieval costumes and majorettes, Arquà Petrarca.

1st Sun Feast of the Rosary, Galzignano Terme (Padua), procession in historical costume recalling the Battle of Lepanto, and a donkey race; *La Barcolana*, massive sailing regatta, Trieste.

2nd Sun Grape festival, Merano, local wines, costumes, and folklore events.

End month Chestnut festival, Drena (Trento); pumpkin festival, Salzano (Venice).

November

1st week Art and antiques show, Bolzano.

Mid-month *Fieracavalli*, major horse fair in Verona (since 1908); *Vino Novello* and food fair, Vicenza; *Fiera di San Martino*, food and crafts fair, Belluno.

21 Feast of Madonna della Salute, Venice, pilgrimage on bridge of boats over Grand Canal.

28–early Dec International Ice Cream Fair, Longarone.

28–mid-Dec *Fiera del Bestiame*, Santa Lucia di Piave (Treviso). Enormous agricultural fair.

December

All month Exhibition of *presepi* (Christmas cribs) in Verona; Christmas markets (throughout Venetia)

First week Fair of San Nicolò, traditional fair in Trieste; Fair of San Nicolò, with a Christmas parade at Vipiteno (Bolzano); Parade of St Nicholas and the Krampus, Tarvisio.

2nd week Regional handicrafts fair, Pordenone; *Festa del Mandorlato*, in honour of nougat, at Cologna Veneta.

2nd–3rd week Radicchio Fair, Castelfranco Veneto (Treviso).

20–31 Nocturnal floating nativity processions, Adria (Rovigo); giant traditional *presepio* and exhibition, Soave.

Tourist Information

Known under various initials as EPT, APT or IAT, Italian tourist offices usually stay open from 8am to 12.30 or 1pm, and from 3 to 7pm, possibly longer in summer. Few open on Saturday afternoons or Sundays. Information booths can also be found at major railway stations and can provide hotel lists, town plans and terse information on local sights and transport. Queues can be maddeningly long. English is spoken in the main centres. If you're stuck, you may get more sense out of a friendly travel agency than an official tourist office. The website for tourism in general is *www.enit.it*. Also try *www.itwg.com* which gives you access to information on all the various regions of Italy as well as train times, flights (from major carriers only) and hotel and car reservations. Or contact the addresses below.

Italian State Tourist Offices

UK, 1 Princes St, London W1B 8AY, **t** (020) 7408 1254, **f** (020) 7853 6464, *www.enit.it*, *www.italiantourism.com*.

USA, 630 Fifth Ave, Suite 1565, New York NY 10111, **t** (212) 245 5618, **f** (212) 586 9249; 12400 Wilshire Blvd, Suite 550, Los Angeles CA 90025, **t** (310) 820 1898, **f** (310) 820 6357; 500 N. Michigan Ave, Suite 2240, Chicago IL 60611, **t** (312) 644 0990/6, **f** (312) 644 3019.

Australia, Level 26, 44 Market Street, Sydney NSW, **t** (612) 926 21666, **f** (612) 926 25745.

Canada, 175 Bloor St East, Suite 907, South Tower, Toronto, **t** (416) 925 4882, **f** (416) 925 4799.

Japan, 2–7–14 Minimiaoyama, Minato-ku, Tokyo 107-0062, **t** (813) 34782 051, **f** (813) 34799 356.

France, 23 Rue de la Paix, 75002 Paris, **t** (33) 1 4266 0396, **f** (33) 1 4742 1974.

N. Zealand, c/o Italian Embassy, 34 Grant Road, Thorndon, Wellington, **t** (04) 473 5339.

Tourist and travel information is also available from **Alitalia** (Italy's national airline) or **CIT** (Italy's state-run travel agency). In the UK, contact the **Italian Travel Centre**, 30 St James's Street, London SW1A 1HB, **t** (020) 7853 6475.

Embassies and Consulates

Foreign Embassies in Italy

UK, Via San Paolo 7, Milan, **t** (02) 723 001 (consulate); Via XX Settembre 80/a, Rome, **t** (06) 422 0001 (embassy).

Ireland, Piazza di Campitelli 3, Rome, **t** (06) 697 9121 (embassy).

USA, Via Principe Amedeo 2/10, Milan, **t** (02) 290 351 (consulate); Via V. Veneto 119/a, Rome, **t** (06) 46 741 (embassy).

Canada, Via Vittorio Pisani 19, Milan, **t** (02) 67581 (consulate); Via Salaria 243, Rome, **t** (06) 854 441 (embassy).

Australia, Via Borgona 2, Milan, **t** (02) 777 041 (consulate); Via Antonio Bosio 5, Rome, **t** (06) 852 721 (embassy).

New Zealand, Via Guido d'Arezzo 6, Milan, **t** (02) 4801 2544 (consulate); Via Zara 28, Rome, **t** (06) 441 7171 (embassy).

Italian Embassies Abroad

UK: 38 Eaton Place, London SW1X 8AN, **t** (020) 7235 9371; 14 Three Kings Yard, London W1K 4EH, **t** (020) 7312 2200; 32 Melville St, Edinburgh EH3 7HA, **t** (0131) 226 3631, *www.embitaly.org.uk*.

Ireland: 63–5 Northumberland Rd, Dublin, **t** (01) 660 1744, *www.ambdublino.esteri.it*; 7 Richmond Park, Belfast, **t** (02890) 668 854.

USA: 690 Park Ave, New York, NY, **t** (212) 439 8600, *www.italconsulnyc.org*; 12400 Wilshire Boulevard, Suite 300, Los Angeles, CA, **t** (310) 820 0622.

Canada: 1100–510 West Hastings St, Vancouver V6B 1L8, **t** 1-604 684 7288, *http://consvancouver.esteri.it*.

Australia: Level 45, The Gateway Building, 1 Macquarie Place, Circular Quay, Sydney 2000, NSW, **t** (02) 9392 7939, *www.conssydney.esteri.it*.

New Zealand: PO Box 463, 34 Grant Rd, Thorndon, Wellington, **t** (04) 473 5339, *www.italy-embassy.org.nz*.

Entry Formalities

Passports and Visas

EU nationals with a valid passport can enter and stay in Italy as long as they like.

Citizens of the USA, Canada, Australia and New Zealand need only a valid passport to stay for up to three months in Italy. A visa in advance is needed for longer stays, available from an Italian embassy.

UK, 38 Eaton Place, London SW1X, t (020) 7235 9371; 32 Melville St, Edinburgh EH3 7HW, t (0131) 226 3631; 111 Piccadilly, Manchester t (0161) 236 9024, www.amblondra.esteri.it.

Ireland, 63–5 Northumberland Road, Dublin 4, t (01) 660 1744, www.ambdublino.esteri.it.

USA, 3000 Whitehaven Street NW, Washington DC 20008, t (202) 612 4400, www.ambwashingtondc.esteri.it. Consulates in Boston, Chicago, Detriot, Houston, Los Angeles, Miami, New York, Philadelphia and San Francisco.

Canada, Consulates in Montreal, Vancouver, Edmonton, Toronto and Ottawa; 275 Slater St, 21st Floor, Ottawa ON K1P 5H9, t (613) 232 2401, www.ambottawa.esteri.it.

Australia, Level 45, The Gateway Building, 1 Macquarie Place, Circular Quay, Sydney 2000, NSW, t (02) 9392 7900.

New Zealand, 34 Grant Rd, Thorndon, PO box 463, Wellington, t (04) 473 5339,www.amb wellington.esteri.it.

France, 17 Rue du Conseiller Collignon, 75116 Paris, t 01 4430 4700, www.italconsulparigi.org.

Germany, Dessauer Strasse 28/29, Berlin, t (030) 254400, www.ambberlino.esteri.it.

Netherlands, 3rd Floor, Vijzelstraat 79, Amsterdam, t (020) 550 2050.

By law you should register with the police within eight days of your arrival in Italy. In practice this is done automatically for most visitors when they check in at a hotel. Don't be alarmed if the owner of your self-catering property proposes to 'denounce' you to the police when you arrive – it's just a formality.

Customs

EU nationals over the age of 17 can now import a limitless amount of goods for personal use. Non-EU nationals have to pass through the Italian customs. How the frontier police manage to recruit such ugly, mean-looking characters to hold the submachine guns and dogs out of such a good-looking population is a mystery, but

they'll let you be if you don't look suspicious and haven't brought along more than 200 cigarettes or 100 cigars, or not more than a litre of hard drink or three bottles of wine, a couple of cameras, a movie camera, 10 rolls of film for each, a tape recorder, radio, record-player, one canoe less than 5½ metres, sports equipment for personal use, and one TV (though you'll have to pay for a licence for it at Customs). You can take the same items listed above home with you without hassle. US citizens may return with $400 worth of merchandise – keep your receipts.

Pets must be accompanied by a bilingual Certificate of Health from your local Veterinary Inspector.

Currency

There are no limits on how much money you can bring into Italy: legally you are not allowed to export more than €10,000, a sum unlikely to trouble many of us, though officials rarely check.

Disabled Travellers

Italy has been slow off the mark in its provision for disabled visitors compared to other European countries. Cobblestones, uneven or nonexistent pavements, appalling traffic conditions, crowded transport and endless flights of steps in many public places are all disincentives.

Progress is gradually being made, however. Venice has added ramps to many bridges; the

Disabled Support Organizations

Royal Association for Disability & Rehabilitation (RADAR), 12 City Forum, 250 City Road, London EC1V 8AF, t (020) 7250 3222, www.radar.org.uk. They provide a guide, Getting There (£5 inc p&p).

SATH (Society for Accessible Travel and Hospitality), 347 Fifth Avenue, Suite 610, New York 10016, t (212) 447 7284, f (212) 725 8253, www.sath.org.

Mobility International, 45 Broadway West, Eugene OR 97401, t (541) 343 1284, www.miusa.org.

Australian Council for the Rehabilitation of the Disabled (ACROD), PO Box 60, Curtin, ACT 2605, t (02) 6283 3200, www.acrod.org.au.

tourist office's Venice-Lido map no.1 indicates the parts of the city accessible by wheelchair. A national support organization in your own country may have specific information on facilities in Venetia, and the Italian tourist office or CIT (travel agency) can also advise on hotels, museums with ramps and so on. If you book rail travel through CIT, you can request assistance.

Helplines: **Coin Sociale, t** (06) 712 9011, *www.coinsociale.it*; *www.italiapertutti.it*, and *www.accessibleurope.com*.

Insurance and EHIC Cards

You can insure yourself for almost any possible mishap – cancelled flights, stolen or lost baggage and ill health. Check any current policies you hold to see if they cover you while abroad, and under what circumstances, and judge whether you need an additional policy for the journey. Travel agencies sell them, as well as insurance companies.

Citizens of EU countries are entitled to reciprocal health care in Italy's National Health Service and a 90 per cent discount on prescriptions: bring a valid **European Health Insurance Card (EHIC)** with you. The EHIC is free but does not cover all medical expenses (no repatriation costs, for example), and it is advisable to take out separate travel insurance for full cover. Citizens of non-EU countries should check carefully that they have adequate insurance for any medical expenses, and the cost of returning home. Australia has a reciprocal healthcare scheme with Italy, but New Zealand, Canada and the USA do not. If you already have health insurance, a student card, or a credit card, you may be entitled to some medical cover abroad.

No specific **vaccinations** are required or advised for citizens of most countries before visiting Italy; the main health risks are upset stomachs and the effects of too much sun. Take a supply of medicaments with you (insect repellent, anti-diarrhœal medicine, sun lotion and antiseptic cream), and any drugs you need to take regularly.

Maps and Publications

The maps in this guide are for orientation only and, to explore in any detail, you should invest in a good regional map, produced by the Touring Club Italiano, and Istituto Geografico de Agostini. You can find them at:

Stanfords, 12–14 Long Acre, London WC2 9LP, **t** (020) 7836 1321, *www.stanfords.co.uk*.

The Travel Bookshop, 13 Blenheim Crescent, London W11 2EE, **t** (020) 7229 5260, *www.thetravelbookshop.co.uk*.

The Complete Traveler, 199 Madison Ave, New York, NY 10016, **t** (212) 685 9007.

Italian tourist offices can often supply good area maps and town plans.

Money

The currency of Italy is the **euro** (€). There are 7 euro notes: 500, 200, 100, 50, 20, 10 and 5; and 8 coins: 2 euros, 1 euro, 50 cents, 20 cents, 10 cents, 5 cents, 2 cents and 1 cent.

It's a good idea to order a wad of currency from your home bank to have on hand when you arrive in the land of strikes, unforeseen delays and quirky banking hours (*see* below). Take great care how you carry it, however (don't keep it all in one place). Obtaining money is often a frustrating business involving much queueing and form-filling. The major banks and **exchange bureaux** licensed by the Bank of Italy give the best exchange rates for currency or traveller's cheques. Hotels, private exchanges in resorts and Trenitalia-run exchanges at railway stations usually have less advantageous rates, but are open outside normal banking hours. A weekend exchange office can be found in Venice at American Express, S. Marco 1471 or CIT, Piazza S. Marco. In addition there are exchange offices at most airports. Remember that Italians indicate decimals with commas and thousands with full points.

You can (for a significant commission) use your major credit card or British bank card (but check at your bank first) to take money out of Italian automatic tellers (**Bancomat**). Some of the older machines are a little unreliable so look for a nice, shiny, new one. Most machines give you the option of instructions in your native language. You need a four-digit PIN to use these. Make sure you read the instructions carefully, or your card may be retained by the machine. Cash machines in Italy accept Cirrus (the foreign version of

Switch UK) allowing cash withdrawals by debit card. Cirrus can also be used in shops, and you don't need to key in your PIN when making a purchase.

Besides traveller's cheques, most banks will give also you cash on a recognized credit card. Large hotels, resort area restaurants, most petrol stations, shops and car hire firms will accept plastic as well; many smaller places will not. Outside the larger cities you might have a problem with American Express cards, so stick with Visa if you can, or change your cash before you leave for rural areas.

You can have money transferred to you through an Italian bank but this process may take over a week, even if it's sent urgent, *espressissimo*. You will need your passport as identification when you collect it.

Since the euro was introduced, Italy is not the bargain it once was.

Getting There

By Air from the UK and Ireland

There are direct flights to Venice, Verona and Trieste from several British airports, with good year-round services, especially to Venice. Most scheduled flights tend to be more expensive than charters, although there are a number of low-cost options to choose from when taking a scheduled flight (*see* opposite).

British Airways and other **scheduled carriers** have simplified their websites, making it easier for customers to pinpoint the cheapest fares. Fares vary wildly, from as little as €40 all the way up to €700, depending on the season and the time of week.

Carriers who don't offer direct flights, such as Sabena and Lufthansa, can offer cheaper fares to Venice (around £180 return), but these often have quite rigid restrictions and involve flying via another European destination such as Brussels. It's worth checking in advance that flights include all airport taxes, as prices can be misleading otherwise.

From Ireland, Aer Lingus operates five direct flights per week from Dublin to Venice. Ryanair also operates regular direct flights to Venice.

Charter Flights

There are many inexpensive charter flights to Venice and Verona available in summer. You may find cheaper fares by combing the small ads in the travel pages, or from specialist agents (use a reputable ABTA-registered one). The main problems with cheaper flights tend to be inconvenient or unreliable flight schedules, and booking restrictions, i.e. you may have to make reservations far ahead, accept given dates and, if you miss your flight, there's no redress. Taking out good insurance, however cheap your ticket, is your only precaution.

By Air from Mainland Europe

Air travel between Italy and other parts of Europe can be relatively expensive, especially for short hops, so check overland options unless you're in a great hurry. As always, it pays to shop around.

Some airlines (Alitalia, Qantas, Air France, etc.) offer excellent rates on the European stages of intercontinental flights, and Italy is an important touchdown for various long-haul services to the Middle or Far East. However, many of these may have inconvenient departure times and there may be booking restrictions. Amsterdam, Paris and Athens are among the best centres for finding cheap flights. A useful website for budget flights in Europe and from Britain is *www.whichbudget.com*.

By Air from the USA and Canada

The main Italian air gateways for direct flights from North America are Rome and Milan; however, if you're doing a grand tour, check fares to other European destinations (Paris or Amsterdam, for example), which may well be cheaper.

Summer round-trip fares from New York cost around US$1,000–1,300. Delta Airlines operate daily flights to Venice. British Airways sometimes run World Offers when prices may drop under the $1,000 mark. Otherwise, it could well be worth your while catching a cheap flight to London (New York–London fares are always very competitive) and flying on from there.

Major Airlines

In the UK and Ireland

Aer Lingus, Dublin, t (00353) 818 365 000; Belfast, t 0845 084 4444, *www.aerlingus.com*.

Alitalia (Italian State Airline), London, t 0870 544 8259; Dublin, t (01) 677 5171, *www.alitalia.co.uk*.

British Airways, t 0870 850 9850, *www.ba.com*.

easyJet, t 0871 244 2366, *www.easyjet.com*. Flies to Venice, Milan and Rimini.

Lufthansa, t 0870 837 7747, *www.lufthansa.com*.

Ryanair, t 0871 246 0000, *www.ryanair.com*. Three daily flights to Treviso (near Venice), and daily to Trieste and Brescia (near Verona). Often cheaper than easyJet but to smaller, less accessible airports.

In the USA and Canada

Air Canada, t 1 888 247 2262, *www.aircanada.com*.

Alitalia (USA), t 1 800 233 5730, *www.alitalia usa.com*; (Canada), t 1 800 361 8336, *www. alitalia.ca*. May offer you a special deal if you're flying on to Verona, Venice or Trieste.

American Airlines, t 1 800 433 7300, *www.aa.com*.

British Airways, t 1 800 AIRWAYS, *www.britishairways.com*.

Delta, t 1 800 221 1212, *www.delta.com*.

KLM, t 1 800 225 2525, *www.klm.com*. Operating from Toronto and Montréal.

Discount Agencies and Youth Fares

In the UK and Ireland

Budget Travel, 134 Lower Baggot Street, Dublin 2, t (00353 1) 631 1111, *www.budgettravel.ie*.

Italiani Nel Mondo, 6 Palace Street, London SW1E 5HY, t (020) 7834 7651, *www.italiani nelmondo.it*.

Magic of Italy, Wigmore House, Wigmore Lane, Luton LU2 9TN, t 0870 888 0228, *www.magic travelgroup.co.uk*.

Trailfinders, 215 Kensington High Street, London W8 6BD, t 0845 058 5858, *www.trail finders.com*.

United Travel, 2 Old Dublin Road, Stillorgan, C. Dublin, t (00353 1) 215 9300, *www.united travel.ie*.

Besides saving 25 per cent on regular flights, young people under 26 have the choice of flying on special discount charters:

STA, 74 and 86 Old Brompton Rd, London SW7 3LQ, or 117 Euston Rd, London NW1 2SX, t 0870 166 2603, *www.statravel.co.uk*.

USIT, 19–21 Aston Quay, Dublin 2, t (00353 1) 602 1904, *www.usitnow.ie*.

In the USA and Canada

Airhitch, Santa Monica, California, *www.airhitch.org*. Website only.

STA Travel, 205 East 42nd Street, New York NY 10017, t (212) 822 2700, *www.statravelgroup.com*.

Travel Cuts, 187 College St, Toronto ON M5T 1P7, t 1 888 FLYCUTS, *www.travelcuts.com*.

Useful Web Addresses

It pays to check the Internet for last-minute bargains, but you will need to have your suitcase packed and ready to go. Some sites, offering a mixture of flights and holiday packages, do often have very cheap deals for Italy.

www.bargainholidays.com
www.cheapflights.com
www.ebookers.com
www.eurovacations.com
www.expedia.com
www.lastminute.com
www.priceline.com (to bid for tickets)
www.travelocity.com

Prices are rather more if you are flying from Canada, so you may prefer to set off from the States. As elsewhere, fares are very seasonal and much cheaper in winter, especially mid-week.

Charters, Discounts and Deals

From North America, standard scheduled flights on well-known airlines are expensive, but reassuringly reliable and convenient.

Resilient, flexible and/or youthful travellers may be willing to shop around for budget deals on consolidated charters, stand-bys or perhaps even courier flights – remember you can usually only take hand luggage with you on the last of these options (*see www.courier.org*).

For discounted flights, try the small ads in newspaper travel pages e.g. *New York Times, Chicago Tribune, Toronto Globe & Mail*.

Numerous travel clubs and agencies also specialize in discount fares, but may require an annual membership fee.

By Train from the UK and Mainland Europe

A train journey from London to Venice used to be something of a nightmare involving ferries and station changes and taking the best part of 24 hours. This experience can still be repeated, should you so desire it, and will cost you around £200 second-class return plus an extra £14 for a couchette. Fast new rail networks throughout Europe are now providing a much more comfortable alternative. Take a **Eurostar** to Paris and a high-speed **EuroCity** train to Italy, and your journey could be reduced by as much as 12 hours. Unfortunately the price will increase substantially. Train travel, at whatever speed, has its benefits – the opportunity to watch the changing scenery, to acclimatize, and relax – but in an age of low-cost airlines, it is not much of an economy.

Rail Europe Travel Centre, (UK), 178 Piccadilly, London W1V 0BA, t 0870 584 8848, *www.raileurope.co.uk*; (USA), t 1 877 257 2887, *www.raileurope.com*.

Eurostar, EPS House, Waterloo Station, London SE1 8SE, t 08705 186 186, *www.eurostar.com*.

The Orient-Express

One supremely luxurious way of reaching Italy by rail deserves a special mention: the Orient-Express whirls you from London to Venice through Paris, Zürich, Innsbruck and Verona, in a cocoon of traditional twenties' and thirties' glamour with beautifully restored Pullman/wagon-lits.

It's fiendishly expensive – and quite unforgettable. Served by exclusive waiters, evening meals are black tie affairs, and you can watch the heart of Europe unfold outside your window.

Several operators offer packages including smart Venice hotel accommodation and flights for the return journey.

Rail Passes and Timetables

Inter-Rail (UK) or **Eurail** passes (USA/Canada) give unlimited travel throughout Europe for one, two or three months. A month's full Inter-Rail pass costs over £300 (see *www.interrail net.com* or *www.interrailer.com*), although it's cheaper for under-26s and if you buy zonal passes.

If you are planning to see just Italy, inclusive rail passes may not be worthwhile. Fares on Trenitalia, the Italian State Railway, are among the lowest in Europe. If you intend travelling extensively by train, one of the special Italian tourist passes may be a better bet.

The Trenitalia Pass allows 3–10 days' unlimited travel within a two month period (remember that you'll have to pay supplements on Eurostar Italia trains, though), and is available for 1st or 2nd class, and with concessionary rates for over-60s and under-26s. Combined France/Italy train passes are available for non-EU passport holders.

A convenient, pocket-sized timetable detailing all the main and secondary Italian railway lines is now available in the UK from Italwings (see below) costing £7 plus 50p postage, but they do have limited stocks and sell out fast. If you wait until you arrive in Italy, however, you can pick up the Italian timetable at major stations and many newspaper vendors for €4.50; detailed online timetables are found at *www.trenitalia.com*.

The indispensable *European Timetable* is published by Thomas Cook and available in bookshops in Britain, or you can order a copy through t (01733) 416 477, *publishing-sales@thomascook.com*.

Useful Addresses

Contact any of the listings below for Inter-Rail passes or other information on rail travel to Italy.

From the USA and Canada, try the US branches of Rail Europe (*see* above).

Rail Choice (rail passes and tickets within Italy), (UK) t 0870 165 7300, *www.rail choice.co.uk*; (USA) t 1 800 361 RAIL, *www.railchoice.com*.

Thomas Cook, any branch.

Italwings, Travel & Accommodation, Cityjet House, 65 Judd Street, London WC1H 9RF, t (020) 7287 2117, *www.italwings.co.uk*.

CITALIA Holidays, (UK), The Atrium, London Road, Crawley, West Sussex RH10 9SR, t 0870 901 4013, *www.citalia.co.uk*; (Canada) 7007 Islington Ave, Suite 205, Woodbridge, ON LYL 4T5, t 1 800 387 0711, *www.cittours-canada.com*.

Venice Simplon-Orient-Express, UK, Sea Containers House, 20 Upper Ground, London SE1 9PF, **t** (020) 7805 5060; USA, **t** (212) 302 5055, *www.orient-express.com*.

By Bus and Coach

Eurolines is the main international bus operator in Europe, with representatives in Italy and many other countries. Regular services run to many northern Italian cities but, needless to say, the journey is long and the saving on price relatively small (a return ticket from London to Venice costs £107; if booked seven days in advance the price drops). It still makes a masochistic choice in comparison with a discounted air fare, or even rail travel, but if you like travelling with your knees tucked under your chin, the service is reliable at least. Within Italy, you can obtain more information on long-distance bus services from any CIT office.

Eurolines, Victoria Coach Station, London SW1W OAG, **t** 08705 808080, *www.nationalexpress.com*, booked through National Express.

By Car

Driving to Venetia from the UK is a lengthy and expensive proposition. If you're only staying for a short period, check costs against airline fly-drive schemes. Plan for the best part of 30 hours' driving time, even if you stick to fast toll roads.

The most scenic and hassle-free route is via the Alps, avoiding crowded Riviera roads in summer but, if you take a route through Switzerland, expect to pay for the privilege (around £14 or SF30 for motorway use).

In winter the passes may be closed and you will have to stick to those expensive tunnels. You can avoid some of the driving by putting your car on the train, though this is scarcely a cheap option. There is a Motorail link from Denderleeuw in Belgium to Venice: contact **Rail Choice**, **t** 0870 165 7300, *www.railchoice. co.uk*. The **Italian Auto Club (ACI)**, **t** toll free 803 116, *www.aci.it*, offers reasonably priced breakdown assistance.

To bring a GB-registered car into Italy, you need a vehicle registration document, full driving licence, and insurance papers – these must be carried at all times when driving. If you have one of the new photo ID driving licences, take that, otherwise you should get an international driving permit, available from the AA.

Non-EU citizens should preferably have an international driving licence, with an Italian translation incorporated. Your vehicle should display a nationality plate indicating its country of registration.

Before travelling, check everything is in perfect order. Minor infringements like worn tyres or burnt-out sidelights can cost you dear in any country. A red triangular hazard sign is obligatory; also recommended are a spare set of bulbs, a first-aid kit and a fire extinguisher. Spare parts for non-Italian cars can be difficult to find, especially Japanese models.

Before crossing the Italian border, remember to fill up with petrol; *benzina* is still very expensive in Italy. It may also be wise to have a clean car when crossing the border if you don't want to stand out.

AA, **t** 0870 6000 371, *www.theaa.com*.

RAC, **t** 0800 550 055, *www.rac.co.uk*.

AAA, **t** regional according to zip, *www.aaa.com*.

For more information on driving in Italy, *see* 'Getting Around: By Car', p.90.

Getting Around

Italy has an excellent network of airports, railways, highways and byways and you'll find getting around fairly easy – until one union or another takes it into its head to go on strike (to be fair they rarely do it during the high holiday season). There's plenty of talk about passing a law to regulate strikes, but it won't happen soon if ever. Instead, learn to recognize the word in Italian: *sciopero* (SHO-pe-ro), and do as the Romans do – quiver with resignation. There's always a day or two's notice, and strikes usually last only a day, just long enough to throw a spanner in the works if you have to catch a plane. Keep your ears open and watch for notices posted in the stations; if you aren't seriously affected, you could take the Italian approach: shrug your shoulders and head for the nearest café.

By Air

Air traffic within Italy is intense, with up to 10 flights a day on popular routes.

Domestic flights are handled by **Alitalia**. Air travel makes most sense when hopping between north and south. Shorter journeys are often just as quick (and much less expensive) by train or even bus if you take check-in and airport travelling times into account. Trieste, Venice and Verona all have direct flights to and from Rome and Milan.

Domestic flight costs are comparable to those in other European countries: a return fare from Rome to Venice costs about £125 including tax. Fares change often, even from hour to hour, if you're checking on the Internet. There are variable discounts for children under 12 and a nominal fee for infants.

Each airport has a bus terminal in the city; ask about schedules when you purchase your ticket, to avoid hefty taxi fares. Baggage allowances vary between airlines. Tickets can be bought at CIT offices and other large travel agencies.

Several other domestic airlines offer very competitive fares, though some don't accept foreign credit cards on their websites:

Air Dolomiti, *www.airdolomiti.it* (Verona-based).

Air One, *www.flyairone.it*.

Alpieagles, *www.alpieagles.com* (Venice-based).

Meridiana, *www.meridiana.it* (all over).

By Train

Rail information from anywhere in Italy, **t** 892 021 (in Italy, land lines only), *www.trenitalia.com*.

Italy's national railway, **Trenitalia** (a division of Ferrovie dello Stato, or FS), is well run, inexpensive (despite recent price rises) and often a pleasure to ride. Some trains are sleek and high-tech, but much of the rolling stock hasn't been changed for 50 years.

Possible unpleasantnesses you may encounter, besides a strike, are delays, crowding (especially at weekends and in the summer), and crime on overnight trains, where someone rifles through your bags while you sleep. The crowding at night, however, becomes much less of a problem. If possible try to avoid travelling by train at 1pm, as the school children all pile into every available space to get home to *Mamma*.

It's best to reserve a seat in advance (*fare una prenotazione*): the fee is small and can save you hours standing in some train corridor. On the more expensive trains, **reservations** are mandatory. Do check when you purchase your ticket in advance that the date is correct; tickets are only valid the day they're purchased unless you specify otherwise. A number on your reservation slip will indicate in which car your seat is – find it before you board rather than after. The same goes for sleepers and couchettes on overnight trains, which must also be reserved in advance. At sleepy rural train stations without information boards, the imminent arrival of a train is signalled by a platform bell.

Tickets

Tickets may be purchased not only in the stations, but at many travel agents in the city centres. Fares are strictly determined by the kilometres travelled. The system is computerized and runs smoothly, at least until you try to get a reimbursement for an unused ticket. You may have to queue but you do get your money eventually, provided you have not stamped your ticket.

If you've bought a ticket for a journey using both InterCity and Eurostar Italia, and the InterCity is over 30 minutes late or the Eurostar Italia is over 20 minutes late, you can claim a third of the fare back. The voucher will be posted out to you in Italy if your claim is valid – claim forms are available at stations.

Be sure you ask which platform (*binario*) your train arrives at; the big permanent boards in the stations are not always correct. Queues for tickets are often extremely long, but there are efficient machines with instructions available also in English. Pay by cash or credit card to book tickets and reservations. If you pay by credit card don't withdraw your card till the ticket has been printed – if you interrupt the transaction your card may be debited but you miss out on the ticket. And if you try to do the transaction again you'll get debited twice and end up with one ticket. Always remember to stamp your ticket (*convalidare*) in the not very obvious yellow machines at the head of the platform before boarding the train, or else you may have to pay a fine. Don't be alarmed if rural stations look uninhabited, or if the ticket office is closed. Tickets can be bought at any tobacconist or café near the station; failing that, honesty is the best approach. If you get on a train without a ticket, you can buy one from the conductor with an added 20% penalty. You can also pay a conductor to move up to first class or get a couchette, if there are places available.

There is a fairly straightforward hierarchy of trains. At the bottom of the pyramid is the humble *Regionale* or *Interregionale* which often stops even where there's no station in sight; it can be excruciatingly slow. When you're checking the schedules, beware of what may look like the first train to your destination – if it's a *Regionale*, it will be the last to arrive. A *Diretto* stops far less, an *Espresso* just at the main towns. *Intercity* trains whoosh between the big cities and *Eurocity* trains link Italian cities with major European centres. Both of these services require a supplement – some 30% more than a regular fare. Sitting on the pinnacle are the true Kings of the Rails, the super-swish and super-fast *Eurostar Italia* trains. These make very few stops, have both 1st- and 2nd-class carriages, and carry a supplement which includes an obligatory seat reservation. So, the faster the train, the more you pay. InterCity trains are cheaper than Eurostar Italia and usually only an hour slower; even 1st-class InterCity is cheaper than 2nd-class Eurostar Italia.

Trains are now almost entirely non-smoking. On Eurostars and InterCities there is one 2nd-class and one 1st-class carriage for smokers; on other trains smoking is banned entirely: steep fines to pay for those who ignore the signs.

Facilities

Refreshments on routes of any great distance are provided by bar cars or trolleys; you can usually get sandwiches and coffee from vendors along the tracks at intermediary stops. Station bars often have a good variety of take-away travellers' fare; consider at least investing in a plastic bottle of

mineral water, since there's no drinking water on the trains.

Besides trains and bars, Italy's stations offer other facilities. Most have a *Deposito*, where you can leave your bags for hours or days for a small fee. The larger ones have porters (who charge a few euros per piece) and some even have luggage trolleys; information offices, currency exchanges open at weekends (not at the most advantageous rates, however), hotel-finding and reservation services, kiosks with foreign papers, restaurants, etc. You can also arrange to have a rental car awaiting you at your destination, *see* p.91.

Beyond that, some words need to be said about riding the rails on the most serendipitous national line in Europe. Be careful of beggars or thieves doing the rounds on the trains; and beware of pickpockets on the platform when you arrive. Trenitalia may have its strikes and delays, its petty crime and bureaucratic inconveniences, but when you catch it on its better side it will treat you to a dose of the real Italy before you even reach your destination. If there's a choice, try for one of the older cars, depressingly grey outside but fitted with comfortably upholstered seats, Art Deco lamps and old pictures of the towns and villages of the country.

Best of all, Trenitalia is relatively reliable, and even if there has been some delay you'll have an amenable station full of clocks to wait in; some of the station bars have astonishingly good food (some do not), but at any of them you may accept a well-brewed cappuccino and look blasé until the train comes in. Try to avoid travel on Friday evenings, when the major lines out of the big cities are packed. Trenitalia is a lottery; you may find a train uncomfortably full of Italians (in which case stand by the doors, or impose on the salesmen in first class, where the conductor will be happy to change your ticket). Now and then, you may just have a beautiful 1920s compartment all to yourself for the night – even better if you're travelling with your beloved – and be serenaded on the platform.

By Coach and Bus

Inter-city coach travel is sometimes quicker than train travel, but also a bit more expensive. Coaches almost always depart from the vicinity of the train station, and tickets usually need to be purchased before you get on. In many regions they are the only means of public transport and well used, with frequent schedules.

If you can't get a ticket before the coach leaves, get on anyway and pretend you can't speak a word of Italian; the worst that can happen is that someone will make you pay for a ticket. The base for all country bus lines will be the provincial capital.

City buses are the traveller's friend. Most cities (at least in the north) label routes well; fares within the city limits and immediate suburbs cost around €1. City bus tickets must always be purchased before you get on, either at a tobacconist's, a newspaper kiosk, in bars, or from ticket machines near the main stops. Once you get on, you must 'obliterate' your ticket in the machines in the front or back of the bus; controllers stage random checks to make sure you've punched your ticket. Fines for cheaters are €50, and the odds are about 12 to 1 against a check, so many passengers take a chance. If you're good-hearted, you'll buy a ticket and help some overburdened municipal transit line meet its annual deficit.

By Car

The advantages of driving in Italy generally outweigh the disadvantages, but, before you bring your own car or hire one, consider the kind of holiday you're planning. For a tour of art cities or a few days lounging on the beach, you'd be better off not driving at all: parking is impossible, traffic impossible, deciphering one-way streets, signals and signs impossible. But for touring the countryside a car gives immeasurable freedom.

Third-party **insurance** is a minimum requirement in Italy (and you should be a lot more than minimally insured, as many of the locals have none whatsoever). Obtain a Green Card from your insurer, which gives automatic proof that you are fully covered. Also get hold of a **European Accident Statement** form, which may simplify things if you have an accident. Always insist on a full translation of any statement you are asked to sign. Breakdown assistance insurance is obviously a sensible investment (e.g. AA's Five Star or RAC's European Motoring Assistance).

Petrol (*benzina*: unleaded is *benzina senza piombo*, and diesel is *gasolio*) is still very expensive in Italy (just under €1.35 per litre; fill up before you cross the border). Many fuel stations close for lunch in the afternoon, and few stay open late at night, though you may find a 'self-service' where you feed a machine nice smooth €5 notes. Motorway (*autostrada*) tolls are quite high. Rest stops and petrol stations along the motorways stay open 24 hours. Other roads – *superstrada* on down through the Italian grading system – are free of charge.

Italians are famously anarchic behind a wheel. The only way to beat the locals is to join them by adopting an assertive and constantly alert driving style. Bear in mind that whoever hesitates is lost (especially at traffic lights, where the danger is less great of crashing into someone at the front than being rammed from behind). All drivers from boy racers to elderly nuns tempt providence by overtaking at the most dangerous bend, and no matter how fast you are hammering along the *autostrada*, plenty will whizz past at apparently supersonic rates.

North Americans used to leisurely speed limits and gentler road manners may find the Italian interpretation of the highway code somewhat stressful. If you are a nervous driver, avoid cities – even parking can seem well nigh impossible. Be careful on motorways when you leave your car at Autogrilles (roadside stops), as thefts are not uncommon. Don't leave anything out that could tempt thieves and park in a well-lit spot as near as possible to the door.

Speed limits (generally ignored) are 130km/h on motorways (110km/h for cars under 1100cc or motorcycles), 110km/h on main highways, 90km/h on secondary roads, and 50km/h in built-up areas. Fines for an offence (*infrazione*) vary from €32 to €1,000.

If you are undeterred by these caveats, you may actually enjoy driving in Italy, at least away from the congested tourist centres. Signposting is generally good although keep your eyes peeled, as the sharper the bend, the shorter the warning you will get. Hairpins abound in the mountains and they are numbered, so you know how many more you have to deal with. Roads are usually excellently maintained; indeed, you will find road crews in the most inaccessible locations, bravely shoring up another collapsed rock face. Some of the roads are feats of engineering that the Romans themselves would have admired – bravura projects suspended on cliffs, crossing valleys on vast stilts and winding up hairpins.

Buy a good **road map**. The Italian Touring Club series is excellent, while the commendable *AA Road Atlas Italy* is available in the UK.

The **Automobile Club of Italy (ACI)** is a good friend to the foreign motorist. Besides having bushels of useful information and tips, ACI can be reached from anywhere by dialling **116** – also use this number if you have to find the nearest service station. If things go seriously pear-shaped and you need major repairs, the ACI can make sure the prices charged are according to their guidelines.

Hiring a Car

Hiring a car, *autonoleggio*, is simple but not particularly cheap – Italy has some of the highest rates in Europe. A small car (Fiat Punto or similar) with unlimited mileage and collision damage waiver, including tax, will set you back around €50 per day although if you hire the car for a week, this will decrease slightly pro rata.

Ordering child seats can be a problem: book these well in advance – or bring your own.

The minimum age limit is usually 25 (sometimes 23) and the driver must have held their licence for over a year – this will have to be produced, along with the driver's passport, when hiring the car. Major rental companies have offices in airports or main stations, though it may be worthwhile checking prices of local firms. If you need a car for longer than three weeks, leasing may be a more economic alternative. The National Tourist Office has a list of firms that hire caravans (trailers) or camper vans. Non-residents are cannot buy cars in Italy.

Taking all things into account, it may make sense to arrange your car hire before leaving home and, in particular, to check out fly-drive discounts. Notwithstanding the convenience of picking up the car when you arrive, it often works out cheaper.

The best deals are often found on the Internet: firms such as Auto Europe (*see above*) have reciprocal arrangements with other companies, making it possible to pick up your car from airports, hotels and many city centres. Ask for a car with the least amount of company stickers on it – hire cars are a prime target for thieves – and when you park always be sure to leave nothing on display.

Hitchhiking

It is illegal to hitch on the *autostrada*, though you may pick up a lift near one of the toll booths. Don't hitch from the city centres; head for suburban exit routes. For the best chances of getting a lift, travel light, look respectable and take off your sunglasses. Holding up a sign indicating your destination in huge letters will vastly improve your chances of getting a lift. Never hitch at points which may cause an accident or obstruction; Italian traffic is bad enough already!

Risks for women are lower in northern Italy than in the more macho south, but it is not advisable to hitch alone. Two or more men are likely to encounter some reluctance from drivers.

By Motorcycle or Bicycle

Mopeds, Vespas and scooters are the vehicles of choice for a great many Italians. You will see them everywhere. In the traffic-congested towns this is a ubiquity born of necessity; when driving space is limited, two

Car Rental Agencies

UK and Ireland

Avis, t 0844 581 0147, *www.avis.co.uk*.
Auto Europe, t 0800 358 1229, *www.auto europe.com*.
Europcar, t 0845 758 5375, *www.europcar.co.uk*.
Hertz, t 0870 844 8844, *www.hertz.co.uk*.

USA and Canada

Avis, t 1 800 331 1212, *www.avis.com*.
Auto Europe, t 1 888 223 5555, *www.auto europe.com*.
Europcar, t 877 940 6900, *www.europcar.com*.
Hertz, t 1 800 654 3001, *www.hertz.com*.
National, t 1 800 CAR RENT, *www.nationalcar.com*.

wheels are always better than four. However, in Italy, riding a two-wheeler often seems to be as much a form of cultural and social expression as a means of getting from A to B.

Italian youths tend to prefer chic Italian lines, Vespas, Lambrettas and the like, which they parade self-consciously through the town's main drags. Older members of society, in the main, plump for mopeds, the type you can actually pedal should you feel so inclined. Choosing your machine, however, is only the first stage of this cultural process; it then becomes necessary to master the Italian way of riding. This means dispensing with a crash helmet (despite the fact that they are compulsory) in order to look as stylishly laid-back as possible while still achieving an alarming rate of speed: riding sidesaddle, or whilst on the phone, or smoking, or holding a dog or child under one arm; all of these methods have their determined and expert adherents.

Despite the obvious dangers of this means of transport (especially if you choose to do it Italian-style), there are clear benefits to moped-riding in Italy. For one thing it is cheaper than car hire – costs for a *motorino* are about €20 per day, scooters somewhat more (around €30), you must be at least 14 – and can prove an excellent way of covering a town's sights in a limited space of time. Furthermore, because Italy is such a scooter-friendly place, car drivers here are more conditioned to their presence and so are less likely to hurtle into them when taking corners.

Nonetheless, you should only consider hiring a moped if you have ridden one before (Italy is no place to learn) and, despite local examples, you should wear a helmet. Also, be warned, some travel insurance policies exclude claims resulting from scooter or motorbike accidents.

Italians are keen **cyclists**, and can be regularly seen racing drivers straight up the Dolomites. If you're not training for the Tour de France consider the topography well before planning a bicycling tour. Much of the Veneto and southern half of Friuli is fairly flat and prime cycling territory, but it can be sweltering in the summer.

Prices for **bike rental** begin at about €10 per day, which may make buying one interesting (€120–200) if you plan to spend much time in the saddle, either in a bike shop or through the classified ad papers put out in nearly every city and region.

Italians have elevated the science of building bicycles to an art form, and makes such as Colnago, Pinarello and De Rosa have been cherished by cyclists the world over. Buy a bike in Italy and you're buying a piece of Italian heritage.

You will see every age group clawing their way up impossible mountains, then having a leisurely lunch before launching themselves back down again. If you bring your own bike, do check the airlines to see what their policies are on transporting them. Bikes can be transported by train in Italy, either with you or within a couple of days – apply at the baggage office (*ufficio bagagli*). Many towns in Venetia hire out bikes by the hour or day; ask at the tourist offices.

Where to Stay

All accommodation in Italy is classified by the Provincial Tourist Boards. Price control, however, has been deregulated since 1992. Hotels set their own tariffs from then on, which means that prices rocketed. After a period of rapid and erratic price fluctuation, tariffs are at last settling down again to more predictable levels under the influence of market forces. Good-value, interesting accommodation in cities can be very difficult to find.

The quality of furnishings and facilities has generally improved in all categories in recent years. Many hotels have installed smart bathrooms and electronic gadgetry. At the top end of the market, Italy has a number of exceptionally sybaritic hotels, furnished and decorated with real panache. Nevertheless, you can still find plenty of older-style hotels and *pensioni*, whose eccentricities of character and architecture (in some cases undeniably charming) may frequently be at odds with modern standards of comfort or even safety.

Hotels and Guesthouses

Italian *alberghi* come in all shapes and sizes. They are rated from one to five stars, depending what facilities they offer (not

Accommodation Price Codes

Prices quoted in the guide represent the cheapest rate you can expect to pay for a double room with bath/shower in high season. Prices will often drop considerably, particularly at the top-end places, in the low season.

luxury	€€€€€	€250 and above
very expensive	€€€€	€160–250
expensive	€€€	€100–160
moderate	€€	€70–100
inexpensive	€	€70 and under

their character, style or charm). The star ratings are some indication of price levels, but don't pay too much attention to them. For tax reasons not all hotels choose to advertise themselves at the rating to which they are entitled, so you may find a modestly rated hotel just as comfortable (or more so) than a higher rated one. Conversely, there are a number of hotels that offer few stars in hopes of attracting budget-conscious travellers, but charge just as much as a higher-rated neighbour.

Pensioni are generally more modest establishments, though nowadays the distinction between these and ordinary hotels is becoming blurred. *Locande* are traditionally an even more basic form of hostelry, but these days the term may denote somewhere fairly chic. Other inexpensive accommodation is sometimes known as *alloggi* or *affittacamere*. There are usually plenty of cheap dives around railway stations; for somewhere more salubrious, head for the historic quarters, although rooms can be small. But whatever the shortcomings of the décor, furnishings and fittings, you can usually rely at least on having clean sheets. Unless it's the winter season, the heating will be off.

Price lists, by law, must be posted on the door of every room, along with meal prices and any extra charges (such as air-conditioning). Many hotels display two or three different rates, depending on the season. Low-season rates may be about a third lower than peak-season tariffs and although the seasons should be clearly marked, it's worth asking, as summer can come amazingly early to some hotels! A number of resort hotels, along with the

resort around them, close down altogether for several months a year.

During high season you should always book ahead to be sure of a room (a fax or email reservation may be less frustrating to organize than one by post). If you have paid a deposit, your booking is valid under Italian law, but don't expect it to be refunded if you have to cancel. Deposits (particularly common in Verona and around Lake Garda in high season) may be debited from credit cards in advance to pay or require wiring money into the account (make sure you get a receipt or email or fax confirmation). Tourist offices publish annual regional lists of hotels and pensions with current rates, but do not generally make reservations for visitors. Major city business hotels may offer significant discounts at weekends.

Main railway stations generally have accommodation booking desks; inevitably, a fee is charged. Chain hotels or motels are generally the easiest hotels to book, though not always the most interesting to stay in. Top of the list is CIGA (*Compagnia Grandi Alberghi*) – now owned by the Starwood Group – with some of the most luxurious establishments in Italy, many of them grand, turn-of-the-century places that have been exquisitely restored. Venice's legendary Cipriani is one of its flagships. The French consortium Relais et Châteaux specializes in tastefully indulgent accommodation, often in historic buildings. At a more affordable level, one of the biggest chains in Italy is Jolly Hotels, always reliable if not all up to the same standard; these can generally be found near the centres of larger towns. Many motels are operated by the ACI (Italian Automobile Club) or by AGIP (the oil company) and usually located along major exit routes.

If you arrive without a reservation, begin looking or phoning around for accommodation early in the day. If possible, inspect the room (and bathroom facilities) before you book, and check the tariff carefully. Italian hoteliers may legally alter their rates twice during the year (although in some hotels they may appear to change daily), so printed tariffs or tourist board lists (and prices quoted in this book!) may be out of date. Hoteliers who wilfully overcharge should be reported to the local tourist office. You will be asked for your passport for registration purposes.

Prices listed in this guide are for double rooms in high season; you can expect to pay about two-thirds the rate for single occupancy, though in high season you may be charged the full double rate in a popular beach resort. Extra beds are usually charged at about a third more of the room rate. Rooms without private bathrooms generally charge 20–30% less, and most offer discounts for children sharing parents' rooms, or children's meals. A *camera singola* (single room) may cost anything from about €40 upwards. A double room (*camera doppia*) is from about €50 to €300 or more. If you want a double bed, specify a *camera matrimoniale*.

Breakfast is usually included in the room rate, with little or no reduction if you don't want it. Many hotels now offer a buffet. If you are given the choice, you can usually get better value by eating breakfast in a local bar or café. In high season you may be expected to take half-board in resorts if the hotel has a restaurant, and one-night stays may be refused.

Hostels and Budget Accommodation

There aren't many youth hostels in Italy (where they are known as *alberghi* or *ostelli per la gioventù*), but they are generally pleasant and sometimes located in historic buildings. The *Associazione Italiana Alberghi per la Gioventù* (Italian Youth Hostel Association, or AIG) is affiliated to the International Youth Hostel Federation. For a full list of hostels, contact **AIG** at Via Cavour 44, 00184 Roma, **t** (06) 487 1152, **f** (06) 488 0492, *www.ostellionline.org*; or see the Italy sections of *www.yha.com* (official hostels) or *www.hostelbooking.com* (includes unofficial hostels). An international membership card will enable you to stay in any of them. You can obtain these in advance from the following organizations (or you can purchase them on the spot in many hostels if you don't already have one):

UK, Youth Hostels Association of England and Wales, Dimple Road, Matlock, Derbyshire DE4 3YK, **t** (01629) 592 600, *www.yha.org.uk*.

USA, Hostelling International USA, 8401 Colesville Rd, Suite 600, Silver Spring, MD 20910, **t** (301) 495 1240, *www.hiayh.org*.

Australia, Australian Youth Hostel Association, 422 Kent St, Sydney, **t** (02) 9261 1111 (branches all over Oz), *www.yha.com.au*.

Canada, Canadian Hostelling Association, 1600 James Naismith Drive, Suite 608, Gloucester, Ontario K1B 5N4, **t** (613) 748 5638.

Religious institutions also run hostels; some are single sex, others will accept Catholics only. Rates are usually somewhere around €15, including breakfast. Discounts are available for senior citizens, and some family rooms are available. You generally have to check in after 5pm, and pay for your room before 9am. Hostels usually close for most of the daytime, and many operate a curfew. During the spring, noisy school parties cram hostels for field trips. In the summer, it's advisable to book ahead.

Villas, Flats and Chalets

If you're travelling in a group or with a family, self-catering can be the ideal way to experience Italy. The National Tourist Office has lists of agencies in the UK and USA which rent places on a weekly or fortnightly basis. CIT offices also rent flats and villas. If you have set your heart on a particular region, write ahead to its tourist office for a list of local agencies and owners, who will send brochures or particulars of their accommodation. Maid service is included in the more glamorous villas; ask whether bed linen and towels are provided. A few of the larger operators are listed in the table overleaf.

Rural Self-Catering

For a breath of rural seclusion, the normally gregarious Italians head for a spell on a working farm, in accommodation (usually self-catering) that often approximates to the French gîte. Often, however, the real pull is a restaurant in which you can sample some home-grown produce (olives, wine, etc.). Outdoor activities may also be on tap.

This branch of the Italian tourist industry is run by a special agency, **Agriturist**, and has boomed in recent years to include two other similar organizations, **Terranostra** and

Turismo Verde. Prices of farmhouse accommodation are still reasonable (expect to pay around €45–50 upwards for a cottage or double room). To make the most of your rural hosts, it's as well to have a little Italian under your belt. You can obtain complete listings compiled by the regional centres.

Veneto: Agriturist Ufficio Regionale, Via Monteverdi 15, Venezia VE, **t** (041) 987 400, *www.agriturist.it*. Terranostra: Via Croce Rossa 32, Padova, **t** (049) 899 7311, *www.terra nostra.it*. Turismo Verde: Via Rizzardi 26, Marghera VE, **t** (041) 538 1999, *www. turismoverde.it*.

Trentino: Associazione Agriturismo Trentino, Via Aconcio Jacopo 13, Trento, **t** (0461) 235 323.

Alto Adige: Alto Adige Promozione Turismo, Piazza Parocchia 11, 39100 Bolzano, **t** (0471) 307 000, **f** (0471) 993 808.

Friuli-Venezia Giulia: Via Daniele Morozz, 33100 Udine, **t** (0432) 202 646, *www.agri turismofvg.com*.

Alpine Refuges

The Italian Alpine Club operates refuges (*rifugi*) on the main mountain trails (some accessible only by *funivie*). These may be predictably spartan, or surprisingly comfortable (as well as richly characterful). Many have restaurants. For an up-to-date list, write to the **Club Alpino Italiano**, Via Petrella 19, Milan, **t** (02) 205 7231, *www.cai.it*. Refuges charge €20–35 per person per night, including breakfast; camping €8 per adult plus €6 per tent. Most are open only from July to September, but those used by skiers are about a fifth more expensive from December to April. Book ahead in August.

Camping

Life under canvas is not necessarily a great bargain, but there are over 2,000 sites in Italy. Unofficial camping is generally frowned on and may attract a stern rebuke from the local police. Camper vans (and facilities for them) are increasingly popular. You can obtain a list of local sites from any regional tourist office.

Campsite charges generally range from about €8 per adult; tents additionally cost about €6 each. Small extra charges may also be levied for hot showers and electricity.

To obtain a camping carnet and to book ahead, write to the **Centro Internazionale Prenotazioni Campeggio**, Casella Postale 23, 50041 Calenzano, Firenze, **t** (055) 882 391, **f** (055) 882 381, *www.federcampeggio.it* (ask for their list of campsites as well as the booking form). The *Touring Club Italiano* (TCI) publishes a comprehensive annual guide to campsites and tourist villages throughout Italy, which is available in bookshops for €20. Write to **TCI**, Corso Italia 10, Milan, **t** (02) 85261, *www.touringclub.it*.

Tour Operators and Special-Interest Holidays

Dozens of general and specialist companies offer holidays in Italy. Some of the major ones are listed below. Not all of them are necesssarily ABTA-bonded; we recommend you check before booking.

UK General

Cosmos, Wren Court, 17 London Road, Bromley, Kent BR1 1DP, **t** 0870 443 5285, *www.cosmos-holidays.co.uk*.

Cresta Italy, Chaler House, Woodlands Road, Altrincham, Cheshire WA14 1EZ, **t** 0870 161 0900, *www.crestaholidays.co.uk*.

First Choice, Diamond House, 2 Peel Cross Road, Salford, Manchester M5 2AN, **t** 0870 850 3999, *www.firstchoice.co.uk*.

Magic of Italy, Wigmore House, Wigmore Lane, Luton LU2 9TN, **t** 0870 888 0228, *www.magic travelgroup.co.uk*.

Page & Moy, 136–40 London Road, Leicester LE2 1EN, **t** 0870 833 4012, *www.page-moy.co.uk*.

Sunvil, Sunvil House, 7–8 Upper Sq, Old Isleworth, Middx TW7 7BJ, **t** (020) 8568 4499, *www.sunvil.co.uk*.

Thomson Holidays, 148 Queensway, Bayswater, London W2 6LY, **t** (020) 7229 2654, *www.thomson.co.uk*.

UK Special-interest

Alternative Travel, 69–71 Banbury Road, Oxford OX2 6PJ, **t** (01865) 315678, *www.atg-oxford.co.uk*. Walking and cycling tours.

Arblaster & Clarke, Clarke House, Farnham Road, West Liss, Hants GU33 6JQ, **t** (01730) 893 344, *www.winetours.co.uk*. Wine tours linked with opera.

British Museum Traveller, 46 Bloomsbury Street, London WC1B 3QQ, **t** (020) 7323 1234, *www.britishmuseumtraveller.co.uk*. Guest lecturers, art and architecture.

Brompton Travel, Brompton House, 64 Richmond Road, Kingston upon Thames, Surrey KT2 5EH, **t** (020) 8549 3334. Tailor-made tours and opera.

Citalia, (UK) The Atrium, London Road, Crawley, RH10 9SR, **t** 0870 901 4013, *www.citalia.co.uk*; (Canada) Toronto, **t** 800 387 0711, *www.cittours-canada.com*. Opera.

JMB, 3 Powick Mills, Old Road, Worcester WR2 4BU, **t** (01905) 422 282, *www.jmb-travel.co.uk*. Opera tours.

Kirker, 4 Waterloo Court, 10 Theed Street, London SE1 8ST, **t** (0870) 112 3333, *www.kirkerholidays.com*. A decent range of city breaks, tailor-made tours and trips to the Verona Opera.

Martin Randall Travel, 10 Barley Mow Passage, Chiswick, London W4 4GF, **t** (020) 8742 3355, *www.martinrandall.com*. Cultural tours led by expert guides: themes include art and architecture, wines, gardens.

Ramblers, Lemsford Mill, Lemsford Village, Welwyn Garden City AL8 7TR, **t** (01707) 331 133, *www.ramblersholidays.co.uk*.

Saga, The Saga Building, Enbrook Park, Folkestone, Kent CT20 5SE, **t** (0800) 096 0074, *www.saga.co.uk*, or *www.sagaholidays.com*. Tours for the over-50s.

Solos, 54–8 High Street, Edgware, Middlesex HA8 7EJ, **t** 0870 0720 700, *www.solosholidays.co.uk*. Singles holidays.

Special Tours, 2 Chester Row, London SW1W 9JH, **t** (020) 7730 2297, *www.specialtours.co.uk*. Escorted cultural tours: principally art, architecture, gardens.

Tasting Places, Unit 108, 40 Buspace Studios, Conlan Street, London W10 5AP, **t** (020) 8964 5333, *www.tastingplaces.com*. Cookery courses near Verona.

Travel for the Arts, 12–15 Hanger Green, London W5 3EL, **t** (020) 8799 8350, *www.travelforthearts.com*. Opera and ballet.

Travelsphere, Compass House, Rockingham Road, Market Harborough, Leicestershire LE16 7QD, **t** (0870) 240 2426, *www.travelsphere.co.uk*. Coach tours.

Venice Simplon-Orient-Express (UK), Sea Containers House, 20 Upper Ground, London SE1 9PF, **t** (020) 7921 4000; (USA) **t** (212) 683 2442, *www.orient-express.com*. Luxury rail tours.

WA Shearings, Miry Lane, Wigan WN3 4AG, **t** (01942) 824 824, *www.washearings.com*. Coach tours.

USA and Canada

American Express Vacations, American Express, PO Box 297812, Ft Lauderdale, FL 33329-7812, **t** 1 800 297 2977, *www.americanexpress.com/travel*. A range of repacked or tailor-made tours.

Dailey-Thorp Travel, PO Box 670, Big Horn, Wyoming, **t** (307) 673 1555 or 800 998 4677, *www.daileythorp.com*. Music and opera tours.

Maupintour, 2688 South Rainbow Blvd, Las Vegas NV 89146, **t** 1 800 255 4266, *www.maupintour.com*.

Travel Concepts, 225 Worcester Rd, Framingham, MA 01701, **t** (508) 879 8600, *www.travelconcept.com*. Wine, food, sport.

Villa Holidays and Self-Catering Tour Operators

In the UK

Individual Travellers Co, Spring Mill, Earby, Barnoldswick, Lancashire BB94 0AA, **t** 0870 078 0193, *www.indiv-travellers.com*.

Inghams, 10–18 Putney Hill, London SW15 6AX, **t** (020) 870 440, *www.inghams.co.uk*.

Interhome, 383 Richmond Road, Twickenham, Middx TW1 2EF, **t** (020) 8891 1294, *www.interhome.com*.

Abercrombie & Kent, St George's House, Ambrose Street, Cheltenham, Gloucestershire GL50 3LG, **t** 0845 700 618, *www.abercrombiekent.co.uk* (UK) or *www.abercrombiekent.com* (USA).

Magic of Italy, Wigmore House, Wigmore Lane, Luton, Bedfordshire LU2 9TN, **t** 0870 888 0228, *www.magictravelgroup.co.uk*.

In the USA

Hideaways International, 767 Islington Street, Portsmouth NH 03801, **t** (603) 430 4433, *www.hideaways.com*.

Hometours International, 1108 Scottie Lane, Knoxville TN 37919, **t** (865) 690 8484.

Rentals in Italy, 700 Main St, Ventura CA 93001, **t** 1 800 726 6702, *www.rentvillas.com*. They also offer car rental schemes.

Practical A–Z

07

Conversions: Imperial–Metric

Length (multiply by)
Inches to centimetres: 2.54
Centimetres to inches: 0.39
Feet to metres: 0.3
Metres to feet: 3.28
Yards to metres: 0.91
Metres to yards: 1.09
Miles to kilometres: 1.61
Kilometres to miles: 0.62

Area (multiply by)
Inches square to centimetres square: 6.45
Centimetres square to inches square: 0.15
Feet square to metres square: 0.09
Metres square to feet square: 10.76
Miles square to kilometres square: 2.59
Kilometres square to miles square: 0.39
Acres to hectares: 0.40
Hectares to acres: 2.47

Weight (multiply by)
Ounces to grams: 28.35
Grammes to ounces: 0.035
Pounds to kilograms: 0.45
Kilograms to pounds: 2.2
Stone to kilograms: 6.35
Kilograms to stone: 0.16
Tons (UK) to kilograms: 1,016
Kilograms to tons (UK): 0.0009
1 UK ton (2,240lbs) = 1.12 US tonnes (2,000lbs)

°C	°F
40	104
35	95
30	86
25	77
20	68
15	59
10	50
5	41
-0	32
-5	23
-10	14
-15	5

Volume (multiply by)
Pints (UK) to litres: 0.57
Litres to pints (UK): 1.76
Quarts (UK) to litres: 1.13
Litres to quarts (UK): 0.88
Gallons (UK) to litres: 4.55
Litres to gallons (UK): 0.22
1 UK pint/quart/gallon =
   1.2 US pints/quarts/
   gallons

Temperature
Celsius to Fahrenheit:
multiply by 1.8 then
add 32

Fahrenheit to Celsius:
subtract 32 then multiply
by 0.55

Italy Information

Time Differences
Country: + 1hr GMT; + 6hrs EST
Daylight saving from last weekend in March
to end of October

Dialling Codes
Italy country code 39
To Italy from: UK, Ireland, New Zealand 00 /
USA, Canada 011 / Australia 0011 then dial 39
and the full number including the initial zero
From Italy to: UK 00 44; Ireland 00 353; USA,
Canada 001; Australia 00 61; New Zealand 00
64 then the number without the initial zero
Directory enquiries: 12
International directory enquiries: 176

Emergency Numbers
Police: 112/113
Ambulance: 118
Fire: 115
Car breakdown: 116

Embassy Numbers in Italy
UK: (06) 422 0001; **Ireland** (06) 697 9121;
USA: (06) 46 741; **Canada** (06) 854 441;
Australia (06) 852 721;
New Zealand (06) 441 7171

Shoe Sizes

Europe	UK	USA
35	2½ / 3	4
36	3 / 3½	4½ / 5
37	4	5½ / 6
38	5	6½
39	5½ / 6	7 / 7½
40	6 / 6½	8 / 8½
41	7	9 / 9½
42	8	9½ / 10
43	9	10½
44	9½ / 10	11
45	10½	12
46	11	12½ / 13

Women's Clothing

Europe	UK	USA
34	6	2
36	8	4
38	10	6
40	12	8
42	14	10
44	16	12

Crime and the Police

Police t 113, Carabinieri t 112.

There is a fair amount of petty crime in Italy, although relatively little in Venetia – purse-snatchings, pickpocketing, minor thievery of the white-collar kind (always check your change) and car break-ins and theft – but violent crime is rare. Nearly all mishaps can be avoided with adequate precautions. Scooter-borne purse-snatchers can be foiled if you stay on the inside of the pavement and keep a firm hold on your property. Pickpockets strike in crowded buses or trams and gatherings: don't carry too much cash, and split it so you won't lose the lot at once. In cities and popular tourist sites, beware groups of scruffy-looking women or children with placards, apparently begging for money. They use distraction techniques to perfection. The smallest and most innocent-looking child is generally the most skilful pickpocket. If you are targeted, the best technique is to grab hold sharply of any vulnerable possessions and shout furiously. Be extra careful in train stations, don't leave valuables in hotel rooms, and always park your car in garages, guarded lots or on well-lit streets, with temptations out of sight.

Purchasing small quantities of soft drugs for personal consumption is technically legal in Italy, though what constitutes a small quantity is unspecified, and if the police don't like you to begin with, it will probably be enough to get you into big trouble.

Political terrorism, once the scourge of Italy, has declined greatly in recent years, mainly thanks to special quasi-military squads of black-uniformed national police, the *Carabinieri*. Local matters are usually in the hands of the *Polizia Urbana*; the nattily dressed *Vigili Urbani* concern themselves with directing traffic, and handing out parking fines.

Eating Out

When you eat out, mentally add to the bill (*conto*) the bread and cover charge (*pane e coperto*), between €1.20 and €4, and maybe a 15 per cent service charge. This is often included in the bill (*servizio compreso*); if not, it will say *servizio non compreso*, and you'll

Restaurant Price Categories

Price of a full meal for one, without wine

very expensive	€€€€	€50 and above
expensive	€€€	€35–50
moderate	€€	€25–35
inexpensive	€	€25 and under

have to do your own arithmetic. Additional tipping is at your own discretion, but never do it in family-owned and -run places.

When you leave a restaurant you will be given a receipt (*scontrino* or *ricevuto fiscale*) which according to Italian law you must take with you out of the door and carry for at least 60 metres. There is a slim chance that the tax police (*Guardia di Finanza*) may have their eye on you and the restaurant, and if you don't have a receipt they could slap a heavy fine on the restaurant.

For further information about eating in Italy, including details of local specialities, wines and a menu decoder, *see* the **Food and Drink** chapter, pp.67–76.

All restaurants listed in this guide are divided into price categories (*see* above).

Electricity

Italy uses 220 volts. Travellers from some countries, including the UK, will need to take an adaptor to use their own electrical gear; these are easily found at airports and shops back home; some Italian plugs and sockets are non-standard however. For details of which plug to use, see *www.kropla.com*.

Health and Emergencies

Fire service (incendio) *t 115.*
Ambulance (ambulanza) *t 118.*

Less serious problems can be treated at a *Pronto Soccorso* (casualty/first-aid department) at any hospital clinic (*ambulatorio*) or at a local health unit (*Unità Sanitaria Locale* – USL). Airports and main railway stations also have first-aid posts. If you have to pay for any health treatment, make sure you get a receipt, so that you can make any claims for reimbursement later (*see* **Planning Your Trip**, p.83).

Dispensing chemists (*farmacie*) are generally open from 8.30am to 1pm and from 4 to 8pm. Pharmacists are trained to give advice for minor ills. Any large town will have a 24-hour *farmacia*; others take turns to stay open (the address rota is posted in the window and in the local papers).

Most Italian doctors speak at least rudimentary English, but if you can't find one, contact your embassy for a list of English-speaking doctors.

Internet

Internet access has become much more widespread in recent years, and most resorts and towns will have an Internet point of some kind. Ask at the tourist office for a list. Costs vary; in some cities there is free access for under-26s or students at information centres. Practically all hotels, and most B&Bs, now have Internet access. The larger hotels are likely to have Wi-Fi access, too.

National Holidays

Most museums, as well as banks and shops, are closed on the following national holidays. In addition to these general holidays, many towns also take their patron saint's day off.

1 January (New Year's Day)

6 January (Epiphany)

Easter Monday

25 April (Liberation Day)

1 May (Labour Day)

15 August (Assumption, the official start of the Italian holiday season)

1 November (All Saints' Day)

8 December (Immaculate Conception)

25 December (Christmas Day)

26 December (St Stephen's Day)

Opening Hours

Although it varies from town to town, most of northeast Italy closes down at 1pm until 3 or 4pm to eat and properly digest the main meal of the day. Afternoon hours are from 4 to 7.30, often from 5 to 8 in the hot summer months. Bars are often the only places open during the early afternoon.

Some cities close down completely during August when locals flee from the polluted frying pan to the hills, lakes or coast. In any case, don't be surprised if you find anywhere in Italy unexpectedly closed (or open for that matter), whatever its official stated hours.

Banks

Banking hours vary, but core times in large towns are usually Monday–Friday 8.30am–1pm and 3–4pm, closed weekends and on local and national holidays (*see* above). Outside these hours, you will usually be able to find somewhere to change money (at disadvantageous rates).

Shops

Food shops usually open Monday–Saturday from 8am to 1pm and 3.30 to 8pm, though hours vary according to season and are shorter in smaller centres. In some large cities hours are longer. Some supermarkets and department stores stay open throughout the day. Clothes shops tend to open at 9am at the earliest (often more like 10am).

Offices

Government-run dispensers of red tape (e.g. visa departments) often stay open for quite limited periods, usually during the mornings, Monday to Friday. It pays to get there as soon as they open (or before) to spare your nerves in an interminable queue. Anyway, take something to read, or write your memoirs.

Museums and Galleries

Many of Italy's museums are magnificent, many are run with shameful neglect, and many have been closed for years for 'restoration' with slim prospects of reopening in the foreseeable future. With two works of art per inhabitant, Italy has a hard time financing the preservation of its heritage; ring the local tourist office to find out exactly what is open and what is closed 'temporarily' before setting off on a wild-goose chase; or look at the useful website *www.musei online.it*. Occasionally, even if a museum is officially closed, you might be able to get one of the 'renovators' to let you in.

Churches

Italy's churches have always been a prime target for art thieves and as a consequence are usually locked when there isn't a sacristan or caretaker to keep an eye on things. All churches, except for the really important cathedrals and basilicas, close in the afternoon at the same hours as the shops, and the little ones tend to stay closed.

Always have a pocketful of coins for the light machines in churches, or whatever work of art you came to inspect will remain clouded in ecclesiastical gloom. Don't do your visiting during services, and don't come to see paintings and statues in churches the week preceding Easter – you will probably find them covered with mourning shrouds.

Sightseeing Tips

In general, Sunday afternoons and Mondays are dead periods for the sightseer – you may want to make them your travelling days. Places without specified opening hours can usually be visited on request, but it is best to go before 1pm. **Entrance charges** vary widely; major sights are fairly steep (€2–12), but others may be completely free. EU citizens under 18 and over 65 get free admission to state museums, at least in theory. Depending on what time of year you're there, you may well have the museum to yourself.

Packing

You simply cannot overdress in Italy; whatever grand strides Italian designers have made on the international fashion merry-go-round, most of their clothes are purchased domestically, prices be damned. Now whether or not you want to try to keep up with the natives is your own affair and your own heavy suitcase – you may do well to compromise and just bring a couple of smart outfits for big nights out. It's not that the Italians are very formal; they simply like to dress up with a gorgeousness that adorns their cities just as much as those old Renaissance palaces. The few places with dress codes are casinos, posh restaurants and the major churches (no shorts, sleeveless shirts or strappy sundresses).

Remember to pack small and light: trans-Atlantic airlines limit baggage by size (two pieces are free up to 1½ metres in height and width; in second-class you're allowed one of 1½ metres and another up to 110cm). Within Europe limits in economy class are by weight; 20kg (44lbs) in second class, 30kg (66lbs) in

first. You may well be penalized for anything larger. If you're travelling mainly by train, you'll want to keep bags to a minimum. Never take more than you can carry; but do bring the following: any prescription medicine you need, an extra pair of glasses or contact lenses if you wear them, a pocket knife and corkscrew (for picnics), a torch/flashlight (for dark frescoed churches, caves and crypts), a travel alarm (for those early trains) and a pocket Italian–English dictionary (for flirting and other emergencies – outside the main tourist centres you may well have trouble finding someone who speaks English). If you're a light sleeper, you may want to invest in earplugs. Your electrical appliances will work in Italy if you convert them to run on 220 AC with two round prongs on the plug.

Photography

Film and developing are much more expensive than they are in either the UK or the USA, though there are plenty of outlets where you can obtain them. Note that you are not allowed to take pictures in most museums and in some churches. Most cities now offer one-hour processing.

Post Offices

Post offices in Italy are usually open from 8am until 1pm (Monday to Saturday), or until 6 or 7pm in a large city. Dealing with *la posta italiana*, the most expensive and slowest postal service in Europe, has always been a risky, frustrating and time-consuming affair. Even buying the right stamps requires dedicated research and saintly patience; Italians view the invention of the fax machine as a gift from the Madonna.

To have your mail sent *poste restante* (general delivery), have it addressed to the central post office (*Fermo Posta*) and expect three to four weeks for it to arrive. Make sure your surname is very clearly written in block capitals. To pick up your mail you must present your passport and pay a nominal charge. Stamps (*francobolli*) may be purchased in post offices or at tobacconists (*tabacchi*, identified by their blue signs with a white T). Prices fluctuate. The rates for letters and postcards (depending how many words you write!) vary according to the whim of the tobacconist or postal clerk. Dimensions of a letter or card affect the price as well as the weight. If you want something to get there fast, use *posta prioritaria* (takes 1 day in Italy, 3 days elsewhere in Europe).

You can also have money telegraphed to you through the post office; if all goes well, this can happen in a mere three days, but expect to pay good commission.

Shopping

'Made in Italy' has become a byword for style and quality, especially in fashion and leather, but also in home design, ceramics, kitchenware, jewellery, lace and linens, glassware and crystal, chocolates, bells, Christmas decorations, hats, straw work, art books, engravings, handmade stationery, gold and silverware, bicycles, sports cars, woodworking, a hundred kinds of liqueurs, aperitifs, coffee machines, gastronomic specialities, and antiques (both reproductions and the real thing). You'll find the best variety of goods in Verona and Venice – in other words, where the money is. Be sure to save receipts for Customs (or tax rebates).

When buying antiques, be sure to demand a certificate of authenticity – Venetia is Italy's top manufacturer of reproductions, and they can be so good that some of the world's

Weekend Antiques Markets

Monthly weekend antique markets are a thriving business, as follows:

First Sunday Battaglia Terme, Vittorio Veneto, Serravalle, Marostica, Noventa Vicentina, Povegliano Veronese, Morgano-Badoere, Udine and Brugine.

2nd Saturday Asolo and Adria.

2nd Sunday Cadoneghe, Noale, Portobuffolè, Asolo, Vittorio Veneto, Roncade, Sacile and Montegrotto Terme.

3rd Saturday and Sunday Verona and Montagnana.

3rd Sunday Padua, Cittadella, Mirano, Soave, Godega di Sant'Urbano, Paese, Este and San Zenone degli Ezzelini.

4th Saturday Monselice.

4th Sunday Treviso, Piazzola sul Brenta, Valeggio sul Mincio, Dolo, Pordenone and San Daniele.

major museums have found that 'antique' armour in their collections is not quite what it seems.

To get your antiques or modern art purchases home, you must apply to the **Export Department** of the Italian Ministry of Education. The seller should have details of export tax.

Sports and Activities

Beaches

Venetia is not remarkable for its beaches, and although you'll find plenty of sand at major resorts – Venice's Lido, Lignano Sabbiadoro, Bibione, Grado and Jesolo – much of the coast is disappointingly flat and dull and many seaside resorts are plagued by that peculiarly Italian phenomenon, the concessionaire, who parks ugly lines of sunbeds and brollies all the way along the best stretches of beach, and charges all comers handsomely for the privilege. During the winter you can see what happens when the beaches miss out on their manicures; many get depressingly rubbish-strewn. Italy is still quite prudish about going topless.

Fishing

You don't need a permit for sea-fishing (without an aqualung), but Italy's coastal waters, polluted and over-exploited, may disappoint. Commercial fishing has depleted stocks to such an extent that the government has begun to declare 2- and 3-month moratoria on all fishing to give the fish a break. Many freshwater lakes and mountain streams are stocked, however, and if you're more interested in fresh fish than the sport of it, there are innumerable trout farms where you can practically pick the fish up out of the water with your hands. To fish in fresh water you need to buy a year's membership card from the **Federazione Italiana della Pesca Sportiva**, which has an office in every province; they will inform you about local conditions and restrictions.

Football

Soccer (*il calcio*) is a national obsession. For many Italians its importance far outweighs tedious issues like the state of the nation – not least because of the weekly chance (slim but real) of becoming an instant millionaire in the *Lotteria Sportiva*. All major cities, and most minor ones, have at least one team of some sort. For league results see *www.fic.it*. The sport was actually introduced by the English, but a Renaissance game, something like a cross between football and rugby, has existed in Italy for centuries. Modern Italian teams are known for their grace, precision and coordination; rivalries are intense, scandals rife. The rewards offered by such big-time entertainment attract all manner of corrupt practices, yet crowd violence is minimal compared with the havoc wreaked by Britain's lamentable fans. Big-league matches are played on Sunday afternoons from September to May. For information, contact the **Federazione Italiana Giuoco Calcio**, Via G. Allegri 14, 00198 Rome, **t** (06) 855 3237, *www.figc.it*. Rugby and baseball are also played in most cities; even American football and basketball have their devotees.

Golf

Italians have been slower than some nationalities to appreciate the delights of biffing a small white ball into a hole in the ground, but they're catching on fast. New courses are now spawning all over the country. For information, contact the local tourist offices or the **Federazione Italiana Golf**, **t** (06) 323 1825, *www.federgolf.it*.

Hiking and Mountaineering

These activities are becoming steadily more popular among native Italians every year. The Dolomites (*see* pp.292–3) have a good system of waymarked trails and mountain refuges run by the **Italian Alpine Club** (CAI). If you are planning to use the more popular routes in summer, write beforehand to reserve beds in refuges. Walking is practicable between May and October, after most of the snow has melted; all the necessary gear is readily available in Italy but for more money than you'd pay at home. Most chairlifts close early to mid-September. For information see *www. infodolomiti.it*, *www.trentino.to*, *www.sued tirol.info*, *www.turismo.fvg.it*, *www.cai.it*; or contact the **Alpine Club** (UK), **t** (020) 7613

0755, *www.alpine-club-org.uk*, (USA) **t** (303) 384 0110, *www.americanalpineclub.org*.

The CAI can put you in touch with alpine guides or climbing groups if you're up for some real adventure, or write to the Italian National Tourist Board for a list of operators arranging mountaineering holidays. Some resorts have taken to offering *Settimane Verdi* (Green Weeks) – good-value accommodation and activity packages for summer visitors.

Hunting

Italy's most controversial sport pits avid enthusiasts against a growing number of environmentalists. The debate is fierce and the start of the season is marked by huge protests. Indiscriminate trapping, netting and shooting is responsible for the decimation of many migrant Mediterranean songbirds. Less controversial, at least from the conservation point of view, is duck, pigeon and wild-boar shooting.

Riding Holidays

Holidays on horseback are now available in many parts of northeast Italy, particularly in the Dolomites, and there are stables in most seaside resorts as well. For more information, contact the **Associazione Nazionale Turismo Equestre e TREC**, Piazza Antonio Mancini 4, 00196 Rome, **t** (06) 3265 0230; or see *www. fiteec-ante.it*.

Rowing and Canoeing

The annual regatta between the four ancient maritime republics of Venice, Amalfi, Genoa and Pisa (held in turn at each city) is a splendidly colourful event. The fast rivers of the mountain areas provide exciting whitewater sport. For information contact **Federazione Italiana Canoa e Kayak**, Via Pietro Della Valle, 00193 Rome, **t** (06) 3322 1200, *www.federcanoa.it*.

Skiing and Winter Sports

Italy still lacks the cachet of neighbouring Switzerland or Austria among the skiing fraternity, but has caught up significantly and now has a better reputation for safety and efficiency, though erratic snow cover is always a problem. Downhill and cross-country (*sci di fondo*) skiing are available in the Dolomites, along with more exotic variants (for experts only) like heli-skiing. The Sella Ronda links several resorts in an exhilarating day's circuit. The Marmolada glacier in Trentino-Adige, and the glacier above the Stelvio pass provide year-round sources of snowy runs. Prices are highest during Christmas and New Year holidays, in February and at Easter. Most resorts offer *Settimane Bianche* (White Weeks) – off-season packages at economical rates. Other winter sports such as ice-skating and bobsleighing are available at larger resorts. For more information, *see* the regional websites under 'Hiking and Mountaineering' above, plus *www.fisi.org*, *www.dolomitisuperski.it* and *www.goski.com*.

Tennis

If soccer is Italy's most popular spectator sport, tennis is probably the game most people actually play. Every *comune* has public courts for hourly hire, especially resorts. Private clubs may offer temporary membership to passing visitors, and hotel courts can often be used by non-residents for a reasonable fee. Contact local tourist offices for information on where you can play.

Water Sports

Despite Italy's notorious coastal pollution, water sports are immensely popular, especially sailing and windsurfing. Lake Garda has well-equipped sailing and windsurfing schools. Waterskiing is possible on all the major lakes, as well as at many coastal resorts. For further information, contact the following organizations:

Federazione Italiana Vela (Italian Sailing Federation), Corso Sardegna 34/1, 16142 Genoa, **t** (010) 514 376, *www.federvela.it*.

Federazione Italiana Motonautica and **Federazione Italiana Sci Nautico** can both be found at Via Piranesi 44b, Milan, **t** (02) 730 535, *www.fimconi.it* and *www.coni.it*.

Telephones

Public telephones for international calls may be found in the offices of **Telecom Italia**, Italy's telephone company. They are the only places where you can make reverse-charge calls (*a erre*, collect calls) but be prepared for a wait, as all these calls go through the operator in Rome. Long-distance rates are among the highest in Europe. Calls within Italy are cheapest after 10pm, international calls after 11pm. Most phone booths take only phone cards (*schede telefoniche*) available for €2.50 and €5 at tobacconists and newsstands – you will have to snap off the small perforated corner in order to use them. In smaller villages, you can usually find *telefoni a scatti*, with a meter on it, in at least one bar (a small commission is generally charged).

Direct calls may be made by dialling the international prefix (for the UK 0044, Ireland 00353, USA and Canada 001, Australia 0061, New Zealand 0064). To call Italy from abroad, dial the country code 0039 and then the whole number, including the first zero.

Time

Italy is on Central European Time, 1 hour ahead of Greenwich Mean Time and 6 hours ahead of Eastern Standard Time. Italian Summer Time runs from the last weekend of March to the end of October.

Toilets

They 'let down their breeches wherever and before whomsoever they please; according all St Mark's Place, and many parts of the sumptuous building, the Doge's Palace, are dedicated to Cloacina, and you may see Votaries at their devotions every hour of the day'. Thus wrote Samuel Sharp in the 18th century. It's not so bad now, although don't expect Italy to makes its conveniences very convenient even in city centres – look for them in places like train and bus stations and bars. Ask for the *bagno, toilette*, or *gabinetto*; in stations and the smarter bars and cafes, there are washroom attendants who expect 20–25 cents for keeping the place decent. Don't confuse the Italian plurals; *signori* (gents), *signore* (ladies). It's a good idea to carry tissues/wipes with you as it's rare to get soap, running water and toilet paper: one is unusual, all three a miracle.

Venice

Venice seduces, Venice irritates, but Venice rarely disappoints. She is a golden fairytale city floating on the sea, a lovely mermaid with agate eyes and the gift of eternal youth. On the surface she is little changed from the days when Goethe called her the 'market-place of the Morning and the Evening lands', when her amphibious citizens dazzled the world with their wealth and pageantry, their magnificent fleet, their half-Oriental doges, their crafty merchant princes, their splendidly luminous art, their silken debauchery and their decline and fall into a seemingly endless carnival.

o8

Don't miss

⭐ **Glorious mosaics**
St Mark's Basilica **p.126**

⭐ **A gravity-defying palace**
The Doge's Palace **p.130**

⭐ **Venice's showpiece artery**
The Grand Canal **p.121**

⭐ **Avant-garde brilliance**
Peggy Guggenheim Collection **p.140**

⭐ **A cathedral of Venetian art**
Galleria dell' Accademia **p.138**

See map overleaf

PONTE DEI
TRE ARCHI

Canale di Cannaregio

Rio della Madonna dell'Orto

Madonna
dell'Orto

Rio della Sensa

Palazzo
Mastelli

CAMPO
DEL
GHETTO

FONDAMENTA DELLA MISERICORDIA

VECCHIO GHETTO

CANNAREGIO

RIO TERRA DI S. LEONARDO

Palazzo Correr
Contarini

Scalzi

LISTA DI
SPAGNA

PONTE DELLA LIBERTA

PONTE DEGLI
SCALZI

Canal Grande

RIVA DI BIASIO

Palazzo
Vendramin
Calergi

Casino

Gesu

Rio di S. Felice

SS. Apostoli

STRADA NUOVA

Canale Grande

Stazione
S.Lucia

FOND. S. SIMEON

S. Simeon
Piccolo

Fondaco
dei Turchi

CAMPO
S. GIACOMO
DELL'ORIO

SANTA CROCE

Ca d'Oro

Rio di

R. di

Stazione
Marittima

Canale della Scomenzera

Bus Station

PIAZZALE
ROMA

Giardino
Papadopoli

FOND. DEI TRE PONTI

FOND. MINOTTO

Rio Nuovo

CAMPO
S. STIN

S. Rocco

Frari

CAMPO
S. POLO

RIO DI S. POLO

RUGA VECCHIA

PONTE DI
RIALTO

CAMPO
BARETERI

RIVA DEL VIN

S.
Salvador

S.
Di

Rio delle Procuratie

Rio S. Margherita

ROSSA FOND.

CAMPO S. MARGHERITA

SALIZADA S.
PANTALON

Rio Co Foscari

SAN POLO

Casa del
Goldoni

Pal. Pisani

Pal. Corner
Spinelli

Pal.
Corner

RIVA DEL CARBON

Pal.
Bembo

MERCER

CALLE DEI FABBRI

Ca' Foscari

Palazzo
Balbi

Palazzo
Mocenigo

Pal.
Fortuny

CAMPO S.
ANGELO

C. DELLA
MANDOLA

FUSERI

Teatro
Goldoni

PIA
M.

CALLE VALLARESSO

Ca' Rezzonico

Palazzo
Grassi

S. Stefano

La Fenice

Giard
Re

CALLE LUNGA S. BARNABA

Rio di S. Barnaba

San
Sebastiano

CAMPO S.
BASILIO

Stazione
Marittima

DORSODURO

Rio Ognissanti

Rio S. Trovaso

PONTE
DELL'ACCADEMIA

Accademia

Grande

S. Moisè

Ca'
Corner

S. Moisè

Rio di

Ca'
Giustinian

Pal.
Pisani

ZATT AI GESUATI

RIO TERRA A TOL

FOND. BRAGADIN

Peggy
Guggenheim
Collection

S. Maria
della Salute

Dogana
di Mare

ZATT AL SP. SANTO

ZATT AL SALONI

Canale della Giudecca

Palazzo
Vendramin

GIUDECCA

Redentore

Don't miss

⭐ St Mark's Basilica **p.126**
⭐ The Doge's Palace **p.130**
⭐ The Grand Canal **p.121**
⭐ Peggy Guggenheim Collection **p.140**
⭐ Galleria dell'Accademia **p.138**

S. Michele

N

500 m
500 yards

uiti

FONDAMENTE NUOVE

S. Apostoli

S Giovanni Crisostomo

SS. Giovanni
e Paolo

APO S.
LOMEO

S. Lio   CAMPO S.
         MARIA FORMOSA
IZZADA
S. LIO   S. Maria Formosa

S. Zulian

Pal. Querini
Stampalia

CAMPO SS
FILIPPO E
GIACOMO

St Mark's
Basilica

IZZA S.
ARCO
Museo
Correr
dini
li

Pal.
Ducale

Rio di S. Francesco

CANALE DELLE GALEAZZE

Scuola di
S. Giorgio
degli Schiavoni

S. Giorgio
dei Greci

ARSENALE

S. Zaccaria

RUGA GIUFFA

Rio di S. Lorenzo

CASTELLO

Rio del Vin

Pal. Dandolo Gritti

RIVA DEGLI SCHIAVONI

S. Pietro

VIA GARIBALDI

Canale di San Marco

S. Giorgio
Maggiore

S. Giorgio
Maggiore

Giardini
della Biennale

S. Elena

S. Elena

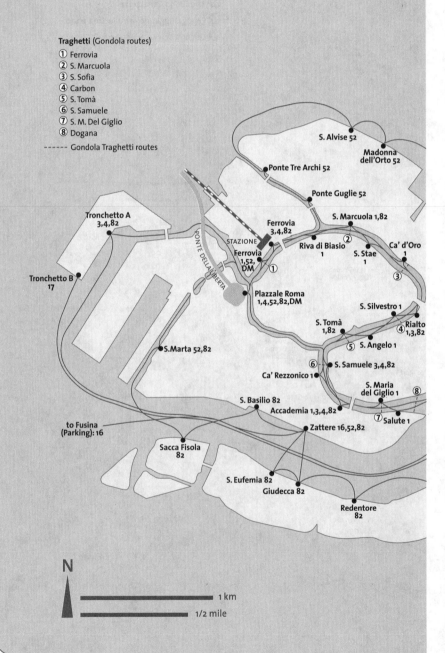

Traghetti (Gondola routes)
① Ferrovia
② S. Marcuola
③ S. Sofia
④ Carbon
⑤ S. Tomà
⑥ S. Samuele
⑦ S. M. Del Giglio
⑧ Dogana
------ Gondola Traghetti routes

S. Alvise 52
Madonna dell'Orto 52
Ponte Tre Archi 52
Ponte Guglie 52
Tronchetto A 3,4,82
S. Marcuola 1,82
Ferrovia 3,4,82
Riva di Biasio 1
S. Stae 1
Ca' d'Oro 1
STAZIONE
Ferrovia 1,52, DM ①
②
③
Tronchetto B 17
Plazzale Roma 1,4,52,82,DM
PONTE DELLA LIBERTA
S. Silvestro 1
S. Tomà 1,82
Rialto ④ 1,3,82
⑤ S. Angelo 1
S.Marta 52,82
⑥ S. Samuele 3,4,82
Ca' Rezzonico 1
S. Maria del Giglio 1 ⑧
S. Basilio 82
Accademia 1,3,4,82
⑦ Salute 1
to Fusina (Parking): 16
Zattere 16,52,82
Sacca Fisola 82
S. Eufemia 82
Giudecca 82
Redentore 82

N

1 km
1/2 mile

08 Venice | Introduction

Regular Lines

1 (*accelerato*) Piazzale Roma–Ferrovia–Grand Canal– San Marco–Lido: stops everywhere
6 (*diretto motonave*) S. Zaccaria–Lido
10 S. Zaccaria–Lido
11 (the 'mixed' line) Lido–Alberoni (by bus)–Pellestrina (by boat)– Chioggia (by boat) (not shown)
13 Fondamenta Nuove–Murano– Vignole–S. Erasmo
14 S. Zaccaria–Lido–Punta Sabbione
17 (car ferry) Tronchetto (Piazzale Roma)– Giudecca–Lido–Punta Sabbione
23 S. Zaccaria–Fondamenta Nuove
52 (green) (*motoscafo*) Lido–S. Zaccaria– Zattere–Piazzale Roma– Ferrovia–Fondamenta Nuove–Lido
41/42 circular route Murano–around Venice– Murano
82 (*diretto*) S. Zaccaria (S. Marco)–Lido–Giudecca–San Giorgio Maggiore
LN Fondamenta Nuove–Murano– Torcello–Burano–Treporti
N (*night service*) Lido–S. Zaccaria–Accademia–S. Toma–Rialto– Piazzale Roma–Zattere–Zitelle–S. Giorgio Maggiore
DM (*direct fast*) Piazzale Roma–Ferrovia– Murano

Summer only

3 Tronchetto–Grand Canal–S. Zaccaria–Tronchetto
4 S. Zaccaria–Grand Canal–Tronchetto–S. Zaccaria
16 (private service) Zattere–Fusina car park

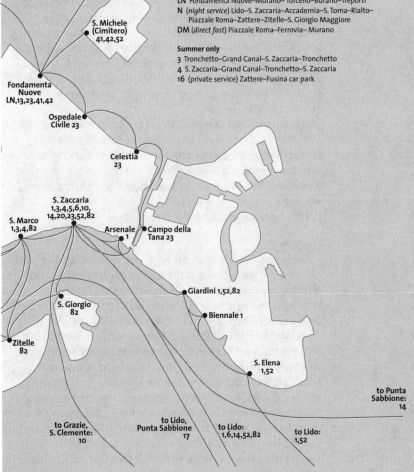

to Murano: LN,13,41,42
to Mazzorbo, Burano, Torcello, Treporti: LN
to Vignole, S. Erasmo: 13

S. Michele (Cimitero) 41,42,52

Fondamenta Nuove LN,13,23,41,42

Ospedale Civile 23

Celestia 23

S. Zaccaria 1,3,4,5,6,10, 14,20,23,52,82

S. Marco 1,3,4,82

Arsenale 1

Campo della Tana 23

S. Giorgio 82

Giardini 1,52,82

Biennale 1

Zitelle 82

S. Elena 1,52

to Punta Sabbione: 14

to Grazie, S. Clemente: 10

to Lido, Punta Sabbione 17

to Lido: 1,6,14,52,82

to Lido: 1,52

One can easily imagine Julius Caesar bewildered by today's Rome, or Romeo and Juliet missing their rendezvous in the traffic of modern Verona, but Marco Polo, were he to return from Cathay today, could take a familiar gondola up the familiar Grand Canal to his house in the Rialto, astonished more by the motorboats than anything else. Credit for this unique preservation goes to the Lagoon, the amniotic fluid of Venice's birth, her impenetrable 'walls' and the formaldehyde that has pickled her more thoroughly than many far more venerable cities on the mainland.

For 1,000 years Venice called herself the Most Serene Republic (*La Serenissima*), and at one point she ruled 'a quarter and a half' of the Roman Empire. The descent to an Italian provincial capital was steep and bittersweet; and sensitive souls find gallons of melancholy or, like Thomas Mann, even death, brewed into the city's canals that have nothing to do with the more flagrant microbes. In the winter, when the streets are silent, Venice can be so evocative that you have to kick the ghosts out of the way to pass down the narrower alleys. But most people (some million or so a year) show up in the summer and, like their ancestors, have a jolly good time. For Venice is a most experienced old siren in her boudoir of watery mirrors.

International organizations pump in the funds to keep her petticoats out of the water and smooth her wrinkles. Notices posted throughout the city acknowledge that she 'belongs to everybody', while with a wink she slides a knowing hand deep into your pocket. Venice has always lived for gold, and you can bet she wants yours – and you might just as well give it to her, in return for the most enchanting, dreamlike favours any city can grant.

History

Venice has always been so different, so improbable, that one can easily believe the legend that the original inhabitants sprang up from the dew and mists on the mud banks of the Lagoon. Historians who don't believe in fairies say that Venice was born of adversity: the islands and treacherous shallows of the Lagoon provided the citizens of the Veneto with a refuge from Attila the Hun and the Arian heresies sweeping the mainland. According to Venetians' own legends, the city was founded at exactly noon, 25 March 413, when the refugees laid the first stone on the Rialto. Twelve Lagoon townships grew up between modern Chioggia and Grado; when Theodoric the Great's secretary Cassiadorus visited them in 523 he wrote that they were 'scattered like sea-birds' nests over the face of the waters'.

In 697 the 12 townships united to elect their first duke, or Doge. Fishing, trading – in slaves, among other things – and their unique knowledge of the Lagoon brought the Venetians their first prosperity, but their key position in between the Byzantine empire and the 'barbarian' kings on the mainland also made them a bone of contention. In 810 the Franks, who had defeated the Lombards in the name of the pope and claimed dominion over the whole of northern Italy, turned their attention to the last holdout, Venice. Doge Obelario de' Antenori, engaged in a bitter internal feud with other Venetian factions, even invited Charlemagne's son Pepin to send his army into the city.

The quarrelling Venetians, until then undecided whether to support Rome or Constantinople, united at the approach of Pepin's fleet, deposed the Doge, declared for Byzantium, and entrenched themselves on the Rialto. The shallows and queer humours of the Lagoon confounded Pepin, and after a gruelling six-month siege he threw in the towel. A subsequent treaty between the Franks and the Eastern Emperor Nicephorus (814) recognized Venice as a subject of Byzantium, with important trading concessions. As Byzantine authority over the city was never more than words, it in effect marked the birth of an independent republic.

The Venetians lacked only a dynamic spiritual protector; their frumpy St Theodore with his crocodile was simply too low in the celestial hierarchy to fulfil the destiny they had in mind. In 829 Venetian merchants, supposedly on secret orders from the Doge, carried off one of the Republic's greatest coups when they purloined the body of St Mark from Alexandria, smuggling him past Egyptian customs by claiming that the saint was pickled pork. To acquire an Evangelist for themselves was, in itself, a demonstration of the Venetians' new ambition.

Marriage to the Sea

As the East–West trade expanded, the Venetians designed their domestic and external policies to accommodate it. At home they required peace and stability, and by the beginning of the 11th century had squelched all notions of a hereditary dogeship by exiling the most hyperactive families; Venice would never have the despotic *signori* who plagued the rest of Italy. Raids by Dalmatian pirates spurred the Venetians to fight and win their first major war in 997, under Doge Pietro Orseolo, who captured the pirates' coastal strongholds. The Venetians were so pleased with themselves that they celebrated the event with a splendidly arrogant ritual every Ascension Day, the Sensa or 'Marriage of the Sea', in which the Doge would sail out to the Lido in his sumptuous barge, the *Bucintoro*, and cast a diamond ring into the sea, proclaiming 'We wed thee, O sea, in sign of our true and perpetual dominion'.

Venice, because of her location and fleet, supplied a great deal of the transport for the first three Crusades, and in return received her first important trading concessions in the Middle East. Archrival Genoa became increasingly envious, and in 1171 convinced the Byzantine Emperor to all but wipe out the Venetian merchants in Constantinople. Rashly, the Doge, Vitale Michiel II, set off in person to launch a revenge attack upon the Empire, and failed utterly, and on his return he was killed by an angry mob. The Venetians learned from their mistakes: the Great Council, the Maggior Consiglio, was created to check the power of the Doge and avert future calamities. Vengeance stayed on the back burner until the next Doge, the spry and crafty Enrico Dandolo, was contracted to provide transport for the Fourth Crusade. When the Crusaders turned up without their fare, Dandolo offered to forgo it in return for certain services: first, to reduce Venice's rebellious satellites in Dalmatia, and then, in 1204, to sail to Constantinople instead of Egypt. Aged 90 and almost blind, Dandolo personally led the attack; Christendom was scandalized, but Venice had gained, not only a glittering hoard of loot, but three-eighths of Constantinople and 'a quarter and a half' of the Roman Empire – enough islands and ports to control the trade routes in the Adriatic, Aegean, Asia Minor and the Black Sea.

To ensure their dominance at home, in 1297 the merchant élite limited membership in the *Maggior Consiglio* to themselves and their heirs (an event known in Venetian history as the *Serrata*, or Lock-out), their names inscribed in the famous Golden Book. The Doges were reduced to honorary chairmen of the board, bound up by an increasingly complex web of laws and customs to curb any possible ambitions; for the patricians, fear of revolution from above was as powerful as fear of revolt from below.

A Rocky 14th Century

First the people (1300) and then the snubbed patricians (the 1310 Tiepolo Conspiracy) rose up against their disenfranchisement under the *Serrata*. Both were unsuccessful, but the latter threat was serious enough that a committee of public safety was formed to hunt down the conspirators, and in 1335 this committee became a permanent institution, the infamous Council of Ten. Because of its secrecy and speedy decisions, the Council of Ten (in later years it was streamlined into a Council of Three) was more truly executive than the figurehead Doge: it guarded Venice's internal security, looked after foreign policy and, with its sumptuary laws, kept tabs on the Venetians' moral conduct as well.

Away from home the 14th century was marked by a fight to the death with Genoa over eastern trade routes. Each republic annihilated the other's fleet on more than one occasion before things came to a head in 1379, when the Genoese, fresh from a victory over the Venetian commander Vittor Pisani, captured

Black Death in Venice

Whenever the 21st century leaves a bad taste in your mouth, give some consideration to the 14th. Things were bad all over Europe then, but in Italy they were so rotten that historians speak of a collective death wish in the 1340s. Calamities of every kind befell the peninsula – earthquakes, floods and some of the worst weather on record; wars raged everywhere (Venice was locked in its death struggle with Genoa) and disorder was a constant threat. Bankruptcies wrecked the economy; in 1346–7 the crops were so poor that thousands of people died of starvation. Even the wine went off.

The Italians were exhausted, and resigned to disaster. As if on cue, the worst epidemic of all, the Black Death, arrived on the scene in October 1347 – brought from the Crimea on Venetian galleys (though the Venetians blame it on the Genoese). As usual Venice suffered the most: as the densely populated chief port of entry from the East, the city had a dire record of 70 major epidemics in 700 years. No wonder the Venetians lived so intensely, when life itself was so precarious.

On 20 March 1348, Doge Andrea Dandolo set up a council to deal with the plague. The dead were taken on special barges to be buried at San Erasmo on the Lido and at a new cemetery at the long-lost San Marco Boccacalme, or simply sunk into the waters of the Lagoon. Beggars were forbidden to exhibit corpses (an old custom) to raise alms. Strict immigration controls were ordered, and all travellers were obliged to spend 40 days in quarantine at Nazarethum Island (its name, later elided to Lazzaretto, became widely used for all such places).

All the measures were too late. At its worst the Black Death killed 600 Venetians a day; the total dead numbered an almost incredible 100,000 (about half the population). Helpless against the epidemic, most doctors in Venice either died or fled in horror. There was one exception, a health officer named Francesco da Roma, who received an annuity of 25 gold ducats as a reward for remaining in Venice during the Black Death. When asked why he stayed when everyone else fled, he replied: 'I would rather die here than live anywhere else.'

Chioggia and waited for Venice to starve, boasting that they had come to 'bridle the horses of St Mark'. As was their custom, the Council of Ten had imprisoned Pisani for his defeat, but Venice was now in such a jam, with half of its fleet far away, that the people demanded his release to lead what remained of their navy. A brilliant commander, Pisani exploited his familiarity with the Lagoon and in turn blockaded the Genoese in Chioggia. When the other half of Venice's fleet came dramatically racing home, the Genoese surrendered (June 1380) and never recovered in the East.

Fresh Prey on the Mainland

Venice was determined never to feel hungry again, and set her sights on the mainland – not only for the sake of farmland, but to control her trade routes into the West that were being increasingly harried and taxed by the *signori* of the Veneto. Treviso came first, then opportunity knocked in 1402 with the sudden death of the Milanese Duke Gian Galeazzo Visconti, whose conquests became the subject of a great land grab. Venice picked up Padua, Bassano, Verona and Belluno, and in 1454 added Ravenna, southern Trentino, Friuli, Crema and Bergamo. In 1489 the Republic's overseas empire reached its greatest extent when it was presented with Cyprus, a somewhat reluctant 'gift' from the king's widow, a Venetian noblewoman named Caterina Cornaro who received the hill town of Asolo as compensation.

But just as Venice expanded, Fortune's wheel gave a creak and conspired to squeeze her back into her Lagoon. The Ottoman Turks captured Constantinople in 1453 and, although the Venetians tried to negotiate trading terms with the sultans (as they had previously done with the infidel Saracens, to the opprobrium of the West), they would be spending the next three centuries fighting a losing battle for their eastern territories. The discovery of the New World was another blow, but gravest to the merchants of Venice was Vasco da Gama's voyage around the Cape of Good Hope to India in 1497, blazing a cheaper and easier route to Venice's prime markets that broke her monopoly of Oriental luxuries; Western European merchants no longer had to pay Venice for safe passage to the East. In just 44 years nearly everything that Venice had worked for, for over 500 years, was undermined.

On the mainland, Venice's rapid expansion had excited the fear and envy of Pope Julius, who rallied Italy's potentates and their foreign allies to form the League of Cambrai to humble the proud Republic. They snatched her *terra firma* possessions after her defeat at Agnadello in 1509, but quarrelled amongst themselves afterwards, and before long all the territories they had conquered voluntarily returned to Venice. Venice, however, never really recovered from this wound inflicted by the very people who should have rallied to her defence, and although her Arsenal produced a warship a day, and her captains helped to win a glorious victory over the Turks at Lepanto (1571), she was increasingly forced to retreat.

A Most Leisurely Collapse

The odds were stacked against her, but in her heyday Venice had accumulated enough wealth and verve to cushion her fall. Her noble families consoled themselves in the classical calm of Palladio's villas, while the city found solace in masterpieces of Venice's golden age of art. Carnival, ever longer, ever more licentious, was sanctioned by the state to bring in moneyed visitors, like Lord Byron, who dubbed it 'the revel of the earth, the masque of Italy'. In the 1600s the city had 20,000 courtesans, many of them dressed as men to whet the Venetians' passion. It didn't suit everyone: 'Venice is a stink pot, charged with every virus of hell,' fumed one Dr Warner, in the 18th century.

In 1797 Napoleon, declaring he would be 'an Attila for the Venetian state', took it with scarcely a whimper, ending the story of the world's longest-enduring republic, in the reign of its 120th Doge. Napoleon took the horses of St Mark to Paris as his trophy, and replaced the old *Pax tibi, Marce, Evangelista Meus* inscribed in the book the lion holds up on Venice's coat-of-arms with 'The Rights of Men and Citizens'. Reading it, a gondolier made the famous remark, 'At last he's turned the page.' Yet while many patricians danced merrily around his Liberty trees, freed at last from responsiblity, the people wept. Napoleon gave Venice to Austria, whose rule was confirmed by the Congress of Vienna after the Emperor's defeat in 1815. The Austrians' main contribution was the railway causeway linking Venice irrevocably to the mainland (1846). Two years later, Venice gave its last gasp of independence, when a patriotic revolt led by Daniele Manin seized the city and re-established the Republic, only to fall to the Austrian army once again after a heroic one-year siege.

Modern Venice

The former Republic did, however, finally join the new kingdom of Italy in 1866, after Prussia had conveniently defeated the Austrians. Already better known as a magnet to visitors than for any activity of its own, Venice played a quiet role in the new state. Things changed under Mussolini, the industrial zones of Mestre and Marghera were begun on the mainland, and a road was added to the railway causeway. The city escaped damage in the two world wars, despite heavy fighting in the environs; according to legend, when the Allies finally occupied Venice in 1945 they arrived in a fleet of gondolas.

But Venice was soon to engage in its own private battle with the sea. From the beginning the city had manipulated nature's waterways for her own survival, diverting a major outlet of the Po, the Brenta, the Piave, the Adige, and the Sile rivers to keep her Lagoon from silting up. In 1782 Venice completed the famous *murazzi*, the 2½-mile-long, 20ft-high sea walls to protect the Lagoon. But on 4 November 1966 a deadly combination of wind, torrential storms, high tides and giant waves breached the *murazzi*, wrecked the Lido and left Venice under record *acque alte* (high waters) for 20 hours, with disastrous results for the city's architecture and art. The catastrophe galvanized the international community's efforts to save Venice. Even the Italian state, notorious for its indifference to Venice (historical grudges die slowly in Italy), passed a law in 1973 to preserve the city, and contributed to the construction of a new flood barricade similar to the one on the Thames.

This giant sea gate, known as 'Moses', has now been completed, but arguments continue over whether it will ever be effective if needed, and what its ecological consequences might be. Venice today is perennially in crisis, permanently under restoration, and seemingly threatened by a myriad potential disasters – the growth of algae in the Lagoon, the effects of the outpourings of Mestre on its foundations, the ageing of its native population, or perhaps most of all the sheer number of its tourists. Proposals have been made to charge admissions at the causeway and limit the number who come in daily. Fears of an environmental catastrophe have, though, receded of late; somehow, the city contrives to survive, as unique as ever, and recent proposals to give it more of a function in the modern world as, for example, a base for international organizations, may serve to give it new life as well.

Architecture

At once isolated but linked to the traditions of East and West, Venice developed her own charmingly bastard architecture, especially in a style called Venetian Gothic, adopting only the most delightfully visual elements from each tradition. Ruskin's *The Stones of Venice* is the classic work on the city's buildings, which harsher critics – and Ruskin was one – disparage for being all artifice and show. The Venetians inherited the Byzantines' love of colour, mosaics, rare marbles and exotic effects, epitomized in the magnificently gaudy St Mark's. Venetian Gothic is only slightly less elaborate, and achieved its best products in the great palaces, most notably the Palazzo Ducale and the Ca' d'Oro, with their ogival windows and finely wrought façades.

The Renaissance arrived in Venice relatively late, and its early phase is called Lombardesque, after the Lombardo family (Pietro and sons Tullio and Antonio) who designed the best of it, including Santa Maria dei Miracoli and the rich Scuola di San Marco.

Later Renaissance architects brought Venice into the mainstream of the classical revival, and graced Venice with the arcaded Piazza San Marco, the Libreria of Sansovino, the San Michele of Mauro Codussi (or Coducci), and two of Palladio's finest churches. Venice's best Baroque works are by Longhena, the spiritual heir of Palladio.

To support all this on the soft mud banks, the Venetians drove piles of Istrian pine 16½ft into the solid clay – over a million posts hold up the church of Santa Maria della Salute alone. If Venice tends to lean and sink, it's due to erosion of these piles by the salty Adriatic, pollution, and the currents and wash caused by the deep channels dredged into the Lagoon for the large tankers sailing to Marghera. Or, as the Venetians explain, the city is a giant sponge.

Most Venetian houses are four to six storeys high. On the tops of some you can see the wooden rooftop loggias, or *altane*, where the Renaissance ladies were wont to idle, bleaching their hair in the sun; they wore broad-brimmed hats to protect their complexions, and spread their tresses through a hole cut in the crown.

Venetian Art

Venice may have been a Renaissance Johnny-come-lately, but the city and its hinterland are rivalled only by Tuscany when it comes

The Face of Venice

Venice stands on 117 islets, divided by over 100 canals that are spanned by some 400 bridges. The longest bridges are the 4.2km rail and road causeways that link Venice to the mainland. The open sea is half that distance across the Lagoon, beyond the protective reefs or *lidi* formed by centuries of river silt and the Adriatic current. The Grand Canal, Venice's incomparable main street, was originally the bed of a river that fed the Lagoon; the other canals, its tributaries (called *rio*, singular, or *rii*, plural), were shallow channels meandering through the mud banks, and are nowhere as grand – some are merely glorified sewers.

A warren of 2,300 alleys, or *calli*, handle Venice's pedestrian-only traffic, and they come with a colourful bouquet of names – a *rio terrà* is a filled-in canal; a *piscina* a filled-in pool; a *fondamenta* or *riva* a quay; a *salizzada* is a street that was paved in the 17th century; a *ruga* is one lined with shops; a *sottoportico* passes under a building. A Venetian square is a *campo*, recalling the days when they were open fields; the only square dignified with the title of 'piazza' is that of St Mark's, though the two smaller squares flanking the basilica are called *piazzette*, and there's one fume-filled *piazzale* (Piazzale Roma), the dead end for buses and cars.

All the *rii* and *calli* have been divided into six quarters, or *sestieri*, since Venice's earliest days: San Marco (by the *piazza*), Castello (by the Arsenal) and Cannaregio (by the Ghetto), all on the northeast bank of the Grand Canal; and San Polo (by the church), Santa Croce (near Piazzale Roma), and Dorsoduro, the 'hard-back' by the Accademia, all on the southwest bank.

Besides these, the modern *comune* of Venice includes the towns on the Lagoon islands, the Lido, and the mainland *comuni* of Mestre and Marghera, Italy's version of the New Jersey Flats, where most Venetians live today. There is some concern that historic Venice (population around 60,000 and falling, down from 170,000 in 1946) may soon become a city of second homes belonging to wealthy northern Italians and foreigners.

08 Venice | Venetian Art

to topnotch painting. Before the 14th century the Venetians excelled primarily in mosaic, an art they learned from the Byzantines, shown at their very best in St Mark's and Torcello. In 1306 Giotto painted his masterpiece in Padua's Cappella Scrovegni and gave local painters a revolutionary eyeful. His naturalism influenced a school of artists in Padua and Paolo Veneziano, the first great Venetian painter of note, although many artists would continue painting decorative Gothic pieces for a long time to come, notably Jacobello del Fiore, Michele Giambono and the Vivarini family.

Things began to change in the mid-15th century, with the advent of two great masters. Andrea Mantegna (1431–1506), trained in Padua, influenced generations with his strong interests in antiquity, perspective and powerful sculptured figures. His more lyrical and humane brother-in-law, Giovanni Bellini (*c.* 1440–1516), founded the Venetian school. Bellini learned the technique of oil painting from Antonello da Messina during his visit in 1475, and he never looked back: his use of luminous natural light and colour to create atmosphere ('tonalism') and sensuous beauty are characteristics all of his followers adopted, if few ever equalled. Meanwhile Giovanni's brother, Gentile Bellini, and Vittore Carpaccio (1470–1523) avoided tonalism altogether in their charming and precise narrative works.

Getting to Venice

By Air

Venice's Marco Polo Airport is 12km north of the city near the Lagoon, and has regularly connections from London, New York (via Milan), Paris, Vienna, Nice, Zürich, Frankfurt, Düsseldorf, Rome, Milan, Palermo and Naples. For **flight information** in Venice call **t** 041 260 9260 or visit *www.veniceairport.it*.

The airport is linked with Venice by **water-taxi** (**t** 041 522 2303), the most expensive option (around €80 for up to four passengers); or by *motoscafi* to San Marco (Zecca) roughly every hour (€12 per person), connecting with most flights (Mar–Oct). Buses take 25mins to the Piazzale Roma and leave every 30mins. Choose between **ATVO buses** (**t** 041 520 5530, *www.atvo.it*; €3) or, cheapest of all, the **ACTV city bus** no.5 (*www.actv.it*; €1).

Some charter flights arrive at Treviso, 30km to the north. If a transfer is not included with your ticket, take a train (15mins to Venice's Santa Lucia station, €2.20). **ATVO buses** (**t** 041 520 5530, *www.atvo.it*; €5) run between Piazzale Roma and Treviso airport to coincide with flights.

By Sea

This is the most thrilling way to approach Venice in all her majesty, although it's only practical if you're coming from the east.

Venicelines (**t** 0871 222 3312, *www.directferries.co.uk*) has a service to Venice from Croatia as far south as Pula. There are also **car-ferries** between Venice, Corfu and Patras, Greece (2 days), and Alexandria, Egypt (3½ days). An easier way to approach Venice on water is by taking the Burchiello from Padua along the **Brenta Canal** (*see* p.187). There is also a summer **hydrofoil** service from Trieste.

By Train

Venice's **Stazione Santa Lucia** (the Ferrovia) is the terminus of the Venice Simplon-Orient-Express and less glamorous trains from the rest of Europe and Italy. Sample journey times: Trieste 2hrs, Padua 30mins, Vicenza 50mins, Verona 1hr 30mins, Bologna 2hrs. From the station you can walk within minutes into the heart of the old city. All trains from Santa Lucia additionally stop in Mestre, where you may have to change for some long-distance services. For **national rail information** call **t** 892021, or see *www.trenitalia.it*.

Water-taxis, *vaporetti* and gondolas (*see* below) wait in front of the station to sweep you off into the city. If you've brought more luggage than you can carry, one of Venice's porters (distinguished by their badges) will take you and your luggage to your hotel (the price for one piece of luggage is around €20 with extra bags at €5; you may need to negotiate). Sometimes you can track down a porter once you disembark at one of the main landings or the Lido.

Porter stands are to be found throughout the city at the main tourist points and vaporetto stops; Accademia, Ferrovia, Piazzale Roma, Rialto, San Marco, etc. You can also call a porter, **t** 041 713 719. Since rates for baggage-handling are unregulated everywhere other than at the station, be sure to negotiate a price in advance. The left luggage office, located near the tracks, charges €3 per bag for each 12hrs.

By Car

All roads to Venice end at the monstrous municipal **parking** towers in **Piazzale Roma**, **t** 041 272 7211, or its cheaper annexe, **Tronchetto**, **t** 041 520 7555, nothing less than the largest car park in Europe. You can leave your car there for €20 a day, or less for longer stays. (Most hotels offer guests a 20% discount on parking charges at Tronchetto.)

In the summer, at Easter and Carnival, when the causeway turns into a solid conga-line of cars waiting to park, consider the Italian Auto Club's three alternative car parks (open to non-members): **Fusina**, **t** 041 523 1337, with a shady, year-round campsite, located at the mouth of the Brenta Canal south of Marghera (*vaporetto* no.16 to Venice); **S. Giuliano**, in Mestre near the causeway (bus service to Venice), and **Punta Sabbioni**, **t** 041 530 0455, in between the Lido and Jesolo (*vaporetto* no.17 from Tronchetto).

Getting around Venice

Vaporetti

Public transport in Venice means by water, on the grunting, canal-cutting *vaporetti* (the all-purpose water-buses), or the sleeker, faster water-taxis. The only canals served by public transport are the Grand Canal, the Rio Nuovo, the Canale di Cannaregio and Rio dell'Arsenale; between them, you'll have to rely on your feet, which is not as gruelling as it sounds, as Venice is so small you can walk across it in an hour.

Single tickets (a flat rate of €5) should be purchased and validated in the machines at the landing stages (random inspections aren't very frequent, but if you get caught you'll have to pay a fine on the spot).

As some landing stages don't sell tickets, it's best to stock up (most *tabacchi* sell them in blocks of ten). You can also buy a single ticket on board, but tell the attendant immediately you get on. There are also family tickets and group tickets which are a bit cheaper. Or, if you intend being on a boat at least three times in a given day, purchase a 24-hour tourist pass, for €12, valid for unlimited travel on all lines, or the 3-day pass, for €25. This does not cover the boat to the airport

Lines of most interest to visitors are listed on pp.108–9; most run until midnight. There is also an all-night line. Precise schedules are listed in the tourist office's free fortnightly guide, *Un Ospite di Venezia*.

At San Marco you can also find a number of **excursion boats** to various points in the Lagoon; they are more expensive than public transport, but may be useful if you're pressed for time.

Water-taxis

These are really tourist excursion boats – they work like taxis, but their fares are de luxe. Stands are at the station, Piazzale Roma, Rialto, San Marco, Lido and the airport. They can hold up to 15 passengers, and fares are set for destinations beyond the historic centre, or you can pay €80 per hour. Within the centre the minimum fare for up to four people is €80; additional passengers are up to €5 each, and there are surcharges for baggage, holiday or nocturnal service (after 10pm), and for using a **radio taxi** (t 041 522 2303 or t 041 723 112).

Gondolas

Gondolas, first mentioned in the city's annals in 1094, have a stately mystique that commands all other boats to give way. Shelley and others have compared them to a funeral barque or the soul ferry to Hades, and not a few gondoliers share the infernal Charon's expectation of a solid gold tip for their services.

Once used by all and sundry, gondolas now operate, frankly, for tourists (and weddings). Official **prices** are €75 for a 45-minute ride (more after 8pm). Be sure to agree with the gondolier on where you want to go and how long you expect it to take, before setting out.

In addition, gondolas retired from the tourist trade are used for gondola *traghetti* services across the Grand Canal at various points between its three bridges – your only chance to enjoy an economical, if brief, gondola ride for €0.50. *Traghetto* crossings are signposted in the streets nearby. For appearance's sake you'll have to stand up.

Hiring a Boat

Perhaps the best way to spend a day in Venice is by bringing or hiring your own motor boat, to drive, or to be chauffeured. Contact any of the following: **Cooperativa San Marco**, San Marco 4267, t 041 522 2303; **Veneziana Motoscafi**, San Marco 4179, t 041 716 000; **Serenissima Motoscafi**, Castello 4545, t 041 522 4281.

The *Cinquecento–Settecento*

For the heavy hitters of Venice's 16th-century Golden Age, however, tonalism was a religion: while other Italians followed the Romans in learning drawing and anatomy, the Venetians went their own way, obsessed by the dramatic qualities of atmosphere. The tragically short-lived Giorgione di Castelfranco (1475–1510) was the seminal figure in the new manner: his *Tempest* in the Accademia is a remarkable study in brooding tension. Giorgione also invented 'easel painting' – i.e. art that served neither Church nor State nor the vanity of the patron, but stood on its own for the pleasure of the viewer.

Giorgione's colleague, Tiziano Vecellio, or Titian (*c.* 1485–1576), was the greatest master of the Venetian school. Known for his bold, spiralling compositions, his rich colours and his luscious mythologies, he was a revolutionary in his old age, using increasingly free brushstrokes and even applying paint with his fingers. Tintoretto

When to Go to Venice

Venice (*Venezia*) is as much a character as a setting, and the same may be said of its weather. In no other city will you be so aware of the light; on a clear, fine day no place could be more limpid and clear, no water as crystal-bright as the Lagoon. The rosy dawn igniting the domes of St Mark's, the splash of an oar fading in the cool mist of a canal, the pearly twilit union of water and sky are among the city's oldest clichés.

If you seek solitude and romance with a capital R, go in January. Pack a warm coat, water-resistant shoes and an umbrella, and expect frequent fogs and mists. It may even snow – in 1987 you could even ski-jump down the Rialto bridge. But there are also plenty of radiant diamond days, brilliant, sunny and chill; any time after October you take your chances.

As spring approaches there is Carnival, a game and beautiful but rather bland attempt to revive a piece of old Venice; Lent is fairly quiet, though in the undercurrent the Venetians are building up for their first major invasion of sightseers at Easter. By April the tourism industry is cranked up to full operational capacity; the gondolas are un-mothballed and the café tables have blossomed in the Piazza. In June even the Italians are considering a trip to the beach.

In July and August elbow-room is at a premium. Peripheral camping grounds are packed, queues for the tourist offices' room-finding service stretch longer and longer, and the police are kept busy reminding the hordes that there's no picnicking in St Mark's Square. The heat can be sweltering, the ancient city gasping under a flood of cameras, shorts, sunglasses and rucksacks. Scores head off to the Lido for relief; a sudden thunderstorm over the Lagoon livens things up, as do the many festivals, especially the Redentore and its fireworks in July. In the autumn the city and the Venetians begin to unwind, as the rains begin to fall, and you can watch them pack up the parasols and cabanas on the Lido with a wistful sigh.

As far as hotels are concerned, high season is from Carnival to mid-November, with prices coming down a bit in midsummer.

(1518–94), of the famously quick brushstrokes, took his Mannerist compositions to unforgettable extremes, while his contemporary, Paolo Veronese (1528–88), painted lavish *trompe l'œil* canvases and frescoes that are the culmination of Venice at her most decorative. This was also the period of Palma Vecchio, the sensuous painter of Venetian blonde goddesses, Cima da Conegliano, author of some of the loveliest landscapes, and Lorenzo Lotto, of the famous psychologically penetrating portraits, who was run out of Venice by Titian and his buddies.

Venetia enjoyed an artistic revival in the twilight years of the 18th century, when its art was in great demand at home and abroad. Much of the thanks goes to Giambattista Tiepolo (1697–1770), the first to cast aside Baroque gloominess to create an effervescent, light-filled, brilliantly coloured style; he was also the last great fresco-painter in Italy. His chief follower was his son Giandomenico, although his influence can also be seen in the luminous palettes of Antonio Canaletto (1697–1768) and Francesco Guardi (1712–93), who produced the countless views of Venice that were the rage among travellers on the Grand Tour; even now most of their works are in Britain and France. Pietro Longhi, their contemporary, devoted himself to genre scenes that offer a delightful insight into the Venice of 200 years ago.

Around the City

The Grand Canal

🚏 **The Grand Canal**

A ride down Venice's bustling and splendid main artery is most visitors' introduction to the city, and there's no finer one. The Grand Canal has always been Venice's status address, and along its looping banks the patricians of the Golden Book, or *Nobili Homini*, built a hundred marble palaces with their front doors giving onto the water, framed by peppermint-stick posts where they moored their watery carriages.

The highlights, from Piazzale Roma to Piazza San Marco, include the 12th-century **Fondaco dei Turchi** (with rounded arches, on the right after the Station Bridge), the Ottoman merchants' headquarters until 1838, and now the Natural History Museum. Nearly opposite, Mauro Codussi's Renaissance **Palazzo Vendramin-Calergi**, where Richard Wagner died in 1883, is now the casino. Back on the right bank, just after the San Stae landing, the Baroque **Palazzo Pésaro** is adorned with masks by Longhena. And then comes the loveliest palace of all, the **Ca' d'Oro**, with a florid Venetian Gothic façade, formerly etched in gold, now housing the Galleria Franchetti (*see* p.145).

Byron Goes Swimming

Byron arrived in Venice in 1816, his heart full of romance as he rented a villa on the Brenta to compose the last canto of his *Childe Harold's Pilgrimage*. The city's canals at least afforded him the personal advantage of being able to swim anywhere (his club foot made him shy of walking); on one occasion he swam a race from the Lido to the Rialto bridge and was the only man to finish.

It wasn't long before the emotional polish of *Childe Harold* began to crack. To Byron's surprise, Venice didn't perfect his romantic temper, but cured him of it. He went to live in the Palazzo Mocenigo on the Grand Canal, in the company of 14 servants, a dog, a wolf, a fox, monkeys and a garlicky baker's wife, La Fornarina, who stabbed him in the hand with a fork – which so angered Byron that he ordered her out, whereupon she threw herself into the Grand Canal. Under such circumstances, all that had been breathless passion reeked of the ridiculous, as he himself admitted:

And the sad truth which hovers o'er my desk
Turns what was once romantic to burlesque.

Venice, its women, its own ironic detachment and its love of liberty set Byron's mind free to write *Beppo: A Venetian Story*, spoofing Venice's *cavalieri serventi* (escort-lovers – even nuns had them) while celebrating the freedom of its people. He followed this with two bookish plays on Venetian themes, *Marino Faliero* and *The Two Foscari*, and most importantly began his satirical masterpiece, *Don Juan*.

Meanwhile debauchery was taking its toll: an English acquaintance wrote in 1818 that 'His face had become pale, bloated and sallow, and the knuckles on his hands were lost in fat'. Byron became infatuated with a young countess, Teresa Guiccioli, and left Venice to move in with her and her elderly husband in Ravenna. But, having tasted every freedom in Venice, Byron once more began to chafe; the *contessa* was 'taming' him. He bundled up the manuscript of *Don Juan* and left, only to die of fever at the age of 36 in the Greek War of Independence.

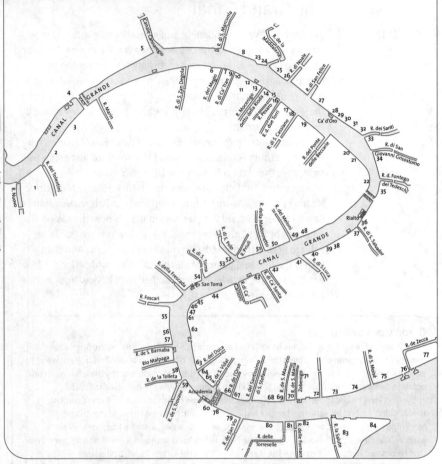

After the Ca' d'Oro Europe's most famous bridge, the **Ponte di Rialto**, swings into view. 'Rialto' recalls the days when the canal was the Rio Alto; originally it was spanned here by a bridge of boats, then by a 13th-century wooden bridge. When that was on the verge of collapse, the Republic held a competition for the design of a new stone structure. The winner, Antonio da Ponte, was the most audacious, proposing a single arch spanning 157ft; built in 1592, it has defied all the dire predictions of the day and still stands, even taking the additional weight of two rows of shops. The reliefs over the arch are of St Mark and St Theodore.

To the right stretch the extensive **Rialto Markets** (*see* p.136), and on the left the **Fondaco dei Tedeschi** (German Warehouse), once the busiest trading centre in Venice, where merchants from all over

Palazzi along the Grand Canal

08 Venice | The Grand Canal

the north lived and traded. The building (now the post office) was remodelled in 1505 and adorned with exterior frescoes by Giorgione and Titian; only fragments survive (now in the Ca' d'Oro).

Beyond the Ponte di Rialto are two Renaissance masterpieces: across from the San Silvestro landing, Sanmicheli's 1556 **Palazzo Grimani**, now the Appeals Court, and Mauro Codussi's **Palazzo Corner-Spinelli** (1510), just before the Sant'Angelo landing stage.

Signs and Directions in Venice

The Venetian language, Venetic or Venet, is still commonly heard – to the uninitiated it sounds like an Italian trying to speak Spanish with a numb mouth – and it turns up on the city's street signs. Your map may read 'Santi Giovanni e Paolo' but you should inquire for 'San Zanipolo'; 'San Giovanni Decollato' (decapitated John) is better known as 'San Zan Degola'. Still, despite the impossibility of giving comprehensible directions through the tangle of alleys (Venetians will invariably point you in the right direction, however, with a blithe *sempre diritto*! – straight ahead!), it's hard to get hopelessly lost in Venice. It only measures about 1 by 2 miles, and there are helpful yellow signs at major crossings, pointing the way to San Marco, Rialto and the Accademia, or the Piazzale Roma and the Ferrovia if you despair and want to go home. When hunting for an address in Venice, make sure you're in the correct *sestiere*, as quite a few *calli* share names. Also, beware that houses in each *sestiere* are numbered consecutively in a system logical only to a postman from Mars; numbers up to 5,000 are not unusual.

A short distance further along the left bank are the **Palazzi Mocenigo**, actually three palaces in one, where Byron lived for two years (*see* p.121). A little way further on the same side, the wall of buildings gives way for the Campo San Samuele, dominated by the **Palazzo Grassi**, an 18th-century neoclassical residence, renovated by Fiat as a modern exhibition and cultural centre.

On the right bank, just after the bend in the canal, the lovely Gothic **Ca' Foscari** was built in 1437 for Doge Francesco Foscari; two doors down, by its own landing-stage, is Longhena's 1667 **Ca' Rezzonico**, where Browning died. Further on the canal is spanned by the wooden **Ponte dell'Accademia**, built in 1932 to replace the ungainly iron 'English bridge'. On the left bank, before the Santa Maria del Giglio landing, the majestic Renaissance **Palazzo Corner** (Ca' Grande) was built by Sansovino in 1550. On the right bank, Longhena's Baroque masterpiece **Santa Maria della Salute** is followed by the Customs House, or **Dogana di Mare**, crowned by a golden globe and weather vane of Fortune, guarding the entrance to the Grand Canal. The next stop is San Marco.

Piazza San Marco

Venice's self-proclaimed Attila, Napoleon himself, described this asymmetrical showpiece as 'Europe's finest drawing-room' and, no matter how often you've seen it in pictures or in the flesh, its charm never fades. There are Venetians (and not all of them purveyors of souvenirs) who prefer it in the height of summer at its liveliest, when Babylonians from the four corners of the earth outnumber even the pigeons, who swoop back and forth at eye level, while the rival café bands provide a Fellini-esque accompaniment. Others prefer it in the misty moonlight, when the familiar seems unreal under hazy, rosy streetlamps.

The piazza and its two flanking *piazzette* have looked essentially the same since 1810, when the 'Ala Napoleonica' was added to the west end, to close in Mauro Codussi's long, arcaded **Procuratie**

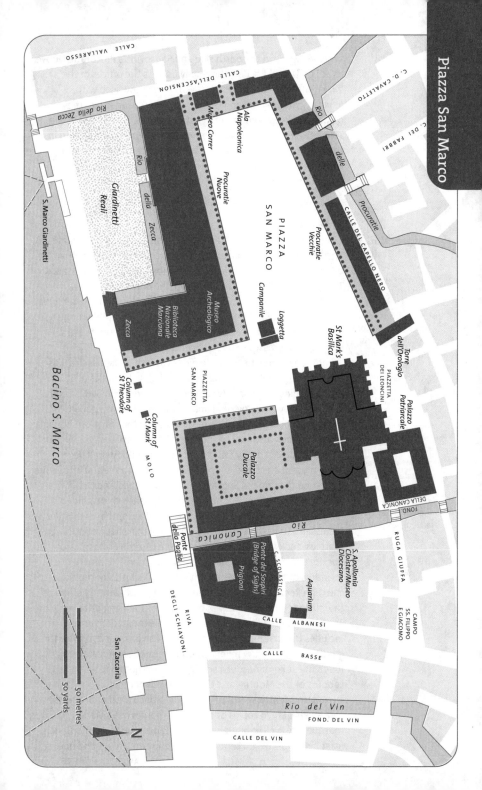

Vecchie (1499) on the north side and Sansovino's **Procuratie Nuove** (1540) on the south. Both, originally used as the offices of the 'procurators' or caretakers of St Mark's, are now filled with jewellery, embroidery and lace shops. Two centuries ago they contained an equal number of coffee-houses, the centres of the 18th-century promenade. Only two survive – the **Caffè Quadri** in the Procuratie Vecchie, the old favourite of the Austrians, and **Florian's**, in the Procuratie Nuove, its décor unchanged since it opened its doors in 1720, although with espressos at more than €3 a head the proprietors could afford to remodel it in solid gold.

St Mark's Basilica

⭐ St Mark's Basilica
open Mon–Sat 9.45–4, Sun 2–4, April–Sept until 5pm; no shorts, and women must have their shoulders covered and a minimum of décolletage, or risk being dismissed from the head of the queue, which can be diabolically long in season; admission is free, but there are separate admission charges for many of the smaller chapels and individual attractions; different sections are frequently closed for restoration; there is disabled access from Piazzetta dei Leoncini

This is nothing less than the holy shrine of the Venetian state. An ancient law decreed that all merchants trading in the East had to bring back from each voyage a new embellishment for St Mark's. The result is a glittering robbers' den, the only church in Christendom that would not look out of place in Xanadu. Yet it was dismissed out of hand for centuries. 'Low, impenetrable to the light, in wretched taste both within and without,' wrote the Président de Brosses in the 18th century.

Until 1807, when it became Venice's cathedral, the basilica was the private chapel of the Doge, built to house the relics of St Mark after the 'pious theft' of his body from Alexandria in 828, a deed sanctioned by a tidy piece of apocrypha that had the good Evangelist mooring his ship on the Rialto on the way from Aquileia to Rome, when an angel hailed him with the famous '*Pax tibi...*' or 'Peace to you, Mark, my Evangelist. Here your body shall lie.'

The present structure, consecrated in 1094, was begun after a fire destroyed the original St Mark's in 976. Modelled after Constantinople's former Church of the Apostles, five rounded doorways, five upper arches and five round Byzantine domes are the essentials of the exterior, all frosted with a sheen of coloured marbles, ancient columns and sculpture ('As if in ecstasy,' wrote Ruskin, 'the crests of the arches break into marbly foam...'). The spandrils of the arches glitter with gaudy, Technicolor mosaics – the High Renaissance, dissatisfied with the 13th-century originals, saw fit to commission new painterly scenes, leaving intact only the *Translation of the Body of St Mark* on the extreme left, which includes the first historical depiction of the basilica itself. The three bands of 13th-century **reliefs** around the central portal, among Italy's finest Romanesque carvings, show Venetian trades, the Labours of the Months, and Chaos in the inner band.

Front and centre, seemingly ready to prance off the façade, the controversial 1979 copies of the bronze **horses of St Mark** masquerade well enough – from a distance. The ancient originals (cast between the 3rd century BC and 2nd century AD, and now inside the basilica's Museo Marciano) were one of the most powerful symbols of the Venetian Republic. Originally a 'triumphal quadriga' taken by Constantine the Great from Chios to grace the Hippodrome of his new city, it was carried off in turn by the artful Doge Dandolo in the 1204 Sack of Constantinople. Another prize from Byzantium are the four porphyry 'Moors' huddled in the corner of the south façade near the Doge's Palace; according to legend, they were changed into stone for daring to break into St Mark's treasury, though scholars prefer to believe that they are four chummy 3rd-century Roman emperors, the Tetrarchs.

The Interior

The best mosaics, most of them from the 13th century, cover the six domes of the **atrium**, or narthex, their old gold glimmering in the permanent twilight. The oldest mosaic in St Mark's is that of the *Madonna and Saints* above the central door, a survivor of the original 11th-century decoration of the basilica. A slab of red marble in the pavement marks the spot where the Emperor Barbarossa knelt and apologized to 'St Peter and his Pope' – Alexander III, in 1177. This, a favourite subject of Venetian state art, is one of the few gold stars the Republic ever earned with the papacy; mistrust and acrimony were far more common.

The interior, in the form of a Greek cross, dazzles the eye with the intricate splendour of a thousand details. The domes and upper vaults are adorned with golden mosaics on New Testament subjects, the oldest dating back to the 1090s, though there have been several restorations since. Ancient columns of rare marbles, alabaster, porphyry and verdantique, sawn into slices of rich colour, line the lower walls; the 12th-century pavement is a magnificent geometric mosaic of marble, glass and porphyry. Like a mosque, the nave is partially covered with carpets.

Baptistry
open only with special permission and prior appt

The first door on the right leads to the 14th-century **baptistry**, much beloved by John Ruskin and famous for its mosaics on the life of John the Baptist, with a lovely Salome in red who could probably have had just as many heads as she pleased. Attached to the baptistry, the **Cappella Zen** was designed by Tullio Lombardo in 1504 to house the tomb of one Cardinal Zen, who had left a fortune to the Republic on condition he be buried in St Mark's. Further along the right transept you can visit the **treasury**, containing the loot from Constantinople that Napoleon overlooked – golden bowls and crystal goblets studded with huge coloured gems, straight from the cavern of Ali Baba. Near the Altar of the Sacrament, at the end of the right transept, a lamp burns 'eternally' next to one pillar: after the 976 fire, the body of St Mark was lost, but in 1094 (after Bari beat Venice to the relics of St Nicolaus) the good Evangelist staged a miraculous reappearance, popping his

Cappella Zen
currently closed

Treasury
open Mon–Sat 9.45–5, Sun 1–5; adm

Note how crooked it is!
In the Middle Ages symmetry
was synonymous with death.

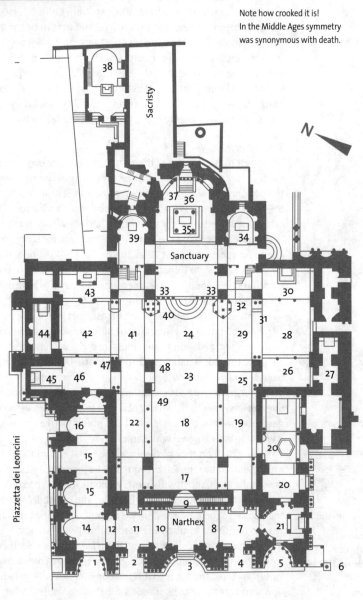

Piazzetta dei Leoncini

Piazza San Marco

St Mark's Basilica

1   *Translation of the Body of St Mark* (1270)
2   *Venice Venerating the Relics of St Mark* (1718)
3   Central door, with magnificent 13th-century carvings in arches
4   *Venice Welcoming the Relics of St Mark* (1700s)
5   *Removal of St Mark's Relics from Alexandria* (1700s)
6   *Pietra del Bando*, stone from which the Signoria's decrees were read
7   *Scenes from the Book of Genesis* (1200) and 6th-century Byzantine door of San Clemente
8   *Noah and the Flood* (1200s), tomb of Doge Vitale Falier (*d.* 1096)
9   *Madonna and Saints* (1060s); red marble slab where Emperor Barbarossa submitted to Pope Alexander III (1177); stair up to the Loggia and Museo Marciano
10 *Death of Noah and the Tower of Babel* (1200s)
11 *Story of Abraham* (1230s)
12 *Story of SS. Alipius and Simon*; and *Tondo with Justice* (1200s)
14 Tomb of Doge Bartolomeo Gradenigo (*d.* 1342)
15 *Story of Joseph*, remade in 19th century
16 Porta dei Fiori (1200s); Manzù's bust of Pope John XXIII
17 *Christ with the Virgin and St Mark* (13th century, over the door)
18 Pentecost Dome (the earliest, 12th century)
19 On the wall: *Agony in the Garden* and *Madonna and Prophets* (13th century)
20 Baptistry, *Life of St John the Baptist* (14th century) and tomb of Doge Andrea Dandolo
21 Cappella Zen, by Tullio and Antonio Lombardo (1504–22)
22 On the wall: *Christ and Prophets* (13th century)
23 In arch: *Scenes of the Passion* (12th century)
24 Central Dome, the *Ascension* (12th century)
25 Tabernacle of the Madonna of the Kiss (12th century)
26 On wall: *Rediscovery of the Body of St Mark* (13th century)
27 Treasury

28 Dome of San Leonardo; Gothic rose window (15th century)
29 In arch: *Scenes from the Life of Christ* (12th century)
30 Altar of the Sacrament; pilaster where St Mark's body was rediscovered, marked by marbles
31 Altar of St James (1462)
32 Pulpit where newly elected doge was shown to the people; entrance to the sanctuary
33 Rood screen (1394) by Jacopo di Marco Benato and Jacobello and Pier Paolo Dalle Masegne
34 Singing Gallery and Cappella di San Lorenzo, sculptures by the Dalle Masegnes (14th century)
35 Dome, *Prophets Foretell the Religion of Christ* (12th century); Baldacchino, with Eastern alabaster columns (*c.* 6th century)
36 Pala d'Oro (10th–14th century)
37 Sacristy door, with reliefs by Sansovino (16th century)
38 Sacristy, with mosaics by Titian and Padovanino (16th century) and Church of St Theodore (15th century), once seat of the Inquisition, and now part of the sacristy: both are rarely open
39 Singing Gallery and Cappella di San Pietro (14th century): note the Byzantine capitals
40 Two medieval pulpits stacked together
41 *Miracles of Christ* (16th century)
42 Dome, with *Life of St John the Evangelist* (12th century)
43 Cappella della Madonna di Nicopeia (miraculous 12th-century icon)
44 Cappella di Sant'Isidoro (14th-century mosaics and tomb of the Saint)
45 Cappella della Madonna dei Mascoli: *Life of the Virgin* by Andrea del Castagno, Michele Giambono, Jacopo Bellini
46 On wall: *Life of the Virgin* (13th century)
47 Finely carved Greek marble stoup (12th century)
48 *Virgin of the Gun* (13th century – rifle ex-voto from 1850s)
49 Il Capitello, altar topped with rare marble ciborium, with miraculous Byzantine Crucifixion panel

08

Venice | Piazza San Marco

Sanctuary
open by prior appointment only

hand out of the pillar during Mass. St Mark is now safely in place in a crypt under the high altar, in the sanctuary. You can't visit his relics, but you can see the altar's retable, the fabulous, glowing **Pala d'Oro**, a masterpiece of medieval gold and jewel work. The upper section may originally have been in the Church of the Pantocrator in Constantinople, and the lower section was commissioned in that same city by Doge Pietro Orseolo I in 976. Over the years the Venetians added their own scenes, and the Pala took its present form in 1345.

In the left transept, the **Chapel of the Madonna of Nicopeia** shelters a 10th-century icon hijacked from Constantinople, the *Protectress of Venice*, formerly carried into battle by the Byzantine Emperors. More fine mosaics are further to the left in the Chapel of St Isidore (Venetian bodysnatchers kidnapped his relics from Chios – and in the mosaic he seems happy to go). In the **Chapel of the Madonna dei Mascoli**, the mosaics on the Life of the Virgin by Tuscan Andrea Castagno and Michele Giambono (1453) were among the first harbingers of the Renaissance in Venice.

Loggia dei
Cavalli
*open daily
9.45–5; adm*

Before leaving, climb the steep stone stair near the west door of the narthex, to the **Museo Marciano**, **Galleria** and Loggia dei Cavalli for a closer look at the dome mosaics from the women's gallery and a visit to the loggia, where you can inspect the replica horses and compare them with the excellently restored, gilded, almost alive originals in the museum.

The Doge's Palace (Palazzo Ducale)

❷ The Doge's
Palace
*entrance on Riva degli
Schiavoni; open
April–Oct daily 9–7;
Nov–Mar daily 9–5.30;
adm exp, includes entry
to the Museo Correr*

What St Mark's is to sacred architecture, the Doge's Palace is to the secular – unique and audacious, dreamlike in a half-light, an illuminated storybook of Venetian history and legend. Like the basilica, it was founded shortly after the city's consolidation on the Rialto, though it didn't begin to take its present form until 1309 – with its delicate lower colonnade, its loggia of lacy Gothic tracery, and the massive top-heavy upper floor, like a cake held up by its own icing. Its weight is partly relieved by the diamond pattern of white Istrian stone and red Verona marble on the façade, which from a distance gives the palace its wholesome peaches-and-cream complexion. Less benign are the two reddish pillars in the loggia (on the Piazzetta façade) said to have been dyed by the blood of Venice's enemies, whose tortured corpses were strung out between them.

Some of Italy's finest medieval sculpture crowns the 36 columns of the lower colonnade, depicting a few sacred and many profane subjects – animals, guildsmen, Turks and Venetians. Beautiful sculptural groups adorn the corners, most notably the 13th-century Judgement of Solomon, near the grand entrance, the 1443 **Porta**

della Carta (Paper Door), a Gothic symphony in stone by Giovanni and Bartolomeo Bon.

Fires in 1574 and 1577 destroyed much of the palace, and at the time there were serious plans afoot to knock it down and let Palladio start again *à la* Renaissance. Fortunately, however, you can't teach an old doge new tricks, and the palace was rebuilt as it was, with Renaissance touches in the interior. Just within the Porta della Carta, don't miss Antonio Rizzo's delightful arcaded courtyard and his finely sculpted stairway, the **Scala dei Giganti**, named for its two Gargantuan statues of Neptune and Mars by Sansovino.

The new ticket office leads you straight into the big courtyard, designed by Antonio Rizzo and containing two of Venice's finest wellheads. First on the tour is the **Museo dell'Opera**, with its rooms full of vast bits of stone capitals, columns, chunks of stonework from the upper loggia, and models of the palace. Then you go back into the courtyard and begin the tour proper by ascending the **Scala dei Censori** to the first floor, or *primo piano nobile*, once the private apartments of the Doge, although its stripped-down unfurnished state offers few clues as to how the Doge lived in this gilded cage of pomp and ritual, leading public and private councils and rites as grand as the 'Marriage to the Sea'. Turn right, and Sansovino's **Scala d'Oro** continues up to the *secondo piano nobile*, from where the Venetian state was governed. After the fire that destroyed its great 15th-century frescoes, Veronese and Tintoretto were employed to paint the newly remodelled chambers with mythological themes and scores of allegories and apotheoses of Venice – a smug, fleshy blonde in the eyes of these two. These paintings are the palace's chief glory, and signboards in each room identify them. Visiting ambassadors and other foreign official guests would be required to wait in the first room, the **Anticollegio**, so the frescoes (Tintoretto's *Bacchus and Ariadne* and Veronese's *Rape of Europa*) had to be especially impressive; in the next room, the **Sala del Collegio**, with several masterpieces by both artists, they would be presented to the hierarchy of the Venetian state.

Tintoretto's brush dominates in the **Sala del Senato** – less lavish, since only Venetians were admitted here – while the main work in the **Sala del Consiglio dei Dieci** is Veronese's ceiling, *Old Man in Eastern Costume with a Young Woman*. Under this the Council of Ten deliberated and pored over the accusations deposited in the *Bocche dei Leoni* – the lions' mouths spread over the Republic. To be considered, an accusation had to be signed and supported by two witnesses, and anyone found making a false accusation would suffer the punishment that would have been meted out to the accused had it been true. Next to the Ten's chamber, the old

Armoury (*Sala d'Armi*) houses a fine collection of medieval and Renaissance arms and armour.

From here the visit continues downstairs, to the vast and magnificent **Sala del Maggior Consiglio**, built in 1340 and capable of holding the 2,500 patricians of the Great Council. At the entrance hangs Tintoretto's crowded, and recently restored, *Paradiso* – the biggest oil painting in the world (23 by 72ft), all the Blessed looking up at Veronese's magnificent *Apotheosis of Venice* on the ceiling. The frieze along the upper wall portrays the first 76 doges, except for the space that would have held the portrait of Marin Falier (1355) had he not led a conspiracy to take sole power; instead, a black veil bears a dry note that he was decapitated for treason. The portraits of the last 44 doges, each painted by a contemporary painter, continue around the **Sala dello Scrutinio**, where the votes for office were counted. Elections for Doge were Byzantine and elaborate – and frequent; the Maggior Consiglio preferred to choose doges who were old, and wouldn't last long enough to gain a following.

At the end of the tour the **Bridge of Sighs** (*Ponte dei Sospiri*) takes you to the 17th-century **Palazzo delle Prigioni**, mostly used for petty offenders. Those to whom the Republic took real exception were dumped into uncomfortable *pozzi*, or 'wells' in the lower part of the Palazzo Ducale, while celebrities like Casanova got to stay up in the *piombi* or 'leads' just under the roof (*see* below).

The Secret Itinerary

The Secret Itinerary
t 041 261 5911; tours 10 and 12; adm includes visiting the state rooms; book at least a day in advance at the director's office on the first floor

In 1984 the section of the palace where the real nitty-gritty business of state took place, a maze of narrow corridors and tiny rooms, was restored and opened to the public. Because the rooms are so small the 1½-hour guided tour, the *Itinerari Segreti* ('Secret Itinerary') is limited to 20 people, and the reason why it's not better known is that it has previously only been available in Italian, but it is now available in French and English too.

The tour begins at the top of the Scala d'Oro, with the snug wood-panelled offices of the **Chancellery** and the 18th-century **Hall of the Chancellors**, lined with cupboards for holding treaties, each bearing the arms of a Chancellor. In the justice department is the **Torture Chamber**, where the three Signori della Notte dei Criminali (judges of the night criminals) would 'put to the question' anyone suspected of treason, hanging them by the wrists on a rope that is still in place. This ended in the early 1700s, when Venice and Tuscany were among the first states in Europe to abolish torture.

Next is the ornate **Sala dei Tre Capi**, the chamber of the three magistrates of the Council of Ten, who had to be present at all state meetings. As this chamber might be visited by foreign dignitaries, it was lavishly decorated with works by Veronese,

Antonello da Messina and Hieronymus Bosch. From here it's up to the notorious **Piombi**, which despite their evil reputation appear downright cosy, as prisons go. Casanova's cell is pointed out, and there's an elaborate explanation of his famous escape through a hole in the roof. Near the end of the tour comes one of Venice's marvels: the attic of the **Sala del Maggior Consiglio**, where you can see how the Arsenale's shipwrights made a vast ceiling float unsupported over the room below; built in 1577, it has yet to need any repairs.

The Campanile

The Campanile
open daily 9–7; adm

St Mark's bell tower, to those uninitiated in the cult of Venice, seems like an alien presence, a Presbyterian brick sentinel in the otherwise delicately wrought piazza. But it has always been there, at least since 912; it was last altered in 1515, and when it gently collapsed into a pile of rubble on 14 July 1902 (the only casualty a cat) the Venetians felt its lack so acutely that they began to construct an exact replica, only a few hundred tons lighter and stronger, completed in 1912. It is 332ft tall, and you can take the lift up for a bird's-eye vision of Venice and its Lagoon; from up here the city seems amazingly compact. Though you have to pay for the view, misbehaving priests had it for free; the Council of Ten would suspend them in cages from the windows. Under the campanile, Sansovino's elegant **loggetta** adds a graceful note to the brick belfry. Its marbles and sculptures glorifying Venice took it on the nose when the campanile fell on top of them, but they have been carefully restored.

The Correr Museum and Clock Tower

Museo Correr
open April–Oct daily
9–7; Nov–Mar daily
9–5; adm, last tickets
90mins before closing;
also incorporates the
Archaeological Museum
and Biblioteca, known
collectively as the San
Marco museums.
Entrance to all except
the Palazzo Ducale is
via the Museo Correr

At the far end of the piazza, in the Procuratie Nuove, the Museo Correr contains an interesting collection of Venetian memorabilia – the robes, ducal bonnets and old-maidish nightcaps of the doges, the 20-inch-heeled *zoccoli*, once the rage among Venetian noblewomen, and a copy of the statue of Marco Polo from the Temple of 500 Genies in Canton. There are also musical instruments, arms and armour, some wonderful old globes and an interesting section called 'Venetian Civilization' with objects from Venetian domestic life: pots and pans, and other domestic artefacts. There are also some antique games – roulette wheel, playing cards, draughts set, jigsaw, children's games (a yo-yo), a bingo set, dominoes – all from the 18th century. Upstairs, the fine collection of Venetian paintings includes two great works by Carpaccio, *The Courtesans* (or Ladies – in Venice it was hard to tell) and *A Visitation*; Ferrarese/Bolognese's *Young Man in a Red Beret*, with his archetypal Venetian face; Antonello da Messina's damaged but luminous *Pietà*, and others by Cosmè Tura and a young Giovanni Bellini; a lively early sculpture by Canova, *Daedalus and Icarus* (1779); and the Bosch-esque *Temptation of St Anthony* by Il Civetta ('the little owl').

At the head of the Procuratie Vecchie two bronze wild men, called the 'Moors', sound the hours atop the clock tower, the newly restored **Torre dell'Orologio**, built to a design by Mauro Codussi in 1499 above the entrance to Venice's main shopping street, the Mercerie. The old Italians were fond of elaborate astronomical clocks, but none is as beautiful as this, with its coloured enamel and gilt face, its Madonna and obligatory lion. The Council of Ten (which actually encouraged fearsome false rumours about itself, to make its job easier) allegedly blinded the builders to prevent them creating such a marvel for any other city. Below, flanking the basilica's north façade, a fountain and two porphyry lions stand in **Piazzetta Giovanni XXIII**, named after the Venetian patriarch who became pope in 1959.

Piazzetta San Marco

To the south of the basilica, the Piazzetta San Marco was the Republic's foyer, where ships would dock under the watchful eye of the Doge. The view towards the Lagoon is framed by two tall Egyptian granite **columns**, trophies brought to Venice in the 1170s. The Venetians had a knack for converting their booty into self-serving symbols: atop one of the columns several Roman statues were pieced together to form their first patron saint, St Theodore with his crocodile (or dragon, or fish), while on the other stands an ancient Assyrian or Persian winged lion, under whose paw the Venetians slid a book, creating their symbol of St Mark.

Biblioteca
*entry via
Museo Correr*

Opposite the Doge's Palace stands the Biblioteca, built in 1536 by Sansovino and considered by Palladio to be the most beautiful building since antiquity, especially notable for the play of light and shadow in its sculpted arcades. Sansovino, trained as a sculptor, was notorious for paying scant attention to architectural details, and the library was scarcely completed when its ceiling collapsed. The goof-up cost him a trip to the Council of Ten's slammer, and he was only released on the pleading of Titian. Scholars with permission from the director can examine such treasures as the 1501 Grimani breviary, a masterwork of Flemish illuminators; Homeric codices, the 1459 world map of Fra Mauro, and Marco Polo's will. But not the famous library Petrarch willed to the Republic – the Venetians misplaced it.

**Archaeological
Museum**
*Piazzetta San Marco
17; entry via
Museo Correr*

Next to the library, Venice's Archaeological Museum is one of the few museums in the city heated in the winter. It has an excellent collection of Greek sculpture, including a violent *Leda and the Swan* and ancient copies of the famous *Gallic Warriors of Pergamon*, all given to the city by collector Cardinal Grimani in 1523. On the other side of the Libreria, by the waterfront, is another fine building by Sansovino, the 1547 **Zecca**, or Old Mint, which once stamped out thousands of gold *zecchini*, and gave English a new word: 'sequin'.

Towards San Polo and Santa Croce

The streets between the Piazza San Marco and the market district of the Rialto are the busiest in Venice, especially the **Mercerie**, which begin under the clock tower and are lined with some of the city's smartest shops. It was down the Mercerie that Baiamonte Tiepolo, miffed at being excluded from the Golden Book, led his rebel aristocrats in 1310, when an old lady cried 'Death to tyrants!' from her window and hurled a brick at his standard-bearer, killing him on the spot, and causing such disarray that Tiepolo was forced to give up his attempted coup. It was a close call that the Republic chose never to forget: the site, above the Sottoportego del Capello Nero, is marked by a stone relief of the heroine with her brick.

The Mercerie continue to the church of **San Zulian**, redesigned in 1553 by Sansovino, with a façade most notable for Sansovino's statue of its pompous and scholarly benefactor, Tommaso Rangone. Sansovino also had a hand in **San Salvatore** in the next *campo*, adding the finishing touches to its noble Renaissance interior and designing the monument to Doge Francesco Venier. An 89-year-old Titian painted one of his more unusual works for this church, the *Annunciation*, which he signed with double emphasis *Titianus Fecit* – '*Fecit*' because his patrons refused to believe that he had painted it. In a chapel north of the altar is the *Supper at the House of Emmaus*, by the school of Giovanni Bellini.

A Doge's Life: Gormenghast with Canals

Senator in Senate, Citizen in City were his titles, as well as Prince of Clothes, with a wardrobe of gold and silver damask robes, and scarlet silks. Once the Doge was dressed, the rest of his procession would fall in line, including all the paraphernalia of Byzantine royalty: a naked sword, six silver trumpets, a damask parasol, a chair, cushion, candle and eight standards bearing the Lion of St Mark in four colours symbolizing peace, war, truth and loyalty. Yet for all the pomp this was the only man in Venice not permitted to send a private note to his wife, or receive one from her, or from anyone else; nor could he accept any gift beyond flowers or rose-water, or go to a café or theatre, or engage in any money-making activity, while nevertheless having to meet the expenses of his office out of his own pocket. Nor could he abdicate, unless requested to do so.

The office was respected, but often not the man. When a Doge died he was privately buried in his family tomb before the state funeral – which used a dummy corpse with a wax mask. First, an 'Inquisition of the Defunct Doge' was held over the dummy, to discover if the Doge had kept to his *Promissione* (his oath of coronation), if his family owed the state any money, and if it were necessary to amend the *Promissione* to limit the powers of his successor still further. Then the dead Doge's dummy was taken to St Mark's to be hoisted in the air nine times by sailors, to the cry of '*Misericordia!*' (Mercy), and then given a funeral service at the church of Santi Giovanni e Paolo.

Campo San Bartolomeo and the Rialto

Humming, bustling **Campo San Bartolomeo,** next on the Mercerie, has for centuries been one of the social hubs of Venice, and still gets packed with after-work crowds every evening. Its centre is graced by the statue of Goldoni, whose comedies in Venetian dialect still make the Venetians laugh; and by the look on his jolly face he still finds their antics amusing.

Follow the crowds up to the Ponte di Rialto (*see* 'The Grand Canal', p.121), the geographical heart of Venice, and the principal node of its pedestrian and water traffic. The city's central markets, the **Rialto,** have been just across the bridge for a millennium, divided into sections for vegetables and for fish. Near the former you may pay your respects to Venice's oldest church, little **San Giacomo di Rialto,** founded perhaps as long ago as the 5th century and substantially reworked in 1071 and 1601. In the same *campo* stands a famous Venetian character, the 16th-century granite hunchback, **Gobbo di Rialto,** who supports a little stairway and marble podium from which the decrees of the Republic were proclaimed.

The Frari and the Scuola di San Rocco

From the Ponte di Rialto, follow the yellow signs to Piazzale Roma, passing the pretty **Campo San Polo** and church of San Polo, with Giandomenico Tiepolo's dramatic *Stations of the Cross* in the Oratory of the Crucifix. The signs next take you before a venerable Venetian institution: the huge brick Gothic church of the Frari, one of the most severe medieval buildings in the city, built between 1330 and 1469. Monteverdi, one of the founding fathers of opera and choir director at St Mark's, is buried here, as is Titian, whose tomb follows the Italian rule – the greater the artist, the worse the tomb (see Michelangelo's in Florence). The strange pyramid with a half-open door was intended by Antonio Canova to be Titian's tomb, but it eventually became the sculptor's own last resting place. The Frari is celebrated for its great art, and especially for the most over-rated painting in Italy, Titian's *Assumption of the Virgin* (1516–18). Marvel at the art, at Titian's revolutionary Mannerist use of space and movement, but its big-eyed, heaven-gazing Virgin has as much artistic vision as a Sunday school holy card.

That, however, is not true of Giovanni Bellini's *Triptych of Madonna with Child and Saints* in the sacristy, or Donatello's rustic statue of *St John the Baptist* in the choir chapel. In the north aisle Titian's less theatrical *Madonna di Ca' Pesaro* was modelled on his wife Celia; the painting had a greater influence on Venetian composition than the *Assumption*. Also note the beautiful Renaissance Tomb of Doge Nicolò Tron by Antonio Rizzo in the sanctuary, from 1476.

San Polo
open Mon–Sat 10–5, Sun 1–5; adm

Frari
open Mon–Sat 10–5; adm

**Scuola Grande
di San Rocco**
open daily 9–5; adm

Next to the Frari, the Scuola Grande di San Rocco was one of Venice's most important *scuole*. San Rocco, renowned for his juju against the Black Death, was so popular among the Venetians that they stole his body from Montpellier and canonized him before the pope did, and his confraternity was one of the city's wealthiest. The *scuola* has a beautiful, lively façade by Scarpagnino, and inside it contains one of the wonders of Venice – or rather, 54 wonders – all painted by Tintoretto, who worked on the project from 1562 to 1585 without any assistance.

Tintoretto always managed to look at conventional subjects from a fresh point of view; while other artists of the High Renaissance composed their subjects with the epic vision of a Cecil B. de Mille, Tintoretto had the eye of a 16th-century Orson Welles, creating audacious, dynamic 'sets', often working out his compositions in his little box-stages, with wax figures and unusual lighting effects. In the *scuola*, especially in the upper floor, he was at the peak of his career, and painted what is considered by some to be the finest painting cycle in existence, culminating in the Crucifixion, where the event is the central drama of a busy human world. Vertigo is not an uncommon response – for an antidote, look at the funny carvings along the walls by Francesco Pianta. In the same room there are also several paintings on easels by Titian, and a Christ that some attribute to Titian, some to Giorgione.

**Scuola Grande di
San Giovanni
Evangelista**
*t 041 718 2347; open
Sun–Mon 10–4; call or
ring the bell*

Just north, beyond Campo San Stin, the Scuola Grande di San Giovanni Evangelista deserves a look for its beautiful Renaissance courtyard and double-ramp stairway (1498), Mauro Codussi's masterpiece, noted for the rhythms of its domes and barrel vaults.

**Galleria d'Arte
Moderna**
*open Tues–Sun
10–5; adm*

**Museum of
Oriental Art**
*open Tues–Sun
9.15–2; adm*

**Natural History
Museum**
*t 041 275 0206; under
restoration; some wings
are open Tues–Fri 9–1
and Sat–Sun 9–4; adm*

From Campo San Stin, if you start along Calle Donà and keep as straight as possible, you should end up at Ca' Pesaro on the Grand Canal, a huge 17th-century pile by Longhena that is occupied by the Galleria d'Arte Moderna, with a collection principally of works exhibited in the Biennale exhibitions. Italian contemporary art, much of it unfamiliar to a foreign audience, is the mainstay, but some international figures are also represented, such as Gustav Klimt. Ca' Pesaro also houses a Museum of Oriental Art, with a higgledy-piggledy collection of Asian artefacts collected in the 19th century. If you really want to escape the crowds, however, head further up the canal to the stuffed Lagoon fowl in the Natural History Museum, in the Venetian-Byzantine Fondaco dei Turchi.

San Marco to Dorsoduro

Following the yellow signs 'To the Accademia' from Piazza San Marco (starting by the tourist office), the first *campo* belongs to Baroque San Moisè (1668), Italy's most grotesque church, with a grimy opera-buffa façade, rockpile and altarpiece. For more opera and less buffa, take a detour up Calle Veste (the second right after Campo San Moisè) to monumental Campo San Fantin and La Fenice (1792), the Republic's last hurrah and one of Italy's most renowned opera houses, which saw the premieres of Verdi's *Rigoletto* and *La Traviata*. In 1996 a fire ripped La Fenice apart, and the opera house remained closed for seven years, with rebuilding delayed by lack of funds and the discovery of Roman ruins beneath the foundations. All ended well, however, with a grand reopening in December 2003 and widespread critical acclaim for the late architect Aldo Rossi's recreation of the original plush interior. Venice has a venerable musical tradition, albeit one that had become more tradition than music by the time of the era of grand opera – although Mozart's great librettist, Lorenzo da Ponte, was a Venetian.

> **La Fenice**
> *t 041 786 511,*
> *www.teatrolafenice.it;*
> *guided tours €7*

Back en route to the Accademia, in the next *campo* stands **Santa Maria Zobenigo** (or del Giglio), on which the Barbaro family stuck a fancy Baroque façade in 1680, not for God but for the glory of the Barbari; the façade is famous for its total lack of religious significance. The signs lead next to Campo Francesco Morosini, named after the Doge who recaptured the Morea from the Turks, but is remembered everywhere else as the man who blew the top off the Parthenon. Better known as **Campo Santo Stefano**, it's one of the most elegant squares in Venice, a pleasant place to sit outside at a café table – particularly at **Paolin**, Venice's best *gelateria*. At one end, built directly over a canal, the Gothic church of **Santo Stefano** has the most gravity-defying campanile of all the leaning towers in Venice (most alarmingly viewed from the adjacent Campo Sant'Angelo). The interior is worth a look for its striking wood ceiling, soaring like a ship's keel, as well as its wooden choir stalls (1488).

The Accademia

> ⭐ **Galleria dell'**
> **Accademia**
> *t 041 520 0345; open*
> *Mon 9–2, Tues–Fri 9–9,*
> *Sat 9am–11pm, Sun*
> *9–8; adm exp; only 300*
> *visitors at a time, so*
> *arrive early or pre-book*
> *a date and time*

Just over the bridge and Grand Canal from Campo Santo Stefano stands the Galleria dell'Accademia, the grand cathedral of Venetian art, ablaze with light and colour. The collection is arranged chronologically, beginning in the former refectory of the Scuola (**Room I**): among them, 14th-century altarpieces by Paolo and Lorenzo Veneziano, whose half-Byzantine Madonnas look like fashion models for Venetian silks. Later altarpieces fill **Room II**, most importantly Giovanni Bellini's *Pala di San Giobbe*, one of the key works of the *quattrocento*: the architecture repeats its original setting in the church of San Giobbe; on the left St Francis invites the viewer into a scene made timeless by the music of the angels at the Madonna's feet. Other beautiful altarpieces in the room are by Carpaccio, Basaiti and Cima da Conegliano (the subtle *Madonna of the Orange Tree*).

The next rooms are small but, like gifts, contain the best things: Mantegna's confidently aloof *St George*, the little allegories and a trio of Madonnas by Giovanni Bellini (including the lovely, softly coloured *Madonna of the Little Trees*) and Piero della Francesca's *St Jerome and Devotee*, a youthful study in perspective. In Room V you will find Giorgione's *La Vecchia*, with the warning 'Col Tempo' ('With Time') in her hand, and the mysterious *The Tempest*, two of the few paintings scholars accept as being indisputably by Big George, but how strange they are! It is said Giorgione invented easel painting for the pleasure of bored, purposeless courtiers in Caterina Cornaro's Asolo, but the paintings seem to reflect rather than lighten their ennui and discontent.

Highlights of the next few rooms include Lorenzo Lotto's *Gentleman in his Study*, which catches its sitter off-guard before he could clear the nervously scattered scraps of paper from his table, and Paris Bordenone's masterpiece, *Fisherman Presenting St Mark's Ring to the Doge* (1554), celebrating a miracle of St Mark.

The climax of the Venetian High Renaissance comes in **Room X**, with Veronese's *Christ in the House of Levi* (1573), set in a Palladian loggia with a ghostly white imaginary background, in violent contrast to the rollicking feast of Turks, hounds, midgets, Germans and the artist himself (at the front, next to the pillar on the left). The painting was originally titled *The Last Supper*, and fell foul of the Inquisition, which took umbrage (especially at the Germans). Veronese was cross-examined, and ordered to make pious changes at his own expense; the artist saved himself both the trouble and the money by simply giving it the title by which it has been known ever since. Room X also contains Veronese's *Annunciation*, and some early masterworks by Tintoretto – *Translation of the Body of St Mark*, and *St Mark Freeing a Slave*, in which the Evangelist, in true Tintoretto-esque fashion, nosedives from the top of the canvas. The last great painting in the room was also the last ever by Titian, the sombre *La Pietà*, which he was working on when he died in 1576, aged about 90, from the plague; he intended it for his tomb, and smeared the paint on with his fingers.

Alongside several more Tintorettos, the following few rooms mainly contain work from the 17th and 18th centuries (Tiepolo, Sebastiano and Marco Ricci, Piazzetta, Longhi, Rosalba Carriera). Canaletto and Guardi, whose scenes of 18th-century Venice were the picture postcards of the British aristocracy on their Grand Tour, are represented in **Room XVII**.

The final rooms of the Accademia were formerly part of the elegantly Gothic church of Santa Maria della Carità, and house more luminous 15th-century paintings by Alvise Vivarini, Giovanni and Gentile Bellini, Marco Basaiti and Crivelli. **Room XX** has a fascinating series depicting the *Miracles of the True Cross* with Venetian backgrounds, painted by Gentile Bellini, Carpaccio and others. **Room XXI** contains the dreamily compelling and utterly charming *Cycle of St Ursula* by Carpaccio, from the former Scuola di Sant'Orsola. Finally, the last room, **Room XXIV**, the former *albergo* of the church, contains two fine paintings that were originally made for it: Titian's striking *Presentation of the Virgin* (1538) and a triptych by Antonio Vivarini and Giovanni d'Alemagna (1446).

Around Dorsoduro

The *sestiere* of Dorsoduro can also boast the second-most-visited art gallery in Venice, the Peggy Guggenheim Collection, just down the Grand Canal from the Accademia in her 18th-century Venetian Palazzo Venier dei Leoni. In her 30 years as a collector, until her death in 1979, Ms Guggenheim amassed an impressive quantity of brand-name 20th-century art – Bacon, Brancusi, Braque, Calder, Chagall, Dalí, De Chirico, Dubuffet, Duchamp, Max Ernst (her second husband), Giacometti, Gris, Kandinsky, Klee, Magritte, Miró, Mondrian, Moore, Picasso, Pollock, Rothko and Smith. Administered by the Solomon R. Guggenheim Foundation in New York, the collection can come as a breath of fresh air after so much high Italian art, and it also sponsors temporary exhibitions, even in winter; look out for posters.

☆ **Peggy Guggenheim Collection**
open Wed–Mon 10–6; 1 April–2 Nov also Sat 10–10; adm exp

From here it's a five-minute stroll down to the serene, octagonal basilica of Santa Maria della Salute ('of Health'), on the tip of Dorsoduro. One of five votive churches built after the passing of plagues (Venice, a busy international port, was particularly susceptible), La Salute is the masterpiece of Baldassare Longhena, its snow-white dome and marble jelly rolls dramatically set at the entrance of the Grand Canal. The interior is a relatively restrained white and grey Baroque, and the **sacristy** contains the *Marriage at Cana* by Tintoretto and several works by Titian, including his *St Mark Enthroned Between Saints*. Almost next to the basilica, on the point, stands the distinctive profile of the **Dogana di Mare**, the Customs House (*see* 'The Grand Canal', p.122).

Santa Maria della Salute
open daily 9–12 and 3–6

The **Fondamenta delle Zattere**, facing away from the city towards the freighter-filled canal and the island of Giudecca, leads around to the **Gesuati**, the only church in Venice decorated by Umbrian artists. For a more elaborate feast, take the long stroll along the Fondamenta (or take *vaporetto* no.5 to San Basegio) to Veronese's parish church of San Sebastiano on Rio di San Basilio. Veronese, it is said, murdered a man in Verona and took refuge in this neighbourhood, and over the next 10 years he and his brother Benedetto Caliari embellished San Sebastiano – beginning in 1555 with the ceiling frescoes of the sacristy and ending with the

San Sebastiano
Rio di San Basilio; open Mon–Sat 10–5; adm

magnificent ceiling, *The Story of Esther*, and illusionistic paintings in the choir (the lights are always lit).

From San Sebastiano you can head back towards the Grand Canal (Calle Avogaria and Calle Lunga San Barnaba); turn left up Calle Pazienza to visit the 14th-century church of the **Carmini** with a landmark red campanile and lovely altars by Cima da Conegliano and Lorenzo Lotto. The Scuola Grande dei Carmini next door was designed by Longhena in the 1660s, and contains one of Tiepolo's best and brightest ceilings, *The Virgin in Glory*.

The Carmini is on the corner of the delightful **Campo Santa Margherita**. Traditionally the main market-place of Dorsoduro, it's a good spot to find relatively inexpensive pizzerias, restaurants and cafés that are not aimed primarily at tourists. It is also close to **Ca' Rezzonico** (Rio Terrà Canal down to the Fondamenta Rezzonico), home to the Museo del Settecento, Venice's attic of 18th-century art, with bittersweet paintings by Giandomenico Tiepolo, some wild rococo furniture by Andrea Brustolon, a pharmacy, genre scenes by Longhi (*The Lady and Hairdresser*), and a breathtaking view of the Grand Canal. The house was owned in the last century by Robert Browning's son, Pen, and the poet died there in 1889. One of the palaces you see opposite belonged to Doge Cristoforo Moro, whom the Venetians claim Shakespeare used as his model for Othello, confusing the Doge's name with his race.

Scuola Grande dei Carmini
open Mon–Sat 9–4, Sun 9–1; adm; sometimes also open for concerts

Museo del Settecento
open Wed–Mon 10–5; adm

San Marco to Castello

From Piazzetta San Marco, the gracefully curving, ever-thronging **Riva degli Schiavoni** took its name from the Slavs of Dalmatia; in 1782 Venice was doing so much business here that the quay had to be widened. A few steps beyond the Palazzo Ducale, one of the city's finest Gothic *palazzi* was converted in 1822 to the famous **Hotel Danieli**, its name a corruption of the 'Dandolo' family who built it. The quay also has a robust **Memorial to Vittorio Emanuele II** (1887), where two of Venice's over 10,000 lions shelter – as often as not with members of Venice's equally numerous if smaller feline population between their paws.

From Riva degli Schiavoni, the Sottoportico San Zaccaria leads back to the lovely Gothic-Renaissance San Zaccaria, begun by Antonio Gambello in 1444 and completed by Mauro Codussi in 1515. Inside, look for Bellini's recently restored and extraordinary *Madonna and Saints* in the second chapel to the right, and the refined Florentine frescoes by Andrea del Castagno in the chapel of San Tarasio. Another church, back on the Riva itself, La Pietà, served the girls' orphanage which the red-headed priest Vivaldi made famous during his years as its concert master and composer

San Zaccaria
open Mon–Sat 10–12 and 4–6, Sun 4–6

La Pietà
open only for concerts

(1704–38). The church was rebuilt shortly afterwards by Giorgio Massari with a remarkable oval interior, in luscious cream and gold with G.B. Tiepolo's extravagant *Triumph of Faith* on top. It has particularly fine acoustics – Vivaldi helped design it.

Due north of La Pietà stands the city's Greek Orthodox church, the 16th-century **San Giorgio dei Greci**, with its tilting tower and scuola, next to the Museo di Icone, run by the Hellenic Centre for Byzantine and Post-Byzantine Studies. Many of its icons were painted in the 16th and 17th centuries by artists who fled the Turkish occupation. In Venice the Greeks came into contact with the Renaissance; the resulting Venetian-Cretan school nourished, most famously, El Greco.

Close by, another ethnic minority, the Dalmatians – present in Venice almost throughout the history of the Republic – began their tiny Scuola di San Giorgio degli Schiavoni in 1451. Its minute interior is decorated with the most beloved art in all Venice: Vittore Carpaccio's frescoes on the lives of the Dalmatian patron saints – Augustine writing, watched by his patient little white dog; Jerome bringing his lion into the monastery; George charging a petticoat-munching dragon in a landscape strewn with maidenly leftovers from lunch; and more. Some of the greatest paintings by Carpaccio's more serious contemporaries, the Vivarini and Cima da Conegliano, hold pride of place in **San Giovanni in Bragora** (between San Giorgio degli Schiavoni and the Riva); the best work, Cima's *Baptism of Christ*, is in the sanctuary.

Museo di Icone
*open Mon–Sat
9–12.30 and 1.30–4.30,
Sun 10–5; adm*

Scuola di San Giorgio degli Schiavoni
*open Tues–Sat
10–12.30 and 3.30–6,
Sun 9.30–12.30; adm*

The Arsenale and Naval History Museum

From the Riva degli Schiavoni, the Fondamenta dell'Arsenale leads to the twin towers guarding the **Arsenale**. Founded in 1104, this first of all arsenals derived its name from the Venetian pronunciation of the Arabic *darsina'a*, or workshop, and until the 17th century these were the greatest dockyards in the world, the very foundation of the Republic's wealth and power. In its heyday the Arsenale had a payroll of 16,000, and produced a ship a day to fight the Turks. Dante visited this great industrial complex twice and, as Blake would later do with his 'dark satanic mills', found its imagery perfect for the *Inferno*. The Biennale has now taken over a vast section of its empty shipyards as a year-round space for exhibitions, arts events, music and the like.

Look at the **Great Gateway** next to the towers. It was built in 1460 – almost entirely from marble trophies nicked from Greece. Among the chorus line of lions is an ancient beast that Doge Francesco Morosini found in Piraeus, with 11th-century runes carved in its back in the name of Harold Hardrada, the member of the Byzantine Emperor's Varangian Guard who was later crowned king of Norway. Other very innocent-looking lions, eroded into lambs, were taken from the island of Delos in 1718 when the Turks weren't looking.

Venice's glorious maritime history is the subject of the fascinating displays in the Museo Storico Navale – most dazzling of all is the model of the Doge's barge, the *Bucintoro*. The museum is just past the gateway to the Arsenale, near the beginning of Via Garibaldi; in a neighbouring house lived two seafarers, originally from Genoa, who contributed more to the history of Britain than that of Venice, Giovanni and Sebastiano Caboto.

Via Garibaldi and Fondamenta Sant'Anna continue to the Isola di San Pietro, site of the unmemorable San Pietro di Castello, until 1807 Venice's cathedral, its lonely, distant site a comment on the Republic's attitude towards the papacy. The attractive, detached campanile is by Codussi and, inside, there is a marble throne incorporating a Muslim tombstone with verses from the Koran, which for centuries was said to have been the Throne of St Peter in Antioch. To the south are the refreshing pines and planes of the **Public Gardens**, where the International Exhibition of Modern Art, or Biennale, takes place in odd-numbered years in the artsy pavilions. This, and the **Parco delle Rimembranze** further on, were a gift to this sometimes claustrophobic city of stone and water by Napoleon, who knocked down four extraneous churches to plant the trees. From here you can take *vaporetto* no.1 or 2 back to San Marco, or to the Lido.

Museo Diocesano to Santi Giovanni e Paolo

The *calli* that lead from the Piazzetta dei Leoncini around the back of San Marco and over the Rio di Palazzo will take you to the Romanesque cloister of Sant'Apollonia and one of Venice's newest museums, the Museo Diocesano, containing an exceptional collection of trappings and art salvaged from the city's churches. Through a web of alleys to the north there's more art in the 16th-century Palazzo Querini-Stampalia, home of the Fondazione Querini-Stampalia, which has an endearing assortment of genre paintings – scenes of 18th-century Venetian convents, dinner parties, music lessons, etc. by Pietro Longhi and Gabriel Bella, as well as works by Bellini, Palma il Vecchio, Vincenzo Catena (a 16th-century merchant and the first known amateur to dabble in painting) and G.B. Tiepolo – all in a suitably furnished 18th-century patrician's *palazzo*.

Santa Maria Formosa, in its charming *campo* just to the north, was rebuilt in 1492 by Codussi, who made creative use of its original Greek-cross plan. The head near the bottom of its campanile is notorious as being the most hideous thing in Venice, while, inside, Palma il Vecchio's *Santa Barbara* is famed as the loveliest of all Venetian blondes, modelled on the artist's own

Museo Storico Navale
open Mon–Fri 8.45–1.30, Sat 8.45–1; adm

San Pietro di Castello
open Mon–Sat 10–5; adm

Museo Diocesano
open Tues–Sat 10–6

Fondazione Querini-Stampalia
open Tues–Sun 10–6, Fri and Sat until 10; adm exp

Santa Maria Formosa
open Mon–Sat 10–5; adm

daughter. Another celebrated work, Bartolomeo Vivarini's *Madonna della Misericordia* (1473), is in the first chapel on the right; the parishioners shown under the protection of the Virgin's mantle earned their exalted position by paying for the painting.

Santi Giovanni
e Paolo
*open daily 7.30–12.30
and 3.30–7.30*

The next *campo* to the north is dominated by **Santi Giovanni e Paolo** (or San Zanipolo), after St Mark's the most important church on the right bank. A vast Gothic brick barn begun by the Dominicans in 1246, this was almost entirely rebuilt after 1333, and finally completed in 1430; no one could accuse it of being beautiful, despite its fine front doorway. San Zanipolo was the pantheon of the doges; all their funerals were held here after the 1300s, and some 25 of them went no further, but lie in splendid Gothic and Renaissance tombs. Scattered among them are monuments to other honoured servants of the Venetian state, such as Marcantonio Bragadin, the commander who in 1571 was flayed alive by the Turks after he had surrendered Famagusta, in Cyprus, after a long siege; his bust sits on an urn holding his neatly folded skin. The adjacent chapel contains Giovanni Bellini's polyptych of *St Vincent Ferrer*, a fire-eating subject portrayed by the gentlest of painters; nearby there's a buoyant Baroque ceiling by Piazzetta in St Dominic's chapel, and a small shrine containing the foot of St Catherine of Siena. The right transept has paintings by Alvise Vivarini, Cima da Conegliano and Lorenzo Lotto; the finest tomb is in the chancel, that of Doge Andrea Vendramin, by Tullio and Antonio Lombardo (1478), while the **Chapel of the Rosary** in the north transept, which was severely damaged by fire in the 19th century, has a ceiling by Veronese from the church of the Umilità, long demolished.

Adjacent to San Zanipolo, the **Scuola Grande di San Marco** has one of the loveliest Renaissance façades in Italy, the fascinating *trompe l'œil* lower half by Pietro and Tullio Lombardo, the upper floor by Mauro Codussi, and finished in 1495. The *scuola* is now used as Venice's municipal hospital, but it is possible to enter to see the lavish coffered ceiling in the library with the permission of the Direttore di Sanità.

Opposite stands the superbly dynamic **Equestrian Statue of Bartolomeo Colleoni**, the *condottiere* from Bergamo (1400–76) who had served the Republic so well on the mainland. In his lifetime proud of his emblem of *coglioni* (testicles – a play on his name), Colleoni envied Donatello's statue of his predecessor Gattamelata erected by the Venetians in Padua, and in his will he left the Republic 100,000 ducats if it would erect a similar statue of him in front of St Mark's. Greedy for the money but unable to countenance a monument to an individual in their sacred Piazza, the wily Venetians put the statue up before the *scuola* of St Mark. Verrocchio, the master of Leonardo and Botticelli, had only finished the plaster moulds when he died in 1488, leaving Alessandro Leopardi to do the casting. Verrocchio never saw a portrait of his subject, and all resemblances to Klaus Kinski are purely accidental.

Cannaregio

Crumbling, piquant Cannaregio is the least visited *sestiere* in Venice, and here, perhaps, more than anywhere else in the city, you can begin to feel what everyday life is like behind the tourist glitz – children playing tag on the bridges, old men in shorts messing around in unglamorous, unpainted boats on murky canals, neighbourhood greasy spoons and bars, banners of laundry waving gaily overhead.

Santa Maria dei Miracoli and the Ca' d'Oro

Santa Maria dei Miracoli
open Mon–Sat 10–5; adm

From Campo San Zanipolo (*see* left), Calle Larga G. Gallina leads to the perfect little Renaissance church of Santa Maria dei Miracoli, built by Pietro Lombardo in the 1480s and often compared to an exquisite jewel box, elegant, graceful and glowing with a soft marble sheen, inside and out. Just to the south are two enclosed courtyards, known as the **Corte Prima del Milion** and the **Corte Seconda del Milion**, where Marco Polo used to live. The latter in particular looks much as it did when the great traveller lived there; 'Million', his nickname in Venice, referred to the million tall tales he brought back with him from China. Nearby, Codussi's **San Giovanni Grisostomo** (1504) was his last work, a seminal piece of Renaissance architecture that contains Giovanni Bellini's last altar painting (*SS. Jerome, Christopher and Augustine*), as well as a beautiful high altarpiece by Sebastiano del Piombo.

Galleria Franchetti
Via 28 Aprile; open Mon 8.15–2, Tues–Sun 8.15–7.15; adm

Further towards the railway station up the Grand Canal, signposted off Strada Nuova, stands the enchanting Gothic **Ca' d'Oro**, finished in 1440 and now housing the Galleria Franchetti. In its collection are Mantegna's stern *St Sebastian*, Guardi's series of Venetian views, an excellent collection of Renaissance bronzes and medallions by Pisanello and Il Riccio, Tullio Lombardo's charming *Double Portrait*, and now sadly faded fragments of the famous frescoes by Giorgione and Titian from the Fondaco dei Tedeschi. Also present are minor works by Titian, including a voluptuous Venus. The building itself is famous for the intricate traceries of its façade, best appreciated from the Grand Canal, and the courtyard, with a beautifully carved wellhead by Bartolomeo Bon.

Gesuiti
open daily 10–12 and 5–7

Due north, near the Fondamenta Nuove, stands the church of the Gesuiti, built by the Jesuits when the Republic relaxed its restrictions against them, in 1714–29: a Baroque extravaganza, full of *trompe l'œil* of white and green-grey marble draperies that would make a fitting memorial for Liberace. A previous church on this same site was the parish church of Titian, to which he contributed the *Martyrdom of St Lawrence* – the saint on a grill revered by Titian's patron, Philip II of Spain.

Madonna dell'Orto to the Ghetto

Madonna dell'Orto
open Mon–Sat 10–5; adm

Northern Cannaregio was Tintoretto's home base, and he is buried in the beautiful Venetian Gothic Madonna dell'Orto. It also contains several of his jumbo masterpieces, such as the *Sacrifice of the Golden Calf*, in which Tintoretto painted himself bearing the idol – though he refrained from predicting his place in the *Last Judgement*, which hangs opposite it. He also painted the highly original *Presentation of the Virgin* in the south aisle, near one of Cima da Conegliano's greatest works, *St John the Baptist*. The *Madonna* by Giovanni Bellini was, alas, stolen some years ago, and all they now have is a photograph.

From the Campo Madonna dell'Orto, take a short walk down the Fondamenta Contarini, where, across the canal, in the wall of the eccentric **Palazzo Mastelli**, you can see one of Venice's curiosities: an old, stone relief of a Moor confronting a camel. There are three more 'Moors' in the **Campo dei Mori**, just in front of the Madonna dell'Orto. The original identities of these mysterious figures have long been forgotten, although a fourth one, embedded in one corner of the square and with a metal nose like Tycho Brahe, is named Signor Antonio Rioba. He featured in many Venetian pranks of yore: anonymous satires or denunciations would be signed in his name, and new arrivals in the city would be sent off to meet him.

Sant'Alvise
open Mon–Sat 10–5; adm

Also in the area is another little church, Sant'Alvise, which must be the loneliest church in Venice. Its main features are a forceful Calvary by Giambattista Tiepolo and a set of charming tempera paintings that Ruskin called the 'Baby Carpaccios', but which are now attributed to Carpaccio's master, Lazzaro Bastiani, as Carpaccio would have been only about eight years old when they were painted.

Three *rii* to the south of Sant'Alvise is the **Ghetto** – *the* Ghetto, that is, for, like Arsenal, the Venetians invented it: *ghetto* derives from the word *getto* meaning 'casting in metals', and there was an iron foundry here which preceded the establishment of a special quarter to which all Jews were ordered to move in 1516. The name is poignantly, coincidentally apt, for in Hebrew '*ghetto*' comes from the root for 'cut off'. And cut off its residents were, for the Ghetto is an island, surrounded by a moat-like canal, and at night all Jews had to be within its windowless walls. Cramped for space, the houses are tall, with very low ceilings, which, as many people have noted, eerily presages ghetto tenements of centuries to come.

But the Venetians did not invent the mentality behind the Ghetto; Spanish Jews in the Middle Ages were segregated, as were the Jews of ancient Rome. In fact, Venetian law specifically protected Jewish citizens and forbade preachers from inciting mobs against them – a common enough practice in the 16th century. Jewish refugees came to Venice from all over Europe; here they were relatively safe, even if it meant that they had to pay for it with high taxes and rents. When Napoleon threw open the gates of the Ghetto in 1797, it is said that the impoverished residents who remained were too weak to leave.

The island of the **Ghetto Nuovo**, the oldest section, is a melancholy place, its small *campo* often empty and forlorn. The **Scuola Grande Tedesca** is the oldest of Venice's five synagogues, built by German Jews in 1528, and is in the same building as the small Museo Comunità Israelitica/Ebraica. The informative tours (in English) organized by the museum visit this synagogue and two others, the **Scuola Spagnola** – an opulent building by Longhena – and the **Scuola Levantina**.

Light years from the Ghetto in temperament, but only three minutes away on foot, the Palazzo Labia (next to the 1580 Ponte delle Guglie), has a ballroom with Giambattista Tiepolo's lavish, sensuous frescoes on the Life of Cleopatra. The *palazzo* is now owned by RAI, the Italian state broadcaster.

Away from the *palazzo* towards the railway station runs the garish, lively **Lista di Spagna**, Venice's tourist highway, lined with restaurants, bars, hotels, souvenir stands and other visitor-related establishments that are not always as cheap as they should be.

Museo Comunità Israelitica/Ebraica *open Sun–Fri 10–6; guided visits on the half-hour summer 10.30–4.30; winter 10.30–3.30; closed Sat and Jewish hols; adm*

Palazzo Labia *t 041 524 2812; open only by prior appt*

The Lagoon and its Islands

Pearly and melting into the bright sky, iridescent blue or murky green, a sheet of glass yellow and pink in the dawn, or leaden, opaque grey, Venice's Lagoon is one of its wonders, a desolate, often melancholy and strange, often beautiful and seductive 'landscape' with a hundred personalities. It is thirty-five miles long and averages five miles across; half of it, the Laguna Morta ('Dead Lagoon'), where the tides never reach, consists of mud flats except in the spring, while the shallows of the Laguna Viva are always submerged, and cleansed by tides twice a day.

To navigate this treacherous sea, the Venetians have developed an intricate network of channels, marked by *bricole* – wooden posts topped by orange lamps – that keep their craft from running aground. When threatened, the Venetians only had to pull out the *bricole* to confound their enemies; and as such the Lagoon was always known as 'the sacred walls of the nation'. Keeping the Brenta and other rivers from silting it up kept engineers busy for centuries.

The city of the Venetians, by divine providence founded in the waters and protected by their environment, is defended by a wall of water. Therefore should anybody in any manner dare to infer damage to the public waters he shall be considered as an enemy of our country and shall be punished by no less pain than that committed to whomever violates the sacred border of the country. This act will be enforced forever.

16th-century edict of the Maistrato alle Acque

'Forever' unfortunately ended in the 20th century. New islands were made of landfill dredged up to deepen the shipping canals, upsetting the delicate balance of lagoon life; outboards and *vaporetti* churn up the gook from the Lagoon and canal beds, and send corroding waves against Venice's fragile buildings. These affect the tide, and increase both the number of *acque alte* and unnaturally low tides that embarrassingly expose Venice's underthings – and let air in where it was never supposed to go, accelerating the rot and the subsidence of its wooden piles and substructures.

Then there are the ingredients in the water itself. The Lagoon is a messy stew of 60 years' worth of organic waste, phosphates, agricultural and industrial by-products and sediments – a lethal mixture that ecologists warn will take a century to purify, even if by some miracle pollution is stopped now. It's a sobering thought, especially when many Venetians in their 50s remember when even the Grand Canal was clean enough to swim in.

And in recent years the Lagoon has been sprouting the kind of blooms that break a girl's heart – algae, 'green pastures' of it, stinking and choking its fish. No one is sure if the algae epidemic isn't just part of a natural cycle; after all, there's an old church on one Lagoon island called San Giorgio in Alga (St George in Algae). Crops of algae are on record in the 1700s and 1800s and at the beginning of the 20th century, at times when water temperatures were abnormally high because of the weather. But other statistics are harder to reconcile with climatic cycles: since 1932, 78 species of algae have disappeared from the Lagoon, while 24 new ones have blossomed, these mostly micro-algae thriving off the surplus of phosphates. These chemicals have now been banned in the Lagoon communities, leading to a noticeable fall in recent algae counts.

Once the largest of the 39 Lagoon islands were densely inhabited, each occupied by a town or at least a monastery. Now all but a few have been abandoned, many tiny ones with only a forlorn, vandalized shell of a building, overgrown with weeds. Occasionally one hears of plans to bring them back to life, only to wither on the vine of Italian bureaucracy. If you think you have a good idea for one, take it up with the Intendenza di Finanza.

San Giorgio Maggiore and the Giudecca

San Giorgio Maggiore
vaporetto no.82; open daily 10–12.30 and 2–7; adm to campanile

The little islet of San Giorgio Maggiore, crowned by Palladio's church of **San Giorgio Maggiore**, dominates the view of the Lagoon from the Piazzetta San Marco. Built according to his theories on harmony, with a temple front, it seems to hang between the water and the sky, bathed by light with as many variations as Monet's series on the Cathedral of Rouen. The austere white interior is relieved by Tintoretto's *Fall of Manna* and his celebrated *Last Supper* on the main altar, which is also notable for the fine carving on the Baroque choir stalls. A lift can whisk you to the top of the **campanile** for a remarkable view over Venice and the Lagoon. The old monastery, partly designed by Palladio, is now the headquarters of the Giorgio Cini Foundation, dedicated to the arts and the sciences of the sea, and venue for frequent exhibitions and conferences.

La Giudecca
vaporetto no.82

La Giudecca actually consists of eight islands that curve gracefully like a Spanish tilde just south of Venice. Prominent among its buildings is a string of empty mills and factories – the product of a brief 19th-century flirtation with industry – and for the most part the atmosphere is relatively quiet and homely. Like Cannaregio, it's seldom visited, though a few people wander over to see Palladio's best church, **Il Redentore**. In 1576, during a plague

Il Redentore
open Mon–Sat 10–5; adm

that killed 46,000 Venetians, the Doge and the senate vowed that if the catastrophe ended they would build a church and visit it once a year until the end of time. The Redentore was completed in 1592, and on the third Sunday of each July a bridge of boats was constructed to take the authorities across from the Zattere. This event, the *Festa del Redentore*, is still one of the most exciting events on the Venetian calendar. The Redentore itself provides a fitting backdrop; Palladio's temple front, with its interlocking pediments, matches its basilican interior, with curving transepts and dome. The shadowy semicircle of columns behind the altar adds a striking, mystical effect, all that survives of Palladio's desire to built a circular church, which he deemed most perfect to worship the essence of God.

The Lido and South Lagoon

The Lido, one of the long spits of land that form the protective outer edge of the Lagoon, is by far the most glamorous of the islands, one that has given its name to countless bathing establishments, bars, amusement arcades and cinemas all over the world. On its seven miles of beach, poets, potentates and plutocrats at the turn of the last century spent their holidays in palatial hotels and villas, making the Lido the pinnacle of *belle époque* fashion, so brilliantly evoked in Thomas Mann's *Death in Venice*, and Visconti's subsequent film. The story was set and filmed in the **Grand Hotel des Bains**, just north of the **Palazzo del Cinema**, where Venice now hosts its Film Festival.

The Lido is still the playground of the Venetians and their visitors, with its bathing concessions, riding clubs, tennis courts, golf courses and shooting ranges. The free beach, the **Spiaggia Comunale**, is on the north part of the island, a 15-minute walk from the *vaporetto* stop at San Nicolò (go down the Gran Viale, and turn left on the Lungomare d'Annunzio), where you can hire a changing hut and frolic in the sand and sea.

Further north, beyond the private airfield, the **Porto di Lido** is maritime Venice's front door, the most important of the three entrances into the Lagoon, where you can watch the ships of the world sail by. This is where the Doge would sail to toss his ring into the waves, in the annual 'Marriage of the Sea'. It is stoutly defended by the mighty **Forte di Sant'Andrea** on the island of Le Vignole, built in 1543 by fortifications genius Sammicheli. In times of danger, a great chain was extended from the fort across the channel.

One of the smaller Lagoon islands just off the Lido, with its landmark onion-domed campanile, is San Lazzaro degli Armeni. It was Venice's leper colony in the Middle Ages, but in 1715 the then-deserted island was given to the Mechitarist Fathers of the Armenian Catholic Church after they were expelled from Greece by the Turks. Today their monastery is still one of the world's major centres of Armenian culture and its monks, always noted as linguists, run a famous polyglot press able to print in 32 languages, one of the last survivors in a city once renowned for its publishing. Tours of San Lazzaro include a museum filled with relics of the ancient Christian history of Armenia, as well as memorabilia of Lord Byron, who spent a winter visiting the fathers and bruising his brain with Armenian. The fathers offer inexpensive prints of Venice for sale; or else they would appreciate a donation.

San Lazzaro degli Armeni
vaporetto no.20 from San Zaccharia at 3.10; tours begin daily at 3.25; adm

Islands in the North Lagoon

Most Venetian itineraries take in the islands of Murano, Burano and Torcello, all easily reached by inexpensive *vaporetti*. Nos.41 and 42 from Fondamenta Nuove to Murano call at the cypress-studded cemetery island of **San Michele**, with its simple but elegant church of San Michele in Isola by Mauro Codussi (1469), his first-known work and Venice's first taste of the Florentine Renaissance, albeit with a Venetian twist in the tri-lobed front. It contains the tomb of

San Michele in Isola
open daily 7.30–12 and 3–4

Fra Paolo Sarpi, who led the ideological battle against the pope when the Republic was placed under the Great Interdict of 1607. Venice, considering St Mark the equal of St Peter, refused to be cowed and won the battle of will after two years, thanks mainly to Sarpi, whose *Treatise on the Interdict* proved it was illegal. In return, he was jumped and knifed by an assassin: '*Agnosco stylum romanae curiae*,' he quipped ('I recognize the method or the "dagger" of the Roman court'). His major work, the critical *History of the Council of Trent*, didn't improve his standing in Rome, but made him a hero in Venice. Sarpi's main interest, however, was science; he supported Copernicus and shared notes with Galileo, then lecturing at Padua, and 'discovered' the contraction of the iris.

Cemetery
open daily April–Sept 7.30–6; Oct–Mar 7.30–4

The **cemetery** itself is entered through the cloister next to the church. The Protestant and Orthodox sections contain the tombs of some of the many foreigners who preferred to face eternity from Venice, among them Ezra Pound, Sergei Diaghilev, Frederick Rolfe (Baron Corvo) and Igor Stravinsky. The gatekeeper provides a basic map.

Murano

Murano
vaporetti nos.41 and 42 from San Zaccaria or Fondamenta Nuove, nos.12, 13 or 14 from Fondamenta Nuove, or the DM, a fast route from Tronchetto, Piazzale Roma and Ferrovia

The island of Murano is synonymous with glass, the most celebrated of Venice's industries. The Venetians were the first in the Middle Ages to rediscover the secret of making crystal glass, and especially mirrors, and it was a secret they kept a monopoly on for centuries by using the most drastic measures: if ever a glass-maker let himself be coaxed abroad, the Council of Ten sent their assassins after him in hot pursuit. However, those who remained in Venice were treated with kid gloves. Because of the danger of fire, all the forges in Venice were relocated to Murano in 1291, and the little island became a kind of republic within a republic – minting its own coins, policing itself, even developing its own list of NHs (*Nobili Homini* – noblemen) in its own Golden Book – aristocrats of glass, who built solid palaces along Murano's own Grand Canal.

But glass-making declined like everything else in Venice, and only towards the end of the 19th century were the forges once more stoked up on Murano. Can you visit them? You betcha! After watching the glass being made, there's the inevitable tour of the 'Museum Showrooms' with their American funeral-parlour atmosphere, all solicitude, carpets and hush-hush – not unfitting, as some of the blooming chandeliers, befruited mirrors and poison-coloured chalices begin to make Death look good. There is no admission charge, and there's not even too much pressure to buy. It wasn't always so kitschy. The **Museo Vetrario** or Glass Museum, in the 17th-century Palazzo Giustinian on Fondamenta

Museo Vetrario
open April–Oct Thurs–Tues 10–5; Nov–Mar Thurs–Tues 10–4; adm included in San Marco museums adm

Cavour, has some simple pieces from Roman times, and a choice collection of 15th-century Murano glass.

Santi Maria e Donato
open daily 9–12 and 3.30–7; adm

Nearby stands another good reason to visit this rather dowdy island, the Veneto-Byzantine **Santi Maria e Donato**, a contemporary of St Mark's basilica, with a beautiful arcaded apse. The floor is paved with a marvellous 12th-century mosaic, incorporating coloured pieces of ancient Murano glass, and on the wall there's a fine Byzantine mosaic of the Virgin. The relics of Bishop Donato of Euboea were nabbed by Venetian body snatchers, but in this case they outdid themselves, bringing home not only San Donato's bones but those of the dragon the good bishop slew with a gob of spit; you can see them hanging behind the altar.

San Pietro Martire
open Sun–Fri 9–12 and 3–6, Sat 3–6

Back on the Fondamenta dei Vetrai, the **San Pietro Martire** has one of Giovanni Bellini's best altarpieces, *Pala Barbarigo* (1484), a monumental *Sacra Conversazione* of the Madonna enthroned with Saints Mark and Augustine, and Doge Barbarigo, that achieves a rare serenity that perfectly suits the subject.

Burano

Burano
vaporetto line LN from Fondamenta Nuove

Burano is the Legoland of the Lagoon, where everything is in brightly coloured miniature – the canals, the bridges, the leaning tower, and the houses, painted with a Fauvist sensibility in the deepest of colours. Traditionally on Burano the men fish and the women make Venetian point, 'the most Italian of all lace work', beautiful, intricate and murder on the eyesight. All over Burano you can find samples on sale (of which a great deal are machine-made

Scuola dei Merletti
Piazza Galuppi; open April–Oct Wed–Mon 10–5; Nov–Mar Wed–Mon 10–4; adm

or imported), or you can watch it being made at the **Scuola dei Merletti**. 'Scuola' in this case is misleading; no young woman in Burano wants to learn such an excruciating art. The school itself was founded in 1872, when traditional lacemaking was already in decline. In the sacristy of **San Martino** (with its tipsily leaning campanile) look for Giambattista Tiepolo's *Crucifixion*, which Mary McCarthy aptly described as 'a ghastly masquerade ball'.

San Francesco del Deserto
visitors welcome daily 9–11 and 3–5; donations appreciated

From Burano you can hire a *sandolo* (small gondola) to **San Francesco del Deserto**, some 20 minutes to the south. St Francis is said to have founded a chapel here in 1220, and the whole islet was subsequently given to his order for a monastery. In true Franciscan fashion, it's not the buildings you'll remember (though there's a fine 14th-century cloister), but the love of nature evident in the beautiful gardens.

Torcello

Torcello
vaporetto line LN from Fondamenta Nuove

Though fewer than 100 people remain on Torcello, this small island was once a serious rival to Venice herself. According to legend, its history began when God ordered the bishop of Roman *Altinum*, north of Mestre, to take his flock away from the heretical

Lombards into the Lagoon. From a tower the bishop saw a star rise over Torcello, and so led the people of Altinum to this lonely island to set up their new home. It grew quickly, and for the first few centuries it seems to have been the real metropolis of the Lagoon, with 20,000 inhabitants, palaces, a mercantile fleet and five townships; but malaria decimated the population, the *Sile* silted up Torcello's corner of the Lagoon, and the bigger rising star of Venice drew its citizens to the Rialto.

Torcello is now a ghost island overgrown with weeds, its palaces either sunk into the marsh or quarried for their stone; narrow paths are all that remain of once bustling thoroughfares. One of these follows a canal from the landing-stage past the picturesque Ponte del Diavolo to the grass-grown piazza in front of the magnificent Veneto-Byzantine **Cathedral of Santa Maria Assunta** with its lofty campanile, founded in 639 and rebuilt in the same Ravenna basilica-style in 1008. The interior (no longer a cathedral, although mass is celebrated every Sunday during the summer) has the finest mosaics in Venice, all done by 11th- and 12th-century Greek artists, from the wonderful floor to the spectacular *Last Judgement* on the west wall and the unsettling, heart-rending *Teotoco*, the stark, gold-ground mosaic of the thin, weeping Virgin portrayed as the 'bearer of God'.

Cathedral of Santa Maria Assunta
open daily 10–5; adm

Next to the cathedral is the restored 11th-century octagonal church of **Santa Fosca**, surrounded by an attractive portico, a beautiful and rare late Byzantine work. Near here stands an ancient stone throne called the **Chair of Attila**, though its connection with the Hunnish supremo is nebulous. Across the square, the two surviving secular buildings of Torcello, the Palazzo del Consiglio and Palazzo dell'Archivio, contain the small **Museo dell'Estuario** with an interesting collection of archaeological finds and artefacts from Torcello's former churches.

Museo dell'Estuario
open Tues–Sun 10–12.30 and 2–5.30; adm

Tourist Information in Venice

(i) **Venice >**
Palazzina dei Santi,
Giardini Reali,
t 041 529 8711,
www.turismovenezia.it;
*smaller offices can be found at **Palazzetto Selva**; the **railway station**; the **Piazzale Roma** bus station; **Marco Polo Airport** at Rotonda Marghera; and the **Lido** at Gran Viale 6*

The main source in English on any current events is the fortnightly magazine *Un Ospite di Venezia*, distributed free at tourist offices and in hotels. Otherwise, the two local daily papers *Il Gazzettino* and *Nuova Venezia* both have listings of films, concerts and so on in Venice and the *terra firma*.

For €15, people between the ages of 14 and 29 can buy a **Rolling Venice** card, which gives discounts on the city's attractions, from films at the Film Festival to museums, hostels, shops and restaurants (and access to the university canteen in Palazzo Badoer, Calle del Magazen 2840). It also allows you to buy a special reduced-price ticket for travelling on the *vaporetti*. Apply at one of the following (take a photo and your passport):

Agenzia Arte e Storia, Santa Croce 659, Corte Canal, t 041 524 0232 (*open Mon–Fri 9–1 and 3.30–7*).

Assessorato alla Gioventù, San Marco 1553, Corte Contarina, t 041 274 7645 (*open Mon–Fri 9.30–1, Tues and Thurs also 3–5*).

Associazone Italiana Alberghi per la Gioventù, San Polo 3101, Calle del

Castelforte, t 041 520 4414 (*open Mon–Sat 8–2*).

Many churches now belong to an association called **Chorus** (t 041 275 0462, *www.chorus-venezia.org*), and a collective ticket for all these churches costs €8. All Chorus churches have the same opening times (*Mon–Sat 10–5*). Tickets are available from the churches, from VELA ticket offices, and from the Venice Pavilion tourist office.

VELA (*www.velaspa.com*), the commercial branch of the ACTV transport company, acts as a ticket office not only for bus and boat tickets but also for concerts, operas, dance events and the Biennale. All are available from main *vaporetto* stops (Accademia, Ferrovia, Rialto, Tronchetto, Vallaresso, San Zaccaria, Lido) and **VELA agencies** (t 041 272 2660, *www.hellovenezia.com*).

For the usual **Internet** services: **The Netgate**, Dorsoduro 3812/A, Crosera, t 041 244 0213.

Venetian Navigator, Castello, Calle Casselleria 5300, t 041 277 1056.

Net House, San Marco, Campo Santo Stefano, t 041 277 1190 (*open until midnight*).

If you lose something in the city, try the **police**, t 041 522 4576; or if you lose it on a train, t 041 785 238; or on a *vaporetto*, t 041 272 2179.

If you have an accident or become seriously ill, go to the Pronto Soccorso department of the city **hospital** in Castello, Campo Santi Giovanni e Paolo, or the Ospedale del Mare, Lido, 1 Lungomare d'Annunzio (t 041 529 5330); if you need a doctor at night or on holidays, ring the **Guardia Medica**, t 041 529 4060.

Ambulance, t 041 118.

Several *farmacie* are open all night on a rotating basis: the addresses are posted in the window of each, or visit *www.farmavenezia.it* for an updated list; *Un Ospite di Venezia* has a list at the back.

Places that **exchange money** outside normal banking hours include:

American Express, San Moisè 1471, t 041 520 0844 (*open summer Mon–Sat 8–8; winter Mon–Sat 9–5*).

Travelex, San Marco 5126, Riva del Ferro, t 041 528 7358, near the Rialto (*open Mon–Sat 9–6, Sun 9.30–5*).

The main **post office** is in the Fondaco dei Tedeschi, near the Ponte Rialto (*open Mon–Sat 8.15–7.25*). There are smaller offices at the foot of Piazza San Marco (Calle dell' Ascensione) and at the western end of the Zattere. You can buy stamps at any tobacconist.

Festivals in Venice

The Venice **Biennale** (*odd-numbered years; June–Sept*) is the most famous contemporary art show in the world (since 1895). The main exhibits of the forty or so countries officially represented are set up in permanent pavilions at the Giardini Pubblici.

The city's other great cultural junket is the **Venice Film Festival** (*late Aug/early Sept*), in the Palazzo del Cinema and the Astra Cinema on the Lido. As well as spotting the stars, you can sometimes get in to see films if you arrive at the cinemas really early.

Venice's renowned **Carnival** (*10 days before Shrove Tues*), first held in 1094, was revived in 1979 after several decades of dormancy. It attracts huge crowds, but faces an uphill battle against the inveterate Italian love of *bella figura* – getting dressed up in elaborate costumes, wandering down to San Marco and taking each other's picture is as much as most of the revellers get up to. Concerts and shows are put on all over Venice, with city and corporate sponsorship, but there's very little spontaneity or serious carousing, and certainly no trace of what Byron called the 'revel of the earth'.

In 1988 Venice revived another crowd-pleaser, *La Sensa* (*first Sun after Ascension Day*), in which the Doge married the sea. Now the mayor plays the groom, in a replica of the state barge or *Bucintoro*. It's as corny and pretentious as it sounds, but on the same day you can watch the gondoliers race in the **Vogalonga**, or long row, from San Marco to Burano and back again.

Venice's most spectacular festival is **Il Redentore** (*third Sun in July*), with its bridge of boats (*see* p.149). The greatest excitement happens the Saturday night before, when Venetians row out for an evening picnic on the water, manoeuvring for the best view of the fabulous fireworks display over the Lagoon. For the thousands of landlubbers the prime viewing and picnicking spots are towards the eastern ends of either the Giudecca or the Zattere.

More perspiration is expended in the **Regata Storica** (*first Sun in Sept*), a splendid pageant of historic vessels and crews in Renaissance costumes and hotly contested races by gondoliers and a variety of other rowers down the Grand Canal.

Another bridge of boats is built on 21 November, this time across the Grand Canal to the Salute, for the feast of **Santa Maria della Salute**, which also commemorates the ending of another plague, in 1631. This event provides the only opportunity to see Longhena's unique basilica as it would have been when it was built, with its doors thrown open onto the Grand Canal.

Shopping in Venice

Since the Middle Ages, Venice has been one of Italy's top cities for shopping, whether you're looking for tacky bric-a-brac (walk down the Lista di Spagna, the Riva degli Schiavoni or through the Rialto) or the latest in hand-crafted Venetian design.

Many Venetian shops neither have nor display a name, and some of those listed below will be mere addresses.

Shops are generally open Monday–Saturday 8–1 or 9–1 and 4–7.30, although many tourist shops have longer hours. Many shops are closed on Monday morning (except grocers). Markets and grocers tend to close Wednesday afternoon.

Art and Antiques
Madera, Dorsoduro 2762, Campo San Barnaba, **t** 041 522 4181, *www. maderavenezia.it*. The contemporary *objets* in this small design shop are all handmade using traditional methods, mostly by young Italian artisans.

Items include jewellery made of Venetian glass beads, beautifully turned wooden bowls and utensils and some Japanese-inspired ceramics.

Sabbie e Nebbie, San Polo 2768A, Calle dei Nomboli, **t** 041 719 073. An interesting little shop with a carefully chosen mix of Japanese ceramics, ethnic papers and ceramics by Italian designers.

Antichità, Dorsoduro 1195, Calle Toletta, **t** 041 522 3159. A squeeze of a shop packed with beautiful antique glass beads, jewellery, lace, children's clothes, and bits and pieces.

Bastianello Arte, San Marco 5042, Campo San Bartolomeo, **t** 041 522 6751. Western and Oriental antiques, as well as Art Nouveau and jewellery.

Pietro Scarpa, San Marco 1464, Campo San Moisè; and San Marco 2089, Calle Larga XXII Marzo. The shops resemble museums; the second one sells old drawings.

Unnamed Shop, Dorsoduro 2609, Fondamenta del Soccorso. A real 'Old Curiosity Shop': from Baroque clocks to bills printed by the 1848 revolutionary government.

Books
Filippi, Castello 5284, Calle del Paradiso, **t** 041 523 6916. This bookshop has the city's best selection of Italian books about Venice, including facsimiles of antique books from the days when Venice was one of Europe's chief printing centres.

Libreria Cassini, San Marco 2424, Calle Larga XXII Marzo, **t** 041 523 1815. Old prints and rare editions.

Libreria Goldoni, San Marco 4742, Calle Goldoni, **t** 041 522 2384. Venice's largest general bookstore. Good for holiday reading.

Mare di Carta, Santa Croce 222, **t** 041 716 304. Sea-related books in all languages.

The Museum Shop, Dorsoduro 710, Fondamenta Venier dei Leoni, **t** 041 240 5410. Next to the Guggenheim. A fine selection of art and photography books, children's books in English, gifts and postcards. Profits go to the museum. *Closed Tues.*

Marco Polo, Salizzada San Lio 5469, Castello, t 041 522 6343. Travel guides and more.

Sangiorgio, San Marco 2087, Calle Larga XXII Marzo, t 041 523 3451. Books in English, especially about Venice, and some hefty art tomes.

Sansovino, San Marco 84, Bacino Orseolo (just outside the Procuratie Vecchie), t 041 522 2623. Art and coffee-table books, and lots of postcards.

Clothes, Accessories and Shoes

Most of the big-name designer boutiques (Gucci, Prada, Versace, Louis Vuitton, Armani) are clustered around the outskirts of Piazza San Marco, along streets such as Mercerie, Frezzeria, Calle dei Fabbri, Calle Larga XXII Marzo and Salizzada San Moisè. Venetians buy their clothes at the COIN department store, while most tourists buy their 'Vuitton' and 'Prada' bags from the street-sellers paving the way to Piazza San Marco along Calle Larga XXII Marzo. Their first offer will be about three times what you should end up paying.

COIN, Cannaregio 5788, Fontego Salizzada San Giovanni Grisostomo, t 041 520 3581. Good department store. *Open daily.*

Emilio Ceccato, San Polo, Sottoportico di Rialto, t 041 531 5301. Gondoliers' shirts, jackets and tight trousers.

Hibiscus, San Polo 1060, Ruga Rialto, t 041 520 8989. Beautiful, colourful silk garments and accessories, and original jewellery.

Kalimala, Castello 5387, Salizzada San Lio, t 041 528 3596. Beautiful and practical handmade leather goods: chunky bags, luggage, belts and other accessories.

Risuola Tutto di Giovanni Dittura, Dorsoduro 871, Calle Nuova Sant'Agnese, t 041 523 1163. The best selection of colourful velvet slippers with cord and rubber soles. Cheaper than markets. Also shoe repairs. *Open daily.*

Rolando Segalin, San Marco 4365, Calle dei Fuseri, t 041 522 2115. 'Il Calzolaio di Venezia' stocks fabulous handmade shoes: from the sublimely elegant to the extraordinarily eccentric. *Open Mon–Fri and Sat am.*

Trois, San Marco 2666, Campo San Maurizio, t 041 522 2905. A Venetian institution, with Fortuny fabrics made to traditional specifications on the Giudecca.

Venetia Studium, San Marco 2403, Calle Larga XXII Marzo; San Marco 723, Merceria San Zulian, t 041 522 9281. Pleated silk Fortuny scarves, Fortuny lamps, *pochettes*, cushions, waistcoats and drawstring bags.

Vogini, San Marco 1253, Calle Larga XXII Marzo 1300, t 041 522 2573. The greatest name in Venetian leather, with articles by Venetian designer Roberta di Camerino.

La Coupole, San Marco 2255, Calle Larga XXII Marzo, t 041 523 1273. Posh shoes by French and Italian designers.

No Name Cobbler, Castello 5268, Calle delle Bande. Old-fashioned shoe repair shop.

Food and Drink

Caffè Costarica, Cannaregio 1337, Rio Terrà San Leonardo, t 041 716 371. Gift packs for Java junkies. *Open Mon–Sat 9.30–1 and 4–7.*

Cantinone già Schiavi, Dorsoduro 992, Fondamenta Priuli, t 041 523 0034. A fine old wine shop.

Panificio Volpe, Cannaregio 1143, Calle Ghetto Vecchio, t 041 715 178. Traditional Jewish pastries.

Pantagruelica, Dorsoduro 2844, Campo San Barnaba, t 041 523 6766; Giudecca 461, Fondamenta Sant' Eufemia, t 041 523 1809. A comprehensive range of cheeses, hams and salamis, pastas, rice, preserves, wines, bread, oils and vinegars, all carefully sourced and much of it organic.

Il Pastaio, San Polo 219, Calle dei Varotari, Rialto markets. Pasta in a score of colours and shapes, including tagliatelle made with cuttlefish ink or curry.

Pastificio Artigiano, Cannaregio 4292, Strada Nuova. Venice's tastiest and most exotic pastas: *al cacao* (chocolate pasta), *al limone* (lemon), or beetroot, garlic, mushroom...

Rizzo Pane, San Marco, Calle delle Botteghe (just off Campo F. Morosini).

Everything you could ever need for a full picnic.

Sacchi, Cannaregio 1815, Rio Terrà San Leonardo. Possibly the best fruit and veg shop in Venice, with a spectacular and mouthwatering display.

Supermercato Coop. Many locations in the *centro storico*.

Unnamed Boat, Dorsoduro, Ponte dei Pugni. Near Campo San Barnaba, this boat has the unusual distinction of housing the very last floating greengrocer's in Venice. *Open Mon–Sat am*.

Glass and Ceramics

L'Arca, Santa Croce 1811, Calle Tintor, t 041 710 427. Intensely coloured, modern ceramic tiles, vases, plates.

CAM, Murano, Piazzale Colonna 1/b, t 041 739 944. One of the largest selections of glassware on Murano. Exceptionally friendly and unpushy.

Carlo Moretti, Murano, Fondamenta Manin 3, t 041 736 588. Contemporary glassware.

Domus Vetri d'Arte, Murano, Fondamenta Vetrai 82, t 041 739 215. A small glass shop with a tasteful selection by some top Italian designers.

Pauly, San Marco 316, Calle Larga San Marco, t 041 523 5484. Classic blown glassware.

San Vio, Dorsoduro 669, Campo San Vio 669. Striking modern designs.

Unnamed Shop, San Marco 1470, Salizzada San Moisè. Some of Murano's most ambitious creations, at astronomical prices.

Jewellery

Jewellers are concentrated in Piazza San Marco and on the Ponte Rialto.

Codognato, San Marco 1295, Calle dell' Ascensione, t 041 522 5042. One of the oldest jewellers in Venice, with rare pieces by Tiffany and Cartier, and Art Deco baubles.

Missiaglia, San Marco 125, Piazza San Marco, near Quadri, t 041 522 4464. Some of the most elegant work by Venetian gold and silversmiths, as well as necklaces, etc.

Nardi, San Marco 69/71, Piazza San Marco 69–71, next to Florian, t 041 522 5733. One of Venice's luxury establishment jewellers, celebrated for its series of 'Othellos', elaborate jewelled pieces of carved ebony, each unique. Past customers include Grace Kelly and Elizabeth Taylor.

Perle e Dintorni, San Marco 3740, Calle della Mandola, t 041 520 5068; San Marco 5468, Calle della Bissa, t 041 522 5624; Cannaregio 5622, Campo Santi Apostoli, t 041 520 6969. Glass beads to buy or have made into necklaces and bracelets in a couple of hours.

Lace

This is fiendishly hard to avoid on Burano, though beware that the bargains on offer are probably neither handmade nor Buranese.

Annelie, Dorsoduro 2748, Calle Lunga San Barnaba, t 041 520 3277. Exquisitely worked items, new and antique. *Closed Sat pm*.

La Fenice Atelier, San Marco 3537, Campo Sant'Angelo, t 041 523 9578. Exquisite bed linens, towels and nightwear in superb silks, satins and cotton lawn, decorated with lace and embroidery. Made-to-measure service.

Jesurum, Cannaregio 3219, t 041 524 540. A vast quantity of lace (tablecloths, lingerie, etc.), plus an array of swimming costumes and summery togs.

Markets

Campo San Maurizio. A flea market appears periodically in this square, in the heart of the principal antiques area. *A week before Easter and Christmas, and third week of Sept*.

Rialto Markets. Venice's major markets, selling everything under the sun on the bridge and in all the streets to the north. There is a fish market, and fruit and veg, in the Peschiera, Fabbriche Vecchie and Fabbriche Nuove. *Open Mon–Sat 7–1 (fruit and veg), Tues–Sat 7–1 (fish, on Ruga degli Specializi)*.

Rio Terrà San Leonardo. Clothes, fish and food. *Open daily*.

Masks and Costumes

Giorgio Clanetti, Castello 6657, Barbaria delle Tole, t 041 522 3110. Fine, traditionally crafted masks. Rarely open, so call ahead.

Mondonovo, Dorsoduro 3063, Rio Terrà Canal, **t** 041 528 7344. Sells some of the best masks in town: camels, sphinxes, moonfaces and everything else in between.

Papier-mâché, Castello 5175; Calle Lunga Santa Maria Formosa, **t** 041 522 9995. Exquisite paintwork and masks decorated in the style of Kandinsky.

Tragicomica, San Polo 2800, Calle dei Nomboli, **t** 041 713 003. Extraordinary variety of wonderfully shaped masks and costumes.

Paper and Stationery

Alberto Valese-Ebrû, San Marco 3471, Campo Santo Stefano, **t** 041 520 0921. Persian/Italian styles in paper-making; also silk ties and masks.

Carta da Cassetti, Dorsoduro 364, **t** 041 523 2804, *www.cartadacassetti. com*. Tucked away in a tiny *piazzetta* between the Salute and the Guggenheim. Original designs: sheets of paper or original gifts.

Legatoria Piazzesi, San Marco 2511, Campiello Feltrina, **t** 041 522 1202. 'The Oldest Paper Shop in Italy': all sorts of gifts and papers.

Paolo Olbi, San Marco 3652, Calle della Mandola (near Campo Sant'Angelo), **t** 041 528 5025. Exquisite handmade paper, blank books and photo albums. Also leather-bound.

Il Pavone, Dorsoduro 721, Fondamenta Venier dei Leoni, **t** 041 523 4517. Paper products covered in unusual designs made on the premises. Bound books and other gifts.

Wood

 ⭐ Cipriani >>

Franco Furlanetto, San Polo 2768, Calle dei Nomboli. A workshop for *'remi e forcole'*, where you can buy gondola oars and oar-locks (more beautiful than practical).

Livio de Marchi, San Marco 3157, Salizzada San Samuele. Internationally renowned for everyday objects sculpted in natural wood – clothes hanging on pegs, benches in the form of giant paintbrushes, desks made from piles of oversized wooden books.

La Scialuppa, San Polo 2695, Calle Seconda dei Saoneri. Beautiful *forcole* (walnut gondola oar-locks), and make-your-own-gondola kits.

Sports and Activities

Aero Club G. Ancillotto, Lido, **t** 041 526 0808, *www.aeroclubvenezia.com*. A flying school that also offers excursion flights over Venice.

Alberoni Golf Course, Lido, Via del Forte Alberoni, **t** 041 731 333. This course on the southern tip of the Lido is among the best in Italy. Non-members are permitted, but need proof of membership of another club. *Open Oct–Mar Tues–Sat 8.30–6; April–Sept Tues–Fri 8.30–6, Sat–Sun 8.30–8.*

Giorgio Barbieri, Lido, Viale S. M. Elisabetta 5, **t** 041 526 1490. Rent a bike, or a touristy tricycle with a canopy, to explore the length of the Lido.

Where to Stay in Venice

Whatever class of hotel you stay in, expect it to cost around a third more than it would on the mainland, even without the often outrageous charge for breakfast. Reservations are near-essential from about April to October and for Carnival; many hotels close in the winter, although many that do stay open offer substantial discounts. Single rooms are always very hard to find. If you arrive at any time without reservations, tourist offices at the station and Piazzale Roma have a free room-finding service. The tourist office in Piazza San Marco has a list of agencies that rent self-catering flats.

Luxury (€€€€€)

★★★★★Cipriani, Giudecca 10, Fondamenta San Giovanni, **t** 041 520 7744, *www.orientexpresshotels.com*. Since 1963 this has been one of Italy's most luxurious hotels, a villa isolated in a lush garden at one end of the Giudecca that's so quiet and comfortable you could forget Venice exists, even though it's only a few minutes away by the hotel's 24-hour private launch service. An Olympic-size pool, sauna, Jacuzzis in each room, tennis courts and a superb restaurant (*see* below) are just some of its facilities. Nowhere could pamper you more.

*****Danieli**, Castello 4196, Riva degli Schiavoni, **t** 041 522 6480, *www.luxurycollection.com*. The largest and most famous hotel in Venice, in what must be the most glorious location, overlooking the Lagoon and rubbing shoulders with the Palazzo Ducale. Formerly the Gothic *palazzo* of the Dandolo family, it has been a hotel since 1822; Dickens, Proust, George Sand and Wagner stayed here. Nearly every room has a story to tell, in a beautiful setting of silken walls, Gothic staircases, gilt mirrors and oriental rugs. The new wing is comfortable, but lacks the charm and the stories.

*****Gritti Palace**, San Marco 2467, Campo Santa Maria del Giglio, **t** 041 794 611, *www.starwood.com/grittipalace*. The 15th-century Grand Canal palace that once belonged to the dashing glutton and womanizer Doge Andrea Gritti has been preserved as a true Venetian fantasy and elegant retreat. All the rooms are furnished with Venetian antiques, but for a real splurge do as Somerset Maugham did and stay in the Ducal Suite. Another of its delights is the restaurant, the Club del Doge, on a terrace overlooking the canal.

⭐ Hotel Flora >>

****Londra Palace**, Castello 4171, Riva degli Schiavoni, **t** 041 520 0533, *www.hotelondra.it*. Tchaikovsky wrote his Fourth Symphony in room 108, and the hotel was also a favourite of Stravinsky. The hotel was created by linking two palaces together, and it has an elegant interior, over half the rooms with a stunning canal view, and exceptionally good service. There is also an excellent restaurant, Les Deux Lions.

****Des Bains**, Lido, Lungomare Marconi 17, **t** 041 526 5921, *www.sheraton.com*. A grand old luxury hotel in a large park designed for dalliance. Thomas Mann stayed here on several occasions, and had Aschenbach sigh his life away on the private beach. It has a saltwater swimming pool, two tennis courts, a private pier and a motorboat service into Venice. There are 190 large rooms, a Liberty-style salon and a breeze-filled veranda dining room. Service is faultless. *Closed Dec–mid-Mar*.

****Kette**, San Marco 2053, Piscina San Moisè, **t** 041 520 7766, *www.hotelkette.com*. Sixty-three elegant rooms with pale striped walls, mezzacorona beds and smart bathrooms; colour schemes are dusty pink and green. Public rooms on the ground floor have been expanded and there are now conference facilities. Air-conditioning in all rooms.

***San Moisè**, San Marco 2058, Piscina San Moisè, **t** 041 520 3755, *www.sanmoise.it*. A major overhaul of this quiet hotel has swept aside the rather cloying Venetian style in favour of a cleaner look. Most bathrooms have a tub. Book early for a room overlooking the canal; there is a little terrace outside on the calle.

Very Expensive (€€€€)

***American**, Dorsoduro 628, Fondamenta Bragadin, **t** 041 520 4733, *www.hotelamerican.com*. An elegant, traditional hotel that has undergone extensive renovation, this overlooks the lovely San Vio canal (the best rooms, with windows on two sides, are 201 and 202). There's a pretty first-floor breakfast terrace and an Internet point for guests' use. Staff are very friendly.

***Hotel Flora**, San Marco 2283/A, **t** 041 520 5844, *www.hotelflora.it*. This hotel is tucked away on a little alley just steps away from San Marco, with an American bar and uniformed staff at your beck and call providing exceptional service. If you want something more modern and ethnic, ask for their sister hotel, Novecento.

***Locanda Cipriani**, Torcello, Piazza Santa Fosca, **t** 041 730 150, *www.locandacipriani.com*. There are only six rooms in this famous yellow-painted, green-shuttered country house hotel, in the most rural and tranquil spot in Venice. Some have views over the garden; you can sleep where Hemingway wrote his Venice novel, *Across the River and into the Trees*. All the rooms are spacious and fresh, and there is an excellent restaurant (*see* below). *Closed Jan*.

***Locanda del Ghetto**, Cannaregio 2892, Campo del Ghetto Nuovo, **t** 041 275 9292, *www.veneziahotels.com*. A delightful hotel with a pretty canal-side breakfast room. Right by the synagogue (one room has a beamed ceiling that was part of the 16th-century version), it has nine stylish bedrooms with parquet floors, pale gold fabrics and smart furniture. Two of the bedrooms have terraces overlooking the *campo*.

(★) Oltre Il Giardino >

***Oltre Il Giardino, San Polo 2542, t 041 275 0015, *www.oltreilgiardino-venezia.com*. Offers just six rooms in a tranquil corner of Venice, near the Frari Church. Owner Lorenzo speaks perfect English and will pamper you like a house guest.

Expensive (€€€)

***Do Pozzi, San Marco 2373, Via XXII Marzo, t 041 520 7855, *www.hotel dopozzi.it*. With 29 rooms on a charming little square where tables are set out for breakfast or a drink. Rooms on two of the floors have been renovated, and there are some in a nearby annexe.

**San Fantin, San Marco 1930A, Campiello Fenice, t 041 523 1 401, *www.hotelsanfantin.com*. Just around the corner from La Fenice in a quiet little *campo*, this simple hotel is a bit of a time-warp, with a reception area a bit like your granny's parlour, dated in a rather refreshing way. The 14 rooms (two without a bath) are pleasant, and the place is spotless.

*Antica Locanda Montin, Dorsoduro 1147, Fondamenta di Borgo, t 041 522 7151, *www.locandamontin.com*. An old-fashioned Venetian hostelry, with ten character-filled rooms, a bohemian atmosphere and an infamous arty restaurant.

Ca' del Dose, Castello 3801, Calle del Dose, t 041 520 9887, *www.cadel dose.com*. One of the new generation of good-value *affittacamere* or small B&Bs in Venice. Just off the Campo Bandiera e Moro, it has six comfort-able rooms furnished stylishly with dark parquet floors and elegant fabrics. One large room at the top of the house has a terrace.

Moderate (€€)

**Hotel Iris, San Polo 2910A, Calle del Cristo, t 041 522 2882, *www.irishotel. com*. The clean, pleasant rooms in this hotel have been recently redecorated; one has a pretty ceiling fresco and is

really quite elegant. All rooms have phone and TV. *Closed Jan.*

*Silva, Castello 4423, Fondamenta del Remedio, t 041 522 7643, *www.locanda silva.it*. A bit hard to find – on one of the most photographed little canals in Venice, between the San Zaccaria *vaporetto* stop and Santa Maria Formosa. Fairly basic, but quiet; the staff are friendly.

Inexpensive (€)

*Casa Boccassini, Cannaregio 5295, Calle del Fumo, t 041 522 9892, *www.hotelboccassini.com*. In a quiet neighbourhood well away from the crowds, this is something of a find. The basic but clean-as-a-whistle rooms have the odd antique piece to add character, and there is a pleasant breakfast room and sitting area, though it's the delightful garden that is the real attraction. All rooms have a phone; three don't have a bath.

*Doni, Castello 4656, Calle del Vin, t 041 522 4267, *www.albergodoni.it*. A basic but clean little family-run hotel on a pretty canal; the best rooms (larger with creaky old wooden floors and overlooking the water) are the three without a bath.

Hostels and Campsites

The tourist office has a list of all inexpensive hostel accommodation in Venice; as sleeping in the streets is now discouraged, schools are often pressed into use to take in the summer overflow, charging minimal rates to spread out a sleeping bag. **Assocamping** (t 041 968 071, *www.cavallino.net*) will supply a list of campsites.

**Fusina, Via Moranzini 79, t 041 547 0055, *www.camping-fusina.com*. At least 1,000 places. Venice is 20mins away by boat; *vaporetto* no.16 from San Zaccaria runs every hour (until 11pm in the summer). It has a restaurant, pizzeria, bar, breakfast bar, public Internet and email terminals, and a marina with slip access so you can yacht off to Greece, leaving your car at Fusina. Tents are €9, plus €9pp; campers/cars plus a tent are €14 per night, then €9pp. There are also small self-catering bungalows for rent. *Open all year.*

Serenissima, Via Padana 334, Oriago, Mira, **t 041 921 850, *www.camping serenissima.com*. Three hundred camping places and 60 bungalows just off the Brenta Canal; bus no.53 connects with Venice every half-hour. *Open April–Oct.*

Foresteria Valdese, Castello 5170, Palazzo Cavagnis, **t** 041 528 6797, *www.diaconiavaldese.org/venezia*. An old *palazzo* converted into a dormitory/*pensione* by the Waldensians. Check-in 9–1 and 6–8. Beds in dorms with bath €22; breakfast included.

Istituto Canossiano, Giudecca 428, Fondamenta del Ponte Piccolo, **t** 041 522 2157. A women-only hostel, run by nuns. It is simple and clean, with 10.30pm curfew. Beds €15.

Ostello di Venezia, Giudecca 86, Fondamenta delle Zitelle, **t** 041 523 8211, *www.ostellionline.org*. One of the most strikingly located youth hostels in Italy, right on the Giudecca Canal, with views of San Marco. No phone reservations, but you can book online if you register; to be assured of a place in July or August, you need to make contact well in advance. At other times, you can chance it and book in person any day after 6pm (doors open for queueing at midday). It's members only, but cards are sold at the door. Doors are open 7–9.30am and 1.30–11pm (curfew is at 11.30pm). Rates are €19.50 a head, with breakfast included, or €24 for a family room.

⭐ The Met >>

Eating Out in Venice

The Venetians are traditionally the worst cooks in Italy, and their beautiful city bears the ignominy of having the highest percentage of dud restaurants *per capita*. Not only is cooking in general well below the norm in Italy, but prices tend to be about 15% higher, and even the moderate restaurants can give you a nasty surprise at *conto* time with excessive service and cover charges. The cheap ones, serving up 500 tourist menus a day, are mere providers of calories to keep you on your feet; pizza is a good standby if you're on a budget.

Very Expensive (€€€€)

Antico Martini, San Marco 1983, Campo San Fantin, **t** 041 523 027, *www.anticomartini.com*. A Venetian classic, all romance and elegance. A Turkish coffeehouse in the early 18th century, but nowadays better known for seafood, a superb wine list and the best *pennette al pomodoro* in Venice. The intimate piano bar-restaurant stays open until 2am. *Closed Tues, and Wed midday.*

The Met, Hotel Metropole, Riva degli Schiavoni, **t** 041 520 5044, *www.hotel metropole.com*. The only Michelin-starred place in Venice, set in a romantic location on the Grand Canal and offering creative specialities with an emphasis on seafood. You'll even find Venetians dining here! Enjoy the bizarre collection of *objets d'art*, from cigarette cases to crucifixes.

Da Fiore, San Polo 2202A, Calle del Scaleter, **t** 041 721 308. People 'in the know' believe this to be the best restaurant in Venice. Food is taken seriously here; the atmosphere is sober without any of the pretentious frills of many other Venetian eateries. You could start with a plate of *misto crudo* or marinated raw fish or scallops *gratinati* in the oven with thyme before moving on to the classic *bigoli in salsa* (handmade spaghetti in a sauce of mashed anchovies and onions), penne with scallops and broccoli, or a wonderful, silky black squid ink risotto. Main courses include *involtini* of sole wrapped round *radicchio*, and a meaty tuna steak flavoured with rosemary. Reservations essential. *Closed Sun and Mon, early Jan and Aug.*

Harry's Bar, San Marco 1323, Calle Vallaresso, **t** 041 528 5777, *www. cipriani.com*. In a class by itself, a favourite of Hemingway and assorted other luminaries, this is as much a Venetian institution as the Doge's Palace, though food has become secondary to its celebrity atmosphere. Best to avoid the restaurant upstairs and just flit in for a quick hobnob while sampling a sandwich or the justly famous cocktails (a Bellini, Tiziano or Tiepolo – delectable fruit juices mixed with Prosecco), at a table downstairs near the bar.

Hostaria da Franz, Castello 754, Fondamenta San Giuseppe, **t** 041 522 0861, *www.hostariadafranz.com*. Booking advised. A fine restaurant well worth the fairly hefty outlay. Eat in the intimate, elegant dining room or outside on the enchanting canal-side terrace. The traditional fish dishes (with creative twists) contain only the freshest ingredients: giant prawns marinated in citrus fruits, ravioli stuffed with fish, and sea bass with fresh herbs. Eels are a speciality; Franz prepares them to a secret recipe. The wine list is excellent. *Closed Jan.*

Harry's Dolci, Giudecca 773, Fondamenta San Biagio, **t** 041 522 4844. Decked out like a *trattoria*, with tiled walls and wooden tables. Similar food to Harry's Bar, but considerably cheaper, with wonderful service and stunning views across the canal. *Closed Tues and Nov–Mar.*

Il Sole Sulla Vecia Cavana, Cannaregio 4624, Rio Terrà SS. Apostoli, **t** 041 528 7106, *www.veciacavana.it*. Traditional and more creative dishes are served at this elegant restaurant, all beautifully presented. The seafood salad with 'pearls' of melon and cucumber makes for an unusual *antipasto*; follow this with 'margherite' (a kind of ravioli) stuffed with sea bass, and wonderful Sicilian-style tuna steaks seared on the grill and served with capers, tomato and oregano. Also some meat dishes. *Closed Mon, and 2 weeks Aug, 2 weeks Jan.*

⭐ **Da Ignazio >>**

Cipriani, Giudecca 10, **t** 041 240 8507, *www.orientexpresshotels.com*. Booking advised. A meal here may not be the ultimate gastronomic experience, but it certainly holds its own with romance and atmosphere, especially in summer when tables are laid on a magical terrace and a piano tinkles in the background. The wide variety of dishes, both local and otherwise, are well prepared and exquisitely presented: an interesting array of *antipasti* to start, fillet of John Dory in a potato crust and served with asparagus, and duck breast with polenta soufflé. No children under eight at dinner. For a less wallet-busting (and far less romantic)

experience, come for lunch at the Cip's club. *Closed Nov–Mar.*

La Fiaschetteria Toscana, Cannaregio 5719 (Salizzada San Giovanni), **t** 041 528 5281, *www.fiaschetteriatoscana.it*. A Tuscan name because it was a Tuscan wine dealer a century ago, but it's strictly Venetian cooking here. Seafood is the speciality, with the likes of stuffed ravioli and homemade *tagliolini*, and fresh fish of the day. The whole family pitches in. Reservations essential. *Closed Tues and July.*

Locanda Cipriani, Torcello, Piazza Santa Fosca 29, **t** 041 730 150, *www.locanda cipriani.com*. In spite of the high prices and merely average food, this is an idyllic place to eat, as Hemingway and Chaplin discovered in their time. Situated off sleepy Torcello's main square, it is rustic and cosy, with a lovely vine-covered terrace. There are six elegant bedrooms above the restaurant (*see* p.159). *Closed Tues and Jan.*

La Corte Sconta, Castello 3886, Calle del Pestrin, **t** 041 522 7024. It may be off the beaten track, but the reputation of this *trattoria* rests solidly on its exquisite molluscs and crustaceans, served in a setting that's a breath of fresh air. Locals claim it's even better in the off-season; be sure to order the house wine. Booking essential. *Closed Sun and Mon, and mid-July–mid-Aug.*

Da Ignazio, San Polo 2749, Calle dei Saoneri, **t** 041 523 4852. Booking advised. Cosy, traditional *trattoria* serving classic Venetian fish dishes for more than 50 years. Also such oddities as *moeche* (small, soft-shelled crabs eaten whole), *castraure* (spring artichokes) and *sparesee* (wild asparagus). Or delicious spaghetti with *vongole veraci* (giant clams). There is a pretty courtyard. *Closed Sat and 3 weeks July–Aug.*

Da Remigio, Castello 3416, Ponte dei Greci, **t** 041 523 0089. A definite neighbourhood favourite, with the freshest of fish dishes. Very popular with the locals. *Closed Mon eve and Tues.*

Expensive (€€€)

Osteria San Marco, San Marco 1610, Frezzeria, **t** 041 528 5242. Plain white walls, exposed brickwork and wooden tables in this stylish new *osteria/ enoteca*. The food is interesting too: gnocchi with crab and rosemary, ravioli stuffed with ricotta and mint and served with a lamb sauce, scallop salad with artichoke hearts, guinea fowl with balsamic vinegar, and fillet steak cooked with coffee (an ancient recipe). *Open all day for a snack and a glass of wine. Closed Sun and Jan.*

Alla Nuova Speranza, Castello 145, Campo Ruga, **t** 041 528 5225. Booking required for dinner (or the cook will go home early). No cards. Simple, friendly *trattoria* with a TV at one end of the wood-panelled room and football coupons on sale from a little booth at the other. Packed with local workmen at lunchtime. Fill up on great-value seafood: fat *capparossoli* (clams) sautéed in garlic and wine or tossed into spaghetti or monkfish. The tourist menu is good value at €15.

Vecio Fritolin, Santa Croce 2262, Calle della Regina, **t** 041 522 2881, *www.veciofritolin.it*. A calm, civilized restaurant with a delightful owner, Irina. The day's catch is cooked without fuss and beautifully presented: baby shrimp on a bed of sautéed artichoke hearts; green *tagliolini* with nettles; courgette flowers and shrimp; steamed fillet of turbot with asparagus in a buttery vinaigrette. *Closed Sun eve and Mon.*

Le Bistrot de Venise, San Marco 4685, Calle dei Fabbri, **t** 041 523 6651, *www.bistrotdevenise.com*. This cosy restaurant presents poetry readings, live music and other cultural events as well as specializing in historical Venetian dishes full of unusual herbs and spices: pumpkin and cheese gnocchi flavoured with cinnamon, spicy pheasant soup, *baccalà* in a sweet and sour sauce, sturgeon cooked with prunes, grapes and balsamic vinegar and Turkish spiced rice pudding. *Open until 12.30am.*

Vini da Gigio, Cannaregio 3628A, Fondamenta San Felice, **t** 041 528 5140, *www.vinidagigio.com*. Booking essential. Small restaurant with views over the canal, always crowded with local foodies. Still has the feel of an old *bacaro* (*see* p.165), with low,

beamed ceilings and rustic tiled floors. Traditional food: fish, game and meat, various kinds of raw, marinated fish, fish soup, *baccalà mantecato* (creamed stockfish), sautéed scallops, duck from the lagoon ('*masorini*') – and the superb wine list features some 600 labels from both Italy and beyond. *Closed Mon, 3 weeks Jan/Feb and 3 weeks July/Aug.*

Ribò, Santa Croce 158, Fondamenta Minotto, **t** 041 524 2486. The young owners of this small restaurant have favoured an elegant, modern look, and food to match: *carpaccio* of octopus with shallot vinegar, risotto with scampi and asparagus, tuna steak with fresh herbs, *tempura* of scallops. There's a delightful garden. *Closed Mon.*

Al Mascaron, Castello 5225, Calle Lunga Santa Maria Formosa, **t** 041 522 5995. A favourite Venetian *osteria*, now somewhat spoilt by too many tourists, but nonetheless full of atmosphere and serving good food. Wine is served out of huge containers in the front and the atmosphere is noisy and unpretentious. Traditional Venetian specialities – both fish and meat – are served at marble-topped tables. Liver and sardines are served *in saor*, that is with pine nuts, raisins and marinated onions. *Closed Sun and Jan.*

L'Incontro, Dorsoduro 3062, Rio Terrà Canal, **t** 041 522 2404. If you can't stand the sight of another fish, head for this reasonably priced Sardinian restaurant where the menu is entirely meat- and vegetable-based: gnocchi with tomato and *pecorino*, ravioli flavoured with saffron, steaks (beef or horse) and roast suckling pig. *Closed Mon and Tues midday.*

Al'Aciugheta, Castello 4357, Campo SS. Filippo e Giacomo, **t** 041 522 4292, *www.aciugheta-hotelrio.it*. One of the best of the cheaper restaurants and bars near Piazza San Marco, with a good atmosphere. It's a touristy pizzeria at the front, but go early to the back room with a local for great *cicheti* (*see* p.165) and wines.

Moderate (€€)

Osteria ai Assassini, San Marco 3695, Rio Terrà dei Assassini, **t** 041 528 7986.

Popular *osteria* on a quiet street north of La Fenice. Fish features on Thursdays and Fridays, the rest of the week is for carnivores. The ambience is rustic (low ceilings, wood panelling and brickwork) and lively, and the place is full of Italians. Snack on *cicheti* if you're not up for a whole meal. *Closed Sat midday and Sun.*

Bancogiro: Osteria da Andrea, San Polo 122, Campo San Giacometto, **t** 041 523 2061. This modern *osteria* enjoys a fabulous position overlooking the Grand Canal. In the street-level bar, excellent wines and snacks are served; above, those who have booked can choose creative dishes such as fish salad with apple and mandarin, roast fresh tuna with pine nuts and gratin of steamed vegetables flavoured with coriander. Booking essential. No cards. *Closed Sun eve and Mon.*

Anice Stellato, Cannaregio 3272, Fondamenta della Sensa, **t** 041 720 744. New-generation, family-run *bacaro/trattoria* near the remote church of Sant'Alvise. Traditional dishes are enlivened by the odd creative twist – spaghetti with *capparossoli* (local clams) or with sardines and balsamic vinegar, tagliatelle with scampi and courgette flowers, *dorade* flavoured with curry. Booking advised. *Closed Mon and 3 weeks Aug/Sept.*

Gam-Gam, Cannaregio 1122, Sottoportico di Ghetto Vecchio, **t** 041 715 284, *www.jewishvenice.org*. No cards. A modern kosher bar and restaurant by the entrance to the ghetto with tables on the canal. Excellent choice of *antipasti* (houmous, baba ganoush, tasty salads, etc.), fish, meat and vegetable couscous, *shawarma* and *latkes*. The odd Italian dish is thrown in too, and there are vegetarian options. *Closed Fri eve and Sat.*

Alla Vedova, Cannaregio 3912, Ramo Ca d'Oro, **t** 041 528 5324. Booking essential. One of the oldest and best-known *bacari* in Venice, where locals crowd round the bar to eat a selection of excellent *cicheti* (including wonderful spicy *polpette* or meatballs) while hungrier punters join a relaxed crowd of tourists at wooden tables in the adjoining room for tagliatelle with duck, *fritto misto* and *fegato alla veneziana* (and vegetarian options). The same family has run the place for some 130 years, and the décor and atmosphere have been carefully preserved. *Closed Tues.*

Mistra, Giudecca 212A, **t** 041 522 0743. Booking advised. First-floor *trattoria* with watery views among boatyards on the south side of Giudecca. Specialities are fish and dishes from Liguria (so expect lots of pesto). *Closed Mon eve, Tues and Jan.*

Ai Quattro Feri, Dorsoduro 2754, Calle Lunga San Barnaba, **t** 041 520 6978. No cards. A new *osteria* run along traditional lines, with excellent *cicheti* and full meals at honest prices: pumpkin soup, spaghetti with artichokes and shrimps, simple grilled fish, seppie with polenta or fresh tuna *in saor*, a speciality of the house. *Closed Sun.*

Al Pantalon, Dorsoduro 3958, Calle del Scalater, **t** 041 710 849, *www.osteria alpantalon.it*. Venetians and tourists alike pile into this popular rustic *osteria* near the Frari. Run by the same team as Alla Patatina (*see* p.166), it has *cicheti* at a front counter and tables in an adjoining room. *Closed Sun.*

Inexpensive (€)

Rosticceria San Bartolomeo, San Marco 5424, Calle della Bissa, **t** 041 522 3569. No-frills *trattoria* with an even cheaper snack bar downstairs. Eat in or take away.

Vino Vino, San Marco 2007A, Calle del Caffettier, **t** 041 241 688, *www.vino vino.co.it*. A pleasant little wine bar near La Fenice, offering some 350 wines from all over Italy and further afield. Choose from snacks at the bar or reasonably priced meals in the adjoining room.

Da Toni, Dorsoduro 1642, Fondamenta San Basegio, **t** 041 528 6899. No cards. Simple local *trattoria* harks back to pre-commercial days: scallops with parsley, garlicky sea snails, and excellent grilled monkfish. *Closed Mon and Tues lunch and 3 weeks Aug.*

Il Réfolo, Santa Croce 1459, Campo San Giacomo dell'Orio, **t** 041 524 0016.

Excellent new pizzeria run by the same team behind the legendary Da Fiore (see p.161). Closed Tues and Dec and Jan.

Cafés and Bars

Between 5pm and dinner is the time to indulge in a beer and tramezzini, finger sandwiches that come in a hundred varieties.

Caffè Costarica, Cannaregio 1337, Rio Terrà San Leonardo. Brews Venice's most powerful espresso and great iced coffee (frappé). Also sells ground coffees and beans. Closed Sun.

Caffè Florian, San Marco 56/59, Piazza San Marco, t 041 520 5641, www.caffeflorian.com. Florian's has a charming and cosy 18th-century décor of mirrors and frescoes, and every Venetian learns to have coffee here rather than at Quadri (see below). The thimblefuls of espresso are good, if outrageously costly, and be warned that sitting on the outside terrace when there is live music carries an extra charge of €4.50 per head.

Gran Caffè Lavena, San Marco 133, Piazza San Marco, t 041 522 4070, www.venetia.it/lavena. Excellent coffee in a beautiful old setting (1750), with fewer tourists and less stinging prices. Open until midnight.

Gran Caffè Quadri, San Marco 120, Piazza San Marco. t 041 522 2105, www.quadrivenice.com. Another of Venice's historic coffeehouses, Quadri fell from grace during the Second World War. It's an elaborate confection of stucco and mirrors. The food in the gorgeous restaurant upstairs is good. There's a charge for music on the terrace. Open until midnight.

Marchini, San Marco 676, Calle Spadaria, t 041 522 9109, www.golosessi.com. The smell of chocolate as you enter is almost overwhelming; it has a mouth-watering range of chocolates, cakes and pastries, all of them beautifully presented, including the prize-winning Torta del Doge. Closed Sun.

Rosa Salva, Castello 6779, Campo SS. Giovanni e Paolo, t 041 522 7949 (also San Marco 4589, Campo San Luca, t 041 522 5385). Have breakfast in one of Venice's best cake shops with tables on the square.

Paolin, San Marco 2962, Campo Santo Stefano, t 041 522 5576. Known as the best gelateria in the city, above all for its divine pistachio.

Il Doge, Dorsoduro 3058, Campo Santa Margherita, t 041 523 4607. No cards. Lively gelateria. Open until midnight.

Gelateria Causin, Dorsoduro 2996, Campo Santa Margherita. Reassuringly old-fashioned caffè/gelateria. Closed Sun.

Nico, Dorsoduro 922, Fondamenta Zattere ai Gesuati, t 041 522 5293. Also a must on anyone's ice-cream tour, if the late-night queues are anything to go by. Try the gianduia dip.

Il Caffè, Dorsoduro 2963, Campo Santa Margherita, t 041 528 6255. Known as Caffè Rosso, 'The Red Bar'. A lively local hang-out. Cocktails, coffee, pastries and snacks. Open until 2am. Closed Sun.

Alla Mascareta, Castello 55183, Calle Lunga Santa Maria Formosa, t 041 523 0744. Enoteca with an exceptional wine list and a wonderful choice of cheeses, hams and salamis. Open 6pm–1am. Closed Sun.

Rizzardini, San Polo 1415, Campiello dei Meloni, t 041 522 3835. No cards. An invitingly old-fashioned pastry shop and caffè (since 1742) with traditional Venetian cakes and biscuits, including marzipan cake and a mean-looking strudel. Closed Tues and Aug.

Dal Mas, Cannaregio 150A, Lista di Spagna, t 041 715 101. The home-made cakes and pastries at this pasticceria are probably the nearest decent sugar fix to the station. Closed Tues and July.

Bacari

The bacaro is Venice's answer to a tapas bar, although many of them also serve complete meals, often at long tables in a back room. Originally drinking places, they come in all shapes and sizes, from gloomy holes in the wall with standing room only to slick, new establishments with trendy décor. They all offer a choice of wines by the glass (un ombra), and an array of cicheti or tasty little snacks which are usually arranged on the counter: anything from fishy tit-bits to grilled vegetables, artichoke hearts, deep-fried courgette flowers, chunks of salami, ham or cheese, or squares of fried polenta. They are often speared with a toothpick off the main serving dish, or you can ask for a selection to be put on a plate, pointing at what takes your fancy even if you have no idea what it is. Prices are not usually displayed on each item so the bill can quickly mount up.

★ Alla Patatina >>

Venice is full of *bacari*, usually hidden away down narrow alleyways. Most are open all day (some have a couple of hours' siesta in mid-afternoon) but close at around 8pm; some of the newer ones stay open late. They rarely accept credit cards.

Al Bacareto, San Marco 3447, Calle della Botteghe, t 041 528 9336. Booking advised. A popular, traditional *bacaro* with a huge variety of excellent *cicheti*, plus some more substantial dishes for hungrier clientele. There's a small terrace too. *Closed Sat eve and Sun, and Aug.*

Al Volto, San Marco 4081, Calle Cavalli, t 041 522 8945. A cosy little *bacaro* near Campo San Luca. Choose a snack and a drink, or one of the handful of daily dishes such as *bigoli in salsa* or *calimari in umido*. *Closed Sun.*

Ai Do Mori, San Polo 429, Calle dei Do Mori, t 041 522 5401. This historic 'locale' occupies a long, rather gloomy, wood-panelled room. There's nowhere to sit, so punters (a mix of locals and clued-up foreigners) prop up the bar. Good wine list, plus *cicheti*. *Closed Sun and 3 weeks Aug.*

Algiubagiò, Cannaregio 5039, Fondamenta Nuove, t 041 523 6084, *www.algiubagio.com*. Right by the *vaporetto* stop for the islands, with a large terrace and friendly staff. Good for a drink, snack or light meal. *Closed Jan.*

Da Codroma, Dorsoduro 2540, Fondamenta Briati, t 041 524 6789. At lunchtime the long communal tables are packed with students. In the evening the atmosphere is smoky and laid-back. *Closed Sun and 3 weeks Aug.*

Vino Vino (*see* under the 'restaurant' section, p.164).

Al Bottegon, Dorsoduro 992, Fondamenta Nani, t 041 523 0034. An old-fashioned wine shop near the Zattere with an 18th-century atmosphere and wine by the glass served with snacks. *Closed Sun afternoon.*

Alla Patatina, San Polo 2741A, Ponte San Polo, t 041 523 7238. A lively place famous for its home-made potato chips. *Closed Sat eve, Sun and 2 weeks in Aug.*

Enoteca Due Colonne, Cannaregio 1814C, Rio Terrà del Cristo, t 041 524 0685. A fun, noisy bar full of Venetians, serving *cicheti*, panini and a wide variety of drinks. *Closed Sun.*

Osteria Al Portego, Castello S. Lio 6015, t 041 522 9038. An authentic *bacaro* where the locals hang out.

Entertainment and Nightlife in Venice

Sadly, in a city that's clearly made-to-order for revelry and romance, life after dark is notoriously moribund. The locals take an evening stroll to their local *campo* for a chat and an *aperitivo* or a late-night ice cream, a Venetian tradition – Campo Santo Stefano and Campo Santa Margherita are popular and lively at night – before heading home; the hot-blooded may go on to bars and discos in Mestre, Marghera or the Lido.

Even so, there are places to go among all this peace and quiet, and there's always Venice's packed calendar of special events. For an up-to-date calendar of current events, exhibitions, shows, films and concerts in the city, consult *Un Ospite di Venezia*, free from tourist offices.

Visitors are left to become even poorer at the **Casinò di Venezia**, Cannaregio 2040, Ca' Vendramin-Calergi, t 041 529 7111, *www.casino venezia.it* (open daily 3pm–2.30am; dress smartly). You might prefer a comparative bargain – a moonlit gondola ride – or you can do as most people do: wander about. Venice is a different city at night.

Opera, Classical Music and Theatre

La Fenice, Campo San Fantin 1965, t 041 786 511, *www.teatrolafenice.it*. After a devastating fire in 1996,

La Fenice is back in all its splendour, with a rich and varied programme of music, opera, ballet, contemporary dance and culture.

Teatro Malibran, Cannaregio 5850, Campo del Milion, **t** 041 786 601. Malibran took centre stage during the reconstruction of La Fenice; thanks to contributions from the Friends of La Fenice, the Malibran has been renovated and now hosts a variety of spectacles.

I Frari, San Polo, Campo dei Frari, **t** 041 272 8611. Regular concerts in this huge church. *Open May–July and Sept–Oct Fri 9pm.*

Palazzo delle Prigioni, Riva degli Schiavoni, **t** 041 984 252, *www. collegiumducale.com*. Venetian Baroque and classical concerts in the ex-prison next to the Palazzo Ducale. *Open Jan–Sept.*

La Pietà, Castello, Riva degli Schiavoni, **t** 041 523 1096. Concerts in Vivaldi's lovely rococo church (*see* p.141). Prices are usually high, but the acoustics are well nigh perfect.

Teatro Goldoni, San Marco 4650B, Calle del Teatro, **t** 041 240 2011, *www.teatrostabileveneto.it*. Italian classics (Goldoni, Pirandello and so on) in a beautiful state-run theatre. Big-name directors and actors appear regularly. Some concerts too.

Jazz, Clubs and Nightspots

Venice's few late-night bars and music venues can be fun, or just posey and dull, and what you find is pretty much pot luck.

Bacaro Jazz, San Marco 5546, Salizzada del Fondaco dei Tedeschi, **t** 041 528 5249. A lively bar where you can eat and drink until late. Jazz and blues sounds, and the occasional live act. *Open Thurs–Tues 11am–2am.*

Caffè Blu, Dorsoduro 3778, Salizzada San Pantalon, **t** 041 710 227. A crowded, smoky bar with live music (blues, Latin, jazz) on Fri evenings (Oct–April). *Open Mon–Fri 8.30am–2am, Sat 5pm–2am.*

Il Caffè, Dorsoduro 2963, Campo Santa Margherita, **t** 041 528 6255. Café-by-day (*see* p.165), open-air nightspot after dark. *Open Mon–Sat 7am–1.20am.*

Casanova Disco, Cannaregio 158A, Lista di Spagna, **t** 041 275 0199. Large classic 'disco' with pop, rock and chart music and some house nights. *Open daily 9pm–4am.*

Da Codroma, Dorsoduro 2540, Fondamenta Briati, **t** 041 524 6789. This popular student eaterie and drinkerie (*see* p.166) turns into a crowded nightspot with live jazz and blues on Tues. *Open Sun–Fri 8am–midnight.*

Al Delfino, Lido, Lungomare Marconi 96, **t** 041 526 1412. An 'American bar' with music, snacks and billiards. *Open until 2am.*

The Fiddler's Elbow, Cannaregio 3847, Campiello Testori, **t** 041 523 9930. An Irish pub behind Palazzo Fontana. *Open daily 5pm–1am.*

Iguana, Cannaregio 2515, Fondamenta della Misericordia, **t** 041 716 722. Latin club with great cocktails (happy hour 7–9), Mexican food and dancing to Latin sounds. Live music Tues. *Open Tues–Sat 6pm–2am.*

Margaret Duchamp, Dorsoduro 3019, Campo Santa Margherita, **t** 041 528 6255. A designer 'disco bar' (as it calls itself); one of the few in Venice and frequented by a trendy mix of Venetians and foreigners. *Open daily 9am–2am (winter closed Tues).*

L'Olandese Volante, Castello 5658, Campo San Lio, **t** 041 528 9349. 'The Flying Dutchman' is a current favourite for young trendies and one of Venice's answers to a pub, open late with snacks. *Open Mon–Sat 10am–midnight.*

Paradiso Perduto, Cannaregio 2540, Fondamenta della Misericordia, **t** 041 720 581. The city's most popular late-night bar/restaurant, with inexpensive food and a relaxed, bohemian atmosphere; live jazz and roots music, parties, exhibitions. *Open Tues–Sun 7pm–1am, Thurs–Sun also 11am–3pm.*

Piccolo Mondo, Dorsoduro 1056, Calle Contarini-Corfù, **t** 041 520 0371. Tiny and rather sleazy, but one of the few real clubs in Venice. *Open Tues–Sun 10pm–4am.*

Sound Code, Mestre, Via delle Industrie 32, **t** 041 524 405. The best disco in the area. *Open Mon–Sat 10pm–4am.*

Teranga, Mestre, Via della Crusca 34, **t** 041 531 7787. A popular and lively club playing mainly African sounds, and with a programme of regular live music. Membership required (about €10). *Open Tues–Sun 10pm–4am.*

Cipriani Hotel, Giudecca 10, Fondamenta San Giovanni, **t** 041 520 7744. The Cipriani has two piano bars: the San Giorgio (*7pm–10pm*); and Bar Gabbiano (*10pm–1am*), where the pianist also sings, and you can dance.

T.A.G. Club, Mestre, Via Giustizia 19, **t** 041 921 970. An excellent little club with live blues, jazz and rock. *Open Fri–Sun 10.30pm–5am.*

Al Vapore, Marghera, Via Fratelli Bandiera 8, **t** 041 930 796. Small venue near Mestre station that is extremely popular for excellent live jazz and blues concerts featuring both known and lesser-known names. *Open Tues–Sun 7am–3pm and 6pm–2am.*

The Veneto

The Veneto is lush and green, plush with art and architecture, and charged with the stuff that dreams are made on. The Bard may never have visited the cities where he set many of his plays, but there's something very Shakespearean about them – something gorgeous and poetic, full of character and Renaissance swagger.

Thousands of villas and gardens, scattered from the foothills of the Dolomites to the plain of the Po, give the Veneto a uniquely rarefied if often daydreamy distinction.

Corsica

Sardinia

09

Don't miss

1 A medieval Sistine Chapel
Cappella degli Scrovegni, Padua **p.173**

2 A Palladian city and villas
Vicenza **p.219**

3 The city of Romeo and Juliet
Verona **p.239**

4 'Madonna blue' waters
Lake Garda **p.260**

5 A magical Renaissance hill town
Asolo **p.209**

See map overleaf

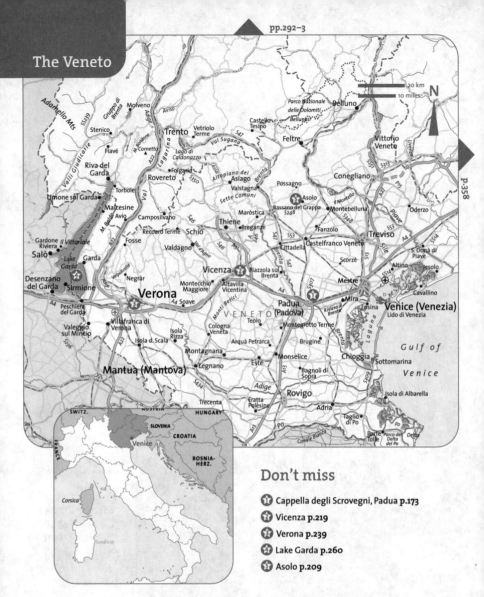

The Veneto

Don't miss

⭐ Cappella degli Scrovegni, Padua **p.173**

⭐ Vicenza **p.219**

⭐ Verona **p.239**

⭐ Lake Garda **p.260**

⭐ Asolo **p.209**

The Veneto has always been one of the wealthiest corners of Italy, and since the war its beauty has often fallen victim to its own prosperity. While car-free in their historic centres, the cities are often engulfed by some powerful sprawl, 'Venetopolis' as regional writer Carlo Pizzati dubbed it.

'Someone from Treviso can have dinner in Venice and an hour later drive to Verona to go listen to *Rigoletto*. A Vicentino, after skiing in Cortina, can drive down to Padua to go to the movies and be back home only 20 minutes after showtime.'

But you'd have to drive like an Italian nun to do it.

Padua

Although only half an hour from Venice, Padua (*Padova*) refuses to be overshadowed by the old dowager by the sea, and can rightly claim its own place among Italy's most interesting and historic cities. Nicknamed *La Dotta*, 'The Learned', Padua is the brain of the Veneto, once home of the great Roman historian Livy and, since 1221, to one of Europe's most celebrated universities, which counts Petrarch, Dante and Galileo among its alumni.

Padua's churches, under the brushes of Giotto, Guariento, Altichiero, Giusto de' Menabuoi and Mantegna, were virtually laboratories in the evolution of fresco. But most of all Padua attracts pilgrims; it is the last resting place of St Anthony of Padua, and his exotic, seven-domed mosque of a basilica is the city's most striking landmark. Padua has more porticoed streets than any city in Italy except Bologna, some of which could easily serve as a setting for *The Taming of the Shrew*, which Shakespeare set in this lively, student-filled city.

History

According to Virgil, ancient *Patavium* was founded in 1185 BC by Antenor, a hero of the Trojan War, giving it a pedigree nearly as hallowed as Rome's. Unfortunately the archaeological record won't have it: Patavium was a simple Palaeoveneto village on a branch of the Brenta river until the 4th century BC, when it became one of the Veneto's capitals. It sided with Rome against the Gauls in 45 BC, and grew into a prosperous Roman *municipium*. In 602 the Lombards burned it to the ground.

From the rubble Padua rose, a slow phoenix, to become an important *comune* by the 12th century. In the 13th century, it hosted one of the best characters of the day, St Anthony, and one of the worst, Ezzelino III da Romano, who robbed Padua of its independence while bleeding it white. In 1259 local *signori*, most importantly the Da Carrara, picked up where Ezzelino left off and fought over the pieces, then lost the city to the Scaligers of Verona in 1328. Doge Francesco Dandolo (after a deal reportedly made under his dining table) returned it to the Da Carrara in 1337, and as a bonus admitted them into Venice's Golden Book. For all the troubles, the 13th and 14th centuries were a golden age for Padua, in art, architecture and technology; it was the time of the famous Latin lecturer Vergerius, who made the university and Padua itself one of the earliest centres of Latin letters, and Giovanni Dondi (1320–89), who built Europe's first astronomical clocks. The Da Carrara, however, had ambitions beyond an entry in the *Libro d'Oro*. Francesco da Carrara allied himself with the king of Hungary and raised himself against Venice; in 1373 the Paduans proudly hung

V. BEZZECCA

VIA FRA PAOLO SARPI

VIA JACOPO AVANZO

Train Station

PIAZZALE STAZIONE

VIA DELLA PACE

VIA NICCOLO TOMMASEO

V. PILADE BRONZETTI

VIA BEATO PELLEGRINO

VIA RAGGIO DI SOLE

PIAZZALE MAZZINI

VIALE CODALUNGA

CORSO DEL POPOLO

VIA U. FOSCOLO

VIA GIOTTO

VIA TRIESTE

Giardini dell'Arena

Canale Piovego

Santa Maria del Carmine

VIA D. CAMPAGNOLA

PZA. PETRARCHA

Cappella degli Scrovegni

CORSO GARIBALDI

Bus Station

Porta Savonarola

VIA SAVONAROLA

RIV. MUGNAI

VIA S FERMO

LARGO EUROPA

Museo Civico

VIA G. B. MORGAGNI

CORSO MILANO

VIA S. PIETRO

VIA DANTE

PZA GARIBALDI

Eremitani

VIA VOLTURNO

VIA NICCOLO ORSINI

RIVIERA S. BENEDETTO

PLA S. BENEDETTO

Scuola di San Rocco/ S. Lucia

PZA INSURREZIONE

Porta Altinate

VIA ALTINATE

Santa Sofia

VIA G.B. BELZONI

Palazzo del Capitano

VIA S. LUCIA

PIAZZA SIGNORI

Caffè Pedrocchi

PIAZZA CAVOUR

VIA DIGLI PONTI ROMANI

Municipio

VIA S. SOFIA

VIA G. FALLOPPIO

VIA MILAZZO

V. DEI TADI

Loggia della Gran Guardia

PZA DELLA FRUTTA

Palazzo della Ragione

RIV. DEI PONTI ROMANI

VIA MARSALA

Duomo

PIAZZA DUOMO

PZA ERBE

Palazzo del Bò

VIA ANTENORE

V. DEL SANTO

VIA EUGANEA

VIA DEL VESCOVADO

VIA S. ROSA

VIA S. G. BARBARIGO

RIV. FITO LIVIO

VIA SAN MASSIMO

Porta San Giovanni

RIVIERA P. PALEOCAPA

PZA CASTELLO

VIA 20 SETTEMBRE

V.S. CHIARA

RIV. RUZANTE

VIA RUDENA

Loggia e Odeo Cornaro

VIA SAN FRANCESCO

V. OSPEDALE CIVILE

VIA G. GIUSTINIANI

VIA CERNAIA

La Specola

PIAZZA DEL SANTO

PZA DEL CESAROTTI

Gattamelata

VIA LOCATELLI

Basilica di Sant'Antonio

VIA GATTAMELATA

VIA A. S. SOGRAFI

VIA P. PAOLI

VIA A. CAVALLETTO

V. R. MARIN

V. CERATO

VIA UMBERTO

RIV. RUZANTE

VIA B. L. BELUDI

Orto Botanico

VIA JACOPO FACCIOLATI

VIA LUIGI CADORNA

VIA S. MARIA

PRAG

VALLE

DELLA

VIA GUGLIELMO

CORSO VITTORIO EMANUELE II

VIA 58 FANTERIA

VIA CAVAZZANA

VIA MICHELE SANMICHELI

VIA ALESSANDRO

VIA GIOTTO

MARCONI

Basilica di Santa Giustina

GIORDANO BRUNO

PIAZZALE S. CROCE

Porta Santa Croce

V.G. FABRICI D'ACQUAPENDENTE

VIA JACOPO CRESCINI

CAVALLOTTI

VIA A. A. COSTA

N

500 metres
500 yards

Getting to and around Padua

Padua is easily reached by **train** from Venice (40mins), Vicenza (45mins) and other cities on the Milan–Venice line. Outside the train station, a booth dispenses tickets and directions for the city buses.

The **bus station** is a 10-min walk away in Piazza Boschetti, Via Trieste 40, **t** 049 820 6844, and has buses every half-hour to Venice, and good connections to Vicenza, Treviso, Este, Monselice, Bassano and Rovigo; **APS city buses** (**t** 049 20111) from the station serve Abano Terme, Montegrotto Terme and Torreglia. **Landomas** (**t** 049 860 1426) has direct connections to Marco Polo or Treviso airports from Padua and the Euganean Hills – they'll pick you up at your door if you book a day in advance. **Radio taxi: t** 049 651 333.

Besides **cruises** along the Brenta Canal (*see* p.188), **Delta Tour** (**t** 049 870 0232, *www.deltatour.it*) also offers mini-cruises around Padua on the Piovego.

The following **car hire** firms can be found in Padua: **Avis**, Piazzale Stazione 1, **t** 049 664 198; **Europcar**, Piazzale Stazione 6, **t** 049 657 877; **Hertz**, Piazzale Stazione 1/VI, **t** 049 875 2202; **Maggiore**, Piazzale Stazione 15, **t** 049 875 8605; **Sevenzee**, Via Venezia 31B, **t** 049 856 1350.

the banner of St Mark as a war trophy in the Basilica of Sant'Antonio. After three decades of the usual betrayals, scheming and conspiring on both sides, Venice besieged Padua, then raging with plague, in 1405; the last of the Da Carrara was heard shouting from the walls, inviting the devil 'to come and get him', as he was captured. He was later strangled in a Venetian prison.

Under the Venetians Padua continued to prosper; its university went on to become one of the chief medical schools in Europe. Many students were involved in the Resistance in the Second World War, and the north part of the city was heavily bombed by the Americans (March 1944). But Padua is hardly one to forget its past – even long-gone buildings and streets are outlined on the pavement, giving the city a curious fourth dimension of time.

Cappella degli Scrovegni and the Museo Eremitani

⭐ Cappella degli Scrovegni and the Museo Eremitani
t 049 201 0020, www.cappelladegli scrovegni.it; open 9–7, until 10 in summer, museum closed Mon; same ticket; adm exp, but Padova Card costs only €2 more. Book in advance for chapel

Padua deserves at least a whole day, but if you only have a couple of hours a short walk from the bus or railway station leads to its gem: Giotto's extraordinary, recently restored, frescoes in the Cappella degli Scrovegni (or Madonna dell'Arena), a pearl sheltered by the crusty shell of Padua's Roman amphitheatre. It is lucky to be there; bombs shattered the surrounding neighbourhood in the last war. In another close call, the Paduans, in a 19th-century fit of 'progress', knocked down the Palazzo Scrovegni and were about to demolish the chapel too, until an opportune campaign by *The Times* saved Giotto's masterpiece.

The Cappella degli Scrovegni

We owe the Arena Chapel to Enrico Scrovegni, who built it in 1303 in expiation for the sins of his father, Reginaldo the usurer, who died shrieking for the keys to his safe to keep anyone from touching his money and who was denied a Christian burial. Fortunately, he left enough of his filthy lucre behind for Enrico to build a chapel and commission Giotto, then at the height of his career, to fresco the interior with a New Testament cycle (1304–07),

Cappella degli Scrovegni

1 St Joachim chased from the temple
2 St Joachim takes refuge among the shepherds
3 The angel appears to St Anne and informs her of her imminent motherhood
4 The angel appears to St Joachim and tells him his prayer will be answered
5 St Joachim's dream
6 The meeting of SS Joachim and Anne by Jerusalem's Golden Gate
7 The birth of Mary
8 The presentation of Mary at the Temple
9 Handing over the rod to St Simeone
10 The prayer for the blossoming of the rods
11 The wedding of Mary and Joseph
12 The Wedding Procession
13 God giving the Archangel Gabriel his orders
14 The Annunciation
15 The Visitation
16 The Nativity
17 The Adoration of the Magi
18 Presentation of Jesus at the Temple

19 The Flight into Egypt
20 The Massacre of the Innocents
21 Jesus among the Doctors of the Temple
22 The Baptism of Jesus
23 The Marriage at Cana
24 The Resurrection of Lazarus
25 The Entry of Jesus into Jerusalem
26 Chasing the Merchants from the Temple
27 Judas receiving the Thirty Pieces of Silver
28 The Last Supper
29 The Washing of the Feet
30 The Kiss of Judas
31 Jesus before Caiaphas
32 Jesus crowned with the Crown of Thorns
33 The Cavalry
34 The Crucifixion
35 The Deposition
36 The Resurrection
37 The Ascension
38 Pentecost

Giotto translated the art of painting from Greek to Latin

Cennino Cennini,
Il Libro dell'Arte (1400)

Nowadays he would not be allowed to paint a tennis court.

Charles (Président) de
Brosses, *Lettres sur l'Italie* (1740)

on the lives of the Virgin and her Son. In sheer power and inspiration these frescoes are the medieval equivalent of the Sistine Chapel, as revolutionary for the 14th century as Michelangelo's would be for the 16th. Giotto's fresh, natural narrative composition, solidly anchoring three-dimensional figures in their setting, derives its power not from divine trappings but sheer moral authority; his gift for portraying meaning and emotion in a glance or gesture conveys the story directly to the heart. Compare these frescoes to the Byzantine mosaics in San Marco, and you'll at once understand what Cennini was talking about.

Giotto's sons worked at his side and, like their father, were remarkably ugly. Their fellow Florentine Dante visited them while they worked, and couldn't help asking Giotto, 'How is it that you make painted figures so well, and real ones so badly?'; Giotto returned at once, 'Because I make the former by day and the latter by night.' Dante laughed and, as a compliment to the artist, placed Reginaldo in the seventh ring of the *Inferno* (Canto XVII). Giotto, however, had no doubt where he was going; you'll find him fourth from the left in the front row of the elect in the powerful *Last Judgement* on the west wall. A delegation from heaven accepts Enrico's offering of the chapel, while on the far left a singularly harrowing pre-Dantesque Inferno is ruled by a big blue Satan munching and excreting sinners. Along the bottom of the frescoes note the monochrome *Vices and Virtues*, painted by Giotto in imitation of stone reliefs – history's first *grisailles* – while the frescoes in the apse, depicting the later career of the Virgin, are a slightly later work by Giotto's followers.

Museo Eremitani

The same ticket gets you into the Museo Eremitani, installed in the adjacent Augustine convent of the Eremitani, with its noteworthy **archaeological collection**: coins, vases and 14 funerary stelae from the 6th to the 1st centuries BC, inscribed in bastard Etruscan. Padua is the only place in northern Italy where such stelae were discovered; apparently the local aristocracy wanted to put on airs by using the Greek alphabet.

The **painting section** houses literally acres of art, not always in chronological order, but a gold mine for connoisseurs of lesser-known painters mingled among the greats. To see Giotto's *Crucifixion*, designed for the altar of the Cappella Scrovegni, you'll need to ignore the guides at the top of the stairs suggesting you turn left and instead make for your right and go to the room at the far end of the corridor. Alongside the Giotto are other fine frescoes by Pietro da Rimini and Giuliano da Rimini, which originally hung in the Convento degli Eremitani. Around the corner to the left highlights are *Portraits of Philosophers* by the prolific Luca

Giordano of Naples and fine works by Francisco Solimenos. Giordano's *Job* may in fact be the best portrayal of a bad smell in Italian painting. Doubling back on yourself, you'll find Giotto's follower Guariento, founder of the Paduan school, who painted the lovely but rather odd series of *Angels*, weighing souls and fighting the devil, each slightly different, as if they were freeze frames from a film.

Moving onwards and upwards, the International Gothic style is represented by Lorenzo Veneziano, Jacopo Bellini (*Christ in Limbo*) and a charming but anonymous millefleurs *Madonna* (1408). The link in Padua from Giotto to the Renaissance was Francesco Squarcione, at least according to art historians; a rather dry polyptych, one of only two documented works by his hand, is here. This is followed by a charming *Expedition of the Argonauts* by Lorenzo Costa of Ferrara, and then a number of 16th-century Paduan paintings showing the influence of Andrea Mantegna (including Bartolomeo Veneto's all-dwarfing *Madonna* and Pietro Paolo Agabiti's *Madonna with SS Peter and Sebastian*, with the face of a Hollywood starlet – Sebastian, that is). Lombard painters check in with Madonnas by Da Vinci's follower Bernardo Luino and Andrea Previtali.

The museum then moves swiftly to the 16th century, starting with an enormous and fantastically detailed Brussels tapestry, *David Ordering Joab to Attack the Ammonites*. Behind this wall, you can find G.B. Tiepolo's *St Patrick Bishop of Ireland*, in a very non-Irish setting, and two paintings by his son Giandomenico. The surrounding rooms are perhaps the most stirring, containing impressive works by Domenico Campagnolo and Giampiero Silvio, both of whom worked in Padua; luminous Dutch art by Lamberto Sustris (1515–95), responsible for some of the frescoes in the Odeo Cornaro (*see* p.182) and splendid paintings by Giambattista Zelotti (1526–78) of the Verona-Mantova school. Il Romanino of Brescia weighs in with his masterpiece, a huge altarpiece of the Virgin and Saints (originally in Santa Giustina) as well as a Last Supper with Judas clutching his money under the table. Other paintings to look for: Tintoretto's *Crucifixion* (with a battle in the background); *Dinner at the House of Simon*; the *Martyrdom of SS Primo and Feliciano*, and a small Crucifixion against a black sky by Veronese; and works by Palma il Giovane (Negretti) and 17th-century painter Il Padovanino (Alessandro Varotari) and his followers.

Close by are works by artists from all over Europe: in the 1600s the nobility in the Veneto began to collect genre scenes and landscapes, attracting foreign artists to cash in. Especially represented here are Eismann and Philip Peter Roos, and the local painters they inspired, such as Antonio Marini of Venice, who specialized in battle scenes. A portrait of Elena Lucrezia Cornaro

Piscopia, painted in 1676 to honour her doctorate from Padua University, shares a room with what must be the campest portrait in all Italy: the 17th-century *Venetian Captain* by Sebastiano Mazzoni, matched only by its frame, carved with cupids, lions and a giant artichoke.

From the same century but from another world are the 'realist' works by Mateo di Pittochi (Matteo of the Beggars); the paintings of tiny people being chased by snails and attacked by crabs by Faustino Bocchi (1659–1741); and the idyllic landscapes by Francesco Aviani (a Venetian proto-hippy, 1662–1715). There are also striking 18th-century *trompe l'œils* by a brother and sister team, Pietro and Caterina Leopoldo della Santa, genre scenes by Pietro Longhi and Rosalba Carriera's *Portrait of a Young Priest.*

Some of the finest paintings are part of the **Quadraria Emo Capodilista**, a private collection donated to the museum in 1864 that includes Giorgione's *Leda and the Swan* and *Country Idyll*; Giovanni Bellini's *A Young Senator* and *Christ's Descent from the Cross*, the latter painted with his father Jacopo; and a Mythological Scene by Titian. In Italy, a bride brought her trousseau in an ornate wedding chest or *cassone*; Titian as a youth decorated two with mythological scenes, shown here. Also worth hunting out are a portrait by Padua's leading female artists of the Renaissance, Chiara Varotari (1584–1663) and a Baroque David and Goliath by Pietro Muttoni della Vecchia. (David, always so young and dashing in Renaissance paintings, has a grey beard here.)

Another donation, the **Museo Bottacin**, has more from the 18th century, and a fabulous coin collection. The *bronzetti* from the 14th–17th centuries that fill the halls were a speciality of Padua, especially those by Andrea Briosco, better known as Il Riccio ('Curly'). His famous *Drinking Satyr* is here, as well as works by Alessandro Vittoria, Niccolò Roccatagliata and a certain Il Moderno, whose name was probably invented by his agent.

The Eremitani, Santa Sofia and the Carmine

Eremitani
open Mon–Sat 8.30–12.30 and 3.30–6, Sun and hols 8.30–12.30 and 4–6; same ticket as the Cappella Scrovegni

Next to the museum, the church of the **Eremitani** (1306) lacked the luck of the Cappella Scrovegni and was shattered in an air raid in 1944. What could be salvaged of the frescoes has been pains-takingly pieced together – frescoes by Giusto de' Menabuoi and Guariento (his *Story of SS Augustine, Philip and James* in the second chapel to the right of the altar), and most importantly the magnifi-cent **Ovetari chapel**, begun by Andrea Mantegna in 1454 at the age of 23. Mantegna was a precocious young man: the pupil and adopted son of Squarcione, he took his master/father to court at age 17 for exploiting him. He also found his unique style at an early age, with its remarkable clarity of line and colour and fascination with antiquity – Squarcione had an archaeological collection, but

09 The Veneto | Padua

another influence on Mantegna was Padua itself, with its university and Latin letters. Painted 150 years after Giotto, *The Martyrdom of St Christopher and St James* still astonishes, thanks to Mantegna's wizardly use of scientific perspective to foreshorten the action from below and his use of Roman architecture to depict the power of the state – massive, hard, polished and pitiless, populated by remorseless, indifferent men.

Padua's oldest church, the 9th-century **Santa Sofia**, is to the east, at the corner of Via S. Sofia and Via Altinate; much rebuilt in the 11th century, it has a lovely Veneto-Byzantine apse and a precious polychrome Pietà (1430) by Egidio da Wienerneustadt. The quarter to the west of the Eremitani, Borgo Molino, was once an 'island' cut off by the Bacchiglione. Its centrepiece, the *Carmine* church, was rebuilt as the headquarters of a confraternity by Lorenzo da Bologna in 1494. Although it was heavily damaged in the air raids, the shells somehow missed the Sacristy and **Scuola del Carmine** (1377), with its interior covered by elegant *cinquecento* frescoes by Domenico Campagnola and Stefano dall'Arzere. Near here, just off Piazza Petrarca, the **Porta di Ponte Molino** and Torre di Ezzelino are leftovers from the 13th-century walls.

To Caffè Pedrocchi and the University

A short walk south from the Eremitani leads into Piazza Garibaldi, site of Padua's oldest surviving gate, **Porta Altinate**, 'captured from Ezzelino da Romano in 1256' as the plaque boasts. The streets all around, however, were torn up in 1926 to create big squares for big buildings flaunting the might of the Corporate State. A whole neighbourhood, Borgo Santa Lucia, was bulldozed to create **Piazza Insurrezione**, sparing the Scuola di San Rocco (1525) which, like the one in Venice, was built by a confraternity focused on plague prevention. Domenico Campagnola and Gualtiero Padovano frescoed it in 1537, although their work seems stale after Tintoretto's fireworks in Venice. Behind the *scuola*, the church of **Santa Lucia** was also spared; founded in the 11th century, it has a fine painting of San Luca by G.B. Tiepolo on the left of the high altar. Via Santa Lucia still has a number of medieval houses; a remarkable one built over Via Marsilio da Padova is remembered as the **Casa di Ezzelino**.

*Scuola di
San Rocco*
*open Tues–Sat 9.30–
12.30 and 3.30–7*

South of Piazza Garibaldi and around the corner from another new square, **Piazza Cavour**, you'll find a stylish Egyptian-revival mausoleum with columned stone porches at either end. This is, in fact, the Caffè Pedrocchi, built in 1831 by Giuseppe Jappelli, and famous in its day for never closing (it couldn't – it had no doors) and for the intellectuals and students who came here to debate the revolutionary politics of Mazzini. You can still get a coffee, as well as visit the upper floor. In Jappelli's adjacent neo-Gothic

Caffè Pedrocchi
*open Tues–Sun
9.30–12.30 and
3.30–7; adm*

Pedrocchino (built to contain the overflow of clients) students turned words into deeds in 1848, clashing with the Austrian police. Look carefully and you can still see the bullet scars.

At the far end of the complex, the 16th-century **Municipio** (the former Palazzo Comunale) hides behind an uncomfortable façade of 1904. Opposite is the seat of the **University of Padua**, Andrea Moroni's 16th-century Palazzo del Bo' ('of the ox', a nickname derived from the sign of a tavern that stood on this site in 1221). The façade, attributed to Vincenzo Scamozzi, opens up to a handsome 16th-century courtyard. Galileo delivered his lectures on physics from an old wooden pulpit, still intact, and counted among his students Sweden's Gustavus Adolphus, who went on to mastermind the Protestant victories in the Thirty Years War. The golden Great Hall is covered with the armorial devices of its alumni; the steep claustrophobic **Anatomical Theatre** (1594) was the first permanent one anywhere, designed by Fabricius, tutor of William Harvey who went on to discover the circulation of blood – only one of scores of Renaissance Englishmen who earned degrees at Padua's School of Medicine. Other professors included Vesalius, author of the first original work on anatomy since Galen (1555), and Gabriello Fallopio, discoverer of the Fallopian tubes.

Palazzo del Bo'
guided tours in summer Mon, Wed and Fri 3.15, 4.15, 5.15; Tues and Thurs 9.15, 10.15 and 11.15; winter hours reduced; adm

Before continuing to the Palazzo della Ragione, duck around the corner of the university to have a look at **Piazza Antenore**, with a pair of sarcophagi for a centrepiece. The one on columns supposedly contains what remains of Antenor, hero of the Trojan War and founder of ancient Patavium; the body was discovered in 1274, although modern scholars have had a peek and say Antenor was really a soldier from the 3rd century AD. The great Roman historian Livy was a son of the nearby Euganean Hills, and the other sarcophagus commemorates his 2,000th birthday. Perhaps he'll get something nicer for his 3,000th.

The Medieval Civic Centre: Palazzo della Ragione and Piazza dei Signori

Directly behind the Municipio (*see* above), the delightful medieval **Piazza delle Erbe** and **Piazza della Frutta** still host a bustling market every morning, divided by the massive, arcaded Palazzo della Ragione. Constructed as Padua's law courts in 1218 and then rebuilt in 1306, its upper storey or *Salone* is one of the largest medieval halls in existence, measuring 260ft by 88ft, with an 85ft ceiling like a 'vaulting over a market square', as Goethe described it. Its great hull-shaped roof was rebuilt after a fire in 1756 – an earlier blaze, in 1420, destroyed most of the frescoes by Giotto and his assistants, although some Virtues by Menabuoi survived. The rest were replaced with over 300 biblical and astrological scenes by Niccolò Miretto – one of the Renaissance's

Palazzo della Ragione
open Feb–Oct 9–7, Nov–Jan 9–6; closed Mon; adm exp during exhibitions

most important glorifications of astrology, which had had its own renaissance in the 13th century under Ezzelino's chief advisor and uncannily accurate astrologer, Guido Bonatto. Many of the later popes had astrologers; Petrarch roundly condemned them. Two exhibits never change, however. One is the *pietra del vituperio*, a cold stone block where the bankrupt had to strip to a loincloth and sit bare-bottomed before the court for three sessions to purge them of the sin of bankruptcy. Leaving any remaining property beside the stone, they were then sent into permanent exile. The second is a giant **wooden horse**, built for a joust in 1466, its fierce glance complemented by testicles the size of bowling balls.

Just to the west, the stately **Piazza dei Signori** saw many a joust in its day, and can boast Italy's oldest astronomical clock, built by Giovanni Dondi in 1344 and still ticking away, set in the tower of the **Palazzo del Capitanio**. On the left is the fine Renaissance-style Loggia della Gran Guardia (or del Consiglio), completed by Giovanni Maria Falconetto in 1523; while behind Dondi's clock you'll find Padua University's Arts Faculty, the **Liviano**, built in 1939 by Gio Ponti. Ponti incorporated the upper floor of the old Da Carrara palace in the Liviano, with its remarkable Sala dei Giganti, named after its huge 14th-century frescoes of ancient Romans and repainted by Domenico Campagnola in the 1530s; Altichiero added the more intimate 14th-century portrait of Petrarch sitting at his desk.

Sala dei Giganti
open for special
winter concerts only

The Duomo and Baptistry

Around the corner from the square stands Padua's rather neglected Duomo, begun in the 12th century, but tampered with throughout the Renaissance – Michelangelo was only one of several cooks who spoiled the broth here before everyone lost interest and left the façade unfinished. The interior is neoclassical and serene, and the most memorable art is new, along the altar, where the smooth white figures of saints and trees melt into the stairs. In the 1370s Giusto de' Menabuoi frescoed the adjacent Romanesque **Baptistry**, with over a hundred scenes; the dome, with its multitude of saints seated in the circles of paradise, is awesome but rather chilling.

Baptistry
open daily 10–6; adm

The 15th-century bishop's palace to the left of the cathedral contains the Pinacoteca dei Canonici with portraits of the bishops by Bartolomeo Mantagnana; a portrait of Petrarch, probably from life, was transferred here from the house he lived in while he served as a canon. Stroll down Via del Vescovado, one of Padua's most characteristic porticoed streets; among the palazzi, No.32, the **Casa degli Specchi** (1502), is especially handsome.

Pinacoteca dei
Canonici
entrance at Via
Dietro Duomo 15

Basilica di Sant'Antonio

Basilica di
Sant'Antonio
*open Mon–Fri
6.30am–7pm, Sat–Sun
6.30am–7.45pm*

One of the busiest and most beloved saints on the calendar, Anthony of Padua, was a Portuguese missionary inspired by the teachings of St Francis. Sailing off to convert the infidels of the Middle East, he was shipwrecked in Italy, where he stayed, preached and was canonized in 1232, only 10 months after his death – an ecclesiastical speed record, which soon led to his nickname: in Padua Anthony isn't merely *a* saint, he is *The* Saint, *Il Santo*. A suitably unique basilica to shelter his mortal remains was begun in the year of his death, according to legend, by a friar who accompanied St Francis to Egypt. For pure fantasy it is comparable only to St Mark's: a cluster of seven domes around a lofty, conical cupola, two octagonal *campanili* and two smaller minarets – perhaps not what a monk vowed to poverty might have ordered, but certainly a sign of the esteem in which his devotees held and continue to hold him; even Francis, the patron saint of Italy, doesn't have anything approaching *Il Santo's* organization. Even the 50 father confessors on duty are often hard pressed to keep up with demand.

Inside pilgrims queue patiently in the **Cappella del Santo** to pray, press a palm against his tomb and study the votive testimonials and photos (happy babies, wrecked cars, including insurance-style charts of the collision), proof of The Saint's interventions. With all this activity surrounding the tomb, no one pays much attention to the 16th-century marble reliefs lining St Anthony's chapel, although they are exquisite works of the Venetian Renaissance: the fourth and fifth are by Sansovino, the sixth and seventh by Tullio Lombardo, and the last by Antonio Lombardo. Behind the saint's chapel the **Cappella di Conti** has richly coloured frescoes on the life of Saints Philip and James by Florentine Giusto de Menabuoi (1382).

The **high altar**, unfortunately dismantled and rearranged over the centuries, is mostly the work of Donatello (1443–50), crowned by his stone *Deposition*, over bronze statues of the Madonna and six patron saints of Padua and dramatic reliefs of the miracles of St Anthony below, each intricately crowded with figures in architectural perspectives that were to be a strong influence on Mantegna. The magnificent bronze **Paschal Candelabrum** (1519) is the masterpiece of Il Riccio, who spent nine years on the project; although it was designed for Easter, Christianity takes a backseat to the myriad satyrs, nymphs and other mythological creatures in relief, immersed in imaginative decorative motifs. Earlier in his career, Il Riccio helped his master Belluno (one of Donatello's assistants) cast the 12 bronze reliefs of Old Testament scenes on the choir walls.

09 The Veneto | Padua

To the left of the altar, at the beginning of the ambulatory, note the **De Marchetti tomb** by Giovanni Comini (1690), an excellent example of the Hallowe'en-style tombs that were the rage in the Baroque era – here a bust of dead man on a stack of books is topped by a skeleton blasting away on the trump of doom. Behind the high altar, in the ambulatory, don't miss the **Treasury** where one of a hundred glittering gold reliquaries holds the tongue and larynx of *Il Santo*, found perfectly intact when his tomb was opened in 1981, the 750th anniversary of his death.

In the right transept, the **Cappella di San Felice** contains more beautiful frescoes and a remarkable Crucifixion, painted in the 1380s by Altichiero, the leading Giotto-esque artist of the day. The basilica complex, big enough to require its own information office, includes several other exhibitions and museums in its cloisters. There's a free audiovisual show (in Italian) on the saint's life, while the Museo Antoniano contains art made for the basilica over the centuries.

Sharing the large piazza in front of the basilica, a bit lost among the pigeons and exuberant souvenir stands, is one of the key works of the Renaissance, Donatello's **Statue of Gattamelata** (1453), the first large equestrian bronze since antiquity and Padua's answer to Rome's Marcus Aurelius. The cool 'Honeyed Cat' was a *condottiere* who served Venice so well and honestly that the republic, in a rare moment of generosity, paid for this monument, which Donatello infused with a serene humanistic spirit, in marked contrast to Verrocchio's Colleoni statue in Venice. As a yardstick of taste, it is interesting to note that only 50 years after its completion the horse was being criticized for its realistic detail.

Flanking the piazza opposite Gattamelata, the Oratorio di San Giorgio was built in 1377, and beautifully frescoed by one of the leading heirs of Giotto, Altichiero of Verona, with help from Jacopo Avanzi. Visit the adjacent Scuoletta del Santo, an old confraternity with paintings on the Life of St Anthony by a variety of artists, some of which are winningly absurd; four, certainly not the best, are attributed to a teenage Titian.

Behind the basilica, at Via Cesarotti 37, the **Loggia** and Odeo Cornaro (1524 and 1530) are two Renaissance gems designed by Giovanni Maria Falconetto of Verona, whose refined use of ancient architectural orders exerted a major influence on Palladio. Built in the gardens of the humanist Alvise Cornaro (*see* opposite), the Odeo was used for concerts and is decorated inside with exquisite stuccoes, while the Loggia saw performances of the plays of Ruzante (Angelo Beolco; *c.* 1496–1542), the Paduan dramatist who invented and played the role of Ruzante, 'the Joker', a satirically minded peasant faced with one catastrophe after another; some of his works prefigure the *commedia dell'arte*.

Museo Antoniano
open Tues–Sun 9–1 and 2–6; audiovisual show 9–12.30, 2.30–6; adm

Oratorio di San Giorgio
ask the guard for permission to enter

Scuoletta del Santo
open Tues–Sun 9–12.30, 2.30–7; adm

Odeo Cornaro
t 049 820 4513, www.padovanet.it/ museicivici; tours in Italian only every 30mins Oct–May 10–1 and 3–6, June–Sept Tues–Fri 10–1, Sat–Sun 10–1 and 3–6; adm

A Patrician's Life

In the 1540s the great humanist Luigi (Alvise) Cornaro (whose beautifully restored villa, the Loggia and Odeo Cornaro, is now open; *see* opposite) wrote a philosophical treatise *On the Sober Life*. Cornaro was 83 at the time, and he was sick and tired of hearing people knock old age. While defending the glories of the golden years, he incidentally left behind one of the best accounts of how a nobleman in the Veneto might expect to spend his time:

'Let them come and see, and wonder at my good health, how I mount on horseback without help, how I run upstairs and up hills, how cheerful, amusing, and contented I am, how free from care and disagreeable thoughts. Peace and joy never quit me... My friends are wise, learned, and distinguished people of good position, and when they are not with me I read and write, and try thereby as by all other means, to be useful to others. Each of these things I do at the proper time, and at my ease, in my dwelling, which is beautiful and lies in the best part of Padua, and is arranged both for summer and winter with all the resources of architecture, and provided with a garden by running water. In the spring and autumn, I go for a while to my hill in the most beautiful part of the Euganean mountains, where I have fountains and gardens, and a comfortable dwelling; and there I amuse myself with some easy and pleasant chase, which is suitable to my years. At other times I go to my villa on the plain. There all the paths lead to an open space, in the middle of which stands a pretty church; an arm of the Brenta flows through the plantations – fruitful, well-cultivated fields, now fully peopled, which the marshes and the foul air once made fitter for snakes than for men. It was I who drained the country; then the air became good, and people settled there and multiplied, and the land became cultivated as it now is, so that I can truly say: 'On this spot I gave to God an altar and a temple, and souls to worship Him.' This is my consolation and my happiness whenever I come here. In the spring and autumn, I also visit the neighbouring towns, to see and converse with my friends, through whom I make the acquaintance of other distinguished men, architects, painters, sculptors, musicians, and cultivators of the soil. I see what new things they have done, I look again at what I know already, and learn much that is of use to me... But what most of all delights me when I travel, is the beauty of the country and the palaces, lying now on the plain, now on the slopes of the hills, or on the banks of rivers and streams, surrounded by gardens and villas...'

Cornaro goes on to say that he has just written his first comedy, then gives practical advice on draining marshlands and preserving lagoons, and writes of the joys of being a grandfather. When he turned 95, Cornaro added a postscript, saying that he owed part of his happiness to the fact that so many people had read his treatise and were now enjoying their old age. He died, well over 100 years old, in 1565.

The Venetians were a famously long-lived race, and Cornaro hints why: their lives were too delightful to give up easily. While other Italians mocked Venetians for being a republic of old men, they were firmly under the thumb of Spain.

Botanical Gardens, Europe's Biggest Square and La Specola

Orto Botanico
open daily summer 9–1 and 3–6, winter Mon–Sat 9–1; adm

A few streets south of the Piazza del Santo, the Orto Botanico was one of Europe's first botanical gardens, established in 1545; it retains the original layout, and even a few original specimens. At 'Goethe's palm', planted in 1585 and still flourishing, the great poet-scientist speculated on his Theory of the Ur-plant, that all plants evolved from one universal specimen.

Beyond, **Prato della Valle** was a swampy meadow converted into a square with a moat by the city's Venetian *procuratore* Andrea Memmo in 1775 to give Padua a new commercial centre. Today it does service as municipal car park, flea market, amusement park and 'theatre of acting statues' for 79 illustrious men associated with Padua (and one woman, the Renaissance poet Gaspara Stampa, who gets a bust at the foot of Il Riccio).

Basilica of Santa Giustina
open daily 7.30–12 and 3–8

On one side stands the 393ft Basilica of Santa Giustina, the 11th-largest church in all Christendom, designed by Il Riccio with an exotic cluster of domes echoing St Anthony's, but the façade is unfinished and the interior stillborn Baroque: the best bits are an altarpiece by Sebastiano Ricci in the second chapel on the left, the large apse painting of the *Martyrdom of Santa Giustina* (1575) by Veronese and the 16th-century choir stalls. The left transept has a beautiful 14th-century tomb, the *Arca di S. Luca*, with alabaster reliefs made in Pisa. A door in the right transept leads to the original church, the 5th-century **Sacellum di San Prosdocimo**, burial place of Padua's first bishop, with a marble iconostasis; remains of the other previous churches lie beyond the monastery gate.

West of the basilicas, in Piazza Castello, Ezzelino da Romano rebuilt a castle in the medieval walls, now used as Padua's prison.

La Specola
accessible off Riviera Tiso da Camposampiero; t 049 829 3469, www.pd.astro.it/museo; guided tours May–Sept Sat–Sun at 6pm; Oct–April Sat–Sun at 4pm; buy tickets in advance from the Oratorio di S. Michele

The tallest and oldest bit, the 144ft Torrelunga (1062), has had a rather more dignified career since 1767, when an astronomical observatory, La Specola, was added to the roof. Padua's massive and well-preserved Renaissance **walls**, considered impregnable in their day, were designed by Michele Sammicheli and finished in 1544. A few of the ornate gates, many in white Istrian stone, survive and are perhaps most easily seen from a bike saddle. The best are the **Porta Portello** (1519) to the northeast; the **Porta San Giovanni** and **Porta Savonarola** (1530, by Falconetto) to the west; and **Porta Santa Croce**, to the south.

Tourist Information in Padua

If you plan to visit more than one attraction in Padua, a Padova Card is a wise investment for €14 (which is only €2 more than the individual ticket price for the Cappella degli Scrovegni, for instance). The card includes admission or discounts at a number of museums and attractions in Padua, as well as discounts on public transport and parking. Validity 48hrs.

Activities in Padua

Every summer a series of concerts, exhibitions, open-air films and shows takes place in Padua. *Padova Today*, available from the tourist office, lists events. The Prato della Valle sees a large general market every Saturday,

(i) **Padua** >
*Train station,
t 049 875 2077,
www.turismopadova.it;
open Mon–Sat
9.15–7, Sun 9–12;
Galleria Pedrocchi,
t 049 876 7927; open
Mon–Sat 9–1.30, 3–7;
www.turismopadova.it*

and an antique market every third Sunday of the month.

Where to Stay in Padua

Padua ✉ 35100

Very Expensive (€€€€)
****Methis Hotel**, Via Mantegna a Riviera Paleocapa 70, t 049 872 5555, *www.methishotel.it*. A trendy new hotel with each floor representing one of the four elements. The top-floor 'air' rooms are all in white and are the most luxurious.

Expensive (€€€)
****Grand'Italia**, Corso del Popolo 81, t 049 876 1111, *www.hotelgranditalia.it*. A fine Liberty building opposite the station, with modern furnishings and attentive service.

Moderate (€€)

***Al Cason**, Via Paolo Sarpi 40, **t** 049 662 636, www.hotelalcason.com. Cheaper and near the station, this hotel will make you feel at home, and fill you up in its restaurant.

****Al Fagiano**, Via Locatelli 45, **t** 049 875 0073, www.alfagiano.it. A friendly, welcoming place just west of the Basilica di Sant'Antonio. All rooms are en suite with air-conditioning. The nicest rooms seem to be on the third floor.

Inexpensive (€)

****Arcella**, Via J. D'Avanzo 7, **t** 049 605 581, www.hotelarcella.com. Situated near the station but on the wrong side of the tracks; friendly owners; limited parking.

Dante, Via San Polo 5, **t** 049 611 756. Very friendly, clean and central. Arrive early to secure a room.

***Junior**, Via L. Faggin 2, **t** 049 811 756. A ten-minute walk from the station, this welcoming little hotel has no en-suite bathrooms, but the easy parking is a bonus.

Ostello Città di Padova, Via Aleardi 30, **t** 049 875 2219, ostellopadova@ ctgveneto.it. A large, pleasant and city-run hostel; IYHF identity cards required. Take bus no.3, 8 or 11 from the station to the Prato della Valle. Book only if you're happy to sleep in a bunk bed.

****Sant'Antonio**, Via S. Fermo 118, **t** 049 875 1393, www.hotelsantantonio.it. Perfectly placed between Piazza della Frutta and the Scrovegni, this place has a friendly atmosphere and air-conditioning. Offers a range of rooms, both en suite or without bath.

Eating Out in Padua

La cucina padovana features what the Italians call 'courtyard meats' (*carni di cortile*) – chicken, duck, turkey, pheasant, capons, goose and pigeon. Pork, rabbit and freshwater fish are other favourites. Try one of the various *risotti* for *primo*.

Expensive (€€€)

Antico Brolo, Corso Milano 22, **t** 049 664 555, www.anticobrolo.com. Not far from the historic centre and occupying an elegant 15th-century building. There's a garden for outdoor dining on Veneto and Emilian specialities. Alternatively, there's a good pizzeria down in the old wine cellar where you'll spend a lot less. *Closed Mon and some of Aug.*

Moderate (€€)

Antica Osteria dal Capo, Via degli Obizzi 2, **t** 049 663 105. Southeast of the cathedral, this simple but popular *osteria* serves up an abundance of delicious fish and meat dishes followed by a range of excellent house desserts. *Closed Sun, Mon lunch and Aug.*

La Corte Dei Leoni, Via Pietro d'Abano 1, **t** 049 875 0083, www. cortedeileoni.com. Come here for a sumptuous meal in a walled courtyard in the historic centre immediately north of Piazza della Frutta. The menu is changed weekly in line with the seasons, while the extensive wine list reflects the best that Italy has to offer. *Closed Sun eve and Mon; good disabled access.*

Giovanni, Via Maroncelli 22, **t** 049 772 620. The crowds venture outside the city walls (bus no.9 from the railway station) for this classic Paduan home cooking, featuring succulent boiled and roast meats. The home-made pasta is good, as are the locally raised capons. *Closed Sun, Mon lunch and Aug.*

Inexpensive (€)

Bastioni del Moro, Via Bronzetti 18, **t** 049 871 0006, www.bastionidel moro.it. A restaurant serving up delicious gnocchi with scallops and *porcini* mushrooms, beyond Padua's western walls (take Corso Milano from the centre). Eat indoors or in the summer garden. Tourist menu. *Closed Sun.*

Godenda Winebar, Via F Squarcione 4, **t** 049 877 4192, www.godenda.it. A stylish but informal wine bar just behind the Piazza delle Erbe, with fine foods arriving on the doorstep daily from all over Italy; desserts, meanwhile, hail from Padua's best *pasticceria*, Graziati. Can get busy. *Closed Sun.*

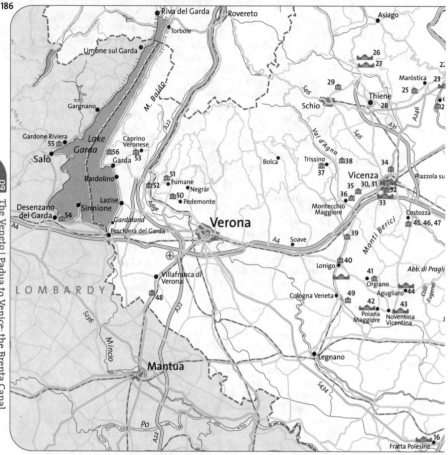

Non-Palladian Villas 🏛

2 Villa Gradenigo, p.188
3 Villa Widmann-Foscari, p.188
4 Villa Nazionale, p.189
5 Villa Foscari-Negrelli-Rossi, p.190
6 Villa Valmarana, p.190
7 Villa Giovanelli, p.190
8 Villa dei Vescovi, p.191
9 Villa Barbarigo, p.192
10 Casa del Petrarca, p.192
11 Villa Emo, p.194
12 Villa Roberti-Bozzolato, p.196
13 Villa Sagredo, p.196
14 Villa Widmann-Borletti, p.196
15 Villa Garzoni-Michiel, p.196
19 Villa Revedin Bolasco, p.202
22 Ca' Rezzonico, p.213
24 Villa Morosini Cappello, p.213
25 Villa Angaran delle Stelle, p.216
28 Villa da Porto Colleoni, p.216
29 Villa Bonifacio Rossi, p.216
32 Villa Valmarana, p.232

34 Villa Trissino, p.236
35 Villa Sale di San Damiano
   Curti, p.237
36 Villa Cordellina-Lombardi,
   p.237
37 Villa Trissino, p.238
38 Villa Piovene-Da Schio, p.238
39 Villa Da Porto, p.234
40 Villa Giovanelli, p.234
41 Villa Fracanzan-Piovene, p.235
45 Villa Trento Carli, p.236
46 Villa Aeolia, p.236
47 Villa da Schio, p.236
48 Villa Canossa, p.254
49 Villa Querini Stampalia, p.256
51 Villa della Torre, p.258
52 Villa del Bene, p.259
53 Villa Carlotti, p.259
54 Villa Romana, p.265
55 Il Vittoriale, p.270
56 Villa Guarienti, p.278
57 Villa Giustinian, p.284

Palladian Villas 🏛

1 La Malcontenta, p.188
16 Villa Badoera, p.199
17 Villa Contarini, p.204
18 Villa Cornaro, p.204
20 Villa Emo, p.203
21 Villa Barbaro, p.206
23 Villa Bianchi Michiel, p.213
26 Villa Godi Valmarana
Malinverni, p.216
27 Villa Piovene Porto Godi,
   p.216
30 Palazzo Barbaran da Porto,
   p.225
31 Palazzo Chiericati, p.226
33 La Rotonda, p.232
42 Villa Pojana, p.235
43 Villa Barbarigo, p.235
44 Villa Saraceno, p.235
50 Villa Serego Alighieri,
   p.258

Venice to Padua: the Brenta Canal

Over the years, the River Brenta made itself universally detested by flooding the surrounding farmland and choking the Lagoon with silt, and in the 14th century the Venetians decided to control its antics once and for all. They raised its banks and dug a canal to divert its waters, and when all the hydraulic labours were completed in the 16th century they realized that the new canal was the ideal place for their summer *villeggiatura*; their gondoliers could conveniently row them straight to their doors, or, as Goethe and thousands of other visitors have done, they could travel there on the *Burchiello*, a water-bus propelled by oars or horses. Over 70 villas and palaces sprouted up along this 'extension of the Grand Canal' and they were famous for their summer parties. Sadly car lights have replaced the fireflies that once made a summer's evening canal ride so magical, casting a glow bright enough to read by.

Getting along the Brenta Canal

In *The Merchant of Venice* Portia left her villa at Belmont on the Brenta Canal and proceeded down to Fusina to save Antonio's pound of flesh. For about the same price you can trace her route on the stately, villa-lined Brenta in a motorized version of the original public **canalboat**, the *Burchiello*, or on the simpler craft of *I Battelli del Brenta*; both make the day-long cruise from March to early Nov on Tues, Thurs and Sat from Venice, and Wed, Fri and Sun from Padua.

The **Burchiello motor-launch** price includes admission to Villa Foscari, La Malcontenta and Villa Widmann (extra charge for Villa Pisani and the return trip to Venice or Padua); book through offices at Via Orlandini 3, Padova, t 049 820 6910, *www.ilburchiello.it* (€62 adult, €31 child; 10% discount with Padova Card). For **I Battelli del Brenta**: Via Porciglia 34, Padova, t 049 876 0233, *www.battellidelbrenta.it*. **Delta Tour**, Via Toscana 2, Padova, t 049 870 0232, *www.deltatour.it*, also run canal tours.

You can follow the Brenta on your own along the SS11 road that follows the canal, by **car** or the half-hourly **bus** to Padua from Piazzale Roma. For La Malcontenta, however, you must take a different bus from Piazzale Roma which leaves only once an hour.

Villas along the Brenta Canal

Sailing up from Venice and Fusina, the first grand sight is Palladio's temple-fronted Villa Foscari, better known as La Malcontenta ① (*see* plan opposite), built in 1560 and as striking as it is

La Malcontenta
t 041 520 3966; open May–Oct Tues and Sat 9–12 or by appt, guided tours; adm exp

simple. Viewed from the canal, it is a vision begging for a Scarlett O'Hara to sweep down the steps – not surprising, as the villa was a favourite model for American plantation builders. Inside are some suitably delicate frescoes by Zelotti, Bernardino India and Battista Franco, one of which shows a sad woman – a possible source of the villa's name, although others say the unhappy one was the beautiful La Foscarina, who hated being cooped up here by her husband, far away from the fleshpots of Venice. Descendants of the original Foscari now own La Malcontenta, and have restored it beautifully.

Further up the canal, Oriago was the scene of early medieval battles between Venice and Padua. It still has the column that once marked their borders, as well as the late 16th-century **Villa Gradenigo** ②, with frescoes on the façade, recently opened to canal-boating visitors. Mira Ponte is the site of the 18th-century

Villa Widmann-Foscari
t 041 424 973; tours April–Sept Tues–Sun 10–6, Oct Tues–Sun 10–5, Nov–Mar Sat–Sun 10–5; adm exp

Villa Widmann-Foscari ③. If you only have time for one villa, don't make it this one – redone in French Baroque soon after its construction, the villa contains some of its original furniture and gaudy murals by two of Tiepolo's pupils.

Mira's post office occupies the Palazzo Foscarini, Byron's address in 1817–19. While living here he composed the fourth Canto of

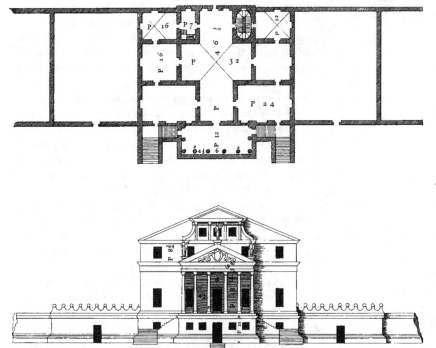

from Palladio's *Four Books of Architecture*

Childe Harold and cut off his last links with perfidious Albion, through his divorce and sale of the family home, consoling himself with a rag-tag collection of gondoliers, waiters, pets and black-eyed contessas who, Shelley sniffed, 'smelled so strongly of garlic that an ordinary Englishman cannot approach them'. You can visit the **Barchessa Valmarana** in Mira, the ornate wings of a demolished 18th-century villa belonging to one of Vicenza's most prominent families, decorated with Baroque frescoes. In Dolo, on the other hand, 16th-century mills are a reminder that life wasn't all fun and games.

'If you've got it, flaunt it,' was the rule in Venice, especially in the 1700s, when one of the grandest villas in all Italy went up at Strà: the **Villa Nazionale** ④ (or Pisani), enlarged by Alvise Pisani, scion of the fabulously wealthy banking family, to celebrate his election as Doge in 1735. The new doge had served as Venice's ambassador in Paris; he suggested that something in the Versailles mould might just do, complete with parterres and canals, and hired an architect

Barchessa Valmarana
Via Valmarana 11,
t 041 426 6387; open
Mar–Oct daily 10–6; in
winter months call

Villa Nazionale
t 049 502 074; hour-
long tours April–Oct
Tues–Sun 8.30–7,
Nov–Mar Tues–Sun
8.30–4; adm

with the delicious name of Frigimelica Preti to do the job. The villa was completed in 1760, but only after the original plans were scaled down. The Pisani sold their brick and mortar dream of grandeur to Napoleon, who gave it to his stepson and viceroy in Italy, Eugène de Beauharnais. In June 1934 Mussolini chose it as the stage for his first meeting with Hitler, where he strutted about in full fig, offering the Führer tips on how to deal with Austria and those pesky socialists. Although most of the villa has been stripped of its decoration, the ballroom makes up with one of Tiepolo's most shimmering frescoes, depicting, what else, the *Apotheosis of the Pisani Family*, who float about on clouds, hobnobbing with virtues and allegories of the continents. Son Giandomenico painted the *chiaroscuro* Roman scenes along the gallery. The vast park (the parterres were replaced in the 1800s with an English-style garden) contains the stables, a veritable equine Ritz, as well as innumerable pavilions and an expert-level box maze of 1721.

Villa Foscari-Negrelli-Rossi
Via Doge Pisani,
t 049 980 0335; open
for visits by appt only

Also on the canal in Strà is the 17th-century Villa Foscari-Negrelli-Rossi ⑤. The architect is unknown and the frescoes are attributed to Pietro Liberi and Domenico de Bruni.

Villa Valmarana
t 049 879 0879; call
in advance; adm exp

South of Strà in Saonara, there's a treat for lovers of Romantic gardens: the Villa Valmarana ⑥, whose *giardino storico* was laid out around a lake in 1816 by Padua's leading architect, Giuseppe Jappelli, with grottoes, waterfalls and statues. **Noventa Padovana**, between Strà and Padua and the *autostrada*, has another collection of villas, notably the Palladian-style **Villa Giovanelli** ⑦ with its statues and temple portico, which is inscribed 'Villaggio S. Antonio'.

Where to Stay and Eat along the Brenta Canal

Dolo ✉ 30031

***Villa Ducale**, Riviera Martiri della Libertà 75, **t** 041 560 8020, *www.villaducale.it* (€€). Sleep here in an antique bed under the frescoes and Murano glass chandeliers, and enjoy the garden setting complete with fountains and lawns which spill down to the Brenta Canal. The villa was built by Count Giulio Rocca in 1884 on the foundations of an 18th-century villa. Just 11 recently restored guest rooms.

Locanda alla Posta, Via Cà Tron 33, **t** 041 410 740 (€€€). Great fish, delicately prepared, and other dishes too. *Closed Mon.*

Mira ✉ 30034

****Villa Franceschi**, Via Don Minzoni 28, **t** 041 426 6531, *www.villafranceschi.com* (€€€€). A 16th-century manor house, lovingly restored and set in a manicured park. Some of the guest rooms have their own private patio.

***Riviera dei Dogi**, Via Don Minzoni 33, **t** 041 424 466, *www.rivieradei dogi.com* (€€€–€€). A less elaborate 16th-century villa overlooking the Brenta Canal, with comfortable modernized rooms.

Nalin, Via Nuovissimo 29, **t** 041 420 083 (€€€–€€). One of the traditional places to round off a Brenta Canal excursion, with a lovely poplar-shaded veranda. The emphasis is on Venetian seafood, finely grilled. *Closed Sun eve, Mon and Aug.*

South of Padua

The landscape south of Padua is as flat as any of the pancake prairies of the Po, with the exception of the lush Euganean Hills: a retreat of poets and the world-weary since Roman times, dotted with villas, spas, trails and country restaurants where Paduans head on Sundays. South of the hills you'll find a handsome trio of medieval towns, Monselice, Este and Montagnana, all 'with pasts', as people used to say of women who dared to have fun.

The Euganean Hills and Around

As soon as you leave Padua you'll spot them: the Euganean Hills or *Colli Euganei*, ancient volcanic islands, once surrounded by sea and now basking in the middle of the Veneto plain. Fertile, well watered by springs and defensible, they were settled early on in the Bronze Age by the Palaeoveneti, who made Este their chief stronghold. Centuries later the Romans discovered the two key secrets of the Euganean Hills: wine (now DOC Colli Euganei) and hot mud. Livy, Suetonius and Martial all recommended the virtues of their mineral springs, which flow from the ground at 87°C, and they have been appreciated ever since: some 130 hotels built over thermal swimming pools provide health or beauty cures at **Abano Terme** (from Aponeus, the Roman god of healing) and **Montegrotto Terme** (ancient *Mons Aegratorum*, 'mountain of the ill'), where the old Roman spa has been excavated. Children love Montegrotto's live butterfly zoo, the **Butterfly Arc**.

Butterfly Arc
La Casa della Farfalla,
t 049 891 0189,
www.butterflyarc.it;
open Apr–Sept
9.30–12.30 and
2.30–5.30; Feb, Mar and
Oct–Nov 9.30–12.30
and 2–4; adm

In the same area, at **Luvigliano** near Torreglia, the vast **Villa dei Vescovi** was designed by Giovanni Maria Falconetto (1579) for holidaying bishops: the interior has fine stuccoes, and the church houses a fine *Pala di San Martino* (1527) by Girolamo Santacroce of Bergamo.

Villa dei Vescovi
t 049 993 3105

From Torreglia, there's a road west to **Teolo**, Livy's birthplace. Here the **Museo di Arte Contemporanea** in the Palazzetto dei Vicari was founded in honour of international art critic Dino Formaggio and houses works from many of Italy's finest living artists. Because of their unusual micro-climate the Euganean Hills are rich in flora, with over a thousand species, protected since 1989 under the auspices of a regional park. In Teolo you can join a 42km circular nature trail around the district or head north to visit the venerable Benedictine **Abbazia di Praglia**, founded in 1117 but given the full Renaissance treatment, with a church by Tullio Lombardo and paintings by Bartolomeo Montagna, Giambattista Zelotti and others. The monks are famous for restoring old manuscripts and singing a mean Gregorian chant.

Museo di Arte Contemporanea
t 049 992 5469; open April–Oct Tues, Thurs and Sun 3–7, Nov–Mar Sun 3–7; adm

Abbazia di Praglia
t 049 999 9300

South of Torreglia, **Valsanzibio** was once the property of the Scrovegni money-bags and still maintains a quiet air of wealth, with an 18-hole golf course and the magnificent park and gardens at the Villa Barbarigo. Set in an enclosed valley, these are the grandest in the Veneto, laid out in the mid-1600s in the style of a Roman water garden (as at Tivoli) with fountains, waterfalls, nymphaea, pools, fish ponds and a domed rabbits' island; it also has one of Italy's finest garden mazes, as devilish to get through as the one at Strà.

Villa Barbarigo
t 049 805 9224, www.valsanzibio giardino.com; open daily Mar–Nov 10–1 and 2–dusk; adm

Arquà Petrarca

Beyond Valsanzibio lies Arquà Petrarca, a jewel of a hill town in a lovely setting (though you will struggle to get there without a car). In 1370, the world-weary Petrarch chose Arquà as his last home, accompanied by his daughter Francesca and her husband and his stuffed cat, Laura II. His charming villa, the Casa del Petrarca, preserves much of its 14th-century structure and furnishings. Petrarch was the artsy trendsetter of the Middle Ages; his presence in Arquà attracted wealthy families from Padua and Venice, who built summer houses in the village – the first example of the lust for *villeggiatura* that would so transform the Veneto landscape over the next four centuries.

Casa del Petrarca
t 0429 718 294; open Tues–Sun summer 9–12 and 3–7; winter 9–12.30 and 2.30–5.30; adm

Getting to and around the Euganean Hills

The spas and towns in the Euganean Hills are easily reached by **bus** from the main station at Piazza Boschetti in Padua.

There are also regular **trains** from Padua to Monselice (23km), Este (32km), Montagnana (52km) and Rovigo (45km), which can take about the same time as the buses, although allow for the vagaries of the Italian train system. You may have to change trains at Monselice.

Buses from Monselice go to Arquà Petrarca once a day, exc. Sun (10km).

The house itself went through a number of owners, one of whom in the 16th century added delightful frescoes illustrating the sonnets (Petrarch chasing a goose, Petrarch being splashed...). With the exception of a radio mast, the view from the poet's study remains the same as it was over 600 years ago, and it isn't hard to imagine the plump old poet laureate sitting there, writing his *Letter to Posterity* (he complains at having to wear spectacles after his 60th birthday). Famous signatures in the visitors' book are on display – Byron and his contessa, Teresa Guiccioli, came in 1818. Petrarch died here in 1374, while reading a book, and now occupies a huge Verona red marble sarcophagus in front of the church. The sarcophagus was opened in the 1970s by scientists from the University of Padua to carry out carbon dating on the remains. Their results did indeed confirm the date if not the identity of the deceased.

Il Catajo
t 049 910 0411, www. castellodelcatajo.it; open Mar–Nov Tues and Sun 2.30–6.30; adm

Museo dell'Aria
t 049 912 5088, www.museodellaria.it; open Tues–Sun 9–12.30 and 2–6; summer 2.30–7; adm exp

Abbazia di Santo Stefano
t 049 911 5027; open Sat 9–12, Sun 2–7

The fourth spa town in the Euganean Hills, **Battaglia Terme**, back on the SS16, is also a small industrial centre, with a severe villa-castle, Il Catajo (1570), the citadel of Venice's *condottiere* Pio Enea I degli Obizzi. Sumptuous on the inside, with lively frescoes by Giambattista Zelotti, it has an English garden with a charming elephant fountain; you can even hire it out for a party. East of Battaglia, two medieval Carrara properties merged to form a single *comune*, **Due Carrare**. The family citadel, **Castello di San Pelagio**, has a sumptuous interior and now a Museo dell'Aria with exhibits dedicated to air travel, from mythology to space exploration. Carrara Santo Stefano is built around the Benedictine Abbazia di Santo Stefano, founded in 1027. Although the abbey was demolished in 1793 the church remains, with its beautiful 11th-century mosaic pavement and 14th-century marble tomb of Marsilio da Carrara.

Monselice, Este and Montagnana

Spilling like an opera set down the southern slopes of the Euganean Hills, the natural citadel of **Monselice** (*Mons silicis*) was first fortified by the Romans. The stone from the hill was used to pave Piazza San Marco in Venice, not once but twice. In its heyday it bristled with five rings of walls and 30 towers, built in 1239 by Ezzelino da Romano to control the road between Padua and Este.

Most of the walls fell victim to medieval Italy's biggest enemy – 19th-century town planners. Nevertheless, the core of the citadel, Ezzelino's Ca' Marcello, was bought up and beautifully restored in the early 1930s by industrialist and art patron Count Vittorio Cini.

The Count made his money mining the stone for which Monselice was famous, selling it for the princely sum of 1,000 pounds sterling per square foot. He left the castle to the city on condition that the collection stays together. Now part of the Castello Monselice, it houses the count's superb collection of medieval and Renaissance arms and antiques, as well as a collection of exquisite candelabra from Holland, Poland and Romania. They say the ghost of Ezzelino's lover Avalda, who died here after a 17-year imprisonment, can be heard wailing if the candles go out. Look out for the collection of crucifixes concealing knives, which captured enemies were made to kiss before they were dispatched.

Castello Monselice
t 042 972 931; open Tues–Sun summer 9–12 and 3–6, winter 9–12 and 2–5; some tours in English; adm

The castle lies near the base of Vincenzo Scamozzi's striking **Via Sacra delle Sette Chiese** (1605), zigzagging up the hill passing the sumptuous **Ca' Nani Mocenigo**, the romanesque **Antica Pieve di Santa Giustina** and seven votive chapels built by Scamozzi and frescoed by Palma il Giovane and Carlo Loth (a mini-version of the Seven Churches of Rome, offering proportionately smaller indulgences). Near the top of the Via Sacra the elegant 16th-century **Villa Duodo** and **Esedra di San Francesco Saverio**, also by Scamozzi, is now a university centre of hydraulic studies.

Mastio Federiciano
t 042 972 931; open April–Oct Tues–Sun; book in advance

Villa Elmo
t 042 978 1970; open April–Nov Sat–Sun 2–7

A path continues up to the Mastio Federiciano (Rocca), built by Frederick II, Ezzelino's boss, over a Lombard fort. Recent finds are being catalogued but pre-Roman remains continue to intrigue. Just north of Monselice in **Rivella**, the late *cinquecento* Villa Emo has an elegant, romantic garden designed by Jappelli in 1816.

Every year on the third Sunday in September Monselice comes alive to the sound of the **Giostra della Rocca**, a medieval festival that dates back to 1239 and the arrival of Emperor Frederick II. The city's nine ancient districts compete in displays of jousting, archery and a horse race, the *quintana*. Each district has its own colours and champions and the entire town and surrounding villages come to the accompanying feast.

Monselice's old rival, **Este** (ancient *Ateste*) is only 9km to the west. This was the capital of the Palaeoveneti and, 2,000 years later, of the powerful 11th-century Lombard lord, Marquess Alberto Azzo II, whose son Guelfo IV became Duke of Bavaria, and whose later descendants included the Electors of Hanover and George I of England (Queen Victoria was proud to say her roots went back to Este); another branch of the family, famous as art patrons in the Renaissance, moved on to Ferrara. Like Monselice, medieval Este was a hotly contested piece of real estate, and bristles with the towers of the **Castello Carraresi**, built by the lords of Padua in 1339 and now put out to pasture in a public garden. There are seven statues depicting notable figures from Este's past, while the empty plinth of Ezzelino still stands as a warning.

Museo Nazionale
Atestino
open daily 9–8; adm

Abutting the garden, the 16th-century Palazzo Mocenigo houses the excellent Museo Nazionale Atestino, its frescoed ceilings gazing down at artefacts from the first Veneto civilization in the 10th century BC up to Roman times. Don't miss the vigorous 9th-century BC rams' heads; the 7th-century BC Situla Benvenuti, a bronze vase decorated with warriors and fantastic animals; a superb collection of 6th- and 5th-century BC bronzes of warriors and horsemen; inscriptions in ancient Venetic, using the Etruscan alphabet; a rare gold medal issued by Augustus; and, a bit out of place, a luscious red-dressed Madonna and Child by Cima da Conegliano. Other highlights are the startlingly tilted 12th-century campanile of **San Martino**, the two grand clock towers in **Piazza Maggiore**, and Giambattista Tiepolo's altarpiece *Santa Tecla verus the Plague* in the **Duomo**. Behind the castle **Villa De Kunkler** was Byron's residence in 1817–18; here Shelley, his guest, wrote 'Lines Written among the Euganean Hills' after the death of his little daughter Clara:

Many a green isle needs must be
In the deep wide sea of Misery,
Or the mariner, worn and wan,
Never thus could voyage on...

Montagnana, 15km west, boasts some of the best-preserved medieval fortifications in Italy, the handiwork of Ezzelino da Romano and the Carrara family. The walls extend for over a mile, defended by 24 intact towers – impressive but not effective; Venice lost and regained the town 13 times during the War of the Cambrai alone. If you're an early riser, watch the walls just after dawn when they change colours from a deep rose to a pale blush. Every September they form a picturesque backdrop to Montagnana's colourful *palio*, inaugurated in 1259 to celebrate the liberation of the city from Ezzelino.

Museo Civico
A. Giacomelli
t 042 980 4128; tours
Sat–Sun at 11, 12, 4, 5, 6;
Wed–Fri at 11am only

Jutting out asymmetrically in the main piazza, the **Duomo** has a portal by Sansovino, a Transfiguration by Veronese, and a huge painting *The Battle of Lepanto* (attributed to Aliense) to which the town contributed so generously with men and money that the Venetians paid for the paving of the piazza (in stone from Monselice) in gratitude. The Museo Civico A. Giacomelli in the recently restored 12th-century **Castello di San Zeno** has exhibits ranging from prehistoric relics to a whole room devoted to two native tenors, Giovanni Marinelli and Aureliano Pertile. Palladio buffs won't want to miss his **Palazzo Pisani**, by the Porto Padova.

Abbazia S. Maria di Carceri
*t 042 961 9777,
www.diweb.it/
pd/carceri; open
Sat–Sun 3–7*

Just south of Este, **Abbazia S. Maria di Carceri/Abbazia Camaldolesi** is a beautiful Augustinian abbey dating from 1189, enlarged during the Renaissance. In 1690 Pope Alexander VIII suppressed the abbey and sold it off at auction; it was bought by a Bergamese noble family and transformed into a farm and summerhouse.

Southeast of Padua

Villa Roberti-Bozzolato
*t 049 580 6768; open
for tours 11.30, 2.30–5.30*

Hardly any tourists make it into this flat country, but if you have a car there are treasures to seek out. In **Brugine**, just off the main Padua–Chioggia road, the 16th-century Villa Roberti-Bozzolato designed by Andrea della Valle (now the Centro Internazionale di Storia dello Spazio e del Tempo) has delightful mythological frescoes by Paolo Veronese and Giambattista Zelotti; on the first Sunday of each month it hosts an antiques fair. **Conselve**, further south, was twice flattened in Venice's wars (1325, versus Padua; 1508, versus Europe) before it became an aristocratic retreat, as recalled in the elegant **Villa Sagredo**, built in the 1660s around a hunting lodge.

Villa Widmann-Borletti
*t 049 538 0008,
www.ildominio
dibagnoli.it*

Villa Garzoni-Michiel
*t 049 534 9602; plans
to open it to the public*

South, **Bagnoli di Sopra** has as its centrepiece Baldassare Longhena's Villa Widmann-Borletti (1656), a vast complex with a villa, a theatre, a church, set out in a green bordered by a party of statues by Antonio Bonazza, and a winery. Best of all, just east of Conselve in **Pontecasale** is Sansovino's Villa Garzoni-Michiel (1536–66), a landmark pre-Palladian work inspired by classical and Roman models.

Another place to aim for is **Piove di Sacco** (it sounds like 'rain sack' but the name is really derived from *Plebs Sacci*, 'taxed people', from the Middle Ages, when this land was the personal property of the emperors). Piove's handsome, much remodelled **Duomo** has a Madonna by Giambattista Tiepolo, a polyptych by Paolo Veneziano and an altar by Sansovino (in the chapel to the left of the main altar), although the best picture in town is yet another Madonna in the 15th-century **Santuario della Madonna delle Grazie**, attributed to Giovanni Bellini.

Where to Stay and Eat in the Euganean Hills

(i) **Abano Terme >**
*Via Pietro d'Abano 18,
t 049 866 9055*

(★) **Hotel Terme Due Torri >**

Abano Terme ✉ 35031
***** Hotel Terme Due Torri, Via P. d'Abano 18, t 049 863 2100, *www.gbhotels.it* (€€€€€–€€€€). Even though it has more than 100 rooms, this hotel can aptly wear the name 'boutique'. Attention to detail and personalised care are the bywords

here, from special meals to any type of health or beauty treatment imaginable. *Closed Jan–Mar.*
***Verdi**, Via F. Busonera 200, t 049 667 600, *www.abanoverdi.com* (€€). A friendly hotel, offering more pools and mud for a quarter of the price. In nearby Torreglia, join the hungry Paduans at some of their favourite country restaurants.
Antica Trattoria Ballotta, Via Carromatto 2, t 049 521 2970,

ⓘ **Montegrotto Terme**
Viale della Stazione 60, t 049 793 384

ⓘ **Este >>**
Via G. Negri 9, t 042 960 0462

ⓘ **Montagnana >>**
Castel S. Zino, t 042 981 320; closed Mon pm and Tues

ⓘ **Monselice >**
Piazza Mazzini, t 042 978 3026

★ **Castello di Lispida >>**

www.ballotta.it (€€). In business since 1605 and one of the oldest restaurants in Venetia, with fine dining inside or in the garden. *Closed Tues and Jan.*

Rifugio Monte Rua, Via Monte Rua 29, t 049 521 1049, *www.monterua.it* (€€). A panoramic location, where dishes change according to season. *Closed Tues.*

Da Taparo, Via Castelletto 42, t 049 521 1060 (€€). This restaurant has a beautiful terrace overlooking the hills to match its delicious Veneto cuisine. *Closed Mon and 15 Jan–15 Feb.*

Teolo ✉ 35037

*Lussana, V. Chiesa Teolo 1, t 049 992 5530, *www.villalussana.com* (€€–€). A charming Liberty-style villa, in the centre of Teolo, with bright rooms and lovely views over a terraced garden and orchard.

Praglia Abbey, t 049 999 9300, *www.praglia.it* (€). If you ring ahead and can behave yourself, try sleeping here – a good way to make sure you catch a Gregorian Mass. There are two dormitories, one just for men inside the abbey, and another for both sexes in the grounds. It's free, but make a donation when you leave, and be prepared to live a day in the life of a monk: wake at 5.15am and lights out at 8.30pm.

Bacco e Arianna, Via Cà Sceriman 784, Vò, t 049 994 0187, *www.baccoe arianna.com* (€). In nearby Vò, stay at this delightful bed and breakfast in the middle of a vineyard.

Arquà Petrarca ✉ 35032

La Montanella, Via Costa 33, t 042 971 8200, *www.montanella.it* (€€€–€€). Near the centre of Arquà, you can enjoy not only the garden and views, but exquisite *risotti* and duck with fruit at this restaurant; select your wine, olive oil and vinegar from the special menus. *Closed Tues eve, Wed, and 2 wks in Aug and Jan.*

Monselice ✉ 35043

****Castello di Lispida, Via IV Novembre 4, t 042 978 0530, *www.lispida.it* (€€€–€€). Starting

out as a monastery in 1150, then a winery – and even King Vittorio Emanuele's headquarters during the First World War – this much-used *castello* is now a luxury country house where some remarkable wines aged in terracotta are produced. Use of barbecue, free pick of the orchards, and an indoor swimming pool add to its patrician charm.

La Torre, Piazza Mazzini 14, t 0429 73752 (€€, €€€ for truffles). An elegant place where funghi fiends can head for gratification. *Closed Sun eve, Mon, and part of July and Aug.*

Venetian Palace Hostel, 'Città di Monselice', Via Santo Stefano Superiore 33, t 0429 783 125, *ostellomonselice@libero.it* (€). For somewhere more stylish try this hostel, once used by the dukes of Padua as a guesthouse. It now offers comfortable rooms and dormitories with modern conveniences. Great value nonetheless.

Este ✉ 35042

**Beatrice d'Este, Viale Rimembranze 1, t 0429 600 533 (€). This hotel has a lovely little *trattoria* attached serving all the usual Veneto standards.

***Castello, Via San Girolamo 7, t 0429 602 223, *www.imieiviaggi.com/ hotelcastello* (€). Enjoy views over the castle and its gardens; well sited for the city centre.

Montagnana ✉ 35044

***Aldo Moro, Via G. Marconi 27, t 0429 81351, *www.hotelaldomoro.com* (€€). Stay in fine rooms beside the Duomo, and visit the restaurant serving local *prosciutto dolce del montagnanese. Closed Mon.*

Rocca degli Alberi Youth Hostel ('Tree Castle'), t 0429 81076 (€). If you are an AIG card-holder, you get to stay in the best location in town, at the Legnano Gate, built in 1362. *Closed mid-Oct–Feb.*

Da Stona, Via Carrarese 51, t 0429 81532 (€). For lunch or dinner, try this excellent *trattoria* with tasty home cooking, *pasta e fagioli, prosciutto dolce*, and a good local wine list; tourist menu. *Closed Mon.*

Little Mesopotamia

About 20km south of Monselice, Rovigo is the capital of the province wedged between Italy's two longest rivers, the mighty Adige and the mightier Po, known as the Polesine or 'Little Mesopotamia'. Like ancient Mesopotamia it has been blessed and cursed by its rivers, which make it fertile but often spill over their banks. Six complete cycles of creation and destruction have moulded the topography of Little Mesopotamia – miles of silt have left its ancient capital Adria high and dry. The main reason for a visit is to explore the Po Delta, a haunting landscape of water, dunes and trees, changing and colour.

Rovigo

The other inhabitants of Venetia may sneer 'Rovigo no m'intrigo' but this prosperous little provincial capital doesn't give a snap. It has the air of a town with ambition and the breeze coming off the Polesine provides a very welcome respite from the sometimes oppressive heat in other parts of the Veneto. For a landmark, Rovigo can match Bologna with its odd couple of leaning towers, the 11th-century **Torri Donà**, one tall, one stubby. Nearby (nothing is far), a lion of St Mark holds court with a statue of Vittorio Emanuele in central **Piazza Vittorio Emanuele II**, a handsome trapezoid dotted with palaces, one containing the Pinacoteca dell'Accademia dei Concordi. Rovigo may be provincial, but it was hardly backward; founded by local scholars in 1580, the academy has over 600 paintings, including Giovanni Bellini's *Madonna* and *Christ Bearing the Cross*; Palma il Vecchio's *Flagellation*; Jan Gossaert's *Venus with a Mirror*; and a 17th-century *Cleopatra*, by Sebastiano Mazzoni, complete with a very realistic asp crawling along her languorous breast. Another section, the Count Silvestri collection, has excellent 17th–18th-century works by Sebastiano Bombelli, Pietro Longhi, Piazzetta, Luca Giordano and Bernardo Strozzi.

Pinacoteca
dell'Accademia
dei Concordi
*www.concordi.it;
open Mon–Sat
9–1.30; adm free*

From adjacent Piazza Garibaldi and its equestrian bronze statue of Italy's most romantic hero, follow Via Silvestri back to Rovigo's most famous church, the octagonal La Rotonda with a detached tower by Longhena. Built in 1603 by Francesco Zamberlan, a not entirely successful engineering pupil of Palladio (the dome had to be demolished the year after it was built), the interior is an art gallery of 17th-century Veneto painting: Pietro Liberi, Antonio Zanchi, Pietro Muttoni, Francesco Maffei and Giambattista Pellizzari all contributed dramatic canvases to the greater glory of Rovigo's *podestà*; the Virgin, angels, virtues and saints stream out of clouds and whirlwinds to pay homage to these robed representatives of Venetian officialdom. At the south end of town (take Corso del Popolo down to Via S. Bellino), the monastery

La Rotonda
*t 0425 24914;
open summer 9–11.30
and 4–7, winter 9–11.30
and 3–6*

Getting around Little Mesopotamia

From Rovigo there are frequent **buses** to Adria and the Delta towns; **trains** also run from Rovigo to Adria and Chioggia (1hr 20mins), or south to Ferrara (30mins) and Bologna (1hr). Rovigo's bus station is on the Piazzale G. Di Vittorio; the railway station is on the Piazza Riconoscenza. Fratta Polesine can be reached by bus from Rovigo (direction Trecenta).

Museo Civico della Civiltà
t 0425 25077; open Mon–Sat 8.30–12.30; other days on request

attached to S. Bartolomeo Apostolo is now the **Museo Civico della Civiltà** in Polesine dedicated to archaeology, ethnography and local history.

Up the Po: Fratta Polesine and Lendinara

The villas of the Po flatlands, the Polesine, are fairly simple compared with their counterparts in the northern Veneto, but have the advantage of being accessible by boat. The most important

Villa Badoera
t 0425 21530; book ahead

one, **Villa Badoera** (1570), is 18km southwest of Rovigo in the centre of **Fratta Polesine**, a building stamped all over with Palladio's signature, from its Ionic temple front over a stately stair to the *barchesse*, perpendicular to the villa but united by curved arcades. Restorations have uncovered original frescoes of pseudo-Roman grotesques by Giallo Fiortino. In the Bronze Age, Mycenaean Greeks founded a trading counter here in Fratta, dealing with caravans that crossed over the Po plain; it thrived from the 11th to the 9th century BC, when it was wiped off the map in a cataclysmic flood.

The other main destination in these parts (although don't expect to see any other tourists!) is **Lendinara** on the left bank of the Adigetto, once the property of the Este family of Ferrara. A miraculous spring flowed here, which is now channelled into the octagonal fountain in the centre of the church of the **Madonna del Pilastrello** (1581) in Piazza Alberto Mario, which has a vast collection of *ex votos*, including one by Paolo Veronese. A rich collection of Renaissance altars and statues fills the **Duomo**; and on Via Garibaldi the **Palazzo Dolfin-Marchiori**, built on a design by Scamozzi, has a garden by Giuseppe Jappelli. In central Piazza Risorgimento you'll find a pair of 14th-century towers left over from the Este castle, and a charming place to sip a cappuccino, the **Caffè Maggiore**, unchanged since 1915.

Adria

The deluge was on such a scale that only in the 6th century BC did people – beginning with the Palaeoveneti and the Etruscans – return to the Po Delta, founding **Adria**, at the time 9km from the sea, but linked to it by an Etruscan canal, the Canale Bianca. They were soon followed by Greek merchants from Corinth, Corfu and Aegina, who lived with the Palaeoveneti and Etruscans in wheeling and dealing harmony; it was praised as 'Shining Adria' by Strabo and 'noble city' by Pliny the Elder. As the Etruscan town of Felsina

(Bologna) became the dominant regional power at the end of the 6th century, Adria lost out to Felsina's port of Spina, although not before Adria gave its name to the sea. The city remained an island of Greekness in the Veneto; in 385–350 BC Syracuse helped to defend it against the Gauls.

After decades of sporadic digging in search of the Etruscan and Greek necropolis, paydirt was struck in 1990 by accident during road work on Via Spolverin. The grave-goods – gold, swords and vases – are now in the Museo Archeologico Nazionale di Adria. Further memories of Adria's glory days in this collection include excellent black-figure Corinthian vases (a beautiful one shows the apotheosis of Hercules); there's also a lovely collection of richly coloured Roman glass and a 3rd-century BC iron chariot of Gaulish workmanship, found entombed with two tiny horses, buried with either a Celtic or Palaeoveneto warrior. Ancient Venetia was famous for its horses in antiquity, although the proof of their value was often demonstrated in the old-fashioned way – sacrificing them at funerals. In the courtyard, a Roman milestone from the Rimini– Aquileia Via Popilla (132 BC) carries the oldest Latin inscription in northern Italy.

Museo Archeologico Nazionale di Adria
Piazzale degli Etruschi, t 0426 21612; open Mon–Sat 9–7, Sun 2–7; adm

The Venice of its day, Adria is now a rather dusty place with only one canal, dominated by a giant radio mast. But it kept its chin up for centuries even after the Romans. The **Duomo Nuovo** in Piazza Garibaldi has as its prize a Coptic relief from the 4th century, made just after the Council of Ephesus agreed on the divinity of the Virgin, showing her between the archangels Michael and Gabriel. The sacristy's lavish Baroque wardrobes by Jacopo Piazzetta (1683) come from the Scuola della Carità in Venice, while a door in the left nave leads to the old Cathedral, with an octagonal baptismal font and remains of the 7th-century crypt that once formed part of the Palaeo-Christian church, its walls decorated with early cartoon-like Byzantine frescoes. The baptismal font of another church, **S. Maria della Tomba**, in Via Angeli, once served in the Roman baths; it also has two fine terracottas, a 14th-century Annunciation and a 15th-century Dormition of the Virgin by Michele da Firenze.

The Po Delta

After travelling over 652km (405 miles), the Po ends its course in a 400-square-mile (1,000 sq km) delta, a marshy fish-filled wonderland of a thousand islets, much appreciated by bitterns, coots, kingfishers, little egrets, herons, terns and migratory birds from the north. Before its current status as the **Parco del Po**, a few resorts mushroomed up along the sandy, pine-shaded shores – namely **Rosolina Mare**, a lovely beach for children, and the exclusive island 'club', **Isola di Albarella**, with its golf course.

Where to Stay and Eat in Little Mesopotamia

ⓘ Rovigo ›
Via J.H. Dunant 10,
t 0425 38611,
www.provincia.rovigo.it

ⓘ Rosolina
Mare ››
Via dei Ligustri 3,
t 0426 68012

Rovigo ✉ 45100

★★★★Villa Regina Margherita, Viale Regina Margherita 6, t 0425 361 540, *www.hotelvillavillareginamargherita.it* (€€). A few steps from the centre, this Liberty-style villa is the most stylish place to stay; bedrooms are well equipped, if lacking the tone of the public rooms.

Tenuta Castel Venezze, San Martino di Vanezze, t 0425 99667, *www.castelvenezze.it* (€€). Some 8km outside Rovigo, this *agriturismo* occupies a reconstructed 15th-century castle, set in extensive parkland with a swimming pool and restaurant. All rooms are carefully furnished with antiques.

Degli Amici, Via Quirina 4, t 0425 91045 (€€€). The best place of all, 8km south of Rovigo in Arquà Polesine, where fish share the menu with duck and goose, prepared in an old wood oven. *Closed Wed, and in summer Sat and Sun lunch.*

Tavernetta Dante dai Trevisani, Corso del Popolo 212, t 0425 26386 (€€€). Here you can try that medieval Veneto favourite, *pappardelle all'anatra* (with duck sauce) as well as other treats. *Closed Aug.*

On the Delta ✉ 45010

Marina 70, t 0426 80080 (€€€). East of Porto Tolle, at Scardovari, this seaside restaurant is devoted heart and soul to fresh seafood, prepared to traditional Italian methods and served on a pretty terrace. *Closed Mon.*

The Po, as it nears the Adriatic, splits into six major branches, each with its own character, including the navigable canal-like Po di Levante; the contorted, lushly overgrown Po di Maistra; and the majestic Po di Pila, which carries 60 per cent of the flow, and has most of the fisheries and bird life, especially around **Rosapineta**. Dogged shepherds and their flocks, thatched houses with great chimneys called *casone* and gypsy shanty towns dot the lonesome shores. If you can, visit the delta in spring, when the colours are fiery and transparent, or at the end of summer, when mists hover over the pools and dunes, tinted scarlet with salicornia and violet with sea lavender, and the reeds and grasses turn to gold. There are several **boat cruises** to choose from which explore the delta and its bird life, most of them departing from **Porto Tolle** or **Taglio di Po**. Other tours include fishing trips and houseboat hire (a fantastic idea given the proximity of Venice, though mosquitoes can be a real problem).

Boat cruises
contact *Delta Tour*,
Padua, t 049 870 0232,
www.deltatour.it; they
offer day-long cruises
with lunch on board

North of Padua

Some of the Veneto's best-known sites are north of Padua, in the charmed foothills of the Dolomites: there's Castelfranco Veneto, birthplace of Giorgione, and Asolo, where the Queen of Cyprus held her fabled Renaissance court. There are also outstanding villas, including Maser, where Palladio and Veronese collaborated to create a unique work of art.

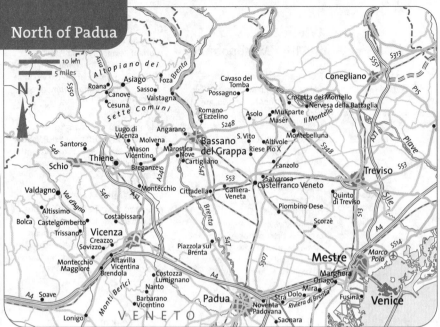

Castelfranco Veneto and Around

Square, walled Castelfranco Veneto was built by Treviso in 1199 to counter the ambitions of Padua, and basks in the glory of having given the world the romantic, enigmatic genius Giorgione, or Zorzon as the locals called him, born here in 1478. Zorzon in gratitude (it seems like a pleasant enough place to have grown up in) left Castelfranco the masterpiece now hanging in the neoclassical **Duomo**: the *Castelfranco Madonna* (1504), a triangular composition of the Virgin, St Francis and the soldier-saint Liberalis, their remote figures inhabiting the same ineffable, dreamlike world as his paintings in the Accademia. The *Castelfranco Madonna* was subject to one of the more spectacular art heists in the 1970s; the thieves' demands for a ransom were repeatedly refused, and the painting was abandoned after a shoot-out with the *carabinieri*. It is now back on view in a glass case, firmly locked to avoid a repeat occurrence.

Next to the Duomo, the **Casa del Giorgione** is in Giorgione's former home. In Via Garibaldi, you can visit the **Teatro Accademico**, an exquisite university lecture theatre, dating from the 1600s. During Zorzon's brief life Castelfranco built its most elaborate gate, the **Porta di Treviso**, with its clock and Venetian lion (1499). From here Borgo Treviso leads to the charming gardens of 19th-century **Villa Revedin Bolasco**. Just west of Castelfranco, near Castello di Godego, a series of prehistoric earthen walls standing between

Duomo
open Mon–Fri 9.30–11.45 and 3.15–5.45

Casa del Giorgione
t 0423 725 022; open Tues–Sun 9–12 and 3–6

Teatro Accademico
open Mon–Fri 9–12 and 2–6; Sat and Sun for special exhibitions

Villa Revedin Bolasco
open mid-Mar–May and mid-Sept–early Nov Tues, Thurs and Sun 10–12.30 and 3–5.30; June–mid-Sept Tues, Thurs and Sun 10–12.30 and 3–7.30; adm

Getting around North of Padua

From Padua there are both **buses** and **trains** to Bassano del Grappa (40mins), via Castelfranco; from Vicenza change trains at Castelfranco, passing Cittadella on the way. From Venice, change in Treviso. Bassano's bus station is in the Piazzale Trento, near the tourist office, t 0424 30850, while the train station is at the top of Via Chilesotti.

Frequent buses from Montebelluna, Bassano or Treviso serve Asolo (14km) and Maser (6km further); others, from Bassano and Vicenza, run to Marostica (20 buses daily), Lonedo di Lugo, Thiene (25km) and Asiago (36km).

6ft and 13ft high form a partially visible rhomboid known as the **Motte**; most have been found to have precise astronomical alignments, although recent measurements now throw some of these findings into doubt.

Cittadella
the North tower is open alternate Sun afternoons

After Treviso built Castelfranco, the Paduans, tit for tat, founded the egg-shaped Cittadella 15km to the west. Its magnificent 13th-century **walls**, surrounded by a moat, are over a mile long and 40ft high. They are made of 'cassalta', basically a mixture of sand, bricks and pebbles from the River Brenta, and have proved remarkably difficult to destroy; during the Second World War they even withstood an air bombardment. One of the 28 towers, the Torre di Malta, contained Ezzelino's infamous torture chamber ('...no man yet was ever sent to Malta/for treachery as foul as his shall be', *Paradiso IX*, 54) but unfortunately it's not open to the public. The Venetians added the fine lion with a kinky tail in the main square.

Villa Emo
t 0423 476 334; open April–Oct 3–6.30, Nov–Mar Mon–Fri 2–4, Sat–Sun 2–5.30; adm exp

From Castelfranco you can also nip up to **Fanzolo**, 5km to the northeast, for another of Palladio's finest, Villa Emo, the only Palladian villa still owned by the family that commissioned it. Villa Emo has the typical Palladian five-part profile, with dovecotes surmounting the ends of the *barchesse*; its temple front, with its tympanum stuccoed by Vittoria, was one of the first to have freestanding columns, not to mention a long ramp that enabled visitors to ride straight up to the door. Unlike many villas, this is still a working farm, and one with a famous pedigree – it was in 1536 one of the first in Europe to grow maize (*granturco* in Italian), used to fatten pigeons before it began to fatten the polenta-mad Venetians. The main rooms have brightly coloured mythologies by Giambattista Zelotti. Palladio also designed the long rows of brick farmworkers' cottages.

Riese Pio X
Museum
t 0423 483 929; open April–Sep daily 8–12 and 3–7, Oct–Mar daily 9–12 and 2–5

Close by, the little village of **Riese Pio X** is named for the Pontiff it produced, Pius X (Giuseppe Sarto, 1835–1914, canonized in 1951), whose home is now a museum. Although his policies were reactionary, he is remembered fondly in the Veneto. The story goes that his housekeeper took to wearing his old stockings, and found that they were not only holey but holy, and miraculously cured her bunions. When she told the pope, he laughed and said, 'They certainly don't do that for me!'

Near Riese, **San Vito** has in its cemetery one of the most striking modern tombs in Italy, designed by Venetian architect Carlo Scarpa (1975) for himself and TV baron Giuseppe Brion. The tomb itself has some similarities with neolithic tombs, both in its structure and styling, which gives it an even grander impression. Although it's been abandoned since the 1700s, you can also have a look at what remains of the once-fabulous castle and gardens that Venice built in 1490 for Caterina Cornaro – the **Barco della Regina Cornaro**, in **Altivole**.

Piazzola sul Brenta and Piombino Dese: Palladian Villas

There's a choice of roads north from Padua, and a choice of villas to see along the way. The SS47 follows the River Brenta to Cittadella, by way of **Piazzola sul Brenta** and the imposing Villa Contarini. Built in 1414, the villa was greatly enlarged in 1564 by Palladio for Marco Contarini, a Procurator of the Republic; later residents added the 17th-century *barchesse*, adorned with the full whack of Palladian statues and balustrades, on grounds that include an arcaded hemicycle, park and lake. The interior is more elaborate than the average villa as well, featuring special Music and Listening Rooms with excellent acoustics. Villa Contarini had an interesting career in the 19th century, when it was purchased by Silvestro Camerini, who made Piazzola into a model industrial/ agricultural estate. In fact, one of its main products, jute, was still being processed in the 1960s.

Villa Contarini
*t 049 559 0238;
garden open Mar–Oct
Thurs–Tues 9–7,
Nov–Feb Thurs–Tues
10–4; adm*

The more easterly SS307 from Padua to Castelfranco Veneto passes near **Piombino Dese**, a sprawling rural *comune*, but a must-see detour for Palladiophiles, for its Villa Cornaro (1553) a block from the Piombino Dese train station. Built in 1553, this is among Palladio's most monumental and well-preserved villas, where he introduced one of his most original features – the two-storey projecting portico-loggia. It's also the only Palladian villa to preserve much of its original *intonaco* cladding and tile floors; another unique feature is the grand Salon, where niches were designed to hold full-length statues of the Cornaro ancestors – a throwback to the ancient Romans, who liked to keep wax models and masks of their forebears around the place. The harmonious interior was only frescoed in 1716 (after the Cornari relocated their famous art collection), when Procurator Andrea Cornaro commissioned 21-year-old Mattia Bortoloni to execute 104 fresco panels in stucco frames, using the newly fashionable 'light manner'. The subjects were carefully chosen by Cornaro, who eschewed the usual mythologies and religious allegories for scenes from the Old and New Testaments. Not what one expects in a country house, although the Bible may have been merely a

Villa Cornaro
*t 049 936 5017;
call in advance*

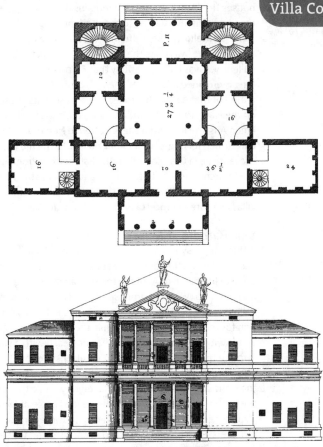

from Palladio's *Four Books of Architecture*

vehicle to smuggle in a forbidden Masonic message: the frescoes on the eastern wall of the main room especially abound with Masonic symbols.

Montebelluna and the Montello

The Roman *Mons Bellonae*, Montebelluno is proud to be the world capital of ski and hiking boots, celebrated in all their glory in the **Museo dello Scarpone**, in one of a score of villas scattered about its hills above Piazza Garibaldi, the Villa Binetti-Zuccareda. Long before ski boots, however, what is now the centre of Montebelluna was an important medieval market; in Piazzetta di Mercato Vecchio a column erected by the Venetians in 1593 honours the commercial concessions Montebelluna enjoyed from the 9th century until 1872. Another country house, the Villa Biagi,

Museo dello Scarpone
Vicolo Zuccareda 1,
t 0423 303 282; open
Tues–Sat 9–12 and 3–6,
Sun 9–12 and 3–7; adm

Museo Civico
*Via Piave 41, t 0423
300 465; open daily
9–12 and 2–5.30; adm*

houses the Museo Civico, with remains of a Palaeoveneti necropolis discovered just to the north of Montebelluna.

The **Montello**, the beautiful hilly district between Montebelluna and the Piave, was once the main source of oak timber for Venetian galleys, yet was cut so carefully that 6,000 hectares of primordial forest remained intact until the 19th century; in this century about a third of that has been reforested. Because of its strategic location on the Piave, the Montello saw heavy action in the First World War, when Austro-Hungarian shells flattened **Nervesa della Battaglia** and turned its 12th-century **Abbazia di S. Eustachio** (where Giovanni della Casa compiled the first Index of Prohibited Books for the Church, in 1555) into the striking ruins that stand to this day. From Nervesa 'La Panoramica' skirts the top of the hills, farms and villas en route to **Crocetta del Montello**, near Maser.

Villa Barbaro at Maser

Villa Barbaro
*t 0423 923 004; open
Mar–Oct Tues, Sat–Sun
and hols 3–6; Nov–Feb
Sat–Sun and hols
2.30–5; guided tours on
request; adm exp*

This unique synthesis of two great talents, Palladio and Veronese, was created in 1568 for two great patrons, the Barbaro brothers, Daniele (Patriarch of Aquileia and humanistic scholar) and Marcantonio (Venetian ambassador and amateur sculptor). Palladio used the Temple of Fortuna Virilis in Rome as his inspiration for the central residence, while the *barchesse* are graceful wings with dovecotes rising at the ends, each with a sundial, forming the five-part profile that would inspire countless buildings (including the United States' Capitol). The horses frisking about the front lawn add to the patrician dignity, while the reliefs on the central pediment – the double-headed eagle of Byzantium (Aquileia, in this case) and two men astride dragons or sea monsters, each holding a woman in one arm and touching the horns of a central ox-head – add an air of mystery. Emblems like this were the rage in the Renaissance, full of puns and allegorical references for those in the know, which unfortunately doesn't include us.

Palladio taught Veronese about space and volume, and nowhere is this so evident as in these ravishing, architectonic *trompe l'œil* frescoes, which repopulate the villa with the original owners and their pets, lingering as if the villa lay under the same spell as Sleeping Beauty's castle – an effect heightened by the slippers passed out to visitors at the door (to protect the original floors). Signora Barbaro and her sons gaze down from painted balconies; a little girl opens a door; a dog waits in a corner; painted windows offer views of imaginary landscapes; the huntsman in the far bedroom is Veronese, gazing across the row of rooms at his mistress. As delightful as these are, one tradition has it that Palladio was miffed that Veronese's *trompe l'œil* detracted from the appreciation of the harmonic proportions of his rooms, and he

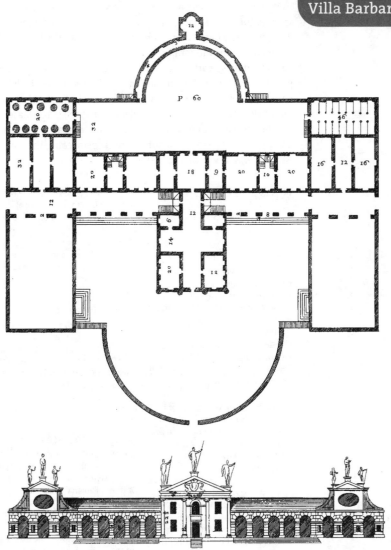

from Palladio's *Four Books of Architecture*

punished the painter by completely snubbing him in the *Quattro Libri*. The back garden is taken up with a nymphaeum, guarded by giants sculpted by Marcantonio Barbaro. The striking, if crumbling, **Tempietto**, just across the road, is a miniature Barbaro pantheon by Palladio in 1580, inspired by his favourite Renaissance building, Bramante's Tempietto in Rome, and decorated with statues by Alessandro Vittoria and Orazio Marinali.

Other villas dot the road between Maser and Asolo, including the 17th-century **Villa Rinaldi**, a grand Baroque stage set. Or there's a longer, enchanting route up through the **Forcella Mostaccin** (take the road into the mountains just south of Villa Barbaro). If you find yourself in these parts on 21 March, you can witness a curious old purification rite: the Trial of the Old Year ('*La Vecia*'), in which the past year is made to answer for all the ills that happened, in an Inquisition-style interrogation, and burned at the stake. **Maser-Muliperte**, **Quinto di Treviso** and **Cavaso del Tomba** are the venues, and if their calendars seem out of whack, it's because the spring equinox was New Year's Day under the *Serenissima*.

Where to Stay and Eat around Castelfranco Veneto

(i) Castelfranco
Veneto >
*Via Francesco Maria
Preti 66,* **t** *0423 491 416*

Castelfranco Veneto ✉ 31033

***Al Moretto, Via S. Pio X 10, **t** 0423 721 313, *www.albergoalmoretto.it* (€€; no restaurant). The oldest hotel in town, set in the centre of Castelfranco and housed in an appealing 17th-century palace.

****Fior, Via dei Carpani 18, **t** 0423 721 212, *www.hotelfior.com* (€€). In the same area, occupying an old villa and park, with tennis, swimming pool and sauna.

***Roma, Via Fabio Filzi 39, **t** 0423 721 616, *www.albergoroma.com* (€€). Situated outside the fortifications of Castelfranco but offering a good view of them; all rooms have TV and air-conditioning.

***Ca' delle Rose, on the Circonvallazione Est, **t** 0423 420 374, *www.barbesin.it* (€). Just northeast of Castelfranco at Salvarosa, you can stay at this remodelled hotel and dine at its famous restaurant (Barbesin, *see* below).

Barbesin, Via Montebelluna 41, Salvarosa, **t** 0423 490 446, *www.barbesin.it* (€€€). The setting is as idyllic as the products of its kitchen, based entirely on fresh, seasonal ingredients; the veal with apples melts in your mouth. *Closed Wed eve and Thurs.*

Palazzino, Via Roma 29, **t** 049 596 9224 (€€€). In Galliera Veneto, between Castelfranco and Cittadella,

in a former patrician hunting lodge. A great place to try traditional Renaissance dishes. *Closed Tues eve, Wed and Aug.*

Alle Mura, Via Preti 69, **t** 0423 498 098 (€€€–€€). An elegant place next to the fortifications, with well-prepared seafood dishes and a garden. *Closed Thurs.*

Fanzolo ✉ 31050

Quinto di Treviso, Locanda Righetto, Via Ciardi 2, **t 0422 470 080, *www.locandarighetto.it* (€; restaurant €€). This historic hotel and restaurant faces the River Sile and is renowned for its freshly caught eel with *polenta*, Sile trout and carp. *Restaurant closed Mon; hotel and restaurant closed first 10 days in Jan.*

Piombino Dese ✉ 35017

Ca' Marcello, Via dei Marcello 13, Levada di Piombino Dese, **t** 049 935 0340, *www.camarcello.it* (€€€€€). A true Palladian villa dating from 1550 and still owned and inhabited by the Marcello family, descendants of the Doge of Venice. Count Jacopo will give you a personal tour of the main part of the villa and grounds, and for a treat, you can stay for a week or more in the four-bedroom apartment with private pool.

Montebelluna and Around ✉ 31044

***San Marco, Via Buziol 19, **t** 0423 300 766, *www.hotelsanmarco.tv.it* (€€; no restaurant). One of the town's many villas makes a pleasant base in the hills.

Maser and Around ✉ 31010

*Locanda alla Posta, Piazza Martiri, 13, t 0423 543 112 (hotel €; restaurant €€€). North of Maser in Cavaso del Tomba, this 17th-century villa with fine panoramic views has seven rooms and serves delicious local fare such as *mousse di caprino* (kid) with pears and *crostini. Hotel closed mid-June–mid-July, restaurant closed 1–15 July, Wed eve and Thurs.*

Da Bastian, Via Cornuda, t 0423 565 400 (€€€). Just up the road from Palladio's villa, dine in enchanting surroundings, where the pâté, *risotto,* Venetian-style snails and desserts are renowned. *Closed Wed eve and Thurs, some of Aug.*

Trattoria Casa Rossa, Via Roma 134/a, Pederobba, t 0423 689 055 (€€€). Order the full selection of *antipasti* and make a meal of it.

⭐ Trattoria Casa Rossa >>

Asolo

⭐ Asolo

The old walled hill town of Asolo was the consolation prize given by Venice in 1489 to Queen Caterina Cornaro after demanding her abdication from the throne of Cyprus. It could have been worse: Asolo, with its benign lush micro-climate, just happens to be one of the most enchanting spots in Italy, and Caterina's Renaissance court lent it a high degree of refinement and art. The handsome young Giorgione strolled through its rose gardens strumming his lute, and the enforced idleness that prevailed in Asolo may have inspired his invention of art for pleasure. The Queen's friend, Cardinal Pietro Bembo, used her court as the setting for his sophisticated dialogues on love, *Gli Asolani* (1512), and created the verb *asolare* to describe the pleasant but meaningless method of passing time that prevailed here.

In the 19th century Asolo came back into fashion when Robert and Elizabeth Barrett Browning chose it as a romantic retreat (Robert entitled his last volume of poems *Asolando* 'for love of the place'; Pippa Passes was set here as well). Their son Pen became something of the town boss, much to the disapproval of the English community who had followed his parents, buying up five houses in town and restarting the old silk and weaving industries. He invited the parents of the great English traveller Freya Stark to move to Asolo, and she described the little hill town: 'The roofs of the town are red, darkened and mottled by centuries of sunlight and rain, for this is the dampest and greenest corner of Italy.'

Pliny wrote that Asolo's Roman incarnation *Acelum* was one of the chief fortified *oppida* of the Roman Tenth Region. Remains of an Imperial-era theatre are currently being investigated beneath the gardens of Freya Stark's former villa. A Roman aqueduct feeds the charming *cinquecento* **Fontana Maggiore**, nicknamed the *Ombelico del Mondo*, 'the navel of the world', the chief ornament in Asolo's central Piazza Maggiore. The **Duomo** just below was built over the Roman baths, finally in 1747, and has fine works by Lotto (*Apparation of the Madonna*, 1506), Jacopo da Bassano and Vivarini.

Imperial-era theatre
to take a peek, ask at the Department of Cultura, Municipio, t 0423 524 637

Just up from the piazza the **Castello della Regina** with its watch tower (in both senses of the word – it tells the time) encloses what little remains of the garden where Queen Caterina lived in 'lace and poetry'. Don't expect much: most of the garden is now privately owned as part of Browning's Villa Beach, and the courtyard hosts a lighted *bocce* court. In 1700 the castle's great hall was replaced with a theatre, but in 1930 the John Deere tractor heir bought it, dismantled it, and rebuilt it in Sarasota, Florida. You could also visit the **house of Gian Francesco Malipiero** in Via Foresto Vecchio for some incredibly ornate frescoes depicting all manner of cherubs looking saintly. The best way of seeing all that Asolo has to offer is to either stay for a few months and let it unfold before you or get a guide from the tourist office (they run English tours as well). At one time every wall of Asolo was covered with frescoes and it must have sparkled like a jewel. Nowadays we are left with tantalising glimpses of what has gone.

House of Gian Francesco Malipiero
t 0423 950 966; call for times; adm

Near the castle, the frescoed **Loggia del Capitano** contains a museum dedicated to Queen Caterina, Browning and La Duse. The portico outside houses a bookshop in summer and photography exhibitions in winter. Alas, not a single slim volume of Browning poetry to be found. Most of the shops are down Via Browning, while next to the Porta Santa Caterina is the charming **Palazzetto di Eleonora Duse**, her last home; the poem engraved on the façade was written by Gabriele D'Annunzio in memory of their love. Continue down narrow Via S. Caterina to the bizarre, rusticated 16th-century **Casa Longobarda**, built by a Lombard architect in the service of Queen Caterina and decorated with grotesques and mysterious reliefs. A lane on the left descends to the cemetery, last resting place of Eleonora Duse and Freya Stark.

Loggia del Capitano
t 0423 952 313; open Sat–Sun 10–12 and 3–7; adm

For the famous views of poet Giosuè Caducci's 'hundred horizons' of Asolo, climb (or drive – the road is halfway down the hill) up to the **Rocca**, constructed over a Palaeoveneti and Roman fort. It's a stiff climb on a hot day but there's usually water on sale at the ticket office.

Rocca
t 0423 524 637, or ask in the tourist office; open Sat–Sun 10–dusk; closed during bad weather; adm

North of Asolo

North of Asolo the foothills are known as the **Colle degli Ezzelini** for the tyrant's first base, a tower reconstructed at Sopracastello. Unfortunately you can't get inside. The main town here, **Possagno**, was the birthplace of Antonio Canova (1757–1822), the ultimate neoclassical sculptor, favourite of Napoleon and several popes. You can visit his house, and his clay and plaster models in the **Gypsoteca**. Most artists leave a work or two for their home towns to remember them by, but Canova designed nothing less than a full-scale model of the Pantheon with the Parthenon stuck on the front as his personal souvenir. The town itself describes the

Gypsoteca
t 0423 544 323; open Tues–Sun 9–12 and 3–6; adm

Where to Stay and Eat in Asolo

ⓘ Asolo >
Piazza G. D'Annunzio
2, t 0423 529 046,
www.asolo.it; closed
Mon afternoon

Asolo ✉ 31011

****Villa Cipriani**, Via Canova 298, **t** 0423 523 411, www.starwood.com/italy (€€€€€). Here Asolo can boast one of Italy's most charming and evocative hotels, in a house dating from the 16th century that belonged to Robert Browning. Overlooking a paradise of hills and cypresses, the hotel has an enchanting garden filled with roses, songbirds and pomegranate trees; some of its 32 rooms are located in garden houses.

★ Al Sole >

****Al Sole**, Via Collegio 33, **t** 0423 951 332, www.albergoalsole.com (€€€€). Also in the historic centre, this celebrated hotel is run by two sisters whose love and charm show in the details. Stay in the suites dedicated to Elonora Duse or Gabriele D'Annunzio. Some of the rooms contain charming

old-fashioned bathtubs. A new restaurant overlooking the *piazza* is a welcome addition.

***Duse**, Via Browning 190, **t** 0423 55241, www.hotelduse.com (€€€, but the cheapest in town). Overlooking Asolo's central *piazza*, with a little garden behind it.

Hosteria Ca' Derton, Piazza D'Annunzio 11, **t** 0423 529 648 (€€€). Set in one of Asolo's oldest houses, featuring traditional specialities to match the setting and attentive service. Very romantic. Book in advance. *Closed Sun eve, Mon.*

Ai Due Archi, Via Roma 55, **t** 0423 952 201 (€€). Wood-panelled, intimate, elegant and antique like Asolo itself, serving up delicious *polenta* in various guises. *Closed Thurs.*

Caffè Centrale, Via Roma 72. Every celebrity that has passed through has had a drink at this historic café. You should, too: it's a great place to watch the world go by.

Tempio
open Tues–Sun summer 9–12 and 3–6, winter 2–5

Tempio as 'one of the greatest monuments that man on earth has ever erected – in praise of God – to himself'. For a small fee you can climb up the dome; or study the detached, leaning campanile and try to figure out if it was built that way for free.

Bassano del Grappa and Around

Sprawled over the foothills of the Alps where the Brenta begins its flow down the plain, the bustling town of Bassano celebrated its first millennium in 1998. Over the past 1,000 years it has given the world lovely ceramics, white asparagus, firewater, tenor Tito Gobbi (1913–84) and a dynasty of painters who adopted Bassano's name as their own and rather sombrely influenced 17th-century painting across Europe. In that same century, Bassano's Remondini family were pioneers in a phenomenon we take for granted – the mass media – churning out thousands of prints of Italian masterpieces, views and holy pictures that were sold around the world. With so many gold stars pasted on its forehead, it's not surprising that Bassano is a town of character, but one wearing a few patches after severe damage in the battles of 1917–18.

The first houses, back in 998, were clustered on a height overlooking the Brenta, around the **Castello Ezzelino**, which bears the name of the famous bad guy who rebuilt it. Most of the action these days happens in Bassano's three central squares: first, the

Castello Ezzelino
t 0424 228 241; visits on request: ask for Ivan

medieval Piazzotto Montevecchio, where the old municipal pawn shop or **Monte di Pietà** is covered with the coats of arms of 120 Venetian *podestà*. This is linked to piquant Piazza Libertà, hogged by the neoclassical façade of the mastodonic church of **San Giovanni**; while the last square, Piazza Garibaldi, is guarded physically and spiritually by the 13th-century **Torre Civica** (with 19th-century battlements) and the Gothic church of San Francesco.

Museo Civico
open Tues–Sat 9–6.30, Sun 3.30–6.30; adm; same ticket for the ceramics museum

San Francesco's cloister contains Bassano's **Museo Civico**, with the excellent Chini collection of vases from Magna Grecia, cartoons and studies by Canova, and paintings with an emphasis on the dark and stormy, especially by the Bassano family, and particularly Jacopo (see his masterpiece, the twilit *Baptism of St Lucia*). Alessandro Magnasco contributes the uncanny *Burial of a Trappist Monk and Franciscan Banquet*, full of racing, wraith-like friars. There are calmer works as well: Michele Giambono's *Madonna* and a beautiful, recently restored *Crucifix* by Guariento.

Palladio designed Bassano's landmark, the **Ponte degli Alpini**, the unique covered wooden bridge that spans the unruly Brenta. First constructed in 1599, the bridge has been rebuilt and repaired several times to the master's design – lastly in 1948 (when it was renamed in honour of Italy's Alpine troops), with more repairs in 1969, 2000 and 2002 after flood damage. At one end, you'll find **Nardini's**, Bassano's oldest distillery. Mingle with the locals and knock back a grappa or a *mezza e mezza* in this tavern, virtually unchanged since the 1700s and with beautiful views over the river. In the Palazzo Beltrame-Menarola, the rival grappa distillery Poli operates a **Museo della Grappa** where you can taste and buy. There

Nardini's
www.nardini.it, for overseas purchases

Museo della Grappa
t 0424 524 426; open 9–7.30; adm free

A Grappa Digression

Although a lot of grappa does come from Bassano del Grappa, its name doesn't derive from the town or its mountains but from *graspa*, the residue left at the bottom of the wine vat after the must is removed; it can be drunk unaged and white, or aged in oak barrels, where it takes on a rich, amber tone. First mentioned in a 12th-century chronicle, grappa, or *aqua vitae* ('the water of life'), was chugged down as a miracle-working concoction of earth and fire to dispel ill humours. In 1601 the Doge created a University Confraternity of Aqua Vitae to control quality; during the First World War Italy's Alpine soldiers adopted Bassano's enduring bridge as their symbol and its grappa to keep them on their feet. One of their captains described it perfectly:

Grappa is like a mule; it has no ancestors and no hope of descendants; it zigzags through you like a mule zigzags through the mountains; if you're tired you can hang on to it; if they shoot you can use it as a shield; if it's too sunny you can sleep under it; you can speak to it and it'll answer, cry and be consoled. And if you really have decided to die, it will take you off happily.

In our peaceful days grappa's fiery spirit is too potent for most: from 70 million litres guzzled in 1970, only 25 million were drunk in 1990, and most of that as a coffee 'corrector', as the Italians quaintly put it. The Veneto with its 20 distilleries is a leading producer, and Bassano is a good place to seek out some of the better, more elusive labels; besides big boy Nardini, look for Poli, Da Ponte, Brunello di Montegalda, Schiavo, Folco Portinari, Maschio, Rino Dal Tosco and Carpenè Malvolti. There are some Friulian brands as well if you're not going to Friuli itself; in particular try Sojno di Deue Domenis. Grappa is as varied as wine; not all of it is as eye-wateringly strong as its reputation suggests.

are methods for drinking grappa, the idea being to take a little to cleanse your tastebuds (or prepare them for the shock) and then to drink the glass. Wincing is not allowed.

Museo della Ceramica
open Tues–Sat and Sun pm April–Oct 9–12.30 and 3–6.30; June–Sept Tues–Sun 10–12.30; Nov–March Fri 9–12.30, Sat–Sun 3.30–6.30; adm

In the mid-17th century, Bassano and the nearby town of Nove became the Veneto's top ceramic manufacturers, a status they maintain to this day, thanks to 55 thriving firms. In the 18th-century Palazzo Sturm, just up Via Schiavonetti from the bridge, the Museo della Ceramica has a fine display of local porcelain knick-knacks and majolica.

Around Bassano, and the Brenta Canal

There are two villas worth seeking out in Bassano's suburbs. From the centre follow Via Roma/Via Beata Giovanna out to early 18th-century **Ca' Rezzonico**, attributed in part to Giorgio Massari. One of the few villas still isolated in the fields, the interior is lavishly stuccoed and decorated with paintings, some by Canova. Three kilometres southwest of Bassano in **Angarano**, Palladio designed **Villa Bianchi Michiel** with his usual lateral *barchesse*, although the 17th-century owners demolished the central body of the villa and replaced it with a loftier, more palatial house, crowned with a tympanum by Longhena. Just south in **Cartigliano**, the striking 16th-century Villa Morosini Cappello, attributed to Palladio's disciple Francesco Zamberlan, is entirely wrapped in loggias and porticoes, and has recently been restored as the town hall. Stop, too, at Cartigliano's parish church for its excellent fresco cycle by Jacopo Bassano.

Villa Morosini Cappello
t 0424 592 696; open Mon–Fri 9–1, Wed 4.30–6.30; otherwise by special arrangement

Grotte di Oliero
t 0424 558 250, www.valbrenta.net; open Oct–April, Sat, Sun and hols 9.30–7; May, June and Sept 9.30–12 and 2–5; July and Aug daily 9.30–6.30; adm

Angarano marks the beginning of Bassano's own **Brenta Canal**, dug in the last century to control the unpredictable river. Unlike its sister to the south, this canal has no villas, but it does have stalactite caves, the Grotte di Oliero, near **Valstagna**. There are four of these, excavated by waters thundering down from the Alpago, and one is open for visits by boat; admission includes a botanical park and speleological museum.

This quiet corner of the Veneto wasn't always so peaceful. Among the nature trails in the area, one of the most beautiful is also one of the most vertical, the **Calà del Sasso** – 4,444 steps leading up to Sasso, on the Asiago plateau (*see* below), chiselled out of the rock in the 15th century by the Venetians. Alongside the steps, they hollowed a chute for the logs from the Asiago's forests; these would be floated down the Brenta to Venice's Arsenale and made into galleys.

Opera Festivals in Bassano del Grappa

Bassano hosts an annual **opera** festival between October and December (call the tourist office for programmes). Meanwhile Opera Estate is in full swing during July and August, with big names in jazz, pop, opera, dance and cinema (*www.operaestate.it*).

Romano d'Ezzelino and Monte Grappa

There in that part of sinful Italy
which lies between Rialto's shores and where
the Piave and the Brenta river spring
rises a hill of no great height from which,
some years ago, there plunged a flaming torch,
who laid waste all the countryside round.

Paradise IX, 25–30 (trans. by Mark Musa)

Dante is referring here to **Romano d'Ezzelino** and its infamous son, known as the 'flaming torch' from a dream his mother had before he was born. Dante already saw Ezzelino down in the Seventh Circle of hell with the other cruel tyrants – although his sister Cunizza, who went through four husbands and at least two lovers, retired in Florence and did good deeds, and met Dante in heaven. These days Romano d'Ezzelino is best known for its striking car museum featuring the best that Ferrari, Alfa Romeo, Lancia and the like have created, the **Museo dell'Automobile Bonfanti**.

Museo dell' Automobile Bonfanti
Via Torino 1, www.museo bonfanti.veneto.it; open Tues–Sun 10–12 and 2–6; adm

The 'Grappa' was added to Bassano's name in 1928, not for its firewater but in memory of the terrible fighting in the First World War at Monte Grappa, where the Italians held the line after Caporetto in 1917–18. The Strada Cadorna from Romano d'Ezzelino up to Monte Grappa (5,824ft) was built during the conflict and ends in a gargantuan trench called Galleria Vittorio Emanuele II, dug by the Italians to shelter their battery of guns. Displays and a

Museum
t 0423 544 840; open daily 8–12 and 1.30–5

museum describe the conflict, while the monumental cemetery holds the remains of 12,615 Italians; the slightly smaller Austro-Hungarian cemetery contains 10,590. Little visited but deeply impressive is the **Museo degli Alpini**, dedicated to the Italian Alpine troops who held the line at Bassano, as well as installing the world-famous 'Via Ferrata' (the system of fixed ladders and walkways embedded into rock faces, enabling them to roam the mountains and cover distances thought impossible at the time) that stretches from Bassano to the Swiss–Austrian border. And for lovers of all things Hemingway, try the **Museo Storico Permanente**, devoted to the American volunteers, Hemingway among them, who provided much needed support to the Italian troops during the First World War, ferrying the wounded away from the front.

Museo degli Alpini
Via Angarano 2, inside Taverna al Ponte on the covered bridge, t 0424 503 662

Museo Storico Permanente
Via Cà Erizzo 7, t 0424 217 807; normally closed, call in advance

Where to Stay and Eat in Bassano del Grappa

ⓘ **Bassano del Grappa >**
Largo Corona d'Italia 35, t 0424 524 351, www.vicenzae.org

Bassano del Grappa ✉ 36061

As you may have noticed wandering through town, dried mushrooms and honey as well as grappa are specialities of Bassano, but it's yet another treat that attracts droves of hungry gourmets every April: *Asparagi DOC di Bassano*, long fat white asparagus, delicate and full of flavour, and perfect for spring-cleaning one's internal plumbing. Legend has it that white asparagus was first stumbled upon by a poor farmer during the 1500s. When his crops were ruined by a hailstorm, he dug underground and discovered the tender white stalks were a delicious improvement on the green ones. Try it the local way: with boiled eggs, mashed with your fork and mixed with olive oil, vinegar, salt and pepper.

★ Villa Ca' Sette >

★★★★Villa Ca' Sette, Via Cunizza da Romano 4, t 0424 383 350, *www. ca-sette.it* (€€€€). The finest hotel in town, set in a villa dating from the 1700s, that has been refitted with stylish modern accents in 19 rooms and suites. The elegant restaurant Ca' 7 spills out onto the garden. Reservations necessary. *Closed Sun eve and Mon.*

★ Al Ponte >>

★ Trattoria del Borgo >>

Villa Brocchi Colonna, Contrà San Giorgio 98, t 0424 501 580, *www. villabrocchicolonna.it* (€€€). An *agriturismo* built in the Tuscan style, just outside Bassano del Grappa, in a green and hilly area called San Giorgio. Family-owned and run, with

large pretty rooms, most containing Jacuzzi bathtubs.

★★★Al Castello, Via Bonamigo 19, t 0424 228 665, *www.hotelalcastello.it* (€€). Bang in the centre, small, friendly and very comfortable. Ask for rooms 10 or 11.

Al Ponte, Via Volpato 60, t 0424 219 274, *www.alpontedibassano.com* (€€€). Set in a prime location along the Brenta river, this stylish restaurant headed by the Strafella family serves regional specialities; don't miss the pigeon. Another must are the homemade chocolates, and you can take home jams and other home-made products. *Closed Mon and Tues lunch.*

Trattoria del Borgo, Via Margnan 7, t 0424 522 155 (€€). Tucked away in a valley within the oldest part of the town, this authentic *trattoria* offers local specialities and interesting wines. There's a little garden, too. *Reservations essential.*

West to Schio and Asiago

In a land rich in clay and water, **Nove** has been known since the 1600s for its majolica, a craft that graduated into fine porcelains in the 1700s. Budding potters learn the ropes at the national ceramics school: part of the complex includes the **Museo Istituto Statale d'Arte per la Ceramica**; the far larger Museo Civico della Ceramica in the 19th-century Palazzo De Fabris has works from the last three centuries by local masters and foreign artists, including Picasso.

Museo Civico della Ceramica *open Tues–Sat 9– 6.30, Sun 3.30– 6.30; adm*

In contrast to workaday Nove, **Marostica**, 7km west of Bassano, is a striking town enclosed in 13th-century walls, its upper castle sprawled over the hill, and a lower castle, once the abode of the Venetian lord, sitting like a giant rook in the main piazza. This provides the perfect setting for the storybook event that has put Marostica on the map: the *Partita a Scacchi*, the human chess match, which takes place on even-numbered years, the second weekend in September. The game, played with its human (and horse) 'pieces' in medieval costume on a 72-square-foot board, commemorates the contest in 1454 for the fair hand of Lionora Parisio, disputed by Rinaldo d'Angarano and Vieri da Vallonara, whom Lionora loved. Her father, the Venetian *podestà*, refused to let the suitors fight the traditional duel for humanitarian reasons 'in sad memory of the unhappy lovers Madame Juliet Capuleti and Master Romeo Montecchio' and even offered the loser the hand of his younger daughter. The level of play matches the gorgeous costumes; each game is a reproduction of a famous grandmasters' duel, although occasionally things go wrong when the pieces misunderstand their commands, announced in archaic Venetic, and move to the wrong square. If you feel like a round yourself, there's a smaller board under the loggia with 3ft chess pieces; if you come at the wrong time of year, all the Renaissance finery is on display in the lower castle in a small **Museo dei Costumi**.

Museo dei Costumi
t 0424 556 008; open on request 9–12 and 2.30–6; adm

West of Marostica, in **Mason Vicentino**, the 18th-century **Villa Angaran delle Stelle** is one of the finest in the region, linked to a Gothic-Renaissance chapel and open for visits. The vines you see growing here go into the bottles of DOC Breganze, produced in seven styles (the red, mostly Merlot, is good), which you can pursue along the scenic, signposted 'Strada del Vino Breganze' through the hills.

Villa Angaran delle Stelle
t 0424 411 456; call in advance

Further west, **Lonedo** (part of **Lugo di Vicenza**, 6km north of Breganze) has two villas by Palladio. The **Villa Godi Valmarana Malinverni** was his very first (1540), noticeably predating his eye-opening visit to Rome. The central portion with its three-opening loggia, usually the most prominent and decorated part of his villas, is recessed behind two large wings, and the windows are asymmetrical, reminiscent of earlier fortress villas. But the loggia (inspired by Palladio's patron, Giangiorgio Trissino) is a first opening to the outside world; there had been no war for 30 years and Venetia was beginning to feel safe. The interior rooms, arranged symmetrically on a central axis, were frescoed by Zelotti, Padovano and assistants, and contain a fossil collection and a big collection of little-known Italian 19th-century painting. You can see Palladio's progress a couple of doors down, in the more classically elegant **Villa Piovene Porto Godi**, set in a neoclassical park; the stair, gate and *barchesse* were added in the 18th century.

Villa Godi Valmarana Malinverni
Via Palladio 44; open Mar–Nov Tues and Sat–Sun 2–6; June–Sept same days 3–7; adm

Villa Piovene Porto Godi
gardens open daily 2–7; adm

In the centre of pleasant **Thiene**, 10km to the west, the *quattrocento* **Villa da Porto Colleoni** is an attractive example of what Palladio was reacting against, with towers, battlements and Venetian-Gothic windows; inside there are frescoes (some by Zelotti), antique ceramics and jumbo paintings of the former residents of the stables; these were especially designed in the 18th century by Francesco Muttoni and quaintly decorated with Cupids to encourage horsey love. Opposite, note the flamboyant little church of the **Natività**, its roofline studded with flames of curly kale. Continue west to **Santorso**, where the **Villa Bonifacio Rossi** was nearly completely redone in the 19th century, but has kept its beautiful park, with century-old trees, a little lake, a butterfly park and a quirky temple in the Pompeii style.

Villa da Porto Colleoni
t 0445 366 015; open mid-Mar–mid-Nov Sun and hols, guided visits only at 3, 4, 5; adm

Villa Bonifacio Rossi
www.oasirossi.it; open Sat–Sun 9.30–7; adm

Schio, west of Santorso, has been the Veneto's main textile manufacturer ever since it became part of the Serene Republic in

1406; 'Italy's Little Manchester' they called it in the late 18th century, after Niccolò Tron, Venetian ambassador to England, brought back the newfangled techniques of the Industrial Revolution. Schio's Lanificio Rossi, founded in 1817, was long the most important woollen manufacturer in the country – Rossi's enormous factory, the **Fabbrica Alta** in Via Pasubio, was finished in 1862 and can be visited on the tourist office's industrial archaeological tour. To house employees, a grid of houses called **Nuova Schio** was laid out with lofty intentions of mixing the various classes together. A project begun in 1990 is trying to bring the neighbourhood back to life. A monument to weavers stands in the main square, along with the **Duomo**, remodelled in the 18th century and containing a Palma il Vecchio in the sacristy. Schio's finest church, however, is the early 16th-century **San Francesco**, located off Via Baratto and frescoed with the story of the Franciscan order.

Asiago and the Altopiano dei Sette Comuni

When the inhabitants of Vicenza need a deep breath of fresh air, they head north of Thiene to the cool green mountain plateau of Asiago (3,258ft). Although inhabited early on by the Palaeoveneti, it was long isolated and cut off from the rest of the Veneto, not only physically but linguistically; later inhabitants were descendants of medieval Bavarian immigrants, and to this day they still speak a Germanic language called Cimbra. Between 1310 and 1807 the seven *comuni* of the plateau, Gallio, Lusiana, Conco, Enego, Fozo, Roana and Rotzo, constituted an autonomous confederated state, the *Spettabile reggenza dei sette comuni*, allied to the Republic of Venice. The Altopiano had the misfortune to find itself on the front lines of the First World War; nearly every building was blown to bits, and only swathes remain of the once-great forests harvested by Venice for her galleys (one of the loveliest walks in the area is the loggers' path down the **Calà del Sasso**, *see* p.213, from the hamlet of Sasso, south of Fozo).

Like the seven comuni that share its lofty pedestal, their capital **Asiago** was totally rebuilt after 1918. The focal point is a massive pink stone **Municipio** (1929), with an enormous tower bearing a winged lion. A delightful mossy fountain featuring Pan and all the animals of the forest splashes by the domed church, containing two mediocre Bassanos. A ghastly number of war dead – 12,795 identified, 21,491 nameless, 19,999 Austro-Hungarians – lie in the hilltop Sacrario, which also houses a small **Museo Storico**.

Museo Storico
open mid-May–Sept 9–12 and 3–6, Oct–mid-May 9–12 and 2–5

The *altopiano* has its share of ski resorts and mountain refuges, but on the whole its green meadows are uncannily quiet. Many *comuni* have their own souvenirs of the war to end all wars, most of all Roana and its hamlets west of Asiago; here in **Canove**, the

Museo Storico della Guerra
Via Roma 30; open mid-June–mid-Sept 10–12 and 3–7

Museo Storico della Guerra 1915–1918 records the destruction of Canove, and contains materials gathered during its reconstruction – unexploded grenades, arms and other equipment left behind by various armies.

Museo dei Cuchi
Via XXV Aprile 16, t 0424 694 283; open daily 9–12.30 and 3–7

On a lighter note, in nearby **Cesuna**, the Valente family has set up part of their home as a Museo dei Cuchi. *Cuchi* are terracotta whistles, in hundreds of imaginative shapes and designs, whose local name is derived from their cuckoo-like sound. Traditionally made in various corners of the world (the oldest ever found were Greek, from the Bronze Age) they have had various uses – not only to imitate birds, but to keep away evil spirits or more mundane crop-stealers – before becoming toys. Whistle-makers, the *maestri cucari*, once thrived around Bassano and Marostica, where they specialized in men riding chickens, referring to some convoluted legend involving Napoleon.

Cesuna is near the deep, steep, glacier-gouged **Val d'Assa**, 'the Sanctuary of Prehistory', rich in rock engravings from 5000 and 3000 BC, most abundantly at Canova di Roana and Tunkelbald and Bostel de Rotzo. You can pick up a map at the Asiago tourist office.

ⓘ **Marostica >**
Piazza Castello, t 0424 72127, proloco@telemar.it

ⓘ **Schio**
Piazza dello Statuto 17, t 0445 691 212, www.vicenzae.org

★ **Due Mori >**

ⓘ **Asiago >>**
Via Stazione 5, t 0424 462 221

Where to Stay and Eat West of Bassano

Marostica ✉ 36063

Marostica is famous for its cherries and a rather unusual dish, *paetarosta col magaragno*, young turkey roasted on a spit and served with pomegranate sauce.

***Due Mori, Corso Mazzini 73, t 0424 471 777, *www.duemori.it* (€€€). Monica and Riadh, a young couple with a passion for hospitality, run this small boutique hotel and restaurant just steps away from the famous Chess Square. Monica is also a licensed guide.

***La Rosina, 2km north in Valle San Florian, Contrà Marchetti 4, t 0424 470 360, *www.larosina.it* (€€). Located in a superb hilltop setting, the restaurant here features traditional specialities; rooms are modern and comfortable. *Closed Aug.*

Castello Superiore, t 0424 73315 (€€). Located in a newly renovated upper castle, there are lovely views and lovely food, with an emphasis on fresh local ingredients. Top it off with a *caffè corretto*, 'corrected' with one of a score of different grappas.

Lugo di Vicenza ✉ 36030

Taverna Torchio Antico, Via Palladio 46 (inside Villa Godi Malinverni), t 0445 36030 (€€). Found in the *foresteria* (guesthouse) of the Villa Godi Malinverni, and serving delicious Veneto cuisine. *Closed Mon, Tues eve exc in summer, and Jan.*

Asiago ✉ 36012

Asiago is synonymous with its low-fat cow's milk cheese with a bit of a bite, one of the few in Italy to achieve DOC status. There are two kinds: fresh *asiago pressato*, delicate and soft, often used in cooking, fried or in salads, and *asiago d'allevo*, ripened like cheddar, and sold *mezzano*, *vecchio* or *stravecchio* (middle-aged, old or extra old), becoming more intensely flavoured with age.

****Sporting Residence Hotel, Asiago corso IV Novembre, t 0424 462 177, *www.sportingasiago.com* (€€€€€). A historic hotel in the centre of town with indoor pool, sauna and American bar. Staff will help organise trekking excursions. Skiing nearby.

***Da Barba, t 0424 463 363, *www.dabarba.it* (€€). A little place in Kaberlaba, 5km from Asiago, offering magnificent views, a warm welcome and good food not far from the pistes. *Closed May and mid-Oct–Nov.*

***Erica**, Via Garibaldi 55, t 0424 462 113, *www.hotelerica.it* (€€). This long-established hotel is a cosy bet for a summer or winter stay. *Closed first half of Oct.*

Lepre Bianca da Pippo (Phil's White Hare), at Camona, t 0424 445 666 (€€, restaurant €€€). Just northeast of Asiago in the *comune* of Gallio. Not only are the rooms cosy, but there's opportunity for memorable dining in an elegant English-style dining room; seasonal dishes, exquisitely fresh seafood (rare up in these hills) and delicate desserts. *Closed Tues lunch in winter, part May and part Nov.*

Vicenza

Vicenza

'The city of Palladio', prettily situated below the Monti Berici, is an architectural pilgrimage shrine and knows it. Where other Italians grouse about being a nation of museum curators, the Vicentini glory in it: Vicenza, after all, is the best example of what a gentry immersed in humanistic thought and classical philosophy could achieve in bricks and mortar. Their pride in their unique city was vindicated in 1994 when UNESCO put Vicenza on its list of World Heritage Sites. If you're coming specifically to see the villas, they tend to be open only from mid-March to mid-November.

History

A Palaeoveneto centre, Vicenza was made a Roman *municipium* in the year 49 BC, and later suffered, like all the towns in the region, invasions by the Eruli, Ostrogoths, Visigoths and the Lombards, who made the town one of their 36 duchies. Later ruled by count-bishops, Vicenza became a free *comune* in 1164, although it wasn't strong enough to fight the neighbourhood bullies – the Da Carrara of Padua, the Scaligers of Verona and the Visconti of Milan. On 28 April 1404 the city offered herself on a platter to Venice, which wasn't one to look a gift horse in the mouth.

Under the Republic, the splendour of Vicenza's architecture earned it the nickname 'the Venice of the *Terra Firma*'. The works by Palladio and his followers drew an impressive list of visitors – among them Montaigne, Inigo Jones, Montesquieu and De Brosses; Goethe wrote that he could easily spend 'a month, following a course of lessons on architecture with old Scamozzi'. During the Second World War, air raids severely damaged the old town centre; restorers repaired all the major monuments and now, in a second wave, are aiming at 'minor' buildings, for these days the roubles roll in Vicenza. The city (pop. 108,000), one of Italy's wealthiest, promotes itself as the *Città d'Oro*, thanks to its 800 gold-working firms (producing half of all Italy's goldwork); it was the birthplace of the inventor of the silicon chip, Federico Faggin, and produces machine tools, textiles, ceramics and shoes.

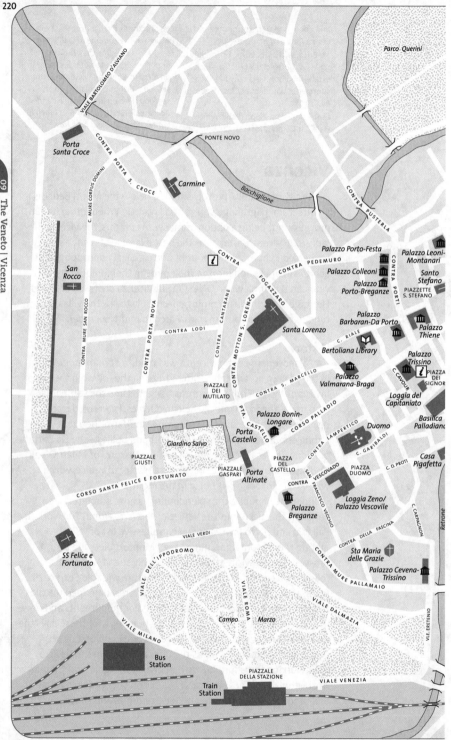

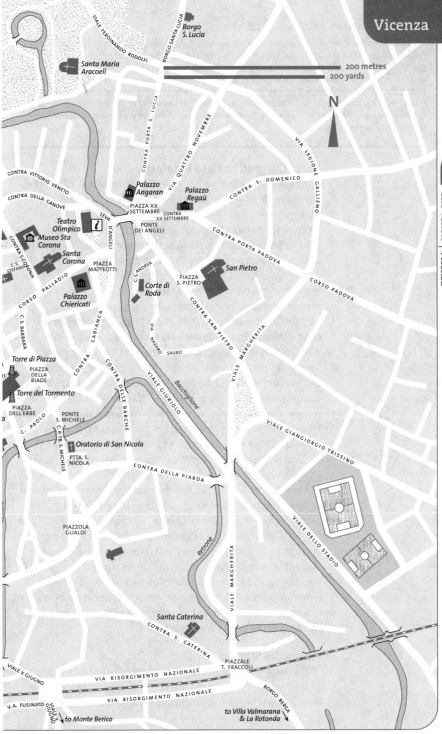

Santa Maria
Aracoeli

Borgo
S. Lucia

200 metres
200 yards

N

CONTRA VITTORIO VENETO

CONTRA DELLA CANOVE

VIALE FERDINANDO RODOLFI

BORGO SANTA LUCIA

CONTRA PORTA S. LUCIA

VIA QUATTRO NOVEMBRE

VIA LEGIONE GALLIENO

CONTRA S. DOMENICO

Palazzo
Angaran

Palazzo
Regaù

PIAZZA XX
SETTEMBRE

CONTRA
XX SETTEMBRE

LEVA
D'ANGELI

PONTE
DEI ANGELI

CONTRA PORTA PADOVA

Teatro
Olimpico

Museo Sta
Corona

Santa
Corona

PIAZZA
MATTEOTTI

C.S. ANDREA

Corte di
Roda

San Pietro

PIAZZA
S. PIETRO

CORSO PADOVA

C.S. STEFANORA

CORSO PALLADIO

Palladio

Palazzo
Chiericati

C.S. BARBARA

CONTRA CABIANCA

VIA
NAZARO
SAURO

CONTRA SAN PIETRO

VIALE MARGHERITA

Torre di Piazza

PIAZZA
DELLA
BIADE

Torre del Tormento

PIAZZA
DELL'ERBE

C. PAOLO

PONTE
S. MICHELE

C.PT.B.S. MICHELE

CONTRA DELLE BARCHE

VIALE GIURIOLO

Bacchiglione

Oratorio di San Nicola

PTTA. S.
NICOLA

CONTRA DELLA PIARDA

VIALE GIANGIORGIO TRISSINO

PIAZZOLA
GUALDI

Retrone

VIALE MARGHERITA

VIALE DELLO STADIO

Santa Caterina

CONTRA S. CATERINA

PIAZZALE
T. FRACCOLI

VIALE X GIUGNO

VIA RISORGIMENTO NAZIONALE

BORGO BERGA

V.A. FUSINATO

VIALE X GIUGNO

VIA RISORGIMENTO NAZIONALE

to Monte Berico

to Villa Valmarana
& La Rotonda

Getting to and around Vicenza

Vicenza is on the main rail line between Verona (45mins), Padua (35mins) and Venice (1hr); there is also a branch line up to Thiene; trains always run, if not on time. The station is on the south side of town, at the end of Viale Roma. The FTV bus station, t 0444 223 111, is alongside it: buses depart from here for Bassano and Marostica as well as to Asiago, Rovigo, Este, Lonigo and other destinations in the region. You can rent a bike at the train station's *deposito bagagli* – part of the deal includes a free map with bike routes.

Leave your car in one of the two attended car parks, one at the west end of the town by the Mercato Ortofrutticolo and the other to the east by the stadium. Both are linked to the centre by a special bus service every five minutes.

Porta Castello to Casa Pigafetta

The Viale Roma, the main road up from the station, enters the city proper through the **Porta Castello**, with its powerful 11th-century tower. It also has one of the most startling palaces in Vicenza: the **Palazzo Breganze**, designed by Palladio and partly built by his pupil Scamozzi before the very monumentality of the design defeated him, leaving only two bays framed by three Corinthian columns the size of sequoias. Scamozzi also built the less exciting **Palazzo Bonin Longare** at No.13, in 1602, after his master's designs; the best part is the inner courtyard.

Contrà Vescovado begins by Palazzo Breganze and leads to the Gothic **Duomo**, its façade decorated with a diamond pattern that was carefully pieced together after the war. The side door on Contrà Lampertico is one of Palladio's few attempts at sacred architecture in Vicenza; he also designed the dome atop Lorenzo da Bologna's graceful tribune of 1482. Of the art, the most notable piece is a polyptych by Lorenzo Veneziano painted in 1356, in the fifth chapel on the right. Excavations have revealed remains of the Duomo's 8th-century ancestor, a stretch of Roman road in the crypt and, out in the square, a **cryptoportico**, a U-shaped subterranean passage under what was once a very large 1st-century AD house.

Opposite the Duomo, slip into the courtyard of the neoclassical Bishop's Palace to see the exquisite **Zeno Loggia** (1494) by Bernardino da Milano. Down Contrà Proti, turn at Via Pigafetta for the delightful Gothic **Casa Pigafetta** (1444), birthplace of Antonio Pigafetta, a local aristocrat who just happened to be in Spain in 1519 when Magellan was setting out on his world tour. Pigafetta went along and, unlike Magellan, survived; and wrote the definitive account of the voyage three years later. His motto '*Il n'est rose sans espine*' is inscribed on either side of the door. Beyond, to the left, lies the Piazza dei Signori.

Piazza dei Signori

This kingly square is the heart and soul of Vicenza, its public forum from Roman times to this day. In the 1540s the Vicentines decided that the piazza's crumbling Gothic Palazzo della Ragione no longer matched their new Renaissance-humanist aspirations and decided to give it a facelift. Having rejected new designs proposed by such luminaries as Sansovino and Giulio Romano, they surprisingly hired the still relatively unknown Palladio to give it a new look in 1549. It was his first big break, and Vicenza would never be the same. The marble loggias he added to the building, ever after known as the **Basilica** ('hall of justice', as in Latin), were to be his only work in stone in the Veneto and would painstakingly remain a work in progress for decades, showcasing Palladio's talents in the heart of his adopted city throughout his life – it was only completed in 1619. The result perfectly fulfils its aims, with two tiers of rounded arches interspersed with Doric and Ionic columns that give an appearance of Roman regularity, although Palladio had to vary the size of the arches to compensate for the irregularities in the trapezoidal structure. The great copper keel of a roof (rebuilt after the war, when it caught fire and collapsed) is concealed behind a balustrade lined with the life-size classical statues that would become a hallmark of Palladio's work; stare at them long enough and the urge to shoot them off like ducks in a penny arcade becomes almost irresistible.

Basilica
open Tues–Sun 9–1 and 3–7; adm

To see what Palladio was disguising, go behind the Basilica to **Piazza delle Erbe**, home to Vicenza's daily food and produce market, and its pleasant-sounding **Torre del Tormento**, the medieval prison. In the adjacent *piazzetta* stands a statue of Palladio, contemplating the basilica with a finger on his chin, as if trying to figure out what he forgot. The truth is it was his favourite work, and he didn't mind saying so himself.

The Basilica shares Piazza dei Signori with two **columns**, as in Piazzetta San Marco in Venice, one topped with the Redeemer (1640) and the other with St Mark's lion (1473), and the needle-like **Torre di Piazza** (or Torre Bissara, after the barons who raised it in the 12th century); in the 14th century the civic authorities tamed it with a mechanical clock and in 1444 added its headdress. Opposite, the 16th-century **Monte di Pietà**, built in two sections, was frescoed in the 1900s with Liberty-style pin-up girls, some of whom still faintly survive. Next to this stands Palladio's **Loggia del Capitaniato**, now the seat of the town council, which was built to celebrate the great victory at Lepanto in 1571; the Contrà del Monte façade is decorated with reliefs of trophies and statues of War (symbolized by Venice) and Peace (Vicenza). If its grand brick columns and arches seem confined in too narrow a space, it's because the loggia was meant to extend over several more bays; the building boom that made Palladio's fortune ended in the late 1560s, leaving most of his designs incomplete. Inside, ask to see the Camera Bernarda, with frescoes transferred from Villa Porto at Torri di Quartesolo.

09 The Veneto | Vicenza

South of the Retrone

From Piazza dei Signori, Via San Michele leads to the Retrone, one of Vicenza's two rivers, spanned here by the **Ponte San Michele** (1620). There are lovely views of the Retrone lapping the houses and, on the opposite bank, the Oratorio di San Nicola. This is remarkable for one of the creepiest altarpieces in Italy, *La Trinità* by the 17th-century Vicentine painter Francesco Maffei, whose feverish brush infected the oratorio's walls as well with the assistance of Giulio Caprioni.

Oratorio di San Nicola
t 0444 543 812; open for concerts and services only

Vicenza's Roman theatre, the 1st-century AD Teatro di Berga, was studied by Palladio but dismantled in the 1700s. Traces of it remain just south of S. Nicola, in and around picturesque **Piazzola Gualdi**. In Contrà Del Guanto, the octagonal Oratorio di Santa Chiara e San Bernardino (1451) is covered with a handsome wooden ceiling and has paintings by Giulio Carpioni.

Oratorio di Santa Chiara e San Bernardino
open summer Mon–Fri 6–8 and 5.30–7, Sat 6–8 and 3.30–5.30; winter Mon–Fri 6–8, Sat 7–8 and 3.30–5.30

Corso Palladio, Contrà Porti and Contrà Riale

Returning to the Piazza dei Signori, step behind the Loggia dei Capitaniato to join **Corso Palladio**, the *decumanus* of ancient *Vicetia* and 'the most elegant street in Europe, not counting the Grand Canal in incomparable Venice'. This famous axis is lined with palaces, including, just to your right, Vincenzo Scamozzi's masterpiece, the **Palazzo Trissino**, with its Ionic portico and superb courtyard (begun in 1592, now the Municipio). A few doors down is the lovely late Gothic **Palazzo Da Schio** (1470s).

Palladio himself is only dubiously linked to a couple of buildings on the street named after him; to find his work, turn up elegant **Contrà Porti** – the Roman *cardo*. One of his earlier works, **Palazzo Iseppo Da Porto** (1552) at No.21, is influenced by Raphael and contains frescoes by Giambattista Tiepolo. Next door, the sombre Gothic **Palazzo Porto-Colleoni** (No.19) hides an internal garden courtyard and an airy asymmetrical loggia; next to it, the late Gothic **Palazzo Porto-Breganze** (No.17) has a beautiful door added in 1481 and a precious mullioned window, the only one in Vicenza with Venetian reversed arches.

While building the Palazzo Porto-Festa, Palladio impressed the plutocrat Marc'Antonio Thiene, who hired him to redo his vast medieval Palazzo Thiene (now the Banca Popolare), a beauty treatment designed to create the most imposing residence in all Vicenza, although the project, like so many of Palladio's, was never completed. The Contrà Porti side of Palazzo Thiene is a fine work by Lorenzo da Bologna; around the corner is Palladio's part which, with its weighty sculpted windows, rustication and Mannerist classicizing, is his homage to Giulio Romano; Lord Burlington declared that it was the most beautiful building in the world.

Palazzo Thiene
t 0444 542 131; open by appt only

Certain parts of the interior retain the original and rather magnificent decoration.

Opposite, on the corner of Contrà Riale, **Palazzo Barbaran-da Porto** was built from scratch by Palladio in 1570 and now holds the Museo Palladiano. Unlike the buildings he merely dressed in new clothes, the Palazzo Barbaran-da Porto is as symmetrical as pie, with two orders on the façade, Ionic on the ground level and Corinthian on the *piano nobile*; some of the frescoes inside are by Zelotti.

Continue down quiet Contrà Riale, where the convent of San Giacomo (1652) is now the Bertoliana Civic Library, repository of 400,000 volumes, 6,000 manuscripts and rare incunabula dating from the 13th to the 19th century, including Francesco Colonna's novel *Hypnerotaumachia Polifilo*, published in 1499 by the famous Venetian press of Aldus. Widely read in Renaissance Vicenza, the *Hypnerotaumachia* was the first antiquity-worshipping hodgepodge fantasy, full of nostalgia for ancient architecture, hieroglyphs and pagan sacrifices; a number of architects based designs on the imaginary buildings in its woodcuts. Have a look down Stradella San Giacomo, with its view of a graceful 18th-century loggetta set amid ivy and a magnolia. Contrà Riale gives onto lively Corso Forgazzaro, where at No.16 Palladio's **Palazzo Valmarana-Braga** (begun in 1566) is distinguished by gigantic pilasters crowned by an attic, framed by two armoured telamones in high relief, symbolically 'imprisoned' and specially designed to be seen in perspective in the narrow street.

Santa Corona, Santo Stefano and Pietro Longhi

In lower Corso Palladio, a square opens by the early Gothic church of Santa Corona, built by the Dominicans in the 1260s to entice the many locals who strayed into the Paterene heresy back to the Catholic fold. In later centuries it was adorned with beautiful art, especially Veronese's *Adoration of the Magi* (1573), the three kings dressed in gorgeous reds and yellows; and Giovanni Bellini's *Baptism of Christ* (1502), a lovely example of his late style set in a rugged, rather un-Venetian landscape. The high altar (1670) is a massive bloom of inlaid marble and mother-of-pearl; the wooden choir stalls (1482–9) are lovely; and the altarpiece of the rococo Cappella Thiene just to the right of the high altar has Giovanni Battista Pittoni's masterpiece *SS Peter and Paul and Pius V Adoring Mary*. Palladio designed the Valmarana Chapel; note how the plan and the front view refer to his Redentore in Venice.

Alongside the church, the Museo Naturalistico Archeologico contains natural history exhibits on the region, as well as Lombard relics, fine Roman mosaics and Vicenza's oldest goldwork – a lamina embossed with Palaeoveneti warriors, *c.* 1500 BC.

Museo Palladiano
t 0444 323 014;
www.cisapalladio.org;
open Mar–Dec Tues–
Sun 10–6; Jan–Feb
Sat–Sun 12–6; other
times by request

Bertoliana Civic Library
www.biblioteca
bertoliana.it;
open Mon–Fri 8–7,
Sat 8–12.30

Palazzo Valmarana-Braga
open Mon–Fri 8–11,
Sat 8–12.30

Santa Corona
open daily 8.30–12
and 2.30–6.30

Museo Naturalistico Archeologico
t 0444 320 440;
open Tues–Sun 9–5,
July–Aug 9–7; adm

Palazzo Leoni Montanari
open Tues–Sun 10–6; adm

The nearby **Palazzo Leoni Montanari**, built 1676–94 (now the Banco Ambrosiano), is one of Vicenza's few Baroque palaces and contains, in the recently restored Sala dell'Antica Roma, an ensemble of 14 paintings by Venetian genre master Pietro Longhi and his school. From San Corona, take Contrà S. Stefano to the Baroque **Santo Stefano** to see one of Palma il Vecchio's most beautiful paintings, *Madonna with SS George and Lucy and Musical Angel*.

Santo Stefano
open Mon–Fri 8.45–10 and 5–6.30, Sat 8.45–10

Palazzo Chiericati: the Pinacoteca

In Piazza Matteotti, at the north end of the Corso, Palladio designed his masterful Palazzo Chiericati (*see* plan opposite), built in 1550 and finished only in 1670. For once not constricted by a narrow street, he created the lightest and airiest palace of the century, extending the double loggias of his villas into a double colonnade of two different orders, playing with voids and solids; the rooms may fulfil his rules on harmonic proportions, but are topsy-turvy compared with previous palaces, running parallel to the façade.

Pinacoteca
open Tues–Sun 10–6, till 7 July and Aug; adm

Since 1855, when a new wing was added, Palazzo Chiericati has been home to the *comune*'s **Pinacoteca**. The ground floor, containing a collection of contemporary Italian works (Carrà, De Pisis, Guidi, Lincini, Maccari, Oppi, Tancredi), retains its original stuccoes and frescoes, including a hilarious ceiling by Domenico Brusasorci, who took it upon himself to portray the sun god and his steeds in the position earthlings would see them at noon – all bums and bellies. The other paintings are in chronological order, with the oldest works in the 19th-century wing: there's a polyptych by Paolo Veneziano, a portrait of Pico della Mirandola by a follower of Bellini, a Calvary by Hans Memling from a triptych, and works by the four top Vicentine painters of the *quattrocento*: Bartolomeo Montagna, Giovanni Buonconsiglio, Marcello Fogolino and Giovanni Speranza; Fogolino's *St Francis Receiving the Stigmata* incorporates another fine view of Vicenza.

The collection continues in the Palladian wing, with one of Bartolomeo Montagna's finest works, the *Madonna in Trono* with saints, and others by Cima da Conegliano and Veronese. The Flemish section includes Van Dyck's *Four Ages of Man* and Jan 'Velvet' Brueghel the Elder's *Madonna*. From the 17th century, there's the irrepressible Francesco Maffei (*Glorification of the Inquisitor Alvise Foscarini*) and Giulio Caprioni, along with Pietro and Marco Liberi and Francesco di Cairo; from the 18th century, Giambattista Piazzetta's *St Francis in Ecstasy*, landscapes by Marco Ricci, paintings by Francesco and Giambattista Pittoni, and two excellent Tiepolos (*Immacolata* and *Time Discovers Truth*) plus other paintings by his son Giandomenico.

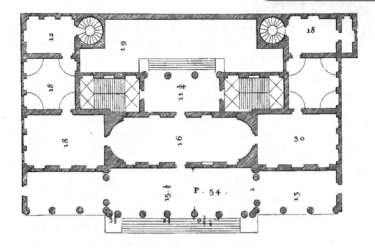

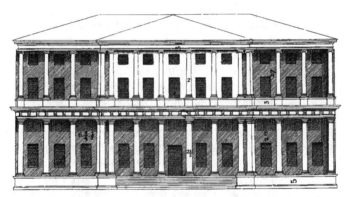

from Palladio's *Four Books of Architecture*

Piazza Matteotti is the showcase for two more fine buildings: the **Palazzetto Giacomazzi-Trevisan**, the only Rococo venture in this *palazzo*-ridden city, and **Palazzo Valmarana-Trento** (1718), a masterpiece by Francesco Muttoni, who kept up a regular correspondence with Lord Burlington to help him further Palladianism in England. Stretching along the north end of Piazza Matteotti, the **Palazzo del Territorio** began as a castle in the 13th century, and expanded to engulf the Teatro Olimpico.

Teatro Olimpico

Teatro Olimpico
t 0444 222 800; open Tues–Sun 10–6, till 7 July–Aug; adm

This was Palladio's swansong, one of the most original works of the Italian Renaissance, as well as the oldest operational indoor theatre in the world (1580). Palladio himself was a member of the group of 25 literati, artists and dilettantes who founded the high-minded 'Olympic Academy' in 1555. The immediate inspiration for the Olimpico was a temporary wooden theatre that Palladio erected in the Basilica in 1561 for an opera, *L'Amor costante*, by Alessandro Piccolomini, and a recital of his patron Giangiorgio Trissino's *Sofonisba* – monochrome frescoes in the Antiodeo show scenes from both works and document the ideas going through Palladio's mind. The architect's triumphant return to Vicenza from Venice in 1579 may have been the impetus to construct a permanent setting for the academy's plays and lectures, on the site of an old prison donated by the *comune*. For the seating and stage, Palladio went back to his Vitruvius and the Roman works he had seen during his sojourns: his cavea has 13 rows of seats arranged in a semi-ellipse, topped by a Corinthian colonnade and a balustrade decorated with statues of members of the Academy.

Palladio died as the outer walls were going up, and the project was inherited by Vincenzo Scamozzi, who designed the rooms for academy use – the Odeo and Antiodeo – and, disregarding Palladio's plans for a stage screen with a triumphal arch and classical statues, built a stucco and wood stage set of a square and streets radiating out in flawless, fake perspective, representing Thebes, for the theatre's inaugural production in 1585, Sophocles' *Oedipus Rex*. But here Thebes has become a pure ideal, a Renaissance dream city, so perfect that no one ever thought to change the set, or bothered later, as the Council of Trent banned theatrical representations soon afterwards. Visitors over the centuries have adored it; William Beckford leapt on stage in 1780 and recited Aeschylus, feeling that he had at last 'penetrated into a real and perfect monument of antiquity'. Another perfect and memorable moment occurred in 1987 during a visit by the Queen Mother, when her bodyguard fell off the stage and penetrated the orchestra pit. From April to June you can catch a series of classical and jazz concerts, and in September it hosts a classical theatre season; book early as tickets sell very fast.

Over the Bacchiglione

Behind the theatre, Ponte degli Angeli crosses over the Bacchiglione to Piazza XX Settembre, site of **Palazzo Angaran** (1480), Vicenza's finest pre-Palladian Renaissance palace; the beautiful ornate late Gothic **Palazzo Regaù** stands nearby, at the beginning of Contrà XX Settembre. This neighbourhood, an old craftsmen's district, is locally known as the 'Republic of San Zulian': on Contrà Sant'Andrea, the **Corte dei Roda** is a traditional complex of artisans' houses and courtyards. Just to the right of the Ponte degli Angeli, Contrà San Pietro leads to San Pietro, the church of a Benedictine monastery from the Carolingian era, rebuilt in the

San Pietro
*t 0444 514 443;
visits on request*

Renaissance. The interior is a colourful gallery of late 16th-century works by the Maganza family of Vicenza, and there's a beautifully decorated cloister of 1427.

From Palazzo Angaran, take Contrà Santa Lucia to Porta Santa Lucia (1369) and turn left for the 1680 church of **Santa Maria Aracœli**, built on a design by the great Baroque genius Guarino Guarini of Turin. The hyper-ornate high altar (1696) explodes around a painting on that favourite Renaissance subject linking Christianity to classical Rome, The Triburtine Sibyl showing the Virgin and Child to Octavian, attributed to Pietro Liberi. Behind the church, Vicenza's prettiest public garden, the **Parco Querini**, is planted with pines and cedars of Lebanon; a statue-lined lane cuts through the lawns to a round island with the landscape designer Antonio Piovene's elegant Ionic temple (1820).

Santa Maria Aracœli
open Sat 10–12 and 3–6

Outside the Historic Centre

North of the Duomo and Corso Palladio, **Corso Fogazzaro** is an ancient, atmospheric street where the porticoes have richly carved Gothic capitals and Vicenza holds a very popular antiques fair in spring and autumn. Here the Franciscan church of **San Lorenzo** (1280) has a grand façade and lovely marble portal, with a lunette of the *Madonna with Child and Saints* by Andriolo de Santi (1334). The interior is filled with sumptuous altars, frescoes and paintings dedicated by the noble families of Vicenza, notably the Pojana altar of 1474 in the right transept, and the chapel just left of the high altar, with a Beheading of St Paul by Bartolomeo Montagna. The 15th-century cloister is charming, and outside the apse you can see bits of Corso Fogazzaro's Roman predecessor. Further on, **Chiesa del Carmine**, a Gothic church with a neo-Gothic façade, is decorated throughout with 15th-century bas-reliefs brought over from another church and altars by Veronese and Jacopo Bassano.

Chiesa del Carmine
open daily 8–12 and 4–7

Beyond the Carmine, Contrà di Porta Santa Croce continues towards the gate of the same name, built during the Scaliger tenure. Following along Contrà Mure Corpus Domini, you come to the area where Alberto della Scala commissioned 'architect Giovanni' to lay out the walled district of **Porta Nuova**, a grid that had broad green spaces inside the blocks, defended by a little fort or **Rocchetta** (1365). **San Rocco** (1530) on Contrà Mure Corpus Domini was, like the Duomo, designed by Lorenzo da Bologna. The walls and the altar are adorned with paintings by Giambattista Zelotti and Alessandro Maganza; don't miss the romantic cloister.

South, just outside Piazza Castello, the English-style **Giardino Salvi** contains a pair of loggias, one Palladian and one by Longhena (1649), reflected in the Seriola. Vicenza's oldest church, **SS. Felice e Fortunato** is a ten-minute walk from here along Corso SS. Felice e Fortunato; built as a simple hall just after Constantine made

Giardino Salvi
open daily 7.30–8pm

SS. Felice e Fortunato
open Mon–Sat 9–12 and 3.30–6.30

09 The Veneto | Vicenza

Christianity the religion of the empire, it was remodelled in 398 with three naves and the Chapel of the Martyrium di Santa Maria Materdomini. Charlemagne visited the Benedictine monastery attached to the church; it was badly damaged by the Hungarians in 899 and rebuilt in the 1160s, with a battlemented bell tower and spire. Over the course of the 20th century, the church was un-restored as much as possible to its 4th-century appearance, revealing the original mosaics in the right aisle and the martyrium. The altarpiece, *St Valentine Healing the Sick* by Alessandro Maganza (1585), is the centre of the local celebrations on 14 February.

Tourist Information in Vicenza

Get hold of a Museum Card at the **tourist office**; it's valid for three days and provides discounted access to Vicenza's museums and *palazzi*.

Where to Stay in Vicenza

(i) Vicenza ›
Piazza Matteotti 12, also Piazza dei Signori, t 0444 320 854, www.vicenzae.org; open Mon–Sat 9–6; Signori office until 6.30

Vicenza ✉ 36100

Vicenza itself has a pretty limited selection of hotels.

****Hotel de la Ville**, Viale Verona 12, t 0444 549 049, *www.boscolo hotels.com* (€€€€). The top hotel in town. Part of the respected Boscolo chain, with a fine restaurant and richly appointed rooms and suites.

****Campo Marzo**, Viale Roma 21, t 0444 545 700, *www.hotelcampo marzio.com* (€€€). Near the railway station, providing modern, comfortable rooms, with air-conditioning, and a garage.

***Cristina**, Corso Santi Felice e Fortunato 32, t 0444 323 751, *hotel. cristina@keycomm.it* (€€). For comfort in a central location; parking.

Due Mori, Contrà do Rode 26 (near the Piazza dei Signori), t 0444 321 886, *www.hotelduemori.com* (€). On a quiet street near Piazza dei Signori, a charming, beautifully furnished bargain – with good disabled facilities and fans in every room.

Eating Out in Vicenza

This is *polenta* and *baccalà* (salt cod) country, whose hearty and filling fare is not the most subtle on the stomach. But the locals beg to differ: their *baccalà alla vicentina* is made of top-quality cod, soaked for 36 hours, sprinkled with cheese and browned in a mix of butter, oil, anchovies and onions, and seasoned with parsley, pepper and milk.

A favourite way to eat *polenta* is sliced and grilled, accompanied with *sopressa* sausage from Valli del Pasubio and Recoaro, or pigeon roasted on embers. Other specialities include potato gnocchi made with cinnamon and raisins, and *bigoli con l'arna*, fat spaghetti with duck sauce, delicious with a glass of red Tocai. Montecchio Maggiore is known for its *mostarda*, a spicy condiment of fruit with mustard.

Nuovo Cinzia & Valerio, Piazzetta Porta Padova, t 0444 505 213 (€€€). For perfectly prepared seafood: *tagliatelle* with salmon, cuttlefish risotto or grilled sole, followed by home-made ice cream and crisp biscuits. *Closed Sun eve, Mon, Aug.*

Principe, Via S. Caboto 16, t 0444 675 131, *hotelprincipe@keycomm.it* (restaurant €€€, hotel €€). A great restaurant and hotel just east of Montecchio Maggiore in Arzignano: a top, French-trained chef prepares superb and imaginative food, accompanied by a selection of home-made breads, a chariot of French cheeses and delightful pastries. *Restaurant closed 10 days in Jan, 10 days in Aug, Sat lunch and Sun; booking obligatory.*

Antica Trattoria Tre Visi, Corso Palladio 25, t 0444 324 868 (€€). A 15th-century palace that was converted into an inn some 200 years ago. With its fireplace and rustic fittings, it is a charming place to enjoy good, high-quality Veneto cooking and home-made pasta dishes. *Closed Sun eve, Mon and July.*

Da Biasio 1848, Via X Giugno 172, t 0444 323 363 (€€). On the way to or from Monte Berico, the perfect place to rest a while. Eat such delicacies as sole spring rolls with an orange salad and walnut cream, followed by sea bass with artichokes or sturgeon with black truffle. *Closed Mon and Sat lunch.*

Antica Casa della Malvasia, Contrà delle Morette 5, near Piazza dei Signori, t 0444 543 704 (€). Lively and deservedly popular, with young,

friendly staff and cheap but delicious food and wine.

Righetti, Piazza Duomo, t 0444 543 135 (€). Extremely busy and full of character – a far cry from a typical self-service – with meat and fish cooked to order on a charcoal grill. *Closed Sat and Sun.*

Vecchia Guardia, Contrà Pescherie Vecchie 11, t 0444 321 231 (€). Located near Piazza dell'Erbe, for pizza and straight-forward meals. *Closed Thurs.*

Antica Offelleria della Meneghi, Contrà Cavour 18. If you need something sweet and stylish, Vicenza has two historic *pasticcerie* near the Basilica: this one, and Sorarù, Piazzetta Palladio 17.

South of Vicenza

Monte Berico, Villa Valmarana and La Rotonda

Just to the south of the city rises Vicenza's holy hill, Monte Berico. Buses make the ascent approximately every half-hour from the bus station, or you can walk up like a good pilgrim by way of Viale Eretenio, running parallel to the Retrone, stopping along the way to look at No.12, the elegant **Palazzo Civena-Trissino** (now the Eretenia Nursing Home), one of Palladio's earliest works (1540), showing the influence of Bramante and Raphael and an interest in their effects of *chiaroscuro* that would become a theme in his later work. Nearby, in Via delle Grazie, the church of **Santa Maria delle Grazie**, rebuilt 1595, contains paintings by Maganza, De Pieri, Marinali and Jacopo and Leandro da Bassano.

At the end of Via Eretenio, turn left in Viale X Giugno and head up through the half-mile-long covered walkway or **Portici**, built in the 18th century to shelter pilgrims, with superb views along the way over the city and the Villa Rotonda, down in the 'Little Valley of Silence'. The Baroque **Basilica di Monte Berico** that crowns the hill commemorates two apparitions of the Virgin in 1428, announcing the end of a plague that devastated Vicenza. It still does a brisk pilgrim trade, its polished, candle-flickering interior presided over by the painted marble statue of the Madonna of Monte Berico, attributed to Antonino da Venezia; Vicenza's goldsmiths have crafted donations by the faithful into her fabulous necklace and a gold crown weighing eight pounds. The church possesses two first-class paintings: *La Pietà* by Bartolomeo Montagna, hanging near the altar, and the *Supper of St Gregory the Great* by Veronese, appropriately hung in the refectory (down the steps to the left), and carefully pieced together on Emperor Franz Joseph's orders

Santa Maria delle Grazie
open Mon–Sat 9–11.30, also Thurs 3–6

Basilica di Monte Berico
open summer Mon–Sat 6.15–12.30 and 2.30–6, Sun 6.15am–7pm; winter 6–12.30 and 2.30–6, weekends 6am–7pm

after Austrian soldiers shredded it with their bayonets during the battle of Monte Berico (10 June 1848), quashing Vicenza's popular revolt that had begun three months earlier. Beyond the church, a pretty walk leads to Giovanni Antonio Selva's 18th-century **Villa Guiccioli**, the people's centre of resistance during the Battle of Monte Berico. Now home to the **Museo del Risorgimento e della Resistanza** it houses documents on the city's history to 1945; the large garden that surrounds it is now a romantic public park.

Museo del Risorgimento e della Resistanza
open Tues–Sun 9–1 and 2.15–5, July and Aug 9–7; adm

Walk back down the Portici as far as Via M. D'Azeglio (alternatively, from the centre of Vicenza take AIM bus no.8 or 13); from here the narrow Stradella S. Bastian leads to the **Villa Valmarana**, nicknamed 'dei Nani' after the stone dwarfs on the wall, arty ancestors of the modern garden gnome. The villa's main attraction, however, is its sumptuous decoration by the Tiepoli, father and son, in frameworks painted by Mengozzi Colonna, master of illusionary architectural perspectives. Giambattista based his frescoes on *The Iliad*, *Orlando Furioso*, *The Aeneid* and Tasso's *Jerusalem Delivered*, concentrating on the scenes where the heroes face the hard choice between duty and love. Duty, of course, always wins out, but Tiepolo's heart is on the side of the nearly sacrificed Iphigenia and the forlorn Angelica, Dido and Armida. Son Giandomenico contributed the ceiling and a landscape in the main villa, and painted his masterpiece in the *Foresteria* (guesthouse): intimate, gently ironical scenes of rural life that seem to undermine his father's Grand Manner right under his nose.

Villa Valmarana
open Tues–Sun 10–12 and 3–6; adm exp

From there, a further five-minute walk along the Stradella Valmarana brings you to the celebrated Villa Almerico-Capra, better known as **La Rotonda**, designed by Palladio for a Monsignor Almerico in 1567 and completed after his death by the faithful Scamozzi. Unlike Palladio's other villas which, under their classical skins, were functional farmhouses, the Villa Rotonda was built for sheer delight, for the Monsignor's garden parties and musical evenings and, although no one knew it at the time, as the perfect setting for Joseph Losey's film *Don Giovanni*. One of the main interests of the Accademia Olimpica was mathematics, and La Rotonda is, if anything, an exercise in geometry – a circle in a cube, complemented by four symmetrical porches: its location is so perfect that one critic wrote that Palladio planned the hill before the villa. The round central hall has stucco decorations and rather overblown frescoes by Alessandro Maganza and Ludovico Dorigny; the four arms contain four identical suites of rooms. Alexander Pope, however, thought it really rather ridiculous:

La Rotonda
gardens open mid-Mar–mid-Nov Tues–Sun 10–12 and 3–6; adm; interior open Wed only, same times; adm exp

> 'tis very fine,
> But where d'ye sleep, or where d'ye dine?
> I find by all you have been telling
> That 'tis a house, but not a dwelling.

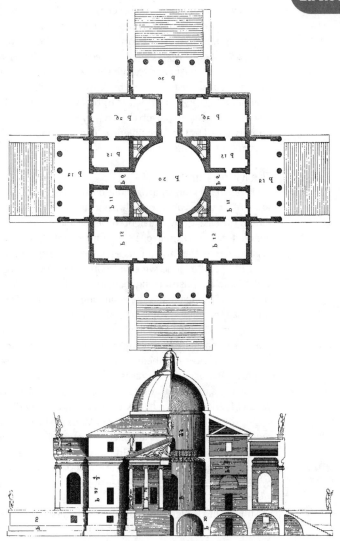

from Palladio's *Four Books of Architecture*

There are two historic churches in the same area, southwest of Vicenza, on the route of AIM bus no.4 (although check at the tourist office for opening hours before setting out). The first, simple single-naved Franciscan **San Giorgio in Gogna** (982) is immersed in the greenery of Monte Berico. It was far enough from the city to be the site of the *lazzaretto* or fever hospital, and to be used for executions by the Austrians. It has only one painting,

The Apparitions of the Virgin to Vincenza Pasini (1620) by Alessandro Maganza, which has a view of Vicenza at the time, as seen from the exact place where San Giorgio stands. The same buses pass by the **Abbey of Sant'Agostino**, 5km southwest of Vicenza (near the Vicenza West *autostrada* exit). Founded by the Lombards in the 7th century, rebuilt in 1357 and restored in 1942 by the parish priest, the church has a façade of tufa and bricks, with an arched portal. The interior has 14th-century frescoes by the Veneto and Emilian schools and a golden polyptych (1404) by Battista da Vicenza, commissioned by Ludovico Chiericati to commemorate Vicenza's peaceful surrender to Venice.

Abbey of Sant'Agostino
t 0444 569 393; open Sat and hols 9–12 and 4–7; other times by request

The Monti Berici

With so many grander attractions on all sides, this clump of hills south of Vicenza is undeservedly neglected. Like Padua's Euganean Hills to the east, the Monti Berici have volcanic origins under a hundred-million-year-old pile of marine sediment, and like the Euganean Hills, they also produce good wines, most famously a red Tocai, the 'pearl' of Berici wines, introduced by a local carpenter drafted into the Austro-Hungarian army in the time of Maria Theresa. La Rotonda marks the beginning of the 78km Colli Berici wine road that ends up at Montecchio Maggiore (*see* p.237).

Although wild and lonely in places, the Monti Berici are in certain spots as immaculate as Tuscany. One such place is **Brendola** (12km southwest of Vicenza) where the historic centre hangs over an amphitheatre of garden terraces and the plain of San Valentino. Guarded by a ruined 11th-century bishops' citadel, the **Rocca dei Vescovi**, Brendola's town hall, occupies a 15th-century villa with a loggia. The 15th-century church, **Santa Maria dei Revese**, has a charming façade formed like a shell, and other villas look on to the prettiest square, **Piazzetta del Vicariato**. Others line the road south towards Lonigo, most theatrically the **Villa Da Porto** (or La Favorita) by Francesco Muttoni (1714), a Palladian revival showpiece located just north of Sarego.

Villa Da Porto
t 0444 623 253; open daily by appointment

In the Veneto **Lonigo** is synonymous with horses and its Horse Fair, held every year since 1486 on 25 March, while its racetrack is used for racing brakeless motorcycles, which seems to be just as foolhardy as it sounds. Originally a possession of the Scaligers of Verona, Lonigo became the stamping ground of one of Venice's noblest families, the Pisani, after 1402. Along the porticoed streets and squares, look for the **Palazzo Pisani** by Sammicheli (1560; now the town hall) and the princely **Villa Giovanelli** with a scenic entrance (now a monastery). Strikingly set on a hill just above Lonigo is Vincenzo Scamozzi's loveliest work, the **Rocca Pisana** of 1576, where he out-Palladios Palladio by perfecting the geometry of La Rotonda: the Rocca has a similar central plan and symmetrical

Rocca Pisana
t 0444 831 104; open April–early Nov by request; groups only

façades (the main entrance distinguished by an Ionic porch), but omits all the stuccoes and frescoes that gild Palladio's lily; note how the Venetian windows were especially designed to frame the spectacular views. Nearby, the Sanctuary of the Madonna dei Miracoli has a charming shell-shaped façade sculpted in the soft stone quarried from the surrounding hills. Its miraculous Madonna has accumulated an impressive collection of *ex votos* dating back to the 15th century, now in an adjacent museum.

Sanctuary of the Madonna dei Miracoli
t 0444 830 502; open by request only

East of Lonigo stretches the **Val Liona**, the largest valley in the Monti Berici, known for its rich deposits of *nummulites* (Eocene fossils). The woods are dotted with medieval mills, stone quarries and the stone houses of stonecutters as well as more villas. **Sossano** to the south is the place to try Berico-Euganean *prosciutto*, while just west in Orgiano Francesco Muttoni's centrally designed **Villa Fracanzan-Piovene** (1710) was one of the first examples of the Palladian revival in the Veneto and has lovely grounds. Unlike most, the family still maintains the villa's original vocation: an extensive collection of antique ploughs, tractors and other agricultural machines fills its Museo della Civiltà Contadina, and the kitchen has all of its original fittings.

Museo della Civiltà Contadina
t 0444 874 589; guided tours Sun and hols by request; adm exp

Further south, **Poiana Maggiore**, named after the family that once owned it, has three of their villas all clustered together, most importantly Palladio's Villa Pojana (1550) with a façade and five round windows inspired by Serlio. The villa featured in his *Quattro Libri* although, like most of his illustrations, it was never completed to the design. **Noventa Vicentina** (from *Nova Entia*, a Benedictine foundation) has for its town hall the **Villa Barbarigo** (1588), with a double portico front, four pointy obelisks on the cornice and *barchesse* decorated with Tuscan porticoes; you can pop in to see the frescoes on weekday mornings, although the best art is nearby in the **Duomo** (1856): Giambattista Tiepolo's luminous *SS Roch and Sebastian*.

Villa Pojana
Via Castello 41

Two other charming villas await just north in **Agugliaro**. Palladio's recently restored Villa Saraceno (1549–68) on Via Finale was another one that featured in his writings, although one of the *barchesse* was never completed; the frescoes inside are by the school of Veronese. Just up the road you can find the same family's former residence, the elegant **Palazzo delle Trombe** with its dovecote attributed to Michele Sammicheli.

Villa Saraceno
t 0444 891 371, www.landmarktrust.org.uk; open Tues–Sun 9–12 and 2–4; owned by the Landmark Trust

North, in the heart of the hills on the ridge called the Riviera Berica, **Barbarano-Vicentino** is the centre of the DOC Colli Berici growing region and hosts a lively wine festival in September. Its Gothic **Palazzo dei Vicari** has a time-clobbered façade covered like a collage with coats of arms. From Barbarano you can visit the solitary **Scudelletta Gorge**, dominated by the church of **San Giovanni in Monte**, or follow the Riviera Berica to **Nanto**, famous

Where to Stay and Eat South of Vicenza

(★) Agriturismo
Palazzetto Ardi >>

Monte Berico ✉ 36100

San Raffaele, Viale X Giugno 10 (through an arch in the Portici), **t** 0444 545 767, *www.albergosanraffaele.it* (€). Situated up on the slopes of Monte Berico: good value, as well as tranquillity and great views.

Lonigo ✉ 36045

La Peca, Via Principe Giovanelli 2, **t** 0444 830 214 (€€€€). Folk drive down from Vicenza and further afield to eat at this ultramodern establishment, owned and run by two young but gifted brother-chefs. You know you're in good hands as soon as you sit down and a basket full of warm home-made bread appears. Innovative recipes, with more than a passing nod at tradition. *Closed Sun eve and Mon,* part of Jan and Aug and Sun lunch also in summer; booking obligatory.

Gambellara ✉ 36053

Agriturismo Palazzetto Ardi, Via Ciron 4, **t** 0444 440 450, *www.palazzetto ardi.com* (€€€). Carlo and Michela are full of enthusiasm for their *agriturismo* – so much so that they named their wine, a wonderful Bordolese, 'Entusiasmo'. Expect cosy rooms, warm hospitality and home-cooked meals at the weekend. You can buy apples and *sopressa* (home-made salami) to take home.

Costozza di Longare ✉ 36023

Taverna Aeolia, Piazza da Schio 1, **t** 0444 555 036 (€€). You can dine, and dine well, in this 16th-century villa frescoed by Zelotti, where the menu changes monthly; their *baccalà alla vicentina* is famous. *Closed Tues, and some of Nov.*

for olive oil, truffles and *nantopietra*, the soft Vicenza stone prized by sculptors. **Lumignano**, in the centre of a group of Palaeolithic caves, is celebrated for its delicate *bisi* (peas).

Returning towards Vicenza, **Costozza di Longare** was a favourite spot for summer villas, and with good reason: its name comes from its *covoli* (caves), which maintain a constant temperature of 13°C, a natural place to keep 'custodia' wines in the Middle Ages, but also to provide air-conditioning to the villas, Renaissance-style. An ingenious system of air ducts links the cellars and rooms of the 17th-century **Villa Trento Carli**; the **Villa Aeolia** (now a restaurant, see above), and the **Villa da Schio**, with a vast Italian garden and stone dwarfs. The Counts da Schio still use their cellars to store wine. Costozza's other caves were the home of the first mushroom-growing business in Italy, and they still sprout *funghi* today.

Villa Trento Carli
t 0444 510 499; guided tours April–Oct, Sun 3–6; adm

Villa da Schio
t 0444 555 032; park and cellars open Tues–Sun 10–6; adm exp

North and West of Vicenza

Cricoli to Montecchio Precalcino

Still privately owned, the **Villa Trissino** where Giangiorgio Trissino met and christened Palladio still stands in **Cricoli**, just outside Vicenza on the Montecchio Precalcino road. Originally a little family castle, Trissino had the idea in 1537 to remodel it as the perfect setting for his 'Accademia Trissiniana', where all the young noblemen of Vicenza came to study from dawn to dusk under a strict regime based on Platonic rules, seeking to become 'universal men'. Moral rectitude and physical cleanliness were deemed essential to the study of Greek and Latin, which Trissino believed would lead his pupils to a mastery of Italian style (one of Trissino's goals was to create a national Italian language, based on Hellenic spelling and pronunciation); other classes were in philosophy, geography, astronomy and music, which Trissino considered the most important of all. As study aids, he covered the walls with Greek and Latin inscriptions extolling Study, Arts and Virtue.

Although neither noble nor young, Palladio attended the classes, but his most important lesson was Trissino's villa itself. In his remodelling Trissino, a keen student of Vitruvius, kept the towers of the original *castello*, linked them with a portico inspired by Falconetto's Loggia Cornaro in Padua and devised a ground plan of rooms according to Vitruvius' concepts of proportion and harmony. This arrangement of rooms was unprecedented, the archetype for Palladio's own villas (*see* pp.59–63).

Keen villa-fanciers will find plenty of less academic 18th-century examples littered along the road from Vicenza to **Montecchio Precalcino** (20km) where the charming Villino Forni Cerato is a fine late 16th-century work based on Serlio's treatises.

Montecchio Maggiore

Vicenza province alone has some 400 villas, and driving along the back roads between Vicenza and Montecchio Maggiore you can see several of them. A few deserve special mention: the bright white *settecento* temple of **Villa Bonini**, near the western *autostrada* exit; in **Altavilla**, Francesco Muttoni's **Villa Valmarana Morosini** of 1724, a curious marriage of Palladian and Baroque now owned by a university; in **Creazzo**, an eclectic 19th-century castle, and Villa Fadinelli Seppiej, built in the 18th-century Palladian revival style; and in **Sovizzo**, the large *cinquecento* Villa Sale di San Damiano Curti, expanded in the 19th century, when the owner added a little classical-style theatre to the garden. Sovizzo also has something far rarer than a villa in these parts: a Copper Age megalithic tomb complex, in a field at San Daniele.

Montecchio Maggiore, 13km west of Vicenza, is defended by two Scaliger castles standing side by side on a hill. In Luigi da Porto's 1529 tale of *Romeo and Juliet* they belonged to the rival clans, the Montecchi and Cappelletti; the view of them from Da Porto's villa was an inspiration for the story. There's a car park by **Castello della Villa** or Romeo's castle, now used for summer performances, and a pretty walk from there to **Castello di Bellaguardia** or Juliet's castle (complete with balcony and the courtyard Ristorante d'Amore).

Just before Montecchio is the Villa Cordellina-Lombardi, built in the Palladian revival style in the 1730s by Giorgio Massari, which

---

Villa Fadinelli Seppiej
Via Pozzetto 38, t 0444 546 824; open July–mid-Oct; booking essential

Villa Sale di San Damiano Curti
Via Roma, t 0444 551 009; open Mon, Wed, Fri, Sat, Sun 10–12 and 3–6; ring ahead

Megalithic tomb complex
Via degli Alpini, t 0444 376 130

Villa Cordellina-Lombardi
Via Lovara 36, t 0444 696 085; open April–mid-Oct Tues–Fri 9–1, Sat–Sun 9–12 and 3–6; adm

was frescoed by a young Giambattista Tiepolo with *The Family of Darius before Alexander* and *The Generosity of Scipio*; the sky Tiepolo painted on the ceiling glows with what would become his trademark luminosity. On Piazza Marconi, another villa houses the **Museo Civico G. Zannato**, which includes a major collection of fossils, finds from the late Roman necropolis at Carpane near a section of the Via Postumia that linked Genoa to Aquileia, and a room of gems and semi-precious stones used in *pietra dura* inlays. West of Montecchio Maggiore you can pick up yet another wine road, the Strada del Vino Recioto DOC Gambellara, which winds through Montorso, Montebello and Gambellara. Unlike the other Reciotos (natural sparkling dessert wines), Recioto di Gambellara is white; they also do a still white Gambellara and Vin Santo.

**Museo Civico
G. Zannato**
Piazza Marconi 15,
t 0444 698 874; open
Mon–Sat 9–12.30 and
2.30–6, Sun 9.30–12.30

Up the Val d'Agno

From Montecchio Maggiore, what is now the SS246 to the Val d'Agno was a favourite Vicentine villa-building alley. One of the first, set in one of the most beautiful landscape gardens in the Veneto, **Villa Trissino** (1718), was struck by lightning and left as a ruin, while the upper villa is by Francesco Muttoni, built over an old tower house. The same family still owns its first Villa Trissino, a Gothic-Renaissance palace on Via Paninsacco. Two kilometres up the road in **Castelgomberto**, the Villa Piovene-Da Schio (1666) has three large mythologies painted by a young Giambattista Tiepolo (1725) for the Palazzo Porto Sandi in Venice. You can't see them, but you can wander around the beautiful period park.

**Villa Piovene-
Da Schio**
t 0445 940 052; open
June–Sept by request
only 9–12; adm

Valdagno, the valley's main town, divides in two; its age-old textile industry on one side of the torrent, and on the other an ambitious 'ideal' industrial town, the **Città Sociale**, built 1927–46, a mix of modernist architecture and traditional building material designed by Gaetano Marzotto, with a school, theatre and sports centre. At the head of the valley, the therapeutic virtues of the waters at **Recoaro Terme** were discovered in 1689; its mineral water, flavoured with sour orange, is sold nationwide.

On the Road to Verona

After Montecchio Maggiore, there's only one real reason to stop between Vicenza and Verona: **Soave**, where the vineyards of the archetype of Italian white wines literally engulf the old town, in a tender landscape that fits its name (the same as the English 'suave', even if it derives from a 6th-century Swabian encampment on the site). In contrast with all the green softness, Soave is crowned by the well-preserved and toothsomely crenellated Castle of the Scaligers, which was first built in the 10th century. *Après* castle, try a Soave Classico or the sweet Recioto di Soave, a dessert wine made from raisins, at the **Enoteca del Castello** on Via Roma.

**Castle of the
Scaligers**
open Tues–Sun 9–12
and 3–6; adm

Where to Stay North and West of Vicenza

Bolzano Vicentino ✉ 36050

***Locanda Grego**, Via Roma 24, t 0444 350 588, *www.locandagrego.it* (€€). In the hills above the Vicenza Nord *autostrada* exit, this hotel occupies an old postal relay station, with well-furnished rooms and a good restaurant. *Closed part of Aug.*

Altavilla ✉ 36077

****Genziana**, Via Mazzini 75, Selva, t 0444 572 398, *www.hotelristorante genziana.com* (€€). Six kilometres west of Vicenza in Altavilla, this hotel is warm and welcoming and full of art; pool too. *Closed part of Aug.*

Verona

 Verona

There is no world without Verona walls

But purgatory, torture, hell itself

Hence banished is banish'd from the world;

And world's exile is death.

Romeo and Juliet, Act III

Well, love does lead one to extremes, and although Verona isn't quite a world on its own, it is one of the choicest morsels on this planet. When Cupid's pilgrims alight here they sigh over 'Juliet's balcony' and other places concocted in response to a desperate need for shrines to the unlucky teenage couple. But the gorgeous rosy-pink city curling along the banks of the Adige has far more to offer than Romeo and Juliet and all the other star-crossed lovers singing their operatic hearts out in the Arena: evocative streets and romantic piazzas, sublime art, magnificent architecture, and all the gnocchi you can eat. According to Goethe, even the wind in Verona 'is charged with fragrance as if it had passed over a hill of roses'.

History

Blessed with a navigable river at the bottom of a busy alpine pass, Verona was favoured by the Romans from the time of its colonization in 89 BC, and returned the favour by giving Rome the architect Vitruvius and the lyrical, lovesick poet Catullus. The city maintained its status as a regional capital under the Ostrogoths and Franks, and in 1107 became a free *comune* in league with Padua, Vicenza and Treviso. Freedom in the case of 12th-century Verona meant a free-for-all, as the city's nobility spiced up the national Guelph and Ghibelline rivalries with a sideshow of purely domestic feuds and vendettas that inspired the original *Romeo and Juliet* (by Luigi da Porto, 1529), and led to the *comune* actually inviting Ezzelino da Romano to take power as *podestà* in 1230. It was under his reign that Pope Gregory IX forced Verona to accept the Inquisition under Dominican Giovanni da Vincenza, who celebrated his arrival in 1233 by barbecuing 60 Cathars outside the Arena.

Ezzelino's successors, the della Scalas or Scaligeri, were a typical late medieval Italian family of exquisite gangsters, softening their lust for power with a refined taste for the arts. Bartolomeo della Scala was one of Dante's first and most generous patrons. His descendants' names were, however, uniquely canine, the better to terrify their opponents. 'Big Dog', Cangrande I (1311–29), was the

VIA MAMELLI

STRADONE
ARCIDIACONO
PACIFICO/VIA SOLE

VIALE DEI MILLE

PIAZZA
VITTORIO
VENETO

VIA EDERLE

VIA ANZANI

PONTE
GARIBALDI

VIA PRATO SANTO

VIA TOMASO DA VICO

VIA RISORGIMENTO

VIA M. TODESCHINI

VIA QUATTRO NOVEMBRE

Fondazione Museo
Miniscalchi-Erizzo

VIA S.
MAMMASO

VIALE DELLA REPUBBLICA

VIA ARSENALE

BORGO TRENTO

Arsenale

PIAZZALE
CADORNA

LUNGADIG PANVINIO

VIA EMILEI

Ca
M

PONTE
RISORGIMENTO

PIAZZA
SACCO E
VANZETTI

PONTE
VITTORIA

VIA DIAZ

CORSO PORTA BORSARI

VIA S. VIASTADE

VIA PONTIDA

Basilica
of San Zeno

PIAZZA
S. ZENO

Adige

Porta dei
Borsari

VIA CATULLO

to Milan

Porta
S. Zeno

VIA PORTA S. ZENO

PIAZZA
CORRUBIO

VIA S. GIUSEPPE

RIGASTE S. ZENO

PONTE
SCALIGERO

S. Lorenzo

Palazzo
Bevilacqua

CORSO CAVOUR

VICOLO TRE
MARCHETTI

VIA SCARSELLINI

VIA ROSMINI

S. ZENO

Arco
dei Gavi

SS. Apostoli

VIA CATTANEO

Arena

STRADONE A. PROVOLO

Castelvecchio

VIA ROMA

Museo
Lapidario

PIAZZA
BRA

Palazzo
Barbieri

VIA S. SILVESTRO

V. MANIN

STRADONE PORTA PALIO

Gran
Guardia

VIA G. MARCONI

VIA VALVERDE

CORSO PORTA NUOVA

VIA MONTANARI

VIA BERTONI

VIA BATTISTI

V.C. TRINITA

CITTADELLA

VIA DEL MINATORE

VIA LOCATELLI

to Mantua
and Airport

Porta
Nuova

Bus
Station

VIA FRANCO FACCIO

Porta Nuova
Train Station

Campo
Sportivo

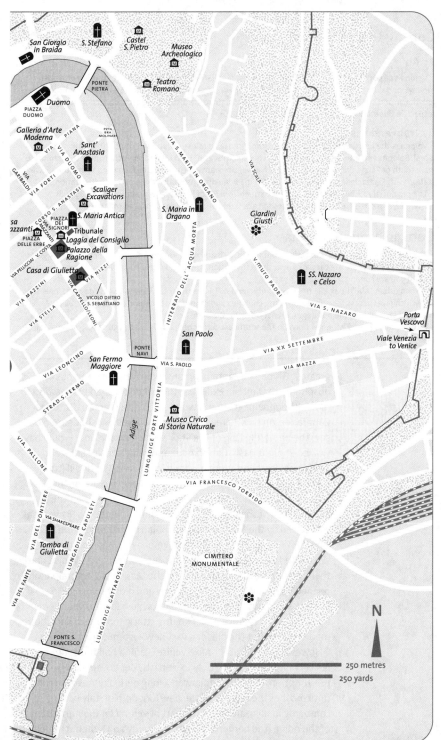

San Giorgio in Braida

S. Stefano

Castel S. Pietro

Museo Archeologico

PONTE PIETRA

Duomo

PIAZZA DUOMO

Galleria d'Arte Moderna

VIA PIANA

Teatro Romano

PZTA BRA MOLINARI

Sant' Anastasia

VIA DUOMO

VIA FORTI

VIA GARIBALDI

VIA S. MARIA IN ORGANO

VIA SCALA

Scaliger Excavations

CORSO S. ANASTASIA

S. Maria Antica

S. Maria in Organo

Giardini Giusti

sa azzanti

PIAZZA DEI SIGNORI

VIA MAZZANTI

Tribunale

Loggia del Consiglio

PIAZZA DELLE ERBE

VIA PELLICCIAI

V. COSTA

Palazzo della Ragione

Casa di Giulietta

VIA NIZZI

VICOLO DIETRO S. SEBASTIANO

INTERRATO DELL' ACQUA MORTA

V. MURO PADRI

SS. Nazaro e Celso

VIA MAZZINI

VIA CAPPELLO/LEONI

VIA STELLA

San Paolo

VIA S. NAZARO

Porta Vescovo

Viale Venezia to Venice

VIA LEONCINO

San Fermo Maggiore

PONTE NAVI

VIA S. PAOLO

VIA XX SETTEMBRE

VIA MAZZA

STRAD. S. FERMO

Adige

LUNGADIGE PORTE VITTORIA

Museo Civico di Storia Naturale

VIA PALLONE

VIA FRANCESCO TORBIDO

VIA DEL PONTIERE

VIA SHAKESPEARE

LUNGADIGE CAPULETI

Tomba di Giulietta

CIMITERO MONUMENTALE

VIA DEL FANTE

LUNGADIGE GATTAROSSA

PONTE S. FRANCESCO

N

250 metres

250 yards

Getting to and from Verona

By Air

Verona's **airport**, Valerio Catullo, to the southwest at Villafranca, has daily flights to London on British Airways, and direct flights to Rome, Naples and Bari. For information, **t** 045 809 5666. Every 20mins buses link the airport to Porta Nuova train station in Verona; there are also three direct connections daily to the respective bus stations in Brescia, Mantua and Trento.

By Train and Bus

Verona is the junction of major **rail** lines from Vicenza (35mins), Padua (1hr), Venice (1hr 45mins), Milan (2hrs), Bologna (1hr 40mins), Trento (1hr) and Bolzano (1hr 40mins). The **station**, Porta Nuova, is a 15-minute walk south of Piazza Brà, along Corso Porta Nuova; alternatively, city buses nos.11, 12 and 13 link the railway station with Piazza delle Erbe and Piazza Brà. A machine dispenses bus tickets opposite the station.

The provincial APT **bus depot** is across the street from Porta Nuova railway station (**t** 045 805 7811, *www.aptv.it*) and has frequent departures to Lake Garda and the mountains, and Mantua (1 hour).

Getting around Verona

The historic centre is closed to traffic from 1.30–4, 6–8 and 10pm–10am with the exception of cars going directly to hotels. There are **car parks** near the train station, Arena and Corso Porta Nuova, the main entry point if you are coming from the A4.

Verona urban (AMT, **t** 045 887 1111, *www.amt.it*) and APT buses offer the **Verona Card** (3 days €12, one day €8), which gives access to various museums, churches and monuments in Verona and AMT public transport (available at the bus depot, tourist office or museums).

Bicycles can be hired (summer only) on the southeast corner of Piazza Brà, **t** 045 582 389. For **taxis** call **t** 045 532 666.

greatest Ghibelline captain in Italy and gave such generous hospitality to Dante in exile that the poet dedicated his *Paradiso* to him (although one may well wonder if Dante's famous 'Letter to Cangrande' on how to read poetry ever arrived; most postmen who saw the name 'Big Dog of the Stair' written on the door would have walked straight past). Cangrande captured Vicenza, Padua and Treviso before dying suddenly aged 41; his heir, Mastino II (the Mastiff), consolidated his gains while his own successor, the fratricidal Cansignorio (Lord Dog, 1359–75), presided over the construction of the family's last great monuments. In 1387 Verona was seized by the Milanese warlord Gian Galeazzo Visconti.

By the time Visconti died in 1402, Verona had had enough of *signori* and annexed itself to Venice. Yet relations with Venice had their ups and downs. In the Wars of the League of Cambrai, Verona opened its gates to the German army and didn't return to St Mark's fold until 1517. The Venetians, who had absolved them of their oath of allegiance under enemy attack, took them back, but made Verona foot the bill for a vast new system of fortifications.

However (and notably unlike Venice) Verona had the spunk to resist Napoleon in 1797 – only to be partly destroyed for its presumption. There then followed a long period of Austrian rule, until most of the city joined the new Kingdom of Italy with Lombardy in 1859, although the part of Verona on the north bank of the Adige (the border between Lombardy and Venetia) remained

Austrian along with Venice until 1866. Bombed in the Second World War, Verona quickly rebuilt itself as suited its rank, not only as a *città d'arte*, but as one of the great postwar economic success stories of modern Italy.

Porta Nuova to the Arena

The first thing most people see of Verona, whether arriving by rail or road, is Sammicheli's Renaissance gate, the **Porta Nuova**, now stranded on a traffic island at the head of the Corso Porta Nuova. This avenue leads straight under another gate, Gian Galeazzo Visconti's **Portoni della Brà**, and into the heart of tourist Verona: the large, irregular **Piazza Brà**, the favourite promenade of the Veronese and tourists, milling about a broad swathe of café-filled pavements (the Liston) curving around the Arena.

Arena
www.arena.it; open Tues–Sun 8.30–7.30, Mon and during opera season 1.30–7.30; adm; for opera information see p.221

Built in the 1st century AD and, after the Colosseum, the best-preserved amphitheatre in Italy, the elliptical Arena measures 456 by 364ft and seats 25,000 – the only substantial change was wrought by earthquakes, which shattered the outer arcade with the exception of the four arches of the wing or *ala*. Dressed in pink and white marble, the Arena is lovely enough to make one almost forget the brutal sports it was built to host. During the Middle Ages, Verona kept up Roman traditions by using it for public executions; in the Renaissance it hosted knightly tournaments, and in the Baroque era it was used for bull-baiting. Since 1913, the death and mayhem has been purely operatic, with sets in Karnak proportions.

Opposite the Arena in Piazza Brà rises the 17th-century **Palazzo della Gran Guardia**, with a Visconti tower peeking over its shoulder; on the corner of Via Roma, the Museo Lapidario Maffeiano,

Museo Lapidario Maffeiano
Via Roma 28; open Tues–Sun 8.30–2, Mon 1.30–7.30; adm

established in 1714, was one of the first museums in the world dedicated to ancient inscriptions. It houses an incredible collection, including some beautiful Roman funeral reliefs, depicting a couple as their children wished them to be remembered, although one wonders whether the memories were particularly fond.

The vegetable market [...] that day was alive with delightful figures of women and girls, with [...] soft appetising bodies, marvellously golden and unashamedly dirty, made for the night far more than the day.
Heinrich Heine

Piazza delle Erbe, Piazza dei Signori and the Scaliger Tombs

From Piazza Brà, **Via Mazzini** (the first street in Italy to ban cars) is the most direct route to the core of medieval and Roman Verona, the **Piazza delle Erbe**.

The **market square** that so entranced Heinrich Heine occupies the old forum and still fulfils its original purpose, selling fast food, souvenirs and overpriced vegetables, although you'd be hard pressed these days to find an unashamedly dirty tomato of any kind. Four monuments on the piazza's spine poke their heads above the rainbow lake of parasols – a Lion of St Mark; a 1368 fountain built by Cansignorio topped by a Roman statue known as the 'Madonna Verona'; a 16th-century loggia called the 'Berlina' where malefactors were tied and pelted with rotten produce; and an elegant Gothic stone lantern.

A colourful panoply of buildings encases the square, including the charming **Casa Mazzanti**, formerly part of a Scaliger palace and brightened with 16th-century frescoes, and the 12th-century Torre dei Lamberti, 275ft high, reached by a lift from the courtyard of the Palazzo della Ragione. The shorter **Torre del Gardello** at the other end of the piazza was another work of Cansignorio. Six ancient gods blithely pose atop the adjacent yellow sandstone **Palazzo Maffei** (1668), while a battlemented red-brick palace, built in 1301 for a merchants' association, still does duty as Verona's Chamber of Commerce after 700 years.

Torre dei Lamberti
*open Tues–Sun
9.30–6.30, Mon
1.30–7.30; adm*

From Piazza delle Erbe, the **Arco della Costa** ('of the rib' – named after a whalebone hung in the arch) leads into stately **Piazza dei Signori**, the civic centre of Verona, presided over by a grouchy statue of Dante (1865). The striped **Palazzo della Ragione** has a lovely Romanesque-Gothic courtyard, the Cortile del Mercato Vecchio, which forms a pretty setting for a series of free summer classical/jazz/blues concerts. Behind Dante, the **Loggia del Consiglio** (1493) is the city's finest Renaissance building, decorated with yellow and red frescoes and statues of five ancient celebrities of Verona (one of whom, Pliny the Elder, was pinched from Como). The adjacent crenellated **Tribunale** (law courts), formerly a Scaliger palace, has a portal by Sammicheli; in the courtyard, and in adjacent Via Dante, you can peer down through glass into Verona's Roman streets, revealed in the 1980s Scaliger excavations. The underground corridors are used for photo exhibitions.

Scaliger excavations
*t 045 800 7490; open
Tue–Sun 10–7*

The arch adjoining the Tribunale leads to the grand Gothic pantheon of the della Scala, the **Scaliger Tombs** or Arche Scaligere, which Ruskin considered the crowning achievement of Veronese Gothic. The three major tombs portray their occupants in warlike, equestrian poses on top, and reposing in death below, although a copy replaces the best one, the horseman atop the Tomb of Cangrande (*d*. 1329), built into the wall of the 12th-century **Santa Maria Antica**. Don't miss the crowned dogs next to Cangrande's effigy, standing like firemen holding up ladders, the della Scala emblem. More ladders adorn the fantastical pinnacles of the tomb of 'Lord Dog' Cansignorio (*d*. 1375), the more sedate one of Mastino II (*d*. 1351), and the web of their wrought-iron enclosure. The rather plain 14th-century house in the same Via delle Arche Scaligere belonged to the Montecchi family (Shakespeare's Montagues), and has been known ever since as the **Casa di Romeo**.

The tour groups, however, are all over the Casa di Giulietta, near the Piazza delle Erbe at Via Cappello 23. Although the association is slim (the 13th-century house was once an inn called 'Il Cappello',

Casa di Giulietta
*open Tues–Sun
8.30–7.30, Mon
1.30–7.30*

reminiscent of the dal Cappello family, the original of the Capulets), it was restored on the outside in 1935 to fit the Shakespearian bill, with lovely windows and *de rigueur* balcony; inside you can peruse lovelorn graffiti of modern youth, ripe postcards, and photos of a more recent Romeo, the American actor Leonardo di Caprio. The well-fondled bronze statue of Juliet in the courtyard is a bit busty for a 13-year-old, but girls grew up faster back then.

Sant'Anastasia, Modern Art and the Duomo

North of the Scaliger Tombs, it's hard to miss Gothic **Sant'Anastasia**, Verona's largest church, begun in 1290 but never completed; in its woebegone façade only the fine portal, with frescoes and reliefs of St Peter Martyr, hints of its builders' good intentions. The interior, however, is beautiful but, just coming in from the bright sun, many people start at what appears to be two men loitering under the holy water stoops; these are the *Gobbi*, or hunchbacks. The three naves are supported by massive marble columns and decorated by an all-star line-up of artists: there's the beautiful Fregoso altar by Sammicheli (the first on the right), and excellent frescoes by Verona native Altichiero from 1390, in the Cavalli Chapel in the right apse (note how the horse-head helmets that the worshippers wear on their backs resemble the dragon head on Cangrande's statue). The next chapel has 24 terracottas by Michele da Firenze on the *Life of Jesus*; paintings by the school of Mantegna fill the Pellegrini chapel and, to the left of the high altar opposite a large 15th-century *Last Judgement*, the tomb of Cortesia Serego (1429) has an equestrian statue by Tuscan Nanni di Bartolo and frescoes by Michele Giambono. Best of all, in the sacristy, there's a fairy-tale fresco, *St George at Trebizond* (1438) by Pisanello, one of his finest works, although his watchful, calculating princess seems more formidable than any dragon. Nearby, in Via Piana, the medieval Palazzo Forti which once lodged Napoleon now houses the **Galleria d'Arte Moderna**, where frequent exhibitions share the walls with Italian masters (Hayez, Fattori, De Pisis, Boccioni, Vedova, Manzù) of the 19th and 20th centuries.

A few streets down Via Duomo, almost at the tip of the river's meander, stands Verona's **Duomo**, consecrated in 1187, Romanesque at the roots and Renaissance in its windows and octagonal crown. The portal, supported on the backs of griffons, was carved by the great 12th-century Master Nicolò of San Zeno (*see* below). Look for the chivalric figures of Roland and Oliver guarding the west door and, on the south porch, a relief of Jonah being swallowed by the whale, and another of a dog biting a lion's buttocks; lastly, be sure to walk around to see the apse, made of volcanic tufa and one of the finest Romanesque works in the Veneto. Inside, there's the

Galleria d'Arte Moderna
t 045 800 1903; hours and adm vary depending on exhibition

beautifully carved Tomb of St Agatha (1353) in the Cappella Mazzanti, and an Assumption by Titian in the first chapel on the left. Painted in 1540, it shows us a very different Virgin from Titian's famous goddess whirlwinding to heaven in Venice's Frari – this one looks down sympathetically at her friends on earth. In the second chapel on the right, Liberale da Verona contributed a delightful Adoration of the Magi, its foreground dominated by frolicking children, rabbits and dogs. A pope is buried in the choir – Lucius III, who preferred Verona to Rome, and made the city the papal seat from 1181 to 1185. The pretty cloister has a few remains of the Duomo's pre-Romanesque predecessor (victim of an earthquake), and in its ancient baptistry, **San Giovanni in Fonte**, there's an eight-sided font big enough to swim in, carved in 1200 from a single piece of marble and decorated with beautiful reliefs. The chapter library, the Biblioteca Capitolare, was founded in the 5th century as a Scriptorium and justifiably claims to be the oldest library still operating in Europe; it contains a magnificent collection of medieval manuscripts.

Biblioteca Capitolare
Piazza del Duomo 10, t 045 596 516; open Mon–Wed, Fri, Sat 9.30–12.30; also Tues, Fri 4–6

Head away from the cathedral, down Stradone Arcidiacono Pacifico/Via Sole to Via S. Mamaso, for the Fondazione Museo Miniscalchi-Erizzo, a private, ecletic collection of furniture, paintings, weapons and more stored in a frescoed 15th-century palace.

Fondazione Museo Miniscalchi-Erizzo
Via S. Mamaso 2A; open Mon–Sat 4–7, Sun 10.30–12.30; adm

North of the Adige: Veronetta

The north bank of the Adige, locally known as 'Veronetta', was that part of the city that remained in Austrian hands until 1866. It's due a whole morning unto itself: if you cross over the Ponte Garibaldi, just down from the Duomo, the first landmark is the large dome of **San Giorgio in Braida** (1477) to your right, worth a closer look inside to see Paolo Veronese's *Martyrdom of St George*. Follow the Adige down to **Santo Stefano**, an important Palaeo-Christian church, pieced together in the 12th century from 5th–10th-century columns and capitals, and brightened with 14th-century frescoes, some by Altichiero. The bridge here, **Ponte Pietra**, was built by the Romans and blown up in the Second World War along with Verona's other bridges. The Veronese dredged up as much of its original stone as they could when they rebuilt it.

In ancient times, the citizens of Verona would trot over the Ponte Pietra to attend the latest plays at the picturesque Teatro Romano. Actually, they still do: the cavea and arches, carved out of the cypress-clad hill of San Pietro in the time of Augustus, are in good enough nick to host a summer theatre season. A lift goes up to the **Archaeology Museum**, occupying a convent built on top of the theatre and containing a collection of small bronzes, portrait busts and a few mosaics. Further up still, the **Castel San Pietro** was built

Teatro Romano
t 045 800 0360; open Tues–Sun 8.30–7.30, Mon 1.30–7.30; adm

by the Austrians over Roman and Visconti-era fortifications, and has famous views over Verona at sunset.

South, on the Interrato dell'Acqua Morta, **Santa Maria in Organo** has a façade (1533) by Fra Giovanni da Verona; the talented friar also made the extraordinary *intarsia* choir stalls, lectern and cupboards (in the sacristy) depicting scenes of old Verona, *trompe l'œil* birds, animals, musical instruments and flowers. Across the street that runs behind the church are the cool Giardini Giusti, described by Thomas Coryate, the court jester of King James I's son Prince Henry, as 'a second paradise, and a passing delectable place of solace'. That was in 1611, the date of the enormous cypresses, formal box hedge parterres, fountains and grotto topped with a leering mask. The hillside was re-landscaped in the 19th century in the more romantic English style, making it a favourite setting for newlywed photos.

Continuing south, **Santi Nazaro e Celso** (1484) on Via Muro Padri contains 16th-century frescoes and a painting of the eponymous saints by Montagna, while San Paolo (rebuilt 1763), on Via San Paolo, boasts Veronese's beautiful *Madonna and Saints*, painted before he had to move to Venice, supposedly on the run after committing murder. On the river bank, at Lungadige Porta Vittoria 9, there's the elegant Palazzo Pompei, built in 1530 by Sammicheli and now housing the Museo Civico di Storia Naturale, with an excellent fossil collection.

San Fermo Maggiore and Juliet's Tomb

From Piazza delle Erbe, Via Cappello/Leoni leads past the picturesque ruins of the 1st-century BC **Porta dei Leoni** (incorporated into a building), marking the beginning of the Roman *cardo maximus*. This leads to the splendid vertical apse of **San Fermo Maggiore**, an architectural club sandwich: it consists of two churches, one built on top of the other. The Romanesque bottom was begun in 1065 by the Benedictines, while the upper Gothic church, with its attractive red and white patterns, was added by the Franciscans in 1320, along with the façade. Walk around to see the apse, a harmonious *mélange* of both styles.

The upper church is covered with a lovely wooden ceiling of 1314 and fine 14th-century frescoes – the *Crucifixion* in the lunette over the door is by Turone. The first chapel on the right has a charming if mutilated fresco of scroll-bearing angels, by Stefano da Verona; in the right transept the Cappella Alighieri has a pair of tombs by Sammicheli; and the left transept has frescoes on the Life of St Francis by Liberale da Verona. The **Cappella delle Donne** contains one of Caroto's best altarpieces (*Madonna and Saints*, 1528) and a beautiful tomb, the *Monumento Brenzoni* (1439) by Florentine Nanni di Bartolo, with statues and a graceful fresco,

Annunciation and Archangels, by Pisanello (1462). The lower
church has more frescoes, columns and capitals inspired by
classical models.

Tomba di Giulietta
*open Tues–Sun
8.30–7.30, Mon
1.30–7.30; adm*

The so-called **Tomba di Giulietta** is back near the river on Via del
Pontiere, not far from the Piazza Brà. Even the Veronese admit no
connection with any tradition here, except that the Romanesque
cloister and the 14th-century red marble sarcophagus would make
a jolly good stage set for Shakespeare's last scene. Be prepared to
queue, nevertheless. A small museum of frescoes is an added
attraction, including lovely 16th-century allegorical and mythological scenes by Paolo Farinati.

Piazza delle Erbe to the Arco Dei Gavi

From Piazza delle Erbe, Corso Porta Borsari leads to an impressive
Roman customs house, the twin-arched **Porta dei Borsari** ('Gate
of the Duty-collectors'), built in the 1st century AD on the Via
Postumia. A small temple to Jupiter stood nearby on Via Diaz, its
foundation now traced in porphyry (the temple itself was relocated
to Verona's Cimiterio Monumentale); bits of the Roman walls are
just to the right.

Back then, once you passed out of the Porta dei Borsari, you'd find
the Via Postumia chock-a-block with tombs, but now this is **Corso
Cavour**, one of Verona's most elegant thoroughfares, embellished
with palaces from various epochs. The best is Sammicheli's refined
if unfinished **Palazzo Bevilacqua** (1588, No.19), with its ornate,
rhythmic alternation of large and small windows, columns and
pediments; at No.44 his **Palazzo Canossa** is from the same period,
but was finished only in 1675.

Opposite Palazzo Bevilacqua, the lovely Romanesque church
of **San Lorenzo** (1117) preserves its upper, women's gallery
(*matroneum*) reached by way of two cylindrical towers. To the left
and a bit back from the Palazzo, another venerable church,
SS. Apostoli, was founded in the 5th century and rebuilt several
times since (especially after the Second World War); the oldest
surviving bit is a votive chapel dedicated in the 6th century to
Saints Teuteria and Tosca, modelled after the Mausoleum of Galla
Placidia in Ravenna. Further down, Corso Cavour opens up into a
small square with yet another Roman arch: the simple but elegant
Arco dei Gavi, designed by Vitruvius in honour of a local family. The
French demolished it in 1805, but in 1932 the local *fascisti* put it
back together again.

Castelvecchio and its Museum of Art

Next to the arch, Cangrande II's fortress of **Castelvecchio** (1355)
has weathered centuries of use by other top dogs, from the
Venetians to Napoleon and the Nazis, to become Verona's excellent

Museum of art
*t 045 806 2611; open
Tues–Sun 8.30–7.30,
Mon 1.30–7.30; adm*

civic **museum of art**. Exhibits are arranged chronologically: among the oldest treasures in the first five rooms you'll find goldwork from the 4th to 7th centuries, a sarcophagus (1179) carved with vivid reliefs of Saints Sergius and Bacchus, the *Archivolto di Peregrinus* (1120), and expressive 14th-century Veronese sculpture, especially a stark, painful Crucifixion by the Maestro di S. Anastasia. Two other statues are attributed to his circle, *St Catherine* and *St Cecilia*, patroness of music, holding her invention – a portable organ – under her arm.

Beyond the collection of old town bells and detached frescoes wait excellent 14th-century paintings: *SS James and Anthony* by Tommaso da Modena, a polyptych by Altichiero, and another by Turone, one of Verona's first documented painters. The museum is especially rich in lovely Madonnas, beginning with two straight out of fairy tales, the *Madonna of the Quail* by Pisanello and the *Madonna of the Rose Garden* by Stefano da Verona; others are by Jacopo Bellini and Michele Giambono. A *Pietà* by Tuscan Filippo Lippi and early Flemish works offer a change of pace, before Room 15 returns to Venetian art with the *Madonna della Passione* by Carlo Crivelli and Andrea Mantegna's *Holy Family*. Local Renaissance painters Liberale da Verona, Francesco Morone and Francesco Bonsignori fill the next rooms, followed by a beautiful Madonna by Giovanni Bellini and Carpaccio's *SS Caterina and Veneranda*.

Next comes Verona's mascot, the striking 14th-century equestrian **statue of Cangrande I** from the Arche Scaligere, displayed outside the first-floor window of the Napoleonic wing. The pyjama-clad steed, complete with an equine hood ornament and deathly eyes, and the moronically grinning 'Big Dog' himself, with his ghastly dragon-helmet slung over his back, make an unforgettable pair, straight out of a malevolent pantomime. But this was the great Ghibelline captain to whom Dante dedicated his *Paradiso*; and, as with the Veneto's other great equestrian statues, of Gattamelata and Colleoni, a physical resemblance to the hero was irrelevant.

Behind the castle, Cangrande II's **Ponte Scaligero** spanning the Adige repeats the attractive 'swallowtail' battlements of the Castelvecchio; like the Ponte Pietra it was blown up in the war and meticulously reconstructed in the 1950s, in the indomitable Italian spirit of *dov'è era, comè era* ('where it was, as it was'), using the original stone.

Basilica of San Zeno Maggiore

**Basilica of
San Zeno Maggiore**
*open summer
Mon–Sat 8.30–6, Sun
1–6; winter Sun 1–5*

A 15-minute walk west from the Castelvecchio, mostly along the riverbank, or bus no.32 or 33 from Corso Porta Borsari, will take you to the superb Basilica of San Zeno, one of the finest Romanesque buildings anywhere. First built in the 4th century next to a

Benedictine monastery (of which only the massive brick tower on the left survives), the basilica took its present form between 1120 and 1398. Its magnificence demanded a legend: beneath its lofty campanile (finished in 1149) lies the tomb of a personage no less than Venice's old nemesis – Pepin the Short, King of the Franks. For centuries San Zeno was the symbol of Veronese liberty, the custodian of its *carroccio* or war wagon. All medieval Italian cities had them to take into battle, drawn by oxen and equipped with altars and priests to pray for their enemy's discomfort, and drums and trumpets to rally their own troops. Capturing another *comune*'s *carroccio* was the most devastating blow an army could inflict. Florence, for instance, got Fiesole's, and the mortified city never recovered.

The rich façade of San Zeno has a perfect centrepiece: a 12th-century rose window, the *Wheel of Fortune* by Maestro Brioloto. Below, the beautifully carved porch (1138) by Masters Nicolò and Guglielmo shows scenes from the months, the miracles of San Zeno, the Hunt of Theodoric (driving a stag straight to Hell) and other allegories. The **bronze doors** with their 48 panels are a 'poor man's Bible' and one of the wonders of 11th-century Italy. Even after a millennium, they have an unmatched freshness and vitality: in the Annunciation scene Mary covers her face in fear and anguish while the angel Gabriel does his best to comfort her; in the Descent into Hell Christ and a large, leering Satan fight a tug-of-war for souls. Other scenes seem strange to us, especially the one of two nursing mothers on the lower left-hand door, one suckling twin children, the other, what look to be twin crocodiles. In the 18th and 19th centuries, Grand Tourists found the doors appalling: 'To this low level did art fall during the Carlovingian decadence and the Hungarian invasions,' sniffed Hippolyte Taine; but Ruskin thought they beat any Renaissance work in Venice hands down.

The vast interior, divided into three naves by Roman columns and capitals, has a beautiful Gothic ceiling, 13th- and 14th-century frescoes and, on the altar, the magnificent triptych *Madonna, Angels and Saints* (1459) by Andrea Mantegna, a work that brilliantly combines the master's love of classical architecture and luminous colouring. Although the French returned the painting after Napoleon carted it off, they kept the predella, and the panels are copies of the originals in the Louvre and Tours. In the crypt below, the body of St Zeno glows in the dark. Also spare a glance for the handsome cloister, completed in 1313.

The Madonna di Campagna

Of the many surviving gates in Verona's walls, the furthest from the centre is the easterly 16th-century **Porta Vescovo** on the far side of the monumental cemetery. Viale Venezia leads out from here to the suburb of **San Michele Extra**, built around a long-gone 8th-century Benedictine monastery. In the 1500s a fresco of the Madonna on a wall performed so many miracles that the bishop commissioned Michele Sammicheli to design a church to house it: this was the round and rather startling **Sanctuario della Madonna di Campagna** (1562), one of Longhena's inspirations for La Salute. It became the aim of a very popular all-night pilgrimage on the first Sunday of each May, until the authorities noticed that the pilgrims were having far too much May Day-style fun along the road, and abolished it all in 1804.

Tourist Information in Verona

⭐ Gabbia d'Oro >>

It is worth noting that on the first Sunday of the month admission is free to the Museo Castelvecchio, the Teatro Romano, Juliet's tomb and the Museo Lapidaro Maffeiano.

Note also that on Monday morning most shops are closed (apart from food shops, which close on Wednesday afternoons).

Festivals in Verona

Verona hosts a **Shakespeare festival** (in Italian) in the Roman Theatre: same address as above for information and tickets. From mid-December to mid-January, the arcades of the Arena are used for a massive show of Christmas cribs (*presepi*) from around the world.

In the spring the city hosts one of Italy's oldest **carnivals**, first recorded in 1530; the last Friday of carnival is known as the 'Bacchanal of Gnocchi', presided over by the Papà del Gnocco who walks about with a giant potato dumpling on a fork.

Contact t 045 806 6485, *www.estateteatraleveronese.it* for details of cultural events.

Where to Stay in Verona

ⓘ Verona >
*Palazzo Barbiera,
Via Leoncino 61,
t 045 800 0861;
Porta Nuova railway
station, t 045 800 861;
both open daily, closed
Sun in winter*
For the province:
*Piazza delle Erbe 38,
t 045 800 6997,
www.tourism.verona.it*
Youth information:
*Corso Porta Borsari 17,
t 045 801 0795*
Internet point:
*IT Verona Arena, Via
Roma 17, open Mon–Fri
10–10, Sat–Sun 2–10*

Verona ✉ 37100

There are plenty of soulless chain hotels on the fringes of the city, but not really enough nice places in the centre, especially during the opera season in July or August, so do book. Rooms are also tight in March, when Verona hosts an agricultural fair, and April, for the Vinitaly Wine Fair.

Luxury (€€€€€)
*****Gabbia d'Oro, Corso Porta Borsari 4/a, t 045 800 3060, *www.hotelgabbiadoro.it*. Just steps away from Piazza delle Erbe, this small ivy-covered *palazzo* is a haven of tranquillity. Rooms are decorated in rich fabrics; one suite has its own secluded outdoor bath tub on the terrace. The Orangerie is open for bistro snacks and there is a secluded library which can be reserved for small gatherings.

Very Expensive (€€€€)
****Accademia, Via Scala 12, t 045 596 222, *www.accademiavr.it*. A restored 16th-century palace houses another excellent, atmospheric choice of places to stay, smack in the centre.

Expensive (€€€)
***De' Capuleti, Via del Pontiere 26, t 045 800 0154, *www.hotelcapuleti.it*. Another good choice in the historic centre, with air-conditioning and satellite TV for news junkies.
*****Colomba d'Oro, Via C. Cattaneo 10, t 045 595 300, *www.colombahotel.com*. Located in a quiet, traffic-free street near the Arena, offering very comfortable air-conditioned rooms behind its old stone façade and secure parking, but no restaurant.
***Giulietta e Romeo, Vicolo Tre Marchetti 3, t 045 800 3554, *www.giuliettaeromeo.com*. Centrally located near the Arena, this recently restored hotel is on a quiet street and offers fine rooms (and parking facilities), but no restaurant.

⭐ Bottega del
Vino >>

***Italia**, Via Mameli 58, **t** 045 918
088, *www.hotelitalia.tv*. On the other
side of the Adige, near the Roman
Theatre: the rooms are tranquil,
modern and comfortable.

***Novo Hotel Rossi**, Via delle Coste 2,
t 045 569 022, *www.novohotelrossi.it*.
Very convenient and *simpatico* if
you're arriving by train; some rooms
fall in the moderate category.

Moderate (€€)

Aurora, Piazza delle Erbe, **t** 045 594
717, *www.hotelaurora.biz*. Right in the
heart of Verona; no frills but friendly
staff and well priced.

Sammicheli, Via Valverde 2, **t** 045
800 3749. About 150 yards from the
Arena, this is convenient for opera-
goers, with easy parking, and TV.

Torcolo, Vicolo Listone 3, **t** 045 800
7512, *www.hoteltorcolo.it*. Friendly and
very close to the Arena with large,
tastefully furnished rooms, all with
air-con. The nicest by far of Verona's
two-star hotels.

Inexpensive (€)

Catullo, Via Catullo 1, **t** 045 800 2786,
locandacatullo@tiscalinet.it. Try this
hotel for cheaper rooms with or
without bath in the centre; some even
have balconies.

Ostello Verona, Via Fontana del Ferro
15, **t** 045 590 360, *www.ostellionline.
org*. If you have an IYHF card, you can't
beat a 16th-century villa with frescoes
just beyond the Castel di San Pietro
(take bus no.73 to the first stop across
the river). Beds are up in the newer
wing. The reception stays open year-
round, 24 hours a day, but you won't
be allowed in until 5pm; get there
early in summer.

Eating Out in Verona

The Veronese have long gastro-
memories. They've been fond of
potato gnocchi (served with melted
butter and sage) since the late 16th
century, when the ingredients were
distributed after a great famine and,
like the Parisians, attribute their
weakness for horsemeat to a siege
when horses were all there was left to
eat; it's served in stew called
pastissada de caval. In summer look
for Italy's finest peaches.

Very Expensive (€€€€)

Arche, Via delle Arche Scaligere 6,
t 045 800 7415. Run by the same
family for over a hundred years, and
located near the Scaliger tombs, a
restaurant which has long been the
classic place to go for a special meal
in an aristocratic setting. The freshest
of fish is brought in daily from
Chioggia and imaginatively prepared
by the maestro in the kitchen.
Excellent wine list. *Closed Sun, Mon
lunch, and part of Jan.*

Bottega del Vino, Via Scudo di Francia
3 (off Via Mazzini), **t** 045 800 4535.
A century-old restaurant, preparing
traditional recipes using organically
grown ingredients, and pasta made
on the premises, all customized to
accompany a huge list of wine from
around the world. *Closed Tues, except
during opera season.*

Il Desco, Via dietro San Sebastiano 7,
t 045 595 358. This king of the
Veronese restaurant scene occupies a
15th-century palace, not far from the
Ponte Nuovo. Expect exquisite dishes
based on seasonal ingredients:
gnocchi with ewe's milk cheese, red
mullet with black olives and rosemary,
goose liver in a sauce of sweet wine
and grapes. *Closed Sun and Mon (exc.
Mon lunch in July, Aug and Dec); also
closed part of Jan and June.*

I Dodici Apostoli, Corticella San Marco
3, **t** 045 596 999. An even older
favourite, located a couple of streets
from Piazza delle Erbe, offering a
traditional Renaissance setting –
complete with frescoes of Romeo and
Juliet. The name is derived from
twelve 18th-century 'apostles' of the
kitchen who gathered here to dine.
Some delicacies are adapted from
Roman or Renaissance recipes; the
salmone in crosta (marinated salmon
in pastry) is famous. *Closed Sun eve,
Mon, two weeks June and July.*

Maffei, Piazza delle Erbe 38, **t** 045 801
0015. Another beauty, both ancient
and elegant, which serves a melt-in-
the-mouth cheese flan and *risotto*
with pumpkin and Amarone. *Closed
Sun, Mon in July and Aug.*

L'Oste Scuro, Via San Silvestro, 10, **t** 045
592 650. A relaxed yet elegant place
specializing in seafood prepared with

creative flair. The fish couldn't be fresher and the desserts are also sure to tempt: try the *pistacchio semifreddo* with fruits of the forest or passion fruit. *Closed Mon lunch, Sun, and part of Aug and Dec.*

Expensive (€€€)

Greppia, Vicolo Samaritana 3, **t** 045 800 4577. Located near Juliet's house and serving up traditional and Veronese favourites in a quiet little square. *Closed Mon and June.*

Moderate (€€)

Alla Pergola, Piazzetta Santa Maria in Solaro 10, **t** 045 800 4744. A traditional and reliable old favourite, housed in a deconsecrated medieval church off Via Garibaldi. *Closed Wed and Aug.*

Alla Strueta, Via Redentore 4 (near the Roman Theatre), **t** 045 803 2462. Prices are lower over the Adige in Veronetta, where this old workers' *osteria* now features delights in the order of smoked goose breast, gnocchi and, yes (or rather, neigh!), *pastissada de caval.* *Closed Mon, Tues lunch and Aug.*

Inexpensive (€)

All'Isolo, Piazza Isolo, 5, **t** 045 594 291. A simple family *trattoria* in a lively square not far from the Giardini Giusti but miles away from the hordes of tourists near the Arena. Dishes include *fettucine* with duck, *baccalà* with *polenta* or soused pike. *Closed Wed and Aug.*

Osteria Morandin, Via XX Settembre 144, just off Interrato dell'Acqua Morta, **t** 045 594 453. This is another old standby in Veronetta, with a good choice of wines and a few dishes to go along. *Closed Sun.*

Antico Cafè Dante, Piazza dei Signori. Stop for a coffee at this historic café.

Cordioli, Via Cappello 39. This takes some beating for traditional Veronese pastries. *Closed Wed.*

Entertainment and Nightlife in Verona

Verona bills itself as the 'city for all seasons' and offers a wide-ranging cultural programme throughout the year.

All listings are printed in the tourist office's free **Passport Verona**. A broadsheet fly-posted weekly in cafés and around town, *Siri-Sera*, has information on discos, films and more casual artistic events.

Opera, Classical Music and Theatre

From December to April there is drama in the **Teatro Nuovo** (*www. teatrostabileverona.it*), while the **Teatro Filarmonico**, sponsored by the Ente Lirico, hosts opera and music.

Stagione Lirica. Big events take place in the Arena, especially this opera and ballet festival, founded in 1913, with performances almost daily in July and August. If you're travelling on a tight schedule, it's best to reserve your seat before coming to Italy. Online booking by credit card (no commission).

Liaisons Abroad, London, **t** 020 7376 4020. Will arrange tickets before you go.

Ente Lirico Arena di Verona, Piazza Brà 28, **t** 045 800 5151, *www.arena.it*. An alternative place to contact for programme details and reservation; tickets sales are next to the Arena at Via Dietro Anfiteatro 6/b. If you get an unnumbered seat, plan on arriving an hour earlier to get yourself situated. And bring a cushion (or you can hire one there).

Art

There are a number of **art galleries** around the Piazza delle Erbe, while the area between the Via Ponte Pietra, Via Duomo, Sottoriva, and Corso S. Anastasia is called the 'little city of antiques'. But buyer beware: the region is Italy's largest producer of reproductions.

Bars

Unlike the Venetians, the Veronese like to be out and about in the evening and have their own expression for pub-crawling, *'andar per goti'* (going Goth-ing), after a memorable binge by Theodoric's gang back in the 5th century. The bars in Piazza Brà and Piazza delle Erbe are the busiest.

Al Carro Armato, Via San Pietro Martire 2a, **t** 045 803 0175. An old-fashioned bar near the Piazza de' Signori, and one of the most atmospheric.

Cappa Café, Piazzetta Brà Molinari 1, **t** 045 800 4516. Outside tables overlooking the Ponte Pietra. *Open day and night.*

Le Vecete, near Piazza delle Erbe at Via Pellicciai 32, **t** 045 594 681. A favourite wine bar and a decent restaurant too. *Closed Sun.*

South of Verona: La Pianura Veronese

Six hundred years ago, Verona's well-watered breadbasket (in this case, rice basket) was crossed by one of the wonders of Europe: the **Serraglio**, a mini-Great Wall of China, built in the mid-14th century by the Scaligers to defend Verona from Mantua and other bullies coming from the south. Stretching 16km, fortified with 200 towers, these thick walls, complete with moats and towers, were the most advanced fortifications of the day. But by the time the Venetians inherited the Serraglio in the 15th century they were not terribly impressed with its ability to stand up to the artillery of the day, and concentrated their defences at Legnano and Peschiera del Garda; now only traces of the great walls remain.

The Serraglio's eastern hub was **Villafranca di Verona**, a town founded by Verona along the road to Mantua in 1185 as an agricultural colony and fortified camp. Laid out in an elongated grid, with an elevated **castle** on one end, its plan is reminiscent of the *bastides* or *villefranches* ('free towns' with tax exemptions to attract settlers) founded by England and France during the Hundred Years War. There were a number of these in the Veneto, but this is the only one to keep its walls intact. Just as impressive, in its way, is the massive **Villa Canossa** at **Grezzano**, 4km southeast, a neo-Palladian ranch built in 1776, in the centre of an enormous rice plantation.

The source of all the moisture in these parts is the Adige and Lake Garda's main drain into the Po, the River Mincio. On its banks, **Valeggio sul Mincio** started out as another Veronese colony and was given a 14th-century castle and a bridge by the Visconti during their brazen attempt to seize all of Italy. Most of all they were interested in the possibilities of diverting the Mincio: they intended either to drain the lakes of Mantua downstream to make it easy to conquer, or to flood the plain inside the Serraglio in case Mantua attacked. In 1393 they invested an enormous sum in the project at **Borghetto** (a *frazione* of Valeggio), building at the end of the Scaligers' Serraglio the 1980ft-long **Ponte Rotta**, a cross between a fortified bridge and a dyke, with a system of portcullises that could be used to shut off the river's flow. It's still there, a bit overgrown but one of the surviving engineering marvels of the

Middle Ages. Nearly six centuries later another Visconti, Luchino, found Borghetto's romantic, 19th-century atmosphere the perfect setting for his film *Senso*.

In fact, everything here is on a big scale. There's the **Cavour Parco Acquatico** south of town, a water fun park in a tropical garden with palms and sandy beaches, set in an enormous botanical park with lakes and beautiful old trees. In Valeggio itself, the old grounds of the Villa Maffe became in the early 19th century the **Sigurtà Gardens**. This was the 40-year project of Dr Count Carlo Sigurtà, 'Italy's Capability Brown' – who, granted water rights from the Mincio, used them to transform a barren waste into 123 acres of Anglo-Italian gardens along a 7km lane; parking areas along the

Cavour Parco Acquatico
www.parcoacquatico cavour.it; open late May–early Sept 9.30–7; adm exp

Sigurtà Gardens
t 045 637 1033, www. sigurta.it; open Mar– Oct daily 9–6; adm

route allow you to get out and walk along the waterlily ponds, topiary gardens and valleys of roses.

One of the strangest encounters of any kind in Italian history occurred just north of Valeggio, in **Salionze**. Word had reached Pope Leo the Great that Attila the Hun had laid waste to the Veneto and was on his way to do the same to Rome. Leo rode forth to prevent Attila from coming any closer and met up with the Hunnish warlord in Salionze. Their meeting is faithfully recorded on Leo's tombstone in St Peter's: the Pope told Attila that he would get a fatal nosebleed if he came any closer. But there was a snag – Attila didn't understand Latin. Fortunately SS Peter and Paul came down from the clouds to translate, and the Hun, suitably impressed, turned on his heel and retreated – it's as good an explanation as any for why Attila suddenly turned back from his stated goal.

The Eastern Plain: Legnano and Cologna Veneta

Halfway between Verona and Rovigo, **Legnano** is the biggest town and industrial centre of the Pianura. Two mighty floods of the Adige and Second World War bombardments have obliterated everything but a 16th-century tower, a last reminder that for a thousand years Legnano was a key in the Veneto's defences and a corner of the Austrian 'Quadrilateral'. It was also the birthplace of Antonio Salieri (1750–1825), the composer and director of the Viennese Opera, who did *not* in point of fact poison Mozart, at least according to the locals (and most historians); Legnano's theatre is named in his honour.

Cologna Veneta, east of the Adige, was another agricultural colony, founded by the Romans this time, back in 170 BC; originally the main crop was hemp, although now the town specializes in *mandorlato* (nougat; try it at Rocco Garzotto & Figlio, Via Quari Destra 57). The historic centre is well preserved, around a picturesque 19th-century cathedral with an altarpiece of the Nativity by Bartolomeo Montagna. The neighbouring **Civico Museo Archeologico** has a good assortment of finds, not only from Roman times but also from the Palaeoveneti and the Bronze Age (8th century BC). In nearby Pressana, **Villa Querini Stampalia** is an example of a villa that expanded over the years into a handsome mix of late Gothic and Renaissance elements.

Civico Museo Archeologico
open Sun only 9.45–12 and 3–6

Where to Stay and Eat South of Verona

This is prime grazing land, for people, that is: Valeggio, famous for its home-made *tortellini*, has over 40 restaurants, and the Pianura has two gourmet shrines.

Valeggio sul Mincio ✉ 37067
Il Borghetto, Via Raffaello Sanzio, 14A Fraz. Borghetto, **t** 045 795 2040, *www.borghetto.it* (€€€). Ten 15th-century watermills have been converted into rooms and apartments in the charming hamlet of Borghetto.

Many of the units still have part of the mill's mechanism imbedded in the walls.

***Al Cacciatore**, Via Goito 31, **t** 045 795 0500, *www.alcacciatore.net* (€€). A pretty country villa converted into a hotel with 19 rooms, country-style furnishings and a restaurant.

***Eden**, Via Don G. Beltrame 10, **t** 045 637 0850, *www.albergoedenvaleggio. com* (€€). A new-ish and stylish hotel, with very comfortable rooms in a quiet setting.

Antica Locanda Mincio, Via Michelangelo 12, Borghetto, **t** 045 795 0059 (€€€). A charming 17th-century inn, adding culinary expertise to a delightful setting – depending on the season you can dine by the fireplace or out on the banks of the Mincio. The dishes have a touch of Mantua in them, which isn't a bad thing. *Closed Wed, Thurs, some of Feb and Nov.*

Borsa, Via Goito 2, **t** 045 795 0093, *www.ristoranteborsa.it* (€€). Many give the *Tortellini di Valeggio* crown to this restaurant, where the river and lake fish make a good *secondo. Closed Tues eve, Wed and mid-July–mid-Aug.*

Isola della Scala ✉ 37063

Gabbia d'Oro ('Gilded Cage'), 6km from Isola at Gabbia south of Verona, **t** 045 733 0020 (€€€). A restaurant occupying an old inn, elegantly restored if not always that easy to find on these arrow-straight country roads. The reward: Veronese regional cuisine at its finest, prepared with the choicest and freshest ingredients, although you may perhaps prefer to avoid some of the fussier dishes on the menu. *Closed Tues and Wed, Jan and Aug.*

Isola Rizza ✉ 37050

Perbellini, Via Muselle 11, **t** 045 713 5352 (€€€€). Lost in the middle of an ugly industrial area north of Legnano, next to a *panettone* bakery, is this island of classic refinement and masterful cuisine, every dish from *antipasti* to dessert a pure delight, with service to match. *Closed Mon, Tues lunch, Jan, June and Aug.*

North of Verona: Lessinia Natural Park

Museo dei Cimbri
open July–Aug Wed–Fri 2.30–6.30, Sat–Sun 9.30–12.30 and 3.30–6.30, Sept–June Wed, Sat and Sun 2.30–6.30; adm

Pesciara Museum
open Tues–Sun; Nov–Feb 10–12 and 2–5; Mar–Oct 9–1 and 2–6.30

Fossil museum
t 045 651 6005, www.lessiniamusei.it; open mid-June–mid-Sept daily 9.30–12.30 and 3.30–6.30; mid-Sept–mid-June Sat–Sun 10–12 and 2.30–4.30

North of Verona, the soft foothills of the Dolomites make up the Lessinia, now a Regional Natural Park, and one famous for rocks, in formations, fossils and flintstones. In the 13th century Lessinia was settled by Bavarians, whose descendants still speak a kind of medieval German, or Cimbra. Although traditionally a poor area, the inhabitants enjoyed a golden age in the 1600s manufacturing flintlocks. You can learn more about them, their folklore, costumes, and the huge *tromboni* (a kind of arquebus) that they blast on holidays at the small **Museo dei Cimbri** in **Giazza**, one of Lessinia's prettiest villages with its medieval German houses. **Bolca**, southeast of Giazza, caused a sensation in the Renaissance when the discovery of a rich bed of fossilized fish was cited as proof of Noah's Flood. As well as interesting, they are also extremely beautiful and delicate, and at **Pesciara**, you can now visit the site where the fossils were found as well as a special museum.

A winding road loops east to the next valley and **Bosco Chiesanuova**, Lessinia's modest winter sports centre. From here, follow the road to **Velo Veronese**, the starting point for a visit to **Camposilvano**, its fossil museum, and the **Valley of the Sphinxes** (Valle delle Sfingi), named for its striking chasms and landforms, made of layer upon layer of red ammonite. In recent years a

Grotta di Rovere 1000
t 045 918 484; open mid-June–Aug Sat–Sun by appointment

beautiful stalactite cave was discovered in adjacent Rovere: Grotta di Rovere 1000.

Another pretty place to aim for is west, at **Molina**, where the Parco delle Cascate has paths along the waterfalls. North, beyond **Fosse**, the slopes of Corno d'Aquilio are pierced by the **Spluga della Preta**, one of the world's deepest chasms, its floor halfway to hell – 2,906ft down. Lessinia's wealth of flint first attracted people in the Lower Palaeolithic age (500,000 BC). Shelters and flint workshops have been discovered on the ridges and in the caves; some can be seen in the prehistory museum at **Sant'Anna d'Alfaedo**, along with a 20ft-long fossilized shark. South of Sant'Anna, not far off the road to Fane, don't miss the **Ponte di Veja**, a spectacular natural 170ft arch, the inspiration for the Malebolge bridge in Dante's *Inferno*.

The region of Valpolicella is sliced by torrents and dotted with Romanesque churches and villas. **Negrar**, one of the main centres, has a handsome 12th-century campanile and park at Villa Rizzardi. Just west in **Pedemonte**, Palladio's **Villa Serego Alighieri** was built in 1565–9, its two prominent wings bearing a continuous double portico of Ionic columns. West, in a hamlet of the same name, the 12th-century church of **San Floriano** is one of the prettiest in the area, with a frieze and an arcade on its tufa façade. **Fumane**, another important wine village to the north, has a number of stately homes and a landmark, the 16th-century **Villa della Torre** (on the road to Cavolo). The name of the architect has been forgotten, although the originality of the design suggests Giulio Romano; based on the concept of an ancient Roman villa, the rooms are off a peristyle court with a fountain. Other features include pools resembling Roman *piscinae*, a little octagonal temple, and towering dovecotes.

Further west, **Sant'Ambrogio** produces Verona's famous red marble in addition to red wine; nearby, in the lovely old hilltop hamlet of **San Giorgio**, the parish church was founded in the 7th century and expanded in the 1100s. The ciborium over the altar also dates from the 600s, and among the frescoes there's a fascinating 11th-century Last Judgement. In such ancient surroundings, perhaps it's not surprising that the parish maintains

Valpolicella

The cherry-scented prince of Veronese wines, Valpolicella was the *vino retico* quaffed by all the emperors from Augustus to Theodoric, and hails from 19 *comuni* west of Verona and south of Lessinia. The Molinara, Rondinella and Corvina grapes that grow so well here are vinified in different ways – the familiar stuff sold in your supermarket at home (Superiore), and three others, made from well-ripened grapes left to dry for several months: Recioto della Valpolicella, a fine dessert wine with a bittersweet aftertaste, not unlike port; DOCG Amarone, left longer in the vat to become a dry, powerful (16°) wine of great character that can be aged up to 20 years, one of the best and most distinctive wines in Italy; and Ripasso, wine fermented on the lees of the Recioto to take on some of nuances of Amarone.

a custom long forgotten elsewhere in Italy: the distribution of fava beans after a funeral, symbolic of the afterlife. North of Sant'Ambrogio on the Adige, **Volargne** merits a detour for its riverside **Villa del Bene**, built in the 1400s and enlarged by Sammicheli in the next century. He enclosed the courtyard at the entrance, and added the portico and loggia to the façade, a second courtyard, and dovecotes; the interior has fine frescoes by Caroto and Domenico Brusasorci, including – rather bizarrely for a villa – scenes of the Apocalypse.

Up the Rear Slopes of Monte Baldo

Just west of Sant'Ambrogio (*see* above) is one of your last chances for a long time to cross the Adige and the A22 into the eastern valleys of Lake Garda's **Monte Baldo** (*see* below). Once over the Adige, turn north at **Affi**, a village made of rounded stones from the Adige, for **Rivoli Veronese**, a small village set in a morainic amphitheatre. This is the origin of the famous Rue de Rivoli in Paris, laid out by Napoleon to celebrate his great victory over the Austrians here on 14 January 1797.

Carry on north for **Caprino Veronese**, a medieval new town and later a favourite area for *villeggiatura*. One summer house, the 17th-century **Villa Carlotti**, is now the town hall and Museo Civico, where you can visit the 'Room of Dreams' with its caryatids and frescoes, and another containing a magnificent 14th-century statue group called *Il Compianto* ('The Lamented One'), where life-size figures of Joseph of Arimathea, St John, Nicodemus and the holy women mourn a strikingly dead cadaverous Christ.

From Caprino you can turn up the sometimes vertiginous road west for **San Zeno di Montagna**, with views over Lake Garda, or meander west towards **Platano**, where an enormous ancient plane tree predates even the 15th-century Palazzo Nichesola, with its high chimneys. The main road continues north by way of the striking **Santuario della Madonna della Corona**, set up on a nearly inaccessible rocky spur under a cliff, where a statue of Our Lady of Sorrows appeared in a blaze of light just as the Turks captured Rhodes from the Knights of St John in 1522, having apparently flown there to escape the infidels. The shrine was built in 1540 and 556 steps were dug out of the side of the mountain for pilgrims; thousands still come to pay their respects on 19 September, although most now drive up the paved road. Further north, **Ferrara di Monte Baldo** was an iron-mining centre and is now an excursion centre, with skiing and a botanical garden sheltering some of the many rare species that thrive in Monte Baldo's unique micro-climate. You won't, however, see the species the Italians like best – black truffles, which thrive under the big mountain's oaks.

Museo Civico
t 045 620 9911; open
Tues, Wed, Fri, Sat 10–12

Tourist Information in Lessinia Natural Park

ⓘ Bosco
Chiesanuova ›
Piazza Chiesa 38,
t 045 705 0088

For guided tours of Lessinia Natural Park, contact **Comunità Montana della Lessinia**, Piazza Borgo 52, Bosco Chiesanuova, t 045 679 9211. Other good sources of information include *www.lessiniapark.it* and *www.verona tuttintorno.it.*

Where to Stay and Eat in Lessinia Natural Park

⭐ Villa Giona ››

⭐ La Magioca ›

Negrar ✉ 37024

La Magioca, Via Moron 3, t 045 600 0167, *www.magioca.it* (€€€€). A bed and breakfast almost too good to be true, with a lawn straight out of *House & Garden*. You'll be fussed over like long-lost relatives and served up home-baked pies and cookies for breakfast.

Pedemonte ✉ 37020

****Villa del Quar**, Via Quar 12, t 045 680 0681, *www.hotelvilladelquar.it* (€€€€€). Not far from Palladio's villa in Valpolicella, this lovely Relais & Châteaux villa in S. Pietro in Cariano has been beautifully restored, with 22 elegant rooms; its restaurant, Arquade, occupies the villa's chapel

and emphasizes the best of the region's cuisine, with the occasional French touch. *Closed Mon out of season, and early Jan–mid-Mar.*

Sant'Ambrogio di Valpolicella ✉ 37010

Groto de Corgnan, Via Corgnano 41, t 045 773 1372 (€€€). Once you've looked at the vines here, stop to sit around the fire and sip them with dishes specially concocted to bring out their best – the wine list includes the finest Amarones. *Closed Sun and Mon lunch.*

S. Pietro in Cariano ✉ 37029

****Villa Giona, Via Cengia 8, t 045 685 5011, *www.villagiona.it* (€€€€). A spectacular villa in the Valpolicella hillside with large rooms, suites and self-catering apartments. The grounds include vineyards partnered with the famous Allegrini winery. Cooking and wine-tasting courses are hosted and a swimming pool is in the works. Guests can dine in the *loggia*.

Bolca/Altissimo ✉ 36070

Casin del Gamba, Via Pizzati 1, Roccolo, t 0444 687 709 (€€€). Just east of Bolca in Altissimo, dine superbly at this old hunting lodge 2km from the centre, where the chef prepares dishes entirely based on the season, accompanied by a great wine list and masterful desserts. *Closed Sun eve and Mon, second half of Jan and Aug.*

Lake Garda

🌟 Lake Garda

*Kennst du das
Land wo die
Citronen blühn?*

Goethe

Garda is the largest of Italy's famous lakes (48km long, 16km across at its widest point) and most the dramatic, its 'Madonna blue' waters, as Winston Churchill described them, lapping at the feet of the Dolomites. Shaped like the profile of a tall-hatted witch, its Latin name *Benacus* is of Celtic origin, a word similar to the Irish *bennach*, 'horned one', describing its many headlands. Two of Italy's greatest poets left their imprint on its shores: ancient, tragic, lovelorn Catullus and that 20th-century Italian fire hazard, Gabriele D'Annunzio.

The other lakes are warm but Garda, Venice's 'little sea', has a genuine Mediterranean climate. Open to the south and blocked off from the cold winds of the north by the Dolomites, Garda's great volume (its average depth is 445ft) make it a giant solar battery,

Arco

Varone

Riva del Garda

Bezzecca

Condino

Molina di Ledro

Torbole

Lake Ledro

Val di Ledro

Valli Giudicarie

Passo de Maniva

Lodrone

Limone sul Garda

Bagolino

Tremosine

Malcesine

Lake Idro

Campione

Anfo

Tignale

Assenza

Lavenone

Idro

Monte Baldo

Brenzone

Gargnano

Lake Garda

Bogliaco

Sabbio

Vobarno

Pai

Toscolano-Maderno

S. Zeno

Gardone Riviera

Caprino

Salò

Is. di Garda

Torri del Benaco

Gavardo

S.Felice del Benaco

Costermano

Garda

Polpenazze

Manerba

Affi

Moniga

Bardolino

Padenghe

Cavernago

Cisano

Lazise

Sirmione

Desenzano del Garda

Lonato

Colombare

Pacengo

Rivoltella

Peschiera del Garda

A4

S. Martino d. Battaglia

Castiglione d. Stiviere

Solferino

Carpenedolo

Sigurta Gardens

Valeggio sul Mincio

A22

N

5 km

2.5 miles

warming the surrounding hills throughout the winter and keeping deadly frosts and clammy mists at bay. For Goethe and generations of chilblained travellers from Middle Europe, its olives, vines, citrus groves and palm trees have long signalled the beginning of their dream Italy. No tourist office could concoct a more scintillating oasis to stimulate what the Icelanders call 'a longing for figs', that urge to go south.

It does have its moods. Sailors and windsurfers come to test their mettle on the winds, first mentioned by Virgil: the *sover* which blows from the north from midnight and through the morning, and the *ora*, which comes from the south in the afternoon and evening. White caps and storms are not uncommon, but on the other hand the breezes are delightfully cool in the summer. The best time to visit is autumn and spring, when temperatures are pleasant and there are not so many tourists about. Although services drop to a minimum, winter is also a good time to visit, when the jagged peaks shimmer with snow and you can better take in the voluptuous charms that brought visitors to Garda in the first place.

Peschiera to Desenzano: the South Shore

The gateway to Lake Garda from the Veneto is **Peschiera del Garda**, an old military town near the mouth of the River Mincio. Its strategic position has caused it to be fortified since Roman times, though the imposing walls that you see today are actually 16th-century Venetian, reinforced by the Austrians when Peschiera was one of the corners of the empire's 'Quadrilateral'. Its massive purifying plant, the ultimate destination of what goes down every drain in every lakeside town (thanks to an underwater pipeline) still helps it to fulfil its ancient role as a defender, this time of the lake's status as the cleanest in all Europe.

Gardaland
t 045 644 9777,
www.gardaland.it;
open April–mid-June
9.30–6.30; mid-
June–early Sept
9.30–midnight; last 3
wks Sept 9.30–6.30; Oct
Sat–Sun 9.30–6;
1st weekend Nov
9.30–6; adm

Here, too, you can treat the children – at **Gardaland**, Italy's largest, and most massively popular, Disney-clone theme park with a green dinosaur named Prezzemolo or 'Parsley' as official mascot. Attractions include the Magic Mountain roller coaster, Colorado boat ride, the Valley of the Kings, an African safari, some fairly scary space rides, a pirate ship, robots, a dolphin show and 'The World Of Barbie' (Her Sublime Plasticity continues to exert a subliminal effect on Italian womanhood: every little Italian girl owns at least ten Barbies). And now there's the new Flying Island, an orbiting space station that offers a wonderful panorama of the lake and surroundings. There are free pushchairs to drive toddlers around the park from the Information Office.

Getting around Lake Garda's South Shore

There are two **train** stations at the southern end of Lake Garda, at Desenzano and Peschiera, both of which are also landings for the lake's **hydrofoils** (*aliscafi*) and **steamers**. **Buses** from Brescia, Trento and Verona go to their respective shores; Desenzano, the gateway to Lake Garda, is served by buses from Brescia, Verona and Mantua. Frequent buses connect Sirmione to Desenzano and Peschiera.

Other local bus lines run up and down the road that winds around the lake shores – a marvel of Italian engineering, called La Gardesana, Occidentale (SS45) on the west and Orientale (SS249) on the east. In summer, however, their scenic splendour sometimes pales before the sheer volume of holiday traffic.

All **boat** services on the lake are operated by **Navigazione sul Lago di Garda**, Piazza Matteotti 2, Desenzano, t 030 914 9511, *www.navigazionelaghi.it*, where you can pick up a timetable; the tourist offices have them as well. The one **car ferry** crosses from Maderno to Torri; between Desenzano and Riva there are several hydrofoils a day, calling at various ports (2hrs the full trip), as well as the more frequent and leisurely steamers (4hrs). Services are considerably reduced from November to March. Full fare on the 4hr sail from Desenzano to Riva on the steamer is €9.30, on the hydrofoil €12.70. Children travel for free (up to 4 years) or at reduced rates (4–11-year-olds). 20% discount for EU over-60s Mon–Fri.

Parco Natura Viva
t 045 717 0113,
www.parconatura
viva.it; open Mar–
Oct daily 9–6; Nov
Thurs–Tues 9–6; Feb
Sun 9–6; adm

Some 5km east of Gardaland there's the Parco Natura Viva, a safari park and breeding centre for endangered animals; with English-speaking guides, it aims to educate and fascinate kids of all ages.

Sirmione

Few towns enjoy the dramatic position of Sirmione, strung out along the narrow 4km-long peninsula that pierces Lake Garda's broad bottom like a pin. Lake views and a lush growth of palms, cypresses and parasol pines keep the medieval core from ever feeling claustrophic, even when it's heaving with people, as it tends to be in season. To find fewer day-trippers and more of the atmosphere that inspired Catullus, Dante, Goethe, Byron, and later Pound and Joyce, who met here, make sure you come before June or after September.

The Rocca Scaligera to the Grotte di Catullo

Rocca Scaligera
t 030 916 468; open
summer Tues–Sun
8.30–7, winter Tues–Sun
8.30–4.30; adm, but
free for under-18s and
over-60s

Large car parks signal the entrance into the historic centre; only the vehicles of residents and hotel guests are permitted into town over the bridge of the fairy-tale castle, the Rocca Scaligera. Built by Mastino I della Scala, *signore* of Verona in the 13th century, it is entirely surrounded by a moat where mallards and swans bob and float. Palms fill the courtyard; Dante slept here; but there's not much to see inside, though the views of lake and town from its swallowtail battlements and lofty tower are lovely. A second set of battlements protect the 15th-century church of **Santa Maria Maggiore**, overlooking a slender beach; note the reused Roman capital on the porticoed façade and the unusual pastel brick ceiling. Nearby begins the *passeggiata panoramica* that skirts the peninsula's east shore.

Rome's greatest lyric poet, Catullus, was born in Verona in 84 BC, only to die some 30 years later in the fever of a broken heart. In between passionate bouts in the Palatine home of his fickle mistress, 'Lesbia', he would cool his heels at the family villa at Sirmione. But chances are the great late 1st-century BC villa at the very tip of the rocky promontory known as the Grotte di Catullo wasn't it – only a millionaire could have afforded such an opulent pleasure dome. The superb site is romantic with a capital R, set among ancient olives and rosemary hedges. Rigidly rectangular, symmetrical and vast (550ft by 310ft), the villa was flanked by porticoes on the east and west (as well as a long underground cryptoporticus on the west), while a belvedere on the north end overlooked the lake. Of this only the supporting hall called the Aula dei Giganti survives, strewn with enormous chunks; some of the ceilings here once stood over 55ft high. Olive trees trace the villa's main residential section which collapsed in the 4th century. A huge cistern, 141ft long, fed the large bath complex and heated pool. A small museum, expanded and reopened in 1999, contains a comprehensive exhibition of fragments of vases, lamps, spearheads and other bits salvaged from the villa's ruins, as well as prehistoric and medieval remains discovered around the peninsula and Lake Garda.

Grotte di Catullo
t 030 916 468; open summer Tues–Sun 8.30–7, winter Tues–Sun 8.30–4.30; adm, but free for under-18s and over-60s

Museum
open same hours as Grotte di Catullo

Near the Grotte di Catullo, standing alone on the peninsula's highest point, the Romanesque **San Pietro in Mavino** was built of scavenged Roman bricks; inside are frescoes from the 13th to the 16th centuries by the school of Verona. Also near here is the thermal **Stabilimento Termale Catullo**, where a pipe brings up steaming sulphuric water from the bottom of the lake, just the thing for respiratory ailments. The medieval lanes in the centre have been given over to boutiques, bars and pizzerias; if you want to escape, there are good places to swim off the rocks along the west shore.

Desenzano del Garda

Lively, colourful and thoroughly pleasant Desenzano del Garda, on a wide gulf dotted with beaches, is Garda's largest town, built up in the 15th and 16th centuries (if you arrive by train, a bus will take you to the centre). Life centres around its busy portside cafés, presided over by a statue of Sant'Angela, foundress of the Ursuline Order, who seems appalled at all the carryings-on; another statue on the lakefront, the whooshing **High Speed Monument**, celebrates an air speed record (709 km/hr) set here in 1934 by Francesco Agello. On the lower end of the technological scale, Desenzano's Bronze Age (2200–1200 BC) inhabitants lived in pile dwellings, recently discovered in the peat bogs southwest of town and yielding the contents of the new **Museo Archeologico Rambotti** in the cloister of Santa Maria de Senioribus. There are models of houses and, amongst the ornaments, little 'pearls' of

Museo Archeologico Rambotti
Santa Maria de Senioribus, Via Anelli 7, t 030 914 4529; open Tues–Sun 3–7

amber: Desenzano was on the ancient trade route between the amber-rich Baltic and the Mediterranean, which endured until the end of the Roman period.

Desenzano, also on the Bergamo–Verona Via Gallica, became a popular resort (read refuge) of the Romans towards the end of the empire, when the rich and powerful retreated from the growing anarchy to their country estates. Incorporating vast agricultural lands, maintained by hundreds of slaves and retainers, these estates were the origins of feudalism. One of the most important was Desenzano's **Villa Romana**, just in from the Lungolago.

Villa Romana
Via Crocifisso 22,
t 030 914 3547; open
Mar–mid-Oct Tues–Sat
8.30–7, Sun 9–5.30;
end Oct–Feb 8.30–
4.30; adm

Although begun in the 1st century BC, the villa was given its present form in the 4th century, fitted with sumptuous heated baths, a triclinium (dining hall) with three apses, and other rooms covered with the most extensive mosaic floors in northern Italy; pick up the free archaeological itinerary pamphlet in English. Nearby, along Via Roma, **Santa Maria Maddalena** has 27 huge canvases by a transplanted Venetian, Andrea Celesti (*d.* 1712), and a strikingly different *Last Supper* by Giandomenico Tiepolo.

The Risorgimento Hills and the Red Cross

Desenzano is the base for visiting not only Lake Garda but the low, morainic amphitheatre of hills to the south. Although famous for battles, perhaps more important for Western civilization was the combat averted in 425, at the twilight of the Roman Empire. Attila the Hun, having devastated northeast Italy, was marching to annihilate Rome when he met Pope Leo I south of Desenzano. The pope, with Saints Peter and Paul as his translators, informed Attila that if he should continue to Rome he would be stricken by a fatal nosebleed, upon which the terrible but superstitious Hun turned aside, sparing central Italy.

Move the clock ahead 1400 years, when Italy, fragmented for all that time, was beginning to reunite in the Risorgimento. In a single day, 24 June 1859, the Italians and their French allies pounded the Austrian occupier twice, when King Vittorio Emanuele II and his Sardinian army crushed the Austrian right wing at San Martino, while Napoleon III defeated Emperor Franz Joseph at Solferino, 11km to the southwest. At **San Martino della Battaglia** the victory is commemorated by a monumental complex. An **ossuary** in a 13th-century chapel contains the bones of 2,619 dead from both sides. At the highest point of the hill the round 213ft **Torre Monumentale** was inaugurated in 1893; a winding ramp inside leads up to the panoramic terrace, passing rooms with frescoes and statues on the events and heroes of the Risorgimento. A museum behind the tower contains portraits, photos, weapons, uniforms, letters and other mementoes from the campaign.

Monumental
complex
t 030 991 0370; open
Oct–Feb Mon–Sat 9–12
and 2–5.30, Mar–Sept
Mon–Sat 9–12.30 and
2.30–7, Sun 9–7; adm

Cappella Ossuaria
*Mar–Sept Tues–
Sun 9–12.30 and
2.30–7; adm*

Solferino saw the single bloodiest battle in the whole war; the Cappella Ossuaria behind the church of S. Pietro contains the remains of 7,000 mostly French and Austrian troops. The **museum** (same hours) traces the history of Italy from 1796 to 1870, and contains weapons, arms and documents from the battle: other memorabilia is housed in Solferino's mighty tower, the **Spia d'Italia** ('Italy's spy'), first built in 1022 by the Scaligers of Verona and restored in the 17th century. Nearby stands a simple **Memorial to**

**Museo della
Croce Rossa**
*Via Garibaldi 50,
t 0376 638 505; open
Tues–Sun 9–12 and 3–7;
donation*

the Red Cross, erected in 1959 to commemorate not only the centenary of the battle, but Henry Dunant's founding of what was first known as the Committee to Aid the Wounded in War. You can learn more about it in the **Museo della Croce Rossa**, Via Garibaldi 50 in **Castiglione delle Stiviere**.

Before inspiring the creation of the Red Cross, Castiglione delle Stiviere witnessed the birth of St Luigi Gonzaga (every great Italian family managed to churn out a saint or two) and built a big Baroque basilica in his honour. His life is chronicled in the **Museo**

**Museo Storico
S. Luigi**
*Via Perati 8, t 0376
638 062; open Oct–May
Tues–Sun 9–11 and 3–5,
June–Sept Tues–Sun
9–11 and 3–6; donations*

Storico S. Luigi, in the early 17th-century convent of the Vergini di Gesù. The museum also holds a ripe bounty of mostly religious Baroque paintings (by F. Bassano, Barocci, Piazza and Guardi), a beautiful, functioning clock of 1567 called the Orologio de San Luigi and an important pewterware collection.

**Fondazione Ugo
Da Como**
*open July–Aug daily
10–12 and 2.30–6.30,
Sept–June Sat–Sun only;
www.fondazioneugoda
como.it; adm*

Lastly, if it's a weekend, stop in **Lonato**, north of Castiglione and only 4km from Desenzano, to visit the **Fondazione Ugo Da Como**. Ugo Da Como was a Brescian scholar and humanist who, when he died in 1941, left his house, furnishings and priceless library of parchments, codices and manuscripts to a foundation for scholars; the house-museum, with its rich, eclectic collection of ancient sculpture, antiques, detached frescoes, Renaissance and Mannerist paintings, ceramics, antique pewter and more, is impressive to stroll through; it becomes even more so when you learn that Da Como bought the house, the 15th-century residence of the Venetian Podestà, in a public auction in 1906 for 1,000 lire!

Activities and Markets on the South Shore

Sirmione is a good place for **windsurfing** over the lake waters: contact Martini, t 320 111 2465, or Lana, t 338 624 3650, *www.lana planet.it*, to rent a board or canoe.

Bar Chocolat, t 030 990 5297, and Sirmiotrans, t 333 270 5604, rent **bikes**; Adventure Sprint, t 030 919 000, rent **car-scooters** for cautious bikers.

In Desenzano you can rent a bike at Girelli, t 030 911 9797, and a charter

boat at South Garda, t 335 630 2142. To **dive** in the lake's cleanest area contact Coltri, t 030 991 0297; Mydive, t 030 999 1541; Dian Sub, t 030 914 4821; or Tritone, t 030 912 0809. To **sail**, contact Fraglia Vela, t 030 914 3343. For **horse riding** contact Spia d'Italia, t 030 913 0235; and for **karting** in Lonato, contact South Garda Karting, t 030 991 9958.

In Sirmione there is a **market** held each Fri at the end of Via XXV Aprile, approaching the peninsula. The city centre piazzas host open-air concerts from Sept to June.

There is a market in Desenzano every Tues on the lake near the Municipio, and another at Rivoltella hamlet on Sun.

Where to Stay and Eat on the South Shore

ⓘ Peschiera del Garda >

Piazza Betteloni 15, t 045 755 1673. See also www.lagodi garda.it, www.garda riviera.com, www.garda informa.com, www. bresciaholiday.com and www.lagodigarda-e.it

Peschiera del Garda ✉ 37019

Ai Capitani, Via Castelletto 2/4, t 045 640 0782, *www.aicapitani.com* (€€€€€). A new luxury boutique hotel set in a historic *palazzo* in the centre of town. The concierge service can hook you up with a yacht, a private wine tasting or a diving trip on Lake Garda. There's an intimate health spa on the top floor.

La Torretta da Alice e Mauro, Via G. Galilei 12, Peschiera del Garda, t 045755 0108 (€€). Situated in the historic centre, this simple restaurant specialises in fresh lake and sea fish, such as fillet of tuna cooked directly on the hearth.

ⓘ Sirmione >

Viale Marconi 2, t 030 916 114

Sirmione ✉ 25019

If you're driving, have the confirmation of your reservation handy to get past the castle guards.

*****Villa Cortine, Via Grotte 6, t 030 990 5890, *www.hotelvillacortine.com* (€€€€€). A neoclassical villa built by an Austrian general and converted into a hotel in 1954. It offers an immersion in romance, and perhaps the rarest amenity in the town – tranquillity. Its century-old garden occupies almost a third of the entire peninsula, with exotic flora, venerable trees, statues and fountains running down to the water's edge. Inside, all is plush and elegant under frescoed ceilings and perhaps a bit too exclusive, but it's ideal for a break from the real world, with private beach and dock, pool and tennis court. Half-board obligatory during high season (Easter and mid-June–Sept). *Open April–mid-Oct.*

*****Grand Hotel Terme, Viale Marconi 7, t 030 916 261, *www. termedisirmione.com* (€€€€€–€€€€). Another top choice, with a private beach, pool, gym and a full health and beauty programme, as well as a lovely lakeside restaurant. *Open Mar–Dec.*

***Catullo, Piazza Flaminia 7, t 030 990 5811, *www.hotelcatullo.it* (€€€). Refurbished in 1991 and situated in the heart of the old town, offering good-sized rooms with beautiful views and all modern amenities. Panoramic terrace and solarium. *Open early Mar–early Nov.*

****Eden, Piazza Carducci 18, t 030 916 481, *www.hoteledenonline.it* (€€€). Also in the centre, in a medieval building. It has been remodelled with fine marbles, and coordinated bedrooms with princely bathrooms, TV and air-conditioning. Unusually, it does not have a restaurant. *Open Mar–Oct.*

***Corte Regina, Via Antiche Mura 11, t 030 916 147, *www.corteregina.it* (€€). In the city centre and recently refurbished, this hotel has all modern amenities and welcomes children (convenient family rooms) and small pets.

***Pace, Piazza Porto Valentino 5, t 030 990 5877, *www.pacesirmione.it* (€€). The family that runs the Catullo also manages this smaller hotel, in the old city centre, with a charming veranda overlooking the lake and nice beginning-of-the-century décor.

**Speranza, Via Casello 6, t 030 916 116, *www.hotelsperanza.sitonline.it* (€€). No lake views, but all the fittings of a three-star hotel, including air-conditioning and marble bathrooms, but at significantly lower prices. *Open Mar–Nov.*

**Grifone, Via Bocchio 4, t 030 916 014 (€). More attractive on the outside than in the rooms, but has a great location overlooking the Rocca Scaligera. *Open April–Oct.*

La Rucola, Via Strentelle 3, t 030 916 326, *www.ristorantelarucola.it* (€€€). An intimate and classy atmosphere to go with its gourmet fish and meat specialities, changing seasonally and according to the genius of young chef and patron Gionata Bignotti, who creatively mixes aromatic herbs and fruit flavours with traditional Mediterranean cuisine. *Menus degustazione* include a 10-dish grand menu. Excellent selection of wines (over 700 labels), whiskies, cognac and grappas. Near the Scaliger castle.

Reserve in advance. *Closed Thurs and Fri lunch.*

Antica Contrada, Via Colombare 23, **t** 030 990 4369, *www.anticacontrada. it* (€€€). A mother-and-son team offer an interesting selection of freshwater fish (caught by members of the same family) and seafood dishes, home-made pastas and desserts. Good selection of wines and grappa. *Closed Mon and Tues lunch, and Jan.*

Risorgimento, Piazza Carducci 5/6, **t** 030 916 325 (€€). Very popular place managed by four young partners, two in the kitchen and two serving at the tables. Dishes range from fish (try the spaghetti with lobster) to meat (*flambé* fillet with *porcini* mush-rooms). *Closed Tues (exc. July and Aug), mid-Nov–mid-Dec and Jan.*

Al Progresso, Via Vittorio Emanuele 20, **t** 030 916 108 (€). Family atmosphere and dishes; also in the city centre. *Closed Thurs.*

Osteria al Torcol, Via San Salvatore 30, **t** 030 990 4605 (€). For a late cold or hot snack or meal and excellent wines – and oils – to taste. Try local cheeses and *affettati* or be treated to home-made pasta or *ravioli al bagoz* close to the old wine press inside or outside, your table placed in the *osteria*'s kitchen garden. *Closed Wed.*

Desenzano del Garda ✉ 25015

(i) Desenzano del Garda >
Via Porto Vecchio 34,
t 030 914 1510

****Piccola Vela, Via T. dal Molin 36, **t** 030 991 4666, *www.gardalake.it/ piccola-vela* (expensive). Only a short walk from the city pier with its own olive grove and views over the lake from the balconies. This offers all modern comforts including air-conditioning, safe, minibar, laundry, garage, swimming pool. It also has apartments with their own kitchen in the back garden; these are particularly suitable for families or those travelling with pets.

***Tripoli, Piazza Matteotti 18, **t** 030 914 1305, *www.hotel-tripoli.it* (€€€–€€). Small, white, lakefront hotel; has renovated, well-equipped rooms in the centre of the action and a garage. *Open Mar–Nov.*

***Piroscafo, Via Porto Vecchio 11, **t** 030 914 1128, *www.hotelpiroscafo.it* (€€). A family-run hotel in the centre of the town, right on the old quay. Rooms are simple, with air-conditioning, and some have nice balconies overlooking the quay. *Open Mar–Nov.*

Alessi, Via Castello 3, **t 030 914 1980, *www.hotelalessi.com* (€). Up in the old city centre and no views, but plenty of family atmosphere – even an ironing table for the hotel guests in the breakfast room. A recently renovated hotel.

***Mayer e Splendid, Via U. Papa 10, **t** 030 914 2253, *www.hotelmayere splendid.it* (€). A venerable hotel situated right by the quay, allowing you to tumble out of bed and onto a steamer; there is parking and rooms have air con. *Open Mar–Nov.*

Esplanade, Via Lario 10, **t** 030 914 3361 (€€€€). Delightful if rather formal with a lovely lakeside terrace, where clients tuck into the likes of a delicate lasagne with seafood infused with wine, or zucchini flowers stuffed with goat's cheese; excellent wine list and desserts. More than 800 Italian and foreign wines. *Closed Wed.*

Cavallino, Via Gherla 30, **t** 030 912 0217 (€€€€). Book a table here for an unforgettable feast. The chef creates imaginative, seasonal dishes based on lake fish and seafood, duck, pigeon (the pigeon stuffed with foie gras is superb) and offal, followed by an excellent cheeseboard and tempting desserts. In the city centre. *Closed Mon, Sun eve and 2 wks in Nov.*

Bagatta alla Lepre, Via Bagatta 33, **t** 030 914 2259 (€€€€–€€€). Classy restaurant with a table full of truffles and delicacies, also for sale, serving creative Mediterranean cuisine. Bagatta Alla Lepre Wine Bar offers cheaper fare in a more informal, if trendy ambiance. *Closed Tues, Wed lunch and 3 wks in Jan.*

Al Portico, Via Anelli 44, **t** 030 914 1319 (€€€). Traditional cuisine is on offer, including lake and sea fish, home-made pasta. *Closed Wed.*

Caffè Italia, Piazza Malvezzi 19, **t** 030 914 1243 (€€). Wine bar and restaurant offering a good selection of hot and cold dishes, including very selected Chianina meat, under the porticoes near the Duomo square. Good selection of wines also by the glass, ideal for breakfast, brunch and late-night snacks as it is open non-stop 7.30am–3am. *Closed Mon.*

Trattoria La Contrada, Via Baratta 12, Desenzano, **t** 030 914 2514 (€€). A romantic restaurant in the historic centre, serving traditional Lombardian-Venetian dishes. The young and creative chef offers a wide range of selections from the lake (such as *polenta* with pike, *tortelli* filled with freshwater fish and perch with citrus fruits). *Closed Wed.*

Entertainment and Nightlife in Desenzano del Garda

There are many trendy wine bars and disco pubs along the lake front in Desenzano – the *passeggiata* is very lively in high season. On summer nights, Desenzano becomes one of the hottest scenes in north Italy.

Art Club, **t** 030 999 1004. Has gay nights. *Open Wed and Fri; closed Nov.*

Back Stage, Disco Live and Dance Bar, in Rivoltella, **t** 030 911 1563. *Open Wed, Fri and Sat.*

Dehor, **t** 030 991 9955. One of the best discos of the Lombardy region, especially lively in the summer. *Open Tues, Fri and Sat.*

Mazoom Le Plasier, less than 1km from the A4's Casello di Sirmione exit, **t** 030 991 0319. Attracts punters from as far as Milan and Venice for their crazy parties with national and international guests, and famous for house music. On Friday expect refined and simple house, on Saturday house music for the real die-hards. *Open Fri and Sat.*

Rising Sun Pub, Via Mantova 53, Lonato, **t** 030 991 9919, opposite the Dehor. Czech beer, spaghetti and live music heat up this vast nightspot. *Open 8pm–3am; closed Mon.*

Sesto Senso Club, Via Dal Molin 99, **t** 030 914 2684. Posing with Italian TV celebs is part of the fun at this Liberty villa. *Open Sat and Sun.*

Salò and Gardone Riviera: the Lombard Shore

The west or Lombard shore of Garda is its most prestigious, with the oldest villas (one, belonging to Gabriele d'Annunzio, is the lake's biggest attraction after Gardaland) and grandest hotels. The climate is especially benign between Gardone Riviera and Limone.

Salò

On the north edge of the Valtenesi, Salò (the Roman *Salodium*) is traditionally Garda's 'capital', the seat of the Venetian magistrates. It enjoys a privileged location, set on a deep bay with a grand promenade, lit by street lamps that resemble Minoan sacral horns. In 1901 an earthquake shook it hard, but architecturally at least it was an auspicious moment for a disaster, and when Salò was rebuilt it was with a Liberty-style flourish. Some fine older buildings survived the quake, including a late Gothic **cathedral** with a Renaissance portal of 1509 stuck in its unfinished façade; among the paintings by Romanino and Moretto there's a golden polyptych by Paolo Veneziano kept securely (but hard to see properly) under glass.

Museo Civico Archeologico
open July–Sept Mon–Sat 9–12.30 and 3.30–6.30, Sun 9.30–12.30

Museo del Nastro Azzurro
t 0365 20804; open summer Tues–Sat 5–7, Sun 10–12.30 and 5–8; adm

The Venetian-style Loggia della Magnifica Patria at Lungolago Zanardelli 55 contains the tourist office. The small **Museo Civico Archeologico**, also housed here, displays items found in Salodium's necropolis. **L'Ateneo**, in the Renaissance Palazzo Fantoni, contains a collection of 13th-century manuscripts and early printed books. At Via Fantoni 49, the **Museo del Nastro Azzurro** is dedicated to 'blue-ribboned' Italian military figures from 1797 to 1945: a collection of uniforms, weapons and portraits, and a room on the Fascist period and the 'Republic of Salò' (or Italian Social Republic) of 1943–5.

Gardone Riviera and D'Annunzio's Folly

North of Salò, sumptuous old villas, gardens and hotels line the lovely promenade at **Gardone Riviera**. Gardone became the most fashionable resort on Lake Garda in 1880, when a German scientist noted the almost uncanny consistency of its climate. One place that profits most from this mildness is the **Giardino Andrea Heller**, named after its new multimedia artist owner. The garden contains many of Heller's works, as well as sculptures by contemporary artists, such as Roy Lichtenstein and Keith Haring.

Giardino Andrea Heller
www.hellergarden.com; open Mar–Oct daily 9–7; April–Sept 8.30–8

Above the garden waits **Il Vittoriale degli Italiani**, the home of Gabriele D'Annunzio (1863–1938, *see* below). This luxurious Liberty-style villa in an incomparable setting, designed for a German family by Giancarlo Maroni, was presented to the extravagant

More Italian than Any Other Italian

Born Gaetano Rapagnetta into a very modest family in the Abruzzo, the self-styled angel Gabriel of the Annunciation (one wonders what he would have thought of Madonna) went on to become the greatest Italian poet of his generation, a leading figure in the *fin-de-siècle* Decadent school who managed to have nearly all of his works placed on the pope's Index. But Gabriele D'Annunzio scoffed at the idea that the pen is mightier than the sword. A fervent right-wing nationalist, he clamoured for Italy to enter the First World War, and when it was over he was so furious that Fiume (Rijeka), a town promised as a prize to Italy, was actually to be ceded by the Allies to Yugoslavia, that he took matters into his own hands and invaded Fiume with a band of volunteers (September 1919). In Italy D'Annunzio was proclaimed a hero, stirring up a diplomatic furore before being forced to withdraw in January 1921.

Luigi Barzini has described D'Annunzio as 'perhaps more Italian than any other Italian' for his love of gesture, spectacle and theatre – what can you say about a man who would boast that he had once dined on roast baby? Yet for the Italians of his generation, no matter what their politics, he exerted a powerful influence in thought and fashion; he seemed a breath of fresh air, a new kind of 'superman', hard and passionate yet capable of writing exquisite, intoxicating verse; the spiritual father of the technology-infatuated Futurists, ready to destroy the old bourgeois *Italia vile* of museum curators and parish priests and create in its stead a great modern power, the 'New Italy'. He lived a life of total exhibitionism – extravagantly, decadently and beyond his means, at every moment the trend-setting, aristocratic aesthete, with his borzois and melodramatic affairs, with 'the Divine' actress Eleanora Duse and innumerable other loves (preferably duchesses). Apparently he thought the New Italians should all be as flamboyant and clever, and he disdained the corporate state of the Fascists. For Mussolini, the still-popular old nationalist was a loose cannon and an acute embarrassment, and he decided to pension him off into gilded retirement on Lake Garda, correctly calculating that the gift of the villa would appeal to his delusions of grandeur.

writer by Mussolini in 1925, ostensibly as a reward from a grateful nation for his patriotism and heroism during the First World War, but also as a sop to keep the volatile, unpredictable poet out of politics. D'Annunzio immediately dubbed his new home 'Il Vittoriale' after Italy's victory over Austria in 1918; with Maroni's help he recreated it in his own image, leaving posterity a remarkable mix of eccentric beauty and self-aggrandizing kitsch.

Where to Stay and Eat on the Lombard Shore

(i) Salò >
Lungolago Zanardelli 52, t 0365 21423

Salò ✉ 25087

****Laurin**, Viale Landi 9, **t** 0365 22022, *www.laurinsalo.com* (€€€€€–€€€). One of loveliest places to stay on the lakes: an enchanting Liberty-style villa converted into a hotel in the 1960s, retaining the elegant period décor in the public rooms. The charming grounds include a swimming pool and beach access. For stylish dining, amid frescoes, Art Nouveau windows and beautifully presented gourmet dishes, indulge at the hotel's restaurant (€€€). *Closed mid-Dec–Jan.*

****Hotel Bellerive**, Via Pietro da Salò 11, **t** 0365 520 410, *www.hotelbellerive. it* (€€€€–€€€). Directly on Lake Garda, this hotel is decorated in relaxing muted tones. Excellent restaurant with local specialities, especially lake fish. Very near the historical Sal area with its labyrinth of tiny streets.

****Duomo**, Lungolago Zanardelli 63, **t** 0365 21026, *www.hotelduomosalo.it* (€€€). The first-floor rooms are the ones to request here – all lead out to a huge geranium-laden balcony overlooking the lake; rooms with no lake view are just within the moderate range. Rooms are big and modern, and there's a fine restaurant. Additional amenities include a sauna, solarium, whirlpool and fitness hall.

***Vigna**, Lungolango Zanardelli 62, **t** 0365 520144, *www.hotelvigna.it* (€€€–€€). Recently refurbished with comfortable and modern rooms, and views that really steal the show. Junior suites are larger, more expensive and with whirlpool bath or shower. *Closed mid-Dec–mid-Jan.*

Il Bagnolo, Bagnolo di Serniga hamlet, **t** 0365 20290, *www.gardalake.it/ ilbagnolo* (€€). A farmhouse situated in the hills above Salò and Gardone di Riviera, halfway between the two. Accommodation is in an old 18th-century *cascina*, just restored, and a newer farmhouse. The restaurant offers milk and meat produced in-house and local wine, oil and cheeses. *Restaurant closed Tues.*

Lepanto, on the lake at Lungolago Zanardelli 67, **t 0365 20428, *hotel. lepanto@libero.it* (€). This is Salò's best-kept secret. The signpost advertises the restaurant, in a nice garden terrace, but there are also six rooms to stay in, all overlooking the lake, for the lucky few who book in advance.

Antica Trattoria delle Rose, Via Gasparo da Salò 33, **t** 0365 43220 (€€€). Run by the same family as the Osteria dell'Orologio (*see* below). Go for *pasta e fagioli*, or lake fish with fresh pasta. *Closed Wed and 2wks in Jan.*

Trattoria alla Campagnola, Via Brunati 11, **t** 0365 22153 (€€€–€€). A beautiful oasis in summer, with a flower-strewn terrace and an *orta* growing fresh vegetables. Home-made pasta, creative use of seasonal produce and charming, knowledgeable staff. A class act. *Closed Tues lunch and early Jan–early Feb.*

Il Melograno, Via del Panorama 5, **t** 0365 520 421 (€€). Another hidden jewel, this time in Campoverde hamlet, south of Salò. The young chef experiments with home-made foie gras dishes with excellent results – try for instance the *scaloppa* filled with foie gras – and also cooks mouth-watering risottos and lake fish soups. Good selection of local wines and

Alsacian wines to go with the foie gras. *Closed Mon eve, Tues and Nov.*

Osteria dell'Orologio, Via Butturini 26, **t** 0365 290 158 (€€). Extremely good value with daily specials and good wine by the glass: an old, beautifully restored inn where you can indulge in local dishes such as *polenta* and gorgonzola, lake fish and skewered wild birds. Very popular so arrive early or book a table or you'll have to wait. *Closed Wed, 2 wks in Jan and July.*

Cantina San Giustina, Salita S. Giustina, **t** 0365 520 320 (€). The place for a cold snack of cheeses and local *affettati*, salted *coregone* or ready-made grilled vegetables, and an excellent selection of local wines. The vaulted *cantina* features books, wines, cheeses and a beautiful old slicing machine. *Open 8pm–5am; closed Mon.*

Pasticceria Vassalli, Via San Carlo 86, *www.pasticceria-vassalli.it*. An essential stop for chocoholics and those with a sweet tooth.

ⓘ **Gardone Riviera >**
Corso Repubblica,
t 0365 20347

Gardone Riviera ✉ 25083

Gardone Riviera and its suburb Fasano Riviera have competing Grand Hotels, both of which are attractive old pleasure domes.

*****Villa del Sogno, Via Zanardelli 107, Fasano, **t** 0365 290 181, *www.villadelsogno.it* (€€€€€). An excellent choice, this was its creator's neo-Renaissance 'Dream Villa' of the 1920s. Immersed in trees, there's a private beach 5mins' walk away and a pool in its flower-filled garden. Also tennis, sauna, two restaurants and bars. *Open April–mid-Oct.*

***Villa Fiordaliso, Corso Zanardelli 132, **t** 0365 20158, *www.villafiordaliso.it* (€€€€€). A Liberty-style palace set in luxuriant gardens directly on the lake. It has only seven rooms, all finely equipped. You can request (for a price) the suite where Mussolini and his mistress Clara Petacci spent their last few weeks. Located in a serene park, with a private beach and pier, it also boasts an elegant restaurant, the best in Gardone, featuring classic Lombard dishes. *Hotel closed Dec–Jan, restaurant closed Mon and Tues lunch, and Nov–mid-Feb.*

*****Fasano Grand Hotel, Corso Zanardelli 190, Fasano Riviera, **t** 0365 290 220, *www.grand-hotel-fasano.it* (€€€€). Fasano's alternative was built in the early 19th century as a Habsburg hunting palace and converted into a hotel around 1900. Surrounded by a large park, it's furnished with *belle époque* fittings; there are tennis courts, a heated pool and private beach with waterskiing and windsurfing, and the restaurant is one of Lake Garda's best. *Open April–mid-Oct.*

****Grand Hotel, Via Zanardelli 84, Gardone, **t** 0365 20261, *www.grandgardone.it* (€€€€). With its 180 rooms this was one of the largest resort hotels in Europe when built in 1881. It is still recognized as a landmark, and its countless chandeliers glitter as brightly as when Churchill stayed there in the late 1940s. Almost all the palatial air-conditioned rooms look onto the lake, where guests can luxuriate on the garden terraces, or swim in the heated outdoor pool or off the private sandy beach. The dining room and delicious food match the quality of the rooms. Also on the lake, the **Villa Principe** is the annexe lodge in the hotel park, recently refurbished, offering even more expensive rooms and more of a country-style stay, with all amenities, and beach.

***Bellevue, Via Zanardelli **t** 0365 290088, *www.hotelbellevuegardone.com* (€€). Above the main road overlooking the lake, with a garden sheltering it from the traffic. It offers modernized rooms, all with private bath, and a swimming pool. *Open April–early Oct.*

***Monte Baldo, Via Zanardelli 110, **t** 0365 20951, *www.hotelmontebaldo.it* (€€). A lakeside, less pricey hotel where a well-aged outer appearance hides a fully refurbished and modern stylish interior. The hotel also has a pool. Breakfast, meals, snacks and drinks are served on tables placed along the lakeside terrace. Nestled in the lakeshore garden is the annexe Villa Acquarone, recently refurbished, which offers more rooms, all with lake views and atmosphere. *Open April–Oct.*

*Hohl, Via dei Colli 4, **t** 0365 20160 (€€–€). Halfway up to Il Vittoriale, this is another atmospheric 19th-century villa in a pleasant garden. The rooms don't have a bath but are quiet, big, with old rather bohemian-looking furniture. *Open 1 Mar–31 Oct.*

Touring, Via Zanardelli 147, t 0365 21031 (€). A modern, solid, year-round budget choice in Fasano, all rooms en suite.

Ristorante Casinò, Corso Zanardelli 42, t 0365 20387 (€€€). Old-style atmosphere and service here, where you can enjoy the lake views from under the portico or eat right on the lake on the front mooring. Lake and sea fish and meat dishes. *Closed Mon and Jan–Feb.*

**Locanda Agli Angeli, t 0365 20832 (€€). Located in Gardone Sopra, the small hamlet of Il Vittoriale, this is a very good family-run restaurant where you can eat home-smoked *magatello di manzo* (beef) with local capers, delicious gnocchi in a *parmigiano* wrap, meat and fish, and local cheeses with red onion sauce and bread with nuts. The *locanda* has also 9 rooms to let (€€), simple but comfortable, some with air-con. *Closed Tues and mid-Nov–early Feb.*

Limone and Riva: the North Shore

The highest mountains embrace northern Lake Garda, and the consistent gusts of wind and air currents make the triangle between Limone, Riva and Malcesine the stuff that windsurfing dreams are made of; world championship meets take place here on a regular basis, and the shores are well supplied with rentals and schools if you're inspired to give it a whirl. Expect to hear a lot of German as sun-starved Austrians, Swiss and Germans pour down here for ersatz Mediterranean weekends among the bougainvillaea and olives.

Limone sul Garda

North of Gargnano the lake narrows, the cliffs plunge sheer into the water and the Gardesana road pierces tunnel after tunnel like a needle. In the morning, when the wind's up, windsurfers flit across the waves like a swarm of crazed one-winged butterflies. On weekends their cars are parked all along the road around **Campione**, a tiny hamlet huddled under the cliffs. For tremendous views, take one of the several turnings inland that wind precipitously up to the cliffs: to peaceful **Tignale**, with its church perched on the edge of a spectacular viewpoint, and **Tremosine**, atop a 1,000ft precipice that dives down sheer into the blue waters below, looking across the lake to mighty Monte Baldo.

The inland route from Tremosine rejoins the lake and La Gardesana shore road at **Limone sul Garda**, a popular resort town with a tiny port and 3km of beach. Its name comes from the Latin *limen* (border), although by happy coincidence Limone was one of the main citrus-producing towns on Lake Garda, and to this day its lemon terraces with their white square pillars are a striking feature of the landscape: D.H. Lawrence, who lived south of Limone for a spell, liked to see them as the ruins of ancient temples.

Riva del Garda and Around

North of Limone the lake enters into the Trentino region, where the charming town of Riva sits snug beneath an amphitheatre formed by Monte Brione. An important commercial port for the bishops of Trento from 1027, it was much sought and fought after through the centuries, ruled at various times by Verona, Milan and Venice before it was handed back to the bishop-princes of Trent in 1521. In 1703, during the War of the Spanish Succession, the French General Vendôme sacked it and all the surroundings, leaving only a ghost of the former town to be inherited by Napoleon in 1796.

With its long beaches and refreshing summer breezes, Riva revived as a resort during the days of Austrian rule (1813–1918) as the 'Southern Pearl on the Austro-Hungarian Riviera', a pearl especially prized by writers: Stendhal, Thomas Mann, D.H. Lawrence and Kafka were among its habitués. The centre of town, Piazza III Novembre, has a plain Torre Apponale (1220), where salt and grain were stored, and the **Palazzo Pretorio**, built by Verona's Cansignorio della Scala in 1376, while the lakefront was defended by the sombre grey bulk of the 12th-century castle, the **Rocca**, surrounded by a swan-filled moat. This now houses Riva's Museo Civico with finds from the Bronze Age settlement at Lake Ledro, and six statue-stelae with human features from the 4th–3rd millennia BC, recently discovered; and from Roman Riva, as well as paintings, detached frescoes and sculpture gleaned from the surroundings. Riva's best church, the **Inviolata** (1603), was commissioned by the princely Madruzzo family of Trento from an unknown but imaginative Portuguese architect, who was given a free hand with the gilt and stucco inside; it also has paintings by Palma Il Giovane.

Only 3km north, a dramatic 287ft waterfall, the Cascata del Varone, crashes down a tight grotto-like gorge by the village of Varone; walkways allow visitors to become mistily intimate with thundering water. From the west side of Riva the exciting Ponale road, a walking path since the recent opening of a gallery, rises to **Lake Ledro** (a 5km walk, but you can also drive), noted not only for its scenery but also for the remains of a Bronze Age settlement (c. 2000 BC) of pile dwellings, discovered in 1929. One has been reconstructed near the ancient piles around **Molina di Ledro**, where the Museo delle Palafitte houses pottery, axes, daggers and amber jewellery recovered from the site; the visit includes the new prehistoric botanical garden, dedicated to the plants cultivated by northern Italian farmers in the Bronze Age. From here you can continue to Lake Idro, through the shadowy gorge of the **Valle d'Ampola**.

One of the most dramatic sights on Garda is just behind Riva, in a natural balcony of hills overlooking the lake: the jagged crag and

Torre Apponale
*t 0464 573 869; open
Mar–Oct Tues–Sun
10–6, mid-July–Aug
daily; adm*

Museo Civico
*same hours as
Torre Apponale*

Cascata del Varone
*www.cascatavarone.
com; open May–Aug
daily 9–7, April and Sept
daily 9–6, Mar and Oct
daily 9–5; adm*

**Museo delle
Palafitte**
*open mid-June–mid-
Sept 10–1 and 2–6; mid-
Sept–mid-June 9–1 and
2–5; closed Mon and
Dec–Feb; adm*

Castello di Arco
lawn open April–Sept 10–7, upper towers 10–6; Oct–Mar 10–4; adm

Castello di Arco, dramatically crowned with ancient, dagger-sharp cypresses and the swallowtail crenellations. Built to defend the Valle di Sarca, the main funnel of northern armies into Italy, it was controlled by the cultured Counts of Arco, who tugged their forelocks at various stages to Verona, Milan and Trento. The path up is lovely if a bit tiring on a hot day and, despite the damage wrought by Vendôme's troops, there are a few frescoes left, including one of a courtly game of chess.

Arco itself, once heavily fortified and moated (the only surviving gate has a drawbridge) became, like Riva, a popular Austro-Hungarian resort in the 1800s, prized for its climate. In the centre, a Baroque fountain dedicated to Moses splashes before the Palladian-inspired **Collegiata dell'Assunta** (1613): another Madruzzo project, this time by Trentino architect Giovanni Maria Filippi, who went on to become court architect of Emperor Rudolph II in Prague. There's a pretty public garden full of Mediterranean plants, near the equally pretty 19th-century **Casino**, while on the edge of town, off Via Lomego, the park laid out at the end of the 19th century by the Habsburg Archduke Albrecht has recently been restored and opened as an **Arboretum**. One kilometre south of Arco, the 15th century church of **San Rocco** at Caneve has fine frescoes by the Veronese school from the early 16th century.

Arboretum
open, summer 8–7; winter 9–4

Dro, up the Sarca valley, is near the small lakes of Cavedine and Toblino, and **Sarche**, where an ancient glacier deposited the *marocche*, a remarkable field of enormous boulders. Olive trees as well as enormous chestnuts grow around **Drena**, at the bottom of Val Cavedine. The landmark here is the stark **Castello**, its keep rising up like a finger accusing heaven. Built by the Counts of Arco in 1175 and ruined by Vendôme in 1703, the lists, where knightly tournaments once took place, have been restored to host congresses and theatrical performances; the keep has splendid views, taking in the mighty *marocche*, and contains a museum of local artefacts, dating from the 18th century bc to the Renaissance.

Castello
open Nov–Feb, Sat and Sun only 10–6; Mar–Oct exc Mon 10–6; adm

Back on Garda's northeast shore, **Monte Baldo** looms over **Torbole**, an old fishing village and pleasant resort and the mouth of the Sarca, the most important river feeding the lake.

Where to Stay and Eat on the North Shore

(i) **Limone sul Garda >**
Via Comboni 15, t 0365 954 070

Limone sul Garda ✉ 25010
****Le Palme**,Via Porto 36, t 0365 954 681, *www.sunhotels.it* (€€€–€€). Housed in a pretty Venetian villa in the historic city centre, preserving much of its original charm alongside modern amenities. Named after its

two ancient palm trees, it has a fine terrace and a good fish restaurant. *Open April–Oct.*

***Hotel Coste**, Via Tamas 11, t 0365 954 042, *www.hotelcoste.com* (€€). In an olive grove 10mins from the city centre, is this family-friendly hotel with its own outside pool, *boules* area and children's playground. Minimum three days stay. *Open April–Nov.*

***La Limonaia**, Via Sopino Alto 3, t 0365 954 221, *www.chincherini.com* (€€). Enjoys a superb position above the centre, and has both an adults' and a children's pool and playground. Needs refurbishing. *Open Mar–Oct.*

****Villa Margherita**, Via Luigi Einaudi 3, t 0365 954 149 (€€). Further out and up from the city centre. Staying here is like entering Ms Margherita's private house, spotless and carefully decorated and furnished. In the olive groves, it is a peaceful retreat with a stunning view of the olive tree slopes and the lake. Rooms each have a different colour and flowery décor; the corner ones are particularly nice with windows on two sides and a private terrace.

****Mercedes**, Via Nanzello 12, t 0365 954 073, *www.mercedeshotel.com* (€). Delightful little hotel in a prime location with wonderful views and extremely friendly owners – a genuine bargain. *Open April–Oct.*

Monte Baldo, Via Porto 29, t 0365 954 021 (€). Spotlessly clean, pretty little hotel, positioned right on the lake. Ask for one of the five rooms with balconies (no en suite). Friendly and very well priced with good *trattoria* below. *Open Mar–Nov.*

Tovo, Via Tamas 17, t 0365 954 064 (€). High above Limone and the Gardesana highway, with a terrace overlooking the lake, this pretty restaurant serves excellent pizzas and local specials. *Closed Mon.*

(i) **Riva del Garda >**
Giardini di Porta Orientale 8, t 0464 554 444. See also www.rivadel garda.com and www.gardatrentino.it

Riva del Garda ✉ 38066

For cheaper accommodation there are also plenty of rooms in private houses in the area. Ask the local tourist office for the list.

****Grand Hotel Liberty**, Viale Carducci 3/5, t 0464 553 581, *www.grandhotelliberty.it* (€€€€). Come here for a stylish stay in a Liberty villa set in its own grounds at the back of the city centre. Indoor pool and whirlpool baths.

****Grand Hotel Riva**, Piazza Garibaldi 10, t 0464 521 800, *www.gardaresort.it* (€€€). A turn-of-the-century hotel majestically positioned on the main square. 87 modern rooms look out over the lake; air-conditioning on lakefront ones only. The rooftop

restaurant combines fine food with incomparable views.

****Hotel du Lac et du Parc**, Viale Rovereto 44, t 0464 566 600, *www.hoteldulac-riva.it* (€€€€). A modernized, spacious hotel set in a large lakeside garden. The many facilities include indoor and outdoor pools, a beach, sailing school, gym, sauna and tennis courts. *Open mid-April–Oct.*

****Sole**, Piazza III Novembre, t 0464 552 686, *www.hotelsole.net* (€€€). Right on the port in Riva's main square. Plenty of atmosphere and a beautiful terrace; all the rooms have private baths.

***Centrale**, Piazza III Novembre 27, t 0464 552 344, *www.welcometo gardalake.com* (€€). Fully equipped, spacious rooms and bathrooms; beside the harbour.

***Portici**, Piazza III Novembre 19, t 0464 555 400, *www.hotelportici.it* (€€). Competely refurbished and with modern rooms, all with bathrooms. *Open April–Oct.*

***Restel de Fer**, Via Restel de Fer 10, t 0464 553 481, *www.restel-de-fer.de* (€€). Built in 1400; only five rooms and a good restaurant, with summer dining in the cloister.

Ostello Benacus, Piazza Cavour 9, t 0464 554 911, *www.ostelloriva.com* (€). Riva's hostel, with beds for €14.50 per night. *Open Mar–Oct.*

***Villa Moretti**, Via Mazzano 7 (3km up in Varone), t 0464 521 127, *www.rivadel garda.com/villamoretti* (€). If you want peace and quiet, a garden and pool in a panoramic spot, this family-run hotel fits the bill.

Villa Negri ai Germandri, Via Bastione 31, t 0464 555 061 (€€€€, evenings only). Overlooking the lake and the city centre and set in the historical villa of Architect Maroni of D'Annunzio's Vittoriale, just below the castle (a shuttle service in golf carts is provided for restaurant guests from Riva's car park). The villa hides an exclusive restaurant, serving a nine-dish menu of local cuisine changed daily. The terrace bistro is less expensive and has an outdoor chef overseeing the grill. Take some time to visit the cellar, with over 800 labels kept in a former First World War shelter excavated in the rocks.

Al Volt, Via Fiume 73, **t** 0464 552 570 (€€€). Located in an old 17th-century palace. The cuisine is a marriage of Trentine and Alsacian dishes, just like the chef and his wife. *Menu degustazione* at €35. *Closed mid-Feb–mid-Mar.*

La Colomberia, Via Rovigo 30, **t** 0464 556 033 (€€). In an 18th-century castle, 500 yards from the lake shore path. The speciality is grilled meats accompanied by home-produced wine. Outside dining with view over the mountains. *Closed Wed.*

Arco ✉ 38062

****Palace Hotel Città, Viale Roma 10, **t** 0464 531 100, *www.welcometo gardalake.com* (€€€–€€). A modern hotel with a balcony for every comfortable, fully equipped room (satellite TV, air-conditioning), a pool, gym, sauna and slimming programme, and an optional vegetarian menu in the restaurant.

***Al Sole, Via Foro Boario 5, **t** 0464 516 676, *www.soleholiday.com* (€€). A popular place to stay, and its excellent restaurant features local produce – try gnocchi with local prunes. *Closed Dec.*

Da Gianni, Via S. Marcello 21, **t** 0464 516 464, *www.dagianni.it* (€€–€). Situated at the foot of the Arco Castle hills, this family-run restaurant offers typical Trentino specialities. They have also 8 guest rooms (€). *Closed Sun eve and Mon.*

Belvedere, Via Serafini 2, in Varignano, **t** 0464 516 144 (€). The best place to eat. The specialities are salted meat and Trentine dishes such as *canederli* (meat and bread dumplings in broth). *Closed Wed, July and Aug.*

Torbole ✉ 38069

****Lido Blu, Via Foci del Sarca 1, **t** 0464 505 180, *www.lidoblu.it* (€€€). On a spit of land with water on either side, this modern hotel is excellent for families: private beach, gym, covered pool and windsurfing school.

****Piccolo Mondo, Via Matteotti 7, **t** 0464 505 271, *www.hotelpiccolo mondotorbole.it* (€€€). Has a very good restaurant with specialities from Trentino. *Closed Tues exc. summer and 2 wks in Feb and Nov.*

Le Terrazze della Luna, **t** 0464 505 301 (€€). You can dine romantically in this 19th-century Austrian fort in nearby Coe. *Closed Mon exc. summer.*

ⓘ **Torbole >>**
Via Lungolago Verona 19, **t** 0464 505 177

ⓘ **Arco >**
Viale delle Palme 1, **t** 0464 532 255

Malcesine to Bardolino: the East Shore

Garda's east shore belongs to the province of Verona. The silvery groves that grace the hills gave it its name, the Riviera degli Olivi, but its most outstanding feature is Monte Baldo, a massive ridge of limestone stretching 35km between Lake Garda and the Adige valley, cresting at 6,989ft. Baldo is anything but bald: known as 'the botanical garden of Italy', it supports an astonishing variety of flora from Mediterranean palms to Arctic tundra; some 20 different flowers first discovered on Monte Baldo bear its name. The southern third of the Riviera degli Olivi is more grapey than olivey, the land of Bardolino.

Malcesine

South of Torbole, the forbidding cliffs of Monte di Nago hang perilously over the lake (but nevertheless attract scores of Lycra-bright human flies) before Malcesine, the loveliest town on the east shore. The Veronese lords always took care to protect this coast and in the 13th century, over the old Lombard castle, they

Getting around the East Shore

APT **buses** run up the east coast from Verona and Peschiera as far as Riva, t 045 805 7811; SIA buses, t 030 377 4237. The car ferry crosses year-round from Torri del Benaco to Maderno.

Rocca Scaligera
t 045 657 0333; open
mid-Mar–early Jan daily
9.30–dusk, early Jan–
mid-March Sat–Sun
10–5; adm

built their magnificent Rocca Scaligera rising up on a sheer rock over the water; inside are natural history exhibits, prehistoric rock etchings and a room dedicated to Goethe, who was accused of spying while sketching the castle. Also note the 16th-century **Palazzo dei Capitani del Lago** at the heart of Malcesine's medieval web of streets.

Cable car
runs daily 8–6;
journey time 10mins;
carries foot passengers
and cyclists; closed
Nov; €14 return

Every half-hour a cable car runs vertiginously up **Monte Baldo**; the views are ravishing, and the ski slopes at the top are very popular with the Veronese. Malcesine also has pretty walks through the olives, and the shore has lovely places to swim and sunbathe, especially around the cove called the **Val di Sogno**.

Torri del Benaco and Garda

Further south, past a steep, sparsely populated stretch of shore, there are two pretty towns, one on either side of Punta di San Vigilio, that played minor roles in the 10th century. The first, laid-back **Torri del Benaco**, owes its name to a rugged old tower in the centre which served as the headquarters of Berengario, the first king of Italy, in his 905 campaign against the Magyars. Later, it was defended by another Scaliger castle (1383), now a museum with displays on olive oil, citrus, fishing, and rock engravings found in the area from c. 2000 BC, similar to those in the Valle Camonica. The church of **Santa Trinità** has good 14th-century Giotto-esque frescoes. One of the many lovely walks in the region is up to the old village of **Albisano**, with beautiful views, then on to Crer and Brancolino, where the largest of Torri's prehistoric etchings can be seen, especially near Crer's church. The first recorded pleasure tourist in Torri was the great Medicean poet Poliziano in the 15th century; more recent fans have included André Gide and Stephen Spender.

Scaliger castle
t 045 629 6111; open
June–Sept 9.30–1 and
4.30–7.30, Jan–May and
Oct 9.30–12.30 and
2.30–6

Laurence Olivier, for his part, preferred enchanting **Punta di San Vigilio** with its Sirens' rocks, occupied by the beautiful **Villa Guarienti** by the great Venetian Renaissance architect Sammicheli, the old church of San Vigilio, and a 16th-century tavern, now an inn (*see* below). In Punta San Vigilio, the Mermaid bay, a private beach accessible by walking through a park shaded with olive trees, has playgrounds for children and two refreshment bars. On the other side of a green soufflé of a headland, the Rocca del Garda, lies **Garda** itself, a fine old town with Renaissance *palazzi* and villas. It gave the lake its modern name, from the Lombard *Warthe*, 'the watch'. After Charlemagne defeated the Lombards, Garda became a county, and in its long-gone castle the wicked Count Berenguer secretly held Queen Adelaide of Italy prisoner in 960, after he murdered her husband Lotario and she refused to marry his son. After a year she was discovered by a monk, who spent another year plotting her escape. She then received the protection of Otto I of Germany, who defeated Berenguer, married the widowed queen, and became Holy Roman Emperor.

Bardolino

To the south, Bardolino is synonymous with its lively red wine with a bitter cherry fragrance that goes so well with fishy *antipasti*; you can learn all you want to know about it at the Cantina Zeni's **Museo del Vino** or by following the wine route through the soft rolling hills, dotted with 19th-century villas. There are two important churches in Bardolino itself: the 8th-century **San Zeno** and the 12th-century **San Severo**, with frescoes and a landmark campanile. **Cisano**, south of Bardolino, has a museum dedicated to the Riviera degli Olivi's other cash crop, the **Museo dell'Olio d'Oliva**.

The next town, **Lazise**, was the main Venetian port and near the harbour retains an ensemble of Venetian buildings, as well as another castle, this one built in the 9th century by the Magyars and taken over and rebuilt by the Scaligers. Also nearby are Gardaland and the Parco Natura Viva (*see* p.262–3).

Museo del Vino
Cantine F.lli Zeni,
t 045 721 0022;
open Mar–Oct daily
9–1 and 2–6

Museo dell'Olio
d'Oliva
Via Peschiera 54,
t 045 622 9047,
www.museum.it; open
Mar–Dec Mon–Sat
9–12.30 and 2.30–7,
Sun 9–12.30

09 The Veneto | Malcesine to Bardolino: the East Shore

Where to Stay and Eat on the East Shore

(i) **Malcesine >**
Via Capitanato 6/8,
t 045 740 0044,
www.malcesine.com

Malcesine ✉ 37018

The town of Malcesine has only 35,000 inhabitants but 17,000 hotel beds. Once a playground for the élite, it is now a typical tourist destination with the obvious consequence that restaurant food is often terribly tourist-oriented.

****Bellevue San Lorenzo**, Via Gardesana 164, t 045 740 1598, *www.bellevue-sanlorenzo.it* (€€€€). Surrounded by olive, cypress and magnolia trees, this delightfully peaceful hotel provides wonderful views of the lake. There are scuplture outside and unusual furniture within. There's a swimming pool, too, and a sauna.

****Querceto**, Campiano, t 045 740 0344, *www.parkhotelquerceto.com* (€€€). Situated south of the centre, this is a romantic place to stay, with lovely views, a pool, garden, and one of the best restaurants in the area. *Open mid-May–Sept.*

***Vega**, Viale Roma, t 045 657 0355, *www.hotelvegamalcesine.com* (€€€). An inviting lakefront hotel in the city centre with big, modern rooms, all with satellite TV, minibar, safe and air-conditioning, and a private beach.

Erika, Via Campogrande 8, t 045 740 0451, *www.erikahotel.net* (€€–€). Just behind the city centre; offers family-run, cosy hospitality. Own garage. *Open end Mar–Oct.*

*Malcesine**, Piazza Pallone, t 045 740 0173, *www.chincherini.com* (€€–€). Beautifully positioned, on the lake in the city centre; has a garden with swimming terrace, average rooms, and an excellent value if average restaurant.

San Marco, Via Capitanato, t 045 740 0115, *www.malcesine.com/sanmarco* (€). Right in the centre, you can sleep where Goethe snoozed in 1786; all simple rooms have bath.

Stella Alpina, t 045 740 0078, *www.malcesine.com/stellaalpina* (€).

Garda >>

*Lungolago Regina
Adelaide 3,
t 045 627 0384*

⭐ Locanda San
Vigilio >>

ⓘ Torri del
Benaco >

*Via Gardesana 5,
t 045 722 5120,
www.torridel
benaco.com*

⭐ Ristorante Ai
Beati >>

In Dosso Ferro hamlet, 500 yards from the city centre. Swimming pool, and parking in a shady garden.

Trattoria Vecchia Malcesine, Via Pisort 6, t 045 740 0469 (€€€€). Ideal for romantic dinners; beautiful sunsets in mid-summer from the terrace. High-quality food cooked by young chef Leandro Luppi and served by his wife Lidia. Leandro's Alto Adige origins make him lean towards smokey flavours and spices like cumin, combined with Garda's best ingredients: try the *canederli di speck* (ham-flecked dumplings), seasoned with Monteveronese cheese from Veneto, or butterfly pasta with *porcini* mushrooms and *ricotta*. Best to reserve. *Closed Wed and lunch exc. Sun.*

Trattoria La Pace, t 045 740 0057 (€€). By the Porto Vecchio; a popular place with outdoor tables for seafood by the lake.

Hippopotamus, Piazza Disciplina, t 045 657 0068 (€). A small wine bar open until late where you can taste and buy a vast array of local wines. *Closed Wed.*

Torri del Benaco ✉ 37010

★★★Gardesana, Piazza Calderini 20, t 045 722 5411, *www.hotel-gardesana. com* (€€€). Right on the harbour with splendid views of the lake, old harbour and castle. All rooms have baths, and breakfast and meals are served on the harbour patio when the weather is good. Vivien Leigh and Laurence Olivier, Maria Callas and French writer André Gide all sojourned there. The fame of the hotel is also due to its restaurant (*open eves only*), the best on the Veronese shore according to many, which serves lake specialities with a creative touch: the soup of Garda lake fish is worth the journey alone. *Open mid-Mar–Oct.*

★★★Al Caval, Via Gardesana 186, t 045 722 5666, *www.alcaval.com* (€€). Near the lake, this plain and simple hotel has a park and windsurf rentals (*closed Jan–mid-Mar*). It has an excellent restaurant (€€), that offers both a vegetarian menu and a *menu degustazione. Closed Wed and lunch.*

Garda ✉ 37016

★★★★Locanda San Vigilio, Punta San Vigilio, t 045 725 6688, *www.locanda-sanvigilio.it* (€€€€€). This little inn hidden out by Sammicheli's villa by a little private harbour has seven romantic rooms and a beach. Dinner in the tavern is a magical experience. *Open Mar–Nov.*

★★Du Parc, Via Marconi 3, t 045 725 5343, *www.chincherini.com* (€€€). A lakeside villa set in its own grounds, which has recently been entirely refurbished and upgraded. The rooms are basic for the price category. *Open July–Aug.*

★★★Flora, Via Giorgione 22 and 27, t 045 725 5348, *www.hotelflora.net* (€€€). An exceptionally well-priced hotel situated slightly above the town and within its own grounds, and slick and modern with pine fittings, spacious rooms, all with balcony, and fantastic amenities – tennis, mini-golf and two pools. No restaurant. *Open mid-May–early Oct.*

★★★★Regina Adelaide, Via Francesco 23, t 045 725 5977, *www.regina-adelaide.it* (€€€). In Garda's centre, with all modern amenities, carefully decorated rooms and a fully equipped health and fitness centre, personal trainer and personalized fitness programmes, indoor and outdoor pool. The annexe is nicely done.

★★★Continental, Via Giorgione 14, t 045 725 5100, *www.hotelcontinental.vr.it* (€€€–€€). Next door to the Flora, this hotel is also in its own grounds and well priced, but not quite as modern or comfortable – and with only one swimming pool. *Open April–Oct.*

★Ancora, Via Manzoni 7, t 045 725 5202, *www.allancora.com* (€). In the centre of the action, and a good-value lakefront option. Clean and comfortable rooms. *Open mid-Mar–late Oct.*

Ristorante Ai Beati, Via Val Mora 57/59, t 045 725 5780 (€€€). This excellent restaurant overlooking Lake Garda will surprise you with its freshwater fish dishes, meats and an interesting wine list. A meal on the lakeside terrace in summer is an unforgettable experience.

Stafolet, Via Poiano 12, **t** 045 725 5427 (€€). On the landward side of Garda; it's worth asking directions to, for its *tagliolini* with truffles and grilled meat and dish. Pizza also available.

Al Pontesel, Via Monte Baldo 109, **t** 045 725 5419 (€). Less distinguished, but good and reasonably priced, featuring stout local cooking.

Costermano ✉ 37010

****Locanda San Verolo**, Località San Verolo, **t** 045 720 0930, *www.san verolo.it* (€€€€). A charming country house in the hills above Garda, owned by the same family as Locanda San Vigilio (*see* above). The cosy rooms offer dramatic views over the countryside. There's an outdoor pool and wonderful restaurant with home-cooked specialities.

Bardolino ✉ 37011

****Color Hotel**, Via S. Cristina 5, **t** 045 621 0857, *www.colorhotel.it* (€€€). Every floor is a different colour, from vibrant red to soothing beige. The suites are the best; very large and all with views of the pools. A new addition is the outdoor lounge with pool and waterfall. The health spa is nearly finished; you can have a Thai massage out on the lawn for now. Restaurants and snack bars, also at poolside.

ⓘ Bardolino >>
Piazzale Aldo Moro,
t *045 721 0078,*
www.info-bardolino.it

The Eastern Veneto

While the western frontier of the Veneto is defined by Lake Garda, the eastern Veneto incorporates the two provinces north of Venice, Treviso and Belluno. The hills get bigger as you head north; much of Belluno province is in the Dolomites (*see* next chapter).

Treviso

Famous for *radicchio*, cherries, Prosecco and Benetton clothes, Treviso is one of the Veneto's best kept secrets, a 'Venice in miniature' laced with little canals (*canagi*) diverted from the River Sile, languorous with willow trees, lazy water wheels, swans, mossy walls, yet all humming with more than a little discreet prosperity. Roman *Tarvisium*, it enjoyed a fairly robust and riotous Middle Ages under its *signori*, the da Camino, some of whom were benign, such as the 'good' Gherard, and some not so nice, such as Riccardo, who was murdered while playing chess in 1312. Despite flirtations with anarchy, the 14th century saw the arrival of one of Giotto's greatest pupils, Tommaso da Modena, who spent most of his life painting in Treviso. After a brief period under the Scaligers, the city and its surrounding Marca were annexed by Venice in 1339, the first of its *terra firma* acquisitions.

Colours were an obsession in Treviso long before Benetton united them. Attractive building stone was scarce, so it became the custom to cover the humble brick walls with plaster and frescoes: in the 1300s with simple colours and patterns, and by the 1500s with heroic mythologies and allegories. Although faded and fragmented since then – Treviso endured 35 air raids during the last war, including a fierce one on Good Friday 1944 that destroyed half

Getting to and around Treviso

Treviso **airport** (t 0422 315 111) is southwest of the town; bus no.6 runs from there to the railway station; Ryanair links it three times a day to London Stansted.

Both the train and bus stations (t 0422 577 311) are in Via Roma south of the centre. **Trains** run from Venice or Mestre to Treviso (30mins) and Belluno (2hrs), either directly or by changing at Padua or Conegliano. One line to Belluno goes via Conegliano and Vittorio Veneto; the other, longer but more scenic, via Montebelluna (also a getting-off point for Maser (see p.206), Asolo (p.209) and Feltre (p.289).

Cars. It's very simple: don't try to take a car into Treviso. In 2000 the council changed the traffic system in and around Treviso and the result is mayhem. There are 35,000 residents and 140,000 commuters in Treviso, and like true Italians, they all drive. Abandon your car at the hotel and walk; many of the surrounding roads are one-way so get a decent map.

---

of the city in five minutes – one of the delights here is to pick out frescoes under the eaves, or hidden in the shadows of an arcade. Another is to take a stroll along the outside of the city walls, along the Sile to the south, and along the various Corsos and moats.

Piazza dei Signori and the Duomo

From the bus or train station, it's a 10-minute walk over the Sile along the Corso del Popolo and Via XX Settembre to the Piazza dei Signori, the heart of Treviso. Here stands the only surviving palace of the old *comune*, the enormous brick **Palazzo dei Trecento**, 'Of the Three Hundred', built in the 1200s and rebuilt after it took a bomb on the nose in the war; Treviso café society shelters underneath its loggia. Adjacent, the **Palazzo del Podestà** was rebuilt in 1877, along with the Torre Civica which looms over its shoulder. Behind the Palazzo dei Trecento is the **Monte di Pietà** (former municipal pawn shop). Just up and around the back of the Palazzo dei Trecento, the church of **Santa Lucia** (1389) has a detached fresco by Tommaso da Modena, the *Madonna delle Carceri*, 'of the prisons', recalling the building that once stood nearby.

The elegant and arcaded main street, the **Calmaggiore**, was Tarvisium's *decumanus*. It leads from the square to the **Duomo**, a Venetian Romanesque building with a cluster of domes, founded in the 12th century; the adjacent baptistry gives an idea of what the cathedral looked like before its many alterations. Besides fine Renaissance tombs of local prelates, much of the cathedral's name brand art is concentrated in the **Cappella Malchiostro**, just right of the altar, designed by Tullio and Antonio Lombardo, with works by Paris Bordone (*Adoration of the Shepherds*) and Girolamo da Treviso the elder (*Madonna del Fiore*). The frescoes are by Pordenone, while his mortal enemy, Titian, contributed *The Annunciation* on the altar; Vasari wrote that Pordenone always painted with his sword at his hip in case Titian showed up while he was working. Behind the cathedral, the Museo Diocesano contains one of Tommaso da Modena's masterpieces, the detached fresco *Cristo Passo*, and fine marble reliefs from the 1200s.

Museo Diocesano
Canoniche del Duomo; open Tues 9–12 and Fri 3–6

Museo Civico and San Nicolò

Casa da Noal
*open for special
exhibitions only*

**Museo Civico
Luigi Bailo**
*closed for restoration;
a large part of the
collection is on show
at Santa Caterina
(see below)*

**Capitolo dei
Domenicani**
*open April–Oct 8–6,
Nov–Mar 8–5.30;
ring the bell at the
porter's lodge*

From the Piazza Duomo, Via Canova leads past the 15th-century Casa da Noal, a reliquary of the city's architecture containing bits and pieces salvaged from her ruins. Via Canova meets Borgo Cavour near the Museo Civico Luigi Bailo.

Borgo Cavour makes a grandiose exit through the great Venetian gate, the **Porta dei Santi Quaranta** (1517), encompassed by an impressive stretch of the ramparts. However, if you turn instead down Via S. Liberale and turn right in Via Absidi, you'll come to Treviso's best church, the enormous Gothic **San Nicolò** with its attractive polygonal apse. The interior is a treasure house of lovely frescoes – from a huge St Christopher on the south wall to the charming pages by Lorenzo Lotto on the monument of Senator Agostino d'Onigo, sculpted by Giovanni Buora. Tommaso da Modena contributed the saints standing to attention on the columns, but even better are his perceptive portraits of 40 Dominicans (1352), some using medieval reading glasses, in the Capitolo dei Domenicani in the adjacent Seminario.

San Francesco

Treviso's east end, the Oltrecagnanàn, is separated from the rest of the city by one of its wider streams, the Cagnàn; on a little islet (take Via Trevisi–Via Pescheria from the Monte di Pietà) the lively **Pescheria**, or fish market, built in 1851 is a colourful, appetizing delight, and open every morning except Sunday. Just up Via S. Parisio from here is San Nicolò's near twin, the tall brick, Romanesque-Gothic San Francesco. This was once the great pantheon and art gallery of Treviso, but the masterpieces have been relocated to the Accademia, leaving only a fresco of the Madonna and Saints by Tommaso da Modena, to the left of the high altar, as well as the tombs of Francesca Petrarch (*d.* 1384) and Pietro Alighieri (*d.* 1364), the children of Italy's two greatest poets. Their final meeting place here in Treviso is mostly a coincidence – Pietro's body was moved here when his original church was knocked over.

Santa Caterina
*t 0422 544 864; open
Tues–Sun 9–12.30 and
2.30–6; adm*

Back along the walls to the east, Viale Burchiellati leads shortly to the city's other great gate, Guglielmo Bergamasco's exotic **Porta San Tomaso** (1518), with its inscription 'The Lord protect you while you go in and out'. From here follow Borgo Mazzini to the ill-starred church of Santa Caterina, built in 1346 on the site of a da Camino palace that was razed in a popular revolt. Closed on the order of the *Serenissima* in 1772, badly bombed in the war, Santa Caterina was pieced together after the war to house Tommaso da Modena's detached frescoes on the Life of St Ursula, a cycle that's just as delightful as Carpaccio's St Ursulas in the Accademia; other beautiful paintings, the *Madonna and Saints* and the *Story of Sant'Eligio*, are attributed to Pisanello. The church complex is now a museum and will house part of the Luigi Bailo collection during its renovation; a permanent sculpture museum is also on the horizon. The other big church in these parts, **Santa Maria Maggiore**, has an attractive late Gothic façade (1473) and a Renaissance *tempietto* in the left nave, sheltering a miracle-working Madonna.

Along the Sile

Treviso's meandering Sile is the longest resurgent river in Italy, and its leafy banks have been made into a park: the **Oasi Naturalistica di Cervara**. In Santa Cristina, just west of Quinto, the parish church houses a Madonna in Trono by Lorenzo Lotto. On the other (east) side of Treviso in **Roncade**, the late 15th-century Villa Giustinian (attributed to the circle of Mauro Codussi) is a key work in the evolution of the villa before Palladio: although built with defence in mind, it is the first case of a secular building decorated with classical elements – in this case a loggia and pediment. The villa is now an *agriturismo*, open for *degustazione*.

Villa Giustinian
*t 0422 708 736,
www.castellodi
roncade.com*

Where to Stay in Treviso

(i) Treviso >
*Piazza Monte di Pietà
8, t 0422 547 632,
www.marcatreviso.it*

Treviso ✉ 31100

****Relais Monaco**, Via Postumia 63, t 0422 9641, *www.relaismonaco.it* (€€€€). This patrician villa was scooped up by Benetton and expanded to meet business needs. The plush rooms overlooking the pool and park are for pleasure, with the conference centre in a separate wing.

****Continental**, Via Roma 16, t 0422 411 216, *www.hcontinental.it* (€€€). A modern hotel near the station.

***Scala**, Viale Felissent 1, near the exit for Conegliano, t 0422 307 600, *www.hotelscala.com* (€€€). Just north of town this attractive patrician hotel has 20 rooms, set in a pretty park.

Relais Villa Annamaria, Via Cavour 12, Pezzan di Istrana, t 0422 832 688 (€€€–€€). A B&B with all the services of a hotel, including sleek modern rooms and exceptional service. In a quiet residential location near Treviso.

***Clarion Hotel River**, Via Callalta 83, t 0422 361 770, *www.clarion-hotel-river.com* (€€). Near the Treviso Sud exchange on the A27: cosy rooms in a restored farmhouse.

Il Focolare, Piazza Ancilotto 4, t 0422 56601, *www.albergocampeol.it* (€€). Smack in the historical centre, a hospitable and long-established hotel with good views. Hot in summer (no air-con) and plagued by mosquitoes.

Locanda La Colonna, Via Campana 27, t 0422 544 804, *www.ristorantela colonna.it* (€€). Small locanda with six frescoed rooms. Central and up-market, with air-con.

Eating Out in Treviso

Cichorium intybus, otherwise known as *radicchio trevigiano*, is not only a local obsession, but a salad vegetable that has the same quality control as wine; to be DOC *radicchio trevigiano* it must have sprouted up in one of eight *comuni* and grown under certain organic conditions. It's at its best in December. Another speciality is *sopa coada*, a baked pigeon casserole.

Alfredo el Toulà, Via Collalto 26, t 0422 540 275, *www.toula.it* (€€€). If money's no object, try *sopa coada* here at Treviso's most acclaimed restaurant, in a lovely, elegant *belle époque* setting. The imaginative menu has an emphasis on seafood. *Closed Sun eve, Mon and Aug; reserve.*

Al Canevon, Piazza San Vito 13, **t** 0422 540 208 (€€€). Creative cooking with sea bass and beef to tempt your palate, and in a lovely square right in the heart of Treviso; sit outside in summer. *Closed Tues.*

Al Cavallino, Porta Santi Quaranta, Via Borgo Cavour 52, **t** 0422 412 801 (€€). In a converted stables dating from 1517, an *enoteca*–restaurant offering staples from the Veneto and excellent wine at reasonable prices. *Closed Tues and Wed lunch.*

Beccherie, Piazza Ancilotto 10, **t** 0422 540 871 (€€). One of Treviso's bastions of local atmosphere and cooking – a great place to try *pasta e fagioli* with *radicchio. Closed Sun eve, Mon and 2 wks in July.*

Toni del Spin, Via Inferiore 7, **t** 0422 543 829 (€€–€). An old favourite for its Veneto dishes (*bigoli, risi e bisi*, etc.) topped off with American apple pie. *Closed Sun and Mon lunch, and mid-July–mid-Aug.*

The Marca Trevigiana

You can drive straight up to the Dolomites in less than two hours from Treviso, or spend a day exploring the fine towns of its province, the 'Joyous' Marca Trevigiana, along the way. At the grave risk of offending local pride, you'll find the Marca's most famous bits – Asolo, Maser and Castelfranco – in the section 'North of Padua' (*see* pp.201–219).

Oderzo and Conegliano

Museo Civico Archeologico
t 0422 713 333; open Wed–Sat 9–12 and 3.30–6.30, Sun 3.30–6.30

Pinacoteca Alberto Martini
t 0422 815 202; same hours as the museum

Casa di Gaia da Camino
Via Businello 2, t 0422 850 088; open Sat 3–7, Sun 10–12 and 3–7

Museum
t 0422 861 544; open 1st Sun of each month 9.30–12.30

A delightful mini-miniature Venice crisscrossed by canals and devoted to wine-making, **Oderzo** may not be a household name, but in its Roman heyday as *Opitergium* it was recorded as far away as Egypt. The main square, Piazza Vittorio Emanuele II, marks its old forum, overlooked by the late Gothic **Duomo**, which contains some intriguing fresco fragments; in Via Garibaldi, Roman finds and mosaics fill the **Museo Civico Archeologico**. Nearby, the **Pinacoteca Alberto Martini** has works by Oderzo-born surrealist painter Alberto Martini, as well as other contemporary Italians, mostly from Oderzo. Make the short detour north of Oderzo to **Portobuffolè**, a picturesque village of frescoed buildings and three funny Venetian lions (especially the spooked one with a pie pan face sticking out its tongue on the 15th-century Monte della Pietà, now the Cassa Marca). The oldest house, 13th-century **Casa di Gaia da Camino**, has a bicycling museum and hosts special exhibitions. A popular antiques market takes place on the second Sunday of each month. Just to the south west, **Piavon di Oderzo** has a lovely little **museum**, dedicated to beekeeping and all things bee-like.

West, **Conegliano** is a town neatly divided into old and new, with the grandiose neoclassical Accademia cinema and its giant sphinxes in the centre. It was the birthplace of Giambattista Cima (1460–1518) – 'the sweet shepherd among Venetian painters' as Mary McCarthy called him – the son of a seller of hides, who often painted his native countryside in his backgrounds. If you haven't

Casa di Cima
Via Cima 24,
t 0438 411 026;
open summer Sat–Sun
4–7, winter on request

Sala dei Battuti
t 0438 22606; open
Sat 10–12, Sun and hols
3–6; otherwise
weekdays on request

seen the originals, reproductions are displayed at his birthplace, the Casa di Cima, on quiet Via Cima. An original and beautiful Cima, a Sacra Conversazione in an architectural setting (1493), is also the altarpiece of the 14th-century **Duomo**; look out as well for Francesco Beccaruzzi's recently restored *SS Marco, Leonardo and Caterina*. In the 16th century two non-Venetians, Ludovico Pozzoserrato of Belgium and Francesco da Milano, collaborated on the 27 Old and New Testament scenes in the adjacent Sala dei Battuti, 'the Hall of the Beaten', i.e. a confraternity of flagellants. Be sure to stroll down arcaded **Via XX Settembre**, lined with old frescoed palaces and porticoes; the **castle** on the hill, begun in the 10th century, has a small **Museo Civico**.

Conegliano has a wine-making school, and produces a delightful Prosecco which you can go a-tasting along the pretty 42km **Strada del Prosecco** – between Conegliano's castle and **Valdobbiadene** to the west, then back east to Vittorio Veneto. On the way have a look at **San Pietro di Feletto**, its exterior richly frescoed in the 15th century by an unknown painter, who pictures Jesus in a unique fashion: lines from his wounds are connected to chickens, wine, people lying in bed, and farm tools.

Vittorio Veneto

The Venetian pre-Alps saw heavy action in the First World War, and the hills around Asiago, Monte Grappa and the Piave are often crowned with dispiritingly huge war cemeteries. Vittorio Veneto, north of Conegliano, was the site of Italy's final victorious battle (October 1918). The name, however, predates the war; in 1866, to celebrate the birth of Italy, the two rival towns Ceneda and Serravalle united and took the name of their royal godfather Vittorio Emanuele II. Since then they've united in sprawl and it's difficult to define where one starts and the other ends.

Battle of 1918
museum
t 0438 57695; open
April–Oct 9.30–12.20
and 4–7, Nov–Mar
9.30–12.30 and 2–5;
closed Mon

Museo Diocesano
t 0438 948 411; open
on request; includes
adm to the small
science museum

Museo del
Cenedese
same hours as Battle
of 1918 museum;
shared ticket

The **Castello di San Martino**, dating back to the Lombards, overlooks Ceneda. The central square, Piazza Giovanni Paolo I, holds the Loggia del Cenedese, designed by Sansovino in 1538, now home to a museum of the Battle of 1918. Albino Luciani (the 'smiling pope', John Paul I), long-time bishop of the diocese, founded the Museo Diocesano in the seminary, with works by Palma il Giovane and Titian. Another church, **Santa Maria del Meschio**, has a beautiful altarpiece of the Annunciation by Andrea Previtali.

A poetic street (Via Dante/Virgilio/Petrarca) links the two halves of Vittorio Veneto. A clock tower announces **Serravalle**, with its old palaces and houses – the setting for Richard Attenborough's film *In Love and War* (1996). The 15th-century **Loggia Serravallese** houses, rather confusingly, the Museo del Cenedese, with a collection of Roman finds, sculpture, and minor paintings; admission also includes the beautifully frescoed (mid-1400s) church of San

Lorenzo. Over the bridge, Serravalle's Duomo has a fine Madonna col Bambino by Titian as well as some wonderful work by Francesco da Milano. A woodsy path leads up to Serravalle's oldest church, hilltop **Santa Augusta**, where, the legend goes, the saint used to distribute bread to the poor until her disapproving father ran her through with his sword. Others say the church marks the site of an old Roman temple dedicated to Octavian Augustus. On 22–23 August the place is packed with pilgrims who don't seem too concerned as to its origins.

Vittorio Veneto's playground, the lovely **Bosco del Cansiglio**, a vast forest of fir, larch and beech on a lofty karstic plateau, was set aside by Venice in 1548 as its 'Forest of St Mark's Oars'; Mount Cansiglio itself offers the closest downhill skiing to Venice.

Bosco del Cansiglio
t 0438 57243; guided tours available; call in advance

Where to Stay and Eat in Marca Trevigiana

(i) **Oderzo >**
Piazza Castello 145, t 0422 815 251

Oderzo ✉ 31046

***Villa Revedin, Via Palazzi 4, t 0422 800 033, www.villarevedin.it (€€). The nicest place to sleep near Oderzo is this 15th-century villa 5km east at Gorgo al Monticano. Rooms are well equipped and the breakfasts superb.
Gellius, Calle Pretoria 6, t 0422 713 577 (€€€€). In the centre, dine in an atmospheric Roman prison. The food has improved dramatically in the last 2,000 years. *Closed Sun eve, Mon, and two weeks in Jan and July.*

Portobuffolè ✉ 31019

****Villa Giustinian, Via Giustiniani 11, t 0422 850 244, www.villagiustinian.it (€€€). A beautiful villa built in 1695 which once belonged to a doge; elegantly furnished, and surrounded by a large park. *Closed part of Aug.*

(i) **Conegliano >**
Via Settembre 61, t 0438 21230

Conegliano ✉ 31015

***Canon d'Oro, Via XX Settembre 131, t 0438 34246, www.hotelcanondoro.it (€€€). Behind an exterior frescoed in the 1500s, this hotel provides a warm welcome and plush modern rooms overlooking the town's main street.
****Relais Le Betulle, Via Costa Alta 56, Conegliano, t 0438 21001, www.relaislebetulle.it (€€€). High in the hills over Conegliano, this hotel makes a wonderful getaway. Designer furnishings with enormous colourful prints on the walls, a restful garden and a trendy wine bar and restaurant.

(i) **Vittorio Veneto >>**
Via della Vittoria 110, t 0438 57243

Al Salisà, Via XX Settembre 2, t 0438 24288 (€€€–€€). An elegant restaurant in a 13th-century building, featuring succulent snails (*lumache*) and game specialities in season, especially venison. There's also a good local wine list, and special menus for lunch. *Closed Tues eve, Wed and Aug.*
Tre Panoce, Via Vecchia Trevigiana 50, t 0438 60071 (€€). A lovely restaurant occupying a *seicento* convent, crowning a hill of vineyards, with outdoor tables in summer (if you're not driving, bus no.1 stops outside). The chef is known for his wizardry with *radicchio. Closed Sun eve, Mon and 3 wks in Jan and Aug.*

Follina ✉ 31051

***Hotel Abbazia, Martiri della Libertà 9, t 0438 971 277, www.hotelabbazia.it (€€€€). On the *Strada del Prosecco* in a 17th-century estate, this elegant hotel has lovely modern rooms with Jacuzzis and an award-winning restaurant. Bike and car hire too.
Gigetto, Via De Gasperi 4, t 0438 960 020 (€€€). Just a hop away in Miane, they will treat you well at this restaurant, featuring the finest dishes the Marca Trevigiana can offer and fantastic list of wines. *Closed Mon eve and Tues, and some of Jan and Aug.*

Vittorio Veneto ✉ 31029

Alice, Via Giardino 94, Loc. Carpesica, t 0438 561173, www.alice-relais.com (€€€). A restored 19th-century farmhouse amidst vineyards on the hills between Conegliano and Vittorio Veneto. Located on the historic wine road of Prosecco, with panoramic views from the large terrace. All 10 rooms are furnished with taste.

Cison di Valmarino ✉ 31030

****CastelBrando**, Via Brandolini 29, t 0438 9761, *www.castelbrando.it* (€€€€–€€€). A medieval castle and hamlet transformed into a resort, complete with health spa, bars and restaurants high on a mountaintop surrounded by acres of forest. Take the scenic cable car up to the hilltop.
Duca di Dolle, Via Piai Orientali 5, t 0438 975 809, *www.bisol.it* (€€€€–€€€) In tiny Rolle, the Bisol

Prosecco makers have restored an old farmhouse to accommodate guests visiting their winery. The *foresteria* has taken off in its own right, offering hospitality typical of the deluxe *agriturismi* of Tuscany, complete with free-form pool and luscious views.
Da Andreetta, Via Enotria 7, Fraz. Rolle, t 0438 85761, *www.andreetta.it* (€€). Exemplary wines, served by owner Alberto, accompany superb local cuisine which varies seasonally. Well positioned in the hills of Prosecco, with a panoramic terrace. *Closed Wed and Thurs lunch, and 2 wks in Jan.*

(★) Duca di Dolle >

Belluno

A provincial capital, strategically located at the junction of the Piave and Ardo rivers, Belluno is one of those small perfectly proportioned Italian cities: urban, urbane, yet never far from magnificent views over the countryside – in this case, of the Venetian Dolomites. Much of the area is covered by the **Dolomiti Bellunesi National Park**, which covers 120 sq miles. There are numerous guided walks, many of which seem to include satisfying stops at bars and restaurants. Parking can be extremely difficult so leave your car at one of the car parks by the river and take the massive escalator into the centre of town.

Inhabited since Palaeoveneto times, the Romans made *Belunum* an important outpost at the foot of the Dolomites, a status continued under the Byzantines. In the late 10th century it came under the rule of bishop-princes and various *signori*; the arrival of Venice in 1404 brought Belluno the peace it needed to thrive. The Bellunesi can be tough, though; when the Nazis invaded in 1943, they put up a stiff fight – 564 were killed in the conflict.

The latter are remembered in the large main square with a fountain that grew up outside the old walls, the **Piazza dei Martiri**, perhaps still better known as the Campedél. It's a short walk from here to the civic and religious centre of town, **Piazza del Duomo**, site of Belluno's finest buildings, the ornate **Palazzo dei Rettori** (1491), residence of the Venetian governors, and the **Duomo**, which for over 20 years was the home church of Pope John Paul I. Founded in the 7th century, and last redesigned by Pietro Lombardo, the cathedral was not finished until the 1600s, and tends to be overshadowed by the magnificent **campanile**, designed by Filippo Juvarra (1742). Around the corner, the Art Deco post office is decorated with reliefs of Hermes and Isis winging letters to their destination (as the Italians say, *magari!*).

Museo Civico
t 0437 944 836; open May–Sept Tues–Sun 10–1 and 4–7, Oct–April Tues–Sat 10–1 and 3–6, Mon 10–1; adm

In Via Duomo, the Museo Civico is a treat for fans of extrovert Baroque painter and inveterate womanizer Sebastiano Ricci, who chased commissions and skirts as far as England; his *Hercules and Omphale* and *The Fall of Phaeton* are among his best works. You can also learn about some interesting if obscure local painters from the 1300–1800s, and there are good sculptures by Il Riccio and native Andrea Brustolon; the antiquities section has finds from the Palaeoveneti necropoli at Mel, which yielded grave goods from the 8th–2nd centuries BC. Via Mezzaterra and Via Rialto follow the ancient Roman *castrum* by way of atmospheric **Piazza del Mercato**, a picture-perfect little square with arcades and a fountain from 1410. To the south Via Mezzaterra ends at the 12th-century **Porta Ruga** and a postcard view of the Piave valley and the mountains. Also have a look at the Gothic **Santo Stefano** (1468) in Via Roma, where a 15th-century relief of the Madonna in her merciful umbrella pose guards the door, leading into a handsome interior.

If you don't have time for a foray into the Dolomites, take the bus to the **Alpe del Nevegal**, 12km south of Belluno, for gorgeous views, skiing in the winter and a chairlift to the Rifugio Brigata Alpina Cadore (5,250ft), with an alpine garden. From the refuge it's an easy three-hour walk up to the **Col Visentin**, site of another refuge that commands a unique panorama: north across the sea of Dolomite peaks and south to the Venetian Lagoon. The hills of the **Alpago** are another popular weekend destination, especially the **Lago di Santa Croce**, a popular windsurfing venue, the focal point for its small villages: aim for **Pieve d'Alpago** in a lovely setting or **Tambre**, on the edge of the forest of Cansiglio.

Feltre: the Dead Man and SS. Vittore e Corona

West from Belluno the SS50 skirts the Piave and the southern flank of the Dolomites on its way to hilltop Feltre. Sacked by the troops of Emperor Maximilian during the War of the League of Cambrai, Feltre was immediately rebuilt and has changed little since, especially the houses along **Via Mezzaterra**, with their faded frescoes and dozens of marble plaques, all hammered into illegibility by someone who had it in for Feltre's memories. The jewel on Via Mezzaterra is the picturesque **Piazza Maggiore**, where a very quizzical Lion of St Mark stands vigil over the castle, the church of **San Rocco** has a fountain by Tullio Lombardo, and the superb 16th-century **Palazzo dei Rettori** (now the Municipio) is decked out with a Palladian portico. Inside, a small wooden theatre built in 1684 saw the production of Goldoni's first plays. In the centre of Piazza Maggiore, a statue honours the great Renaissance educator Vittorino da Feltre, whose famous school in Mantua taught the sons and daughters of the nobility sent from all over Italy and Europe, as well as the gifted poor. Vittoriano was the first

Museo Civico

Via L. Luzzo 23, t 0439 885 242; open April–Oct Tues–Fri 10.30–12.30 and 4–7, Sat–Sun 9.30–5.30; Nov–Mar Tues–Fri 10.30–12.30 and 3–6, Sat–Sun 9.30–10.30; adm

Galleria d'Arte Moderna Carlo Rizzarda

Via del Paradiso 8, t 0439 885 234; same hours as Museo Civico above; adm

Sanctuary of SS. Vittore e Corona

t 0439 2115; open May–Oct 9–12 and 3–7, Nov–April 9–12 and 3–6

in modern times to elevate gymnastics to the status it held in ancient Greek times – an equal to languages, arithmetic and logic.

The Palazzo Villabuono, by the east gate, houses the Museo Civico which has among its archaeological collection an altar to the *anna perrena* (the year), and among its paintings works by Gentile Bellini, Cima da Conegliano and Feltre's own contribution to the Renaissance, Lorenzo Luzzo, better known by his nickname 'Il Morto da Feltre', the Dead Man of Feltre (he had an unusual pallor). *The Transfiguration*, the Dead Man's most acclaimed work, is nearby in the sacristy of the church of **Ognissanti**. Back towards the centre, the Galleria d'Arte Moderna Carlo Rizzarda features a collection of beautiful works in wrought iron, much of it from the forge of the local master Carlo Rizzarda (1883–1931).

Five kilometres from Feltre, signposted off the Treviso road (SS473), the Romanesque Sanctuary of SS. Vittore e Corona sits on **Monte Miesna**. Built in 1100 and almost unchanged since, it shelters the remains of Vittore, a Roman soldier martyred in Syria in 171, and Corona (Stephania), who converted at the sight of his martyrdom and got the same treatment. For such early saints, their story is very well documented and is illustrated by the frescoes in the cloister; they spent a few centuries on Cyprus before the Venetians brought the relics here in 1096. The little apse is filled with their elevated sarcophagus, decorated with windblown acanthus; behind, look for the capitals inscribed with red Kufic script, reading 'The Universe is God'. The bishop's throne was carved from a single block and the frescoes go back to the 1200s, by the schools of Tommaso da Modena and Giotto. A number of figures are copied directly from Padua's Scrovegni Chapel – Giotto himself sold the reproduction rights. Don't miss the *Last Supper*, where the artist tried to paint prawns but drew scorpions instead.

Where to Stay and Eat around Beluno

(i) Belluno >

Via Rodolfo Pesaro 21, t 0437 940 084; for information on the National Park: t 0439 3328, www.infodolomiti.it

(i) Feltre >>

Piazza Trento-Trieste 9, t 0439 2540

Belluno ✉ 32100

***Astor**, Piazza dei Martiri 26-E, t 0437 942 094, www.astorhotel belluno.com (€€). Good value and comfortable, central rooms.

***Delle Alpi**, Via J. Tasso 13, t 0437 940 545, www.dellealpi.it (€€). Close to the station, with large rooms and one of the best restaurants in town, specializing in seafood ferried up from the coast. *Closed Sun and some of Aug.*

Al Borgo, Via Anconetta 8, t 0437 926 755 (€€). An 18th-century villa south of the Piave, and another favoured place to eat. *Closed Mon eve and Tues.*

Pieve d'Alpago ✉ 32010

Dolada, Via Dolada 9, t 0437 479 141 (€€€€). One of the top restaurants in all Venetia, overlooking Lago di Santa Croce. Wood panelling, candlelight and romance accompany inspired dishes in the best Italian tradition: home-made pasta, the celebrated *zuppa dolada*, superb fish, duck and lamb dishes and an exceptional wine list. *Closed Mon, and Tues lunch.*

Feltre ✉ 32032

***Doriguzzi**, Viale del Piave 2, t 0439 2902, www.hoteldoriguzzi.it (€€). Set in a historic *palazzo* close to the station, with modern facilities, parking and a private park.

The Dolomites

There are mountains, and then there are the Dolomites. 'The most beautiful construction in the world', Le Corbusier called the range, made by the tiniest of architects – corals, billions upon billions of them, labouring in the primordial ocean 250 million years ago. Their masterpiece was thrust up from the sea bed 60 million years ago, to be honed and sharpened by aeons of ice and storms. Otherworldly peaks claw at the sky, each monumental sculpted range a petrified tempest of jagged needles, cloud-stabbing pinnacles and tremendous sheer walls, dyed a glowing rose by the dawn and blood-red by the setting sun.

10

Don't miss

See map overleaf

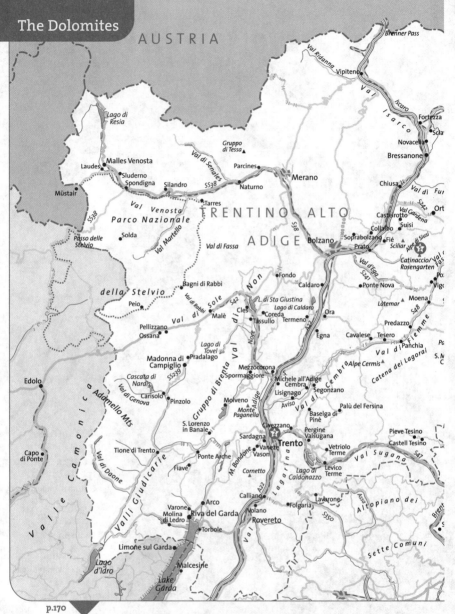

AUSTRIA

p.170

The Dolomites, most romantic of mountains, were named after a wandering French mineralogist with a fantastical name, Dieudonné Sylvain Guy Tancrède de Gratet de Dolomieu, who in 1789 was the first to describe their mineral content. Marmolada (10,961ft) is the highest peak in a range that has glaciers even in summer (17 other peaks top 10,000ft), but elsewhere the snowfields convert in July to a massive bouquet of wild flowers,

20 km
10 miles

N

AUSTRIA

Valle Aurina

Riva di Tures

Campo Tures

Chienes
Brunico
Val di Tures
Valle di Anterselve

Val
Pusteria
S244
Monguelfo
Rienza
Dobbiaco
Sesto
V. di Landro
Val di Sesto

Carbonin
Comelico Superiore
Rif. Auronzo
Lago di Misurina
Misurina
Auronzo di Cadore
Sto Stefano di Cadore
Sappada

Carnia Mountains

La Villa
Vallunga
S244
S. Cassiano
Tofane
S48
Cortina d'Ampezzo
S48
M. Agudo

Passo di Sella
Corvara
Col di Lana
Cinque Torri
S638
S51
S. Vito di Cadore
Calalzo di Cadore
Forni di Sopra
Lago di Sauris
Ampezzo
Tolmezzo

Arabba
S48
Andraz
Selva di Cadore
Borca di Cadore
Lumiei
Socchieve

Campitello di Fassa
Canazei
Marmolada
Caprile
Colle Sta Lucia
Boite
Neve di Cadore
Forni di Sotto

zza di Fassa
o di Fassa
Alleghe
M. Civetta
Cencenighe
Dont
Valle di Zoldano

S346
Canale d'Agordo
S203
M. Pelmo
Boite

Palcade
Cordevole
S203
Paneveggio
Agordo
Longarone
Lago del Vaiont
M. Toc

sso di Rolle
Martino di astrozza
Cole di S. Martino
S347
Frassene
M. Dolada
Val Cellina
Lago di Barcis

Fiera di Primiero
delle Dolomiti,
Parco Nazionale
Belluno

Bellunesi
S. Daniele di Friuli
Tagliamento
S13
A23

Gemona di Friuli
P.358

Feltre
VENETO
Bosco del Consiglio
Polcenigo
FRIULI-VENEZIA GIULIA

Vittorio Veneto
Caneva
Livenza
Sacile
Pordenone
S13

Valdobbiadene
S551
S313
A28

M. Grappa
Conegliano
P5

Bolagna
Romano d'Ezzelino
S248
Asolo
Maser
Montebelluna
A27

Bassano del Grappa

p.170

SWITZ.
AUSTRIA
HUNGARY
A4
FRANCE
SLOVENIA
CROATIA
SS14
BOSNIA-HERZ.
Corsica
Sardinia

Don't miss

Getting around the Dolomites

Even the heirs of the Romans can only make the **trains** go so far in the mountains. The line north from Venice, Treviso and Belluno passes through Pieve di Cadore before petering out in Calalzo di Cadore, 35km from Cortina d'Ampezzo (2½ hours from Venice). The western Dolomites are linked by the main line between Verona and Munich, by way of Trento (1½ hours) and Bolzano (2½ hours) to the Brenner Pass (4 hours). Other lines run from Bolzano to Merano and Malles Venosta, to the west, and from Fortezza (near Bressanone) to Brunico, Dobbiaco and San Candido, to the east.

To make up for the lack of trains, the Dolomites are exceptionally well served by three **bus** companies – in the east, **Dolomiti-Bus, t** 0437 941 167, *www.dolomitibus.it* (with, for example, daily routes to Agordo, Arabba, Falcade and Colle S. Lucia from Venice); in the west, the cheerful but still **SAD Buses, t** 800 846 047, *www.sad.it*; and **Atesina** in the Trentino area (*see* p.310). A SAD bus service connects Dobbiaco with Cortina. The companies add special scenic tours from the major centres in July and August.

> *For Beauty's nothing/but beginning of Terror we're still just able to bear*
> Rainer Maria Rilke,
> *The Duino Elegies*

streaked with blue gentians, yellow Alpine poppies and buttercups, edelweiss and pink rhododendron. The air and light in autumn are so sharp and fine they can break your heart.

Prices skyrocket in the Dolomites during the high season. To avoid the crowds and high prices, visit in June, early July, late September or October, when the Alpine refuges are open but not packed to the gills. For skiing, the best time to visit is immediately after the New Year holidays, when the resorts offer big discounts.

The Dolomites of the Veneto: The Cadore

Although mostly Italian-speaking, much of the Cadore, the district north of Belluno along the upper Piave, was incorporated into Italy only after the First World War. Its somewhat overripe, fashionable, but beautifully positioned heart is Cortina d'Ampezzo, host of the 1956 Winter Olympics, which did much to introduce the Dolomites to the world.

The Piave Valley

The roads north along the River Piave from Belluno (SS50) and Treviso (SS51) meet at the junction of Ponte nelle Alpi before continuing up through scenery marked by the steep pyramids of Monte Dolada and Piz Gallina. A less benign mountain, Toc (6,303ft), looms over the town of **Longarone**. In 1963 a landslide from its slopes crashed into the local reservoir, Lake Vaiont, creating a 'tidal' wave that killed nearly two thousand people in Longarone; a memorial church, unfortunately resembling a parking garage, has photos, scale models and a few poignant pieces salvaged from the mud. A road runs along the path of the disaster, the lofty and narrow **Gola del Vaiont**, to the lake, 6km to the east.

From Longarone there's also the option of turning west on the SS251 for the **Val Zoldana**, a lovely valley lining the River Maè, on its

10 km
5 miles

N

AUSTRIA

Brunico
Monguelfo
Dobbiaco S. Candido
Val Pusteria
S244
Lago di Dobbiaco
Sesto
Val di Sesto

TRENTINO-ALTO ADIGE

V. di Landr
Parco Regionale Dolomiti di Sesto
Val Fiscalina

Tre Cime di Lavaredo

Carbonin
Rif. Auronzo
Comelico Superiore
S. Nicolo' Comelico
S. Pietro di Cadore
Cimasappada

S. Cassiano
Cristallo
Lago di Misurina
Misurina
Auronzo di Cadore
Sto Stefano di Cadore
Sappada

Boite
Tofane
S48
S48
Cortina d'Ampezzo
S48
M. Agudo

S244
Passo di Falzarego
Tondi di Falória

Cinque Torri
S638
Sorapiss
Sauris di Sopra

Andraz
Passo di Giau
S551
S. Vito di Cadore
Lumiei

Pieve di Livinallongo
Selva di Cadore
Antelao
Calalzo di Cadore
Forni di Sopra
Lago di Sauris
Ampezzo

Caprile
Colle Sta Lucia
Borca di Cadore
Pieve di Cadore
Forni di Sotto

S48
M. Pelmo
Boite

Alleghe
VENETO
Valle di Zoldo

Canale d'Agordo
S203
M. Civetta
FRIULI-VENEZIA-GIULIA

S346
Cencenighe
Dont
Passo Duran

Cordevole
S203
Maniago

Agordo
Cimolais
Claut

Frassene
Longarone
Lago del Vaiont

Gosaldo
M. Toc
Meduno

Parco Nazionale delle Dolomiti
Val Cellina

M. Dolada

way past the stunning peaks of Civetta and Pelmo to Selva di Cadore (*see* p.302). Dotted with hamlets in wood and stone and huge barns under rusting corrugated roofs, the Val Zoldana is Italy's *gelato* centre; nearly all of Europe's great home-made ice cream makers are natives, and every November they return for the annual International Ice Cream Fair at Longarone to compare notes, techniques and new flavours.

The main road from Longarone skirts the high banks of the Piave north to the foothills of the Antelao range, 'the King of Cadore', en route to **Pieve di Cadore**. *Pieve* means parish, and from Roman times on this was the most important one in the Cadore, a status that grew with the reputation of that mighty wielder of brush, Tiziano Vecellio (Titian), born here *c.* 1483. His statue stands in the main piazza, and his birthplace, the **Casa Natale di Tiziano**, contains drawings, studies and some original furnishings. In the

Casa Natale di Tiziano
t 0435 32262; open June–Sept Tues–Sun 9.30–12.30 and 4–7, Aug also Mon; outside these times call in advance

Mountain Sports in the Dolomites

Hiking

One is tempted to lapse into Italian hyperbole about hiking in the Dolomites – but suffice to say it's as close as some of us will ever get to heaven. There are routes for everyone from semi-couch potatoes to rock-grappling daredevils, and eight **High Trails of the Dolomites** (*Alte Vie delle Dolomiti*) designed for those 'vagabonds of the path' who fall in between the two extremes. The trails range from 120 to 180km in length, and take the average walker two weeks.

The High Trails have the virtue of keeping you on top of mountains and plateaux for most of their length. While they do not require special climbing skill, they do demand a stout pair of hiking boots with good rubber soles and protection against sudden storms, even in the middle of summer. A telescopic walking stick and a mobile phone in case of emergencies are also recommended.

There are two good sets of maps that include the *Alte Vie* and other paths as well, and point out the location of the Alpine refuges: *Carta dei Sentieri e Rifugi*, *Edizioni Tabacco Udine*, and *Maps Kompass-Wanderkarten*, Edizioni Fleishmann-Starnberg. Both are scale 1:50,000, and are readily available at newsstands in the region. The relevant tourist offices have maps and booklets on each trail in English that contain all the basic information, including phone numbers of the refuges. They also give a good idea of the level of difficulty of each trail. The chairlifts stop in early September.

Strategically placed *rifugi alpini* provide shelter, but if you come when they are closed you'll need to carry camping gear. With a few rare exceptions, the refuges are open from mid-June to mid-September; in July and August it's wise to book a bed in advance. They vary dramatically. Many are owned by the Italian Alpine Club; others are privately owned, primarily by ski resorts. Some are along trails; others may be reached via cable car. All offer bed and board; nearly all now require that you bring a sleeping sheet, or buy one on the site. Prices differ mainly according to altitude: the higher up and more difficult the access, the more expensive. Besides these refuges, there are the *baite* (wooden huts), *casere* (stone huts) and bivouacs (beds but no food) found along some of the higher trails: they generally have no custodians but offer shelter.

For more information contact the **Italian Alpine Club** (CAI), Via Petrella 19, 20124 Milan, **t** 02 205 7231, *www.cai.it*; or contact local tourist offices, whose websites have sections on refuges, guides, walking and climbing: *www.suedtirol.info*, *www.trentino.to*, *www.infodolomiti.it*, *www.guidecortina.com*; also see *www.sat.tn.it*, *www.alpenverein.it*, *www.clubalpino.it*.

Skiing

The Dolomites are like a candy shop for winter sports junkies. On the sunny side of the Alps, they enjoy good clear weather, and when it snows, it falls delightfully dry and powdery.

There is a variety of slopes of all levels of difficulty, and country trails, toboggan and bobsled runs, ice rinks and speed-skating courses; if all of the ski runs were ironed out flat they would stretch all the way from the Brenner Pass to Reggio di Calabria. There are other bonuses as well: ski schools in July, and indoor heated pools in the middle of winter.

Write ahead to the tourist offices in Belluno, Trento or Bolzano, or book a week's *Settimana Bianca* package (a week's room and board at a hotel, ski pass and instruction) from CIT (Citalia) or other travel offices all over Italy. If you want to try as many resorts as possible, the *Dolomiti Superski pass*, 'the world's most extensive ski pass', gives unlimited access (for €32 a day) to 450 lifts and 1,220km of ski runs for periods of one, two or three weeks.

For the latest information and prices, visit *www.dolomitisuperski.com*.

church of Santa Maria Nascente, the last chapel on the left holds his Madonna with SS Andrew and Titian, starring his own family – his daughter as the Virgin, his son as Titian the Bishop, his brother as St Andrew, while Titian himself looks in from the left, holding a staff. You can illuminate the painting for a small fee and a little bit of faith; pay on the right-hand side by the side entrance.

Palazzo della Magnifica Comunità Cadorina
same hours as Casa Natale di Tiziano, above

Museo dell' Occhiale
t 0435 500 213; open July–Aug Mon–Sat 8.30–12.30 and 4.30–7.30, Sept–June Mon–Sat 8.30–12.30; adm

The most important building in Pieve doesn't leave room for any false modesty: the Palazzo della Magnifica Comunità Cadorina. Built in 1525, it now houses the local historical museum, with pre-Roman weapons, 2nd-century BC bronze figurines, and more. Towards Tai, at the crossroads, the Museo dell'Occhiale contains a rare collection of antique spectacles. But what Pieve is proudest of is Babbo Natale (the Italian Santa Claus), who has made the town his home, with a Christmas-letter answering service for children.

The road follows the Piave north past the end of the rail line at **Calalzo**, with buses for **Santo Stefano di Cadore**, the old capital of the federated Cadore villages, now thoroughly converted to its new tourism vocation. Just up from Santo Stefano, in **San Pietro di Cadore**, you'll find something unique in the mountains: a Veneto-style villa, **Palazzo Poli** (1665), designed by Longhena and now the town hall; you can step in to see the frescoes.

Also 5km north of Santo Stefano di Cadore, in little **San Nicolo' Comelico**, there is a small church built in 1199 and frescoed by Gianfrancesco da Tolmezzo in 1482. If you get there in February, you may be able to join the locals in the *maskarade*. A Ladin festival dating from the Middle Ages, it tends to become an extended celebration of the local produce, especially grappa.

At San Pietro you can make a detour up the charming wooded **Valle Visdende**, or continue up the Piave to the popular (if a bit overbuilt) resort of **Sappada**, which hosted the World Snowboard Championships in the winter of 2001. **Cimasappada**, another 4km up the road, has kept more of its traditional mountain character. A road from Cimasappada follows the Piave up to its source.

From Pieve di Cadore there is also a direct road to Cortina d'Ampezzo, the SS51, which winds through the **Valle del Boite** with its many rustic wooden chalets, between the Antelao massif and **Monte Pelmo**, one of the most unusual and striking peaks in the Dolomites. The road passes through **Borca di Cadore** and the more important resort of **San Vito di Cadore** with its lake, an excellent base for ascending Pelmo.

Where to Stay and Eat in the Piave Valley

ⓘ **Sappada >**
Borgata Bach 9, t 0435 469 131; Santo Stefano di Cadore: Piazza Roma 37, t 0435 62230

Sappada ✉ 32047

***Haus Michaela, Borgata Fontana 40, t 0435 469 377, www.hotelmichaela.com (€€€–€€). The emphasis here is on fitness, with an indoor pool, sauna and gym. *Open mid-Dec–end Mar and mid-May–end Sept.*

***Bellavista, Via Cima, t 0435 469 175, www.albergobellavista.com (€€). Located in Cimasappada, 4km from

Sappada, with lovely views and mountain bikes for hire. *Open Dec–Easter and mid-June–Sept.*

***Belvedere, Piazza Cima 93, t 0435 469 112, www.hotelbelvederesappada.it (€€). Also in Cimasappada, this hotel has only 14 rooms, but does have its own sauna and a good restaurant (open to non-residents): mountain specialities include variations on venison and tasty desserts. *Open Dec–mid-April and mid-June–mid-Sept.*

**Corona Ferrea, Borgata Kratten 11, t 0435 469 442, www.corona-ferrea.it

(€€–€). A cheaper choice, with comfortable rooms, all with en-suite bathrooms. *Open mid-June–mid-Sept and mid-Dec–Mar.*

***Siera Hof**, Via Soravia 68, **t** 0435 469 110, *www.sierahof.com* (€). A small place, near the centre of the village.

Laite, Borgata Hoffe 10, **t** 0435 469 070 (€€€). Inside an old wooden chalet; the standard of cooking is extremely high with delicious mountain specialities such as quail stuffed with *foie gras* and tarragon, and guinea fowl with mountain *radicchio. Closed Wed, Thurs lunch, June and Oct.*

Baita Mondschein, Via Bach 96, **t** 0435 469 585 (€€). For some really authentic cooking try this pretty Alpine chalet situated at the bottom of Sappada's slalom course. Serving wonderful grills and some interesting desserts, as well as home-made ice cream. *Closed Tues, June and Nov.*

Pieve di Cadore ✉ 32044

Al Pelmo, Via Nazionale 60, **t** 0435 500 900, *www.pelmo.it* (€€). There are not all that many choices in Pieve di Cadore, but this hotel offers nice rooms with stunning views over the valley and a good, reasonably priced restaurant. They also have a reciprocal arrangement with the nearby Croda Bianca thermal centre, which should cure any aches and pains you might be suffering.

San Vito di Cadore ✉ 32046

****Marcora**, Via Roma 28, **t** 0436 9101, *www.corahotel.it* (€€€). The best of a number of comfortable hotels here, in a fine setting with a pool. *Open end June–Aug and mid-Dec–mid-Mar.*

***Cima Belprà**, Via Calvi 1, at Chiapuzza, **t** 0436 890 441, *www.hotelcimabelpra.com* (€€). A welcoming place with the best restaurant in the whole area, La Scaletta (open to non-guests), with beautiful views, and serving traditional polenta and beef dishes. *Closed Mon out of season, and part of Nov.*

ⓘ **San Vito di Cadore »**
Via Nazionale 9,
t 0436 9119

ⓘ **Pieve di Cadore ›**
Piazza Venezia 20,
t 0435 31644

Cortina d'Ampezzo

🏔 **Cortina d'Ampezzo**

Cortina is the sort of place where David Niven and Audrey Hepburn would sit about in a café in turtlenecks and sunglasses, but it also enjoys the best location in the Dolomites: a lofty, sunny, cross-shaped meadow at the junction of the Boite and Bigontina valleys, in the centre of a ring of extraordinary mountains – Tofane, the great 'mount owl' (scene of the 1997 World Championship); Cristallo, the 'crystal' mountain; Sorapis, licked by stony flames; and the Cinque Torri, the 'five towers'.

Devoted heart and soul to the sporting life, Cortina is almost as well known for its night-time activities in winter, when the *après ski* crowd fills its clubs to trip the light fantastic until the small hours of dawn. But whatever worldly pleasure and delight this snowy fleshpot offers, it comes at a price, rating right up there with Venice herself on the bottom line of the tab. Bear in mind, too, that Cortina essentially closes in April and May and from September to November, though the 14 of the town's 64 hotels that do stay open offer low-season tariffs.

The Sporting Life

The 1956 Olympics endowed Cortina with superb winter sports facilities; here you can ski-jump, speed-skate, fly down bobsled and

Getting to and around Cortina d'Ampezzo

Cortina's **bus** station is just off Via Marconi, and is served by SAD covering the Alto Adige, **t** 800 846 047, *www.sad.it*; and Dolomiti-bus covering Veneto, **t** 0437 941 167, *www.dolomitibus.it*. Services are greatly augmented from June to September, when buses serve virtually every paved road in the region. There's one bus a day direct from Venice via Treviso (**t** 0436 867 921).

The nearest **train** stations are Dobbiaco, 32km north (on the Bolzano–Lienz line; reached from Verona or Innsbruck to Fortezza, then change – note there is no ticket office at Dobbiaco but you can make reservations at the bus station information office in Cortina), or Calalzo di Cadore, 35km south; both have regular bus connections to Cortina.

luge runs, and cut figures of eight in the ice stadium, not to mention the thousand and one downhill and cross-country ski runs in the vicinity. In the summer, it's an excellent base for hiking, rock climbing, delta-planing, torrentialism and more, while in town there's a riding school, tennis, summer/winter swimming pools, and activities like the Ice Disco Dance in the Olympic Ice Stadium.

Cortina has its share of trendy shops, and a museum of contemporary art you can take in if it rains – the **Museo Ciasa de Ra Regoles** has sections on palaeontology and ethnography, and art by De Pisis, Morandi, De Chirico and others.

Two cable cars from Cortina wait to whisk you up to the mountains, both at the end of the town's bus lines: in the north, near the Olympic stadium, to Tofana di Mezzo (10,640ft) where there are privately run Alpine refuges, and in the west, to Tondi di Faloria (7,687ft).

Museo Ciasa de Ra Regoles
Via del Parco; open mid-June–mid-Sept Tues–Sun 10.30–12.30 and 4–7.30 (till 8 in July and Aug), Christmas–Easter 4–7; adm

Tourist Information in Cortina d'Ampezzo

ⓘ Cortina d'Ampezzo >
Piazzetta S. Francesco 8, near Piazza Venezia, t 0436 3231, www.infodolomiti.it; for local guides contact Gruppo Guide Alpine, Corso Italia 69, t 0436 868 505, www.guidecortina.com; open July–Sept

The tourist office provides an accommodation service, good trail maps, information about excursions and the Dolomiti Superski pass.

Where to Stay in Cortina d'Ampezzo

Cortina d'Ampezzo ✉ 32043

Expect to run up against the full- or half-board requirement nearly everywhere in Cortina in its high season (it's an old tradition in these parts: the ancient Greek writer Polybius wrote that in Cisalpine Gaul travellers at inns always requested the price for their whole stay, rather than have itemized accounts as elsewhere – history's first full-board arrangements). It may be mortifying to the pocketbook, but not to the flesh; the local cuisine is usually as *haute* as the price. Visit the tourist office for lists of self-catering flats and homestays.

Luxury–Very Expensive
(€€€€€–€€€€)
*****Miramonti Majestic, Via Peziè 103, **t** 0436 4201, *www.getur hotels.com*. If you're putting on the dog in Cortina, this is the place to do it. Warm, traditional and rustic, it has pretty wooden balconies affording magnificent views. The well-designed rooms have all imaginable creature comforts, and there's an indoor pool, tennis courts, golf, exercise facilities and sauna. *Open mid-Dec–Mar and mid-June–Aug.*

****De La Poste, Piazza Roma 14, **t** 0436 4271, *www.delaposte.it*. If you'd rather be in the centre of the action, try this large, historic Alpine chalet with classy rooms and balconies. The Poste's terrace and bar see much of Cortina's social round, especially in the evening; half-pension mandatory in high season. *Open mid-Dec–mid-April and mid-June–mid-Oct.*

Very Expensive (€€€€)

****Corona**, Via Val di Sotto 12, t 0436 3251, *www.hotelcoronacortina.it.* Another Alpine chalet, close to the centre, down at the bottom of the valley beside the river. Memorable for a modern art collection even more extensive than the one in the museum; it's also more convenient than most for the ski lift. *Open July–early Sept and Dec–mid-April.*

***Da Beppe Sello**, Via Ronco 68, t 0436 3236, *www.beppesello.it.* Award-winning, warm and welcoming, with some of the best food in Cortina. *Open Dec–Mar and mid-May–mid-Sept.*

Expensive (€€€)

****Astoria**, Largo delle Poste 11, t 0436 2525 (hotel), t 0436 863 828 (restaurant). A friendly little hotel right in the centre with only 7 rooms and an excellent restaurant (Pontejel). Eat *cappellotti* ('little hat' pasta) with figs and potato, *camoscio* or steak, followed by peaches and *amaretti*. *Open mid-June–mid-Oct and mid-Dec–mid-April. Restaurant closed Tues.*

****Impero**, Via C. Battisti 66, t 0436 4246, *www.hotelimperocortina.it.* An unpretentious hotel with no restaurant but adequate rooms, all with bath. *Open all year.*

****Menardi**, Via Majon 110, t 0436 2400, *www.hotelmenardi.it.* A charming 800-year-old farmhouse that's been run as an inn by the same family for the past century, furnished with antiques and bedecked with fresh flowers. *Open June–mid-Sept and mid-Dec–Mar.*

****Montana**, Corso Italia 94, t 0436 860 498, *www.cortina-hotel.com.* As a second choice try here. *Open Dec–May and July–Oct.*

Eating Out in Cortina d'Ampezzo

Pontejel (€€€); *see* Astoria, above.

Tivoli, Via Lacedel 34, t 0436 866 400 (€€€€). Its rival, northeast of the centre, offers lovely views and innovative, ultra-refined cuisine. *Open Dec–Easter and mid-June–Sept, closed Mon in low season.*

El Toulà, Via Ronco 123, near Pocol, t 0436 3339 (€€€). An elegant place to eat. A refurbished wooden farmhouse, specializing in perfect grilled meats, roast lamb, and desserts with a Tyrolean touch, accompanied by a renowned wine list. *Open Christmas–Easter and mid-July–end Aug; closed Mon in Jan.*

Excursions from Cortina

Situated at a major crossroads, Cortina offers numerous forays into the surrounding mountains. For the classic Great Dolomites Road between Cortina and Bolzano, *see* p.341.

Lake Misurina and Around

For a beautiful short trip from Cortina, take the SS48 and SS48b over the lofty Tre Croci pass to **Lake Misurina**, shimmering below the jagged peaks of Sorapis and the remarkable triple-spired **Tre Cime di Lavaredo**, 15km northeast of Cortina. The colours of Misurina are so brilliant they look touched up on postcards; as a resort it makes a quiet alternative to Cortina, especially if ice-skating is your sport. From Misurina it's a magnificent 7km drive up to the **Rifugio Auronzo**, located just beneath the Tre Cime di Lavaredo, where you can make the easy walk to the 1916 **Bersaglieri Memorial**, honouring Italy's famous sharpshooters.

Circular Routes from Misurina to Cortina

There are two possible circular routes from Misurina back to Cortina that make rewarding, full-day excursions. Both begin to the east on the SS48 via **Auronzo di Cadore**, past a peak known as the Corno del Doge for its resemblance to the doge's horned bonnet. Auronzo, on the shores of an artificial lake, surrounded by fragrant spruce forests, makes another good alternative base, and has a cable car and chairlifts up **Monte Agudo**.

From Auronzo you can circle south around Pieve di Cadore and the Valle di Boite (161km altogether; *see above*, pp.295) or take the longer route around to the north (224km) through **Comelico** and the beautiful **Val di Sesto**, an area noted for its traditional wooden houses. Just south of the modern village of **Sesto** a short branch valley, the **Val Fiscalina/Fischleintal**, is one of the most dramatic in all the Dolomites, skirting the edge of the **Parco Naturale Dolomiti di Sesto**. The Val Fiscalina is nicknamed 'Sesto's Sundial'; from here the peaks – from One to Nine – are divinely arranged to catch the sun and tell the hour. It's all true and remarkably accurate: there is a pleasant, valley circular stroll of about an hour from the end of the road.

At Sesto the route passes into the Alto Adige, passing by way of **San Candido/Innichen**, a pretty resort on the River Drava; it has a Benedictine monastery and a lovely Romanesque church, the early 13th-century **Collegiata SS. Candidus e Corbinian** on Via Alto, decorated with works from the period: a superb Crucifixion in polychrome wood, Gothic frescoes in the tribune, and sculptures in the recently restored crypt. The Collegiate's treasure and manuscripts are in an adjacent museum. Another museum in San Candido, the **Museo Mineralogico Dolomythos**, is devoted to the bizarre geological history of the Dolomites.

Collegiata SS. Candidus e Corbinian
t 0474 913 149; open 15 July–31 Aug Tues–Sat 10–11, Tues also 8–10

Museo Mineralogico Dolomythos
Villa Wachtler, Via Peter Paul Rainer 9, www.dolomythos.com; open Mon–Sat 10–12 and 3–7, Sun also mid-July–mid-Sept

Museo Gustav Mahler
4km from the centre at Casa Trenker, www.gustav-mahler.it; open Tues and Sat 11–12

The turn back to Cortina (SS51) is at **Dobbiaco/Toblach**, one of the original Dolomite resorts thanks to its magnificent setting, a lake, and a railway station built by the Habsburgs. The large **castle** in the old town was built for Venice's arch-enemy Emperor Maximilian in 1500. In mid-July–August Dobbiaco holds a series of concerts in honour of Mahler, who spent three summers here; in summer, too, you can visit the little **Museo Gustav Mahler**. From Dobbiaco, the road heads south to Cortina past the wooded Lago di Dobbiaco, then enters the dramatic **Val di Landro**, with the Cristallo group looming ahead over **Carbonin/Schluderbach**. Beyond are a pair of little lakes, the Black and the White, and the lonely ruins of the **Castel Sant'Umberto**. The road then circles around castle-crowned **Podestagno**, before descending into the Ampezzo with the Tofane group storming up to the right.

Cortina to Colle Santa Lucia and Agordo

There are two routes to these mountains southwest of Cortina: the main one follows the Great Dolomites Road (*see* p.341) through the Falzarego Pass before taking the SS203 southwards at Andraz, while a lesser-known but equally pretty route takes the smaller SS638 road through the **Passo di Giau**, where some of the most important mesolithic tombs in Europe (5000 BC) were discovered.

Museo Civico
t 043 752 1068; closed for restoration at the time of writing

The remains and artefacts of 'Mondeval man' can be seen down in **Selva di Cadore**, in the Museo Civico, along with a reconstruction of the tombs. Selva is a growing resort in the lovely Val Fiorentina, where a road crosses into the Valle di Zoldana and ends up at Longarone (*see* pp.294–5). Above Selva, **Colle Santa Lucia** is a pretty place with its old agricultural hamlets and a beautiful belvedere (31km from Cortina).

Continuing south from Colle Santa Lucia, the road passes **Caprile** and the mighty north wall of Civetta en route to **Alleghe** with its lovely lake, formed in 1771 by a landslide from Civetta. At **Cencenighe** you have the option of turning off for Falcade and San Martino di Castrozza (*see* p.317), or continuing on to **Agordo** (45km), an attractive town and resort along one of the principal branches of the Piave.

Where to Stay and Eat around Cortina

Misurina ✉ 32040

***Lavaredo**, Via Monte Piana 11, t 0435 39227, www.lavaredohotel.it (€€). Offers tennis courts and a good restaurant. *Closed Nov–mid-Dec and mid-April–mid-May.*

Dolomiti des Alpes, Via Monte Piana, t 0435 39031, www.dolomitidesalpes.com (€). Situated just above the lake, with a sauna-solarium. *Open Dec–April and June–Sept.*

*Sport**, Via Monte Piana 18, t 0435 39125 (€). Overlooking Lake Misurina; simple rooms. *Open Dec–April and June–Sept.*

ⓘ San Candido >>
Piazza del Magistrato 1, t 0474 913 156, www.altapusteria.info

Auronzo di Cadore ✉ 32041

***Auronzo**, Via Roma 30, t 0435 400 202, www.dolomitihotel.com (€€). Auronzo has far more choices: this is a cosy old place with tennis and a park on the lake shore. *Open Jan–Mar and May–Sept.*

ⓘ Auronzo di Cadore >
Via Roma 10, t 0435 9359

Dal Cavalier, on the road east of Auronzo at Cima Gogna, t 0435 9872 (€€). Serving delicious suckling pig

and risotto with herbs or mushrooms, amid traditional, wood-panelled décor. *Closed Wed.*

Vienna, Via Verona 2, t 0435 9394 (€). Near the lake with good views of the mountains. *Open June–Sept.*

San Candido/ Innichen ✉ 39038

***Orso Grigio**, Via Rainer 2, t 0474 913 115, www.orsohotel.it (€€€). This award-winning hotel has charming, modern rooms in a handsome 18th-century building. *Open mid-June–Sept and Dec–Mar.*

***Posthotel**, Via Sesto 1, t 0474 913 133, www.posthotel.it (€€€). Central, traditional, and offering plenty of activities, including a childrens' games room, a Turkish bath and solarium, and excellent local and international dishes in its restaurant. *Open mid-June–Sept and mid-Dec–Mar.*

Uhrmacher's Weinstube, Via Tintori 1, t 0474 913 158. A special treat for wine or spirit lovers; visit the cellar and choose a wine to go with a snack, or try a glass from one of the thirty or so bottles they open every day. *Closed Wed, exc summer.*

ⓘ **Dobbiaco** >
Via delle Dolomiti 3,
t 0474 972 132,
www.dobbiaco.info

ⓘ **Alleghe** >>
Piazza Kennedy 17,
t 0437 523 333; **Agordo:**
Via XXVII Aprile 5A,
t 0437 62105

Dobbiaco/Toblach ✉ 39034

****Cristallo**, Via S. Giovanni 37, t 0474 972 138, *www.hotelcristallo.com* (€€€). Since 1911, the same family has run this fine resort hotel. Located in a beautiful setting, with an indoor pool and sauna. *Open Christmas–Easter and mid-June–early Oct.*

Winkelkeller, Via Conte Künigi 8, t 0474 972 022 (€€). Dine here on refined mountain cuisine. *Closed Wed, Thurs and Oct.*

Selva di Cadore ✉ 32020

***Giglio Rosso**, at Pescul, t 0437 720 310, *www.hotelgigliorosse.it* (€€). A fine place both to stay and to eat. The kitchen does a fine mulberry risotto

and turkey in beer. *Closed early Jan–Mar.*

Alleghe/Caprile ✉ 32022

****Alla Posta**, Piazza Dogliani 19, in Caprile, t 0437 721 171, *www.hotel posta.com* (€€). This 130-year-old hotel is the most prestigious in the area, with pool, sauna and restaurant. *Open 23 Dec–Mar, mid-June–end Sept, Easter.*

***Coldai**, Via Coldai 26, t 0437 523 305, *www.hotelcoldai.com* (€€–€). A hotel with lovely views over the lake and pleasant rooms. *Closed May–mid-June, Oct and Nov.*

Marmolada, Corso Veneto 27, t 0437 721 107 (€). Simple, but who wants to be indoors anyway? *Closed May, Oct.*

The Western Dolomites: Trentino

The autonomous, exceptionally well-organized and beautiful province of Trentino encompasses the western Dolomites, including the stunning Val di Fassa and the Brenta Group, majestically isolated from its sisters west of the Adige. Unlike the Alto Adige/Süd Tirol further north, Trentino is mostly Italian in language and heritage, sprinkled with a Ladin minority in the valleys. Trento itself is a fine little art city, worth a day on its own.

From Verona to Trento: Up the Val Lagarina

From Verona, the A22 and SS12 follow the Adige up through the Valpolicella and the Monti Lessini, and enter Trentino near **Avio**, dominated by the proud 14th-century **Castello di Sabbionara**. This is only one of 29 castles that guarded the Val Lagarina, one of the main routes through to northern Europe. Its owners, the Counts of Castelbarco, gave it to Venice in 1411, but after the Republic enlarged and decorated it, Emperor Maximilian snatched it in 1509, in the War of the Cambrai. The guardhouse preserves a wonderful 14th-century fresco of battling knights, the *Parata dei Combattenti*, while the keep has frescoes of courtly love, divided by fur hangings.

Castello di Sabbionara open Mar–Sept Tues–Sun 10–6, Oct–mid-Dec and Feb Tues–Sun 10–5; adm

Rovereto, the 'Athens of the Trentino'

Further up the Adige, Rovereto is an evocative old place swimming in a sea of vineyards. It has a hallowed scholarly tradition: in the 1750s it had its own Academy, with a funny name, *degli Agiati*, 'of the slowcoaches' and in 1769 it became the first city in Italy to hear the young Mozart play (hence the **Mozart festival** in summer); it was also the birthplace of philosopher Antonio

Mozart festival www.mozartitalia.org

N

10 km
5 miles

Parco Nazionale

Val di Fassa

TRENTINO-ALTO
ADIGE

M. Cevedale

della Stelvio

Appiano

Fondo
Passo di
Mendola

Bagni di Rabbi

Caldaro sulla Strada del Vino

Val di Rabbi

Peio

Val

di

Sole

S42

Romeno

L. di Sta Giustina

Lago di
Caldaro

Malè

Cles

S. Romedio

Val

Sanzeno

di

Coreda

Termeno

Pellizzano

Folgarida

Tassullo

Tueno

Taio

Ossana

Marillevà

Non

Val

di

Brenta

Ton

Lago di
Tovel

Pradalago

Madonna di
Campiglio

Campo Carlo
Magno

Spormaggiore

Mezzocorona

S.
Michele all'Adige

Cembra

Persanella

Cascata di
Nardis

SS239

C. Tosa

Fai della
Paganella

Andalo

Lisignago

Val

Aviso

di

Val di Genova

Carisolo

Pinzolo

Gruppo di Brenta

Molveno

Monte
Paganella

Adige

Baselga di
Pinè

Adamello Mts

Lago di
Molveno

S. Lorenzo
in Banale

Cast. Toblino

Civezzano

Sardagna

Pergine
Valsugana

Stenico

Sarche

Lago di
Toblino

Vaneze

Trento

Tione di Trento

Ponte Arche

Vason

M. Bondone

Val di Daone

Dasindo

Fiavè

Lago di
Cavedine

Cornetto

Lago di
Caldonazzo

Drena

Dro

Valli Giudicarie

Arco

Cascata

Caneve

Varone

Villa
Lagarina

Calliano

Cast. Beseno

Folgaria

Riva del Garda

Volano

Castèl Pietra

Molina
di Ledro

Lago
di Ledro

Torbole

Isera

Rovereto

Cast. Dante

Limone sul Garda

Val

Lagarina

Tremosine

Malcesine

Campione

Camposilvano

Lago
d'Idro

Lago
di
Garda

Avio

Gargnano

Ferrara di
M. Baldo

Recoaro
Terme

Selva
Corvara
Passo di Gardena
Gruppa di Sella
Arabba
Col di Lana
S48
Soprabolzano
Siusi
Fiè all Sciliar
Alpe di Siusi
Campitello di Fassa
Passo Pordoi
Pieve di Livinallongo
Andraz
Bolzano
Prato
Val di Tires
Tires
Catinaccio/ Rosengarten
Canazei
Caprile
Val d'Ega
Nove Levante
Val di Fassa
Pozza di Fassa
Marmolada
Laives
S241
Ponte Nova
S. Giovanni
Vigo di Fassa
Caldaro
Lago di Carezza
Passo di Costalunga
S346
SS203
Ora
Làtemar
Moena
Falcade
Canale d'Agordo
Cencenighe
Cordevole
S203
Egna
S48
Predazzo
Parco
Paneveggio
Pale di S. Martino
S347
Cavalese
Tesero
Panchia
Val di Fiemme
Passo di Rolle
Regionale
Frassene
Segonzano
Alpe Cermis
Catena dei Lagorai
S. Martino di Castrozza
Gosaldo
di
Cembra
Paneveggio-Pale di S. Martino
Parco
Palù del Fersina
Fiera di Primiero
Passo di Cereda
Nazionale
delle Dolomiti
Bellunesi
Borgo Valsugana
Villa Ivano-Fracena
Pieve Tesino
Vetriolo Terme
Castello Tesino
Feltre
L. di Levico
Val Sugana
S47
Levico Terme
Lavarone
Assa
Altopiano dei
Brenta
VENETO
S350
Cavaso del Tomba
Roana
Asiago
Foza
Possagno
Canove
Sasso
Villa Barbaro
Muliparte
Cesuna
Valstagna
Asolo
Masèr
Sette Comuni
Romano d'Ezzelino
Montebelluna
S46
Lugo di Vicenza
Angarano
S248
Altivole
Santorso
Molvena
Marostica
Bassano del Grappa
S. Vito
Schio
Thiene
A31
Riese Pio X

The Western and Brenta Dolomites

Getting around Trentino

Frequent **trains** and **buses** follow the Adige from Verona to Trento, stopping at the main towns.

Rosmini in 1797. Piled on top of the town, its landmark **Castello** was first built by the Castelbarco family, then rebuilt with its fat towers in 1416–87 by the Venetians, when Rovereto formed the northern extent of the *Serenissima*; they lost it after a 40-day siege by the Austrian Archduke. This area was also hotly contested in the First World War, as remembered in the castle's extensive **War Museum**. Below the castle in Piazza del Podestà, there's a spooky fascist memorial to the Legione Trentini and local war heroes, as well as a handsome Venetian Municipio, originally the Palazzo Pretorio (1417). The other thing the Venetians did for Rovereto was introduce silkworms and mulberry trees into the economy; it was especially big in the 16th–18th centuries, when Italy had its own 'silk routes' just like China; picturesque **silk houses**, which provided the power to run the mills, overhang the River Leno below the castle.

A former resident of Rovereto, the Futurist Fortunato Depero (1892–1960), worked for many years in the town, and bequeathed to it the **Museo Depero**. This perfect and rather striking little museum was designed by the artist himself as a showcase for his tapestries, puppets and paintings, dedicated to 'the Futurist reconstruction of the Universe'. This uniquely Italian school of the 20th century, which blindly believed in progress and speed and wanted to blow up St Mark's and ban spaghetti, produced some memorable works in spite of itself. The spanking new **Museo di Arte Moderna e Contemporanea** (MART) of Trento and Rovereto houses the Archivio del '900. Strikingly modern, in glass and stone, it hosts permanent and seasonal exhibitions as well as a major summer arts festival, attracting local and international talent.

Another local lad, the great archaeologist Paolo Orsi, willed his private collection of statues, busts and vases from Magna Graecia to the city's **Museo Civico**; admission includes the **Cinema Archeologico**, Europe's most complete archive of archaeological documentaries. Now installed in its new headquarters, this is the third oldest museum in Italy, founded in 1851. Besides archaeology, other exhibitions are on the natural sciences and the old silk industry, and the stars – in the new planetarium.

Cannons from each of the 19 belligerents in the First World War were melted down to make the largest ringing bell in the world, the **Campana dei Caduti**, or Maria Dolens. Located on the Colle di Miravalle in the southern quarter of Rovereto, it rings a hundred times in memory of the victims of all wars every day at sundown. Just southeast of Rovereto, at **Lavini di Marco**, near the cylindrical First World War ossuary and ruined Castle Dante (where the poet

War Museum
*www.museodella
guerra.it; open
July–Sept Tues–Fri 10–6,
Sat–Sun 9.30–6.30,
Oct–June Tues–Sun
10–6; adm*

Museo Depero
*Via della Terra 53,
t 800 397 760; closed
for restoration at the
time of writing*

**Museo di Arte
Moderna e
Contemporanea**
*Corso Bettini 43,
t 800 397 760;
www.mart.trento.it;
open Tues–Thurs and
Sat–Sun 10–6, Fri 10–9*

Museo Civico
*Palazzo Parolari,
Borgo S. Caterina 43,
www.museocivico.
rovereto.tn.it; open
Tues–Sun 9–12 and 3–6,
also Fri and Sun
8–10pm in summer*

Path of the Dinosaurs
contact Museo Civico, above, for details

sojourned in 1303) you can follow the 'Path of the Dinosaurs', marked by Jurassic footprints planted 200 million years ago. It reveals traces of 150 different dinosaurs, carnivores and herbivores.

Up the Val Lagarina from Rovereto

Across the Adige from Rovereto, **Isera** is the centre for the production of Marzemino, one of Trentino's finest red wines – Mozart found it 'excellent' and the Romans liked it too – a 1st-century AD winemaking villa is currently being excavated. Nearby, the little town of **Villa Lagarina** has a surprisingly rich Baroque chapel in its parish church, and there is a road up to two pretty woodland lakes and the picturesque 13th–15th century Castel Noarna. Decorated with frescoes glorifying the owners, victories over the Turks, and views of other Trentino castles by a follower of Michelangelo, in the 17th century the castle was the rather nasty scene of numerous witchcraft trials.

Castel Noarna
t 0464 413 295, www.castelnoarna.com; call in advance

Just north of Rovereto, in **Volano**, is the Gothic church of **San Rocco**, every square inch brightly frescoed by painters from Verona in the 15th and 16th centuries. Visible from the road, the imposing Castel Beseno is the largest castle in the Trentino, built by the Counts of Castelbarco and inherited by the Tyrolean von Trapp family in 1460, who were responsible for most of the Renaissance improvements and the large space devoted to knightly tournaments. It has a number of well-preserved military exhibits and a room frescoed with scenes of the months. In nearby **Calliano**, the atmospheric 13th-century Castelpietra was a bulwark of Beseno; it once had a great wall along the Adige and controlled the road by means of an enormous iron door, which impressed Machiavelli but not Napoleon, who knocked it all down. The main Sala del Giudizio has some fascinating frescoes on hunting scenes and the *Judgement of Solomon*, and one of a man and a magpie – the former in a cage, much to the bird's amusement.

Castel Beseno
t 0464 834 600, www.buonconsiglio.it; open daily June–Oct 10–6, Mar–May 9.30–5; adm

Castelpietra
t 0464 835 044; call in advance

Two small resorts on a 3,280ft meadowland below Monte Cornetto can be reached by the SS350 from Calliano: **Folgaria**, with the restored 17th-century Maso Spilzi; and **Lavarone**, near the crystal-clear Lago di Lavarone, where Freud spent three summers. The Austro-Hungarians heavily fortified this frontier with Italy between 1908 and 1914. Their 'iron curtain of the highlands' had seven forts: one, Forte Belvedere, built around a huge three-storey pillbox with enough storage space to support 200 people for three months, has been restored as a museum – only the domes that once housed the three 100mm howitzers have been replaced. According to some historians, the first artillery shots were fired from here against the Italians in 1915. The 'Path of Peace' (*Sentiero della Pace*), a month-long walk along the front lines of the First World War, begins near here and continues to the Stelvio pass.

Maso Spilzi
open June–Sept

Forte Belvedere
open July and Aug daily 10–6; April–June Tues–Sun 10–12 and 2.30–6; adm

ⓘ **Rovereto** >
Corso Rosmini 6a,
t 0464 430 363,
www.aptrovereto.tn.it

ⓘ **Lavarone** >>
Via Roma 67,
t 0464 721 133,
www.montagna
conamore.it

Where to Stay and Eat in the Val Lagarina

Rovereto ✉ 38068

***Rovereto**, Corso Rosmini 82/d, t 0464 435 222, *www.hotelrovereto.it* (€€€). A fine central hotel, with comfortable air-conditioned rooms, and an excellent restaurant, **Novecento** (€€), featuring regional dishes, delicious home-made pasta, and light fish dishes. *Closed Sun, Jan and Aug.*

Youth hostel, Via della Scuola 18, t 0464 486 757, *www.ostellorovereto.it* (€). A good, modern hostel near the railway station.

Osteria del Pettirosso, Corso Bettini 24, t 0464 422 463 (€€). This *enoteca* offers a good selection of regional and international wines. Downstairs, in the small but lovely restaurant, you can pair wines with traditional Trentino dishes and a wide variety of cheeses and cold meats. *Closed Sun.*

San Colombano, Via Vicenza 30, t 0464 436 006 (€€). Beyond the centre, not far away from the castle, this simple restaurant will serve you good traditional Italian dishes. Friendly staff. *Closed Sun eve and Mon.*

Lavarone/Folgaria ✉ 38046

***Hotel al Lago**, Vialago 21, Lavarone, t 0464 783 222, *www.hotelallago.com* (€€). Freud stayed here. An indoor swimming pool and tennis courts in addition to its pretty setting on the lake make it a fine place to forget your neuroses.

***Caminetto**, near the chairlift Bertoldi, t 0464 783 214 (*inexpensive*). Lots of wood and flowers give this hotel its cosy charm. *Open Dec–Easter and June–Sept.*

L'Antica Pineta, Via de Gasperi 66, in Folgaria, t 0464 720 327 (*moderate*). A good place to dine and try polenta laden with melted Asiago cheese. *Closed Wed exc. in summer.*

Trento

Lying at the foot of Monte Bondone, between the banks of the Adige and the Fersina, the friendly capital of the Trentino owes much of its charm to the powerful bishop-princes who ruled it for centuries, most notably art patron Bernardo Cles (1514–39). The heritage they left behind is a delightful art city, perhaps in the second division in Italy, but one that would be near the top in any other country in the world. The bishop-prince's Castello del Buonconsiglio has a fresco cycle of the months that is worth the trip alone, while the *centro storico*'s gently winding streets are merry with colourful *al fresco* frescoes.

Bernardo Cles was also behind the event that put Trento on the map, when he lobbied for it to become the venue of the great Counter-Reformation council of the Church (*see* pp.57–9). His successor, Bishop-prince Cristoforo Madruzzo (1539–67), nearly bankrupted his wealthy self in entertaining the dignitaries, but his hard work paid off in other ways, especially in promoting Madruzzo interests throughout Trentino and making the office of bishop-prince a private preserve of his own family for three generations.

To the Duomo

Trento's points of interest can easily be seen on foot. Piazza Dante, in front of the station, is a convenient place to start (and find a place to park); the statues of the eponymous poet and other

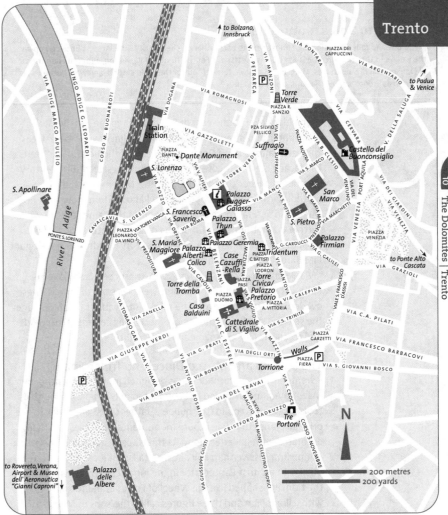

↑ to Bolzano, Innsbruck

to Padua & Venice

to Ponte Alto Cascata

to Rovereto, Verona, Airport & Museo dell' Aeronautica "Gianni Caproni" ↓

PIAZZA DEI CAPPUCCINI

VIA PONTARA

VIA ARGENTARIO

V. F. PETRARCA

VIA MANZONI

VIA ROMAGNOSI

Torre Verde

PIAZZA R. SANZIO

VIA B. CLESIO

VIA CERVARA

V. DELLA SALUGA

VIA DOGANA

VIA GAZZOLETTI

PZA SILVIO PELLICO

PIAZZA DEL SUFFRAGIO

VIA DEL SUFFRAGIO

PIAZZA MOSTRA

Suffragio

Castello del Buonconsiglio

Train Station

LUNGO ADIGE G. LEOPARDI

VIA ADIGE MARCO APULEIO

CORSO M. BUONARROTI

PIAZZA DANTE

Dante Monument

VIA ALFIERI

VIA TORRE VERDE

S. Lorenzo

VIA POZZO

VIA S. MARCO

PIAZZA S. MARCO

San Marco

VIA S. MARIA MADDALENA

VIA MARCHETTI

PORT AQUILA

VIA VENEZIA

VIA DEL GIARDINI

VIA VENEZIA

S. Apollinare

River Adige

PONTE S. LORENZO

CAVALCAVIA S. LORENZO

VIA TORRE VANGA

Palazzo Sugger-Galasso

i

S. Francesco Saverio

Palazzo Thun

VIA ROMA

VIA ORFANE

VIA S. PIETRO

VIA MANCI

S. Pietro

VIA S. PIETRO

Palazzo Firmian

PIAZZA VENEZIA

PIAZZA LEONARDO DA VINCI

S. Maria Maggiore

Palazzo Alberti Colico

Palazzo Geremia

Case Cazuffi-Rella

VIA PREPOSITURA

VIA BELENZANI

VIA OSS MAZZURANA

VIA G. CARDUCCI

PIAZZA C. BATTISTI

Tridentum

VIA G. GALILEI

VIA GRAZIOLI

Torre della Tromba

Casa Balduini

VIA CAVOUR

PIAZZA PASI

PIAZZA DUOMO

PIAZZA LODRON

VIA MANTOVA

Torre Civica/ Palazzo Pretorio

VIA CALEPINA

Cattedrale di S. Vigilio

PIAZZA A. VITTORIA

VIA C. ESTERLE

VIA S.S. TRINITÀ

VIALE S. FRANCESCO D'ASSISI

VIA C.A. PILATI

PIAZZA GARZETTI

VIA FRANCESCO BARBACOVI

VIA ZANELLA

VIA TOMASO GAR

VIA GIUSEPPE VERDI

VIA G. PRATI

VIA DEGLI ORTI

Walls

PIAZZA FIERA

P

VIA S. GIOVANNI BOSCO

VIA INAMA

VIA ANTONIO ROSMINI

VIA BORSIERI

Torrione

P

VIA BOMPORTO

VIA DEL TRAVAI

VIA S. CROCE

VIA XXIV MAGGIO

CORSO 3 NOVEMBRE

Tre Portoni

N

VIA GIUSEPPE GIUSTI

VIA CRISTOFORO MADRUZZO

VIA MONS CELESTINO ENDRICI

Palazzo delle Albere

200 metres
200 yards

Italian celebrities were erected here amid the public gardens in 1896, by Trento's Irredentist societies in defiance of their Austrian rulers. Next to the station itself, the attractive 12th-century collegiate church of **San Lorenzo** stands in a sunken lawn.

From San Lorenzo, both Via Andrea Pozzo and Via delle Orfane lead to pink **Santa Maria Maggiore** (1520), an elegant barrel-vaulted Renaissance church commissioned by Bernardo Cles who had seen Leon Battista Alberti's famous S. Andrea in Mantua, and wanted one for Trento. It was large enough to be used for several sittings of the Council of Trent, and has a beautiful organ gallery by Vincenzo Grandi (1534) and, among the paintings, the *Dispute with the Doctors* by Giambattista Moroni, the 16th-century master from Bergamo.

Getting to and around Trento

The bus and railway station are almost next to each other on the Piazza Dante. Atesina **buses** go up all the valleys in the Trentino, t 0461 821 000, *www.ttspa.it*. For the Trento-Malè station, with **trains** up the Val di Non and Val di Sole to Cles, Malè and Marilleva, turn left out of the main station, and walk 500m to Via Secondo da Trento 7, t 0461 821 000, *www.ttspa.it*.

One block over to the east of S. Maria Maggiore runs Trento's most important street, **Via Belenzani**. It is lined with fine palaces: the best, **Palazzo Pona Geremia**, was one of the first built in Trento; the façade is entirely covered with recently restored 16th-century frescoes of the locals receiving Emperor Maximilian and mythological subjects. Opposite, the **Palazzo Thun** (now the Municipio) is a far more severe work from the same century, while further down there's the luxurious **Palazzo Quetta**, actually two palaces linked behind a single 16th-century façade, and the elegant late Baroque **Palazzo Malfatti Ferrari**.

Via Belenzani ends by the handsome porticoed **Casa Cazuffi-Rella**, decorated with monochrome frescoes from the 1530s. These overlook Piazza Duomo and the 18th-century fountain of Neptune, the sea-god symbol of the region – focus on the trident he wields and recall the city's Roman name, *Tridentum*.

The Duomo and Museo Diocesano Tridentino

Trento's majestic cathedral was designed in the 13th century by Maestro Adamo d'Arogno but completed only in 1515. Although it took 300 years to build (the builders, rather unusually, stuck to the original plans), the style is pure monumental Romanesque, richly decorated with galleries along its three apses and dome. The whole is more impressive than any of the details, but look at the main door, with a Christ Pantocrator in the lunette, the rose window in the transept shaped like the Wheel of Fortune, and the apse door, with a lion porch and three figures called the 'sons of Maestro Adamo'. The Council of Trent held its major sessions here, and its decrees were promulgated before the huge crucifix in a right-hand chapel. Also to the right is the Renaissance tomb of Bernardo Cles. Excavations in 1977 unearthed a 6th-century basilica under the Duomo, original home of the relics of Trento's patron saint, Vigilio.

Museo Diocesano
Tridentino
t 0461 234 419,
www.museodiocesano
tridentino.it; open
Wed–Mon 9.30–12.30
and 2–5.30; adm

Next to the cathedral, the **Palazzo Pretorio**, crowned with swallowtail battlements and a medieval Torre Civica, houses the excellent Museo Diocesano Tridentino, renovated and opened by John Paul II in 1995. This contains the Duomo's Treasure and items from churches throughout Trentino. The paintings of the Council of Trent look like class photos; also note a 16th-century portrayal of a Mass of St Gregory, its nonchalant congregation sitting next to a band of pious skeletons. Other artefacts include three pretty 12th-century ivory caskets made by Islamic craftsmen; an unusual

12th-century enamelled reliquary case, and four charming 15th-century wooden altarpieces from the church of San Zeno in the Val di Non, portraying three martyrs in scenes watched by a man in a beaver hat. The museum's greatest treasure, a cycle of six early 15th-century Flemish tapestries by Peter Van Aelst, woven masterpieces of portraiture and detail, were purchased and brought to Trento by Bernardo Cles. The ticket also includes the excavations of the 6th-century basilica.

East of the Cathedral

In the 12th century, this was the first extension of Trento beyond the walls, and it's still called Borgo Nuovo today. Its main attraction is the Mannerist-Baroque **Palazzo Sardagna** on Via Calepina, frescoed inside with a zodiac by Marcello Fogolino, court painter to Bernardo Cles, visible along with the **Museo Tridentino di Scienze Naturali**. Its collections date back to the 16th century 'Room of Wonders' accumulated by the Madruzzo bishop-princes, and has fossils of the little Tridentinosaurus antiquus, a 260-million-year-old reptile that once stalked the Trentino.

Nearby Via Mantova leads to Piazza Cesare Battisti, where you'll find the visitors' entrance to the recently excavated ruins of the Roman city of **Tridentum**, which feature city walls, buildings and a stretch of road.

Museo Tridentino di Scienze Naturali
www.mtsn.tn.it; open Tues–Sun 10–6

Tridentum
t 0461 230 171; open June–Sept Tues–Sun 9.30–1 and 2–6, Oct–May Tues–Sun 9–1 and 2–5.30; adm

Castello del Buonconsiglio and its Museums

Beginning at Via Belenzani, Via Manci was the *decumanus* of Tridentum and is graced with another conspicuous house, the late Mannerist **Palazzo Fugger Galasso**, locally known as the Devil's Palace; the story goes that the Fuggers enlisted Satan's aid and had it built in a single day. Via Manci leads straight to the residence of the bishop-princes, the **Castello del Buonconsiglio**. Because of Trento's location on the road to Rome, the medieval German Emperors courted the bishops by granting them a regal status that they retained until Napoleon. Originally their home was known as

Castello del Buonconsiglio
t 0461 233 770, www.buonconsiglio.it; open June–Oct Tues–Sun 10–6, Nov–May Tues–Sun 9.30–5; adm exp

Vigilio and the Ciusi–Gobj Masquerade

Vigilio was a Roman patrician who studied in Athens, then moved to Trento with his family, where he was made bishop. His persuasive powers were good enough to convert his diocese, but when he went further afield to the Val Rendena and tipped over a statue of Saturn he was stoned to death. He is celebrated every 20–26 June with an enthusiastic *Palio dell'Oca*, in which teams from each of the city's districts don 17th-century costumes and race down the Adige on rafts, trying to slip a ring over the neck of a papier-mâché goose suspended over the river. The climactic moment comes on 26 June, commemorating the same day back in the Middle Ages when Trento hired workers from Feltre to reinforce the town walls. Food supplies being low, Trento's bishop realized that the city could not afford to feed the workers and sent them home – only the Feltrese returned in the night to raid the stores. The ensuing battle is re-enacted in costume in the Piazza Duomo – the Ciusi are from Feltre, and they have five chances to break the ranks of Trento's Gobj to make off with the prize: a pot of hot, bubbling *polenta*.

Malconsiglio (from the German *mahl* – meal, or banquet), but as this means 'Bad Counsel' in Italian it engendered too many jokes and was discreetly changed.

Buonconsiglio is one of the finest castle-residences in Italy. It consists of two buildings – the 13th-century Castelvecchio that once guarded the road, with its Venetian-Gothic loggia, and the Magno Palazzo, added by Bernardo Cles in 1528–36. Today both house the provincial museum of art: a fine collection of medieval manuscripts, music codices, wooden sculptures from the 15th and 16th centuries, and paintings, although these are overshadowed by the castle's own decoration commissioned by Bishop Cles: excellent 16th-century frescoes by Marcello Fogolino, Gerolamo Romanino and Dosso Dossi. The latter painted the Olympian gods on the vault, who had to conform to Counter-Reformation modesty levels – gods model turn-of-the-20th-century bathing costumes, and the goddesses look like Tarzan's Jane. Best of all are the ravishing, detailed *Frescoes of the Months* in the Torre dell'Aquila, painted around the year 1400. While the nobility sport and flirt in the foreground, peasants perform their month-by-month labours, tending their flocks, making cheese, planting and harvesting, making wine. One scene has the oldest-known depiction of Trento, dominated by the castle itself. Another tower, the Torre Falco, is frescoed with hunting scenes (1530–39).

Buonconsiglio also has a historical collection from the Napoleonic era to the Second World War, including a startling Art Deco painting commemorating that important event, the *Allegory of the Annexation of Trentino to Italy* by Luigi Bonazzo. The idea for this museum was suggested back in 1903 by local patriot Cesare Battisti, who had no idea that 13 years later he would be imprisoned, tried and executed for high treason in this same castle by the Austrians, along with his companions Fabio Filzi and Damiano Chiesa. Their cells, the courtroom where they were tried and the ditch where they were executed, are shrines. You've probably already noticed Battisti's prominent memorial, a marble circle of columns on the hill of Doss Trento just across the Adige. The present is served by the Galleria Civica d'Arte Contemporanea, hosting changing exhibitions.

Galleria Civica d'Arte Contemporanea
Via Belenzani, www.workart online.net; open Tues–Sun 10–6; adm

More Museums: Art, Planes and Saucepans

Cles' successor, bishop-prince Cristoforo Madruzzo, did not feel quite at ease at Buonconsiglio, and built himself a suburban residence on the Adige where he could get away from it all. This, the **Palazzo delle Albere**, 'of the poplars', named after the trees that once lined the road, has some not very serious towers and a moat, and the MART. The 19th- and 20th-century art, mostly Italian and with a high concentration of Futurists, offers a stark contrast to the

MART
Via R. da Sanseverino 45, www.mart.trento.it; open Tues–Sun 10–6; adm

Renaissance frescoes by Marcello Fogolino on the Months, the Ages of Man, the Seven Liberal Arts, and the Virtues.

The Museo dell'Aeronautica Gianni Caproni, by Trento's airport, began in 1929 as the private collection of Gianni Caproni, a native of Trentino and one of Italy's leading aviation engineers in the 1910s and 20s; the museum contains a number of unique planes, as well as a model of Leonardo da Vinci's flying machine. Lastly, in the suburb of Ravina – head southwest, over the river and under the highways – the Museo del Rame is a 'Milky Way of Copper' in a 16th-century farmhouse, the private collection of Signor Navarini, supplier of copper saucepans to Italy's master chefs. The collection goes back to the Renaissance, and among the pudding moulds there's one with Pope Pius IX's face on it, which must have made for an appetizing dessert. You can order a replica of this (or one with your own features) from the adjacent shop. For more museum-browsing, try the small Museo Storico delle Truppe Alpine, dedicated to the Alpini, in the suburb of Doss Trento (across the Adige), and the Museo della Società Alpinisti Tridentini, about climbing in the Trento region.

Around Trento: Monte Bondone

The slopes of Trento's own mountain, Bondone, can be easily reached by mountain road or cable car, departing from the Ponte di San Lorenzo in Trento (behind the bus station) and climbing as far as Sardagna. At least three buses a day continue from here up to Vaneze and Vason, Monte Bondone's ski resorts; from Vason another cable car ascends to one of Bondone's three summits (6,884ft). Further along, Viotte is the site of an Alpine refuge and excellent Botanical Garden, one of the richest in Europe, founded in 1938 on the banks of two artificial lakes, and planted with over two thousand species of high-altitude flora from around the world. Keep your eyes peeled for the pair of golden eagles who have recently nested nearby.

Museo dell'Aeronautica Gianni Caproni
Via Lidorno 3, t 0461 944 888; open Tues–Fri 9–1 and 2–5, Sat–Sun 10–1 and 2–6

Museo del Rame
Via Val Gola 22, t 0461 923 330; open Mon–Sat by ringing ahead

Museo Storico delle Truppe Alpine
t 0461 827 248; open Tues–Thurs 9–12 and 1.30–4.15, Fri 9–12

Museo della Società Alpinisti Tridentini
Via Manci, t 0461 982 804; open Tues–Fri 3–7

Cable car
t 0461 232 154; open daily 7–10.30, every 15mins peak times, otherwise every 30mins

Botanical Garden
t 0461 948 050; open July–Aug 9–12 and 2–6; June and Sept 9–12 and 1–5

ⓘ **Trento >**
Corner of Via Belenzani and Via Manci 2, t 0461 216 000, www.apt.trento.it; Trentino regional information, Via Romagnosi 3, t 0461 405 405, www.trentino.to

10 The Dolomites | Trento

Where to Stay in Trento

Expensive (€€€)

****Accademia**, near Santa Maria Maggiore at Vicolo Colico 4/6, t 0461 233 600, www.accademiahotel.it. Some of the Cardinals attending the Council of Trent are said to have slept at the predecessor of this hotel. The panelled rooms are comfortable and air-conditioned with high ceilings; the restaurant is excellent, with a menu that changes each month, and an inner courtyard for summer dining.

****Grand Hotel**, Via Alfieri 1/3, t 0461 271 000, www.boscolohotels.com. A luxury fin-de-siècle hotel in the heart of the Trentino Alps. Situated in the historic centre of Trento, it boasts 136 rooms of varying types, all furnished in luxury turn-of-the-century style, all exceptionally spacious. There's a car park and and a good restaurant open to non-guests.

Moderate (€€)

***America**, Via Torre Verde 50, t 0461 983 010, www.hotelamerica.it. A very comfortable and good-value choice within walking distance of Trento's train station.

★★★Garnì San Giorgio della Scala, Via Brescia 133, **t** 0461 238 848, *www.garnisangiorgio.it*. A delightful and charming *Garni* situtated on a hillside just outside the city centre. There's a warm atmosphere and rooms are decked out with lots of wooden furniture. Great views from the breakfast room. Car parking available.

⭐ Villa Madruzzo >

★★★Villa Madruzzo, 3km east of Trento in Cognola, Via Ponte Alto 26, **t** 0461 986 220, *www.villamadruzzo.it*. If you have a car, one of the nicest places to stay is this charming 19th-century villa located in a leafy park. It has modern, comfortable rooms, fine views and a very good traditional restaurant. *Closed Sun.*

Inexpensive (€)

⭐ Hotel Lillà >

★★★Hotel Lillà, at Terlago Loc. Travolt, **t** 0461 868 027, *www.hotellilla.com*. Situated 10km outside Trento, on Terlago Lake, this family-run hotel is the ideal place to relax in full contact with nature. Friendly atmosphere, bright and clean rooms, and best of all, hand-made pastries for breakfast. Great value.

Venezia, Piazza Duomo 45, **t** 0461 234 144, *www.hotelveneziatn.it*. Small, basic rooms with bath, some with views of the Duomo. No lift. The same family lets some rooms on Via Belenzani 70 (**t** 0461 234 559), Trento's prettiest street.

Eating Out in Trento

Trentino cuisine is basically Alpine: popular dishes include *canederli*, gnocchi made from breadcrumbs, egg, cheese and bacon; *patao*, a minestrone of yellow flour and sauerkraut; *osei scampadi*, veal 'birds' cooked with sage; and *carne salada e fasoi* (salted and seasoned meat with herbs and beans).

Chiesa, Via Marchetti 9, Parco San Marco (in the 17th-century Palazzo Wolkenstein, near the Castello del Buonconsiglio), **t** 0461 238 766 (€€€€). Trento's most celebrated restaurant is famous for its 'Apple Party Menu' in which Trentino's favourite fruit appears in every course; other choices include smoked trout and a tempting cheese strudel, or even a 1500s menu based on the preferred dishes of Bernardo Cles, accompanied by an extensive wine list and scrumptious desserts. Reservations essential. *Closed Sun.*

Osteria a Le Due Spade, Via Don Rizzi 11, **t** 0461 234 343 (€€€€). In business since 1545, serving refined dishes in a delightful dining room, decorated with mosaics; off Via Giuseppe. *Closed Sun and Mon lunch.*

Lo Scrigno del Duomo, Piazza Duomo 29, **t** 0461 220 030, *www.scrignodel duomo.com* (€€€). A stylish wine bar in a Renaissance *palazzo* with a sumptuous restaurant down in the cellar. Excellent wines accompany pigeon *carpaccio* with mountain honey and *porcini*. *Closed Mon, Sat lunch and Aug.*

Al Vo', Vicolo del Vo' 11 (off Via Torre Verde), **t** 0461 985 374 (€€). Serving good regional dishes and unusual specialities, but can creep into the *expensive* category if you aren't careful. *Closed Sun and two weeks in July.*

Forst, Oss Mazzurana 38, **t** 0461 235 590 (€). Located in the middle of Trento, in a 16th-century palace. A popular place to drink beer and Trentino's wines, eat a *pizza tirolese* (with mushrooms and speck) or a *piatto trentino* (a mixture of local specialities). *Closed Mon and July.*

East of Trento

The magic mountains wait, whether you turn east, west or north of Trento. San Martino di Castrozza and Paneveggio National Park are the main attractions in the Dolomites to the east, but there's plenty to see along the way.

The Valsugana

The emerald Valsugana follows the course of the Brenta, and was a busy place even in prehistoric times, as the main road from the Adriatic to the Danube. The Romans, of course, paved it (the Via Claudia Augusta Altinate), and the bishop-princes built along it. At **Civezzano**, within easy striking distance from Trento, Bernard Cles commissioned Antonio Medaglia, architect of Santa Maria Maggiore, to rebuild the **Pieve dell'Assunta** in an elegant late Gothic-early Renaissance style, while the Madruzzos commissioned the stained glass and paintings by Jacopo and Francesco Bassano. The fancy houses nearby were built to lodge dignitaries attending the Council of Trent. Above Civezzano rises the high plateau of **Pinè**, with its glacial lakes that turn into skating rinks in the winter. There are some exceptionally lively German and Italian Renaissance frescoes in **San Mauro** south of **Baselga di Pinè**; it also has a beautiful late Gothic triptych, with doors, and a fancypants Baroque high altar.

Pergine, the capital of the Valsugana and one of the largest towns in the province, owes its elegant streets, especially Via Maier, to money made in the surrounding mines. A stiff walk (or drive) will take you up to the **castle**, with views taking in the whole valley – a lovely sight in spring, when the cherries are in blossom. You can visit the pretty Gothic chapel, the prison infamous for its water torture, and even hang about for lunch (*see* below); it also holds concerts and art exhibitions.

Pergine Castle
open April–Oct Tues–Sun 10.30–10, Mon 5–10; guided tours June–Sept on Thurs at 6

From Pergine, you can take a detour north into the **Valle dei Mòcheni**, a linguistic island, settled in the 16th and 17th century by Germans who worked the silver and copper mines, and over the centuries developed their own language, Mòcheno. At **Palù del Fersina** you can see their traditional houses; one, at **Tolleri**, is now a museum and cultural institute. The *comune* has established one of the mines by the lake at Erdemolo as a museum, the **Grua va Hardömbl**.

Tolleri
open Mon–Fri 8–12 and 2.30–5.30

Grua va Hardömbl
t 0461 550 053; open May–Oct Sat–Sun 10–5.15; Wed–Mon in July and Aug; adm

A few kilometres from Pergine, **Lago di Caldonazzo** has been 'Trento's Lido' since the 1950s (it's surprisingly warm for an Alpine lake, averaging 24°C in the summer) and fine for sailing and windsurfing. From **Vetriolo Terme** nearby you can hike up to the summit of Panarotta for splendid views over Caldonazzo, as well over neighbouring (and equally warm) **Lake Levico**. This was long a favoured place, with its own aristocratic spa, **Levico Terme**, and ruined castle, where the bishop-princes once lodged in grandeur, with 60 horses parked in their stable.

Just above Levico Terme, the ruins of an ancient Rhaetian walled village lie near the church of **San Biagio**, with fine frescoes from the 14th–16th centuries.

The eastern Valsugana is decidedly more arid. **Borgo Valsugana** (the Roman *Ausugum*) was a prize fought over by every Tom, Dick and Harry who passed through, from the Bishops of Feltre to the Scaligers, Counts of Tyrol, the da Carrara, the Visconti and Venetians before passing to Trento after the War of Cambrai. Many buildings in the *centro storico* have a Venetian touch; the 11th-century church, **Natività di Maria**, has a lavish Baroque interior, while **San Rocco**, like every church dedicated to the saint in Trentino, was frescoed in the early 16th century. Above Borgo, the 13th-century **Castel Telvana** has spectacular views, on a site first fortified by the Romans and conquered by the Lombards in 590 (the precious Lombard 'prince's tomb' was excavated nearby); it is now the town council chambers and you can have a nose about. To the north is the wild Lagorai range, where Italian and Austrian trenches from the war are still visible, or south into the pretty **Valle di Sella**. Here a pagan temple underlies **San Lorenzo all'Armentera**, its interior frescoed from the 12th century with scenes of Lawrence's life and martyrdom on the grill.

Further up the Valsugana, the picturesque **Castel d'Ivano Fracena** guarded the Via Claudia Augusta Alinate in the Middle Ages, and has had more than its share of history; most recently, in 1984, it saw the wedding of Carlo Alberto Dalla Chiesa, whose battles against the Mafia in Palermo earned him a brutal assassination. Now a Cultural Institute, and open for concerts and exhibitions.

North, the gentle wooded Tesino valley has two fine old towns, whose enterprising natives travelled the world in the 1600s, from Russia to America, selling prints of Italian masterpieces from the Remondini Press in Bassano del Grappa (*see* pp.211–13). **Pieve Tesino**, set in a green amphitheatre, has a number of 15th-century buildings, and a grand 18th-century fountain. The second town, **Castello Tesino**, has ruins of its Roman predecessor, next to the *quattrocento* church of **S. Ipolito**, with frescoes on the story of St Julian, who beheaded his parents when he found them in his bed, thinking they were his wife and a lover. Two kilometres away, along the Brocòn road, the Grotta di Castello Tesino is one of the largest stalactite caverns in Italy; the Pro Loco can arrange guided tours.

*Grotta di Castello Tesino
t 0461 594 136;
call in advance*

Where to Stay and Eat in the Valsugana

ⓘ Pergine Valsugana >
*Via 3 Novembre 15,
t 0461 531 258*

Pergine Valsugana ✉ 38057
***Al Ponte**, at Maso Grillo 4, t 0461 531 317, *www.hotelalponte.net* (€€). One of two places to stay and/or eat in Pergine: this modern, up-to-date hotel has a glass gallery, pool, and a good restaurant.

*Castel Pergine, t 0461 531 158, www.castelpergine.it (€€). This place is not as comfortable as Al Ponte – and what's more it's haunted by a 'white lady'. If you're not too spooked, you'll find that it boasts an innovative chef who knows what's what in the kitchen, and who bases his dishes on regional ingredients. *Open April–Oct; restaurant closed Mon.*

San Martino di Castrozza and Around

 Pale di San
Martino

The stunning, pinnacle-crowned **Pale di San Martino** (10,470ft),
the natural Gothic 'altars of St Martin', is the principal mountain
group of the southern Dolomites, and **San Martino di Castrozza**,
dramatically lying at its foot, is the biggest and best-equipped
winter resort south of Cortina d'Ampezzo. The village is of recent
construction – the Austrians demolished the medieval town in the
First World War, leaving only the ancient church. San Martino also
makes a superb base for summer climbing and walking. Among
the most popular excursions (be sure to pick up the map at the
tourist office) is the ascent by cable car and chairlift to the summit
of **Rosetta**. Most of the Pale is for experienced climbers; if you're
not among them, the less demanding walks in the area include the
path up Monte Cavallazza, facing the Pale (3hrs); or, closer at hand,
to the Col Fosco or, more ambitiously, to Paneveggio.

Paneveggio National Park and the 'Forest of Violins'

Much of the best scenery around San Martino lies within the
Parco Naturale Paneveggio–Pale di San Martino, a superb
wilderness of venerable woods, emerald meadows, rushing
streams, wild flowers and wildlife. Access to the park is from the
visitors' centre in **Paneveggio**, a few kilometres north of San
Martino, beyond the Passo di Rolle. There are two splendid paths
that take in tremendous vistas, not only of the Pale di San Martino,
but also the distinctive peaks of Marmolada, Pelmo and Civetta. In
past centuries the forests here provided Venice with the timber for
its fleet; the Venetians not only replanted the trees a certain
distance apart, to make sure the trunks were tall and straight for
masts, but punished tree poachers with death. Another source of
income came from Stradivarius, Amati, Guarneri and other violin
makers in Cremona, who insisted on resonant Paneveggio spruce
for their instruments. Rules are still strict: there are only a few
campsites and no one may stay longer than 24 hours.

The Pale di San Martino is encircled by a road of scenic grandeur.
The northern part of the route (SS346 and SS203) on the way to
Agordo (*see* p.302) passes through the villages of **Canale d'Agordo**
and **Falcade**, with ski facilities. The southern route, also via Agordo
(SS347), passes through **Frassene**, a summer resort, then climbs
through the forests of Gosaldo to the **Passo di Cereda** and 15th-
century town of **Fiera di Primiero**. Like Cortina, Fiera stands at the
crossing of two valleys, the Cismon and the Canali, and has good
skiing; in the summer a popular outing is the hour's walk up to the
sinister ruined **Castel di Pietra**, precariously balancing on a jagged
rock with the Pale di S. Martino as a backdrop – built, according to
legend, to withstand Attila the Hun.

Where to Stay and Eat around San Martino di Castrozza

(i) San Martino >
*Via Passo Rolle 165,
t 0439 768 867,
www.sanmartino.com.*

San Martino di Castrozza
✉ 38058

****Des Alpes**, Via Passo Rolle, t 0439 769 069, *www.hoteldesalpes.it* (€€€). The place to soak up turn-of-the-century Dolomite atmosphere. *Open mid-Dec–Easter and July–mid-Sept.*

***San Martino**, Via Passo Rolle 279, t 0439 68011, *www.hotelsanmartino.it* (€€€). Has an indoor pool, tennis courts and sauna.

***Venezia**, t 0439 68315, *www.albergovenezia.it* (€€). Sits astride the Passo di Rolle north of San Martino, with fantastic views stretching across the valley. Provides a great base for the National Park.

Suisse, Via Dolomiti 1, t 0439 68087, *www.hotelgarni.it* (€). Five minutes' walk up the hill behind San Martino brings you to this simple but comfortable bed and breakfast.

Malga Ces, Loc. Malga Ces, t 0439 68223 (€€). The best dining around; specialities include *canederli, polenta* with venison, village cheeses and fruits of the forest. *Open Dec–Easter and mid-June–Sept.*

Fiera di Primiero ✉ 38054

****Park Hotel Iris**, Via Roma 26, t 0439 762 000, *www.parkhotel iris.com* (€€€– €€). Tranquil and rather grand, with one of the best restaurants in the area, serving not only Trentino's traditional cusine (*gnocchetti* in venison sauce) but some more exotic recipes such as Primiero's speciality, *tosèla*, slices of fresh cow's-milk cheese fried in melted butter, and served piping hot with *polenta* or mushrooms. Well worth stopping by. *Open Christmas–mid-April and June–Sept.*

Val di Fassa and Val di Fiemme

These two northeasternmost valleys of Trentino, running between the Pale di San Martino, Rosengarten and the western slopes of Marmolada, are among the most stunning and most independent-minded, and well loved by cross-country skiers.

Val di Fassa

If you're approaching from San Martino, you can join the Val di Fassa by way of the SS346 from Falcade to **Moena**. Moena is a winter sports centre, and the 'boundary' between the Fassa and Fiemme valleys. It has two churches of note: the large 12th-century **San Vigilio**, with paintings by local artist Valentino Rovisi, a pupil of Tiepolo; and small **San Volfango**, richly decorated with 15th-century frescoes by one of the anonymous, itinerant artists who travelled around the Trentino. A path above Moena takes in not only majestic scenery, but traces of the First World War.

Seven *comuni* in the valley preserve their Ladin language and culture, especially **Vigo di Fassa**, 6km north of Moena, site of the Majon di Fashegn (Ladin Cultural Institute) and several *tabià* – the Ladini's traditional wooden cabins. A 20-minute walk leads up to the pretty Gothic church of **Santa Giuliana a Vigo**, with frescoes from the 1400s honouring the valley's patron saint. In the nearby hamlet of **San Giovanni**, dominated by the large Gothic church of the same name, is the Museo Ladino di Fassa, dedicated to

Museo Ladino
di Fassa
*t 0462 764 267,
www.istladin.net;
open Tues–Sat 3–7
and 10–12.30, July–
mid-Sept daily*

archaeology and ethnography. Seek out the **Casa Soldà**, built in the 1500s by a soldier who made a fortune in the Turkish wars and invested his loot on decorating his house with frescoes. For a big thrill, take the three chairlifts from nearby Pozzo di Fassa up the flanks of Rosengarten, leaving you at the path to the **Torri del Vaiolet**, a strikingly sheer triple pinnacle.

Campitello di Fassa, the next town up the Val di Fassa, has a pretty church frescoed inside and out, and a *funivia* to the **Col Rodella** (8,153ft), a famous viewpoint and winter sports wonderland; the lower station's Museo degli Sci has a collection of ski gear and accessories from the early 20th century. Campitello has two frescoed churches from the 1400s, one devoted to the subject of Sabbath-breaking. Further up the valley, **Canazei** is the main base for exploring the other magnificent peaks in the area – Marmolada, Sassolungo and Sella. Canazei was rebuilt after 1912, when it was destroyed by fire, but the church in the nearby hamlet of Gries escaped, along with its paintings by Valentino Rovisi of Moena. The passes above Canazei lead towards Arabba and Cortina (*see* p.341) or north into the Val Gardena in the Alto Adige (*see* pp.342–4).

Museo degli Sci
t 0462 750 261; open Dec–April daily 8–6.30

Val di Fiemme

The Val di Fiemme begins west of Moena (*see* above). Less densely Ladin than the Val di Fassa, it was nevertheless virtually independent for centuries, a 'Magnifica Comunità' under the auspices of the bishop-princes of Trent. The lake-spangled mountains south of the valley, the **Catena dei Lagorai**, are one of the least developed areas in the Dolomites, and for the most part accessible only by foot.

Civico Museo di Geologia
t 0462 501 237; closed for restoration at the time of writing

In **Predazzo**, the Civico Museo di Geologia was founded in 1899 and takes the subject of Dolomitic rocks and marine fossils in hand; the museum has set up a marked half- or full-day geological path at Doss Cappèl, reached by the Predazzo chairlift.

Down the valley, **Panchià** has a pretty covered bridge spanning the Avisio while another, from the 15th century, does the same work in **Tesero**, a delightful village that hasn't surrendered its soul to tourism, where furniture- and instrument-makers still ply their old trades. Perhaps too well. The chapel of **San Rocco** (1528) is frescoed with yet another 'Sunday Christ', surrounded by all the tools that are taboo on the Sabbath, which makes one wonder: were the Trentini of old inveterate workaholics or merely avoiding the collection plate?

At **Cavalese**, the capital of the Val di Fiemme, the *Regolani* elected to govern the valley held their parliament in the park of the parish church; you can still see their circle of stone benches, the Banc de la Reson. The *Magnifica Comunità* of Cavalese still has considerable local say, governing the Val di Fiemme from the grand old **Palazzo della Comunità**, rebuilt in the 1500s by bishop-princes Bernardo Cles and Cristoforo Madruzzo and frescoed with scenes dominated by the central figure of St Vigil. On the second floor a museum charts Fiemme's proud past and has works by the 17th- and 18th-century Fiemme school, a group of harmless painters who travelled about the smaller courts of Europe, led by Giuseppe Alberti, Orazio Giovannelli and the Unterpergers. Local rule had its disadvantages for some: in nearby Doss delle Strie, 11 witches were burnt alive in 1505. A cable car from Cavalese ascends to Mount Cermis (7,313ft).

Magnifica Comunità Museum
t 0462 340 365,
www.magnifica
comunitafiemme.it;
closed for restoration at
the time of writing

ⓘ Moena >
Piazza C. Battisti 33,
t 0462 609 770,
www.fassa.com

ⓘ Cavalese >>
Via F.lli Bronzetti 60,
t 0462 241 111,
www.valdifiemme.info

ⓘ Canazei >
Via Streda de Dolèda
10, t 0462 609 500,
www.fassa.com

Where to Stay and Eat in Val di Fassa and Val di Fiemme

Moena ✉ 38035

Moena is famous for its *puzzone* or 'stinky cheese' which, in spite of its name, tastes pretty good with toasted *polenta*.

***Catinaccio Rosengarten, Via Someda 6, t 0462 573 235, *www.hotel cr.com* (€€€). Plenty of mountain atmosphere; pool. *Open early Dec–mid-April and June–mid-Sept.*

****Monzoni, t 0462 573 352, *www.hotelmonzoni.it* (€€€). Up at Passo di San Pellegrino, this old mountain refuge has been converted into a splendid hotel. *Open Christmas–mid-April and early July–Aug.*

***Post Hotel, Piazza Italia, t 0462 573 760, *www.posthotelmoena.it* (€€). A sure, classy bet, with fine rooms and a good restaurant, Tyrol. *Open Dec–Easter and mid-June–mid-Sept.*

Malga Panna, Via Costalunga 29, t 0462 573 489 (€€€). Long one of the best restaurants in the region, offering a *menu degustazione* of trout, rabbit, *tortelli ai porcini*, speck, venison and strawberries. *Open Dec–mid-May and mid-June–Oct; closed Mon.*

Canazei ✉ 38032

***La Perla, Via Pareda 103, t 0462 602 453, *www.hotellaperla.net* (€€€). In a panoramic position near the ski slopes; a comfortable spot, with a gym, indoor pool and sauna. *Open Dec–mid-April and mid-June–Oct.*

***Bellevue, Streda Dolomites 124, t 0462 601 104, *www.unionhotels*

canazei.it (€€€–€€). Great mountain views and pleasant rooms. *Open throughout the year.*

**Dolomites Inn, Via Antersies 3, at Penia, t 0462 602 212, *www.dolomites inn.com* (€€). This little place has a fitness centre and squash courts. *Open mid-Dec–mid-April, June–Sept.*

El Ciasel, Via Col de Pin 15, t 0462 602 190 (€€€). If you have yet to try *strangolopreti* ('priest-stranglers'), they're one of the specialities at this restaurant, along with game dishes and *polenta. Closed Mon.*

Cavalese ✉ 38033

***San Valier, Via Marconi 7, t 0462 341 285, *www.hotelsanvalier.com* (€€). Located in a pretty setting with an indoor pool, fitness centre and sauna. *Closed Oct–Nov and May.*

***Sporting-Club Grand Chalet des Neiges, t 0462 341 650, *www.chalet desneiges.it* (€€). Right on the pistes of Mt Cermis, superbly positioned at 6,562ft, this hotel has a pool and sauna to go with its magnificent views. *Open mid-Dec–mid-April.*

***Villa Trunka Lunka, Via De Gasperi 4, t 0462 340 233, *www.trunkalunka.it* (€€). One of the nicest hotels, with the funniest name, and 24 rooms, a sauna and solarium.

Cantuccio, Via Unterberger 14, t 0462 235 040 (€€€–€€). Restaurants sometimes have *caronzèi*, the valley's unique ravioli, filled with potatoes, *puzzone* cheese, nutmeg and chives. Here mushrooms are king, and they make a mean rabbit in garlic cream and artichokes. *Closed Wed eve and Thurs out of season.*

Towards Trento: the Val di Cembra and its Pyramids

Val di Cembra
www.aptpinecembra.it

From Cavalese, the road follows the river Avisio through the steep, vine-terraced Val di Cembra, a valley where the inhabitants have always struggled to make a living. One of the main sources of income is porphyry, quarried with less than environmental correctness since the Second World War. The road then passes through a striking region of rocks eroded into spiky 'pyramids' near **Segonzano**. The highest ones stand over 150ft tall, and many are crowned with porphyry boulders, like natural umbrellas. Students of Dürer might recognize the medieval 'Roman' tower that inspired a pair of his watercolours, made during the artist's first trip to Venice. **Cembra** to the south on the other bank of the Avisio has two frescoed churches: **San Pietro** is especially interesting for its *Life of Jesus* (1500s) and a grand if rather unthreatening Last Judgement by Valentino Rovisi. Other frescoes, *quattrocento* this time, are in little San Leonardo, in **Lisignano**, just south of Cembra: here the artist used his licence to include St Paul at the Last Supper, joining the other apostles at a feast of fish and pretzels to create a weird three-headed figure of the Trinity.

West of Trento: the Brenta Dolomites

The Brenta Group, separate from the other Dolomites, is just as marvellous and strange, and a challenge for experienced Alpinists. The Adamello-Brenta Park is the last refuge of brown bears in the Alps, but you'd have to be very lucky to see one: there are only about a dozen. The following section circles the park clockwise – a 175km round trip from Trento.

Around Monte Paganella

Museo degli Usi e Costumi della Gente Trentina
t 0461 650 314, www. museosanmichele.it; open Tues–Sun 9–12.30 and 2.30–6; adm

Cantine Mezzacorona
Via del Teroldego, t 0461 616 300, www.gruppomezza corona.it; open Mon–Fri; call in advance

To reach Monte Paganella, the eastern flank of the Brenta group facing Trento, first head north along the Adige to **San Michele all'Adige**, home to the Museo degli Usi e Costumi della Gente Trentina, a fascinating ethnographic collection occupying 40 rooms in a 12th-century Augustin monastery. Nearby **Mezzocorona** is the producer of the 'prince of Trentino wines', Teroldego, as well as spumante; it also lies at the beginning of the wine road to Bolzano (*see* pp.333–4). Stop at Cantine Mezzacorona not only for tastings but to see the remains of a 1st-century Roman farm, discovered during the excavations of the modern wine cellars.

From Mezzocorona, follow the signs to the Paganella high plateau, the 'green island' in the mountains. Its three well-equipped resorts are served by six buses a day from Trento: **Fai della Paganella**, **Andalo** (both with cable cars to the summit of Monte Paganella – 6,972ft) and **Molveno**, near Lago di Molveno.

Activities around Monte Paganella

Molveno makes a wonderful base from which to explore the surrounding area, and there are a number of active ways to spend your day near the clear waters of the lake. Guides can be hired all year from **Brenta Est** mountaineering school (**t** 0461 586 409) to show you the varied delights of the Brenta Group; the same people can help with any of your outdoor requirements.

There are plenty of camping and caravaning spaces available all year in all three resorts; indeed it would be difficult to visit and not fill your lungs with the fresh (if sometimes damp) air. A wonderful way to see the massif is by horseback – the **Brenta Club** (**t** 0461 585 377) caters for all styles, including Western. You can also take a tour by horse-drawn coach (*conostoga*) if you can gather a small group.

If you're visiting during the winter, you will find 300km of pistes, some kept alive by snow cannons but with good skiing nonetheless.

Fai has beautiful views over the Adige valley, while Andalo is known for its traditional farmhouses (*masi*); a pretty hour-and-a-half's walking trail, the *giro dei masi*, will take you past many of them. Lake Molveno is a favourite for windsurfers, swimmers and sailors. An hour's path from Lake Molveno's shore leads to a 16th-century Venetian sawmill (**Segheria Veneziana**), still remarkably intact, next to its old water wheel. From Molveno the road continues south to **Ponte Arche**, passing Fiavé, where a 5,000-year-old settlement of lake dwellers was discovered. East of Ponte Arche is picture postcard **Lake Toblino**, with its 12th-century **castle** (now an excellent restaurant) beautifully set on a tiny peninsula amid trees planted by Attila the Hun. Or so they say.

The Valli Giudicarie

The Brenta Group's southern peaks rise over Giudicarie Valleys, a network encompassing several rivers and torrents, running from lake to lake – from Molveno down to Idro. Just south of Molveno, **San Lorenzo in Banale** has a road rising north up the **Val d'Ambiez** and the Rifugio al Cacciatore, providing a quick route for hikers to approach the highest peaks of the Brenta group. Further along, the Giudicarie is defended by the lovely Castel Stenico, founded in the 12th century as an administrative centre for the bishop-princes. It retains some faded but good Renaissance frescoes; part of it now houses the archaeological collections of the Trentino provincial museum. South of Stenico, in one of the Giudicarie's branch valleys, there's a surprise: the parish church of **Dasindo**, rebuilt in 1596 by home-town boy Giovanni Maria Filippi, who went to study Palladio's churches in Venice and incorporated the hemispherical dome and other things he learned in this, his first project; Filippi later became court architect to Emperor Rudolph in Prague. The main valley road next passes Lake Ponte Pia, where a detour leads to the narrow, unpopulated **Val d'Algone**, with a waterfall near Airone and another track into the Brenta.

Just outside **Tione**, the rather dull yet fuctional capital of the valley, the cemetery church of **San Vigilio** was frescoed with a giant

Castel Stenico
*t 0465 771 004,
www.buonconsiglio.it;
open Nov–May daily
9.30–5, June–Oct
daily 10–6*

St Christopher in 1474, the only authenticated work by Cristoforo Baschenis, member of a large clan of itinerant painters from Bergamo. Tione stands at the crossroads to the **Valle del Chiese**, where the river flows south into one of the smaller Italian lakes, Idro; Trentino's most rugged scenery lies along the upper Chiese in the **Val di Daone**, by the artificial lakes of Malga Boazzo and Malga Bissina under lofty Mount Fumo (11,215ft).

The Valle Rendena

The main road around the Brenta group, the SS239, heads north of Tione into the Valle Rendena along the River Sarca, one of the favourite stomping grounds of the Baschenis family. The attractive town of **Pinzolo** makes a good base for exploring the glacier-clad Brenta and Adamello mountains, with their scores of lakes. The exterior of its cemetery church, **San Vigilio**, was frescoed in 1539 by the most accomplished of all the Baschenis, Simone, portraying a vividly eerie medieval-style *Dance of Death*. Placid, business-like skeletons conduct princes, popes, soldiers and everyone else to their end, with a couplet of elegant poetry for each. More of Simone Baschenis' precise, luminous work (on the life of St Vigil) can be seen inside the church. Twenty years before, Simone had his go at a *Danse Macabre* on the façade of Santo Stefano at **Carisolo**, 2km up the road; inside are frescoes on Charlemagne's (probably legendary) visit to the Valle Rendena.

Carisolo stands at the entrance to the lovely **Val di Genova**, one of the most beautiful in the entire Alps, once the haunt of ogres and witches, all of whom were turned to stone after the Council of Trent. Now part of the **Parco Naturale Adamello-Brenta**, the Val di Genova is graced by the lofty **Cascate di Nardis** (4km from Carisolo), a woodland waterfall flowing from the glacier on **Presanella** (10,676ft) – in Pinzolo you can find a guide to make the ascent. To the east a chairlift (the world's fastest, they claim, so hold on to your hat) rises to the lower slopes of **Cima Tosa**, the highest peak of the Brenta Dolomites.

The Dolomites | West of Trento: the Brenta Dolomites

Where to Stay and Eat around Monte Paganella

(i) Molveno >>
t 0461 586 924

San Michele all'Adige ☑ 38010

Da Silvio, Via Nazionale 1, Masetto de Faedo, t 0461 650 324 (€€). Combines a modern setting with an imaginative kitchen; try the delicious *Altamira*, a selection of mixed meats grilled directly at your table. *Closed Sun eve and Mon, part of Jan and June.*

Molveno ☑ 38018

***Belvedere**, Via Nazionale 9, t 0461 586 933, www.belvedereonline.com. (€€€). Fine rooms with exquisite views over the lake and mountains, an indoor pool, fitness centre and solarium. *Open Christmas, Feb and April–Oct.*

***Miralago**, Piazza Scuole 3, t 0461 586 935, www.miralagohotel.com (€€). An older hotel, offering an outdoor heated swimming pool, garden and a superb terrace among its amenities.

ⓘ Pinzolo ››
t 0465 501 007

★ Castel
Toblino ›

★ Da Cipriano ›

Alpotel Venezia, Via Nazionale 8, **t** 0461 586 920 (€€–€). Good Trentino home cooking in the *centro storico*; try their *strangolapreti alla trentina*.

Castel Toblino ✉ 38070

Castel Toblino, Via Caffaro 1, Sanche (TN), **t** 0461 864 036, *toblino@techno progress.it* (€€). Dine, and dine well, in this romantic 12th-century castle on its little peninsula in the lake, with a beautiful courtyard. Food and setting combine to create a truly unique experience. The menu is fresh and imaginative, incorporating such treats as fresh pike *noisettes* and *osetto* (barley risotto). Wines include the justifibly famous Vino Santo. *Open Mar–Oct, closed Tues.*

Calavino ✉ 38072

Da Cipriano, Via Graziadei 13, **t** 0461 564 720 (€€). A must for traditional

Trentino dishes and wines. The owner is a true gentleman and the setting familiar and romantic, especially in the small side rooms. *Closed Wed.*

Pinzolo ✉ 38086

***Centro Pineta, Via Matteotti 43, **t** 0465 502 758, *www.centropineta.com* (€€). A pleasant, medium-sized hotel, warm in the winter and cool in the summer, and pine-scented year-round, with good home cooking. *Open Dec–April and June–Sept.*

F. lli Salvaterra, Via Marconi 44, **t** 0465 501 171 (€). A delightful place, offering wonderful rooms in a quiet street, at prices that will make you smile.

Weinstube Al Gardo, Via Manci 22, **t** 0465 502 580 (€). Near the Salvaterra is another little haven serving classic mountain dishes to fill you up, such as *fondue, raclette* and fine grills.

Madonna di Campiglio

From Pinzolo the SS239 zigzags up to the most important resort in the Brenta Dolomites, the superbly sited Madonna di Campiglio, 'the Empress' gardens' where Emperor Franz Josef brought his beloved Sissi to pick herbs and wild flowers in 1890, a memory Madonna di Campiglio evokes each year with its 'Habsburg Carnival' and costume ball.

Madonna is more than ready for visitors the rest of the year as well; its winter sports facilities include a ski jump, 31 ski lifts, speed-skating, a regular skating rink and an indoor swimming pool. It has hosted the world snowboarding championship, and is home to a dog-trekking school for children.

In the summer Madonna offers experienced climbers the chance to try their mettle on ice and wild, rocky terrain; for inexperienced walkers it has the most scenic trails in the group – the walk to the **Cascate Valesinelle** is especially lovely. Even if you only have enough spunk to get into a chairlift and a funicular, you can enjoy the marvellous views from the **Passo del Grostè**, some 7,415ft above Madonna to the east, or from **Pradalago** to the west.

Get the tourist office's footpath map to take Madonna's classic walk through the beautiful **Val di Brenta** and **Valsinella** just to the south. A more difficult path, the fabulous **Via Bocchette**, takes in the region's most bizarre naked pinnacles and fantastic cliffs, but should only be attempted with proper equipment by seasoned mountain maniacs.

Getting around Madonna di Campiglio

Besides the usual efficient Dolomiti and SAD bus services, Madonna di Campiglio runs a special *pista a pista* **shuttle bus** service for skiers arriving at Verona or Brescia airport; the buses run every Saturday from mid-December to early April, with additional services over the Christmas period. For more information call **t** 0461 391 111, or visit *www.trentinoviaggi.net*.

Madonna does go a bit quiet out of season, during which time it gears itself up for the influx that follows the first snow falls. Even so, there are enough hotels and bed and breakfasts to make the drive worthwhile.

North of Madonna the road passes through **Passo Campo Carlo Magno**, named after Charlemagne, who supposedly stopped here on his way to Rome to receive the Emperor's crown. If it's cable cars you're looking for, Carlo Magno, although soulless, can whisk you up to the incomparable mountains in no time.

Folgarida, beyond the mountain pass, is another well-endowed winter resort.

10 The Dolomites | West of Trento: the Brenta Dolomites

Where to Stay and Eat in Madonna di Campiglio

(i) **Madonna di Campiglio >** *Via Pradalago 4,* **t** 0465 447 501, *www.campiglio.net*

Madonna di Campiglio
✉ 38084

Madonna di Campiglio is the one resort in the Brenta Dolomites with the accommodation and facilities to please the most demanding customers, and prices are correspondingly high.

****Golf**, Via Cima Tosa 3 (up at the Passo Carlo Magno), **t** 0465 441 003, *www.golfhotelcampiglio.it* (€€). You can shoot high-altitude drives while staying at the one-time summer residence of the Habsburg emperors, now beautifully converted into a hotel. *Open Dec–mid-April and July–Aug.*

****Gianna**, Via Vallesinella 16, **t** 0465 441 106, *www.hotelgianna.it* (€€€). This hotel is a family-run bargain among the pine trees, with a bus service running every half-hour to town and the ski lifts. *Open late June–Sept and Dec–late April.*

****Spinale Club**, Via Monte Spinale 39, **t** 0465 441 116, *www.effetravel.com* (€€€). Situated down in Madonna di Campiglio itself, the Spinale Club is a very attractive, elegantly appointed hotel with a large indoor pool and other sporting facilities; they also take special care of children. *Open July–early Sept and Dec–mid-April.*

****Hermitage**, Via Castelletto 69, **t** 0465 441 558, *www.chalet hermitage.com* (€€). A small and cosy hotel, with a fine panoramic terrace and good food. Recently restored and refurnished with eco-friendly materials. *Open July–early Sept and Dec–April.*

***Palù**, Via Vallesinella 4, **t** 0465 441 695, *www.hotelpalu.com* (€€). An older hotel, with air-conditioning in summer and a blazing fireplace to sit around in the winter. *Open mid-June–Sept and Dec–mid-April.*

Artini, Via Cima Tosa 47, **t** 0465 440 122 (€€€). For a special meal, you won't go far wrong with this modern and luminous restaurant, specializing in lovely mushroom dishes. *Open Dec–April and July–Sept.*

Lorenzetti, Via Dolomiti 119, **t** 0465 441 404, (€€€). Spectacular views, excellent cooking and a friendly atmosphere.

Malga Montagnoli, at Montagnoli, **t** 0465 443 355 (€€). Dine here on such fare as venison with redcurrant compote or risotto with mushrooms.

Along the Noce: the Val di Sole and Val di Non

The northern flank of the Brenta group is marked by the river Noce, descending from the Trentino sector of the Stelvio National Park (see p.355). On the way it passes through the Val di Sole and its natural extension, the Val di Non, where apples are king. This was a major route of the mule trains that once travelled between the Adriatic into Lombardy – hence all the fortified manor houses, nearly all of which are still privately owned.

Val di Sole

Italy's 'Sun Valley' of soft green meadows and villages, with the lofty peaks of Monte Cevedale as a backdrop, has a name that may sound like a recent invention by the Trentino tourist board, but was first recorded back in 1071.

Coming up from Madonna di Campiglio, turn left for the upper valley's most up-to-date winter sports facilities at **Marilleva**. The men here were regular slugabeds – the name *Marì levà* comes from 'Husband, get up!' In summer the main sport is whitewater canoeing down 25km of the River Noce, a wild enough adventure to make it the scene of the world canoeing championships in 1993. Many churches in the valley have charming exterior frescoes by the Baschenis family, notably *La Natività di Maria* at **Pellizzano**, with a beautiful *Annunciation* by Simone (1524).

Whitewater canoeing
www.avventura rafting.it

Ossana, a bit further west, was an important frontier post for the bishop-princes; its 12th-century **Castel San Michele** is currently being restored by the province. At Ossana you can follow the **Val di Peio** north into Stelvio National Park (see p.355); the village of **Peio** at the top of the valley has an enormous Baschenis St Christopher for good luck.

In the lower Val di Sole, you'll find **Malè**, the valley's chief market town and home to an ethnographical museum, the Museo della Civiltà Solandra, with handicrafts and agricultural and domestic implements. Malè is still an important woodworking centre. There are some fine examples in the parish church, which also has a curious chapel in front, dedicated to S. Valentino, open on three sides, and used during times of plague when people feared to be indoors. From Malè you can visit **Val di Rabbi**, one of the least changed valleys in the Dolomites, dotted with venerable *masi*. Like the Val di Pejo it extends into Stelvio National Park, which has a summer visitors' centre in the spa of **Bagni di Rabbi**. If you have time, make the short trip up the valley, as it suffers from a condition common in these parts – schizophrenia. It really can't decide whether it's in Italy or Switzerland. Just east of Malè, the

Museo della Civiltà Solandra
t 0463 901 780; open mid-June–mid-Sept Mon–Sat 10–12 and 4–7

13th-century **Castello Caldès** with its frescoed rooms, old graffiti and other fittings, is open for special exhibitions.

Cles and the Val di Non

The wooded Val di Non, the enchanting valley running north–south along the lower course of the River Noce, is the most populous and wealthy in Trentino, in no small measure thanks to Italy's finest apples, especially Golden Delicious and 'Renetta del Canada', which look more like potatoes. Come in the spring, when its apple blossoms, emerald meadows and snow-clad mountains glow with colour.

The large artificial lake of **Santa Giustina** divides the two valleys. **Cles**, on the west bank, has been the capital of the Val di Non since at least AD 46, when the emperor Claudius granted the city its rights, which are still recorded in the *tabula clesiana*. Bishop-prince Bernardo Cles was born here, in the 11th-century lakeside Castello Cles, which he thoroughly remodelled and decorated. The town is divided into six distinct neighbourboods called *colomelli*; the *colomello* Pés has several Renaissance buildings, especially the Palazzo Assessorile and the Pieve dell'Assunta. The older, smaller church of **San Vigilio** is coated inside with frescoes, including a good *Last Supper* by a follower of Giotto, and a *Last Judgement*, with St Peter kindly taking the Elect by the hand while unlocking the gates of Paradise.

Sanzeno, across the lake, is one of the Dolomites' holy vortices: in 397 St Vigil sent three missionaries, Sisinio, Martirio and Alessandro, to convert the locals. They were martyred for their trouble; the handsome parish church dedicated to them has 13th-century frescoes, while the town hall has a room of archaeological finds, not only from the pagans who did them in, but going back to Bronze Age Rhaetians (1300 BC). Then there's the most remarkable church in the whole of Trentino, 6km up a narrow gorge: the

Santuario di San Romedio
open daily 8–6

Santuario di San Romedio; if you're without a car, get a bus from Cles to San Zeno and then walk 2km. The spot where the hermit Romedio lived as a kind of Alpine St Jerome with his pet bear grew into an isolated but popular pilgrimage shrine. The sanctuary consists of chapels in different styles stacked one atop another down the rock over the centuries, the end result somewhat resembling a doll's house in the forest. Don't miss the 11th-century barbaric reliefs on the portal or the disarming home-made *ex votos*, or the ghastly souvenir shop.

The main road from Sanzeno leads to **Fondo**, a quiet summer resort in the upper Val di Non. On the way, stop at **Romeno** to see the frescoes on Sant'Antonio Abate telling the story of the Hanged Man, one of the key miracles that happened along the pilgrimage road to Compostela. Fondo itself is known for the musical bells in

Getting to the Val di Non

Besides the usual **buses**, the Val di Non is served by a little privately run **train** running from Trento to Malè; call **t** 0463 901 150.

its campanile, and more frescoes on the houses of the *centro storico*, relating to Compostela (*ex votos*, apparently, thanking St James for chasing away an epidemic); one house shows the siege of Troy. From Fondo a scenic road rises to the **Passo della Mendola** (4,472ft), with extensive views over the Adige Valley.

South of Lago di Santa Giustina in the Val di Non

South of Cles, the classic excursion is to **Lago di Tovel** (15km south; buses from Cles in July and Aug), lying deep in the folds of the Brenta Dolomites. Unlike other lakes celebrated for their sapphire hue, Tovel was famous for its ruby redness at certain periods, when a rare algae, *Glenodinium sanguineum*, covered its surface. Nowadays Tovel is perhaps the only case in the world where one regrets to say that pollution has made the water turn blue. There is a lovely walk around the lake's perimeter, lasting about one hour, and passing two little bars seemingly placed with great care. Bears are occasionally spotted in the area, although you would have to be very lucky to catch sight of one.

In the main valley, the area south of photogenic **Tuenno** is apple heaven; near orchard-engulfed **Tassullo** you'll find another church, **S. Vigilio**, frescoed within by the Baschenis clan. The village's landmark, the well-preserved **Castel Valèr**, stands on the old Roman road: the 130ft polygonal tower is made of granite especially brought into the area. Amid the orchards just south of Tassullo, the square Renaissance **Castel Nanno** was built as a summer residence by the Madruzzo family in the 16th century, according to legend, after a plan by Palladio.

The main road follows the east bank of the Noce (there's a bridge just north of Tassullo). Aim for **Córedo**, once more important than the farming village of 1,300 souls that it is now, with a fancy bishop's palace, Venetian house and **Palazzo Nero**, named 'black' after it was burned in a peasants' revolt in 1477. It was the local seat of justice – if found guilty the culprit would be burned at the stake in the square just outside, although the frescoes inside, on the life of the French queen St Geneviève de Brabante (who was falsely accused of adultery) were meant to remind the judges to take care. Near the Palazzo Nero, the 13th-century **Castel Bragher**, surrounded by woods and orchards, is one of the best preserved in the whole of Trentino, though still privately owned. Down on the main road, there's **Taio**, a place that frowns on the movement to ban performing animal acts – it's Europe's main producer of circus

Segno Museum
t 0463 468 248; open June–Sept Tues–Sun 2.30–6.30

whips. The nearby hamlet of **Segno** has a museum on the Piazza Padre Eusebio Chino devoted to its hero of the same name, who left home in 1678 to preach to the Indians of Mexico, founding churches and missions, and spending much of his time in the saddle – as he is depicted in the statue outside the museum. Apparently there is also a statue of him in Washington DC.

Castel Thun
t 0461 657 816; open April–June Tues–Sun 9–12 and 2–5.30, July and Aug Tues–Sun 9.30–5.30

Prominent in the lower Val di Non, at **Vigo di Ton**, the Castel Thun was transformed in the 16th century from a military fortress into the most sumptuous palace in the province by the Thun (or Tono) family, hobnobbers with Emperors from the days of Henry IV (1190). Their palace is being restored by the province and will open as a museum, although no one can be sure as to when; the paintings in the gallery, long ignored, were recently found to be major early 17th-century works by Crespi and the Bologna school.

Bear sanctuary
Via Alt Spaur 82, t 0461 653 637, www.proloco spormaggiore.tn.it; open early June–mid-Sept daily 9.30–6.30

If you've gone all around the Brenta group and have yet to spot a bear, you have one last chance at **Spormaggiore**, on the west bank of the Noce: a large, fenced area in a natural setting has been set up as a kind of halfway retirement house for bears from zoos and circuses who couldn't survive on their own in the wild.

Further south are the impressive ruins of the **Castel Belfòrt** (1311) in a beautiful setting overlooking the Val di Non.

Where to Stay and Eat along the Noce

(i) Fondo >>
Via Roma 21, t 0463 830 133, www.valledinon.tn.it; Malè: Viale Marconi 7, t 0463 901 280, www.valdisole.net

Marilleva ✉ 38020
***Sporting Ravelli**, Marilleva 900, t 0463 757 159, www.sportinghotel ravelli.it (€€). Primarily devoted to fun, this complex comes complete with a disco, taverna and games room; it's also one of the more reasonably priced hotels in the area. *Open mid-June–mid-Sept and Dec–early April.*

Cles ✉ 38023
***Punto Verde**, Via S. Vito 20, t 0463 421 275, www.punto-verde.net (€€). A resort hotel with tennis, indoor pool, and sauna. *Open all year.*
*Antica Trattoria**, Via Roma 13, t 0463 421 631, anticatrattoria@email.it (€€). In a historic building, with simple rooms and the best restaurant in Cles, serving Trentino specialities. *Closed Fri eve and Sun, part of June and July.*

Val di Rabbi ✉ 38020
***Albergo Miramonti**, S. Bernardo di Rabbi, t 0463 985 119, www.albergo miramonti.info (€€). About halfway up the Val di Rabbi is this wonderful hotel boasting a swimming pool, sauna and incredible views from all rooms, as well as friendly and helpful staff. The rooms are comfortable and well appointed. *Open June–Sept and Christmas–mid-April.*

Fondo ✉ 38013
***Lady Maria**, Via Garibaldi 20, t 0463 830 380, www.ladymaria hotel.com (€€). Family-run, recently renovated and located in the centre; a Weinstube and pastries and desserts baked every day on the premises are other pluses. *Open all year.*
***Lago Smeraldo**, t 0463 831104, www.hotellagosmeraldo.it (€€). A restored, fortified manor overlooking Lago Smeraldo. Large, comfortable rooms with modern amenities and friendly staff make this a great place to stay. Starting beneath the hotel, and reached via a small weir and some steps, is a fantastic path leading past medieval mills, one of which has been lovingly restored. This well-lit route allows you to stroll into the middle of town in about 15mins without encountering traffic.

Alto Adige/Süd Tirol

Everything has two names on the sunny side of the Alps, in the
bilingual province of Alto Adige/Süd Tirol. In mountain valleys
people speak German and very little Italian, while others still
converse in Ladin (Romansch), a language that owes its origins to
the days when Druso, stepson of Augustus, conquered the region
(15 BC) and Emperor Tiberius sent his soldiers to crush the Celtic

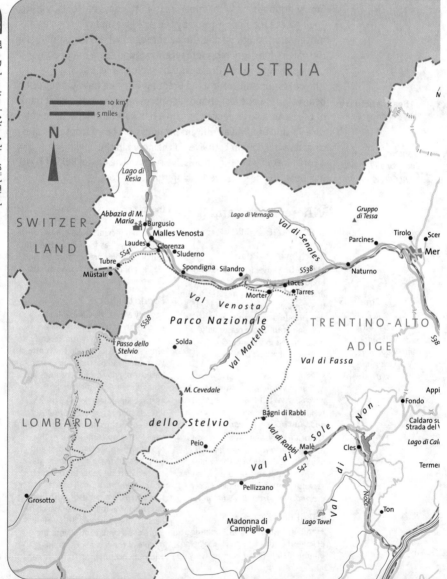

resistance of the mountain valleys of Switzerland and the Tyrol. Some of the soldiers stayed behind in Raetia, as the Romans called the province, and their 'Latin' descendents, the Ladini, still speak Ladin, a nearly incomprehensible linguistic fossil midway between Latin and mountain Celtic. In 590, after the fall of Rome, Rezia formed part of the duchy of Burgundy; in 901 King Lodovico donated Rezia to the bishop of Sabbiona near Bressanone. Although they counted among the great peers of the Holy Roman

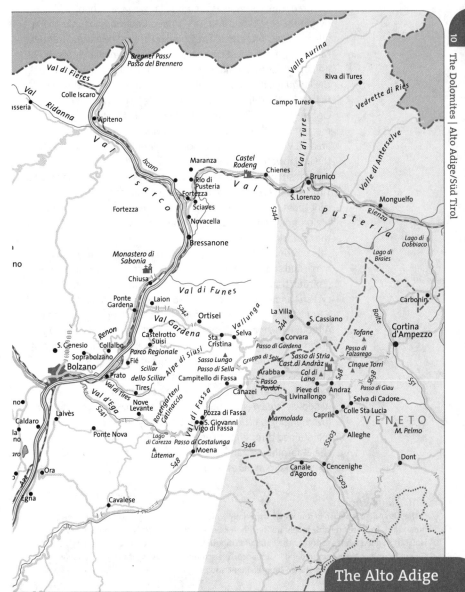

The Alto Adige

Empire, the bishop-princes of Bressanone nevertheless had much of their authority usurped in the 13th century by the counts of Tyrol in Merano, and then by the Habsburgs after the abdication of the 'Ugly Duchess', Margaret of Tyrol, in 1363. Hence, when Napoleon alloted the Süd Tirol to Austria the region had no objection – unlike Italian Trentino, which yearned to join Venetia. Indeed Süd Tirol is far more Austrian than Italian. Forget your typical Italian dishes and customs: here it's schnitzel and strudel that rule the menus. Children learn German as their first language in school.

After the First World War Italy gained Trentino, and in the 1920s absorbed the lands up to the Brenner Pass as the natural frontier. Mussolini, a dedicated cultural imperialist, immediately invented Italian names for all the towns in the Alto Adige and tried to stick the language down the inhabitants' throats, until Hitler told him to lay off. Still, things were so bad that in 1939, when German citizenship was offered to anyone who didn't want to be Italian, most of the people left, leading to severe depopulation of rural areas. It was hardly an auspicious beginning, and if it weren't for the Italian vote from Trentino, the southern half of the region, separatism would have been a serious problem. Even today the Süd Tirol is 69 per cent German-speaking, 27 per cent Italian and 4 per cent Ladin. In recent years Rome has done much to mollify the region, granting it a great deal of autonomy and placing it among the country's wealthiest areas.

Its position at one of the great historical crossroads between north and south, its brilliant Dolomite scenery, its winter sports (Bolzano traditionally produces some of Italy's top skiers and cyclists) and renowned climatic spa at Merano, made the Süd Tirol a tourist destination long before the other Dolomite provinces. Although the mountains steal most of the thunder, the region is a goldmine for early medieval art, with an exceptional collection of sacred and profane frescoes, and exquisite sculpted wooden altarpieces, often with carved shutters, by masters such as Michael Pacher – a local speciality in the Renaissance. Houses with old lead windows, *Stuben* (snug panelled rooms with wood stoves), *Erker* (overhanging balconies) or outer stairways have been carefully maintained through the centuries. Memories are long too – old chalet farmhouses are called *masos*, similar to the Provençal *mas*, from the Roman *mansio*. Some go back to the 14th century, and

Alto Adige Wines

The Alto Adige is awash in fine wines, especially whites – there are some 40 vines for every inhabitant. The most reliable labels are Herrnhofer, Bellendorf, Kehlburg, von Elzenbaum and Hofstatter; good whites to try are the light and smooth Riesling Renano, dry and snappy Gewürztraminer, Weissburgunder (Pinot Bianco), Welschriesling (Riesling Italico), Sylvaner (with a dry, delicate perfume) and Müller-Thurgau (light and fruity).

over 1,200 offer inexpensive *agriturismo* lodgings. You'll also find *Buschenschank* (or *Hofschank*) – farm restaurants, similar concept to *agriturismo* with ingredients from their own produce (*see www.gallorosso.it* for a full list of members).

San Michele all'Adige to Bolzano: the Wine Road

Folks on the west bank of the Adige between Trento and Bolzano were making wine before the Romans, and this lovely **Strada del Vino/Weinstrasse** through the vine-carpeted hills is so well known that most of the villages along it have taken its name. The first place to see something besides vineyards, however, is **Egna/ Neumarkt** on the east bank, a handsome market town founded in 1189 by the bishop of Trento, its streets lined with porticoes. Gothic architect Meister Konrad von Neumarkt built one of his finest works, the 13th–15th-century church of **Nostra Signora**, in nearby **Villa**. From here, it's a short drive up to the **Parco Naturale del Monte Corno**, a gorgeous place in early summer – botanically it's the most diverse park in the Alto Adige. Further up the Adige, **Ora/Auer** has another fine Gothic church, but there's an even better one up on the hill, 14th-century **San Daniele am Kiechlberg**, frescoed by an itinerant Lombard painter.

Cross the Adige for **Termeno sulla Strada del Vino/Tramin an der Weinstrasse**, a town that owes its fame to its blood-heating wine, Gewürztraminer Aromatico, an aphrodisiac; try it, if you have company, at the **Cantina Hofstätter**, home of Gewürztraminer wine, which claims to possess the largest wine cask in Europe. Termeno's neo-Gothic church conserves a mighty 15th-century bell tower and choir coated with elegant Renaissance frescoes by the Bolzano school. Wine paraphernalia, and items relating to Termeno's ancient carnival, are in the **Museo Civico**. Just outside town, rising out of a sea of vineyards, tiny **San Giacomo/St Jakob** in **Castelaz** has extraordinary frescoes spanning the 13th–15th centuries, including some wonderful medieval monsters.

Further north, the Alto Adige's winemaking capital **Caldaro sulla Strada del Vino/Kaltern an der Weinstrasse** overlooks Lago di Caldaro, which is warm enough for a dip from May to September. Besides the grand old homes of the lords of the vine and their sumptuous neoclassical parish church, Caldaro has the regional **Museo Enologico SüdTirolese**, in Castel Ringberg, full of vinous lore and carved barrels, a local speciality. The museum itself, while fascinating, lacks much in the way of English information, a plight often suffered in these German-speaking areas of Italy.

Cantina Hofstätter
*t 0471 860 161,
www.tramin.com*

Museo Civico
*Via Municipio 9; open
Easter–1 Nov Tues–Fri
10–12 and 4–6,
Sat 10–12*

**Museo Enologico
SüdTirolese**
*Castel Ringberg,
t 0471 963 168; open
April–7 Nov Tues–Sat
9.30–12 and 2–6, Sun
and hols 10–12; book
ahead for wine tastings*

Appiano sulla Strada del Vino/Eppan an der Weinstrasse, the next *comune*, has no fewer than 40 castles and manor houses, many owned by wealthy abbeys further north. Perched above is the restored Castle Leuchtenberg. Occasionally the castle owners went on the offensive, most notably Federigo d'Appiano, lord of **Castel d'Appiano**, who in 1158 had the cheek to hijack a treasure the pope was sending to the Holy Roman Emperor. Not long after, the pope and emperor obliterated his castle. The current castle was rebuilt next to the original chapel, Santa Caterina, left untouched by the holy army, with its beautiful frescoes from the dawn of the 13th century, depicting both religious and hunting scenes.

Santa Caterina
open April–1 Nov,
closed Wed

Castel Moos-
Schulthaus
Via Palù 4, t 0471 660
139, guided tours
Easter–1 Nov, Tues–Sat
10, 11, 4, 5; adm

Another of Appiano's castles, Castel Moos-Schulthaus, began as a fortified Tyrolean hunting lodge, and houses not only antique furnishings but a collection of regional paintings from the first half of the 20th century. The *comune*'s most attractive Renaissance-era houses, half-Italian and half-German, are in **San Michele d'Appiano**, where the castle has walls 16ft thick. San Michele also has a far older citadel, one of the best-preserved Bronze Age structures in northern Italy, with a megalithic corridor directed towards the spring equinox.

Where to Stay and Eat on the Wine Road

Caldaro sulla Strada del Vino/ Kaltern an der Weinstrasse ✉ 39052

****Kartheiner Hof**, Kartheinerstrasse 22, t 0471 968 000, *www.kartheiner hof.it* (€€€). There's undoubtedly no lack of places in the Alto Adige's wine headquarters, including this stylish modern hotel in the traditional style, overlooking the lake, with indoor and outdoor pools as well, and every other comfort.

***Goldener Stern**, Via Hofer 28, t 0471 963 153, *www.goldener-stern.it* (€€). Centrally located this hotel offers good-value rooms; the restaurant is under separate management. *Open end-Mar–early Nov.*

Ritterhof, Strada del Vino 1, t 0471 963 330 (€€€–€€). The best dining along the Weinstrasse, this also has lovely views over the vineyards. It's also one of the few places in these mountains that serves fish dishes as well as game. *Closed Mon, and some of July and Aug.*

Appiano sulla Strada del Vino/Eppen an der Weinstrasse ✉ 39057

****Schloss Korb**, Via Castel d'Appiano 5, Missiano, t 0471 636 000, *www.schlosskorb.com* (€€€€–€€€). A fairy-tale 11th-century castle close to Bolzano and surrounded by vines. Spacious rooms, heated outdoor and indoor pools, tennis, and a fine restaurant. *Open Easter–Oct.*

***Castel Aichberg**, Via Monte 31, Aichberg, Appiano, t 0471 662247, *www.aichberg.com* (€€). Set amongst acres of vines, a friendly, family-run hotel in a 17th-century castle with wine cellar, swimming pool and lovely views. *Open Mar–mid-Nov.*

Zur Rose, Via Josef Innerhofer 2, San Michele, t 0471 662 249 (€€€€). Book here for a gourmet epiphany based on Tyrolean traditions in a 12th-century house. *Closed Sun, Mon lunch and July.*

Stroblhof, Via Piganò 25, San Michele, t 0471 662 250 (€€). In a mansion, this *osteria* serves tasty *Schlutzkrapfen* filled with seasonal treats and other regional specialities to accompany their Pinot Nero. *Closed Sun and part Jan and June.*

Bolzano/Bozen

Bolzano, the lively, cultured capital of Alto Adige with its high, narrow gabled houses, beer cellars and arcaded streets, is an excellent base for visiting the mountains on either side. Located on the banks of the Isarco and Talvera, which merge just downstream to form the Adige, Bolzano has been an important market town since the Middle Ages. And since March 1998, the city has had a new mascot, although one far, far older than itself: Ötzi the Ice Man. A huge industry has grown up around Ötzi, and the man continues to amaze, impress and stun into silence the crowds who queue to see him.

Piazza Walther, the Duomo and Via dei Portici

Bolzano's cultural fusion manifests itself unexpectedly in the town's pretty parlour, Piazza Walther. In the centre stands a statue of one of the greatest German *minnesingers*, Walther von der Vogelweide (1170–1230) and at his feet slouch travellers from around the world. In front of Walther stands Bolzano's Gothic Duomo, with its lovely green and yellow roof and pretty tower. The big art, however, is a block behind the cathedral, in the church of the **Domenicani**, now the Music Conservatory, where the chapels of San Giovanni and Santa Caterina contain lovely 14th-century Giotto-esque frescoes by artists from Padua, the best medieval work in the Alto Adige.

Domenicani
open Mon–Sat 9.30–5, Sun 12–5

From the Domenicani, Via Goethe leads up to jovial **Piazza delle Erbe**, Bolzano's commercial hub, where Neptune with his trident (nicknamed *Gabelwirt*, 'Mine host with fork') guards the daily fruit and vegetable market. On Via Argentieri, off Piazza delle Erbe, the 18th-century Palazzo Mercantile or merchants' centre has a lovely courtyard and hall of honour; it now houses a **Museo Mercantile**, where a collection of period furniture and paintings attests to Bolzano's business acumen. If you need more evidence, return to Piazza delle Erbe and stroll up the city's main street, **Via dei Portici**, lined with smart shops under its Tyrolean arcades, *Erker* and pretty stucco decorations. Via dei Portici passes the old heart of the city, **Piazza del Grano** (which was the former cornmarket) and ends in **Piazza Municipio**, where the ornate neo-Baroque Town Hall of 1907 holds court.

Museo Mercantile
open Mon–Sat 10–12.30; adm

From here Via dei Bottai, with its beer cellars and old shops, leads to the Casa di Massimiliano (1512), the old Imperial customs house and now the **Museo Provinciale di Scienze Naturali**, with a large aquarium and absorbing displays on the region's geology. From here Via Vintler leads around to Piazza della Madonna and Via dei Francescani, where the church and convent of the **Francescani** has a pretty Gothic cloister, a 14th-century fresco of the Franciscan

Museo Provinciale di Scienze Naturali
t 0471 412 960, www. naturmuseum.it; open Tues–Sun 10–6; adm

Francescani
open Mon–Sun 8.15–12 and 2.30–7

Getting to Bolzano/Bozen

Trains for Trento to the south, Bressanone, Vipiteno, Brenner and Innsbruck, to the north; Merano and Malles/Venosta, to the northwest; and for Brunico, Dobbiaco and Lienz, to the east via Fortezza, all depart from the rail station, a short distance from Piazza Walther down Viale Stazione.

The **bus** station is across Via Garibaldi, t 0471 450 111, with connections twice daily to Cortina and to nearly every town and many villages in the Alto Adige. For more information, visit *www.sii.bz.it.*

Doctors and a beautiful altarpiece of the Nativity, by woodcarver Hans Klocker (1500). The street leads back to Piazza delle Erbe.

Museo Archeologico dell'Alto Adige: The Ice Man Cometh

Museo Archeologico dell'Alto Adige
Via Museo, nr Piazza delle Erbe, www. archaeologiemuseum.it; open Tues–Sun 10–5.30, daily July–Aug and Dec; audio guides in English available; adm exp

You might recall this sensational discovery from newspaper headlines and the subsequent television documentaries. In 1991 Erika and Helmut Simon were walking along the Similaun glacier northwest of Merano when they happened across a body. There hadn't been an accident or murder there in years. The man they found mummified in the ice had died 5,300 years ago, at the start of the Copper Age.

It was the first time ever that scientists had such an ancient body in such good condition and, after years of study and analysis, Ötzi, as he's been baptised, has become the centrepiece of this museum. Videos show how he was brought in from the cold, and follow all the innumerable autopsies performed on his person. He was about 46 years old, they estimate, an experienced mountaineer who appears to have met a violent end (a stone arrowhead was found embedded in his shoulder). He had tattoos on his torso and legs, which might have served as a kind of acupuncture map. A room reproducing the cold and humidity of the glacier was specially built to house him. And a curious, rather poignant sensation it is, peering through the window at the body of a man who could be one's grandfather, 250 generations removed.

Ötzi, in short, was a lot like us. They've made a model of what he looked like, dressed in all his gear, which is spread out in the next case. His clothing is cunningly designed for the weather, using the few materials at hand in 3700 BC, from bearskin hat to goatskin underwear, and a mantle woven of grasses to keep off the rain; he had a bow and arrows, a flint dagger, and carried bone tools and lucky talismans.

If you don't speak either Italian or German, splash out on the audio tour as there is absolutely no information in English; but the museum itself is well laid out and clear even without linguistic help. Get there early if you can, as tour groups can mitigate the effect Ötzi has on you. While the museum's other exhibits, prehistoric to Roman, tend to pale somewhat after the Ice Man, don't miss the statue stelae carved by his near contemporaries, the cast of the Mithraic altar of Bressanone (*see* p.345–6) or the display of delicate pre-Roman brooches.

Museo Civico and Over the Talvera to Gries

Museo Civico
*t 0471 974 625; open
Tues–Sat, Wed
10–8; adm*

Near here, on the corner of Vias Museo and Cassa di Risparmio, the Museo Civico houses Gothic altarpieces by locals masters, including more by Hans Klocker and Michael Pacher. Via Museo ends at the bridge over the Talvera, a river lined with the parks and promenades; to the right, in its own field, the stout-towered 13th-century **Castel Mareccio** no longer guards Bolzano, but hosts conventioneers.

Just across the Talvera, the imposing Fascist **Monumento alla Vittoria** celebrates Italy's victory in the First World War and was purposefully placed where the Austrian monument was slated to go, had their side won; in 1978 Tyrolean nationalists attempted to blow it to smithereens. Now on Saturday morning the area hosts a peaceful but enormous market.

Corso Libertà leads through Mussolini's planned industrial suburb (1937), purposely built as a contrast to old Bolzano and everything it stood for, then ends up in **Gries**, an old health resort with two important churches – the imposing Baroque **Abbazia dei Benedettini** in the main piazza, with 18th-century frescoes by Tyrolean artist Martin Knoller, and the old parish church of Gries, housing a beautifully carved Gothic wooden altar with doors by Michael Pacher (1475) and a masterful 13th-century crucifix. Bus no.10 travels back from here to the centre.

Gries
*open April–Oct
Mon–Fri 10.30–12
and 2.30–4*

Around Bolzano

There are two beautiful paths around Bolzano. Beyond the Gries parish church, at the end of Via Knoller, begins the 1½km **Passeggiata del Guncina**, with an inn at the top for refreshments. A bit longer but more dramatic, the **Passeggiata Sant'Osvaldo** begins near the train station at Via Renico and descends along the rushing Lungotalvera. Further upriver, **Castel Roncolo/Schloss Runkelstein** has guarded the passage on its impregnable red crag since 1237; it preserves fascinating frescoes, painted on the orders of two extremely wealthy merchants, Niklaus and Franz Vintler, who purchased it in 1385. To compensate for their lack of noble titles, they had the interior and courtyard walls covered with robust frescoes of scenes of chivalry, with an emphasis on the story of Tristan and Isolde. One series contrasts good and bad knightly behaviour; there are exotic animals, and scenes with naked figures, because the artist never finished them. In 1508, the city gave the castle to Emperor Maximilian, but afterwards it suffered grievously from explosions and fire, leaving it one of the Dolomites' top romantic ruins. Yet, somehow, most of the frescoes have survived,

Castel Roncolo
*t 0471 329 808; open
Tues–Sun 10–6*

Modern art museum
Via Sernesi,
www.museion.it;
open Tues–Sun 10–6,
Thurs 10–8

Cable cars
7am–8pm daily

and they're more beautiful than ever, especially after a decade-long restoration. In the historic centre, you'll find a new modern art museum.

Three cable cars ascend from Bolzano, Kolhern, San Genesio and Ritten, the most rewarding one from Via Renon, near the station – it climbs 4,006ft up the slopes of Bonzano's playground, **Mount Renon/Ritten** to **Soprabolzano/Oberbozen**. The views are splendid, stretching across to Rosengarten, but for a truly strange sight continue from Soprabolzano on the rack railway up to **Collabo/ Klobenstein**, and follow the path to the **Longomoso Pyramids** – rocks eroded to form bizarre stone drapery pierced by a dense forest of needles, some crowned with rock hats.

Where to Stay in Bolzano/Bozen

(i) **Bolzano >**
Piazza Walther 8,
t 0471 307 0001,
www.bolzano-bozen.it;
Alto Adige/Süd Tirol
regional office:
Piazza Parrochia 11,
t 0471 999 999,
www.altoadige.com;
Alpine Information
Service, t 0471 993 809

Bolzano/Bozen ✉ 39100

Note that in the summer you may want to base yourself higher up; the humidity in the valley can turn Bolzano into a sauna.

****Parkhotel Laurin, Via Laurin, t 0471 311 000, *www.laurin.it* (€€€€). The best here: a lavish hotel built at the turn of the century in Viennese Jugendstil, located in a fine old park and rose garden near the centre. It has a heated swimming pool, and the public areas are furnished with antiques clustered around black marble fireplaces; don't miss the beautiful frescoed bar and exquisite dining in the restaurant Belle Époque.

****Luna-Mondschein, Via Piave 15, t 0471 975 642, *www.hotel-luna.it* (€€€). A modern hotel, also in the centre, set next to a park, with cosy rooms, parking garage, and indoor/outdoor restaurant serving Tyrolean classics.

***Stadt Hotel Città, Piazza Walther 21, t 0471 975 221, *www.hotelcitta.info* (€€€). In the very heart and soul of Bolzano, with parking.

***Eberle, Passeggiata Sant'Osvaldo 1, t 0471 976 125, *www.eberlebnis.com* (€€). Outside the centre, this 11-room hotel offers guests peace and quiet, a pool, tennis, sauna and gym, in addition to cosy rooms; there's also an excellent restaurant.

**Feichter, Via Grappoli/Weintrauben-gasse 15, t 0471 978 768, *www.hotel*

feichter.it (€€). A wonderful choice for a place to stay, right in the centre of town. It has fine rooms, all with balconies, and a nice *fin-de-siècle* feel about the place.

*Albergo Gatto Nero, Schwarze Katz, S. Maddalena 2, t 0471 975 417 (€). This good-value hotel is just a 15-minute walk from the city centre.

*Klaushof, Colle 14, t 0471 329 999 (€). For peace and quiet, take the Colle cable car (Italy's oldest) from the opposite bank of the Isarco (bus no.11 or a short walk from the train station) up to the refreshing breezes of Colle, where you can find this old farmhouse of 10 rooms, all en suite.

Eating Out in Bolzano/Bozen

Like the language, the cuisine of Alto Adige/Süd Tirol is a bit more than half Austrian – instead of *prosciutto*, expect *speck* (smoked Tyrolean ham). Other specialities are *Wiener schnitzel*, *sauerkraut*, goulash, *knodel* (breadcrumb dumplings), *Terlaner* (wine soup) with apple, cheese, and poppy-seed strudels, *Sachertorte*, and rich mousse for dessert.

Pra Meisa, Via Dr. Streiter 21, t 0471 972 263, *www.prameisa.com* (€€€). This elegant restaurant offers creative dishes from the Ladin tradition combined with *mitteleuropean* and Mediterranean ingredients, such as risotto with Prosecco and golden delicious apples, and braised beef cheek in LaGrein wine. *Closed Sun.*

Batzen Hausl, Andreas Hofer Str, t 0471 050 950 (€€). The oldest hostelry in Bolzano is now a beer cellar and wine bar. Also puts on theatre, cabaret and music events. *Closed Tues.*

Da Cesare, Via Perathoner 17, t 0471 976 638 (€€). Situated in the centre, and a fine place to tuck into fresh pasta and succulent grilled meats.

Patscheiderhof, at Signato, t 0471 365 267 (€€). A favourite of many Sunday lunchers, but the food – pure traditional home cooking – is perhaps better on other days when they aren't so rushed; tasty pasta and roast pork dishes, topped off with poppy-seed cake. *Closed Tues and July.*

Cavallino Bianco/Weisses Rossel, Via dei Bottai 6, t 0471 973 267 (€). This jovial 400-year-old place is still extremely popular, with an eclectic menu stretching from ham and eggs to *Bolognerschnitzel* and a very tasty onion soup. *Closed Sat eve and Sun.*

East of Bolzano towards Rosengarten

The two valley roads southeast of Bolzano eventually meet west of Rosengarten, one of the Dolomites' biggest celebrities, and deservedly so. The stunning road down the Valle d'Ega is the more travelled as part of the famous Great Dolomites Road.

Laviès/Leifers and Nova Ponente

South of Bolzano, Laives/Leifers is one of the principle fruit-growing centres of Alto Adige. For great views of the valley, stop by the **Cappella di San Pietro**, which is all that remains of an old castle destroyed back in the 13th century. To the east, **Nova Ponente/ Deutschnofen** enjoys a fantastical setting, framed by the pinnacles of Sciliar Làtemar, and Rosengarten. Its **Museo Territoriale di Nova Ponente** has a collection of sacred art from the region, although the best works are still in the churches: reliefs (1425) on the altar of **SS Ulrico and Volfango**, and beautiful frescoes from 1410 in the 12th-century church of **S. Elena**, outside Nova Ponente.

Museo Territoriale di Nova Ponente
Via Castel Thurn 1; open Wed and Fri 3–6

The Val d'Ega to Catinaccio/Rosengarten

From Bolzano, the main road to Rosengarten (SS241) begins at Cardara/Kardaun, just east of town, and passes through the breathtaking, narrow, deep red gorge – Mother Nature's sore throat – of the **Val d'Ega**. As the road nears the valley's main settlement and resort, **Nova Levante/Welschnofen**, the craggy peaks of the **Làtemar** group loom up to the right and the rosy pinnacles of Rosengarten soar up to the left. (In summer the clouds are low in the morning but are burned away by the sun by late afternoon.) You can reach the slopes from here or from the Passo di Costalunga, near gorgeous aquamarine Lake Carezza, a popular roadside stop. For an even more spectacular, magical approach, continue along the SS241 to **Pozza di Fassa**, situated on the eastern slopes of Rosengarten.

⭐ **Catinaccio/ Rosengarten**

The sheer walls and crests of **Catinaccio/Rosengarten** (9,781ft) are not only enchanting, but enchanted. The poetic German name first appears in a 13th-century Tyrolean epic: King Lauren of the Dwarves was made prisoner and dragged away from his mountain realm. Furious, the king put a curse on the roses that had betrayed him, that no one would ever see them again, neither by night nor by day. But he neglected to mention the dawn or the twilight, when the spellbound roses make the stony face of Rosengarten blush a deep red.

Sciliar and the Alpe di Siusi

The tangle of valleys between Rosengarten and the Val Gardena encircle the rocky mesa of the Sciliar massif (8,409ft) and the **Parco Naturale dello Sciliar**, the oldest in the Alto Adige. A geological odd man out in the Dolomites, Sciliar is spectacularly coloured, a mélange of red and white rock against the deep green trees. From Lake Carezza, the road skirts Rosengarten's west face then descends into the **Val di Tires/Tierser Tal** with magnificent views; the parish church in the town of **Tires** has early 15th-century frescoes on the *Life of St Catherine* by the Bolzano school.

At Prato all'Isarco/Blumau, on the banks of the Isarco, the road continues around Sciliar by way of **Fiè all Sciliar/Völs am Schern**, now a popular resort town that has all but erased its infamous history as the first place in the Tyrol to hold a witchcraft trial – in 1510, under its baron Leonardo di Völs. He contributed the fine altarpiece in the parish church and remodelled his imposing 12th-century **Castel Presule/Prösels**, a short drive above Fiè, giving it seven towers and a pretty loggia; it now contains a collection of Risorgimento weapons, as well as paintings from Bolzano's Ca' de Bezzi, a 19th-century rendezvous for artists and intellectuals.

Castel Presule/
Prösels
*t 0471 601 062;
tours June and Sept 11,
2, 3, 4; July and Aug 10,
11, 3, 4, 5; May and
Oct 11, 2, 3; adm*

The road continues up to the major resort town of **Siusi**, with another frescoed church (the splendidly situated **S. Valentino**, 14th century) and the ruins of the **Castelvecchio**, the residence of Oswald von Wolkenstein (1377–1445), the well-travelled diplomat, linguist, lyric poet and songwriter in several languages. On Thursdays after sunset you can also visit the area's one astronomical observatory and look through the telescope.

Astronomical
observatory
t 0471 377 024

The **Alpe di Siusi/Seiseralm**, the local playground, is a magnificent plateau under Sciliar's jagged jawbone, the Denti di Terrarossa, noted for its sunny skiing, world-class ski schools and endless meadows of flowers in the late spring; there are numerous cable cars waiting to take you up.

A classic but not strenuous hike from Siusi is the four-hour trek up **Monte Pez**, with an overnight stay at one of the grand dames of 19th-century Alpine refuges, the **Rifugio Bolzano**. **Castelrotto/Kastelruth** just north of Siusi is the third holiday centre in the area, an ancient Ladin village with a pretty historic centre.

The Great Dolomites Road: Bolzano to Cortina d'Ampezzo

ⓘ Great Dolomites Road

The road from Bolzano through the Val d'Ega to Rosengarten and Pozza (*see* above) is the first leg of the fabled 110km *Grande Strada delle Dolomiti*, or Great Dolomites Road, laid out between 1895 and 1909. It's torture, it really is, to have to keep your eyes on this Alpine Amalfi Drive, so linger for as long as you like at the passes and other belvederes to drink in the views. A chauffered convertible would do nicely.

After Pozza di Fassa the road (now the SS48) continues up Trentino's Val di Fassa to **Canazei**, the best base for the ascent of the Dolomites' mightiest peak, **Marmolada** (10,965ft). The road from Canazei climbs past the peculiar tower of **Sassolungo** and Sella glowering on the left, on its way to the **Passo Pordoi**, affording stupendous views of Sella and Marmolada.

From the pass the road writhes down towards **Arabba**, a ski resort dwarfed by Sella, and **Pieve di Livinallongo**, below the odd-shaped **Col di Lana**, its summit blown off by an Italian mine in the First World War. The road then climbs again, past the haunting, eroding **Castello d'Andraz**, to the **Sasso di Stria** (Witch's Rock) and the tunnel at **Passo di Falzarego**, where a cable car on threads ascends the vertiginous cliffs. The road then begins the descent to Cortina, with views of the strange **Cinque Torri** (Five Towers, though one collapsed in 2004) and vertical slopes of Tofane, before reaching the top of the beautiful Boite valley.

10

The Dolomites | East of Bolzano towards Rosengarten

Where to Stay and Eat East of Bolzano

ⓘ Nova Levante/ Welschnofen >
Via Carezza, t 0471 613 126, www.carezza.com

Nova Levante/Welschnofen ✉ 39056

****Posta Cavallino Bianco/Weisses Roessel**, Via Carezza 30, **t** 0471 613 113, *www.postcavallino.com*. (€€€–€€). The name of this hotel recalls the former postal relay station, though its facilities – indoor and outdoor swimming pools, spa centre, tennis, stables with horses, free ski-bus to the slopes and much more – are up to date. *Open mid-Dec–mid-April and mid-June–Oct.*

★ Romantik Hotel Turm >

Fiè allo Sciliar ✉ 39050

****Romantik Hotel Turm**, Piazza Chiesa 9, **t** 0471 725 014, *www.hotel turm.it* (€€€€). This imposing hotel is set in a series of old towers and studded with art (keep an eye out for

the original Picasso in the salon). Stefan works magic in the kitchen, taking Tyrolean specialities to the next level. Guest rooms are a relaxing mix of boutique and Tyrol, while the health spa is a must.

Siusi/Seis ✉ 39040

***Bad Ratzes**, Via Ratzes 29, **t** 0471 706 131, *www.badratzes.it* (€€). A lovely place to relax, in a sunny meadow in the centre of the park. There is also an indoor pool. *Open early Dec–mid-April and mid-May–early Oct.*

***Schlosshotel Mirabell**, Via Laranza 1, **t** 0471 706 134, *www.hotel-mirabell. net* (€€). Early in the 20th century a Russian nobleman built a villa in Siusi, which was converted into this stylish hotel after the Bolsheviks took power. Comfortable and family-run, and equipped with an outdoor pool and sauna. *Open mid-Dec–mid-April and June–mid-Oct.*

Castelrotto/Kastelruth
✉ 39040

****Cavallino d'Oro**, Piazza Kraus, **t** 0471 706 337, *www.cavallino.it* (€€€–€€). Situated in the heart of the village, and built in the 14th century. Its spacious rooms and huge bathrooms have recently been renovated, including two of the original Stuben. *Closed Nov.*

Belvedere-Schönblick, Via O. Wolkenstein 49, **t** 0471 706 336, *www.hotelgarni-belvedere.com* (€€).

Located just south of the village, this is a simple and friendly place with pretty views. *Open mid-Dec–Easter, June–mid-Oct.*

Tschötscherhof, Sant'Osvaldo 19, **t** 0471 706 013, *www.tschoet scherhof.com* (€). Again just outside Castelrotto, this must be one of the province's most charming *masi*, with *agriturismo* rooms as well as an excellent restaurant serving hearty dishes made from ingredients fresh from the farm. Good value. *Closed Dec–Feb.*

Northeast of Bolzano: the Val Gardena

More stunning mountains loom east of Bolzano over the Val Gardena, including the mighty pinnacles of Pelmo, Civetta and Marmolada. Scores of Alpine refuges, chairlifts and cable cars, and fast buses from Bolzano to towns and funicular stations, make access easy. The Val Gardena is a great place to overhear a conversation in Ladin; since 1989 it has been the official administrative language, sparking a little Ladin literary movement for the first time ever. For more information on Ladin, or to learn this complex language for yourself, you can speak to the **Union di Ladins de Gherdeina**.

Union di Ladins de Gherdeina
t 0471 796 870

Along the Valley Road

Lying between the Alpe di Siusi and the jagged Odle group, the Val Gardena is off the *autostrada* northeast of Bolzano. The main valley road, the SS242, begins at **Ponte Gardena/Waidbruck**, under the 11th–16th-century **Castel Trostburg** which is perched on a crag and was where the *minnesinger* Oswald von Wolkenstein once lived. It has a Gothic and late Renaissance décor, including a vaulted Gothic *Stube* and a collection of castle models.

Castel Trostburg
t 0471 654 401,
www.burgeninstitut.
com; guided tours
Easter–31 Oct Tues–Sun
at 11, 2 and 3, plus
10 and 4 July and Aug

Just above Ponte Gardena, near Laion, **Vogelweiderhof** is one of the three disputed birthplaces of one of the first and greatest of all wandering *minnesingers*, Walther von der Vogelweide (*c.* 1170–1228), whose innovation in the art of courtly poetry was to introduce heartfelt love lyrics; patronized by emperors, he was equally well known for his 'didactic poetry' that was so critical of the pope that he has been acclaimed a proto-Protestant by some.

The capital of the Val Gardena, elegant **Ortisei/St Ulrich**, or Urijëi in Ladin, and the next two villages, **Santa Cristina** and **Selva di Val Gardena/Wolkenstein**, are all well-equipped resorts with cable cars to the Alpe di Siusi; skiers shouldn't miss the Saslonch-Ruacia piste which passes right below the 17th-century **Castel Fischburg**.

Getting around the Val Gardena

Buses run along the Val Gardena late June–Sept daily 7.15–5.30, every 15mins.

Above Selva is the little chapel of **St Sylvester** at Vallunga dedicated to the patron saint of cattle, restored in 1993 to reveal some 300-year-old frescoes by itinerant artists.

Museo de Gherdëina

Via Rezia 83, t 0471 797 554; open June, Sept–mid-Oct Tues–Fri 2–6, Thurs 10–12 and 2–6; July and Aug Mon–Fri 10–12 and 2–6, Sun 2–6; adm

Ortisei's **Museo de Gherdëina** in the Cësa Ladins has displays on the valley's history from the Stone Age to the present. On the second Monday of October they have a vast street market, the **Blättermarkt**, which sells just about anything you could want, from pet birds to *Wienerschnitzel*; don't pass up the opportunity to try the local honey. Santa Cristina has lifts into the Odle group and up to the wall of spiralling, dream-like **Sassolungo** (10,434ft) to the south. For astronomical interest, have a look at the **Monte Pana** sundial (call the tourist board for buses): a fine example of a spherical equatorial sundial, though without a sunny day it lacks a certain something.

From the crossroads in Selva di Val Gardena you have a choice of two spectacular routes: either south over the fabulous **Passo di Sella** to Canazei in Trentino, where you can pick up the Great Dolomites Road, or over the stunning **Passo di Gardena** down into the **Alta Badia** to the east, another beautiful valley that has retained its Ladin culture. **Corvara in Badia** and **La Villa/Stern**, one-time host of the Alpine Ski World Cup, are the main resorts. From La Villa you can take a detour into the **Valle di San Cassiano**, named after its chief settlement and site of an ornate Baroque parish church, which was built in the 18th century when the valley had a thriving mining industry. The geology of the Dolomites, popular art and fossils – including the remains of a giant prehistoric bear – are

Pic' Museo Ladin

t 0471 849 505; open Tues–Fri 4–7, Sun 4.30–7.30

the subjects of San Cassiano's **Pic' Museo Ladin**. Another treat in the Alta Badia is the famous **Sella Ronda**, a circuit of the entire Sella group that can be made entirely on skis, thanks to a series of refuges and lifts. To the north, the SS244 leads to San Lorenzo near Brunico, while to the south the road descends to Arabba.

The Woodcarvers of the Val Gardena

Ortisei has specialized in woodcarving for centuries, and if you're buying you'll find a wide range of works to choose from, from the artistic to cheesy Alpine *schlock*, some of it just awful. Farmers took up carving to while away the long winter evenings, using soft pine from the valley's slopes. In the 1640s some began to neglect their land to hike over the mountains, selling carved toys, ornaments, household furniture and implements. By 1820, 300 craftsmen were working in the valley, and a school was set up in 1872 to consolidate skills and encourage trade.

Today over 3,000 woodcarvers whittle away in the Val Gardena. Ask the tourist office for their list of workshops, and stop by Ortisei's parish church and museum (*see* above) to look at permanent exhibitions of their craft created over the past three centuries. If you're inspired, Ortisei's school of woodcarving holds weekly courses in July and August: contact the tourist office for details.

(i) **Ortisei** >
Via Rezia 1, t 0471 796 328, www.valbadia.it

(i) **Santa Cristina** >>
Via Chemun 9, t 0471 793 046, www.valbadia.it.

(i) **Selva di Val Gardena** >
Via Meisules 213, t 0471 795 122, www.valbadia.it.

(★) **Art Hotel Cappella** >>

Where to Stay and Eat in the Val Gardena

Ortisei/Sankt Ulrich in Gröden ✉ 39046

****La Perla**, Strada Digon 8, t 0471 796 421, *www.laperlahotel.info* (€€€€). Located just outside town, and a year-round pleasure to visit, with its park and indoor pool. *Open mid-May–mid-Oct and early Dec–early April.*

***Hotel Snaltnerhof**, Piazza San Antonio 142, t 0471 796 209, *www.snaltnerhof.it* (€€€–€€). Just a stone's throw from the museum, the rooms here are modern and tend to overlook the main square.

Selva di Val Gardena/ Wolkenstein in Gröden ✉ 39048

*****Alpenroyal**, Via Meisules 43, t 0471 795 555, *www.alpenroyal.com* (€€€€€). Small but very comfortable, and one of the few hotels in the area that is open all year, with plenty of facilities to keep its guests fit and happy – indoor pool, whirlpool baths, sauna, solarium, beauty centre and fitness room. *Open June–Oct and Dec–mid-April.*

Europa, Via Nives 50, t 0471 795 157, *www.europa-dolomiti.com* (€€€). A typical little family-run mountain

hotel. *Open Dec–mid-April, late June–Sept.*

****Freina**, Via Freina 23, t 0471 795 110, *www.hotelfreina.com* (€€€–€€). Another choice convenient for the slopes, with 12 rooms with bath. At least half-board is required, but the food is excellent – stop here to eat if you're just passing through.

Santa Cristina in Valgardena/ Sankt Christina in Gröden ✉ 39047

***Cendevaves**, t 0471 792 062, *www.cendevaves.it* (€€€). There are several hotels up at Monte Pana: this one has an indoor pool and good views. *Open early June–early Oct and early Dec–early April.*

****Diamant**, Via Skasa 1, t 0471 796 780, *www.hoteldiamant.it* (€€€). Lovely mountain views, an indoor pool and sauna, and tennis courts, all in a quiet park. *Open June–mid-Oct and Dec–early April.*

Colfosco ✉ 39030

****Art Hotel Cappella**, Pecei 17, t 0471 836 183, *www.hotelcappella.com* (€€€€€–€€€€). An attractive Tyrolean structure dating from 1912 and decorated with artwork from all over the world. There are two restaurants, a health spa, and the slopes right at your feet.

North towards the Brenner Pass

North of Bolzano and Ponte Gardena lies the Val Isarco/Eisacktal, the traditional 'spine' of the Süd Tirol and main highway between the Germanic world and the Mediterranean since Roman times. The modern road, known as the Kuntersweg after the merchant who began it, was drilled through the rock-bound valley in 1314 using gunpowder – the first time it was used in the west for a civil engineering project.

Chiusa/Klausen and the Monastero di Sabiona

On the way up from Bolzano, the first stop north of the Val Gardena was the ancient town of **Chiusa**, its steep houses stretched out along the road. Travellers in days of yore would have to go through customs here, as they passed into the territory of the bishops of Bressanone, who kept an eye on things through their cliff-top **Monastero di Sabiona**. Founded in the 4th century, this is the 'Tyrol's Cradle of Christianity'; the dramatic setting was immortalized in the detailed landscape of Albrecht Dürer's superb engraving, *The Great Fortune (Nemesis)*, c. 1497. In the 5th century it was the home of a wonderful bishop named Lucano, who was denounced by Pope Celestine I for letting his congregation eat dairy products on Friday. Lucano justified himself in a way no other bishop has ever done since: he rode a bear to Rome (bear-back, one presumes) and then, in case that didn't astonish the pope enough, he took off his cloak and hung it on a sunbeam. Nearly all rebuilt in the 17th century after a fire, much of the monastery is now occupied by cloistered Benedictine nuns, but you can visit the uppermost church, Santa Croce, which has vestiges of its palaeo-Christian origins and curious *trompe l'œil* frescoes of landscapes and architecture painted in 1679.

Santa Croce
open daily 2–6

Chiusa became something of an art town in the early 19th century; its **Convento dei Cappuccini**, founded in 1701 by Maria Anna, Queen of Spain, now contains the Museo Civico with Romantic landscapes and other paintings by the local school, and the so-called Loreto treasure (16th–17th century) of goldwork and paintings by Flemish, Spanish and Italian workshops. Up from the main library is a working **water wheel**, some 14 feet across and still turning at alarming speed. It is easy to lose hours listening to its strange rhythms and creakings. Orphan sculptures from surrounding churches have found a home in the somewhat nondescript 15th-century parish church, **S. Andrea**. The village itself is wonderfully tranquil, with the garden of the library making a particularly restful spot from which to escape the heat of the day.

Museo Civico
t 0472 846 148; open Tues–Sat end March–end July 10–12 and 4–7, Aug–Sept 9.30–12 and 3.30–6

Above Chiusa, a bridge conveniently crosses the Isarco for a visit to **Gudon**, the medieval 'village of seven hills' at the bottom of the quiet **Val di Funès**, enjoying lovely views of the bright white towers of the Gruppo delle Odle. Alternatively, take a side road up to the 16th-century Castel Velturno, the elegant summer residence of the bishop of Bressanone, decorated with frescoes and wood *intarsio*, all meticulously restored in the 1980s and used as a setting for art exhibits and theatre.

Castel Velturno
t 0472 855 525, info@felthurns.com; guided tours Mar–Nov Tues–Sun at 10, 11, 2.30, 3.30; adm

Bressanone/Brixen

Now a popular resort beneath Monte Plose, Bressanone is a charming ensemble of frescoed medieval buildings and arcaded streets. Capital of the region for a millennium, and founded in 901, it was the seat of a powerful bishop who was continually at odds with the Counts of Tyrol. In 991, when the bishopric was transferred here from Sabiona, a religious city grew up in the centre of Bressanone – a northern version of the great cathedral complex in Pisa.

Unfortunately, the **Duomo** was metamorphosed into a dull Baroque church in the 18th century, although the frescoes (1745–54) in the vault are Tyrolean Rococo master Paul Troger's finest work. Fortunately, the remodellers never got around to the superb Romanesque cloister, rebuilt after a fire in 1174 and frescoed in the 1390s by followers of Michael Pacher – Leonardo da Bressanone (look for the signature scorpions of his nickname, the Maestro dello Scorpione), Giovanni, Cristoforo and Erasmo of Brunico and others, and the 11th-century Baptistry S. Giovanni Battista, with even earlier and rather unusual frescoes of the Throne of Solomon and Seat of Wisdom.

Cloister
open Easter–1 Nov Mon–Sat, visits at 10.30 and 3

S. Giovanni Battista
same opening times as the cloister, above

Just north of the Duomo stands the parish church of **San Michele**, which was originally a cemetery chapel; rebuilt in 1503, it preserves its older campanile, while the interior was given a Baroque once-over by the apprentices of the cathedral masters. Flanking San Michele, the 16th-century **Casa Pfaundler** is the handsomest palace in town.

The bishops' 13th-century palace has a princely three-storey Renaissance courtyard with terracotta statues in the niches, but instead of prelates it houses the Museo Diocesano. Here you'll find the best part of the cathedral treasure of precious artefacts and sculptures from the Middle Ages up to the 19th century – works by Michael Pacher, Lucas Cranach, Paul Troger, Giambattista Tiepolo, and a fine collection of over 10,000 *presepi* (Christmas crib) figures. Beside the Museo Diocesano there's an old kitchen garden which opens on to a delightful café-restaurant Kutscherhof, run by the Hotel Dominik.

Museo Diocesano
open mid-March–end Oct Tues–Sun 10–5, Dec and Jan 2–5

Three kilometres north of Bressanone at Varna, the fortified, winemaking **Abbazia di Novacella**, was founded by the Bishop of Bressanone in 1142. The abbey is a study in the evolution of architecture, with its 12th-century tower, Baroque church, beautiful frescoed 14th-century cloister, and the round, crenellated 12th–16th century chapel of San Michele, all duly fortified in the late 1400s against the Ottomans – just in case they ever got this far. The one time the defences were tested, in the peasant uprising of 1525, they failed miserably. The Napoleonic deconsecration of the abbey wreaked havoc on its rich collections, but the tour still offers a small gallery of art, with a beautiful altar by Leonardo da Bressanone, and a rococo library of medieval manuscripts, although most of the books ended up in Innsbruck.

Abbazia di Novacella
t 0472 836 189; guided tours in season at 10, 11, 2, 3 and 4; adm

Also just north of Bressanone, the **Altopiano Naz-Sciaves** is nicknamed 'Apple Plateau': planted with thousands of fruit trees, it keeps the bees busy. If you happen to be there in October, you can tuck into various treats made with the stuff during the annual honey week.

Where to Stay and Eat in Chiusa/Klausen and Bressanone/Brixen

If you come between September and late November, you can join in with the locals in their *Törggelen* (from the Latin *torculum*, or wine press) – going from *maso* to *maso* to try the unfermented grape juice (*Sußer*) and the new wine (*Nuie*), with roast chestnuts, speck, rye bread, and smoked salami (*Kaminwurz*), sometimes accompanied by music. But beware: if alcohol is not your forte, take lots of water with you, this stuff isn't for children.

Chiusa ✉ 39043

***Posta**, Piazza Tinne 3, **t** 0472 847 514, *www.parkhotel-post.it* (€€). Central, traditional with comfortable rooms as well as a summer pool in the pretty garden.

Unterwirt, **t** 0472 844 000 (€€). In the centre of Gudon, this family-run hotel dates from 1370, with panelled rooms, a 400-year-old *Stube*, a pretty garden and home-made pasta dishes. *Closed Sun, Mon and Dec–Mar.*

(★) Sunnegg >>

(i) Bressanone >
Viale Stazione 9,
t 0472 836 401,
www.brixen.org

Bressanone ✉ 39042

****Dominik**, Via Terzo di Sotto 13, **t** 0472 830 144, *www.hoteldominik. com* (€€€€). Stay in the lap of luxury at a prestigious Relais & Châteaux hotel; these spacious rooms have lovely views, and there's an indoor pool and sauna. *Closed late Dec–mid-Feb.* The restaurant, one of the best in the entire region, serves regional and Italian specialities. *Closed Tues.*

****Elephant**, Via Rio Bianco 4, **t** 0472 832 750, *www.hotelelephant.com* (€€€€). This hotel recalls a gift from the King of Portugal who, in 1550, sent an Indian elephant to Emperor Maximilian for his menagerie. En route, the pachyderm spent a week in Bressanone's post house, so impressing the locals that they had its portrait done, and there it remains to this day, on the front of this old Renaissance inn. Only the fresco remains, but inside, the ceilings and walls still have antique panelling and beautiful tile stoves. Many of the lovely rooms are furnished with antiques, though no one remembers which one the elephant slept in. There's also a pool, tennis and pleasure garden, as well as a dairy and vegetable garden that provides many of the ingredients for the Tyrolean dishes served in the restaurant. *Open Mar–early Nov and late Nov–early Jan; restaurant closed Mon out of season.*

***Cavallino d'Oro**, Via Brennero 3, **t** 0472 835 152, *www.goldenesroessl.it* (€€€). A comfortable 350-year-old hotel with a swimming pool, and blessed with wonderful views.

***Pension Mayrhof**, Via Tratten 17, **t** 0472 836 327, *www.mayrhofer.it* (€€). Small but very cosy, this *pensione* is very central with a quiet sunny garden. *Closed early Nov–mid-Dec.*

Sunnegg, Weinberg Strasse 67, **t** 0472 834 760, *www.sunnegg.com* (€€). A Tyrolean-style restaurant with good solid food and delicious wines in a beautiful panoramic setting surrounded by vineyards. *Closed Wed, Thur Lunch, Jan–mid-Feb and July.*

Fink, Via Portici Minori 4, **t** 0472 834 883 (€€–€). The old walls are ringed with cafés. This one, a century old, has a restaurant upstairs, serving traditional Südtirolese cooking: saddle of venison, *polenta nera* (made from buckwheat) and a wide variety of cold meats and cheeses, as well as vegetarian dishes. Simpler, less pricey dishes are served downstairs in the Arkade. *Closed Tues eve, Wed, May and 1 wk in Jan.*

The Val Pusteria

Castel Rodeng
t 0472 454 056;
guided tours mid-
May–mid-Oct Tues–Sun
at 11 and 3

The Val Pusteria, the wide and pleasant valley running east from Bressanone along the River Rienza, is dotted with typical Tyrolean villages and castles. The first, the mighty 12th-century **Castel Rodeng**, stands just east of the crossroads of the Pusteria and

Isarco valleys (take the road up from Sciaves or Rio di Pusteria). During restorations in 1973, rare frescoes on the *Legend of Iwein* (derived from a poem by Chrétien de Troyes) were discovered on the ground floor and have been dated to around the year 1200, making them among the oldest secular pictures in Europe. If you're in the area in mid-September, take the cable car from Rio di Pusteria to the old hamlet/new ski resort of **Maranza/Meransen**, for the festival of Aubet, Cubet and Quere, three virgin daughters of the King of Burgundy, a curious cult with pre-Christian origins.

Continue up the Val Pusteria to **San Sigismondo**, where the parish church has fine late-Gothic frescoes on its exterior, and then to **Chienes**, where the Counts Künigl gave their 12th-century fortress Casteldarne/Ehrenburg some of the first Renaissance trimmings in the region, then Baroqued the interior. They were so pleased with the result that they never remodelled it again; all the original family furnishings, tapestries and other decorations are still intact. Many churches in the Val Pusteria contain works by the valley's 15th-century master woodcarver and painter Michael Pacher; the 13th-century parish church of **San Lorenzo di Sebato** has his **Madonna with Grapes** on the high altar. Prominent nearby, the 11th-century convent of **Castel Badia/Sonnenburg** is now a hotel; you can visit the crypt and collection of prehistoric finds.

The capital of the Pusteria, medieval **Brunico/Bruneck**, is the hub of the region. Two lovely old gates guard the town, along with a 13th-century bishop's castle at the highest point. Among the elegant shops along Via di Città, even the city pharmacy has frescoes – as does the 15th-century church by the gate, **Salvatore alle Orsoline**: three beautiful painted reliefs from the same century decorate its neo-Gothic altar. You can also find a wonderful collection of art mainly from the 1920s and 1930s, as well as some work by Friedrich Pacher and Albrecht Dürer, in the Museo Civico di Brunico.

Two kilometres away in Teodone, a handsome old manor houses the **Museo Provinciale degli Usi e Costumi**, Via Duca Teodone 24, devoted to traditional arts and crafts, which includes reconstructions of various mills and farm buildings. Not far away is the **Museo Etnografico di Teodone**, which houses another collection of agricultural implements, as well as a small collection of prints showing the development of the valley.

Brunico stands at the entrance to the heavily wooded **Val di Tures/Taufers**. The main town, **Campo Tures**, is clustered under the baronial **Castel di Tures**, guarding the entrance to the Val Aurina. Tours take in the hall of mirrors, two dozen rooms of tapestries, a chapel frescoed in 1482 by the school of Pacher and beautiful library. Glacier Alpinists come here for the **Vedrette Giganti** (or di Ríes) reached from Riva di Tures (with a waterfall), while extremists

Casteldarne/ Ehrenburg
t 0474 565 221; guided tours April, May, Oct Wed at 3; June–Sept Mon–Sat at 11 and 3, also at 4 in July–mid-Sept; adm

Castel Badia
open daily 10–6

Bishop's castle
t 0474 555 722; open early July–mid-Oct 10–6; closed Mon exc Aug

Museo Civico
Via Bruder-Willramstrasse 1, t 0474 553 292; open Tues–Fri 3–6, Sat–Sun 10–12; July–Aug also 10–12

Museo Provinciale
Via Duca Teodone 24, open Easter Mon–Oct Tues–Sat 9.30–5.30, Sun 2–6; adm

Museo Etnografico
Via Herzog Diet 27; open mid-April–end Oct Tues–Sat 9.30–5.30, Sun 2–6, Mon also in Aug

Castel di Tures
tours Jan–mid-June Tues, Fri and Sun at 4; mid-June–Oct 10, 11, 2, 3.15, 4.30; mid-July–Aug 10–5 every 30mins; adm

may carry on north up the narrow but dramatic Val Aurina to **Casere** and its hamlet, **Pratomagno**, with the northernmost houses in Italy.

East of Brunico, off the main Val Pusteria near Valdàora, the **Valle di Anterselva** is one of the most beautiful in the Alto Adige, growing ever narrower and narrower as it passes Lake Anterselva en route to the Parco Naturale Vedrette di Ríes, rising above a lush shawl of firs. Further east, **Monguelfo/Welsberg** was a favourite 19th-century Middle European resort (poet Hugo van Hoffmansthal spent time here) under a picture postcard 12th-century castle, rebuilt in the 1400s. In 1698 Rococo painter Paul Troger was born in Monguelfo; he left three altarpieces in the parish church. From here a road turns south into the Val di Braies, where the **Lago di Braies**, fast in the Dolomites' embrace, is celebrated for its perfect stillness and intense green colour. East of Monguelfo the road continues east to Dobbiaco (*see* p.301).

Tourist Information in the Val Pusteria

There is a useful independent website for information on the Val Pusteria, with links to all the hotels in the area, a winter sports section with ski-lift opening hours, route maps and transport links: *www.pustertal.com*.

Brunico >>
Via Michael Pacher 11/A, t 0474 555 447, www.kronplatz.com

Where to Stay and Eat in the Val Pusteria

Rio Pusteria/Mühlbach
✉ 39037

***Hotel Corso, 16 Bastioni, Brunico **t** 0474 554 434, *www.hotelcorso.com* (€€€€–€€€). Small, central and friendly hotel with 26 rooms, a Viennese restaurant and local wine tastings.

***Erika, t 0472 520 196, *www.hotel erika.it* (€€). Above Rio Pusteria, near the *funivia* station in Maranza, this little hotel is a perfect base for a sporty stay, run by an Olympic skier, with an indoor pool, tennis and other sports. *Open mid-Dec–mid-April, June–mid-Oct.*

***Masl, t 0472 547 187, *www.hotel-masl.com* (€€–€). In Valles, 7km up the same narrow valley. A delightful hotel, with similar facilities and great food in the restaurant. *Open mid-Dec–mid-April, early May–early Oct.*

Ansitz Strasshof, Via Spinga 2, **t** 0472 886 142 (€€). A family-run *trattoria* where you can taste authentic south Tyrolean dishes. *Closed Wed.*

Brunico/Bruneck and Around
✉ 39031

****Royal Hunter Hinterbuber, t 0474 541 000, *www.royal-hinterhuber.com* (€€€€). For real luxury in a large park, head up 3km to this hotel at Riscone/Reischach. With indoor and outdoor pools, tennis and other sports. *Open early Dec–mid-April, June–early Oct.*

***Andreas Hofer, Via Campo Tures 1, **t** 0474 551 469, *www.andreashofer.it* (€€€). A hotel with a summer pool, gym and satellite TV, and a good restaurant.

***Windschar, Via Ulrich V. Tauffers 3, **t** 0474 504 123, *www.windschar.com* (€€€). In Gais, just up the Val di Tures. A large Tyrolean-style place in a lovely garden setting, with indoor and outdoor pools. *Open mid-Dec–mid-Mar and early May–early Nov.*

*Oberraut, t 0474 559 977, *gasthof. oberraut@dnet.it* (€€). In Ameto, a hamlet just outside of Brunico, this rural *maso* built in 1368 is the home of a cosy little hotel owned by a good chef. Open to non-guests, and serving home-made cheeses, pasta, and sausages; unusual Pusteria specialities available on request. *Closed Thurs exc in season, and Jan.*

The Upper Val Isarco to the Brenner Pass

Between Bressanone and the Pass, the big news is colourful **Vipiteno/Sterzing**, a medieval company town that belonged to the Fuggers, one of Europe's greatest banking dynasties. The attraction it held for them was its mines, especially silver; although abandoned in 1979 they were lucrative enough in the Renaissance to employ 10,000 miners and for the residents to build splendid battlemented houses after a fire devastated Vipiteno in 1443. The tall **Torre di Città** was built to celebrate the reconstruction.

Municipio
open Mon–Thurs
8.15–12.15 and 5–5.30,
Fri 8.15–12.15

The best houses are along Via Città Nuova; pop into the courtyard of the Municipio to see an impressive Mithraic altar from the 3rd century BC, with a cycle of myths carved around the main scene of Mithras sacrificing the bull.

Museo Multscher
open April–Oct
Tues–Sat 10–12 and
2–5; adm

In Piazza Città, the Museo Multscher is devoted to a handful of elegant works by the 15th-century painter Hans Multscher. Vipiteno itself consists primarily of one main street filled with all the usual shops.

Castel Tasso
guided tours Easter–
1 Nov Sat–Thurs at
10.30, 2 and 3; adm

Three kilometres southeast the Counts Thurn und Taxis' magnificent 11th–14th century Castel Tasso has some of the best art in the province in its frescoed rooms, late Gothic decorations and a 12th-century Stube.

Museo Provinciale della Caccia e della Pesca
t 0472 758 121; open
April–15 Nov Tues–Sat
9.30–5.30, Sun 1–5; adm

Other excursions around Vipiteno include the scenic Val Ridanna to the west, with a waterfall near Stranghe and the Castel Wolfsthurn at Mareta. This castle with its 365 windows is considered the most beautiful Baroque building in the whole Tyrol – you can examine the interior while perusing the collection of stuffed deer and fish belonging to the Museo Provinciale della Caccia e della Pesca.

Museo Provinciale Della Miniere
t 0474 651 043; open
April–Oct Tues–Sun
9.30–4.30, Thurs
9.30am–10pm

At **Maiern**, at the top of the Val Ridanna, you can visit the Museo Provinciale Della Miniere, complete with a mining demonstration and a little train which will take you, in matching yellow waterproofs, to the silver lode beneath the Picco Rosso; you can carry on to San Martino Monteneve, the highest former mining town in Europe.

San Martino Monteneve
t 0473 647 045; guided
tours to Monteneve
mid-June–mid-Oct

The main road north of Vipiteno continues to **Colle Isarco/ Gossensass**, a resort and spa that was a favourite of Henrik Ibsen (hence the tiny museum to Ibsen here), with skiing and hiking on Cima Bianca and in the **Val di Fleres**, the Fuggers' silver lode; the cemetery church at **Colle Isarco** has a beautiful late Gothic altarpiece in the miners' chapel, Santa Barbara.

Beyond this lies the **Brenner Pass** (4,511ft), the lowest of the Alpine passes, and the route of countless invaders from the north; during the Second World War it was heavily bombed. From here it is 125km to Innsbruck.

Where to Stay and Eat in the Upper Val Isarco

Vipiteno/Sterzing ✉ 39049

****Aquila Nera**, Piazza Città 1, t 0472 764 064, *www.schwarzeradler.it* (€€€). You can relax in the heart of town in this 16th-century hotel and take a dip in the indoor swimming pool.

***Albergo Post**, Città Nuova 14, t 0472 766 664, *www.highlight-*

hotels.com/post (€€). Located between the two towers that mark the length of the main street. The rooms are wood lined with creaky floorboards but comfortable and all have TV.

Pretzhof, t 0472 764 455, 8km away in Tulve (€€). A favourite place to eat, which will fill you up on delicious traditional dishes, prepared with ingredients from the family's farm. Also has rooms. *Closed Mon, Tues, some of June and July.*

The Upper Adige

A celebrated spa, a dense carpet of vineyards and enough castles for 30 games of chess appear as you follow the road up to the Resia Pass, near the Austrian and Swiss frontiers.

Merano

Just 28km up the Adige from Bolzano, Merano is an attractive town of gardens and flowers, a favourite spa since the 1830s for elderly and sedate central Europeans with respiratory complaints. Basking in a sheltered, balmy micro-climate and endowed with radioactive waters, Merano enchanted Franz Kafka: 'Everlasting snow and rocky areas surrounded by storm overlook subtropical paradises, a small representation of all the continent from Scandanavia to the Riviera, from ice deserts to sweet lands in bloom.' The benefits of the waters, clean air and graded mountain walks are complemented by specific cures, such as the famous grape cure in September–October (in juice form the other months); eating two pounds of Merano grapes a day, taking care to chew them well, apparently keeps the doctor away.

Apart from possibly inflicting digestive disorders, Merano does have other attractions: along the Adige, there's the striking Liberty-style Casino and **Kursaal** topped with dancing Graces, now a Congress Centre. Two streets back, the arcaded Via dei Portici was the main street in the medieval town, and has, at No.68, the Evelyn Ortner Museum where you can see what dedicated female followers of fashion have been wearing over the past century. The stern 15th-century Gothic **Duomo** contains International Gothic frescoes in the style of Trento's Castello del Buonconsiglio.

Via Cassa di Risparmio leads back to the little 15th-century Castello Principesco, built by Archduke Sigismond and containing Gothic furnishings, arms and swords. Opposite, you can take a chairlift up to Tirolo (*see* below) or pick up the 4km **Passeggiata Tappeiner**, the Meraners' favourite promenade, a botanical wonderland overlooking the city. Created by Franz Tappeiner in 1893, the many varieties of plants make a delightful botanical lesson, each labelled and marked on a map available from the tourist office. At the top is **Castile San Zeno** offering fantastic views over the valley. The next street over, the Museo Civico has four Bronze Age *statue stelae*, some fine Gothic sculptures, and a *Pietà* by the school of Michael Pacher.

Museo Civico
Via delle Corse 42,
t 0473 236 015; open
Tues–Sat 10–5, Sun 10–1

In the heart of old Merano is the **Museo Ebraico e Sinagoga**, which holds a fascinating collection of Judaica, including silver work dating from the 13th century. It also has a worthy section dedicated to the fate of the Merano Jews during the Holocaust, none of whom survived the German occupation during the Second World War.

Museo Ebraico
e Sinagoga
Via Schillar 14, t 0473
236 127; open all year,
exc. Jewish festivals,
Tues–Wed 3–6pm,
Thurs–Fri 9–12

For centuries, the landowners of these valleys were generally left alone to govern and defend their turf, and as a result the area bristles with a large proportion of the Alto Adige's 350-plus castles. The big cheese, however, lived just above Merano in **Tirolo**, at Castel Tirol balanced on the precipice. The castle gave its name to the region and to this day remains its symbol: it was the headquarters of the independent Counts until 1363, when Margherita di Maultasch, the 'Ugly Countess', ceded Tyrol to the Habsburgs. Adorned with a fine set of medieval monsters and frescoes, it houses different exhibitions every year. There is also the **Centro Recupero Avifauna** at Castel Tirol (known locally as Guffy Land) which aims to treat injured birds and release them back into the wild. While they are recovering it makes a fun afternoon for children, and children at heart, to wander among the coloured plumes of the convalescing birds.

Castel Tirol
t 0473 220 221,
www.schlosstirol.it;
open Tues–Sun 10–5

Centro Recupero
Avifauna
t 0473 221 500,
www.gufyland.com;
open April–early Nov
10.30–5, early Nov–Mar
Sun 1.30–4.30; adm

Also in Tirolo, the **Agricultural Museum of Brunneburg** is a rather imaginative reconstruction of a 12th-century castle, with a collection of farm instruments and memorabilia related to the poet Ezra Pound (*d.* 1972), who was found too crazy to stand trial for treason (he made pro-Mussolini radio broadcasts during the war) and retired here in 1958 after his release from a Washington hospital. The village facing Tirolo, **Scena/Schenna**, has a round 12th-century church, **San Giorgio**, with good frescoes, and the **Castel Scena**, built in 1346 and still owned by the Counts of Meran with original furnishings, frescoes and armour.

Agricultural
Museum of
Brunneburg
May–Nov Wed and
Mon 10–5; adm

San Giorgio
open daily 10–12

Castel Scena
www.schloss-schenna.
com; guided visits week
before Easter–Oct Mon–
Sat 10.30, 11.30, 2, 3; adm

The Val Venosta

West of Merano, the Val Venosta follows the Adige towards Austria. One of the first villages, **Parcines**, was the home of Peter Mitterhofer, inventor of the typewriter; the **Museo della Macchina da Scrivere** is dedicated to the history of the machines, concentrating on Mitterhofer's prototypes and perhaps most importantly the layout of the QWERTY keyboard. At **Naturno**, the

Museo della
Macchina
da Scrivere
Piazza Chiesa 10,
t 0473 967 581; open
April–Oct Mon and Fri
3–6, Tues–Thurs 10–12
and 3–6, Sat 10–12;
Nov–Mar Tues 10–12

little church of **San Procolo** has some fresco fragments that go back to the 8th century, the oldest, in fact, in any German-speaking territory.

A little way west on the SS38, a narrow but very scenic road digresses north up a majestic gorge into the **Val di Senales/ Schnalstal**, on the western edge of the **Parco Naturale Gruppo di Tessa**, the largest park in the Alto Adige, a rocky wilderness of 10,000-ft peaks – an eyrie where the likes of Reinhold Messner, the Südtirolean master of mountain derring-do, feels perfectly at home; his 13th-century Castel Juvale, located at the entrance to the valley, houses his collection of findings from Tibet, masks from around the world, and more, including photographs from his many expeditions up the world's highest peaks. (He is the only man to have done so without oxygen and unaided.) Most unusual is the collection of yeti artefacts, acquired over many years as a result of exhaustive and exhausting research into the myths and legends of the yeti. (Shuttle buses go to the castle, where there is no parking, from the car park in Stava.) Up the valley, there's **Certosa/Karthaus**, a 14th-century charterhouse delightfully converted into a hamlet after it was suppressed in 1782, as well the little **Lago di Vernago**. Funivias from the top of the valley go over the mountains into Austria. In **Val di Senales/Schnalstal** the celebrated Ice Man's body was found, a remarkably well-preserved prehistoric corpse that was one of the great archaeological discoveries of recent years. Here at the Madonie de Senales/Unser Frau Archeoparc is a fascinating archaeological park recreating his environment and lifestyle.

Back on the main Adige road, the 13th-century cragtop Castello di Castelbello guards the entrance in **Laces/Latsch**, a tourist centre with the only all-year skiing in this area. It has two interesting churches: the first, Santa Trinità (1337), features some pretty frescoes, while the second, **Santo Stefano**, is on the way out of town. It is empty and stripped of all internal fittings but there are some wonderful frescoes on the bell tower of the Virgin Mary and cherubs.

Just southeast, **Tarres/Tarsch** is a picturesque medieval hamlet, while on the other end of Laces the confines of Stelvio National Park (see p.355) begin at Morter and incorporate the entire **Val di Martello**, a wooded valley south of the Val Venosta. It is worth making the trip up the valley, which opens out like a magician's palm to reveal a wide Alpine meadow. At the top you will find, somewhat strangely, a solitary parking ticket machine amidst the stunning splendour. (It's best to pay the price because the risk of getting clamped up here doesn't bear thinking about.) **Paradiso del Cevedale** (6,851ft) at the top of the valley has magnificent views over the stupendous amphitheatre formed by **Cevedale** (12,327ft)

Castel Juvale
t 0473 221 852; guided tours April–June and Sept–Nov daily 10–4; closed Wed; adm

Archeoparc
www.archeoparc.it; open April–early Nov Tues–Sun 10–6; daily mid-July–Aug; adm

Santa Trinità
key available from the house behind; follow signs

10 The Dolomites | The Upper Adige

and surrounding peaks. Back down on the main road **Silandro** has cobbled streets aplenty and some fine hotels. It makes a useful base from which to explore this beautiful valley.

In the upper valley, an hour's drive from Merano, **Sluderno/ Schludrens** is sheltered enough to support orchards and even vineyards. As with the whole valley, expect *schnitzel* not pasta as this valley wears its Austrian heritage proudly. It was long ruled by the Trapps, whose magnificent 13th–16th-century Castel Coira/Churburg has gloriously painted Renaissance loggias, frescoes dedicated to the greater glory of the Trapp family, and the largest private collection of armour in all Europe, with pieces going back to the 13th century. A great place for keeping children enthralled: they will stare in awe at the only complete horse armour in Europe; guided tours are available in English. The counts' tombs fill the 16th-century church of Santa Caterina; the **Museo della Val Venosta** features archaeology, art, and displays on the valley's pedlars.

Castel Coira/ Churburg
*www.churburg.com;
open late Mar–1 Nov
Tues–Sun 10–12 and
2–4.30; adm*

Museo della Val Venosta
*Via Merano 1, t 0473
161 5590; open
April–Oct Tues–Sun
10–12 and 3–6*

Nearby, **Glorenza/Glurns** was given its city status back in 1304, but was razed to the ground in 1499 by the Swiss. Rebuilt in 1555 by Jörg Kölderer, Emperor Maximilian's architect, it stands unchanged – nothing less than the smallest walled city in Europe. There are signs in English, all numbered as you follow a self-guided walk through the history of the town. The walk conveniently pauses outside one of the many cafés, where you can find refreshment in the form of home-made grappa and a local liqueur made from lemons. One item the Swiss missed in their rampage was the church of **S. Pancrazio**, on a hill just south of Glorenza, with a Last Judgement of 1496 frescoed on the campanile. Two kilometres from Glorenza, **Làudes/Laatsch** is one of the best-preserved medieval villages in the Alto Adige, with a striking and finely decorated church of 1408, its choir buttressed against a crag.

Both towns lie at the foot of the lush **Val Monastero/Münstertal** (SS41), 9km from Switzerland; on the way to the border, in the old frescoed village of **Tubre/Taufers**, many houses still retain their traditional exterior stairs. At the entrance to the village, the 13th-century church-hospice **S. Giovanni** was built over the ruins of a Carolingian church; the striking frescoes in the choir, painted around 1220, show the influence of Venice even here. The church in **Müstair**, just over the Swiss border, has what are generally acclaimed the finest Carolingian frescoes in all Europe.

San Benedetto
*t 0473 831 190;
open Mon–Sat
10–11.30am; adm*

Abbazia di Monte Maria
*t 0473 831 306; tours
July–Sept Mon–Fri 10, 11,
3, 4, Sat 10, 11; May, June,
Mon–Fri 10.45, 3, Sat
10.45; phone day before
to book; Nov–April by
appointment only*

Nearly as good, however, are those up the main valley in **Malles Venosta**, 'the town of five towers' in the chapel of **San Benedetto**, built under the direct patronage of Charlemagne himself. Just up in Burgusio, the beautiful 17th-century Benedictine **Abbazia di Monte Maria/Marienberg** forms a gleaming white crown of towers and gables in a woodland setting; the crypt from the original church has rare, excellently preserved 12th-century frescoes of Jerusalem.

On the way to Austria, the road passes the romantically ruined castle of **Lichtenburg** and the artificial **Lago di Resia**, with the church spire of a submerged village poking above its surface. The village (Veccio-Curon, first recorded in 1147) was submerged in 1950 after a long-running campaign by the locals to resist the plan. They held the last Feast of Santa Anna there in 1949, and in March 1950, 72 families (500 people) were moved from their homes. Now all that remains is the church tower (consecrated in 1838 and built in the classical style) and some haunting sculptures by a local artist, made out of pine and larch, and facing the water, like totem poles in North America.

Lago di Resia
t 0473 633 126; boat tours of the lake during high season at 3, 4 and 5pm, winter at 3pm, depending on the number of passengers

South of the Val Venosta: Stelvio National Park

The SS38 at Spondigna (just before Sluderno) is one of the main roads into **Stelvio National Park**, the largest in Italy, administered by the provinces of Sondrio, Trento and Bolzano, all of which have visitors' centres that can tell you where to find the marked trails, Alpine refuges, and the best flowers and wildlife, including chamois, marmots, eagles, and the ibex, reintroduced in 1968.

Stelvio National Park
Visitors' Centre: Via 4 Novembre 4, Malè, t 0463 903 046, www.stelviopark.it; open Mon–Fri 8–12, 2–5

As well as offering endless possibilities for climbers, the park also encompasses 50 lakes, 100 glaciers (a tenth of the park's 134,620 hectares is ice) and Europe's second-highest pass, the **Passo dello Stelvio**, open June through October. In the Alto Adige section of the park **Solda/Sulden**, set in a beautiful mountain-rimmed basin, has most of the hotels and sports facilities, and year-round *funivias* up to the Città di Milano refuge, offering grand views over Gran Zebrù (12,635ft).

Where to Stay and Eat in the Upper Adige

ⓘ Merano ›
Corso Libertà 45, t 0473 272 000, www.meraninfo.it

Merano ✉ 39021

As one might expect of an old-world spa like Merano, there are a good number of luxury hotels, but not much in the lower ranges.

****Castel Fragsburg**, Via Fragsburg 3, t 0473 244 071, *www.fragsburg.com* (€€€€€–€€€€). A small, family-owned ex-hunting lodge way up on a mountaintop with breathtaking views. Pamper yourself at the spa, or enjoy the private sunbathing cabins. Pure luxury!

⭐ Meisters Hotel Irma ›

****Meisters Hotel Irma**, Via Bella Vista 17, t 0473 212 000, *www.hotel-irma.it* (€€€€). Don't let the plain name fool you – the Meister family has owned this property for generations. Services include an extensive spa and a 'Sleep Doctor', who will quiz you about your nightly troubles before providing a remedy. Rooms range from traditional to *über*-chic.

****Castello Labers**, Via Labers 25, t 0473 234 484, *www.castellolabers.it* (€€€€€–€€€). Set among the vines above Merano, a castle-villa from the 1200s. Has a pool and views. *Open April–Nov.*

****Westend**, Via Speckbacher 9, t 0473 447 654, *www.westend.it* (€€€–€€). Another atmospheric choice, this one near the centre: 22 lovely rooms in a 19th-century villa, tucked back in a pleasant garden.

*Pension Tyrol, Via 30 Aprile 8, **t** 0473 449 719 (€€). A quiet hotel near the spa, in a big attractive garden, with free parking.

Sissi, Via Galilei 44, **t** 0473 231 062 (€€€). One of the best restaurants in town, up by the Castello Principesco, where the delicious food has a Piemontese touch. *Closed Mon and Feb.*

Laubenkeller, Via dei Portici 118, **t** 0473 237 706 (€€). Merano's restaurants are concentrated around this street: try this one for *typische Südtiroler* cooking. *Closed Thurs.*

(i) **Naturno >**
Via Municipio,
t 0473 666 077

Naturno ✉ 39025

***Hotel Lamm, Via Compaccio 16, **t** 0473 666 344, *www.hotel-lamm-naturns.it* (€€€€). You'll receive a warm welcome at this quiet village hotel, which is well situated for an assault on the Val Venosta (about half a kilometre out of town in the direction of Sliderno). The rooms are palatial, the service friendly and they make their own grappa on the premises. If you ask nicely they may give you a quick masterclass. They also have a restaurant which serves wholesome Austrian fare as well as classic Italian dishes.

Màlles Venosta/Mals im Vinschgau ✉ 39024

***Plavina, 3km out of the centre in Burgùsio, **t** 0473 831 223, *www. mohren-plavina.com* (€€€–€€). Occupying a building dating back to the 16th century, this hotel has typical rooms with mountain views, indoor pool and sauna. The restaurant, Moro, has been in the same family since 1665, serving seasonal dishes, *schlützkrapfen* (little ravioli) with melted butter, great roast potatoes and game in the autumn. *Closed Tues and Wed lunch, mid-April–mid-May and early Nov–Chrismas.*

Solda/Sulden ✉ 39029

***Eller, Via Principale 15, **t** 0473 613 021, *www.hoteleller.com* (€€€–€€). The oldest hotel in the valley, in business in 1865, so the family knows what they're about; rooms have been recently updated. *Open mid-Nov–April and July–mid-Sept.*

***Gampen, Via Principale 39, **t** 0473 613 023, *www.gampen.it* (€€€–€€). This cosy place is another of Solda's old timers, complete with knockout mountain views. *Open Nov–April and end June–mid-Sept.*

Friuli-Venezia Giulia

For many travellers this bit of the Big Boot, spilling over like a thick lumpy sock to the east, is terra incognita, with a jumbly name that may ring a bell only because it often turns up on the wine list in Italian restaurants. Trieste, at the far end of Italy, evokes cloudy images of pre- and post-war intrigue, a kind of Third Man on the Mediterranean. And in between Trieste and Venice the imagination fails.

Still, the region is a melting pot, Italian-style, and one that is becoming spicier all the time: the reopening of Central and Eastern Europe in the 1990s means that Friuli-Venezia Giulia is no longer Italy's dead end, but an important link to its future.

Corsica

Sardinia

11

Don't miss

⭐ Roman mosaics
Aquileia p.367

⭐ Secrets and charms
Udine p.383

⭐ Long sandy beaches
Grado p.369

⭐ Dark Age wonders
Cividale del Friuli p.386

⭐ Italy meets Mitteleurope
Trieste p.371

See map overleaf

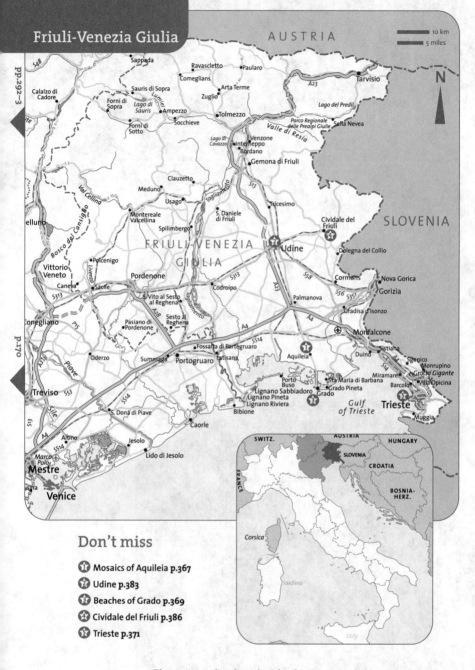

AUSTRIA

10 km
5 miles

N

SLOVENIA

Sappada
Ravascletto
Paularo
Comeglians
Calalzo di Cadore
Arta Terme
Tarvisio
Sauris di Sopra
Zuglio
Forni di Sopra
Lago di Sauris
Ampezzo
Tolmezzo
Lago del Predil
Lunìei
Forni di Sotto
Socchieve
Parco Regionale delle Prealpi Giulie
Sella Nevea
Valle di Resia
Lago di Cavazzo
Interneppo
Venzone
Bordano
Gemona di Friuli
Clauzetto
Meduno
Usago
S. Daniele di Friuli
Tricesimo
Cividale del Friuli
Montereale Valcellina
Spilimbergo
Dolegna del Collio
FRIULI-VENEZIA GIULIA
Udine
elluno
Val Cellina
Bosco del Cansiglio
Polcenigo
Pordenone
Cormans
Nova Gorica
Vittorio Veneto
Caneva
Sacile
Livenza
S. Vito al Sesto al Reghena
Codroipo
Gorizia
Palmanova
S58
S56
S351
Conegliano
Pasiano di Pordenone
Sesto al Reghena
Gradisca d'Isonzo
Oderzo
Summaga
Fossalta di Portogruaro
Latisana
Portogruaro
Monfalcone
Duino
Sistiana
Aquileia
Sgonico
Monrupino
Grotto Gigante
Miramare
Vila Opicina
Barcola
Treviso
Piave
Sile
Porto Buso
Sta Maria di Barbana
Grado Pineta
Grado
Trieste
Lignano Sabbiadoro
Lignano Pineta
Lignano Riviera
Gulf of Trieste
Muggia
S. Donà di Piave
Bibione
Caorle
Altino
Jesolo
Marco Polo
Lido di Jesolo
Mestre
Venice

Don't miss

⭐ Mosaics of Aquileia p.367
⭐ Udine p.383
⭐ Beaches of Grado p.369
⭐ Cividale del Friuli p.386
⭐ Trieste p.371

SWITZ.
AUSTRIA
HUNGARY
SLOVENIA
FRANCE
CROATIA
BOSNIA-HERZ.
Corsica
Sardinia
Sicily

The region is burdened with a history as messy as its name. In Roman days Aquileia was the most important city and became seat of the oldest patriarchate outside Rome. Its ecclesiastical and temporal authority was gradually usurped by Cividale del

Friuli, the Lombard capital in the Dark Ages, and then in the Middle Ages by Udine, before all was snatched away by the Venetians in the 14th century. Trieste was sometimes under the doges' thumb, sometimes Venice's bitter rival under the Counts of Gorizia or the Austrians.

Napoleon threw Friuli-Venezia Giulia in with his 'Kingdom of Illyria', a piece of real estate subsequently picked up by the Austro-Hungarian Empire until 1918, when Italy inherited it along with the easternmost bit of Venice's old *terra firma* empire – all of Istria except for Fiume (modern Rijeka), an error of omission that Gabriele D'Annunzio personally went over to rectify (*see* p.270).

If Italian nationalists were pleased, their Slavic counterparts were outraged. Although Istria was given a certain amount of autonomy in 1924, order was asserted only by brutal repression of the Slavic majority by Mussolini's government, especially once the Duce dictated that everyone had to speak Italian. When the Germans moved in on the scene in 1943 they gave the region a new name, Adriatische Küsterland, and in Trieste set up a concentration camp, the only one on Italian soil.

After the Second World War Istria was ceded to Yugoslavia, while Tito, whose partisans had helped to take Trieste from the Germans, angled for the big port city itself. The Allies forced him to leave, then occupied the city as a neutral free port until 1954, when it was readmitted into Italy. The region's troubles were hardly over: two disastrous earthquakes in 1976 killed a thousand people, levelled entire towns, and left 70,000 buildings in need of structural repair.

Weary of being marginal, Friuli-Venezia Giulia is now creating an identity of its own, although at times this seems like putting together pieces from several different jigsaw puzzles. The population in the east speaks Slovenian, while the Carnia and Julian Alps have a sizeable German minority. Trieste has large Jewish, Greek and Serb minorities, and in the middle, around Udine, you have the Friulians themselves, who speak a language similar to the Swiss Rhaeto-Romance.

Southern Friuli-Venezia Giulia: Along the Coast

From Venice to Lignano-Sabbiadoro

Altino and Caorle

The SS14 from Venice first passes Marco Polo airport and then **Altino**, the modern name of the Roman city of *Altinum*. Once renowned for its wealth and villas, it was sacked by Attila the Hun

Getting to and around Caorle and Lignano-Sabbiadoro

Trains from Venice along the coast run roughly every two hours (journey time to Trieste two hours). **Buses** are less frequent, though Caorle can most easily be reached by direct bus from Venice. An alternative is to take the train to S. Donà di Piave and the local bus to Caorle from there. For Lignano-Sabbiadoro, take the train to Latisana, linked by bus to the coast in about 30mins.

Museo Archeologico Nazionale
t 0422 829 008; open daily 9–7; adm

– the first of many hardships that led its inhabitants to give up and found a new city on the island of Torcello in the Venetian Lagoon. Indeed Attila was busy sacking many of the towns in this area. They took along with them whatever Attila and the Lombards didn't wreck, so that all that remains in the Museo Archeologico Nazionale are mosaics, items from tombs and odds and ends.

The route continues over the Piave near **San Donà di Piave**, a town that had to be completely rebuilt after the First World War; it was near here that Ernest Hemingway, an ambulance driver for the Red Cross, was wounded in 1918, an experience that became the germ of *A Farewell to Arms*. From San Donà you can make a detour to the brightly painted old fishermen's town and modern seaside resort of **Caorle**, originally Roman *Caprulae*, the port of Concordia Sagittaria. One of its landmarks is the church-lighthouse on its isthmus, and another is its cathedral, built in 1038, with a distinctive cylindrical campanile and a splendid Venetian *Pala d'Oro* (12th–14th centuries) on the altar. Wildfowl flock along the coast in the **Valle Grande** (a water valley, that is, on the inner lagoon), which preserves a relic of the primordial pine woods that once scented the shore from Grado to Ravenna. **Bibione**, to the east, is an even bigger resort, with a long strand of sand.

Portogruaro and Around

East of San Donà, the various *autostrade* and highways come together at **Portogruaro**, a seductive old town of porticoed streets, frescoed *palazzi* and sparkling canals, dreaming away under its palm trees and jauntily tilted 193ft campanile (leaning by more than three feet from the bell tower at the last check), built in the 12th century. The Duomo is a wallflower by Veneto standards, but the neighbouring 14th-century **Loggia Comunale** (now the Municipio) is one of the most striking civic buildings in the region, shaped like a mountain crested with fantail Ghibelline battlements, which lend it a curiously organic appearance. There is a small **palaeontology museum** in the town hall. Don't miss the well (1494) in the piazza, crowned with a pair of cranes (*gru*) that gave the town its name. In Via Seminario, the **Museo Nazionale Concordiese** is a church crowded with an assortment of bronzes and coins, some of which are quite stunning, among other finds excavated in **Concordia Sagittaria**, just south of Portogruaro. This was a glass- and arrow-(*sagitta*)- manufacturing Roman colony. Its

Museo Paleontologico
t 0421 277 340; open Mon–Fri 10–12.30 and 3–5.30

Museo Nazionale Concordiese
t 0421 72674; open daily 9–7

Romanesque cathedral standing next to the ruins of a basilica (389) conserves part of its pavement; adjacent stands a frescoed Byzantine baptistry of 1089. There is also a small museum in Via Roma, which is often the initial home of new archaeological finds. Local farmers leave Roman remains piled in the corners of the fields for the curators to pick up and classify, and new finds tend to appear weekly. If you have the time, ask to see the remains beneath the **Banca FriulAdria** on Via 1 Maggio. These date from the end of the 1st century BC to approximately the 2nd century AD. There are three paved rooms, one in mosaic and the other two tiled; the remains of a bath house are just about recognizable.

Museum
Via Roma,
t 0421 270 360; call for
opening hours

In **Summaga**, 3km west of Portogruaro, the Benedictine abbey of Santa Maria Maggiore was built around a 6th-century votive chapel. The walls are covered with a fascinating cycle of 12th- and 13th-century frescoes, all recently restored; in the votive chapel, don't miss the fighting griffins and lions, chivalrous deeds, and virtues and vices. More fond old things await in **Sesto al Règhena**, 9km north of Portogruaro, a quaint medieval village with a moat in the centre, originally part of the defences of Santa Maria in Silvis, an abbey of Lombard foundation that grew to become one of the most powerful in Friuli. The current Romanesque-Byzantine basilica dates from the 11th century and has both a vestibule (with 11th-century frescoes of *St Michael*, and later ones of the *Inferno* and *Paradiso*) and an atrium with three naves. Among the bas-reliefs is a beautiful 13th-century Annunciation, while the vast crypt contains an 8th-century Lombard-Byzantine sarcophagus of St Anastasia. Lastly, at **Fossalta di Portogruaro**, by the little church of Sant'Antonio in Vilanova, grows one of the oldest oak trees in Europe, 300 years old – when they signed the Magna Carta.

Santa Maria Maggiore
t 0421 205 126; call for
opening hours

Santa Maria in Silvis
t 0434 699 014;
open daily Oct–Mar
8–12 and 3–6

Lignano-Sabbiadoro

East of Concordia Sagittaria, **Latisana** was once an important port of the patriarchate, and has only one good reason to detain you: Paolo Veronese's *Baptism of Christ* (1567) in the Duomo. From Latisana, the SS354 branches off to the coast: you can follow the crowds south to the Laguna di Marano and the fastest-growing resort area on the Adriatic, **Lignano-Sabbiadoro**, the 'Austrian Riviera'. Set on the tip of the peninsula, with a lovely 9km sandy beach and scores of new hotels, Lignano-Sabbiadoro and its two adjacent resorts of **Lignano-Pineta** (the prettiest section, under the pinewoods) and smart **Lignano Riviera**, offer fun in the sun and Viennese sausages just like Mutter makes. Some of the smaller islands are dotted with *casoni*, steep thatched fishermen's cottages; some real, some recreated for visitors. Non-native birds seem to like Lignano too – of the 165 species that have been sighted in Italy, 141 have been seen in the Laguna di Marano.

Where to Stay and Eat in Caorle and Lignano-Sabbiadoro

In the beach resorts, high season prices run from mid-June to the end of August; book ahead, especially for the first three weeks of August. Expect the freshest fish, landed daily. In the evenings the docks are awash with squid ink: squid dishes feature heavily in local menus.

(i) Caorle >
Calle delle
Liburniche 16,
t 0421 81085,
www.caorleturismo.it

Caorle ✉ 30021

***Garden**, Piazza Belvedere, t 0421 210 036, www.hotelgardencaorle.com (€€€). Immersed in pines, right by the beach, with a pool, tennis and sauna; nearly all rooms have balconies. Open April–Sept.

***Diplomatic**, Via Strada Nuova 19, t 0421 81087, www.diplomatic.it (€€€). A comfortable hotel, set on its own little port. Featuring the area's best restaurant, **Duilio**, justifiably celebrated for its succulent seafood in the antipasti, with the pasta, and as the main course. A charming setting, a huge wine list and reasonably priced menus are added attractions. Closed Mon, Jan.

(i) Lignano-
Sabbiadoro >
Via Latisana 42,
t 0431 71821,
www.aptlignano.it

Lignano-Sabbiadoro ✉ 33054

****Miramare**, Via Aquileia 47/B, t 0431 71260, www.miramare.com (€€€). Built up in the last 25 years, Lignano-Sabbiadoro is a good place to look for self-catering bungalows as well as hotels, although none really stands out. For comfortable rooms try this place with parking and a garden, as well as its own beach. Open early April–Sept.

****Eurotel**, Calle Mendelssohn 13, t 0431 428 991 (€€€). A fashionable hotel in Lignano Riviera, enjoying perhaps the most beautiful setting in the area and offering lovely rooms, a heated pool and more. Open mid-May–mid-Sept.

****Medusa Splendid**, Raggio dello Scirocco 33, t 0431 422 211, www.hotel medusa.it (€€€). This slightly more intimate hotel also has a pool, excellent rooms and a garden. Open May–mid-Sept.

***Vittoria**, Lungomare Marin 28, t 0431 71221, www.hotel-vittoria.net (€€€). A fine older hotel, which has recently had a facelift. Open mid-May–Sept.

Al Bancut, Via Friuli 32, t 0431 71926 (€€€). In the centre of town, featuring fine grilled fish, traditionally prepared. Closed Wed, mid-Dec–mid Jan.

Bidin, Via Europa 1, t 0431 71988 (€€€). Good restaurants include this small but convivial place, with a separate menu degustazione for either fish or meat. Closed Wed.

Pordenone and its Province

The River Tagliamento divides Friuli in two: the fairly flat western part, de là da aghe (literally 'that side of the water'), has a strong Venetian identity and speaks a similar dialect.

Pordenone

Hemingway poked fun at it and, to be honest, there's not a lot more to say about Pordenone, provincial capital and manufacturer of Zanussi fridges and washing machines. Overlooking the Noncello, it does have a handsome if somewhat over-restored main street, Corso Vittorio Emanuele, lined with porticoes and palaces, some with frescoes from the 14th–17th centuries. The end of the Corso is closed off by the bijou **Palazzo Comunale**, where a Venetian clock tower topped by two bell-ringing Moors was superimposed on a graceful 13th-century building.

If Pordenone is known at all outside Italy, it's primarily due to the self-taught artist Giovanni Antonio de Sacchis (1483–1539), who adopted the town's name and whose works hang in the frescoed rooms of the **Museo Civico d'Arte**, housed opposite the Palazzo Comunale in the pretty 15th-century Palazzo Ricchieri. Other paintings – Pordenone's odd masterpiece, the *Madonna della Misericordia* (1515), his unfinished high altarpiece, and frescoes – decorate the salmon-pink **Duomo**. The 236ft campanile is the town landmark, a refined tower of Romanesque brickwork of 1347. The **Museo Civico delle Scienze** has a room of birds, archaeological finds and a reconstruction of a Renaissance scientific cabinet or *studiolo*.

The washing machine works are actually just outside Pordenone in **Porcìa**, which has a well-preserved *centro storico* with a castle and an unusual 15th-century campanile. If you have the time, there is the **Museo Diocesano d'Arte Sacra**, dedicated to sacred clothing and artefacts in the region from the 4th century to the present day (just about). There are some wonderful sculptures and illuminated texts, and it's free.

Museo Civico d'Arte
t 0434 392 312; open Tues–Sat 3–7, Sun 10–1 and 3–7; adm

Museo Civico delle Scienze
Via della Motta 22 open Tues–Sat 3–7, Sun 10–1 and 3–7; adm

Museo Diocesano d'Arte Sacra
Via Revedole 1, t 0434 524 340; open Tues and Sat 9–1, Wed–Fri 3–6.30

The Pedemontana and Valcellina

If you want to escape the crowds, you can't do better than the foothills or Pedemontana on the western frontier of Friuli. Hanging over the willowy banks of the Livenza, **Sacile**, the main town in these parts, is famous for its bird festival (the *Sagra dei Osei*), held on the last Sunday in August ever since 1351. Thousands of songbirds are assembled at dawn in the main piazza, and prizes are awarded to the birds and the person who can best imitate their songs. Sacile was the 'Garden of the *Serenissima*' and, like many well-watered towns of the *terra firma*, has that dreamy Venetian air to it. There are several attractive *palazzi* and a 15th-century Lombard-style **Duomo**, restored after the 1976 quake; it has modern frescoes, and paintings by Francesco Bassano and Palma il Giovane in the sacristy.

Just north of Sacile, small medieval **Caneva** huddles under the ruins of an 11th-century castle, although the castle chapel of **Santa Lucia** preserves charming frescoes. For fans of cycling, inside the Municipio you can find the **Museo del Ciclismo** dedicated to Toni Pessot and containing bicycles and team clothing from his long and illustrious career. Another 10km north, **Polcenigo** on the Livenza has a Venetian core. There's a NATO air base just east, near the thousand-year-old **Castel d'Aviano**, partly rebuilt by the Venetians in 1432. Just outside the town walls, the 13th-century cemetery church of **Santa Giuliana** has Venetian-Byzantine frescoes; on the other side of Aviano near the train tracks, **San**

Museo del Ciclismo
t 0434 797 411; open Mon–Fri 2–6

Gregorio has a fetching 15th-century fresco cycle by Gianfrancesco da Tolmezzo.

From Aviano it's only 14km up to the forest known as the Bosco del Cansiglio (*see* p.287) and Monte Cavallo (7,380ft), where the up-and-coming ski resort at **Piancavallo** recently hosted the skiing world cup and has wide views over the plain below. Alternatively, if you've found the other Dolomites too busy, continue north into the Valcellina and the **Parco Naturale della Dolomite Friulina**. After Montereale Valcellina, the road passes through a steep, almost claustrophobic **Forra del Cellina**, like one of the valleys in Dante's *Inferno*, before reaching Lago di Barcis and the little mountain resorts of **Claut** and **Cimolais**. Don't miss the stupendous 700ft monolithic pinnacle called the **Campanile** in the Val Montanaia.

The largest town in the region, **Maniago**, with its enormous market square, has made daggers for the Venetian army and knives and cutlery in general since the 14th century. One of the town's 250 firms specializes in antique armour, in great demand in Hollywood; the replicas are so accurate that they have to stamp each piece to keep it from being sold off to museums.

Along the River Tagliamento

East of Pordenone and not far from the wide bed of the Tagliamento, the handsome market town of **San Vito** was the birthplace of Fra Paolo Sarpi. It still has three tower houses, a porticoed Piazza del Popolo and a **Duomo** with a number of good Renaissance paintings, but the best art is in the former church of **S. Maria dei Battuti** – a cycle of 16th-century frescoes by Pompeo Amalteo, a painter from Treviso of whom Vasari made much in his *Lives of the Artists*. Just over the big river in **Codroipo**, the Villa Manin (1738) is the biggest villa in all Venetia, the swan song – or swan blast, rather – of Venice's *dolce vita*. When owner Ludovico Manin was elected Doge in Venice, his chief rival declared, 'A Friulian as Doge! The republic is dead.' The prediction was soon proved correct, and to add insult to injury, Napoleon parked himself at this ranch as a guest, if not a welcome one, in 1797. A painting by David hangs in the room he slept in; also to see are rooms of frescoed fluff, an elegant horseshoe exedra (a secular version of Bernini's colonnade at St Peter's), the armoury, map salon, a museum of carriages, a handsome park (a great place for a picnic) and a contemporary art centre. From here it's 20km to Udine.

Villa Manin
t 0432 906 509,
www.villamanin
contemporanea.it;
open summer Tues–Sun
10–7, winter Tues–Fri
9–12.30 and 2.30–6,
Sat–Sun 10–6;
closed Oct and Mar

If you're not in a hurry, however, there's more to see along the Tagliamento. North of San Vito, **San Giorgio della Richinvelda** has more fine frescoes by Gianfrancesco da Tolmezzo (1496) in the parish church at Provesano. Further north, medieval **Spilimbergo** is a town of discreet charm and more than its share of churches – the best of these, the Gothic cathedral, has a Romanesque portal and paintings by Pordenone. On the edge of town, the pretty 12th-century 'painted' **castle** has exterior frescoes, while in the centre there's a mosaic school, founded in 1922 to renew the great art of Aquileia and Ravenna; graduates have worked as far away as Japan. Under the porticoes of the loggia is the old *maccia*, a length measurement used to ensure that no one was being ripped off in their dealings with the local traders. Even if you don't need anything from the tourist office, pay it a visit as it is in the old **dungeon** of the castle. They use one of the cells for storage.

Scuola Mosaicisti del Friuli
*t 0427 2077,
www.scuolamosaicisti
friuli.it; open July–Aug
Mon–Fri 8–12,
Sept–June 1–3;
reservations only*

Near Clauzetto, the Grotte Verdi di Pradis is uncannily green, thanks to the sun filtering through the limestone – uncanny enough to be made into a church, the 'National Temple of Speleology'. Walkways follow the torrent Cosa that sculpted it up a high narrow gorge. In **Usago** a megalithic structure of cyclopean stones called the Cjadin is attributed to the Palaeoveneti; in nearby **Meduno** a monolithic altar has a primitive carving of a bull.

Grotte Verdi di Pradis
*open daily July–Aug
11–12.30 and 3–6; sunny
Sundays only other
months; call t 0427
80323 to check
conditions; adm*

Surrounded by fields of maize and *prosciutterie*, the most famous town in these parts is **San Daniele del Friuli**, the 'Siena of Friuli', an ochre-tinted market town east of the Tagliamento, famous for its sweet-cured hams. If you find yourself approaching the town at 10pm, the castle bells should be ringing. These were used to tell pilgrims still out on the road that a town was nearby. Don't miss the recently restored frescoes by Pellegrino di San Daniele in the church of **Sant'Antonio Abate**: his masterpiece, painted between 1498 and 1522, and the finest Renaissance cycle in all Friuli. Pellegrino's real name was Martino da Udine, but he spent so much time in San Daniele that he became known as the town's pilgrim. To the right of the Duomo, with its entrance designed by Palladio, the Biblioteca Guarneriana was founded by a canon of Aquileia, Guarnerio d'Artegna (*d.* 1467) and has lovely medieval manuscripts in a historic setting. It's the oldest library in Friuli, established in 1466. But culture is only a sideline in ham-ville, especially in August during the *Aria di Festa*, when the town parties, producing hundreds of hams and bottles of wine.

Biblioteca Guarneriana
*Via Roma 1, t 0432 957
930; open Tues and Fri
9–12 and 3–6*

Where to Stay and Eat in Pordenone and its Province

ⓘ Pordenone >
*Corso V. Emanuele II
38, t 0434 21912,
www.comune.
pordenone.it*

Pordenone ✉ 33170

****Villa Ottoboni**, Piazzetta Ottoboni 2, t 0434 21967, *www.geturhotels.com* (€€€). This elegant hotel is right near the centre and offers fully furnished rooms; the restaurant dates from the late 15th century.

****Park**, Via Mazzini 43, t 0434 27901, *www.bestwestern.it* (€€€). For modern, comfortable rooms and a good, central choice.

****Antica Trattoria La Primula**, Via San Rocco 47, t 0434 91005 (€€€). Some 9km north of Pordenone, at San Quirino, this hotel has for six generations served up the best food (€€€) in the province, superb, classic and simply prepared, from the *antipasti* through the fresh seafood to the elegant desserts, served in the simple but elegant dining room. It has 7 rooms in case you over-indulge (though you will need to book).

Gildo, Viale Marconi 17, in Porcia, 4km west, t 0434 921 212 (€€€). Head out to this imposing Venetian palace in a large park. The menu is equally divided between meat and fish dishes; prices are considerably lower at lunch. *Closed Sun eve, Mon, Aug.*

Osteria Alle Nazioni (€€€). Next to the Antica Trattoria hotel (*see* above) and run by the same folks, this has sensibly priced food. *Closed Sun eve, Mon, part of Jan and Aug.*

Da Zelina, Piazza San Marco, t 0434 27290 (€€). Set in an early Renaissance palace, and serving succulent meat dishes and pizzas in the evening. *Closed Sat lunch, Mon, part of Aug.*

Al Gallo, Via San Marco 10, t 0434 520 996 (€€). Right in the centre of town – the traditional meeting point for locals. Specialities include game fowl and home-made pasta alongside a good wine list. *Closed Sat, Tues lunch.*

(i) **Spilimbergo** >
Piazza Castello,
t 0427 2274

Spilimbergo ✉ 33097

**Michielini, Viale Barbacane 3, t 0427 50450, *michielini@libero.it* (€). An old family-run hotel in the centre of town, with restaurant.

La Torre, Piazza Castello 8, t 0427 50555 (€€€). Alternatively, dine in this castle on the likes of ravioli filled with pumpkin in mushroom sauce and strudels. Anyone fond of wine will have a field day with the selection in its cellar. *Closed Sun eve and Mon.*

Enoteca La Torre, Via di Mezzo 2, t 0427 2998, (€). If you're looking for something lighter try this place, located in the castle gatehouse. It has

a wonderful cellar of Friulian wines and of course San Daniele ham. Staff are friendly and helpful and more than happy to guide you through the Friulian vineyards. *Open 11–2.30 and 6–12, later at weekends; closed Mon.*

Osteria Al Bachero, Via Pilacorte 5, t 0427 2317 (€). The authentic taste of Friulian dining. Try the *baccalà e trippe con polenta* (salted cod and tripe with polenta) or any number of local dishes, and dine around an open fire with simple wooden furniture. They have one menu in English but you won't have to wait for it. *Closed Sun.*

San Daniele del Friuli ✉ 33038

***Alla Torre, Via del Lago 1, t 0432 954 562, *www.hotelallatorre.com* (€€). Fairly new and nice, occupying an old building in the historic centre, with a good buffet breakfast.

Antico Caffè Toran, Via Umberto 1, t 0432 957 544, *www.anticocaffe toran.it* (€). Among the *prosciutterie*, this one has simple meals as well as tasty nibbles. *Closed Mon.*

Pasiano di Pordenone ✉ 33087

****Villa Luppis, Via Martino 34, t 0434 626 969, *www.villaluppis.it* (€€€€). Sixteen kilometres west of Pordenone, set off in a five-hectare park. A Camaldolesi monastery in the Middle Ages, before it became a patrician's villa and finally one of the best hotels in Friuli: 21 rooms furnished with Louis XVI antiques. It's best to book well in advance, especially in season. The restaurant is equally prestigious; try pasta with scampi and courgette flowers. The hotel also runs a shuttle bus to Venice, 40mins away.

Palmanova, Aquileia and Grado

In a beeline from north to south, you have a remarkable planned military town, a superb Roman site, and the only seaside resort in the Adriatic facing entirely south.

Palmanova

In the Renaissance, despite all its theories on planning, only a handful of entirely new towns were ever constructed. One that has survived, Palmanova, was built in 1593 by the Venetians as their

Getting to and around Palmanova, Aquileia and Grado

For Aquileia and Grado, take the **train** to Cervignano del Friuli and then a **bus**, or take a direct bus from Trieste. There is a frequent bus from Trieste aiport to Grado via Aquileia and Cervignano del Friuli train station. Buses also link Palmanova with Aquileia and Grado.

Museo Storico
Borgo Udine 4, t 0432 929 106; open June–Sept Thurs–Tues 9.30–12.30 and 4–6, Sun 9.30–12.30; Oct–May 9.30–12.30; adm

eastern bulwark against the Austrians and Turks and populated by 'volunteers'. Perhaps because it was never actually needed for anything, Palmanova remains intact, a perfect example of 16th-century 'ideal' radial military planning and a geometrical *tour de force*: the star formed by its walls has nine points, while the large, eerie central piazza, which originally contained the arsenal, is a perfect hexagon. Even though most of the walls and moat are now overgrown, their stone softly moulded into serpentine hills and gullies, they are still defended by young conscripts. At the Museo Storico, ask about the July torchlight tour of the walls.

Aquileia

⭐ Aquileia

...the greatest city in the West
Emperor Justinian (6th century)

If Palmanova is unique in its plan, Aquileia is unique in that it was the only great Roman city in Italy to die on the vine; all the others not buried in volcanic mud have evolved into towns or cities. But Aquileia, once the proud capital of the *X Legio Venetia et Histria*, has dwindled from 200,000 to 3,500 inhabitants, who no longer receive emperors but tend to the vineyards and tourists who flock to see the most important archaeological site in Northern Italy.

Founded as a Roman colony in 181 BC, Aquileia was renamed when eagles flew over the town while plans were being laid for Augustus' German campaign. They proved to be a good augury. Augustus himself was in and out of Aquileia and received Herod the Great here. Christianity found an early foothold in the city; the Patriarchate of Aquileia was created in 313, the very same year that Constantine the Great issued the Edict of Milan, and its patriarch was given jurisdiction that extended to the Ukraine. It didn't last; after Aquileia was sacked by Attila (452) and the Lombards (568), it lost most of its territory and the patriarch moved to a safer home in Grado, an island on the outer port of Aquileia. When Aquileia wanted the title back in the 7th century Grado refused to surrender it, and for 400 years rival patriarchs sat in Grado and in Cividale del Friuli, the Lombard capital. When they were reconciled in 1019, Aquileia's great basilica was remodelled; in 1077 the Patriarch received an added boost from Emperor Henry IV, who donated all the lands from Cadore to Istria to the Patriarchate. For Aquileia itself, though, it was the beginning of the end. Its port on the Natissa silted up, malaria chased out the population, and the patriarchate moved to Cividale, and then Udine.

The Basilica

The Basilica
t 0431 919 719; open
winter 9–1 and 2–5,
summer 9–7

Aquileia's magnificent **basilica** and its lofty campanile are a landmark on the Friulian plain for miles around. It was founded and built in 313 by the first Patriarch, Theodore, but wrecked by Attila in 452; rebuilt in the same shape, it was given a Romanesque facelift by Patriarch Poppone (1020–31) and took its final form under the Venetians. One of the basilica's unique features is right outside the entrance – a loggia leads from the façade to the 9th-century 'Pagan Basilica', a kind of waiting room adjacent to the octagonal baptistry, where the pagan taint would be washed away.

When Poppone remodelled the basilica he thought Theodore's floor was a mite old-fashioned and covered it up, nicely preserving it for its rediscovery in 1909. At 837 square yards, this is nothing less than the largest **Palaeo-Christian mosaic** in the west, a vivid and often whimsical carpet of portraits, animals and geometric patterns happily mingling with Christian and pagan scenes and dominated by story of *Jonah and the Whale* (upper) and the *Good Shepherd* (bottom right). On the right, the Cappella di Sant'Ambrogio contains the tombs of four patriarchs and a polyptych by Pellegrino da San Daniele (1503); the last chapel to the right of the altar has some of the Cathedral's oldest bits, 9th-century Lombard *plutei* (reliefs) and detached 4th-century frescoes. Frescoes from 1031 survive in the apse, showing Patriarch Poppone dedicating the basilica, accompanied by Emperor Conrad II and Gisela of Swabia. The tribune (1491) in between the altar steps is by the Tyrolean Bernardino da Bissone.

Set next to the left wall of the nave, the 11th-century white marble Santo Sepolcro is a reproduction of the Holy Sepulchre in Jerusalem. It marks the entrance to the so-called **Cripta degli Scavi** (the excavations carried out in 1917–20 around the bell tower) containing mosaics from Roman times to the 8th century. The crypt proper under the altar is adorned with colourful 12th-century Byzantine-style frescoes. The new **Museo del Patriarcato** opposite the basilica contains fancy medieval reliquaries and other works from the basilica: a *Madonna del Rosario* by Giovanni Antonio Guardi and bas-reliefs of *Christ with St Thomas of Canterbury*, carved only a few years after his martyrdom, showing just how fast news of church politics travelled in the 1170s.

Museo del
Patriarcato
open only for
exhibitions

The Museo Archeologico

Museo
Archeologico
Open Tues–Sun
8.30–7.30, Mon
8.30–2; adm

On the same road, but down to the left, a villa houses artefacts from pre-Christian Aquileia (ring the bell to enter). There's a fine set of highly individualized Republican portrait busts; unlike the Greeks, who idealized themselves in marble (or perhaps were just better looking), the Romans insisted that all their warts, cauliflower ears and crumpled Roman noses be preserved for posterity. Tiberius, Augustus (young and old) and Trajan are among the celebrities. Among the bas-reliefs, there's a charming one of a smith with his tools; also amber and gold ornaments, glass, an enormous collection of coins, one of only two intact Roman chandeliers in the world (the other's in Alexandria) as well as a thousand and one household items that breathe life into ancient Aquileia. There's evidence of the Aquileians' lighter side: there are flies made of gold, and a tiny bronze figurine of a springing cat.

The Excavations

A circular walk, beginning on the Via Sacra behind the basilica, takes in what remains of the ancient city; an unfortunate proximity to a quarrying magpie called Venice has shorn them of most of their grandeur. The Via Sacra passes **Roman houses** and **palaeo-Christian oratories** (some with mosaics intact), then continues up through the considerable ruins of the **harbour**, marked by cypresses: in the 1st century AD this was a bustling commercial port.

Continue straight and bear right after the crossroads on modern Via Gemina to the Palaeo-Christian Museum, with reliefs and sarcophagi, and a walkway over the undulating mossy mosaics of a huge 4th-century basilica; ancient Aquileia required not one but two enormous churches. Return by way of Via Gemina to Via Giulia Augusta (the main Cervignano–Grado road). To the right you can see the old Roman road and, to the left, the **Forum** with its re-erected columns. Just off a fork to the right, the **Grand Mausoleum** (1st century AD) was brought here from the suburbs. The meagre ruins of the amphitheatre, the baths and the **Sepolcreto** (five Roman family tombs) are on Via XXIV Maggio and Via Acidino, north of the village's central Piazza Garibaldi.

Palaeo-Christian
Museum
open daily 8.30–1.45

Grado: Up to Your Neck in Sand

🔞 Grado

Aquileia had an inner port and an outer port, or *grado*, on the island that still bears its name. Today Grado is linked to the mainland by a causeway, and reigns as the queen of its own little lagoon. Hotels and other seaside amenities engulf the narrow alleys or *calli* of the old town, the Castrum Gradense and the **Duomo** (Basilica of Sant'Eufemia), seat of the 6th-century Patriarch of Nova Aquileia, as he fashioned himself. Inside, Corinthian capitals sit atop exotic marble pillars, and the 11th-century domed pulpit is carved with four Evangelists; the painted baldachin could easily be the tent of the sheikh of Araby. The mosaic floor dates from the 6th century, although its scriptural adages and geometrical patterns seem austere after the garden of delights in Aquileia's basilica; note the scene in front of the altar, a map of

Castrum Gradense and its islands. In the back glows a silver *pala* donated by the Venetians in 1372. An alley of sarcophagi separates Sant'Eufemia from its octagonal 5th-century baptistry, with a full-immersion font, and another, smaller basilica, the 5th-century **Santa Maria delle Grazie** with its original altar screeens and mini-theatre for the clergy behind the altar – a common feature of early Byzantine basilicas.

Grado owes its origin as a beach resort to medicine. Keen to bring tubercular children to the seaside, doctors sought a freshwater spring on the peninsula. In 1892 they duly discovered one, and Emperor Franz Josef at once included Grado on his official list of curative resorts in the Habsburg empire. A new town grew up to accommodate the nobility, who have since been replaced by athletes, models and business people all undergoing specific treatments, including the 'sand cure' – being buried up to one's neck in warm sand full of benevolent mineral salts and micro-organisms. If you are keen to try out some of the cures, the **Thermal Bath and Theraputic Department** would be more than happy to help.

Thermal Bath and Theraputic Department
t 0431 889 309

If the free beaches are too crowded, walk east to **Pineta**, or catch the boat to Barbana, an island in the lagoon with a resident Franciscan community; on the first Sunday in July, for the *Perdon de Barbana*, a colourful procession of boats sails to the monastery. There are also daily sea connections in summer to Trieste and the Istrian coast and to the fishing village of **Porto Buso**. Grado's **lagoon** is a major bird-watching area, and now, with the recent introduction of white horses from the Camargue in Provence, you can see them from the saddle (*ask in the Grado tourist office, see below, for details*).

Barbana
frequent daily boats in summer; Nov–May weekends only

Where to Stay and Eat in Palmanova, Aquileia and Grado

ⓘ **Aquileia** ›
Piazza Capitolo, t 0431 919 491; closed Dec–Mar

ⓘ **Grado** ››
Viale Dante Alighieri 72, t 0431 877 111, www.gradoturismo.info

Aquileia ✉ 33051
***Patriarchi**, Via Giulia Augusta 12, t 0431 919 595, www.hotelpatriarchi.it (€€€). Overlooking the Roman excavations; air conditioned.

*Aquila Nera, Piazza Garibaldi 5, t 0431 91045, www.hotelaquilanera.com (€). An old hotel in the quiet main square, offering small rooms. The restaurant is traditional and full of warmth, serving a range of recommendable gnocchi and basic meat dishes.

La Colombara, Via S. Zilli 34, t 0431 91513, www.lacolombara.it (€€). Set on

the Trieste road, and specializing in fine seafood prepared in various ways, accompanied by good wines from the Collio. *Closed Mon, Jan.*

Grado ✉ 34073
****Savoy**, Via Carducci 33, t 0431 897 111, www.hotelsavoy-grado.it (€€€€). Has a pool, garden, parking and comfortable rooms. On the resort side of town, but not actually on the sea. *Open June–Oct.*

***Antica Villa Bernt**, Via Colombo 5, t 0431 82516, www.hotelbernt.it (€€€). A refurbished villa from the 1920s with 22 lovely rooms, all with bath, air-conditioning and TV. *Open April–Oct.*

***Cristina**, Viale Martiri della Libertà 11, t 0431 876 448, www.hotelcristina grado.com (€€). A little way in from the beach but in a shady garden. *Open May–Oct.*

Albergo Ambriabella, Riva Slataper 2, t 0431 81479, *www.hotelambriabella.it* (€€). This hotel faces the Isola della Schiusa and has some welcome personal touches.

Mensa, Casa del Pellegrino, at Barbana, t 0431 80453 (€). For tranquillity, you won't do much better than this simple pilgrims' hostel, managed by friars. Book in advance.

All'Androna, Calle Porta Piccola 4, t 0431 80950, *www.androna.it* (€€€). In the winding streets around the cathedral, with a daily-changing menu of fish, and home-made bread and pasta. *Closed Tues, Jan and Feb.*

De Toni, Piazza Duca D'Aosta 37, t 0431 80104, *www.trattoriadetoni.it* (€€). Right by the old quarter; this restaurant offers fresh fish prepared in a variety of local styles, and a long wine list. *Closed Wed, Dec and Jan.*

Trieste

 Trieste

Once the main seaport of the Austro-Hungarian Empire, two world wars left Trieste a woebegone widow of the Adriatic, a grandiose neoclassical city shorn of its *raison d'être*. With the fall of the Berlin Wall, all this has changed: Trieste is now a very merry widow, courted across Central Europe and quickly regaining its old cosmopolitan lustre, something that the inhabitants accept as simply another twist in a knotted history. The streets and shops bubble with a babel of Slovene, Serbo-Croat, German, Hungarian and Czech, and cars bearing an exotic bouquet of numberplates clog up the straight, central European 19th-century streets. Trade is picking up, too: not from tourists who once passed through on their way to points east, but from Slovenes and Hungarians flashing new-found wealth, and Austrian and Czech businessmen seeking new Mediterranean markets.

Don't come to Trieste for art or beautiful buildings: its profits have been firmly invested in banks, shipping lines and stocks. Instead, come to sense the energy and excitement of a city shaking off decades of nostalgic sloth, and picking up from where it left off, in the vibrant days just before the First World War.

History

Trieste's first visitors were apparently Jason and the Argonauts, who came this way on their journey home from the Danube. The Celtic port of *Tergeste* (from *terg*, or market) traded with the Phoenicians. The annexation of the city and its Istrian inhabitants by the Romans was violent, unlike the peaceful acquisition of the Veneto, but by the time of Augustus, Tergeste was an important imperial port. From the 9th to the 13th centuries the city maintained a precarious independence under its bishop-princes, often quarrelling with Venice (and losing). After Venice's victory at Chioggia in 1382, Trieste was compelled to sign a treaty of allegiance with Leopold of Austria to keep from being submerged by the *Serenissima*. Rivalry with Venice only increased, especially in

Getting to Trieste

By Air

Trieste's **airport**, served by daily flights from Rome and Milan, and daily flights from London on Ryanair, is at Ronchi dei Legionari, t 0481 773 224, 30km to the north near Monfalcone; the airport bus departs from the main bus station in Piazzale Libertà. For information, call t 0481 593 511, *www.aptgorizia.it*. Most of Trieste's **car hire** agencies are at the airport, with some running an office in Piazza Libertà as well: Avis, airport, t 0481 777 085, or Stazione Marittima, t 040 300 820; Hertz, airport, t 0481 777 025, or Stazione Marittima, t 040 322 0098; Europcar, airport, t 0481 778 920, or Stazione Marittima, t 040 322 0820; Maggiore, railway station, t 040 421 323.

By Sea

There are daily **ferries** to and from Muggia, Grado and Monfalcone with Delfino Verde, t 335 548 1327. For up-to-date information on other routes, call t 040 303 540. Livenza, t 340 762 8893, and Mamàca Dreams, t 333 331 0503, serve various destinations for tour groups only.

By Rail

There are frequent **trains** from Venice (2hrs), Gorizia (50mins) and Udine (1hr 20mins), as well as to Austria, Slovenia and other destinations in Eastern Europe, to the Stazione Centrale on Piazza della Libertà 8.

By Long-distance Bus

The main **bus station** is in front of the Stazione Centrale, in Piazza della Libertà, t 040 425 020, *www.triestetrasporti.it*. It has bus services from Venice, Treviso, Padua, Belluno, Trento, and Cortina and Sappada in the Dolomites; long-distance coaches from Milan, Mantua and Genoa; international services from Ljubljana, Rijeka, Zagreb, Athens, Istria and more.

Getting around Trieste

Trieste's long, straight Habsburger streets mean that finding one's way around **on foot** is relatively simple, although use the crossings carefully, as these streets can make even Rome appear pedestrian. City **buses** are frequent, and most routes run from or by the central bus station; for information, t 800 01 6675, *www.triestetrasporti.it*. A **funicular railway** (*tranvia*) runs every 22mins from Piazza Oberdan to Villa Opicina above the city.

Cars have been banished from the city centre and **parking** can be diabolical; it's best to just surrender your *macchina* to one of the garages or car parks (near Piazza della Libertà and Piazza Unità d'Italia) and get it over with. Radio taxi, t 040 307 730.

---

the salt trade, and in the mid-5th century it was the personal intervention of Pope Pius II which kept the Venetians from wiping the city out altogether.

Austria, always longing for a port, appeared on the scene in 1552 and, after a good deal of political instability, Charles VI granted it free port status in 1719. This initiated a golden age for Trieste: the Austrian emperors poured money into the city, in particular Maria Theresa, who gave it a new neoclassical core. Trieste returned to Austrian rule after the fall of Napoleon in 1815, although minus free-port status. The subsequent fall in income, aggravated by heavy-handed policies from Vienna, turned the majority Italian population into ardent Irredentists ('the Unredeemed'), turbulently desiring union with Italy. The Irredentists had some interesting company. Sir Richard Burton, translator of the *Arabian Nights*, was British consul here from 1870 until his death in 1890. James Joyce, after eloping with Nora Barnacle, taught English in Trieste from 1904 to 1915 and in 1919–20; he wrote *Dubliners* and *Portrait of the Artist as a Young Man* here. Joyce befriended and translated Ettore Schmitz, a member of the city's Jewish community, better known by his *nom-de-plume* Italo Svevo, 'the Italian Swabian'. And unknown to either of them, Rainer Maria Rilke was staying and working nearby at Duino.

Italian troops were welcomed in 1918, but Italian government all too soon proved to be another disappointment for Trieste. Mussolini tried to force the heterogeneous population into a cultural strait-jacket, before Hitler's Nazis went a step further, imprisoning and executing Jews and Slavs in the Risiera death camp. Another disaster came in the aftermath of the war, when Trieste found itself permanently divorced from its Istrian hinterland. Tito's Yugoslavia only gave up its last claims to Trieste itself in 1954, and the border question was not settled finally until 1975. In the mid-1960s, the city, seeking a new identity, decided to create a new role for itself as a scientific and research centre, which has paid off: Trieste now has an important institute of theoretical physics at Miramare (run by Nobel prize winner Abdus Salem) as well as departments of genetic engineering, experimental geophysics and marine biology.

Along the Port to Piazza dell'Unità d'Italia

If you only have an hour or two at Trieste's train or bus station you can take Corso Cavour into the **Borgo Teresiano**, formerly the city saltpans and now Trieste's business hub, thanks to Maria Theresa's planners, who laid out the streets with a pair of rulers, and planted them with neoclassical architecture. The Corso passes over the **Canale Grande**, an inlet with moorings for small craft; the adjacent Piazza Ponterosso is the site of the daily market. At the head of the canal stands the neo-Palladian church of **Sant'Antonio** complete with a temple front, and near it, the blue-domed Serbian Orthodox **Santo Spiridone**, an exotic orchid in this regimented Habsburg garden. Just over the canal, overlooking the sea on Riva Tre Novembre, Trieste's oldest coffee house, **Caffè Tommaseo** (1830), has recently been restored, complete with its *belle époque* fittings.

Next along the waterfront opens Trieste's whale of a heart, **Piazza dell'Unità d'Italia**, framed by weighty neoclassical piles: the hefty **Palazzo del Comune**, topped by two Moors who ring the bell over the clock, the **Palazzo del Governo** glowing in its bright skin of mosaics, and the huge, brooding palace of Lloyd Triestino, now the seat of Friuli-Venezia Giulia's regional government. In the summer flowers brighten the piazza, while in winter purple cabbages hold pride of place, unless they are cowering beneath the *bora*, the northeast wind that whips over the Carso. The memorably graceless **Fountain of the Four Continents** was built in the 1750s to commemorate Trieste's new waterworks. A good antidote would be a drink at the piazza's **Caffè degli Specchi** (1839), once a famous Irredentist meeting place.

Trieste keeps its art collections a few blocks south of Piazza Unità d'Italia, around Piazza Venezia. The recently remodelled Museo Revoltella was founded by Baron Pasquale Revoltella, one of the financiers of the Suez Canal (which was also a big boon to Trieste's port). Full of original furnishings, it contains 18th- and 19th-century paintings by Triestine artists that evoke the city's golden days, as well as modern works by Morandi, De Chirico and Canova. From July to September the gallery stays late into the evening when concerts are held.

Up a block from the sea, on Largo Papa Giovanni XXIII and occupying an 18th-century villa, the Museo Sartorio offers another glimpse into Triestine bourgeois life in the 19th century, along with a mix of art, including a triptych by Paolo Veneziano, a collection of drawings by Giambattista Tiepolo, and Italian ceramics. It also houses a wonderful collection of miniatures in surprising poses.

Museo Revoltella
Via Diaz 27, t 040 675 4350, www.museo revoltella.it; open Sept–mid-July Wed– Mon 9–1.30 and 4–7, Sun 10–1 and 3–7; mid-July–Aug Thurs and Sat 9–1.30 and 4–11, Sun 9–2; adm; for concerts call in advance

Museo Sartorio
t 040 301 479 or 040 310 500; closed at time of writing

Up the Capitoline Hill

Catch bus no.24 from the station or Piazza dell'Unità to ascend Trieste's very own Capitoline Hill, the nucleus of the Roman and medieval city. In the fifth century the Triestini raised the first of two basilicas here to their patron San Giusto, a martyr drowned during the persecution of Diocletian. An adjacent basilica was built in the 11th century, linked to the earlier church 300 years later and given an enormous campanile – hence the five asymmetrical naves of the Basilica Cattedrale of San Giusto. The doorway, under a splendid Gothic rose window, is framed by the fragments of a Roman sarcophagus: six funerary busts gaze solemnly ahead like a corporate board of directors, while, embedded in the adjacent squat campanile, a Roman frieze resembles a fashion plate for armour. The interior has some beautiful mosaics, especially the early 13th-century *Christ with SS Giusto and Servulus*, and the 11th-century gold-ground *Madonna with Archangels and Saints*, made by Venetian artists and similar to the Virgin in Torcello, but softer in mood. The oldest frescoes are 12th century, while the newest were added in 1932. Buried on the right is Don Carlos, the Great Pretender of Spain's Carlist Wars, who died in Trieste in 1855.

San Giusto
t 040 309 666; open Mon–Sat 7.30–12 and 2.30–6.30, Sun 8–1 and 3.30–7

Next to San Giusto are bits of the Roman forum and a 1st-century basilica, of which two columns have been re-erected. The excellent view over Trieste from here is marred by a 1933 war memorial by Attilo Selva, extolling the principal Fascist virtues of strength, brutality and vulgarity. The 15th-century **Castello di San Giusto** (closed at the time of writing) was begun by the Venetians during

Museo Civico
t 040 309 362; open
April–Sept daily 9–7,
Oct– Mar daily 9–5

Civico Museo di
Storia ed Arte e
Orto Lapidario
Via Cattedrale 15,
t 040 308 686; open
Tues–Sun 9–1,
Wed till 7; adm

their brief tenure, over in 1508–09, and finished by the Austrians. It offers more views from its ramparts and a small **Museo Civico**, full of armour and weapons. The Castle's Cortile delle Milizie is a favourite setting for summer concerts, which are well worth the trip, if only for the setting.

Just down the lane from the cathedral is the **Civico Museo di Storia ed Arte e Orto Lapidario**, housing intriguing finds from *Tergeste* and a famous fifth-century deer's-head silver *rhyton* or drinking vessel, imported from Greek Tarentum (modern Taranto). The 'stone garden' contains Roman altars, stelae, a red granite Egyptian sarcophagus and the tomb of J.J. Winckelmann (1717–68), son of a poor German cobbler who became an archaeologist and the father of modern art history when he wrote his revolutionary *Reflections on the Painting and Sculpture of the Greeks* in 1755. While staying at a hotel in Trieste, he showed a fellow guest a few ancient gold coins, and was murdered for them by an eaves-dropping Tuscan cook. On the way down to the city, have a look at the **Roman Theatre** on Via del Teatro Romano, built during the reign of Trajan, and remarkably intact. Occasionally there is still the odd performance, but call the tourist office for up-to-the-minute details.

More *Caffès* and Museums

The Grand Cafés, once the symbol of Triestine society and filled with fervent cross-cultural conversation, ideas and spies, still serve delicious cakes and pastries as well as dollops of nostalgia. Joyce was a habitué of the **Caffé Pirona**, Largo Barriera Vecchia 12, north of the castle hill and south of Piazza Goldoni (at the bottom of the 'Giant's Stair' from the Castello); the locals claim he conceived Ulysses over its *pinzas* and *putizzas*. On the other side of Piazza Goldoni, at Via Cesare Battisti 18, is **Caffè San Marco**, opened in 1914 but rebuilt after it was blown up in the First World War, complete with Venetian murals that betrayed the owner's pro-Italian sentiments. According to the Triestini, the masked carnival figures in the oval over the bar portray Vittorio Emanuele and Mussolini, and you won't find a classier joint in which to shoot a round of pool or sit at a marble table throwing back a micro-cappuccino.

One street away, on Via S. Francesco, stands the most beautiful **synagogue** in Italy and the largest in Europe, built in 1912 on ancient 4th century Syriac models to seat 1,500 people. The Jewish population of Trieste was granted the freedom of the city as far back as 1680 in reward for funding the city's various causes. Many of the city's banking and insurance companies, from which Trieste still draws the bulk of its wealth, were originally set up by the Jewish community. The synagogue is beautifully decorated with copper and black and white marble, but unfortunately is not open.

Risiera di San Sabba
Ratto della Pileria 43,
t 040 826 202; bus
no.20, 21, 23 or 19;
open daily 9–7

In sombre counterpoint stands the only concentration camp in Italy to be used for mass exterminations, the Risiera di San Sabba at the southern extreme of the city, an old rice-husking factory that was taken over by the Nazis in September 1943 to 'process', among others, at least 837 Triestine Jews in its crematorium. The actual number may be far higher, as it has recently been confirmed that 22 trains left for Auschwitz from Trieste between September 1943 and November 1944. A national monument since 1965, the building now houses a small museum. Non-denominational services are held at the beginning of each month to commemorate those who passed through or died during the Holocaust.

Museo del Mare
Via Campo Marzio 5,
t 040 304 987; open
Tues–Sun 8.30–1.30

Museo Ferroviario
Via G Cesare 1,
t 040 379 4185;
open Tues–Sun 9–1

Ipanema Rovis
Via Romagna 6,
t 040 372 4602,
www.ipanema
rovis.com; open
Tues–Sat 9–1
and 4–7.30

On a far lighter note and in the same area the Museo del Mare has ships' models and other salty exhibits; the Museo Ferroviario, in the old train station in the Campo Marzio, has a display of retired locomotives. It also runs frequent summer excursions in period trains: three-hour electric train journeys around the city on the Transalpina, and day-long steam train excursions around the region and neighbouring countries; call for schedules. There's also the Ipanema Rovis (Mineral Museum), a veritable treasure trove. This is the personal collection and passion of a former coffee importer from Istria, whose love for minerals developed amidst the coffee plantations of Brazil. It has enormous amethyst druses and geodes, giant petrified tree trunks as well as hundreds of other exquisite crystals and fossils.

Where to Stay in Trieste

(i) **Trieste >**
Via San Nicolò 20,
t 040 679 6111,
www.trieste.com
Piazza Unità d'Italia,
t 040 347 8312
***Friuli regional tourist office**, Via G. Rossini 6,*
t 040 363 952

(★) **Alla Posta >>**

Trieste ✉ 34100

As with all of Trieste it's best to leave your car in one of the big garages, otherwise check with your hotel whether they have parking.

Luxury (€€€€€)
****Duchi d'Aosta**, Piazza dell'Unità d'Italia 2, t 040 760 0011, *www. magesta.com*. The city's finest hotel on Trieste's finest square, in a neo-Renaissance palace erected in 1873. Now owned by the CIGA chain, it exudes a dignified *belle époque* ambience; upstairs, the luxurious rooms are fitted with all modern comforts. It has an excellent restaurant, Harry's Grill, and there is parking outside or in the garage.

Expensive (€€€)
***Al Viale**, Via Nordio 5, t 040 348 0838, *www.hotelalviale.it*. Just a short

walk from Teatro Rossetti and the train station, this hotel has attractive rooms with air-conditioning and Jacuzzi showers.

****Nuovo Hotel Daneu**, Via Nazionale 11, t 040 214 214, *www.hoteldaneu. com*. If you don't like the hurly-burly of a big city, take the tram up to Opicina where this hotel has a good restaurant and indoor pool.

***Alla Posta**, Piazza Oberdan 1, t 040 365 208, *www.albergopostatrieste.it*. This refined hotel makes use of the latest hi-tech gizmos. Room types are divided between business and pleasure. A hearty breakfast is served up each morning.

***San Giusto**, Via dell'Istria 7, t 040 764 824, *www.hotelsangiusto.it*. By the historic hill, a modern hotel with everything you need.

Moderate (€€)
Hotel James Joyce, Via dei Cavizzeri 7, t 040 311 023, *www.hoteljamesjoyce. com*. This small, cosy hotel has just 12

rooms and is only a couple of minutes' walk from Piazza Unità d'Italia. Friendly and popular.

> *Capitelli*

★ Capitelli >

*Capitelli, Via Capitelli 23, t 040 305 947, www.hotelcapitelli.it. Located next to the enormous Piazza Unità d'Italia, and with only nine rooms, so booking is recommended. Recently renovated.

Inexpensive (€)

There are many inexpensive choices in central Trieste – head for Via Roma, Via della Geppa, or Via XXX Ottobre.

Youth Hostel, Viale Miramare 331, t 040 224 102, www.ostellotergeste.it. Idyllically but inconveniently placed overlooking the sea, 8km north of Trieste near Miramare. Take bus no.36.

Around Trieste

***Duino Park**, near the old citadel, t 040 208184, info@duinoparkhotel.it (€€€). Along the coast, at Duino, this modern hotel has its own pool and a private piece of beach.

***Lido**, Via Battista 22, t 040 273 338, hotellidomuggia@tiscalinet.it (€€). Another modern hotel in Muggia on the edge of town and the sea, with a good restaurant serving local seafood.

★ Buffet da Pepi >>

Belvedere, t 040 299 256, www.hotelbelvedere.ts.it (€). With a garden and views over the sea.

Eating Out in Trieste

★ Re di Coppe >>

Trieste is a good place to eat dumplings instead of pasta – Slovenian and Hungarian influences are strong in the kitchen. A famous first course is *jota*, a bean, potato and sauerkraut soup, or you could try *kaiserknödel* (bread dumplings with grated cheese, ham and parsley). For *secondo*, there's a wide variety of fish like *sardoni* (big sardines), served fried or marinated. Goulash, roast pork and *stinco* (veal knuckle) are also popular. The middle-European influence is especially noticeable in the desserts: the lovely strudels, the *gnocchi di susine* (plums), or *zavate*, a warm cream pastry.

Expensive (€€€)

Al Cantuccio, Via Cadorna 14a, t 040 300 131, www.alcantuccio.com (€€€). A haven of creative food beside the seafront. Try scallops with pine nuts

and balsamic vinegar, risotto with prawns and Prosecco or chicken with black grapes. *Closed Sun.*

Antica Trattoria Suban, Via Comici 2, t 040 54368. The place to partake of *cucina Triestina* is this wonderful old inn in the suburb of San Giovanni (with fine views over Trieste). It offers a famous *jota*, *sevapcici* (Slovenian grilled meat fritters), sinful desserts and good wines. Readers warn, however, that the quality depends on the presence of the regular chef. *Closed Mon lunch, Tues, part of Aug.*

Moderate (€€)

Scabar, Via dell'Istria at Erta di S. Anna 63, t 040 810 368, www.scabar.it. Take a taxi into the hills for gourmet fish and mushroom dishes here; the day's special is usually fantastic. *Closed Mon, Tues, Feb, mid-July–Aug.*

Città di Cherso, Via Cadorna 6, t 040 366 044. Convenient to Piazza Unità d'Italia: delicious seafood Friuli-style, topped off with heavenly desserts. *Closed Tues, end July–end Aug.*

Inexpensive (€)

Buffet da Pepi, Via Cassa di Risparmo 3, t 040 366 858. Founded in 1897 and thriving ever since, serving up Trieste's specialities. *Closed Sun, half of July.*

Birreria Forst, Via Galatti 11 (near Piazza Oberdan), t 040 363 486. Another old favourite, serving goulash and lots of beer. *Closed Sun.*

Re di Coppe, Via Geppa 11, t 040 370 330. The waiters still write the orders on the tablecloths here. Enjoy a classic *jota* or boiled meats. *Closed Sat, Sun, part of Aug.*

Entertainment in Trieste

The **opera** season at Trieste's Teatro Comunale Verdi runs from January to September; in summer the theatre and the Sala Tripcovich, in Piazza della Libertà, host an International Operetta Festival (for schedules and bookings, call t 040 672 2249, or visit www.teatroverdi-trieste.com).

Carnival is celebrated with a Venetian flair in Muggia, with a lavish parade that's well beyond what you would expect in a small town.

Excursions from Trieste

You can't go too far from Trieste without running into Slovenia. For a short jaunt, take the **Opicina Tranvia** (the funicular, built in 1902) up the cliffs from Piazza Oberdan for the fine panorama from the **Vedetta d'Opicina**. Another popular excursion is to **Miramare**, some 7km up the beach-lined Riviera di Barcola, jam packed in the summer (bus no.36 from Piazza Oberdan or Stazione Centrale). On the way, watch for the **Faro della Vittoria**, a lofty lighthouse and 1927 war memorial to sailors, crowned by yet another heavy-sinewed, big-busted Valkyrie in a majorette's costume.

Miramare: Habsburg Folly by the Sea

Castello Miramare
*t 040 224 406,
www.castello-
miramare.it; open
April–Sept daily 8–7,
Mar and Oct daily 8–6,
Nov–Feb daily 8–5;
Miramare Park open
daily 10–sunset;
adm for castle*

Towering up on its own little promontory above the sea, the castle of Miramare hides a dark history behind its white 19th-century façade. It was built by the Habsburg Archduke Maximilian, and visitors are greeted by a stone sphinx with a cryptic smile that seems to ask the world why on earth Maximilian left this pleasure palace and like a *dummkopf* allowed Napoleon III's financiers to con him into becoming Mexico's puppet emperor in 1864, and why he lingered around there to face a firing squad three years later. Was he an idealist, as his apologists claim, or too much of a Habsburg to know any better?

Carlotta, the archduke's Belgian wife, after trying desperately to rally European support for her husband, went mad after his execution and survived him for another 50 years back in Belgium. In the meantime Miramare acquired the ominous reputation of laying a curse on anyone who slept within its walls, after another Habsburg – the Archduke Ferdinand – stayed here on his way to assassination in Sarajevo. The Nazis made it their headquarters in 1943; when the Americans occupied the palace in 1946, their commander insisted on sleeping out in the park in a tent.

Inside, the palace retains its original overblown Victorian-era décor, some rather cosy rooms designed like ship cabins, a never-used throne, a historical hall (with a painting of the Argonauts) and, upstairs, 1920s furnishings brought in by the Duke of Aosta, who made this his base. Miramare's magnificent **park** was designed by Maximilian, who made a better botanist than the emperor of Mexico; the gardens and coastal waters are now managed by the World Wildlife Federation and shelter the rare Stella's otter and marsh harriers. The renovated stables are used to stage exhibitions.

The Carso

Most of Trieste's province is occupied by the Carso, a slender 25km ribbon of karst. Karst is pliable limestone, easily eroded by the rain into remarkable shapes – and here into white cliffs that form Italy's most dramatic Adriatic coastline north of Monte Còrnero. Inland, the karst has been buffeted by the 90mph *bora* wind into petrified waves of rock dotted with *dolinas* (swallow holes) while, underground, aeons of dripping water have formed vast caverns, subterranean lakes and rivers. Vineyards grow wherever there's room, and elsewhere the landscape is dominated by sumac, which autumn ignites into a hundred shades of scarlet. Autumn is also the season to look for farms with leafy branch signs; these are *osmizze*, a local peculiarity from the days of the Austro-Hungarian Empire, and are permitted to produce and sell wine directly to the consumer.

Between Miramare and the industrial shipbuilding town of Monfalcone lies the fishing village of **Duino**, with its two castles: the ruined **Castello Vecchio** and the 15th-century **Castello Nuovo**, perched on a promontory over the sea. Castello Nuovo has long been owned by the Princes von Thurn und Taxis, who hosted D'Annunzio, Liszt, Richard Strauss and, most famously, Rainer Maria Rilke. The castle lays on a sound and light show from mid-July to late August (call for programme) of the whole sad story of Miramare's Imperial dream. You can follow the beautiful (and easy) 2km **Rilke walk** along the promontory, beginning in nearby **Sistiana**, a pretty resort with a yacht harbour in its own little bay; peregrine falcons nest on the cliffs.

Born in a karstic abyss in Slovenia, the **Timavo river** continues underground for 30km before reappearing by the winsome Romanesque church of **San Giovanni in Tuba**, just above Duino. The Romans were fascinated with the Timavo – Virgil mentioned it in *The Aeneid* – and their temple to Spes Augusta lies under San Giovanni; you can still see a portion of the mosaic floor (5th

Castello Nuovo
t 040 208 120,
www.castellodiduino.it;
open Mar–Sept
Wed–Mon 9.30–5.30,
Oct Wed–Mon
9.30–4.30, Nov–Feb
Sat–Sun 9.30–4

11

Friuli-Venezia Giulia | Excursions from Trieste

The Duino Elegies

When Princess Marie von Thurn und Taxis left Rilke alone in the castle that winter of 1910–11, the poet was in a restless mood. One day he received a nasty business letter, and despite the blustery winds he went for a walk along the castle bastions to sort out his thoughts before replying. In the wind and waves crashing far below he heard a voice: 'Who, if I cried, would hear me among the angelic orders?' It was the muse Rilke had anxiously been waiting for; he jotted the words down, and by the evening the first of his ten 'Duino Elegies' was finished. Another followed, but 11 years and the terrible war intervened before his 'voice' returned and he completed the Elegies.

As the expression of Rilke's very personal and prophetic vision of reality, the Elegies were notoriously as difficult to write as they are to read. Rilke felt that in the 20th century it was impossible to find adequate external symbols to express our inner lives and, like Blake, he used angels in a highly personal way. On one level, as he wrote to his Polish translator, Rilke felt a responsibility and foreboding that many Europeans of his generation dimly understood. 'Now there comes crowding over from America empty, indifferent things, pseudo-things, dummy life... The animated, experienced things that share our lives are coming to an end and cannot be replaced. We are perhaps the last to have still known such things. On us rests the responsibility of preserving not merely their memory (that would be little and unreliable), but their human and laral worth...' Hence, in part, the Elegies.

century) from the original church. Of the caves, the most famous, the stalactite-encrusted **Grotta Gigante** near Opicina, is the easiest to visit. The name for once is no exaggeration: this is the largest cavern in the world open to visitors (since 1908); its main hall could swallow the entire basilica of St Peter and is graced by a pair of record-breaking 346ft pendulum stalactites. The ceiling is so high that drops of water disintegrate before reaching the floor, forming curious leaf-shaped stalagmites. In 1996 a new path was created, past a belvedere overlooking a vertiginous sheer 360ft drop.

Grotta Gigante
t 040 327 312, www.grottagigante.it; bus no.42 every half-hour from Piazza Oberdan; guided tours April–Sept 10–6, Mar and Oct 10–4, Nov–Feb 10–12 and 2–4; closed Mon exc. July and Aug; adm exp

The Grotta Gigante is near **Monrupino** and its castle, first built by the Romans, where the people of Trieste later took shelter when the Turks raided the coast. The Romans had a second castle at Grisa, a spot now topped with the unexpected pyramid of the **Santuario de Monte Grisa**, an essay in triangular concrete modules finished in 1967. Sgonico, also here, has a beautiful botanical garden, the **Carsiana**, in a sheltered karstic valley where wild Mediterranean herbs grow next to Alpine ferns, and nearly extinct blind amphibians called rosy olms hide in the rocky shelters by the pools; a path runs from Opicina to Monrupino.

Carsiana
t 040 229 573, www.carsiana.it; bus no.42 or 44 from Trieste to Prosecco, then bus no.46; or take the Villa Opicina tram to Villa Opicina itself, and change for bus no.42; open late April–mid-Oct Tues–Fri 10–12, Sat–Sun 10–1 and 3–7

South of Trieste, bus No.40 from Piazza Oberdan offers an excursion to the dramatic white karstic cliffs, pierced with caves and hanging over the **Val Rosandra**, where the locals practise their rock-climbing and where you can visit the lowest Alpine refuge in Europe, only a few miles from the sea. Bus No.20 heads south along the coast from Trieste to **Muggia**, a higgledy-piggledy Venetian fishing port at the end of Italy. The lion in its square looks very disapproving and holds a closed book – although who knows what Muggia did to offend the bosses. The pretty tri-lobed **Duomo** has a peculiar relief over the door, of God holding a grown-up Jesus on his lap; the frescoes inside date from the 13th century. The best views around are enjoyed by the Basilica di Santa Maria Assunta, a 10th-century frescoed church overlooking Muggia and the sea.

Inland Friuli-Venezia Giulia

Gorizia and the Collio

The frontier town of Gorizia was for centuries ruled by a powerful dynasty of counts who, with the winking approval of the kings of Hungary, were always ready to stir up trouble against Venice. When the last count died without an heir in 1500, the city was briefly controlled by Venice before being taken over by the Habsburgs. As in Trieste, the Austrians gave Gorizia broad, straight boulevards and parks and pronounced the result an 'Austrian Nice' (minus the seashore, that is).

The city saw fierce fighting in the First World War, but it was after the Second World War that Gorizia became the Mediterranean's Berlin, cut in two between Italy and Yugoslavia (now Slovenia) in such a thoughtless manner that it almost choked. Life improved in Nova Gorica and Gorizia only in 1979, when residents on either side of the barbed-wire fence were granted a 16km zone to conduct their affairs freely. In 1991 Gorizia saw the first shots of the new Balkan War, when Slovenia declared independence and the Yugoslav army was sent in to wrest back the lucrative border posts. Today, as Slovenia prospers in its independence, the town is a peculiar jumble of flashy boutiques catering for border traffic.

Borgo Castello

Borgo Castello
t 0481 535 146; open April–Sept Tues–Sun 9.30–1 and 3–7.30, Oct–Mar 9.30–6; adm

Crowning Gorizia with its wide straight streets is its medieval core, the Borgo Castello, enveloped by a Venetian fortress of 1509. In the centre, the Castle of the Counts of Gorizia was first mentioned in 1001, but had to be completely rebuilt after its pummelling in the First World War. It now houses the **Museo del Medioevo Goriziano** (same hours as the castle) with a display dedicated to Gorizia's history, and a few antiques and paintings.

Museo Provinciale
open summer Tues–Sun 10–7, winter Tues–Sun 10–1 and 2–7; adm

Just below stands the pretty church of Santo Spirito (1386) and the Casa Formentini, now the **Museo Provinciale** featuring an exhibition on textiles, the city's old bread and butter, and local artists, especially Giuseppe Tominz, master portrait painter to the bourgeoisie of Gorizia and Trieste (*d.* 1866), who is admired for getting their clothes just right. One of his best efforts is a self-portrait with his full-grown brother sitting on his lap, about to receive Giuseppe's fully laden palette on the back of his nice frock coat. There is also an altarpiece by Antonio Guardi, in which the usual saints hanging about the Madonna have, for once, better things to do than stand around and pose.

Museo della Grande Guerra
t 0481 533 926; open Tues–Sun 9–7; adm

Perhaps best of all is the **Museo della Grande Guerra** dedicated to the First World War and the Isonzo front, which evoke the horror and some of the black humour of the Great War, during which much of Gorizia was destroyed. There's a fascinating exhibition of photographs showing the rebuilding of the city and the size of the task undertaken.

Modern Gorizia

Gorizia's **Duomo** is the dull result of tinkering since the 14th century, but has an altarpiece by Tominz. Gorizia once had a prominent Jewish community that lived in a ghetto north of the cathedral. In 1943 nearly all were taken to the concentration camp in Trieste. None returned. The **synagogue** in Via Ascoli was built in 1752, burned by the Nazis but rebuilt and reopened in 1984, and now houses a museum of the community and paintings by its

Gorizia Synagogue
Via Ascoli 19, t 0481 33226; open Tues and Thurs 5–7, second Sun of month 10–1

11

Friuli-Venezia Giulia | Gorizia and the Collio

most famous member, philosopher Carlo Michelstaedter, who committed suicide at the age of twenty-three.

Villa Coronini Cronberg
Viale XX Settembre 14,
t 0481 533 485,
www.coronini.it; open
July–Aug Tues–Sat 10–6,
Sun 10–7; Sept–June
Tues–Sat 10–6

In 1990 Guglielmo Coronini, the last Count of Gorizia, died, and now his home, the Villa Coronini Cronberg (1594), is open to the public. Rooms include the bedroom where Charles X, the last King of France, died in 1836; the impressive library; and the Count's collections – paintings by Tintoretto, Strozzi, Magnasco, Rubens, Monet, Rosalba Carriera, and of course Giuseppe Tominz; prints by Titian and Rembrandt and Japanese masters, and more. The small but very interesting Museum of Fashion and Applied Arts houses all manner of clothing and jewellery, as well as an incredible circular silk-twisting machine from the late 18th century. (It still works apparently, but needs a day or two to get up to speed.) Silk became the mainstay of the local economy early in the 18th century, so much so that laws stated that harming silkworms was a punishable offence.

Museum of Fashion and Applied Arts
Borgo Castello 13,
t 0481 533 926; open
Tues–Sun 9–7; adm

Wine around Gorizia

The hills around Gorizia, the **Collio**, look like a patch of Tuscany that got away. This has been Friuli's most prestigious wine region since the Middle Ages, and these days it is especially known for its Tocai Friulano and Ribolla Gialla. Its centre, the pleasant, leafy town of **Gradisca d'Isonzo**, straddles the blue-green River Isonzo, neat and tidy with pastel houses and little 17th-century *palazzi*, and the **Enoteca Regionale Serenissima**, in business since 1965, where you can taste any or all of Friuli's wines. Medieval **Cormòns**, another major Collio wine town, was the only one in Italy to erect a statue to Emperor Maximilian. Visit its **Cantina Prodottori Vini del Collio e Isonzo**, which produces a Vino della Pace, made from vines gathered from around the globe and sent out annually to the world's heads of state. Just north of Cormòns, San Giovanni al Natisone, Manzano and Corno di Rosazzo are the magic triangle of something a bit less glamorous, but eminently useful – chairs. Some 20 million are cranked out annually.

Enoteca Regionale Serenissima
t 0481 99598; open
Tues–Sun 10–2
and 5–10.30

Cantina Prodottori Vini del Collio e Isonzo
t 0481 60579,
www.cormons.com;
open Mon–Sat

Where to Stay and Eat in Gorizia and the Collio

(i) **Gorizia >**
Corso Italia 9,
t 0481 535 764,
www.gorizia.org

Gorizia ✉ 34170

★★★★**Golf**, Via Oslavia 2, **t** 0481 884 051, *www.golfhotelformentini.it* (€€€). Just north of Gorizia at San Floriano del Collio, this 17th-century manor house has 15 rooms furnished with antiques and every amenity; pool, tennis and golf too.

★★★**Vinnaeria La Baita**, Via degli Alpini 2, at Capriva del Friuli, **t** 0481 881 021,

(★) **Vinnaeria La Baita >**

www.vinnaerialabaita.it (€€€–€€). Owned by famous vinter Jerman, this is a small hotel with 12 rooms and a wine theme. The rooms are large with stylish furnishings, and the restaurant is a must.

Lanterna d'Oro al Castello, t 0481 82007 (€€). In Borgo Castello, you can sup here in medieval splendour. The menu features Friuli specialities such as *prosciutto di San Daniele*, and well-prepared dishes of venison, kid and boar. *Closed Sun eve, Mon.*

Cormòns ✉ 34071

***Felcaro, Via S. Giovanni 45, **t** 0481 60214, *www.hotelfelcaro.it* (€€€–€€). The nicest place to sleep in the Collio. This hotel began life as an Austrian villa and has since spread out over several buildings, with a swimming pool, tennis courts, fitness centre, and a fine restaurant, specializing in game dishes to go with its enormous wine list. *Closed Mon, Jan, 1 wk in June and Nov.*

⭐ La Subida ›

La Subida, Monte 22, **t 0481 60531, *www.lasubida.it* (€€€–€€). In a charming rural setting on a hill, with a handful of rooms, many sleeping up to five, with a pool, tennis and riding. The restaurant, Il Cacciatore (€€€–€€), serves excellent regional dishes, with extensive borrowings from nearby Slovenia: the cold breast of pheasant in mushroom cream is a popular

summer dish. Excellent Collio wines. *Closed Tues, Wed, 2 wks in Feb and July.*

Al Giardinetto, Via Matteotti 54, **t** 0481 60257 (€€€). Accomplished twin chefs have put this restaurant firmly on the gastronomic map with their innovative Friulian dishes – *millefoglie di polenta* and gnocchi with crinkly cabbage and game sauce. *Closed Mon eve, Tues, July.*

Dolegna del Collio ✉ 34070

Castello dell'Aquila d'Oro, Via Ruttars 11, **t** 0481 61255 (€€€€–€€€). A 13th-century castle with one of Italy's best wine cellars, and beautiful refined food on a menu that changes frequently with the chef's inspiration. An ultra-refined setting, down to the last detail. Located just outside Dolegena, in between Gorizia and Udine. *Closed Sun, Mon, 2 wks in Jan and Aug.*

Udine

🎯 Udine

Legend states that Udine's castle sits on a mound erected by Hunnish warriors, who carried the soil to the site in their helmets so that their commander Attila could watch the burning of Aquileia. The story has a ring of prophecy to it, as Udine, granted important market concessions by the Patriarch in 1223, went on to take Aquileia's place as seat of the patriarch from 1238 to 1751. Udine's chief rivals were Gorizia and Cividale until 1385, when the powerful local family, the Savorgnans, took control and brought it into the Serene Republic in 1420. During the Second World War it was the last city to be liberated in Italy (May 1945).

Udine is a charmer, and not half as well known as it deserves to be. Its old streets are interwoven with little canals; it's also the centre of Friulian nationalism, and you're likely to hear people in the streets conversing in Friulian. Venice left its handprint on the architecture, while lagoonland's last great painter Giambattista Tiepolo brightened many of the walls, thanks to his first important patron, Patriarch Dionisio Delfino, who kept him here with commissions between 1726 to 1730, a period when he left his early sombre palette behind and took up the brilliant colours that became his trademark.

Piazza della Libertà and the Castello

The heart of Udine, Piazza della Libertà, has justifiably been called 'the most beautiful Venetian square on the *terra firma*'. Its striking, candy-striped **Loggia del Lionello** – a mini-Doge's palace –

Getting to and around Udine

Udine's **railway station** (with connections to Venice, Trieste and Gorizia) is on Viale Europa Unità; a private local railway links Udine station with Cividale (20mins). The **bus station** is not far away on the other side of the same street, t 0432 504 012, *www.saf.ud.it.*

was built by a goldsmith in 1448 and faithfully reconstructed after a fire in 1876; a second loggia, the **Loggia di San Giovanni** (1533), integrates an earlier clock tower designed by Raphael's student, Giovanni da Udine, where the bell is rung by two Venetian-style Moors. There is the usual column topped by a Lion of St Mark (a bit of nostalgia in this case, from 1883), accompanied by statues of Hercules and Cacus (better known locally as Florean and Venturin), Peace and Justice, the latter from the 1600s and sporting Bette Davis eyes. The **Municipio**, all in white Istrian stone, is a bravura piece of Art Deco by Raimondo D'Aronco (1910–31) that manages to blend right in with all the rest.

Palladio designed the rugged **Arco Bollari** (1556), the gateway to the sweeping portico, built in 1487 to shelter visitors to the **Castello**, once seat of the Patriarch and the Venetian governor. Rebuilt in 1517 and restored in 1990 after the earthquake, it houses the **Civici Musei**; sections include archaeology; photos, especially of Friuli; designs and prints (by Tiepolo and Dürer, among others); and a notable collection of paintings, beginning in the impressive **Salone del Parlamento**, built in 1560 by Giovanni da Udine and frescoed by Pomponio Amalteo and Giovanni Battista Grassi, with monochromes by G.B. Tiepolo. Among the highlights are Carpaccio's *Christ with the Instruments of the Passion*, Giambattista Tiepolo ('*Guardian Angel and Strength and Wisdom*') and a bird's-eye view of Udine by local boy Luca Carlefarijs (1662–1730). The castle shares the hill with **S. Maria di Castello**, a church founded in the sixth century and topped with a giant bronze archangel in the late 18th century. There are fine views over the city from here and from the adjacent 16th-century Venetian **Casa della Contadinanza**, where petitions to the Friuli parliament were processed; it also houses an excellent *enoteca* and shop. Have a look at the small **Museo della Città** on Via Zanon. From the top floor of the gallery there is a good view of the city.

Civici Musei
t 0432 271 591; open Tues–Sat 9.30–12.30 and 3–6, Sun 9.30–12.30; adm, free Sun am

Museo della Città
Via Zanon 24; open for special exhibitions only

Down in the City

Just east of Piazza Libertà, along Via Vittorio Veneto, the oft-altered **Duomo** has a charming 14th-century lunette over the door of the *Coronation of the Virgin and Saints*, with figures so weathered they look like gingerbread. The interior, a dignified Baroque symphony of grey and gold, has frescoes by Tiepolo in the first two altars on the right and in the Cappella del Sacramento. In

Museo del Duomo
t 0432 506 830;
open Tues–Sat 9–12
and 4–6, Sun 4–6

the heavy-set campanile, the small **Museo del Duomo** is adorned with excellent 1349 frescoes of the *Funeral of St Nicholas* by Vitale da Bologna, and a 14th-century sarcophagus. Even after Tiepolo became world famous he never forgot his first patrons in Udine, and in 1759, when he was at the height of his powers, he returned to decorate the adjacent **Oratorio della Purità** (1680), originally a little theatre, with a masterful, partly frescoed, partly painted and recently restored Assumption on the ceiling and an altarpiece of the Immaculate Conception; the *chiaroscuro* frescoes on the walls are by his son Giandomenico.

Oratorio della Purità
t 0432 506 830;
ask at the cathedral sacristy to see inside, or phone in advance

Near the Duomo (down Via Calzolai) on Piazza Venerio, the austere 14th-century **San Francesco** has good 14th-century frescoes by an unknown Venetian. From here take a left on Via Savorgnana for the more ornate **San Giacomo**, with its clock tower and life-size figures gazing over the arcaded **Piazza Matteotti**, Udine's centuries-old market square. Note the outdoor altar on the balcony over the door of San Giacomo, used to celebrate mass on market days – as convenient for shoppers in its day as a drive-in church in a California mall.

From here, Via Sarpi leads around to join the Riva Bartolini with Palladio's **Palazzo Antonini** (now the Banca d'Italia). The Tiepolo trail, however, continues in the other direction: from the Piazza Libertà, take Via Manin through a gate to the Piazza Patriarcato and the Palazzo Arcivescovile, now the **Museo Diocesano**, with sacred works and an entire gallery of Old Testament scenes (*The Fall of the Rebel Angels, Rachel Hiding the Idols, Judgement of Solomon*) beautifully frescoed by Tiepolo – his first major commission. More recent art (Arturo Martini, Severini, Carrà, De Chirico, De Kooning, Segal, Lichtenstein, Dufy, and works by the brothers Afro, Mirko and Dino Basaldell, natives of Udine) is on display in the excellent **Galleria d'Arte Moderna**, located on the northern fringes of the old town. To get there, follow Riva Bartolini to Via Palladio, then go straight on Vias Mazzini, Mantica and A.L. Moro, or take bus no.2 directly from the station or Piazza 1 Maggio.

Museo Diocesano
t 0432 25003; open Wed–Sun 10–12 and 3.30–6.30; adm

Galleria d'Arte Moderna
t 0432 295 891; open Tues–Sat 9.30–12.30 and 3–6; Sun 9.30–12.30; adm

11 Friuli-Venezia Giulia | Udine

Where to Stay and Eat in Udine

(i) Udine >
Piazza 1 Maggio 7,
t 0432 295 972,
www.turismo.fvg.it

Udine ✉ 33100
****Astoria Hotel Italia**, Piazza XX Settembre 24, t 0432 505 091, *www.hotelastoria.udine.it* (€€€€–€€€). The *grande dame* of the city's hotels, located in the heart of town; it has air-conditioning, a garage with plenty of parking, rooms with all mod cons, and a fine restaurant

specializing in Venetian meat and fish dishes. Ask to have a peek in the frescoed conference room, designed by Jappelli in 1833.
***La' di Moret**, just north of the centre at Viale Tricesimo 276, t 0432 545 096, *www.ladimoret.it* (€€€). This elegant turn-of-the-century hotel has won plenty of awards in its time for its rooms; the restaurant, one of the best in the region, features seafood Friuli-style. *Closed Sun eve and Mon lunch.*

⭐ **Villa Gallici Deciani** >

⭐ **Suite Inn** >

Villa Gallici Deciani, Via Gallici 27, **t** 0432 851 487, *www.deciani.it* (€€€). An exquisite villa still lived in by Count Luigi Deciani, a tireless host, who will really make you feel at home. The rural kitchen and dining rooms are decorated in typical country style, while the swimming pool and grounds are sure to take your breath away. Best to stay during the week, when things are quiter.

***Suite Inn**, Via di Toppo 25, **t** 0432 501 683, *www.suiteinn.it* (€€€–€€). A family-run hotel, recently restored, with a warm and familiar atmosphere. Located within walking distance of the town centre, it has 13 rooms furnished in a simple style with the use of natural wood and delicate pastel tints. Objects recalling past Friulian celebrities are scattered around the rooms, giving a little insight into the unique culture of this corner of Italy.

***Cristallo**, Ple. D'Annunzio 43, **t** 0432 501 919, *www.cristallohotel.com* (€€). Located between the station and the city centre, this modern hotel is well priced and very comfortable with secure parking.

Trattoria Agli Amici, Via Liguria 250, at Godia, **t** 0432 565 411, *info@agliamici.it* (€€€). This *trattoria* 6km north of Udine has been popular with locals and visitors alike since it opened way back in 1887. Still managed by the same family, the food here represents a good blend of traditional and contemporary cuisine. Book in advance. *Closed Sun eve, Mon, 1 wk in Jan.*

Vitello d'Oro, Via Valvason 4, **t** 0432 508 982, (€€€). A historic inn serving a wide range of traditional specialities, with an emphasis on fish and seafood. *Oct–May closed Mon lunch and Wed, June–Sept closed Sun and Mon lunch.*

Caffè Contarena, Piazza Libertà, **t** 0432 512 741 (€). Owned by the Enoteca Regionale La Serenissima, this beautiful Stilo Liberty bar is the perfect place to while away the hours. Locally brewed beer, the finest wines in Friuli, tasty nibbles and knowledgeable staff make this a great place to stop by. *Closed Mon.*

Osteria di Villafredda, Via Liuti 7, loc. Loneriacco, Tarcento (nr Udine), **t** 0432 792 153 (€€). Between Udine and Tarcento this popular *osteria* serves delicious local specialities such as *frico e frittata alle erbe*, vegetable and basil soup, veal with sage, veal kidneys with mustard and, to finish, mouthwatering desserts such as blueberry strudel with cinnamon ice cream. *Closed Sun eve, Mon.*

Vecchio Stallo, Via Viola 7, **t** 0432 21296 (€) This charming restaurant offers the best value for money in Udine; good food, and wine by the glass. *Closed Sun.*

Cividale del Friuli

🎯 **Cividale del Friuli**

Only a hop and a skip from Udine in the valley of the Natisone, Cividale del Friuli has an impressive pedigree. Julius Caesar founded it in 50 BC and named it after his family, *Forum Iulii*, a name condensed over the centuries into 'Friuli'. The Lombards invaded in 568, liked what they saw, and made Cividale the capital of their first duchy. The Patriarchate of Aquileia (*see* below) was moved here in 737, initiating a magnificent period documented by the surprising works of Lombard art, and by Paulus Diaconus, the Lombard historian born in Cividale and one of the brightest beams of light we have on the 'Dark Ages' in northern Italy.

Nowdays Cividale is a little jewel of a city, well worth making a detour for.

Getting to Cividale del Friuli

A private local **railway** links Udine station with Cividale (20mins).

The Duomo and Archaeology Museum

Duomo
open daily 9.30–12 and 3–6.30

Museo Cristiano
t 0432 731 144; open Nov–Mar Mon–Fri 9.30–12 and 3–6, April–Oct Mon–Fri 9.30–12

Museo Archeologico Nazionale
open Tues–Sun 8.30–7.30, Mon 8.30–2; adm

The centre of Cividale is a series of squares around the old forum. In the most important, Piazza Duomo, you'll find the rebuilt 13th–15th-century **Palazzo Comunale**, a statue of Caesar, and the **Duomo**, begun in 1453 and given its plain but attractive Renaissance façade by Pietro Lombardo. It contains unique treasures: the 12th-century silver altarpiece, the *Pala di Pellegrino II*, with its 25 saints and two archangels; a fine gilded equestrian monument (1617) and the Renaissance sarcophagus of Patriarch Nicolò Donato. Off the right aisle, the **Museo Cristiano** contains two masterpieces from the 8th century: the octagonal **Baptistry of Callisto** and the **Altar of Ratchis**, dating back to 749, a period when there was still considerable confusion about lion anatomy (the one on the Baptistry is part fish, part hedgehog) and exactly how hands and arms are attached to the human form. In the scene of the Magi, Mary and baby Jesus frown as if they didn't like their presents – what's a baby going to do with a pot of myrrh anyhow? (Yet compare its barbaric charms with the stuccoes in the Tempietto, below.)

Next to the Duomo, the **Museo Archeologico Nazionale** is housed in Palladio's Palazzo Pretorio. This vast treasure trove has an enticing range of Roman relics, notably the unique bronzes from Zuglio – an enormous shield with a man's portrait in the centre, of uncertain date, as well as objects found in hundreds of Lombard tombs in the 6th and 7th centuries – crosses, fibulae, swords and shield-holds (*ambone*), all that survives after the wood and leather have rotted away. The sarcophagus of the 6th-century Lombard Duke Gisulphus produced a fibula, cross and ring all wrought in gold. There are ivory pieces for a game called *ad tabulam* from a knight's tomb, the 8th-century Carolingian *Pax del Duca Orso*, adorned with an ivory crucifix in a golden frame and studded with jewels; a 1400 embroidered altar cover, a fifth-century *Evangelical of St Mark*, autographed by Lombard nobles, who thought it was written in the apostle's own hand; the Pulfero treasure of bronze axes from 2000 to 200 BC, discovered in 1997; and bits from the Romanesque Duomo – mermaids, monsters, and a man in a funny hat.

The Ipogeo Celtico and Tempietto Longobardo

Corso Ponte d'Aquileia descends to the Natisone (a pretty turquoise because of the limestone, like many rivers in the area) and the lofty 1442 **Ponte del Diavolo**, with its view of the mountains. In the Middle Ages, it was a common folk belief that bridges were magical, and many stories grew up on how they were erected overnight by the Devil himself, in exchange for the first soul that ventured across in the morning. But Satan is a sucker in every instance; the wily Cividalesi outsmarted him by the usual ploy of sending over a cat at dawn.

Ipogeo Celtico
*Via Monastero 6,
t 0432 710 360; open
April–Sept 9.30–12.30
and 3–6.30, Oct–Mar
9.30–12.30 and 3–7*

Just up from the bridge is the mysterious **Ipogeo Celtico** on Via Monastero. This dripping, creepy pit, the perfect setting for a nasty cult, may have served as a funeral chamber in the 3rd century BC, although no one's sure, because there is nothing to compare it to. Later the Romans and Lombards used it as a prison, where unfortunates would have to look at the three monstrous, carved heads that peer out of the walls, seemingly from the dawn of time itself. The entrance is unassuming in the extreme: a perfectly ordinary door from the street leads into what looks like the top of someone's cellar, but a few steps down and you're into another world completely.

**Tempietto
Longobardo**
*open Oct–Mar
Mon–Sat 9.30–12.30
and 3–5, Sun 9.30–12.30
and 2.30–6; April–Sept
Mon–Sat 9.30–12.30
and 3–6.30, Sun 9.30–1
and 3–7.30; adm*

Perched by the Natisone river (reached via the little lane that snakes its way northwest, just behind the cathedral) is the **Tempietto Longobardo**, the finest work of the eighth century in Italy, despite the fact that it had to be restored in the 13th century after an earthquake shattered three-quarters of its ornamentation and all of its mosaics. The stuccoes that remain, however, are a love letter from the Dark Ages: ravishing, uncanny, and perhaps even miraculous, a sextet of gently smiling saints and princesses in high relief. Standing at either side of a beautiful and intricately carved window, they are all positioned over an even more intricately carved arch with a vine motif. Artistically, Europe wasn't to see the like again for 400 years. Under the stuccoes the carved and inlaid wooden choir dates from 1371, and you'll also find some frescoes of the same period, replacing the mosaics; the *Adoration of the Magi* is lovely.

Where to Stay and Eat in Cividale del Friuli

(i) **Cividale del
Friuli** >
*Corso Paolino
d'Aquileia 10,
t 0432 731 461,
turismo@cividale.net*

Cividale del Friuli ✉ 33043

***Locanda al Castello, Via del Castello 12, **t** 0432 733 242, *www. alcastello.net* (€€€–€€). Slightly outside Cividale del Friuli in the suburb of Fortino, this ivy-covered hotel is not in a castle but a former fortified Jesuit seminary. Cividale's most atmospheric rooms, as well as a fine restaurant with views from the balcony.

***Roma, Piazza Pico 17, **t** 0432 731 871, *www.hotelroma-cividale.it* (€€). Other choices are in the centre and include this modern hotel without a restaurant but with parking.

Locanda Pomo d'Oro, Piazza S. Giovanni 20, **t 0432 731 489, *www. alpomodoro.com* (€€–€). A romantic place set in an 11th-century hostel.

Al Fortino, Via Carlo Alberto 46, **t** 0432 731 217 (€€). Also pleasant, with typical Friulian fare and home-made pasta. *Closed Mon eve, Tues.*

Alla Frasca, Via di Rebeis 10, **t** 0432 731 270 (€€). A restaurant with a charming Renaissance atmosphere and tasty Friulian dishes, including a *menu di funghi* that offers truffles and mushrooms with everything. *Closed Mon, part of Jan and Feb.*

Il Cantiniere Romano, Via Ristori 31, **t** 0432 732 033 (€€). As well as a fine array of salumi, cheese and wines, there's excellent cooked food such as asparagus flan, steamed sea bass,

chicory soup, couscous with fish and a tempting choice of sweets. *Closed Sun and Mon eve.*

Trattoria Al Paradiso, Via Cavour 21, **t** 0432 732 438 (€). Behind the Duomo in Cividale and always full of locals. *Closed Mon.*

North of Udine: the Julian Alps and the Carnia

The mountainous region to the north of Udine is linked to the city itself by a bright new *autostrada*, one of Italy's recent engineering marvels. It has yet to bring in the crowds. The valleys, especially those in the eastern Julian Alps (named, of course, after Julius Caesar), are Slovenian-speaking, their church towers crowned with colourful garlic domes. If the peaks lack the romance of their Dolomite neighbours, they also lack their crowds, lofty prices and resorts.

Towards the Julian Alps (the Alpi Giulie)

Just off the *autostrada*, 20 minutes north of Udine, Gemona and Venzone were the epicentre of the 1976 earthquake. Rather than move on, both were rebuilt with meticulous care. Set in the Julian foothills, **Gemona del Friuli**'s gem is a 13th-century cathedral, its façade decorated with a beautiful carved portal and a remarkable *St Christopher*, sculpted by a Nordic artist in 1331.

Venzone, a smaller, double-walled town that began as a rest stop on the Julia Augusta road, was made a national monument in 1965. An exhibit under the painted ceiling of the loggia has astonishing before and after photographs. The Municipio had to be totally rebuilt not once, but twice: first in the 1950s after it was razed in the Second World War.

Just west, **Bordano** and **Interneppo** by Lake Cavazzo are two villages always covered with butterflies – painted on the walls. There is a local story that Picasso once painted a butterfly here but the authorities didn't recognise its 'beauty' and the following year it was painted over. Each spring new butterflies appear on the walls so that they never fade.

Venzone lies within the **Parco delle Prealpi Giulia**, a natural park extending to the east, with a large population of marmots, deer and ibex, recently reintroduced; its centre is the **Valle di Résia**, just north of Venzone, where in the 6th century a wandering band of folk from Poland got stuck in its dead end and stayed; to this day they speak ancient Slavonic and preserve customs long forgotten in Poland itself.

The *autostrada* continues northeast into the Julian Alps, the most densely forested region in all Italy, where even the beech trees, overmolested by loggers to the south, still stand tall amid spruce, white and black pines and larches, the haunt of brown bears, lynx and eagles. If you are driving, try the road from Chiusaforte up the Canale di Raccolana past Sella Nevea. It takes you through the heart of the forest and, if you are there during autumn, the colours are truly breathtaking.

The mountains around the pass at **Tarvisio** (near the Austrian and Slovenian frontiers) cradle the up-and-coming resort of **Sella Nevea**, south of Tarvisio, beyond the two pretty duck-filled lakes at the natural park in **Fusine**. You can get a ski pass here, good for the nearby resorts in Austria and Slovenia.

One of the prettiest excursions around the Tarvisio pass is up to **Lago del Predil**, under Monte Magante on the Slovenian border; another is to take the speedy *cabinova* up to the **Santuario del Monte Santo di Lussari**, where a Gothic Madonna has received pilgrims for many centuries.

The Carnia

The Carnia mountains rise to the west, next-door neighbours and cousins to the Dolomites.

Tolmezzo, an 18th-century producer of damasks and taffetas, is its main town and transportation hub of the Carnia mountains. First settled in the late 11th century, the town really developed in 1356 when the Patriarch Nicolo di Lussemburgo declared it the capital of Carnia. In 1741 the **Palazzo Linussio** was built as a factory for a textile magnate and the town never looked back. Its old prosperity shows up in its stately streets and the rococo parish church with a giant archangel on the campanile. In a 16th-century palace the **Museo Carnico delle Arti Popolari** has an exceptional ethnographic collection, covering mountain life from the 14th to the 19th centuries.

Museo Carnico delle Arti Popolari
Via della Vittoria 2,
t 0433 43233;
open Tues–Sun 9–1
and 3–6; adm

Beyond Tolmezzo the scenery grows increasingly delightful. **Arta Terme** to the north is a spa known since antiquity for its sulphurous waters, where Roman matrons came for beauty treatments and legionaries to soak their wounds. *Julium Carnicum*, the local Roman capital, stood at modern **Zuglio** just down the road from Arta; remains of the basilica and forum can still be seen, and finds are displayed in the lovely **Civico Museo Archeologico**, 'Iulium Carniicum'. Note that some of the finest pieces, the bronzes, are in the museum at Cividale.

Civico Museo Archeologico
Via G. Cesare, t 0433 92562; open 1 Oct–31 May Fri–Sun 9–12 and 3–6; 1 June–30 Sept Fri–Sun 9–12 and 3–6, Wed and Thurs 9–12; adm

Further north, the district around Paularo is especially rich in *casolari*, traditional wooden multi-storeyed chalets that resemble walk-up barns. Northwest of Tolmezzo, the stone village of **Ravascletto** is the capital of the Valcalda and a ski resort; from

Comeglians in the north of the valley there is a lovely scenic road up to Sappada in the Cadore (*see* p.297).

West of Tolmezzo, along the valley of the Tagliamento, **Socchieve** has one of the artistic jewels of the Carnia region: the little 14th-century church of **San Martino**, with frescoes by Gianfrancesco da Tolmezzo (1493).

Further west, **Ampezzo**, the second town of the Carnia, is where you can turn off on a road (only finished in 1950) that winds through the deep and spectacular gorge of the Val Lumiei to **Sàuris**, now a small resort by a beautiful turquoise lake. Famous for its smoked hams, Sàuris (both Upper and Lower) was isolated for so long that it has preserved its medieval dialect as well as its medieval houses.

The road west up the Tagliamento crosses over the 'Pass of Death', where in 1848 volunteers from the Cadore heroically took on the Imperial army. Beyond is another typical Carnian church, with frescoes by Gianfrancesco da Tolmezzo, followed by **Forni di Sotto**, a village rebuilt after the Nazis burnt it to the ground in 1944 in reprisal for its partisan activities. They spared **Forni di Sopra**, the upper hamlet with stupendous front-row views of the eastern Dolomites. Its Romanesque church of **San Floriano** is covered with Gianfrancesco's very best frescoes, painted in 1500, and has a striking 15th-century polyptych by Bellunello.

From Forni di Sopra the road crosses the Passo della Màuria into the Cadore (*see* pp.294–303).

Tourist Information in the Julian Alps and the Carnia

(i) **The Carnia >**
t 800 249 905,
www.carnia.it.

(i) **Arta Terme >>**
Via Umberto I 15,
t 0433 929 290,
www.termediarta.it

For information on the Carnia region in general (and the Julian Alps), visit the Info Carnia website: *www.carnia.it*. The website also includes contact details of tourist offices in towns and villages not listed below.

Where to Stay and Eat in the Julian Alps and the Carnia

(i) **Tarvisio >**
Via Roma 10,
t 0428 2135,
www.tarvisiano.org

Tarvisio ✉ 33018

***Valle Verde**, Via Priesnig 12, t 0428 2342, *www.hotelvalleverde.com* (€€). Handily sited near the ski lifts, this hotel has pretty views and a good restaurant that is open to non-guests. In autumn, the menu features a rich spread of local game and mushroom dishes. *Closed Mon, Nov–mid-Dec.*

Arta Terme ✉ 33022

***Poldo**, Piano d'Arta, t 043 392 056, *www.albergopoldo.it* (€€). Enjoys a peaceful setting in the trees, with an exotic garden and views down into the valley. It is also a centre for the treatment of obesity and dietry disorders, so it might not suit everyone. *Open mid-July–mid-Sept and Christmas.*

Salon, Via Peresson 70, t 043 392 003, *www.albergosalon.it* (€€–€). This hotel has basic rooms and an excellent restaurant, where mushrooms and fresh herbs are particularly plentiful; it's well worth a stop here if you're just passing through. *Open mid-July–mid-Sept and Christmas; other times on request.*

(i) **Ravascletto** >
Piazza Divisione Julia,
t 0433 66477

(i) **Sauris** >>
Sauris Disotto 91,
t 0433 86076

Ravascletto ⊠ 33020

***Valcalda**, Viale Edelweiss 8, **t** 0433 66120, *h.perla@jumpy.it* (€€). Ravascletto is famous for its *cjarsons*, the favourite sweet and sour pasta of the Carnia: this is a good place to try it, and to sleep in the able hands of a family in a business that is now well over 60 years old. The seductive views are a plus.

Sauris ⊠ 33020

***Garnì Plùeme**, Sauris di Sotto 42/A, **t** 0433 866 374, *plueme@tiscali.it* (€€–€). A charming old barn, beautifully converted by the Schneider family into an intimate hotel. A warm and inviting atmosphere with wide use of natural wood. There is Internet and satellite TV in all the rooms.

Language

The fathers of modern Italian were Dante, Manzoni and television. Each played its part in creating a national language from an infinity of regional and local dialects; the Florentine Dante, the first to write in the vernacular, did much to put the Tuscan dialect into the foreground of Italian literature. Manzoni's revolutionary novel, *I Promessi Sposi*, heightened national consciousness by using an everyday language all could understand in the 19th century. Television in the last few decades has performed an even more spectacular linguistic unification; many Italians still speak a dialect at home though.

Perhaps because they are so busy learning their own beautiful but grammatically complex language, Italians are not especially apt at learning others. English lessons, however, have been the rage for years, and at most hotels and restaurants there will be someone who speaks some English. In small towns and out of the way places, finding an Anglophone may prove more difficult. The words and phrases below should help you out in most situations, but the ideal way to come to Italy is with some Italian under your belt; your visit will be richer, and you're much more likely to make some Italian friends.

Note that in the big northern cities, the informal way of addressing someone as you, *tu*, is widely used; the more formal *lei* or *voi* is commonly used in provincial districts.

Pronunciation

Italian words are pronounced phonetically. Every vowel and consonant except 'h' is sounded. The stress usually (but not always!) falls on the penultimate syllable. Accents indicate if it falls on the last syllable (as in *città*); accents serve no other purpose, except to distinguish between *e* (and) and *è* (is).

Consonants

Consonants are the same as in English, with the following exceptions:
C when followed by an 'e' or 'i', is pronounced like the English '*ch*' (*cinque* thus becomes cheenquay).
G is also soft before 'i' or 'e' as in *gira*, or jee-rah.
Z is pronounced like '*ts*'.

Look out too for the following consonant combinations:
Sc before the vowels 'i' or 'e' become like the English '*sh*' as in *sci*, pronounced 'shee'.
Ch is pronouced like a 'k', as in *Chianti*, 'kee-an-tee'.
Gn is pronounced as '*nya*' (thus *bagno* is pronounced ban-yo).
Gli is pronounced like the middle of the word *million* (so *Castiglione* is pronounced Ca-steel-yoh-nay).

Vowels

A is pronounced as in English *father*.
E when unstressed is pronounced like 'a' in *fate*; when stressed it can be the same or like the 'e' in *pet*.
I is like the 'i' in *machine*.
O has two sounds, 'o' as in *hope* when unstressed, and usually 'o' as in *rock* when stressed.
U is pronounced like the 'u' in *June*.

Useful Words and Phrases

yes *sì*
no *no*
maybe *forse*
I don't know *Non (lo) so*
I don't understand (Italian) *Non capisco (l'italiano)*
Does someone here speak English? *C'è qualcuno qui che parla inglese?*
Speak slowly *Parla lentamente*

Could you help me? *Potrebbe aiutarmi?*
Help! *Aiuto!*
Please *Per favore*
Thank you (very much) *Grazie (molte/mille)*
You're welcome *Prego*
It doesn't matter *Non importa*
All right *Va bene*
Excuse me *Permesso/Mi scusi*
I'm sorry *Mi dispiace*
Be careful! *Attenzione!/Attento!*
Nothing *Niente*
It is urgent! *È urgente!*
How are you? *Come sta/stai?*
What is your name? *Come si chiama?/ ti chiami?*
Hello *Salve* or *ciao* (both informal)/ *Buongiorno* (formal)
Good morning *Buongiorno*
Good afternoon/evening *Buonasera*
Goodnight *Buonanotte*
Goodbye *ArrivederLa (formal), Arrivederci/Ciao (informal)*
What do you call this in Italian? *Come si chiama questo in italiano?*
What? *Che?*
Who? *Chi?*
Where? *Dove?*
When? *Quando?*
Why? *Perché?*
How? *Come?*
I am lost *Mi sono perso*
I am hungry/thirsty *Ho fame/sete*
I am tired *Sono stanco*
I feel unwell *Mi sento male*
Leave me alone *Lasciami in pace*
good *buono*
bad *cattivo*
well *bene*
badly *male*
hot *caldo*
cold *freddo*
slow *lento*
fast *rapido*
up *su*
down *giù*
big *grande*
small *piccolo*
here *qui*
there *lì*
too (excessively) *troppo*
lots/a lot *molto*
OK *d'accordo*
Is that OK with you? *ti* (formal: *le*) *va bene?*

That's OK, thanks *Va bene così, grazie*
I'm OK (I don't need any) *Io sono a posto*
address *l'indirizzo*

Time

What time is it? *Che ore sono?*
day *giorno*
week *settimana*
month *mese*
morning *mattina*
afternoon *pomeriggio*
evening *sera*
yesterday *ieri*
today *oggi*
tomorrow *domani*
soon *fra poco*
later *dopo/più tardi*
It is too early/late *È troppo presto/tardi*
spring *la primavera*
summer *l'estate*
autumn *l'autunno*
winter *l'inverno*

Months

January *gennaio*
February *febbraio*
March *marzo*
April *aprile*
May *maggio*
June *giugno*
July *luglio*
August *agosto*
September *settembre*
October *ottobre*
November *novembre*
December *dicembre*

Days

Monday *lunedi*
Tuesday *martedi*
Wednesday *mercoledi*
Thursday *giovedi*
Friday *venerdi*
Saturday *sabato*
Sunday *domenica*

Numbers

one *uno/una*
two *due*
three *tre*

four *quattro*
five *cinque*
six *sei*
seven *sette*
eight *otto*
nine *nove*
ten *dieci*
eleven *undici*
twelve *dodici*
thirteen *tredici*
fourteen *quattordici*
fifteen *quindici*
sixteen *sedici*
seventeen *diciassette*
eighteen *diciotto*
nineteen *diciannove*
twenty *venti*
twenty-one *ventuno*
thirty *trenta*
forty *quaranta*
fifty *cinquanta*
sixty *sessanta*
seventy *settanta*
eighty *ottanta*
ninety *novanta*
hundred *cento*
one hundred and one *centuno*
two hundred *duecento*
one thousand *mille*
two thousand *duemila*
million *milione*

Transport

airport *aeroporto*
bus stop *fermata*
bus/coach *autobus*
railway station *stazione ferroviaria*
train *treno*
platform *binario*
taxi *tassì/taxi*
one ticket to xxx *un biglietto per xxx*
one way *semplice/andata*
return *andata e ritorno*
first/second class *prima/seconda classe*
I want to go to... *Desidero andare a...*
How can I get to...? *Come posso andare a...?*
Do you stop at...? *Si ferma a...?*
Where is...? *Dov'è/Dove sono...?*
From where does it leave? *Da dove parte?*
How far is it to...? *Quanto siamo lontani da...?*
What is the name of this station? *Come si chiama questa stazione?*

When does the next ... leave? *Quando parte il prossimo...?*
How long does the trip take? *Quanto tempo dura il viaggio?*
How much is the fare? *Quant'è il biglietto?*
Have a good trip! *Buon viaggio!*
near *vicino*
far *lontano*
left *sinistra*
right *destra*
straight ahead *sempre diritto*
north/south/east/west *nord/sud/est/ovest*
crossroads *bivio*
street *strada*
road *via*
square *piazza*
bicycle/motorbike *bicicletta/motocicletta*
petrol *benzina*
diesel *gasolio*
garage *garage*
This doesn't work *Questo non funziona*
map/town plan *carta/pianta*
breakdown *guasto*
driving licence *patente di guida*
speed *velocità*
danger *pericolo*
parking *parcheggio*
no parking *sosta vietata*
narrow *stretto*
bridge *ponte*
toll *pedaggio*
slow down *rallentare*

Shopping, Services, Sightseeing

I would like... *Vorrei...*
How much is it? *Quanto costa?*
open *aperto*
closed *chiuso*
cheap *a buon prezzo*
expensive *caro*
bank *banca*
entrance *ingresso*
exit *uscita*
hospital *ospedale*
money *soldi*
credit card *carta di credito*
newspaper *giornale*
pharmacy *farmacia*
police station *commissariato*
policeman *poliziotto*

post office *ufficio postale*
shop *negozio*
supermarket *supermercato*
tobacconist *tabaccaio*
WC *toilette/bagno/servizi*
men *Signori/Uomini*
women *Signore/Donne*

Useful Hotel Vocabulary

I'd like a double room, please *Vorrei una camera doppia (matrimoniale), per favore*
I'd like a single room *Vorrei una camera singola*
...with/without bath *...con/senza bagno*
...for two nights *...per due notti*
We are leaving tomorrow morning *Partiamo domani mattina*

May I see the room, please? *Posso vedere la camera?*
Is there a room with a balcony? *C'è una camera con balcone?*
There isn't (aren't) any hot water, soap, light, toilet paper, towels *Manca/Mancano acqua calda, sapone, luce, carta igienica, asciugamani*
May I pay by credit card? *Posso pagare con carta di credito?*
May I see another room please? *Per favore, potrei vedere un'altra camera?*
Fine, I'll take it *Bene, la prendo*
Is breakfast included? *È compresa la prima colazione?*
What time do you serve breakfast? *A che ora è la colazione?*
How do I get to the town centre? *Come posso raggiungere il centro città?*

Glossary

atrium entrance court of a Roman house or early church.

badia abbazia, an abbey or abbey church.

baita traditional wooden Alpine hut.

baldacchino baldachin, a columned stone or fabric canopy above the altar of a church.

barchesse wings of a Veneto villa orginally used as farm buildings, for storing grain or other supplies.

basilica a rectangular building, usually divided into three aisles by rows of columns. In Rome this was the common form for law courts and other public buildings, and Roman Christians adapted it for their early churches.

Calvary chapels a series of outdoor chapels, usually on a hillside, that commemorate the stages of the Passion of Christ.

campanile a bell tower.

cardo transverse street of a Roman castrum-shaped city.

cartoon the preliminary sketch for a fresco or tapestry.

caryatid supporting pillar or column carved into a standing female form; male versions are called telamons.

castrum a Roman military camp, always nearly rectangular, with straight streets and gates at the cardinal points. Later the Romans founded or refounded cities in the form, hundreds of which survive today (Verona and Padua are clear examples).

cavea the semicircle of seats in a classical theatre.

cenacolo fresco of the Last Supper, often on the wall of a monastery refectory.

centro storico historic centre.

ciborium a tabernacle; the word is often used for large, free-standing tabernacles, or in the sense of a *baldacchino*.

chiaroscuro the arrangement or treatment of light and dark in a painting.

comune commune, or commonwealth, referring to the governments of the free cities of the Middle Ages. Today it denotes any local government, from the *Comune di Roma* down to the smallest village.

condottiere the leader of a band of mercenaries in late medieval and Renaissance times.

confraternity a religious lay brotherhood, often serving as a neighbourhood mutual aid and burial society, or following some specific charitable work (Michelangelo, for example, belonged to one that cared for condemned prisoners in Rome).

cupola a dome.

decumanus street of a Roman castrum-shaped city parallel to the longer axis, the central, main avenue called the Decumanus Major.

doss hill, in Trentino.

duomo cathedral.

erker covered overhanging balcony, common in the Süd Tirol.

forum the central square of a Roman town, with its most important temples and public buildings. The word means 'outside', as the original Roman Forum was outside the first city walls.

fresco wall painting, the most important Italian medium of art since Etruscan times. It isn't easy: first the artist draws the *sinopia* (q.v.) on the wall. This is covered with plaster, but only a little at a time, as the paint must be on the plaster before it dries. Leonardo da Vinci's endless attempts to find clever shortcuts ensured that little of his work would survive.

Ghibellines one of the two great medieval parties, the supporters of the Holy Roman Emperors (*see* also Guelphs).

gonfalon the banner of a medieval free city; the *gonfaloniere*, or flag bearer, was often the most important public official.

grotesques carved or painted faces used in Etruscan and later Roman decoration; Raphael and other artists rediscovered them in the 'grotto' of Nero's Golden House in Rome.

Guelphs (*see* also Ghibellines): the other great political faction of medieval Italy, supporters of the pope.

intarsia work in inlaid wood or marble.

intonaco the stucco-like material covering the brick substructure of Palladio's villas.

malga Alpine hut.

maso traditional stone and wood Alpine farmhouse complexes.

monte di pietà municipal pawn shop.

narthex the enclosed porch of a church.

palazzo not just a palace, but any large, important building (though the word comes from the Imperial palatium on Rome's Palatine Hill).

palio a banner, and the horse race in which city neighbourhoods contend for it in their annual festivals.

Pantocrator Christ 'ruler of all', a common subject for apse paintings and mosaics in areas influenced by Byzantine art.

piano upper floor or storey in a building; *piano nobile*, the first floor.

pieve a parish church, especially in the north.

podestà a mayor or governor from outside a *comune*, usually chosen by the emperor or overlord like Venice, although sometimes a factionalized city would itself invite a *podestà* in for a period to sort it out.

polyptych an altarpiece composed of more than three panels.

predella smaller paintings on panels below the main subject of a painted altarpiece.

presepio a Christmas crib.

putti flocks of plaster cherubs with rosy cheeks and bums that infested Baroque Italy.

quadriga chariot pulled by four horses.

quattrocento the 1400s – the Italian way of referring to centuries (*duecento*, *trecento*, *quattrocento*, *cinquecento*, etc.).

rocca a citadel.

Sacra Conversazione Madonna enthroned with saints.

scuola the headquarters of a confraternity or guild, usually adjacent to a church.

sinopia the layout of a fresco (q.v.), etched by the artist on the wall before the plaster is applied. Often these are works of art in their own right.

stube traditional Tyrolean panelled room, usually with a woodstove.

terra firma Venice's mainland possessions.

thermae Roman baths.

tondo round relief, painting or terracotta.

transenna marble screen separating the altar area from the rest of an early Christian church.

triptych a painting, especially an altarpiece, in three sections.

trompe l'œil art that uses perspective effects to deceive the eye – for example, to create the illusion of depth on a flat surface, or to make columns and arches painted on a wall seem real.

tympanum the semicircular space, often bearing a painting or relief, above a portal (doorway).

Further Reading

Barzini, Luigi, *The Italians* (Athenaeum, 1996). A perhaps too clever account of the Italians by an Italian journalist living in London in the 1960s, but one of the classics.

Belfrage, Nicholas, *The Wines of North Italy* (Mitchell Beazley, 1999). One of an acclaimed series of guides on world wines: northern Italy is unexplored wine territory for many and frequently a revelation.

Black, Jeremy, *Italy and the Grand Tour* (Yale University Press, 2003). Lively read on Grand Tourists – such as Byron and Goethe – 'doing' Italy, with ample attention to Venice.

Burckhardt, Jacob, *The Civilization of the Renaissance in Italy* (Phaidon, 1995). The classic on the subject (first published 1860), the mark against which scholars still level their poison arrows of revisionism.

Calvino, Italo, *Invisible Cities* (Harcourt Brace, 1986). Provocative fantasies woven around Marco Polo and Kublai Khan that could only have been written by an Italian. Something even better is his compilation *Italian Folktales*, a little bit Brothers Grimm and a little bit Fellini.

Cole, John W. and Wolf, Eric R., *The Hidden Frontier: Ecology and Ethnicity in an Alpine Valley* (University of California Press, 2000). Cultural and political analysis of an appropriated region: two Alpine villages in the same valley in Alto Adige, only a mile apart yet with an entirely different identity.

Dante, Alighieri, *The Divine Comedy* (trans. by Mark Musa, 1971–84, Penguin). Few poems have ever had such a mythical significance for a nation. Anyone serious about understanding Italy and the Italian world view will need more than a passing acquaintance with Dante.

Del Conte, Anna, *The Classic Food of Northern Italy* (Pavilion Books, 1999). Page after page of delicious recipes from oop north.

Goethe, J. W., *Italian Journey* (Penguin Classics, 1992). An excellent example of a genius turned to mush by Italy; brilliant insights and big, big mistakes.

Ginsborg, Paul, *Italy and its Discontents 1980–2001* (Penguin, 2003). Provides an academic, historical analysis of Italy in the two decades before Berlusconi's second stint as premier.

Grubb, James S., *Provincial Families of the Renaissance: Private and Public Life in the Veneto* (Johns Hopkins University Press, 1996). Fascinating minutiae of everyday life in Verona and Vicenza from the perspective of several merchant families.

Hale, J. R. (ed.), *A Concise Encyclopaedia of the Italian Renaissance* (Thames & Hudson, 1981). An excellent reference guide, with concise, well-written essays.

Jones, Tobias, *The Dark Heart of Italy* (Faber and Faber, 2003). Well-written introduction to Italian politics and society deemed highly controversial in Italy.

Lane, Frederic C., *Venice, A Maritime Republic* (Johns Hopkins, 1973, out of print). The most thorough history of the republic in English.

Lauritzen, Peter and Wolf, Reinhart, *Villas of the Veneto* (Pavilion, 1988). Lush pictures and light descriptions.

Lavant, Mary, *Virgins of Venice* (Penguin, 2003). Fascinating insight into the lives of Venetian women in the 16th and 17th centuries, many of whom were forced into convents at an early age.

Levy, Michael, *Early Renaissance* (1967) and *High Renaissance* (1975), both by Penguin. Old-fashioned accounts of the period, with a breathless reverence for the 1500s – and full of intriguing interpretations.

Littlewood, Ian, *A Literary Companion to Venice* (St Martin's Press, 1995). Concentrated dose of Venetian inspiration.

McCarthy, Mary, *Stones of Florence and Venice Observed* (Penguin, 1986). Brilliant evocations of Italy's two greatest art cities, with an understanding that makes many other works on the subject seem sluggish.

Morris, Jan, *Trieste* (Faber and Faber, 2001). Highly acclaimed look at this frontier-city, from ethnic tensions to political intrigue.

Morris, Jan, *Venice* (*The World of Venice* in the USA, Harcourt Brace, 1995). A beautifully written classic on the World's Most Beautiful City; also *The Venetian Empire* (Penguin, 1990).

Muir, Edward, *Mad Blood Stirrings: Vendetta in Renaissance Italy* (Johns Hopkins University Press, 1998). The true tale of a bloody massacre amongst Udine's aristocracy during Carnival, 1511, and the intrigues which led up to it.

Murray, Linda, *The High Renaissance* and *The Late Renaissance and Mannerism* (Thames & Hudson, 1983). Excellent introduction to the period.

Norwich, John Julius, *A History of Venice* (Penguin, 1983). A classic, wittily written account of *La Serenissima*.

Norwich, John Julius, *Paradise of Cities* (Viking, 2003). Companion guide to Norwich's *History of Venice*, focusing on the legions of distinguished visitors that have visited *La Serenissima* over time.

Parks, Tim, *Italian Neighbours* (1993) and *An Italian Education* (1995) (Grove/Avon Books). Humorous accounts of real life in Montecchio near Verona by a scholar-novelist from Manchester married to an Italian.

Petrarch, Francesco, *The Canzoniere*, or *Rerum vulgarium fragmenta*; bilingual verse translation with notes and commentary by Mark Musa (Indiana University Press, 1996). Among the most influential works in Western literature; Petrarch, 'the first modern man', created the archetype of the hapless lover among many other things.

Plant, Margaret, *Venice – Fragile City* (Yale University Press, 2003). A lushly illustrated love affair with Venice and the arts.

Plotkin, Fred, *Italy for the Gourmet Traveller* (Little Brown and Co, 1996). For travellers whose prime concern is satisfying their taste-buds, this is a highly readable description of typical regional fare with recipes to boot.

Plotkin, Fred, *La Terra Fortunata: Food and Wine of Friuli-Venezia Giulia* (Broadway Books, 2001). This is an excellent guide to one of Italy's most prestigious regions in terms of food and wine.

Procacci, Giuliano, *History of the Italian People* (Penguin, sadly out of print). An in-depth view from the year 1000 to the present – also an introduction to the wit and subtlety of the best Italian scholarship.

Richards, Charles, *The New Italian* (Penguin, 1995). A very readable look at Italian culture and society and what makes Italians tick.

Rilke, Rainer Maria, *Duino Elegies* (translated by C. V. MacIntyre, University of California, 1989). With helpful hints.

Ruskin, John, *The Stones of Venice* (abridged paperback edition: Da Capo Press, 2003). Heavily abridged version of Ruskin's weighty tome: the original is over one million words long. An Arts & Crafts view of Venetian architecture.

Steer, John, *A Concise History of Venetian Painting* (Thames and Hudson, 1984). A well-illustrated introduction.

Vasari, Giorgio, *Lives of the Artists* (Oxford World Classics, 1998). Readable, anecdotal accounts of the Renaissance greats by the father of art history, also the first professional Philistine.

Wills, Gary, *Venice – Lion City* (Simon and Schuster, 2003). Beautiful book about Venice from the Middle Ages to the late Renaissance.

Wittkower, Rudolf, *Art and Architecture in Italy 1600–1750* (Pelican, 1992). The classic on Italian Baroque. Also *Architectural Principles in the Age of Humanism* with lots of insights into Palladio's villas (John Wiley and Sons, 1998).

Zorzi, Alvise, *Venice: City–Republic–Empire* (Sidgwick & Jackson, 1980). Beautifully illustrated, with a large section on Venice's dealings in the Veneto and eastern Mediterranean.

Index

Main page references are in **bold**. Page references to maps are in *italics*.

About the Updater

Viviana Fontana is from a town near Trento where she has a dream job: she organizes classic convertible car rentals and tours in the north of Italy. With work as an excuse, she gets to travel throughout Northeast Italy and meet people from all over the world, often collaborating with her American friend Sharla in the discovery of authentic experiences and great food and wines. Viviana speaks three languages, is an expert on wine, and loves dogs, especially Paco, her sweet pug.

Fourth edition published 2007

Cadogan Guides
2nd Floor, 233 High Holborn,
London WC1V 7DN
info@cadoganguides.co.uk
www.cadoganguides.com

The Globe Pequot Press
246 Goose Lane, PO Box 480, Guilford,
Connecticut 06437–0480

Copyright © Dana Facaros and Michael Pauls
1999, 2001, 2004, 2007
Updated by Viviana Fontana 2007

Cover photographs: © Jon Arnold Images / Alamy;
   David Noton Photography / Alamy
Introduction photographs: p.1 © David R. Frazier
   Photolibrary, Inc./Alamy; pp.3, 5, 8, 15 © OLIVIA;
   p. 4 © CuboImages srl/Alamy; pp. 6, 9, 10-11, 12, 13,
   16 © Fototeca ENIT; pp.9, 14 © Kicca Tomassi;
   pp.10-11 © Fototeca Trentino S.p.A.; p.13 © Cephas
   Picture Library/Alamy; p.15 © AA World Travel
   Library/Alamy
Maps © Cadogan Guides, drawn by
   Maidenhead Cartographic Services Ltd

Art Director: Sarah Gardner
Managing Editor: Antonia Cunningham
Editor: James Alexander
Assistant Editor: Nicola Jessop
Proofreading: Daphne Trotter
Indexing: Isobel McLean

Printed in Italy by Legoprint
A catalogue record for this book is available
   from the British Library
ISBN-13: 978-186011-356-7

The author and publishers have made every effort to ensure the accuracy of the information in this book at the time of going to press. However, they cannot accept any responsibility for any loss, injury or inconvenience resulting from the use of information contained in this guide.

Please help us to keep this guide up to date. We have done our best to ensure that the information in this guide is correct at the time of going to press. But places and facilities are constantly changing, and standards and prices in hotels and restaurants fluctuate. We would be delighted to receive any comments concerning existing entries or omissions. Authors of the best letters will receive a Cadogan Guide of their choice.

CADOGANguides ITALY

'Excellently written,
bursting with character'
– *Holiday Which*

Venice, Venetia &
The Dolomites touring atlas

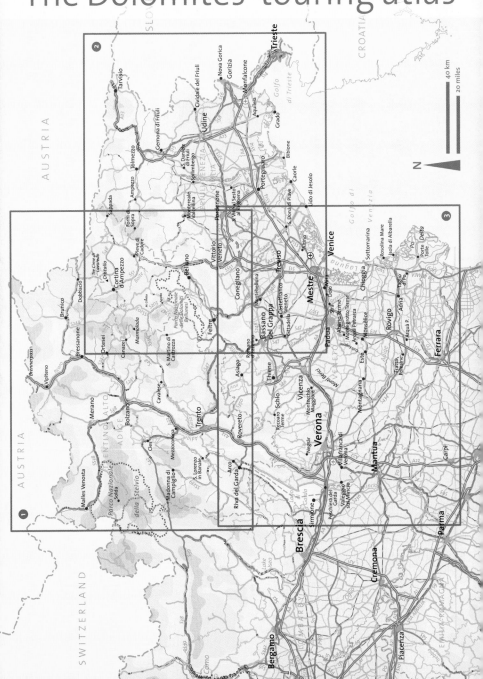

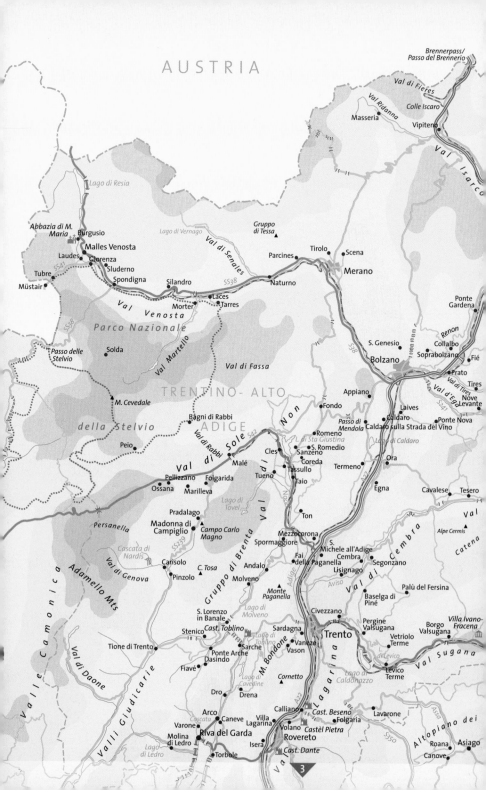

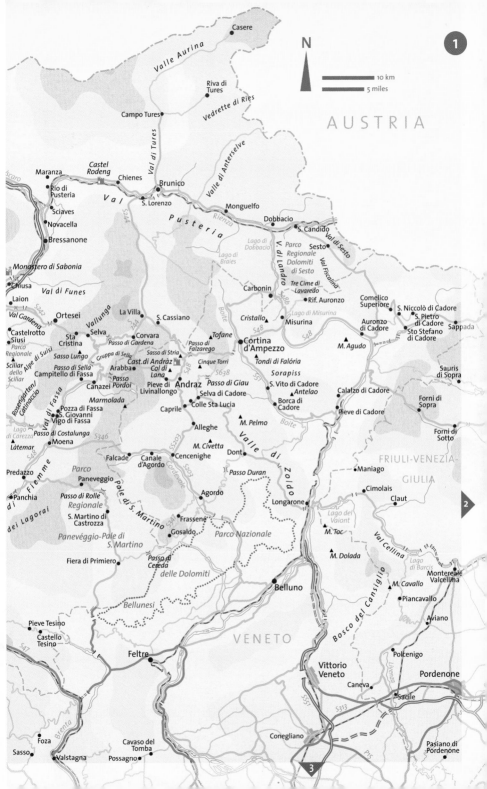

AUSTRIA

Ravascletto
Paularo
Comeglians
Arta Terme
Zuglio
Tolmezzo
Socchieve

Tarvisio

A23

Lago del Predil

Parco Regionale
delle Prealpi Giulie
Sella Nevea

Valle di Resia

N
10 km
5 miles

Lago di
Cavazzo
Interneppo
Bordano
Venzone

Gemona di Friuli

Clauzetto

Usago

S. Daniele
di Friuli
Spilimbergo

S13

Tricesimo

Cividale del Friuli

SLOVENIA

FRIULI-VENEZIA-
GIULIA

Udine

Dolegna del Collio

Tagliamento

S13

Codroipo

Cormans

Nova Gorica

Gorizia

S8

A23

Palmanova

S6

S351

S. Vito al Sesto
al Reghena

Gradisa d'Isonzo

Sesto al
Reghenal

A4

Monfalcone

Fossalta di Portegruaro

SS14

Sistiana

Sgonico

Monrupino
Grotto Gigante

Portegruaro
Latisana

Aquileia

Duino

Summaga

Miramare

A4

Barcolo

Opcina

Porto
Buso

Sta Maria di Barbana

S14

Lignano Sabbiadoro
Lignano Pineta
Lignano Riviera
Bibione

Grado
Grado Pineta

Trieste

Golfo
di Trieste

Muggia

Caorle

CROATIA

"Drive Italy."

Venice, Venetia and the Dolomites – with so many great places to see and surrounded by mountains, why not rent a car and hit the road. Rich in renaissance culture, wonderful food, beautiful churches and Europe's romantic centre. There's no better reason to drive Italy.

Consistently low rates with exceptional quality of service.
Over 2,700 locations in 115 countries.

Budget

Car Rental

Reservations:
0844 581 9998
www.budget.co.uk